SPELLBOUND IN DARKNESS

Ernst Lubitsch (with megaphone) directs one of his social satires, SO THIS IS PARIS (1926). This famous German director, working in Hollywood, bit deep into contemporary foibles. Here he guides the Charleston contest sequence, in which the chorus of two musical shows then playing on the stage in Hollywood participated.

SPELLBOUND IN DARKNESS

A History of the Silent Film

GEORGE C. PRATT

New York Graphic Society Ltd.
Greenwich, Connecticut

International Standard Book Number 8212-0486-6 Cloth edition
International Standard Book Number 8212-0489-0 Paperback edition
Library of Congress Catalog Card Number 72-80412

First published 1966 by the University of Rochester,
Rochester, New York

Revised edition published 1973 by
New York Graphic Society Ltd.,
140 Greenwich Ave., Greenwich, Conn., 06840

All illustrations courtesy of International Museum of Photography at George Eastman House,
Rochester, New York.

Designed by Joseph A. Romeo

Manufactured in the U.S.A.

GRATEFULLY,
FOR
JAMES CARD

ACKNOWLEDGMENTS

I have some personal debts of gratitude which it is a pleasure to acknowledge. First of all, the International Museum of Photography at George Eastman House has provided not only film screenings, but also long runs of periodicals drawn on for reprint, all the stills that appear as illustrations, and the scenario for SATAN McALLISTER'S HEIR.

Successive members of the administration and staff of the Micro-text Room at the University of Rochester were continuously helpful through extended periods of research. I also thank various divisions of the Rochester Public Library, and especially Pat Black, who was then in the Art Department. Liam O'Laoghaire gave help from London and Dublin, and John B. Kuiper, Head of the Motion Picture Section of the Prints and Photographs Division of the Library of Congress, gave help from Washington. More help came from Kevin Brownlow in London.

Beaumont Newhall, then Director of Eastman House, was always encouraging, and allowed me to print hitherto unpublished study notes which he had written when 19. Henri Langlois of the Cinémathèque Française in Paris has made more me conscious of certain unique elements in American film-making of the silent period.

Robert Johnson and Winn McCray acted as sounding boards for ideas bounced off them during what seemed a hundred coffee breaks, especially through my final winter of collecting data. A timely gift to Eastman House from Kathy and Paul Jessup of Scottsville, New York, provided me with one of the readings in Chapter 21.

Eileen Bowser, Associate Curator of the Department of Film at the Museum of Modern Art, New York, Russell Merritt of the University of Wisconsin, and Henry L. Mueller of the University of Illinois have offered suggestions about the manuscript. Emma Wright, secretary to James Card at Eastman House, Alberta and Burrill Phillips of Naples, and Anne Ludlow and Ann McCabe revived my spirits with such regularity during the endless hot summer when the book was drawing to a close, and later during the period of revision, that I owe them a special tribute.

Molli Martin typed the original manuscript; Melissa Reed and Dennis Longwell helped me check the revision. I pay particular thanks to Don Gunn of Chicago, who confirmed the important Eidoloscope reference for me.

University School of the University of Rochester covered certain expenses in connection with the publication of a provisional first edition, for which I am most grateful. Three people especially acted as unofficial press agents for the book: Louise Brooks, Pauline Kael, and Richard Schickel, in particular Mr. Schickel, through whose efforts the book now appears in a regular trade edition.

And Samuel J. Ricotta has been not only an excellent projectionist but an admirable friend.

For kind permission to reprint material, I would like to thank the Quigley Publishing Company, Inc., for those articles and reviews I have reprinted from *The Moving Picture World, Moving Picture News, Motion Picture News* and *The Motion Picture Almanac,* 1929; and the Macfadden-Bartell Corporation for what I have reprinted from *Photoplay Magazine* and *Motion Picture Magazine,** as well as material that appeared in *Classic*** and *Motion Picture Classic.* Material that appeared in the old *Life* magazine between

1920 and 1927 is reprinted by courtesy of Mr. Henry T. Rockwell; that from *The National Board of Review Magazine* is reprinted with the permission of the National Board of Review of Motion Pictures.

The three articles by Iris Barry that were published originally in *The Spectator* (London) have been included by courtesy of that publication; the Stravinsky-CALIGARI review is included by permission of *High Fidelity/Musical America;* the review of Garbo's LOVE is reprinted by permission from *Time* The Weekly Newsmagazine; Copyright Time Inc., 1927.

G. Schirmer, Inc., has granted permission to reprint the Foreword and Instructions from their *Motion Picture Moods* (1924); and J. S. Watson Jr. has granted permission to reprint an excerpt from *The Dial,* a published letter of his, and introductory comments on his then partially finished film (permission also obtained from The Society of Motion Picture and Television Engineers).

I thank the New York Times Company for sixty-two articles and reviews carried in part or in full, © 1913-1929 by the New York Times Company. Reprinted by permission.

The quotation from Constant Lambert's *Music Ho!: A Study of Music in Decline,* copyright 1934 by Faber and Faber Ltd., is included by permission of the publisher. James Card's comments on the silent film appear by his kind permission.

George C. Pratt

Victor, New York, May 7, 1972

*pp. 195-6, 198, 201-2, 245-6, 247-8, 250, 257-8, 269-70, 272-4, 278, 321, 331-2, 337-8, 340, 359, 453-6.
**pp. 336-7, 372-3, 483-8.

THREE WARNINGS

Some attempt has been made to regularize the spelling and the punctuation in these readings, but in many cases what you see is what appeared there originally.

Foreign films are dated here according to the year in which they arrived in this country. Some arrived at once, others were delayed.

Actors, actresses and directors are notoriously shy about remembering their birth dates. Those that appear here are, to the best of my knowledge, accurate.

CONTENTS

INTRODUCTION

I would like to note at the outset that this book includes no bibliography in the usual sense. This is because I feel emphatically that the very substance of the book stands as its own truest "bibliography." It is a compilation of original readings from contemporary sources, pertaining to films both produced in and imported into the United States during the major period of Silent Films—i.e. the period from 1896 through 1929, by which time it was plain that sound had arrived to stay. My selection of the readings, after a survey of much material over a period of years, is intended to provide a connected narrative throughout this time span. We can never afford to disregard eyewitness reports. Here they are, and as the years stretch away from them, they remain a fascinating and an appropriate form of documentation.

In this country we have lately witnessed a resurgence of interest in and enthusiasm for the works of this by-gone era (an enthusiasm which, as will be seen, often stands in marked contrast to the reception granted the same works at the time of their release). The increasing number of film festivals during the past decade or so, and now, very recently, the warm-hearted acclaim accorded Charlie Chaplin on the occasion of his historic return, encourage the feeling a collection of this kind will find audience not only among aficionados, but in the general movie-going public as well.

My earliest chapters deal with those pioneer directors who had to struggle to express themselves coherently in their storytelling on the screen; by the end of the book we reach the complexities of the imports from Russia, and of such a film as Dreyer's THE PASSION OF JEANNE D'ARC.

My comments simply bind the chapters together. Otherwise the book rests upon reviews of the films themselves: reviews which describe ambition, progress, experiment, entertainment, synthesis of attitudes, and the whole gamut of variation in the medium. I have also included general considerations by various writers, accounts of directors at work, two literary sources from which D.W. Griffith derived a famous one-reel film (A CORNER IN WHEAT; 1909), a 1914 scenario for a two-reel Western produced under the supervision of Thomas H. Ince, and—as films got longer and the Teens became the Twenties—glimpses of F. Scott Fitzgerald in Hollywood, plus a revealing series of articles on Hollywood and its product, written by that battler from Britain, the late John Grierson. Almost everything, with very few exceptions, was written in America, but there are three pieces from Iris Barry in London, for example, and a report on Charlie Chaplin from Rome.

This book is emphatically not intended as an encyclopedic record of the time, but the major directors will be encountered—either in person, or through their films, or both—as well as some minor figures in the field, and many of the stars.

Despite some excerpting, which was unavoidable because the span of time, although not long, was so crowded with activity, much of the material I have chosen appears intact, drawn from newspapers, magazines, a few books, and several censor reports. Film credits appear as they are carried in the original sources.

Not all of the films named or reviewed here have survived: deteriorating film stock, neglect, ruinous fires, and deliberate destruction have been their enemies; but fortunately a good many have been retrieved from every conceivable kind of situation and printed on long-lasting film stock for present and future re-examination. Some circulate, others can be examined only in the world's film archives. However, to have omitted reference to certain films that have eluded rescue would have been to damage the historical record; accordingly, they too are here.

Despite my reluctance to offer any conventional bibliography, a few books from the considerable literature in the field should certainly be cited. No book on the silent film, even now, can fail to benefit from two influential predecessors: Paul Rotha's *The Film Till Now* (the first of several editions appeared in 1930) and Lewis Jacobs' *The Rise of the American Film* (1939). No one who writes about the silent period can be unaware of Arthur Knight's *The Liveliest Art* (1957). Of the more recent large-scale works, perhaps only Kevin Brownlow's *The Parade's Gone By* (1968) balances contemporary, recollective and eye-witness views. Interested readers will want to consult the writings of the Russian film-maker Pudovkin, and probably the more difficult writings of his colleague Eisenstein. Theodore Huff has dealt simply but expressively with a single figure in his *Charlie Chaplin* (1951), and Jay Leyda has dealt with a single country in his *Kino*, a history of the Russian and Soviet film (1960). Some of us learned to observe more sharply through the eyes of Rudolf Arnheim, thanks to his *Film* (1933, later revised and re-issued as *Film as Art*), and we continue to learn from the works of the French critic André Bazin, which are gradually being translated into English.

Lest there be a great crowding together at one end of the table and cries of "No room! No room!" (as at a certain Mad Tea Party) over the appearance of yet another book on the silent film, I would like to reply with Alice: "There's *plenty* of room!" I know of no other book that allows the period's own view of its films throughout.

Had there been such a book I would have used it for my course in film history at the University of Rochester, Rochester, New York, instead of preparing my own, which I finally did at the suggestion of the late Arthur L. Assum, at that time Dean of the University School there. His encouragement was of the utmost importance at every stage of the book's preparation. *Spellbound in Darkness* reflects a good many of the discussions I had with Dean Assum about films. It also reflects the almost daily conversations I have had with James Card, Director of the Department of Film, International Museum of Photography at George Eastman House. It was Mr. Card who founded the Motion Picture Department there in 1948, who welcomed me when I joined the staff in 1953, and who has given me many private and innumerable public opportunities to view films in the Dryden Theatre of Eastman House, where he remains in charge of its vast collection.

As explanation for my own personal attraction to the world of film, I can only say that when I was a boy, I was not allowed to go to the movies except on Saturday afternoons, which meant that I missed a great deal that played on school-nights during the week, and I must have decided subconsciously that if it were ever possible to catch up, I would.

We were all movie-mad. I can remember my sister Suzanne's pencil drawings of Mary Pickford in ROSITA and Alice Terry in SCARAMOUCHE, copied from fan magazines. She liked costume films and so did I. I couldn't always get to them, however: they were forbidden if they included torture scenes. Probably my father and mother were right, since I could work up a pretty good nightmare on the sheer strength of my own imagination about what might happen on that unobserved screen; in any case it was not until years later that I saw ROBIN HOOD and THE HUNCHBACK OF NOTRE DAME.

My earliest film recollections are of two moments in HUCKLEBERRY FINN (1920), with Lewis Sargent, which I saw from my father's shoulder across a crowded lobby in my hometown—La Grange, Illinois—because the first show was sold out, and we were waiting for the second. My next recollection is of Mae Marsh's death in THE BIRTH OF A NATION (that would have been its 1921 revival).

Except for seeing as many films as I could, I didn't do anything practical about my infatuation until 25 years later, in Chicago, when Mr. Assum and I co-founded the Roosevelt College Film Society. This absorbed me for five years, until I left Chicago for Rochester.

The time of the silent film is over, but what was produced then is, at its best, no more dead than Post-Impressionism is dead because no one paints that way now, or the early ballets of Stravinsky are dead because he went on to compose in a different manner, or *Ulysses* is dead because James Joyce later wrote *Finnegan's Wake*. These early excitements in other arts all appeared when the silent film was current, and each, like the silent film, represents an achieved goal, not merely a step towards something more recent and thus automatically superior. In 1948 James Agee still found THE BIRTH OF A NATION the single example of a great epic film tragedy, and two decades later Pauline Kael was calling INTOLERANCE the greatest movie ever made. Art is a matter of accumulated resource, but at a very particular time. Otherwise all our masterpieces could be achieved only in the present.

It is always rather difficult to make a sweeping statement about the film field, for no one person may ever see it all. . . .

"Reviews of Feature Films," *The New York Dramatic Mirror,* Vol. 73, No. 1893, March 31, 1915, p. 35.

It is a silly attitude to say that the movies cannot do great things. . . . The film GREED is one of the momentous things in any medium, and so is THE CABINET OF DR. CALIGARI and some of Chaplin's films. . . .

Theodore Dreiser, in "The Story That Cost $93,000," Esther Carples, *Motion Picture Magazine,* Vol. 32, No. 1, August 1926, p. 107.

The nineteenth century was to carry this smug attitude one stage further. The eighteenth-century masters [of music] were admired not so much for their own sake as for being precursors of the Romantic school which through its sheer position in time was naturally an improvement. Once Beethoven's Symphonies were accepted they were considered as being superior to Mozart's in the way that a six-cylinder car is preferred to a four-cylinder car, or a talking to a silent film. Schumann, it is true, admired Scarletti, but with a touch of the patronage displayed by a Lady Bountiful visiting the village, and Clara Schumann simply could not understand how Brahms could take any interest in composers earlier than Bach. Wagner's followers did not look upon *The Ring* as a way of writing operas that was different from Bellini's, but as a way that clearly was a much better one.

Music Ho! A Study of Music in Decline, Constant Lambert, Faber & Faber, 1934, p. 44.

The silent photoplay attracted over eighty million spectators each week in the United States.

Every two months the entire population of the globe was exceeded in number by the total of all who visited the world's silent movies.

More human beings alive today have received their impressions of social behavior, moral justice and poetic expression from the motion picture than from painting, the theatre, or literature.

In less than an average life-time, this monster medium evolved from a peep-show novelty to the dominant cultural force of the mechanized world.

Reviewing the cinema's past is an experience rich in nostalgia for those who lived through its formative years.

Serious students may find close to the surface of the movies, eloquent clues to the special hopes and dreams of the people for whom they were made. For unlike the arts of individual expression, the aim of the film has been to reflect in pictures, the universal longings of the multitude.

"The Silent Drama, 1915-1928," James Card, Dryden Theatre Motion Picture Lecture Programs, George Eastman House, Rochester, New York, Winter-Spring, 1952.

CHAPTER 1

In the Beginning:
"A Magic Lantern Run Mad"

COMMENTARY

Just short of a year after Nathaniel Hawthorne had written the following entry in his diary in late August, 1838, concerning a primitive travelling diorama in Shelburne Falls, Massachusetts, the world was to learn the details about Daguerre's invention in France of the daguerreotype process. This, you might say, began the history of photography.

What gave Hawthorne a shock of amusement at the very end of the diorama showing was not so much the effect of movement after a parade of motionless views (for the enlarged live hand of the exhibitor had already been at work pointing out aspects of the views), as it was the unexpected looming of the boy's head in enormous increase of scale. The face confronts with greater intensity as a "gigantic detail" than the eyeless hand.

Many years afterward, at least one American lecturer was to use a similar live close-up of his hand alone, in conjunction with exhibiting lantern slides of photographs, but full exploitation of the device of arresting an audience by sudden enlargement of scale had to await the motion picture, which by the mid-1890s had become a reality.

Hawthorne himself was interested in photography, at least to the extent of making the young hero of his novel, *The House of the Seven Gables* (**1851**), a daguerreotypist.

1838   **Nathaniel Hawthorne and a Close-up**

Excerpts from *Passages From The American Note-Books,* Nathaniel Hawthorne, Vol. 18 of *The Complete Writings of Nathaniel Hawthorne,* Graylock Edition, Houghton Mifflin Company, Boston and New York, no date, pp. 212-215.

Friday, August 31. A drive on Tuesday to Shelburne Falls, twenty-two miles or thereabouts distant. Started at about eight o'clock in a wagon with Mr. Leach and Mr. Birch. Our road lay over the Green Mountains, the long ridge of which made awful by a dark, heavy, threatening cloud, apparently rolled and condensed along the whole summit. As we ascended the zigzag road, we looked behind, at every opening in the forest, and beheld a wide landscape of mountain swells and valleys intermixed, and old Graylock and the whole of Saddleback. Over the wide scene there was a general gloom; but there was a continual vicissitude of bright sunshine flitting over it, now resting for a brief space on portions of the heights, now flooding the valleys with green brightness, now making out distinctly each dwelling, and the hotels, and then two small brick churches of the distant village. . . .

The top of this Hoosic Mountain is a long ridge, marked on the country map as two thousand one hundred and sixty feet above the sea; on this summit is a valley, not very deep, but one or two miles wide, in which is the town of L————. Here there are respectable farmers, though it is a rough, and must be a bleak place. The first house, after reaching the summit, is a small, homely tavern. We left our horse in the shed, and, entering the little unpainted barroom, we heard a voice, in a strange, outlandish accent, exclaiming "Diorama." It was an old man, with a full, gray-bearded countenance, and Mr. Leach exclaimed, "Ah, here's the old Dutchman again!" And he answered, "Yes, Captain, here's the old Dutchman,"—though, by the way, he is a German, and travels the country with this diorama in a wagon, and had recently been at South Adams, and was now returning from Saratoga Springs. We looked through the glass orifice of his machine, while he exhibited a succession of the very worst scratches and daubings that can be imagined,—worn out, too, and full of cracks and wrinkles, dimmed with tobacco smoke, and every other wise dilapidated. There were none in a later fashion than thirty years since, except some figures that had been cut from tailors' showbills. There were views of cities and edifices in Europe, of Napoleon's battles and Nelson's sea-fights, in the midst of which would be seen a gigantic, brown, hairy hand (the Hand of Destiny) pointing at the principal points of the conflict, while the old Dutchman explained. He gave a good deal of dramatic effect to his descriptions, but his accent and intonation cannot be written. He seemed to take interest and pride in his exhibition; yet when the utter and ludicrous miserability thereof made us laugh, he joined in the joke very readily. When the last picture had been shown, he caused a country boor, who stood gaping beside the machine, to put his head within it, and thrust out his tongue. The head becoming gigantic, a singular effect was produced. . . .

COMMENTARY

In response to a controversy about animal locomotion, which aroused San Francisco in the spring of 1872, the British photographer Eadweard Muybridge (1830-1904) photographed the separate phases of a horse's gait at Sacramento, California. He was trying to prove that a trotting horse at one point pulled all four feet off the ground and he successfully demonstrated that it did, but when he began his experiments he was handicapped by the prevailing process of wet-plate photography, which was too slow to register brief exposures, so he was only able to obtain a "silhouette portrait." (1)

Later, his task was simplified by the more rapid dry plates, and the systems which he successively adopted in working out his problem eventually led to motion pictures.

Muybridge attempted to group his first photographs in sequence, to illustrate "the consecutive phases of a complete stride; this, however, in consequence of the irregularity of their intervals, he was unable to satisfactorily accomplish." (2)

His work was then resumed under the sponsorship of Governor Leland Stanford of California, who granted permission for him to photograph at the Stanford stock farm in Palo Alto. By 1878, Muybridge was employing 12 cameras ranged along the track; afterward, he doubled the number of cameras, and placed them at intervals of 12 inches. He expanded his repertory of subjects to include running dogs, birds in flight, and the acrobatic feats of human beings, and finally he got what he wanted. Transferring his sequence photographs spirally to glass plates, so that the still photographs, rapidly succeeding each other on the screen, gave the impression of movement, he exhibited them to an audience at a program of the San Francisco Art Association, on May 4, 1880.

Muybridge took the long way around to New York, first exhibiting his photographs before very distinguished audiences in Paris, London and the London provinces, on a projector which he had begun by calling a Zoögyroscope and now called a

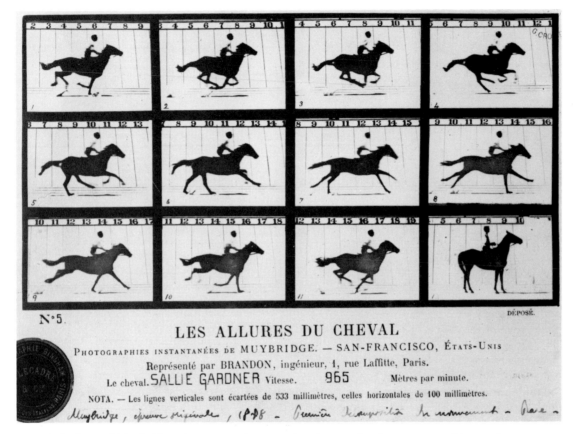

1. Eadweard Muybridge: Sequence photographs of a running horse, secured by twelve cameras, June 19, 1878, Palo Alto, California. Such Muybridge photographs travelled the world. This is what the French saw.

Zoöpraxiscope. He then returned in triumph to the States in 1882. In November of that year he lectured before the New York Turf Club. His principal concern seemed to be a denunciation of most depictions of the horse in painting and sculpture, but he was foresighted enough to describe what he had accomplished as "simply preliminary results." (3)

The first of the following three passages describes Muybridge at the Parisian home of the painter Meissonier (whose own very celebrated paintings of animals were subsequently to fall under good-natured attack as a consequence of Muybridge's revelations). The second presents excerpts from a speech in London; and the third documents his address to an audience of fewer than 40 people in New York: all the members of the Turf Club who cared to challenge the bad weather that evening.

"MR. MUYBRIDGE'S PHOTOGRAPHS OF ANIMALS IN MOTION"   1882

Excerpts from "Mr. Muybridge's Photographs of Animals in Motion," "X," *The American Register,* reprinted in *The Scientific American Supplement,* Vol. 13, No. 317, January 28, 1882, pp. 5058-5059.

One of the latest topics of Parisian conversation has been the magnificent entertainment at the residence of M. Meissonier, where we had the pleasure of meeting a large number of the most eminent artists, scientists, and literati of Paris.

The object of the renowned artist was to introduce to his friends Mr. Muybridge, of California, and afford them an opportunity of witnessing a very remarkable exhibition.

From time to time rumors have reached Europe of certain original and remarkable experiments in animal photography carried on by Mr. Muybridge at Palo Alto, in California, the residence of Governor Stanford, who had placed at Mr. Muybridge's disposition an exercising track and the use of his magnificent stud of horses, and was encouraging the investigations in a variety of other ways. During a visit to Paris last year, Mr. Stanford called upon Meissonier and exhibited to him a few specimens of the photographs. The great artist was immediately impressed with their value as an assistance to art, and they were a ready passport to his favor.

. . . [From] the far-off land of California comes a man who is welcomed by the most eminent of living painters, accorded his friendship, and introduced by him, with a generosity equalled only by the greatness of his renown, to an assemblage of eminent men, such as is seldom found within the walls of one room. [Among those present were the artists Gérôme, Cabanel, Léon Bonnat and Détaille; Alexandre Dumas; the playwright Emile Augier; and Charles Garnier, the architect of the Paris Opera House.]

Of the exhibition itself we need say but little; the applause which greeted the pictures renders it almost unnecessary for us to add our tribute to their praise. . . .

A magnificent supper was provided for the guests, who, after the intellectual feast, were prepared to do ample justice to the more substantial matters of taste which were placed before them. . . .

"THE ATTITUDES OF ANIMALS IN MOTION"   1882

Excerpts from "The Attitudes of Animals in Motion," Eadweard Muybridge, a paper read before the Society of Arts, London, April 4, 1882, *The Scientific American Supplement,* Vol. 14, No. 343, July 29, 1882, pp. 5469-5470.

The attempts to depict the attitudes of animals in motion probably originated with art itself, if, indeed, it was not the origin of art; and upon the walls of the ancient temples of Egypt, we still find pictures of, perhaps, the very earliest attempts to illustrate animal motion. But artists of all ages seem to have followed peculiar grooves in this matter, and to have adopted uniform notions as to the movement of animals. How inaccurate these notions have been, I shall endeavor to demonstrate to you this evening. I will commence, however, by showing you the apparatus by which the photographs were made; you will then better understand the pictures themselves. Here is the apparatus, consisting of an ordinary camera, in front of which is a strong framework, inclosing a couple of panels, each with an opening in the center, sliding one up and one down. In connection with it is an electromagnet, which, on completion of a circuit of electricity, causes a hammer to strike and release a catch which holds the shutters in position; the back shutter is then drawn upward by a strong India-rubber spring, and the front shutter is simultaneously drawn downward. Here is a photograph of three shutters in position, one showing the panels before exposure, one during exposure and a third after exposure. The next picture shows the arrangement in front of the cameras. Here are a series of strong threads stretched across the track, each of which being pressed forward, causes two metal springs to touch, and thereby completes the electric circuit. These threads are arranged at a distance of 12 in. from each other, and as the horse passes along he thrusts the strings, one after the other, completes an electric circuit, which operates the shutter of the particular camera which he is passing at the moment.

Twenty-four cameras are arranged parallel with the direction of the animal. The next picture shows the entire photographic arrangements. The track is covered with India-rubber, to prevent dust flying from the horse's hoofs; and there are here five cameras arranged in a semicircle, the object of which I will explain presently. The result is this: A horse, in his progress over the track, comes in contact with these threads successively, and is photographed in the position in which he happens to be when he strikes the thread; then he moves 12 inches, and of course assumes another position, and is so photographed, then another 12 inches, and so on; in this way we have several positions assumed by an animal during an entire stride. The time of exposure, I may say, is the one five-thousandth of a second. . . .

Here are photographs of a horse . . . walking, photographed simultaneously from five different points of view, according to the arrangement of the cameras I referred to just now. Next, we have a photograph showing the regular series of positions taken by a horse while walking. Of course, in every thousandth part of an inch a horse really gets into a different position, but these are all the positions of a stride which are worth illustrating. . . .

When these photographs were first made, some experts had doubts as to their accuracy. We have here a little instrument called the Zoöpraxiscope, with which we can throw the various positions in rapid succession on the same spot on the screen, and thus produce apparently the real motion, and you will readily understand that if any of the positions were incorrect, it would upset the experiment altogether. . . .

Here are a series of photographs of a horse trotting at about ten miles an hour, showing all the various positions at the different periods of the stride. Now, to me it appears almost incomprehensible, but until these experiments were made, it was a question with some very experienced horse drivers whether a horse was entirely clear of the ground during a trot. Some imagined that he always had one foot on the ground, though I cannot see how it was possible for them to come to that conclusion. Even at a moderate rate, in trotting, the weight of the body is entirely unsupported by the feet, though they may drag along the ground at a certain portion of the stride, no matter how slow the pace. This being about ten miles an hour, the horse is entirely clear. . . .

. . . You may think it a very easy thing to watch an animal, and see how it walks, but it is very difficult. There is as much difficulty in watching the massive movements of an elephant as the more light and rapid movements of the horse. I am not quite satisfied in my own mind yet whether an elephant is upon diagonals during a walk or not; I know he is on laterals, but during half an hour's observation I could not really positively say whether he was supported by the diagonals alone or not. With the hippopotamus I know that to be the case, but I almost question really whether an elephant in walking is supported entirely by diagonals. Here again we have a picture of an ox, by Rosa Bonheur. This is a very celebrated picture in the Luxembourg. Those two oxen are represented in a manner that no oxen would ever think of getting into. You might get a cord, and pull their feet into that position, but it would be strongly against their will. There is another one here by the same artist which is more nearly correct, but not quite. . . .

. . . The next is a wild bull; he was really wild enough for a Spanish bull fight; we had to build a long lane in order to get him to run straight, and we had three or four men ready to catch him in case he should make for the cameras. The bull gallops pretty much like a horse. Next we have a set of photographs of the pig. I thought I would attempt the pig, not that I hoped to gather much information from his movements. The principal event of our experiment was the difficulty we had in inducing him to go forward; of course we followed the old principle of drawing him backwards. . . .

"REALITIES OF ANIMAL MOTION"   1882
From *The New York Times,* November 18, 1882, p. 2.

Professor Muybridge's explanation of his discoveries through his Zoöpraxiscope

Prof. Eadweard Muybridge, whose success in instantly photographing the motion of the horse in running has overturned all previous ideas on the subject, lectured last evening in the Turf Club Theatre under the auspices of the Turf Club, whose members had previously been supposed to care very little what motions a horse made in running so that he brought himself under the wire ahead. Prof. Muybridge's subject was "The Romance and Reality of Animal Motion," and he illustrated his lecture upon a large screen by means of a Zoöpraxiscope, which an eminent English writer describes as "a magic lantern run mad." With this instrument the professor produced upon the canvas, first stationary figures of the horse in the different positions assumed in the walk, the pace, the rack, the canter, and the gallop, and afterward displayed the figure of the animal, first at a walk across the canvas, then pacing, cantering, galloping, and even jumping the hurdle. The effect was true to life, and the spectator could almost believe that he saw miniature horses with their riders racing across the screen. A photograph of Rosa Bonheur's celebrated painting, "The Horse Fair," was thrown upon the canvas, and the lecturer explained where the positions of the animals were incorrect, and demonstrated why their attitudes were impossible. He also displayed and criticized several of Meissonier's masterpieces, and said that the great painter himself acknowledged that the positions of his horse figures were incorrect. Photographs of the equestrian statues of Marcus Aurelius in Rome, and of Washington, in Boston and in Union-square, were exhibited and the attitudes of the horse pronounced impossible. There were also displayed representations of ancient paintings and statues of different countries, in most of which the horse was incorrectly portrayed. One mural painting of the horse at Pisa, of the fifth century of the Christian era, was strictly correct the Professor said, and for that reason the name of the painter had been forgotten. The Greeks, he said, created an era of art which was modified by truth, but their example had been wholly disregarded by the most distinguished artists of modern times. The Professor produced on the screen, by means of his Zoöpraxiscope, a running bull, a goat and a deer, all of which were put through their paces and made to walk, run and jump. The figure of a man was made to walk, run, jump a hurdle, and turn a somersault, and the motions were explained at length. The audience was very enthusiastic, and the wonderful effects produced by the Zoöpraxiscope were repeatedly applauded.

COMMENTARY

The Edison Kinetoscope (1894) provided an intermediate step between Muybridge's glass discs, and films projected for an audience. However, a step forward in one direction was a step backward in another: Kinetoscope pictures, although secured on short strips of film, could be viewed by only one person at a time peering into a peepshow box.

The Kinetoscope was a Thomas A. Edison workshop product on which the inventor W. K. L. Dickson seems to have done most of the work. While Edison acknowledged the inspiration of the achievements of Muybridge "and others," Dickson was careful to point out in print that "It must be understood that only one camera is used for taking these [Kinetoscope] strips, and not a battery of cameras, as in Mr. Muybridge's photographs of *The Horse in Motion*." (4)

On February 27, 1888, Edison and Muybridge consulted as to the possibility of combining the Edison phonograph with the Muybridge Zoöpraxiscope to "reproduce simultaneously in the presence of an audience, visible actions and audible words." (5) When the Kinetoscope appeared commercially six years later, however, it was far from having achieved this visionary goal: there was no sound, only pictures alone, but even though Edison regarded this as a transitional stage, he said with pride that already "every change of facial expression can be recorded and reproduced life size." (6)

What gives particular interest to the first of the three passages below about the Kinetoscope, is the heading "The Fine Arts" under which *The Critic* carries its description. To be called an art was a distinction for which photography had been battling intermittently since its disclosure in 1839, and here, at one stroke, the Kinetoscope is rolled in to glory.

Brander Matthews' "The Kinetoscope of Time" is a fanciful story which appeared in *Scribner's Magazine* for December, 1895, the text overprinted on a drawing on each page. On the final page, in the final sentence, a drawing intervenes in the text, and the last words identify both the subject of the portrait and the proprietor of the hall of visions. Even though the work is offered as imaginative writing, it predicts with all accuracy filmed versions of The Dance of Salome, *The Scarlet Letter, Uncle Tom's Cabin, A Doll's House, The Iliad, Don Quixote, Faust* and the Custer massacre.

The last passage about the Kinetoscope, from a small town newspaper in Upper New York State, indicates that in 1896 subjects were still being manufactured for this peepshow device, in the Edison "Black Maria" studio. Even then the Kinetoscope was outmoded by projectors for screenings to group audiences. The "last week" reference to the Vitascope exhibitions initiated in New York City on April 23 indicates that this report was written shortly thereafter, although it did not reach public print until June 10.

1894   "THE FINE ARTS: THE KINETOSCOPE"

From *The Critic,* Vol. 24, No. 638, May 12, 1894, p. 330.

The Kinetoscope, Edison's latest toy, is a development of that marvel of our youth, the Thaumatrope. But it may be applied to uses which the earlier toy could not subserve. A number of instantaneous photographs illustrating all the important phases of a single action or series of actions are set on a wheel which is made to revolve very rapidly by a small electric motor, which also supplies the light by which they are seen, the whole thing being enclosed in a dark box. By this means the action which is analyzed in the series of photographs is reconstituted, and stage performers dance or go through their contortions, Sandow's muscles swell and relax, fighting-cocks fight, and the organgrinder's monkey snatches off the small boy's hat. The element of color, only, is needed to complete the illusion, and it is possible that that may be supplied. As it stands, the machine should be of great service to artists and others in studying action. Separate instantaneous photographs, as is now well known, are of no value to artists, but the Kinetoscope presents the action as it is seen by the eye, and presents it, in all respects the same, as often as may be desired. If the figures were thrown upon a screen there would be many advantages in working from them rather than from a tired model. It is possible that we may yet see this done, and, with the assistance of the perfected phonograph, that we may witness and hear shadow-plays in which the only real performer will be the electro-magnetic motor behind the scenes. The new invention is exhibited on Broadway above 26th Street.

"THE KINETOSCOPE OF TIME" 1895

By Brander Matthews, *Scribner's Magazine,* Vol. 18, No. 6, December, 1895, pp. 733-744.

As the twelfth stroke of the bell in the tower at the corner tolled forth slowly, the midnight wind blew chill down the deserted avenue. Then it was that I found myself just inside a large circular hall. Letting the hangings fall behind me, I took three or four irresolute paces which brought me almost to the centre of the room. I saw that the walls were continuously draped with the heavy folds of soft velvet, so that I could not even guess where it was I had entered. The rotunda was bare of all furniture; there was no table in it, no chair, no sofa; nor was anything hanging from the ceiling or against the curtained walls. All that the room contained was a set of four curiously shaped narrow stands, placed over against one another at the corners of what might be a square drawn within the circle of the hall. These narrow stands were close to the curtains; they were perhaps a foot wide, each of them, or it might be a little more: they were twice or three times as long as they were wide; and they reached a height of possibly three or four feet.

Going toward one of these stands to examine it more curiously, I discovered that there were two projections from the top, resembling eye-pieces, as though inviting the beholder to gaze into the inside of the stand. Then I thought I heard a faint metallic click above my head. Raising my eyes swiftly, I read a few words written, as it were, against the dark velvet of the heavy curtains in dots of flame, that flowed one into the other and melted away in a moment. When this mysterious legend had faded absolutely, I could not recall the words I had read in the fitful and flitting letters of fire, and yet I retained the meaning of the message; and I understood that if I chose to peer through the eye-pieces I should see a succession of strange dances.

To gaze upon dancing was not what I had gone forth to do, but I saw no reason why I should not do so as I was thus strangely bidden. I lowered my head until my eyes were close to the two openings at the top of the stand. I looked into blackness at first and yet I thought that I could detect a mystic commotion of the invisible particles at which I was staring. I made no doubt that if I waited, in due season the promise would be fulfilled. After a period of expectancy which I could not measure, infinitesimal sparks darted hither and thither, and there was a slight crackling sound. I concentrated my attention on what I was about to see; and in a moment more I was rewarded.

The darkness took shape and robed itself in color; and there arose out of it a spacious banquet-hall, where many guests sat at supper. I could not make out whether they were Romans or orientals; the structure itself had a Latin solidity, but the decorations were Eastern in their glowing gorgeousness. The hall was illumined by hanging lamps, by the light of which I tried to decide whether the ruler who sat in the seat of honor was a Roman or an oriental. The beautiful woman beside him struck me as Eastern beyond all question. While I gazed intently he turned to her and proffered a request. She smiled acquiescence, and there was a flash of anticipated triumph in her eye as she beckoned to a menial and sent him forth with a message. A movement as of expectancy ran around the tables where the guests sat at meat. The attendants opened wide the portals and a young girl came forward. She was perhaps fourteen or fifteen years of age, but in the East women ripen young, and her beauty was indisputable. She had large, deep eyes and a full mouth, and there was a chain of silver and golden coins twisted into her coppery hair. She was so like to the woman who sat beside the ruler that I did not doubt them to be mother and daughter. At a word from the elder the younger began to dance; and her dance was oriental, slow at first, but holding every eye with its sensual fascination. The girl was a mistress of the art; and not a man in the room withdrew his gaze from her till she made an end and stood motionless before the ruler. He said a few words I could not hear, and then the daughter turned to the mother for guidance; and again I caught the flash of triumph in the elder woman's eye and on her face the suggestion of a hatred about to be glutted. And then the light faded and the darkness settled down on the scene and I saw no more.

I did not raise my head from the stand, for I felt sure that this was not all I was to behold; and in a few moments there came a faint glow that grew until I saw clearly as in the morning sun the glade of a forest through which a brook rippled. A sad-faced woman sat on a stone by the side of the streamlet, her gray garments set off the strange ornament in the fashion of a single letter of the alphabet that was embroidered in gold and in scarlet over her heart. Visible at some distance was a little girl, like a bright-apparelled vision, in a sunbeam, which fell down upon her through an arch of boughs. The ray quivered to and fro, making her figure dim or distinct, now like a real child, now like a child's spirit, as the splendor came and went. With violets and anemones and columbines the little girl had decorated her hair. The mother looked at the child and the child danced and sparkled and prattled airily along the course of the streamlet, which kept up a babble, kind, quiet, soothing, but melancholy. Then the mother raised her head as though her ears had detected the approach of some one through the wood. But before I could see who this new-comer might be, once more the darkness settled down upon the scene.

This time I knew the interval between the succeeding visions, and I waited without impatience; and in due season I found myself gazing at a picture as different as might be from any I had yet beheld.

In the broad parlor of a house that seemed to be spacious, a middle-aged lady of an appearance at once austere and kindly, was looking at a smiling gentleman who was coming toward her pulling along a little negro girl about eight or nine years of age. She was one of the blackest of her race; and her round, shining eyes, glittering as glass beads, moved with quick and restless glances over everything in the room. Her woolly hair was braided in sundry little tails, which stuck out in every direction. She was dressed in a single filthy ragged garment, made of bagging; and altogether there was something odd and goblin-like about her appearance. The severe old maid examined this strange creature in dismay and then directed a glance of inquiry at the gentleman in white. He smiled again and gave a signal to the little negro girl. Whereupon the black eyes glittered with a kind of wicked drollery, and apparently she began to sing, keeping time with her hands and feet, spinning round, clapping her hands, knocking her knees together, in a wild fantastic sort of time; and finally, turning a somersault or two, she came suddenly down on the carpet, and stood with her hands folded, and a most sanctimonious expression of meekness and solemnity over her face, only broken by the cunning glances which she shot askance from the corners of her eyes. The elderly lady stood silent, perfectly paralyzed with amazement, while the smiling gentleman in white was amused at her astonishment.

Once more the vision faded. And when, after the same interval, the darkness began to disappear again, even while everything was dim and indistinct I knew that the scene was shifted from the South to the North. I saw a room comfortably furnished, with a fire burning in a porcelain stove. In a corner stood a stripped Christmas-tree, with its candles burnt out. Against the wall between the two doors was a piano, on which a man was

9

playing—a man who twisted his head now and again to look over his shoulder, sometimes at another and younger man standing by the stove, sometimes at a young woman who was dancing alone in the centre of the room. This young woman had draped herself in a long party-colored shawl and she held a tambourine in her hand. There was in her eyes a look of fear, as of one conscious of an impending misfortune. As I gazed she danced more and more wildly. The man standing by the porcelain stove was apparently making suggestions, to which she paid no heed. At last her hair broke loose and fell over her shoulders; and even this she did not notice going on with her dancing as though it were a matter of life and death. Then one of the doors opened and another woman stood on the threshold. The man at the piano ceased playing and left the instrument. The dancer paused unwillingly, and looked pleadingly up into the face of the younger man as he came forward and put his arm around her.

And then once more the light died away and I found myself peering into a void blackness. This time, though I waited long, there were no crackling sparks announcing another inexplicable vision. I peered intently into the stand, but I saw nothing. At last I raised my head and looked about me. Then on the hangings over another of the four stands, over the one opposite to that into which I had been looking, there appeared another message, the letters melting one into another in lines of liquid light; and this told me that in the other stand I could, if I chose, gaze upon combats as memorable as the delectable dances I had been beholding.

I made no hesitation, but crossed the room and took my place before the other stand and began at once to look through the projecting eye-pieces. No sooner had I taken this position than the dots of fire darted across the depth into which I was gazing and then there came a full clear light as of a cloudless sky and I saw the walls of an ancient city. At the gates of the city there stood a young man, and toward him there ran a warrior, brandishing a spear, while the bronze of his helmet and his armor gleamed in the sunlight. And trembling seized the young man and he fled in fear; and the warrior darted after him, trusting in his swift feet. Valiant was the flier, but far mightier he who fleetingly pursued him. At last the young man took heart and made a stand against the warrior. They faced each other in fight. The warrior hurled his spear and it went over the young man's head. And the young man then hurled his spear in turn and it struck fair upon the centre of the warrior's shield. Then the young man drew his sharp sword that by his flank hung great and strong. But by some magic the warrior had recovered his spear; and as the young man came forward, he hurled it again and it drove through the neck of the young man, at the joint of his armor, and he fell in the dust. After that the sun was darkened; and in a moment more I was looking into an empty blackness.

When the next scene grew slowly into view the country I beheld was soaking in the hot sunlight of the South, and I saw a mounted knight in armor. He was old and thin and worn; and his armor was broken and pieced; and his helmet was but a barber's basin; and his steed was a pitiful skeleton. His countenance was sorrowful indeed; but there was that in his manner which would stop any man from denying his nobility. His eye was fired with a high purpose and a lofty resolve. In the distance before him were a group of windmills waving their arms in the air; and the knight urged forward his wretched horse as though to charge them. Upon an ass behind him was a fellow of the baser sort, a genial, simple follower, seemingly serving him as his squire. As the knight pricked forward his sorry steed and couched his lance, the attendant apparently appealed to him, and tried to explain, and even ventured on expostulation. But the knight gave no heed to the protests of the squire, who shook his head and dutifully followed his master. What the issue of this unequal combat was to be I could not see, for the inexorable veil of darkness fell swiftly.

Even after the stray sparks had again flitted through the blackness into which I was gazing, daylight did not return; and it was with difficulty I was able at last to make out a vague street in a mediaeval city, doubtfully outlined by the hidden moon. From a window, high above the stones, there came a faint glimmer. Under this window stood a soldier, worn with the wars, who carried himself as though glad now to be at home again. He seemed to hear approaching feet, and he withdrew into the shadow, as two others advanced. One of these was a handsome youth, with an eager face, in which spirituality and sensuality contended. The other was older, of an uncertain age, and his expression was mocking and evil; he carried some sort of musical instrument, and to this he seemed to sing while the younger man looked up at the window. The soldier came forward angrily and dashed the instrument to the ground with his sword. Then the newcomers drew also, and the elder guarded while the younger thrust. There were a few swift passes, and then the younger of the two lunged fiercely and the soldier fell back on the stones wounded to the death. Without a glance behind them the two who had withstood his onslaught withdrew, as the window above opened and a fair-haired girl leaned forth.

Then nothing was visible; until after an interval the light once more returned and I saw a sadder scene than any yet. In a hollow of the bare mountains a little knot of men in dark blue uniforms were centred about their commander, whose long locks floated from beneath his broad hat. Around this small band of no more than a score of soldiers, thousands of red Indians were raging, with exultant hate in their eyes. The bodies of dead comrades lay in narrowing circles around the thinning group of blue coats. The red men were picking off their few surviving foes, one by one; and the white men could do nothing, for their cartridges were all gone. They stood at bay, valiant and defiant, despite their many wounds; but the line of their implacable foemen was drawn tighter and tighter about them, and one after another they fell forward dying or dead, until at last only the long-haired commander was left, sore wounded but unconquered in spirit.

When this picture of brave men facing death fearlessly was at last dissolved into darkness like the others that had gone before, I had an inward monition that it was the last that would be shown to me; and so it was, for although I kept my place at the stand for two or three minutes more, no warning sparks dispersed the opaque depth.

When I raised my head from the eye-pieces, I became conscious that I was not alone. Almost in the centre of the circular hall stood a middle-aged man of distinguished appearance, whose eyes were fixed upon me. I wondered who he was, and whence he had come, and how he had entered, and what it might be that he wished with me. I caught a glimpse of a smile that lurked vaguely on his lips. Neither this smile nor the expression of his eyes were forbidding, though both were uncanny and inexplicable. He seemed to be conscious of a remoteness which would render futile any effort of his toward friendliness.

How long we stood thus staring the one at the other I do not know. My heart beat heavily and my tongue refused to move when at last I tried to break the silence.

Then he spoke, and his voice was low and strong and sweet.

"You are welcome," he began, and I noted that the accent was slightly foreign, Italian perhaps, or it might be French. "I am glad always to show the visions I have under my control to those who will appreciate them."

I tried to stammer forth a few words of thanks and of praise for what I had seen.

"Did you recognize the strange scenes shown to you by these two instruments?" he asked, after bowing gently in acknowledgment of my awkward compliments.

Then I plucked up courage and made bold to express to him the surprise I had felt, not only at the marvellous vividness with which the actions had been repeated before my eyes, like life itself in form and in color and in motion, but also at the startling fact that some of the things I had been shown were true and some were false. Some of them had happened actually to real men and women of flesh and blood, while others were but bits of the vain imagining of those who tell tales as an art and as a means of livelihood.

I expressed myself as best I could, clumsily, no doubt; but he listened patiently and with the smile of toleration on his lips.

11

"Yes," he answered, "I understand your surprise that the facts and the fictions are mingled together in these visions of mine as though there was little to choose between them. You are not the first to wonder or to express that wonder; and the rest of them were young like you. When you are as old as I am—when you have lived as long as I—when you have seen as much of life as I—then you will know, as I know, that fact is often inferior to fiction, and that it is often also one and the same thing; for is not what might have been quite as true as what actually was?"

I did not know what to say in answer to this, and so I said nothing.

"What would you say to me," he went on, and now it seemed to me that his smile suggested rather pitying condescension than kindly toleration, "what would you say to me, if I were to tell you that I myself have seen all the many visions unrolled before you in these instruments? What would you say, if I declared that I had gazed on the dances of Salome and of little Pearl? That I had beheld the combat of Achilles and Hector and the unequal duel of Faust and Valentine?"

"You are not Time himself?" I asked in amaze.

He laughed lightly and without bitterness or mockery.

"No," he answered, promptly, "I am not Time himself. And why should you think so? Have I a scythe? Have I an hour-glass? Have I a forelock? Do I look so very old then?"

I examined him more carefully to answer this last question, and the more I scrutinized him the more difficult I found it to declare his age. At first I had thought him to be forty, perhaps, or of a certainty less than fifty. But now, though his hair was black, though his eye was bright, though his step was firm, though his gestures were free and sweeping, I had my doubts; and I thought I could perceive one after another many impalpable signs of extreme old age.

Then, all at once, he grew restive under my fixed gaze.

"But it is not about me that we need to waste time now," he said, impatiently. "You have seen what two of my instruments contain; would you like now to examine the contents of the other two?"

I answered in the affirmative.

"The two you have looked into are gratuitous," he continued. "For what you beheld in them there is no charge. But a sight of the visions in the other two or in either one of them must be paid for. So far, you are welcome as my guest; but if you wish to see any more you must pay the price."

I asked what the charge was, as I thrust my hand into my pocket to be certain that I had my purse with me.

He saw my gesture and he smiled once more.

"The visions I can set before you in those two instruments you have not yet looked into are visions of your own life," he said. "In that stand there," and he indicated one behind my back, "you can see four of the most important episodes of your past."

I withdrew my hand from my pocket. "I thank you," I said, "but I know my own past and I have no wish to see it again, however cheap the spectacle."

"Then you will be more interested in the fourth of my instruments," he said, as he waved his thin delicate hand toward the stand which stood in front of me. "In this you can see your future!"

I made an involuntary step forward; and then, at a second thought, I shrank back again.

"The price of this is not high," he continued, "and it is not payable in money."

"How then should I buy it?" I asked, doubtingly.

"In life!" he answered, gravely. "The vision of life must be paid for in life itself. For every ten years of the future which I may unroll before you here, you must assign me a year of your life—twelve months—to do with as I will."

Strange as it seems to me now I did not doubt that he could do as he declared. I hesitated and then fixed my resolve.

2. Thomas A. Edison's "Black Maria" studio, West Orange, New Jersey. Fighting cocks and Sandow's muscles were filmed here for showing in the Kinetoscope, a peep-show invention which could be watched by only one person at a time.

"Thank you," I said, and I saw that he was awaiting my decision eagerly. "Thank you again, for what I have already seen and for what you proffer me. But my past I have lived once and there is no need to turn over again the leaves of that dead record. And the future I must face as best I may, the more bravely, I think, that I do not know what it holds in store for me."

"The price is low," he urged.

"It must be lower still," I answered, "it might be nothing at all; and I should still decline. I cannot afford to be impatient now and to borrow knowledge of the future. I shall know all in good time."

He seemed not a little disappointed as I said this.

Then he made a final appeal, "Would you not wish to know even the manner of your end?"

"No," I answered. "That is no temptation to me, for whatever it may be I must find fortitude to undergo it somehow, whether I am to pass away in my sleep in my bed, or whether I shall have to withstand the chances of battle and murder and sudden death."

"That is your last word?" he inquired.

"I thank you again for what I have seen," I responded, bowing again; "but my decision is final."

"Then I will detain you no longer," he said, haughtily, and he walked toward the circling curtains and swept two of them aside. They draped themselves back and I saw before me an opening like that through which I had entered.

I followed him and the curtains dropped behind me as I passed into the insufficiently illuminated passage beyond. I thought that the mysterious being with whom I had been conversing had preceded me, but before I had gone twenty paces I found that I was alone. I pushed ahead, and my path twisted and turned on itself and rose and fell irregularly like that by means of which I had made my way into the unknown edifice. At last I picked my steps down winding stairs and at the foot I saw the outline of a door. I pushed it back and I found myself in the open air.

I was in a broad street, and over my head an electric light suddenly flared out and whitewashed the pavement at my feet. At the corner a train of the elevated railroad rushed by with a clattering roar and a trailing plume of white steam. Then a cable-car clanged past with incessant bangs upon its gong. Thus it was that I came back to the world of actuality.

I turned to get my bearings that I might find my way home again. I was standing almost in front of a shop the windows of which were filled with framed engravings.

One of these caught my eye, and I confess that I was surprised. It was a portrait of a man—it was the portrait of a man with whom I had been talking.

I went close to the window that I might see it better. The electric light emphasized the lines of the high-bred face, with its sombre searching eyes and the air of old-world breeding. There could be no doubt whatever, that the original of this portrait was the man from whom I had just parted. By the costume I knew that the original had lived in the last century; and the legend beneath the head, engraved in a flowing script, asserted this to be a likeness of Monsieur le Comte de Cagliostro.

Visiting the Edison Studio 1896

Excerpts from "The Wizard at his Work—A West Bloomfield Girl Visits Edison and Sees His Laboratory," Clara A. Shepard, *The Ontario County Times*, Canandaigua, New York, June 10, 1896, p. 3.

Just at the foot of Orange Mountain and opposite one of the side entrances to Llewellyn Park, where he has his beautiful home, is a group of buildings, secured by locked gates, interesting as being the birthplace of so many of our newest and most wonderful inventions—the electrical laboratory of Thomas Edison. By a courtesy and marked kindness on the part of the great inventor, permission was accorded us to take our class in physics through the laboratory and inspect the electrical apparatus.

We were a party of eighteen who rang the bell before the high gate one Wednesday afternoon and entered the usually forbidden precincts in an awed silence. We were conducted first to the library. . . .

The warehouse was first in our way, and it is almost impossible to tell what was not there. . . .

Beyond the store room we came upon the dynamos, which generate the power throughout the building.

An adjoining building is the studio where the photographs are taken for the Kinetoscope. The structure is arranged on wheels so that it can travel about in the well-worn circular track, and thus have the sunlight at any hour of the day. Here "Buffalo Bill's" cowboys and broncos have not *sat*, but performed for their portraits, which we so often see in the Kinetoscope when we "drop a nickel in the slot." Many of the prize fighters and noted horsemen have visited Mr. Edison here and their performances have been perpetuated in this invention which seemed most wonderful until he surpassed it by the more recent Vitascope, in which the figures are life-size. Mr. Edison exhibited this new wonder some days ago to a few favored friends, and last week the first public exhibition was made at Koster & Bial's Music Hall, in New York. . . .

COMMENTARY

Since 1895, a race to achieve screen projection had been under way in at least four countries: England, France, Germany and the United States. That year, Latham's Eidoloscope played a week's run beginning Aug. 26, at the Olympic, a Chicago variety theater. This antedates the earliest known commercial public projections in Europe.

Because he was experiencing difficulty perfecting a projector, Edison arranged to exhibit, as his own invention, the Vitascope, a device actually constructed by the American inventor, Thomas Armat. This was shown at Koster and Bial's Music Hall, New York, on April 23, 1896. The films were tinted by hand, but the Vitascope which projected them was hardly in league with Roentgen rays.

The "similar exhibition" which had set London and Paris agog was the Cinématographe of Louis and Auguste Lumière. This opened a New York engagement on June 29, 1896, with a program which included two of the most famous of the brief early Lumière films: THE SPRINKLER SPRINKLED and THE ARRIVAL OF THE MAIL TRAIN.

The Lumière brothers had been spurred on to the invention of their Cinématographe, a combination camera-printer-projector, by the display of the Edison Kinetoscope in France, where, as well as in England, it enjoyed a short vogue.

The Illustrated American notes the "startling suddenness" with which the Lumière views follow each other, as if popular belief had it that they had to be summoned and "set," as for a stage performance. Even this early, the feeling persists that nature is a trickier subject than people: the Rochester Post-Express considers the shrubbery waving in the breeze perhaps more remarkable than the family at breakfast al fresco, and sixteen years later, a New York audience unused to films was to break into applause at every outdoor scene in a screen version of THE PRISONER OF ZENDA (1913).

1896   "EDISON'S VITASCOPE"

From The New York Dramatic Mirror, Vol. 35, No. 904, April 25, 1896, p. 20.

The Vitascope, on which Thomas A. Edison has been working for years, and which he   15 has at last perfected, will be exhibited at Koster and Bial's, beginning some time during the present week. It is a combination of the most important principles of the Kinetoscope and the Roentgen rays, by which large figures are thrown upon a screen. The figures move as in actual life, and every color and change of expression is shown. London and Paris are going wild over a similar exhibition, the rights to which have been secured by F. F. Proctor.

"EDISON'S VITASCOPE"   1896

From *The New York Dramatic Mirror*, Vol. 35, No. 905, May 2, 1896, p. 19.

The latest invention of Wizard Edison, which he calls the Vitascope, was placed on exhibition for the first time, at Koster and Bial's on Thursday evening last *[April 23]*.

The exhibition was a success in every way, and the large audience testified its approval of the novelty by the heartiest kind of applause.

The Vitascope is nothing more or less than an enlarged Kinetoscope. Those who are familiar with the workings of the Kinetoscope will understand what the Vitascope is, when it is explained that the pictures are thrown upon a screen, and that the figures move as they do in the Kinetoscope. They appear with all the colors of the original, too, which adds greatly to the effect.

The first picture shown was the Leigh Sisters in their umbrella dance. The effect was the same as if the girls were there on the stage; all of their smiles and kicks and bows were seen. The second picture represented the breaking of waves on the seashore. Wave after wave came tumbling on the sand, and as they struck, broke into tiny floods just like the real thing. Some of the people in the front rows seemed to be afraid they were going to get wet, and looked about to see where they could run to, in case the waves came too close. The third picture showed a burlesque boxing match between Walton and Mayon, the long and short comedians. Then followed in quick succession a scene from A MILK WHITE FLAG, in which a couple of dozen people appeared; a serpentine dance with all the colored calcium effects, and an amusing picture showing an argument between John Bull and Uncle Sam.

The Vitascope is a big success, and Mr. Edison is to be congratulated for his splendid contribution to the people's pleasure.

"THE CINEMATOGRAPHE AT KEITH'S"   1896

Excerpt from "The Cinématographe at Keith's," *The New York Dramatic Mirror*, Vol. 36, No. 914, July 4, 1896, p. 17.

The Lumière Cinématographe which is the feature of the bill at Keith's Union Square Theatre this week, was exhibited at a special morning matinee for the press on Saturday *[June 28]*.

A large number of newspaper men gathered, and watched the pictures as they were thrown upon a screen. Some of them were so life-like that the blasé scribes were moved to applaud.

The Cinématographe is worked in the same way as the Vitascope and the Eidoloscope, but the pictures are clearer and there is less vibration, so that the pictures are not so trying to the eyes as those produced by other machines.

The first view was A DIP IN THE SEA, and showed several little boys running along a plank on stilts, and diving into the waves, which dashed upon the shore in the most natural manner. The second picture showed a lawn with a gardener using a hose to sprinkle it. A bad boy steps on the hose, causing the water to squirt into the gardener's face. He drops the hose, runs after the boy, and gives him a sound thrashing.

A street scene in London was very realistic, and THE CHARGE OF THE SEVENTH FRENCH CUIRASSIERS was very inspiring.

The best picture was THE ARRIVAL OF THE MAIL TRAIN. The train came into the station, passengers alighted, met their friends and walked about, and all the bustle incident to affairs of this kind was shown to perfection. . . .

1896   "KEITH'S UNION SQUARE"

Excerpt from "Keith's Union Square," *The New York Dramatic Mirror,* Vol. 36, No. 915, July 11, 1896, p. 17.

Lumière's Cinématographe created a decided sensation here last week [at Keith's Union Square Theatre]. It was fully described in last week's *Mirror,* and it is only necessary to add that the audiences were very enthusiastic over the new discovery. The depot picture with its stirring arrival of an express train, and the charge of the French hussars were wildly applauded and each of the pictures came in for its share of approval. A new picture was shown which represented the noonhour at the factory of the Messrs. Lumière in Lyons, France. As the whistle blew, the factory doors were thrown open and men, women and children came trooping out. Several of the employees had bicycles, which they mounted outside the gate, and rode off. A carryall, which the Lumières keep to transport those who live at a distance from the factory, came dashing out in the most natural manner imaginable. A lecturer was employed to explain the pictures as they were shown, but he was hardly necessary, as the views speak for themselves, eloquently. . . .

1896   "SOME MUSIC-HALL MORALITIES"

Excerpt from "Some Music-Hall Moralities," Henry Tyrrell, *The Illustrated American,* Vol. 20, No. 335, July 11, 1896, p. 76.

. . . Edison's Vitascope and the various other "scopic" adaptations of instantaneous photography are enjoying continuous runs at half a dozen different places in New York. . . . Besides the Vitascope and the Eidoloscope, there has been imported the *Lumière Cinématographe,* which is the European version of practically the same device. The pictures shown are not only popular object-lessons in modern science, but they are charming in themselves, and for the images they evoke in the imagination. Sea-waves dash against a pier, or roll in and break languidly on the sandy beach, as in a dream; and the emotion produced upon the spectator is far more vivid than the real scene would be, because of the startling suddenness with which it is conjured up and changed, there in the theatre, by the magic wand of electricity. Street scenes, railway-trains in motion, boxing-bouts, bull-fights and military evolutions are projected in life-like animation upon the luminous screen, while the audience sit spellbound in darkness. . . .

1897   **The Cinématographe in Rochester, New York**

Excerpt from *The Post-Express,* Rochester, New York, February 6, 1897, p. 14.

The Lumière Cinématographe will begin its fifteenth consecutive week at the   17

Wonderland [Theatre] next week, continuing what was long ago the longest run ever made by any one attraction in this city. People go to see it again and again, for even the familiar views reveal some new feature with each successive exhibition. Take, for example, BABY'S BREAKFAST, shown last week and this. It represents Papa and Mamma fondly feeding the junior member of the household. So intent is the spectator usually in watching the proceedings of the happy trio at table that he fails to notice the pretty background of trees and shrubbery, whose waving branches indicate that a stiff breeze is blowing. So it is in each of the pictures shown; they are full of interesting little details that come out one by one when the same views are seen several times. . . .

Running a Film Backward   1897

Excerpt from *The Post-Express,* Rochester, New York, February 20, 1897, p. 14.

There will be plenty of fun at [the] Wonderland [Theatre in Rochester, New York] next week. In one of the cinematographic views to be shown the machine will be run backward. The scene selected for this curious experiment is the one representing the crossing of the Saône River by the mounted French dragoons. After the troopers reach the other side of the stream the picture machine will be reversed and the men and horses will immediately start backward across the river, the scene closing with the horses backing up the steep bank down which they had plunged but a few moments before. Whatever else it may prove the experiment will at least be a curious novelty and one which everyone who has seen the Cinématographe will be desirous to witness. . . .

COMMENTARY

The Biograph, another American projector, differed from the Vitascope and the Cinématographe in that, among other things, it used film which was considerably larger. It was demonstrated publicly in New York on October 12, 1896, having made its debut in Pittsburgh about a month earlier.

From the start, "improvements" were the order of the day: the Lumière mail train had been seen arriving at a discreet diagonal across the screen; now the Biograph Empire State Express seemed to come straight out at the audience. Friends and casual passers-by had been commandeered as actors for the Lumière films, whereas Biograph presented the great Joseph Jefferson himself in scenes from his greatest role, Rip Van Winkle.

The film taken from the front of a moving train in Conway, North Wales, illustrates an early use of the mounted camera. This particular type of view, with the camera travelling along like a god sweeping low over the earth, was sometimes called a "phantom ride." In the press-agent blurb describing it, we already find exactly the kind of commentary which more than sixty years later could still be heard accompanying a scenic film.

As the American Biograph Company advertised at the end of 1900: "Our Films Are Seven Times the Size of Others, We Show Twice as Many Pictures Per Second, and Our Pictures on the Canvas are LARGER, BRIGHTER, STEADIER and More INTERESTING Than Others. . . . We Have a Stock of Over Three Thousand Subjects and They are Coming all the Time from Europe, Asia, Africa and America. . . ." (7)

During the Gerty MacDowell episode in *Ulysses,* after Bloom discovers Gerty is lame, James Joyce mentions Biograph Mutoscope pictures (their own brand of peep-show device): WILLIE'S HAT, a Biograph subject which dated from 1897, but was considered too risqué for the regular catalogue and therefore was carried only on their special "Club" list.

3. *The Lumière Cinématographe, on display here in a modern setting, in front of a poster for their THE SPRINKLER SPRINKLED. Paris and London were reported "going wild" over the Lumière screenings, and a little later, New York was very impressed.*

"THE AMERICAN BIOGRAPH" **1896**

From *The Illustrated American,* Vol. 20, No. 355, Nov. 28, 1896, p. 735.

Koster and Bial's Music Hall, in West Thirty-fourth street, New York, has in its day offered many attractions to an appreciative public. One of its latest novelties is "The American Biograph," a recent invention by Herman Casler of Canastota, New York. (7a)

Upon the same general principles of the Kinetoscope, Mr. Casler's clever machine has, nevertheless, attractions of its own that give it great popularity. When this part of the performance takes place, the house is darkened, and, like the old-fashioned magic-lantern, the picture is projected upon a screen. But instead of a dull, lifeless scene, there is shown the actual movement of life, realistic to a degree positively startling.

The scheme is, of course, successive photographs of action, following one another with such rapidity as to deceive the eye and make the motion seem continuous. There was a revolving toy, with jumping figures, in vogue some years ago, that gave this effect.

In the Biograph, the inventor has accomplished the feat of passing from 40 to 100 photographs per second before the eye. To realize the rapidity of this motion, try and see how far you can count in a second. To get these pictures, there must be a camera with an arrangement to take photographs at the same ratio. Between each negative there must be a pause, infinitesimal, but still long enough to prevent the whole work being a mere blur.

Taking each plate [frame] as at least two inches wide, there are, in a second, 80 inches of film—for negatives are all taken on a gelatine film—and consequently, in half a minute, the usual duration of the view, 2,400 inches, or 200 feet, of film must be exposed and put out of the way.

Just how this is accomplished is the secret of the American Mutoscope Company, who control the patent. But the camera that is used in the work resembles more than anything else a cedar clothes-chest some five feet long and two feet wide, the only photographic evidence being a suggestive lens poking out of one end. Its weight is about 300 pounds.

The development and printing of this film of 3,000 to 5,000 pictures is only less remarkable than the invention itself. It is done automatically, of course. One spoiled plate [frame] would ruin the entire lot, and to take the series is a matter of much expense. A most ingenious system of cylinders is employed to bring out the results. Positives are made, also automatically, from these negatives.

The film prepared, it is more or less of a simple affair to pass it by electricity before the lantern-lens, whence the pictures are projected on the big screen to delight an appreciative audience. Among the astonishing scenes are: The Empire State Express—one can see the train in the distance coming straight toward the spectator, a wonderfully realistic sight; Major McKinley at home; a fire-engine passing Herald Square, and Joseph Jefferson as Rip Van Winkle. As an interesting spectacle the Biograph is remarkable; as a recorder of history its value cannot be overestimated.

The "Greatest" Biograph Ever **1898**

Excerpt from *The Post-Express,* Rochester, New York, October 1, 1898, p. 4.

. . . Manager Moore [of the Cook Opera House, Rochester, New York] has secured the greatest Biograph picture ever taken. It is a panoramic view of Conway, England, taken from the front of an express train. The film is 750 feet long and is the longest film in existence. . . .

[This week's views will include:]

1. CONWAY, ENGLAND—Panoramic view, taken from the front of an express train, showing tubular bridge, castle built by King Edward I and station. This is the most celebrated picture ever taken on the Biograph. The film is 750 feet in length. . . .

1898   **and "the most perfect"**

Excerpt from *The Post-Express,* Rochester, New York, October 4, 1898, p. 9.

CONWAY is the special attraction at the Cook Opera House this week. It is the most perfect Biograph ever exhibited. Thirty-seven miles southwest from Liverpool in Carnarvonshire, North Wales, near the mouth of the Conway River, lies the ancient and picturesque town of Conway, or Aberconway. There is the beautiful village nestling between the rugged hills, and there are the walls and fortress and castle, with the beautiful cylindrical towers, as they were erected by Edward I, in 1284. For three minutes the spectator is permitted to view this panorama, and all is so real that he feels that he is sitting on an observation car pushed by an engine, at the rate of thirty or forty miles an hour, and, with constantly increasing delight, drinking in, with wide open eyes, one of the most fascinating scenes in the world; nature and art being harmoniously blended. . . .

4. Georges Méliès: *A TRIP TO THE MOON* (1902) — Scene 1: Excitement at the Astronomic Club. This celebrated French film derives from both Jules Verne and H.G. Wells, and proved so popular that it was frequently seen in pirated copies.

CHAPTER 2

Georges Méliès and Edwin S. Porter

COMMENTARY

Two men whose example hastened production of the story film, as opposed to slight screen tales of tiny incidents, or simple reports on news of the day, were Georges Méliès, in Paris, and Edwin S. Porter, in New York.

Méliès (1861-1938), magician and theatrical producer, was present at the Grand Café des Capucines in Paris when the Lumière Cinématographe began its first series of public screenings. He obtained a projector from London, converted it into a camera and began producing films in 1896. Although he was capable of reconstructing his own versions of the destruction of the "Maine," or the events of the Dreyfus affair, he found his real specialty in trick films, and spectacles which resemble filmed theater. He was skillful at multiple exposures, at dissolves, and at halting the camera so that an actor could disappear, change sex, or suddenly be transformed into some unrelated object, but unfortunately the brilliant and unrelieved rain of tricks at times becomes tedious.

The grand list of Méliès spectacles, with costumes and sets meticulously copied from his own designs, began to unroll around the turn of the century: a CINDERELLA in 20 scenes (1899), JOAN OF ARC (1900), RED RIDING HOOD (1901), BLUE BEARD (1901), ROBINSON CRUSOE (1902), FAIRYLAND (1903), THE DAMNATION OF FAUST (1903, for the Berlioz Centenary), FAUST AND MARGUERITE (1904) and AN IMPOSSIBLE VOYAGE (1904).

His best-known work is A TRIP TO THE MOON (1902). It is based partly on Jules Verne's science-fiction novel, *From the Earth to the Moon* (1865), but it also derives from H. G. Wells' *The First Men in the Moon,* another piece of fantasy-fiction which in 1900-1901 ran serially in *The Cosmopolitan Magazine,* with some illustrations that may well have given Méliès a few ideas for his film.

A TRIP TO THE MOON, and apparently almost all the Méliès films, both major and minor, were shown in the United States, but since Méliès did not begin to take out American copyrights until 1903, he was one of the foremost victims of the film "dupers."

Explaining just such a situation, an early film catalogue comments: "In the moving picture business a "dupe" is a duplicated film; that is, one manufacturer copies a film made by another, saves the expense of posing the original, and offers it to the public as his own.

"The method of making a duplicate, or 'dupe,' is as follows: the manufacturer buys a film which is not copyrighted, usually made in Europe, and photographs it, the result being a 'dupe' negative. Film positives are printed from this negative, and offered for sale as originals. The copyist saves the heavy expense of making an original negative, as well as the necessity of invention.

23

"Without going into the question of morals involved, the fact which concerns the exhibitor most is the quality of the 'dupe.' The copy is never as good as the original and in many cases it is very poor. A 'dupe' has lost all the delicate photographic tone of the original; the finer shadows are missing, the whites and blacks are intensified, producing a blotchy effect which makes it impossible to project a view with maximum definition upon the curtain. The best lenses are of no value in projecting 'dupes,' the results being the same as when using a cheap lens." (8)

A TRIP TO THE MOON appears in the Philadelphia catalogue of the American producer Sigmund Lubin, for January, 1903, under the title: A TRIP TO MARS although, curiously, Mars is not even mentioned in the very full synopsis reprinted here. The titles of the scenes are given from a description in another catalogue.

An earlier Méliès film, THE FOUR TROUBLESOME HEADS (1898), appears in the same Lubin catalogue as FOUR HEADS ARE BETTER THAN ONE.

FOUR HEADS ARE BETTER THAN ONE   **FILM 1898**

From *Complete Catalogue, Lubin's Films,* S. Lubin, Philadelphia, Pa., January, 1903, p. 25. Code for ordering: *Unclose.* About 65 feet.

Here is a film that will keep you guessing. A man is seen to lift his head from off his shoulders and places it on the table by his side. He does this three times, and seating himself on a stool with a banjo in his hands proceeds to sing and play; the three heads, all counterparts of the one on his shoulders, accompanying him. The heads annoy him so that he cannot proceed, and using the instrument as a club he smashes two of them to pieces and throws his own away. He is now left without a head. Taking one from the table which he had allowed to remain he tosses it in the air and it lands in the proper place, when he bows to the audience and vanishes. Wonderful!

A TRIP TO THE MOON   **FILM 1902**

From "Feature Films: Legendary—A TRIP TO THE MOON," *Complete Illustrated Catalogue of Moving Picture Machines, Stereopticons, Slides, Films,* Kleine Optical Company, Chicago, Ill., November, 1905, pp. 256-257.
Length 845 feet. Code *Foi.* Price $150.00

The original of this film was made in Paris, and proved so successful that it has been extensively copied in America. The length and price given cover an original print, which will be imported on order; time required about four weeks, cash in full in advance. An American copy, 800 feet in length, costs $96.

An extraordinary and fantastical film in thirty scenes.

> Scene 1. The Scientific Congress at the Astronomic Club.
> Scene 2. Planning the Trip. Appointing the Explorers and Servants. Farewell.
> Scene 3. The Workshops: Constructing the Projectile.
> Scene 4. The Foundries. The Chimneystacks. The Casting of the Monster Gun.
> Scene 5. The Astronomers Enter the Shell.
> Scene 6. Loading the Gun.
> Scene 7. The Monster Gun. March Past the Gunners. Fire!!! Saluting the Flag.

Scene 8. The Flight Through Space. Approaching the Moon.

Scene 9. Landed Right in the Eye!!!

Scene 10. Flight of the Shell into the Moon. Appearance of the Earth from the Moon.

Scene 11. The Plain of Craters. Volcanic Eruption.

Scene 12. The Dream (the Great Bear, Phoebus, the Twin Stars, Saturn).

Scene 13. The Snow Storm.

Scene 14. 40 Degrees Below Zero, Descending a Lunar Crater.

Scene 15. In the Interior of the Moon, The Giant Mushroom Grotto.

Scene 16. Encounter with the Selenites. Homeric Fight.

Scene 17. Prisoners!!

Scene 18. The Kingdom of the Moon. The Selenite Army.

Scene 19. The Flight.

Scene 20. Wild Pursuit.

Scene 21. The Astronomers find the Shell again. Departure from the Moon.

Scene 22. Vertical Drop into Space.

Scene 23. Splashing into the Open Sea.

Scene 24. At The Bottom of the Ocean.

Scene 25. The Rescue. Return to Port.

Scene 26. Great Fete. Triumphal March Past.

Scene 27. Crowning and Decorating the Heroes of the Trip.

Scene 28. Procession of the Marines and the Fire Brigade.

Scene 29. Unveiling of a Commemorative Statue by the Mayor and Council.

Scene 30. Public Rejoicings.

FILM 1902   A TRIP TO MARS (A TRIP TO THE MOON)

From *Complete Catalogue, Lubin's Films,* S. Lubin, Philadelphia, Pa., January, 1903, pp. 7-9.

Code for ordering: *Unferno* 800 feet

The astronomers are assembled in a large hall embellished with instruments. The President and members of the Committee enter. Everybody takes his seat. Entrance of seven men-servants carrying the telescopes of the astronomers. The President takes his chair and explains to the members his plan of a trip to the moon. His scheme is approved of by many, while one member violently opposes same. The President after some argument throws his papers and books at his head; the protesting party finally being thrown out of the club room amidst general disorder.

Upon order being restored, the trip proposed by the President is voted by acclamation, but at the moment of leaving nobody has the courage to accompany him. At this stage five learned men make up their minds to go with him; their colleagues break out in applause, the men-servants bring travelling suits, and the six astronomers exchange their gala robes for appropriate dress for the trip.

President Barbenfouillis selects to accompany him, five colleagues Nostradamus, Alcofrisbas, Omega, Micromegas and Parafaragaramus to pay a visit to the construction workshops of the projectile destined to carry them to the moon. They enter the interior of the workshops, where smiths, mechanics, weighers, carpenters, upholsterers, etc., are working hard at the completion of the machine. Micromegas accidentally falls into a tub of nitric acid. After the termination of the inspection, a workman descends from the

25

top of the roof and informs the astronomers that if they would ascend to the roof they would witness a splendid spectacle; the casting of the gun. The astronomers hasten to a ladder and climb on to the roof, where they finally arrive. Against the horizon the chimneys are seen belching forth volumes of smoke. Suddenly a flag is hoisted by order of the President. At the signal a mass of molten steel is directed from each furnace into the model for the gun. The mold pours forth flames and vapor. This causes much rejoicing among the enthusiastic astronomers.

On the top of the roofs of the town pompous preparations have been made; the shell is in position ready to receive the travellers. These arrive, respond to the acclamations of the crowd, and enter the shell. Marines close the breech through which they have passed.

A number of gunners are now pushing the shell up an incline into the mouth of the gun (of which only the back part is visible).

In the next scene the cannon is fully visible in the distance. It is loaded, the breech is closed; everyone is anxiously waiting for the signal which starts the shell on its voyage. Arrival of marine artillery, commanded by an officer. The officer gives the signal; the gunner occupies his post, and at the word of command, the gun is fired. The crowds flock together from all parts and gaze at the shell as it disappears into space.

In the midst of the clouds the moon is visible at a distance. The shell coming closer every minute, the moon magnifies rapidly until finally it attains colossal dimensions. It gradually assumes the shape of a living, grotesque face smiling sanctimoniously.

Suddenly the shell arrives with the rapidity of lightning, and pierces the eye of the moon. The face at once makes horrible grimaces, whilst enormous tears flow from the wound.

The picture changes and shows the immense lunar plains with their seas, amphitheatres and craters. The shell comes down with a crash. The astronomers get out, and are delighted at the landscape which is new to them, whilst against the horizon the earth is rising slowly into space, illuminating the picture with a fantastic light.

The astronomers inspecting the strange country see craters everywhere. One of them suggests descending a crater into the interior, but just as they are about to carry out their intention, an eruption takes place, the unfortunate men being violently thrown in all directions.

The astronomers show signs of fatigue after the rough trip which they have just had. They stretch themselves out on the ground and go to sleep. In their dreams they see passing in space, comets, meteors, etc.—seven gigantic stars, representing the great bear, appear slowly, and out of the stars come faces of women who seem annoyed at the presence of these intruders in the moon. Then the stars disappear in space and are replaced by a lovely vision of Phoebus on the crescent, of Saturn in his globe surrounded by a ring, and of charming young girls holding up a star. They all discuss the arrival of the terrestials in the moon and decide to punish them in an exemplary manner.

By order of Phoebus, snow is falling from all quarters, covering the ground with its white coat; the astronomers are comically agitated under the covers with which they have wrapped themselves in order to sleep.

The cold becomes terrible. The unfortunate voyagers wake up half frozen, and decide without hesitation and in spite of the danger, to descend into the interior of a great crater, in which they disappear one by one, whilst the snow storm is still raging.

The astronomers arrive in the interior of a most curious grotto filled with enormous mushrooms of every kind. One of them opens his umbrella in order to compare its size with a mushroom, but the umbrella suddenly takes root and transforming itself into a mushroom starts growing gradually, attaining gigantic proportions.

The astronomers suddenly notice strange beings coming out from underneath the mushrooms and approaching them, while making singular contortions. These are the Selinites or inhabitants of the moon. These fantastical beings rush on an astronomer,

26

5. Edwin S. Porter: *THE GAY SHOE CLERK* (1903) — *The close-up: The clerk gets nervous when his customer draws up her skirt. The adjective of the title is applied in its ancient sense, meaning the clerk is a reckless young whippersnapper.*

who defends himself, and with a stroke of his umbrella he knocks a Selinite down, who bursts into a thousand pieces. A second suffers the same fate, but the Selinites are arriving in numbers. The terrified astronomers, to save themselves, take flight, with the Selinites in pursuit.

Succumbing to numbers, the astronomers are captured, bound and taken to the palace of the King of the Selinites.

On a splendid throne, surrounded by living stars, the Selinite King is seated. He commands that the inhabitants of the earth, who have dared penetrate into his state, be fetched, and suggests sacrificing them before the united Selinite army. The astronomers are making superhuman efforts to free themselves of their impediments. President Barbenfouillis makes a dash for the King of the Selinites, and lifting him like a feather, throws him violently on the ground. The unfortunate King burst like a bomb-shell. The astronomers run away in the midst of the general disorder. The Selinite army is pursuing them.

The astronomers run at full speed, turning around each time they are pressed too closely, and reducing the fragile beings to dust, who continue to chase, but, single handed, are not capable of attack as all their force lies in their number.

The still increasing number of Selinites obliges the astronomers to take desperately to flight again, and as they pass through fantastical, picturesque landscapes, still pursued by the Selinites, amongst them they institute a regular massacre.

At last the astronomers have found their shell and quickly shut themselves in the interior; thanks to the advance they have succeeded in gaining over their adversaries. Only one, the President, has been left behind. He arrives, closely pressed by two Selinites. He causes the first to burst by striking him with his hands and kicking the other violently with his feet, he despatches him into space, where he also bursts, then he rushes to the rope which hangs from the point of the shell balanced on the edge of the moon, and letting himself slide down the rope, he gives it an impetus which causes the shell to precipitate itself into space. A Selinite who at this moment clings to the shell in order to hold it back is being drawn with it, and hanging on to the projectile, accompanies it in its drop.

The shell falls with sickening rapidity. Barbenfouillis clinging to the rope underneath tries to enter the projectile, whilst the unfortunate Selinite, half mad, clings desperately to the shell to save himself from falling off.

The Sea appears. The waves break into foam, the shell is attaining a white heat by the friction with the air in its maddening drop and dashes right into the sea, causing enormous columns of water to gush up. The sea closes over the shell again, and a thick vapor is rising, caused by the scorching hot metal dropping into the water.

We continue following the course of the shell into the depths of the ocean, where amongst the debris of ships, marine plants, the medusae, corals and fishes of all kinds, the projectile reaches land at last. Enormous bubbles of air escape from the bottom of the sea and reach the surface. The shell balances, and, thanks to the hermetically sealed air in its interior, is rising slowly to the surface to the bewilderment of the fishes.

The shell is being picked up by a mail steamer, which, taking it in tow, returns to port. The Selinite is still seen clinging to the shell.

In the market place of the town the authorities are assembled, the crowd awaiting the appearance of the astronomers. The procession arrives; the municipal band advances, followed by marines drawing the decorated shell. Finally the astronomers arrive amidst a general ovation.

The Mayor congratulates the astronomers on their happy return. Crowning them, he confers upon them the Order of the Moon.

The march past of the fire brigade and marines takes place. On the square appears the commemorative statue of the trip, representing President Barbenfouillis vanquishing the moon, with this device: "Labor Omnia Vincit."

The marines, the astronomers, the crowd, the Mayor and councillors join in chorus dancing around the statue to the President.

COMMENTARY

When Edwin S. Porter (1870-1941) filmed THE GREAT TRAIN ROBBERY in 1903, he gave the world its most famous motion picture before D. W. Griffith's THE BIRTH OF A NATION (1915).

Through a succession of jobs in his boyhood, Porter had learned about selling newspapers, telegraphy, plumbing, tailoring, theater management, and the circus, before he enlisted in the Navy. He left the Navy in the spring of 1896, and then "assisted" at the historic occasion of the first Vitascope screenings in New York. From the following fall until the summer of 1897, Porter travelled with a projector through the West Indies and South America, and upon his return to the States, began to manufacture cameras and projectors himself. After his business was wiped out by a fire in 1900, the Edison Company engaged him to design and build projectors, but shortly afterward, because a combination camerman and producer was needed, Porter was put in charge of their skylight studio at 41 East Twenty-first Street. Eventually, late in 1909, he moved on to several other companies, but for over nine years at the Edison Company, he "made all the pictures, built and designed cameras, wrote many scenarios, staged all the productions and operated the camera. He did, in fact, produce the pictures." (9)

His THE LIFE OF AN AMERICAN FIREMAN (1903) is somewhat crude, but is nevertheless important as an example of the manner in which Porter tried to edit his material into a coherent narrative. He may have seen the 1901 film FIRE!!! by the British director James Williamson; in any case, the Edison Supplement description of the film, reprinted here, indicates that Porter was striving for refinements that certainly are not apparent in the film: perhaps this text was intended for adaptation as a running commentary while the film was being shown—a favorite device of the early period.

The "Close View of a New York Fire Alarm Box," which comprises all of Scene 2, has occasioned much comment, but while it deserves points for having occurred so early in American films, it is otherwise a pretty impersonal affair, with an anonymous "hand of destiny" flashing about its business of turning in an alarm.

The Supplement synopsis of the film indicates dissolves between the scenes; they will not be found in all prints, but could have been supplied originally in the printing.

FILM 1903   LIFE OF AN AMERICAN FIREMAN

From *Edison Films,* Supplement 168, Edison Manufacturing Company, Orange, New Jersey, February, 1903, pp. 2-3.
Code Word for ordering *Upblowing.* Length 425 feet. Class A. $63.75

In giving this description to the public, we unhesitatingly claim for it the strongest motion picture attraction ever attempted in this length of film. It will be difficult for the exhibitor to conceive the amount of work involved and the number of rehearsals necessary to turn out a film of this kind. We were compelled to enlist the services of the fire departments of four different cities, New York, Newark, Orange, and East Orange, N.J., and about 300 firemen appear in the various scenes of this film.

From the first conception of this wonderful series of pictures it has been our aim to portray LIFE OF AN AMERICAN FIREMAN without exaggeration, at the same time embodying the dramatic situations and spectacular effects which so greatly enhance a motion picture performance.

The record work of the modern American fire department is known throughout the universe, and the fame of the American fireman is echoed around the entire world. He is

29

known to be the most expert, as well as the bravest, of all fire fighters. This film faithfully and accurately depicts his thrilling and dangerous life, emphasizing the perils he subjects himself to when human life is at stake. We show the world in this film the every movement of the brave firemen and their perfectly trained horses from the moment the men leap from their beds in response to an alarm until the fire is extinguished and a woman and child are rescued after many fierce battles with flame and smoke. Below we give a description of each of the seven scenes which make up this most wonderful of all fire scenes, LIFE OF AN AMERICAN FIREMAN.

SCENE 1.—THE FIREMAN'S VISION OF AN IMPERILLED WOMAN AND CHILD. The fire chief is seated at his office desk. He has just finished reading his evening paper and has fallen asleep. The rays of an incandescent light rest upon his features with a subdued light, yet leaving his figure strongly silhouetted against the wall of his office. The fire chief is dreaming, and the vision of his dream appears in a circular portrait upon the wall. It is a mother putting her baby to bed, and the inference is that he dreams of his own wife and child. He suddenly awakes and paces the floor in a nervous state of mind, doubtless thinking of the various people who may be in danger from fire at the moment. Here we dissolve the picture to the second scene.

SCENE 2.—A CLOSE VIEW OF A NEW YORK FIRE ALARM BOX. Shows lettering and every detail in the door and apparatus for turning in an alarm. A figure then steps in front of the box, hastily opens the door and pulls the hook, thus sending the electric current which alarms hundreds of firemen and brings to the scene of the fire the wonderful apparatus of a great city's fire department. Again dissolving the picture, we show a third scene.

SCENE 3.—THE INTERIOR OF THE SLEEPING QUARTERS IN THE FIRE HOUSE. A long row of beds, each containing a fireman peacefully sleeping, is shown. Instantly upon the ringing of the alarm the firemen leap from their beds and, putting on their clothes in the record time of five seconds, a grand rush is made for a large circular opening in the floor, through the centre of which runs a brass pole. The first fireman to reach the pole seizes it and, like a flash, disappears through the opening. He is instantly followed by the remainder of the force. This in itself makes a most stirring scene. We again dissolve the scene, to the interior of the apparatus house.

SCENE 4.—INTERIOR OF THE ENGINE HOUSE. Shows horses dashing from their stalls and being hitched to the apparatus. This is perhaps the most thrilling and in all the most wonderful of the seven scenes of the series, it being absolutely the first motion picture ever made of a genuine interior hitch. As the men come down the pole described in the above scene, and land upon the floor in lightning-like rapidity, six doors in the rear of the engine house, each heading a horse-stall, burst open simultaneously and a huge fire horse, with head erect and eager for the dash to the scene of the conflagration, rushes from each opening. Going immediately to their respective harness, they are hitched in the almost unbelievable time of five seconds and are ready for their dash to the fire. The men hastily scamper upon the trucks and hose carts and one by one the fire machines leave the house, drawn by eager, prancing steeds. Here we dissolve again to the fifth scene.

SCENE 5.—THE APPARATUS LEAVING THE ENGINE HOUSE. We show a fine exterior view of engine house, the great doors swinging open, and the apparatus coming out. This is a most imposing scene. The great horses leap to their work, the men adjust their fire hats and coats, and smoke begins pouring from the engines as they pass our camera. Here we dissolve and show the sixth scene.

SCENE 6.—OFF TO THE FIRE. In this scene we present the best fire run ever shown. Almost the entire fire department of the large city of Newark, N.J., was placed at our disposal and we show countless pieces of apparatus, engines, hook-and-ladders, hose towers, hose carriages, etc., rushing down a broad street at top speed, the horses

6. Edwin S. Porter: *THE GREAT TRAIN ROBBERY* (1903)—Scene 1: *Exactly at nine o'clock, the telegraph operator—doubly covered by bandits—is forced to signal the train to stop and take on water. This famous old thriller ends with a stirring close-up.*

straining every nerve and evidently eager to make a record run. Great clouds of smoke pour from the stacks of the engines as they pass our camera, thus giving an impression of genuineness to the entire series. Dissolving again we show the seventh scene.

SCENE 7.—THE ARRIVAL AT THE FIRE. In this wonderful scene we show the entire fire department, as described above, arriving at the scene of action. An actual burning building is in the centre foreground. On the right background the fire department is seen coming at great speed. Upon the arrival of the different apparatus, the engines are ordered to their places, hose is quickly run out from the carriages, ladders adjusted to the windows and streams of water poured into the burning structure. At this crucial moment comes the great climax of the series. We dissolve to the interior of the building and show a bed chamber with a woman and child enveloped in flame and suffocating smoke. The woman rushes back and forth in the room endeavoring to escape, and in her desperation throws open the window and appeals to the crowd below. She is finally overcome by the smoke and falls upon the bed. At this moment the door is smashed in by an axe in the hands of a powerful fire hero. Rushing into the room he tears the burning draperies from the window and smashing out the entire window frame, orders his comrades to run up a ladder. Immediately the ladder appears, he seizes the prostrate form of the woman and throws it over his shoulder as if it were an infant, and quickly descends to the ground. We now dissolve to the exterior of the burning building. The frantic mother having returned to consciousness, and clad only in her night clothes, is kneeling on the ground imploring the firemen to return for her child. Volunteers are called for and the same fireman who rescued the mother quickly steps out and offers to return for the babe. He is given permission to once more enter the doomed building and without hesitation rushes up the ladder, enters the window and after a breathless wait, in which it appears he must have been overcome by smoke, he appears with the child on his arm and returns safely to the ground. The child, being released and upon seeing its mother, rushes to her and is clasped in her arms, thus making a most realistic and touching ending of the series.

COMMENTARY

1903 was Edwin S. Porter's banner year. After completing THE LIFE OF AN AMERICAN FIREMAN, presented to the public in January, he went on about his business of turning out more films, including THE GAY SHOE CLERK—short as a sneeze—which contains that perfect close-up of a young lady's leg with the hands of a clerk fluttering nervously around it.

UNCLE TOM'S CABIN, a swift and well-mounted replica of the most popular American play of the nineteenth century, followed in September. Porter, or someone, could not decide whether the moonlight race between the "Robert E. Lee," and the "Natchez" (shown in miniature) should occur as Scene 5 (before Uncle Tom rescues Eva from having fallen into the water) or as Scene 10 (after the murder of St. Clare in the barroom). Different synopses show it in different positions. As Scene 5, it implies a connection with the characters—as if they had been on the victorious boat. As Scene 10, it has no connection with the characters whatsoever. There are no close-ups, and the novelty of subtitles between scenes in place of dissolves was stressed by the advertisements.

Porter's use of the direct cut from scene to scene in THE GREAT TRAIN ROBBERY, (released in December, 1903) establishes a far better transition than he could have achieved with dissolves, and sustains the vigor of the film; except for the interminable Scene 6, where the passengers are lined up and relieved of their money and valuables, the film's movement is brisk throughout. (The passenger who tries to escape, and is shot

down, is Gilbert M. Anderson: "Broncho Billy," hero of numerous subsequent Westerns.)

The "life size picture" which concludes the film, of the bandit leader firing, head-on, might easily have been used, as you will notice from the catalogue description, "either to begin the subject or to end it." Again, they couldn't quite decide, but a close-up at the end (or a final, better look at a pivotal character) was a formula which pleased Porter. He preferred it there rather than elsewhere in the film, because he seemed to find that its change in scale was disturbing. In later years he often avoided the close-up entirely, placing "his camera at a considerable distance from his actors" so that there would be no "abnormality of size." (10)

"About Moving Picture Films" furnishes a 1904 report on the change in a public now "educated to appreciate . . . long films which tell an interesting story," and it cites THE GREAT TRAIN ROBBERY as a prime illustration of the new demand. On another page of the same publication from which this article is taken, THE GREAT TRAIN ROBBERY is referred to as "the most popular film that has ever been made."

Porter's later films for the Edison Company include a two-reel PARSIFAL (1904, based on Wagner's opera), THE EX-CONVICT (1904, "A Beautiful Pathetic Story in Eight Scenes"), THE WHITE CAPS (1905, which bears the same name as an Owen Davis melodrama and deals with "outlaws and the criminal classes in general") and THE DREAM OF A RAREBIT FIEND (1906), a virtuoso trick film about a wild, nightmare ride through the sky over New York City. THE KLEPTOMANIAC (1905) struggles to point out social injustice by the contrasting stories of a rich woman who is a kleptomaniac, but is dismissed by the court with apologies, and a poor woman, who steals out of hunger and is clapped into jail. However, the film is so crowded and confusing that its moral is lost, despite Blind Justice as the finale, and when Porter, in 1912, named what he considered to have been his significant films, he made no mention of THE EX-CONVICT, THE WHITE CAPS or THE KLEPTOMANIAC. These are the works which, among film historians, have earned him the attribute of a social conscience, but he himself was prouder of THE "TEDDY" BEARS (1907), on which he had labored "eight hours a day for a straight week" to get only ninety feet of stop-motion film. (11)

One of the actors who came to work for Porter was David Wark Griffith, presently to become director at the rival Biograph Company and, not long after, the foremost figure in the entire world of silent film.

FILM 1903   THE GAY SHOE CLERK

From *Edison Films,* Supplement No. 185, Edison Manufacturing Company, Orange, New Jersey, October Supplement, 1903, p. 20.
Code Word *Utrinde.* Length 75 feet. Class B. $9.00

Scene shows interior of shoe-store. Young lady and chaperone enter. While a fresh young clerk is trying a pair of high-heeled slippers on the young lady, the chaperone seats herself and gets interested in a paper. The scene changes to a very close view, showing only the lady's foot and the clerk's hands tying the slipper. As her dress is slightly raised, showing a shapely ankle, the clerk's hands become very nervous, making it difficult for him to tie the slipper. The picture changes back to former scene. The clerk makes rapid progress with his fair customer, and while he is in the act of kissing her the chaperone looks up from her paper, and proceeds to beat the clerk with an umbrella. He falls backward off the stool. Then she takes the young lady by the arm, and leads her from the store.

UNCLE TOM'S CABIN   **FILM 1903**

From *Edison Films,* Supplement No. 185, Edison Manufacturing Company, Orange, New Jersey, October Supplement, 1903, p. 5.
Code word *Utopical.* Length 1,100 feet. Class A. $165.00

Prologue. Scene takes place on a plantation about ten miles from the Ohio River, Kentucky. George Shelby, owner of the plantation and a large number of slaves, owing to business difficulties, is forced to sell some of his slaves to a trader named Haley. Among Shelby's slaves is a faithful old negro called Uncle Tom, to whom Haley takes a fancy, thinking he can get a large purse for him at auction in the New Orleans market. After a great deal of persuasion Haley induces Shelby to part with him. The following scenes are then shown:

> 1st. Eliza Pleads With Uncle Tom to Run Away.
> 2nd. Tavern. Phineas Outwits the Slave Traders.
> 3rd. Eliza Escapes Across the River on Floating Ice.
> 4th. Rocky Pass. Reunion of Eliza and George Harris.
> 5th. Steamboat Race Between the Robert E. Lee and Natchez.
> 6th. The Rescue of Eva.
> 7th. Welcome Home of St. Clare, Eva and Tom.
> 8th. Eva and Tom in the Garden.
> 9th. Death of Eva.
> 10th. Bar-room. St. Clare Defends Uncle Tom.
> 11th. The Auction of St. Clare's Slaves.
> 12th. Cotton Picking. Tom refuses to Flog Emaline.
> 13th. Mark Avenges the Death of St. Clare and Uncle Tom.
> 14th. Death of Uncle Tom. Tableau.

The photographic and dramatic qualities of our latest moving picture production, UNCLE TOM'S CABIN, are excellent. We offer this film as one of our best creations and one that will prove a great headline attraction. The popularity of the book and play of the same title is a positive guarantee of its success. The story has been carefully studied and every scene posed in accordance with the famous author's version.

In this film we have made a departure from the old method of dissolving one scene into another by inserting announcements with brief descriptions as they appear in succession.

Sold in one length only.

THE GREAT TRAIN ROBBERY   **FILM 1903**

From *Edison Films,* Supplement No. 200, Edison Manufacturing Company, Orange, New Jersey, January Supplement, 1904, pp. 5-7.
Sold in one length only.
Code word *Vacunaban.* Length 740 feet. Class A. Price $111.00

This sensational and highly tragic subject will certainly make a decided "hit" whenever shown. In every respect we consider it absolutely the superior of any moving picture film ever made. It has been posed and acted in faithful duplication of the genuine "Holds Ups" made famous by various outlaw bands in the far West, and only recently the East has been shocked by several crimes of the frontier order, which fact will increase the popular interest in this great *Headline Attraction.*

SCENE 1.—INTERIOR OF RAILROAD TELEGRAPH OFFICE. Two masked robbers enter and compel the operator to set the "signal block" to stop the approaching train, also making him write a fictitious order to the engineer to take water at this station, instead of at "Red Lodge," their regular watering stop. The train comes to a standstill; conductor comes to the window, and the frightened operator delivers the order while the bandits crouch out of sight, at the same time keeping their revolvers trained on him. No sooner does the conductor leave than they fall upon the operator, bind and gag him, then hastily depart to catch the moving train.

SCENE 2.—AT THE RAILROAD WATER TANK. The bandit band seen hiding behind the tank as a train stops to take water (according to false order). Just before she pulls out they stealthily board the train between the express car and the tender.

SCENE 3.—INTERIOR OF EXPRESS CAR. Messenger is busily engaged with his duties. Becoming alarmed at an unusual sound, he goes to the door, and peeping through the keyhole, discovers two men trying to break in. He starts back in a bewildered manner. Quickly recovering, his first thought is of the valuables in the strong box, which he hastily locks, and throws the key through the open side door. Pulling his revolver, he fortifies himself behind a pile of trunks, etc. In the meantime, the two robbers have succeeded in effecting an entrance. They enter cautiously. The messenger opens fire on them. A desperate pistol duel takes place, in which the messenger is killed. One of the robbers stands watch while the other tries to open the treasure box. Finding it locked, he searches the messenger for the key. Not finding it, he blows the safe up with dynamite. After securing the valuables and mail bags, they leave the car.

SCENE 4.—THE FIGHT ON THE TENDER. This thrilling scene was taken from the mail car showing the tender and interior of locomotive cab, while the train is running forty miles an hour. While some of the bandits are robbing the mail car, two others are seen climbing over the tender. One of them holds up the engineer, and the other covers the fireman. The latter secures a coal shovel and climbs up on the tender, where a desperate fight takes place with the outlaw. They struggle fiercely all over the tank, having several narrow escapes from being hurled over the side of the tender. Finally they fall, with the robber on top. He grabs a lump of coal, and strikes the fireman on the head, rendering him senseless. He then hurls the body from the swiftly moving train. The bandits then compel the engineer to bring the train to a stop.

SCENE 5.—THE TRAIN UNCOUPLED. Shows the train coming to a stop. With the robbers' pistols close to his head, the engineer leaves the locomotive, uncouples it from the train, and pulls ahead about one hundred feet.

SCENE 6.—THE EXTERIOR OF PASSENGER COACHES. The bandits compel the passengers to leave coaches with hands aloft, and line up along the tracks. One of the robbers covers them with large pistols in either hand, while the others ransack travelers' pockets. A passenger makes an attempt to escape, but is instantly shot down. After securing everything of value, the band terrorize the passengers by firing their revolvers in the air, and then make safe their escape on the locomotive.

SCENE 7.—THE ESCAPE. The desperadoes board the locomotive with their booty, command the engineer to start his machine, and disappear in the distance.

SCENE 8.—OFF TO THE MOUNTAINS. The robbers bring the engine to a stop several miles from the scene of the "Hold Up," and take to the mountains.

SCENE 9.—A BEAUTIFUL SCENE IN A VALLEY. The bandits come down the side of a hill on a run and cross a narrow stream. Mounting their horses, which were tied to nearby trees, they vanish into the wilderness.

SCENE 10.—INTERIOR OF TELEGRAPH OFFICE. The operator lies bound and gagged on the floor. After a desperate struggle, he succeeds in standing up. Leaning on the table, he telegraphs for assistance by manipulating the key with his chin, and then faints from exhaustion. His little daughter enters with his dinner pail. Discovering his condition, she cuts the ropes, and, throwing a glass of water in his face, restores him to consciousness. Arousing in a bewildered manner, he suddenly recalls his thrilling experience, and rushes forth to summon assistance.

SCENE 11.—INTERIOR OF A DANCE HALL. This typical Western dance house scene shows a large number of men and women in a lively quadrille. A "Tenderfoot" appears upon the scene. He is quickly spotted, pushed to the center of the hall, and compelled to dance a jig, while the bystanders amuse themselves by shooting dangerously close to his feet. Suddenly the door opens and the half dead telegraph operator staggers in. The crowd gather around him, while he relates what has happened. Immediately the dance breaks up in confusion. The men secure their guns and hastily leave in pursuit of the outlaws.

SCENE 12.—THE POSSE IN PURSUIT. Shows the robbers dashing down a rugged mountain at a terrible pace, followed closely by a large posse, both parties firing as they proceed. One of the desperadoes is shot and plunges head first from his horse. Staggering to his feet, he fires at his nearest pursuer, only to be shot dead.

SCENE 13.—BATTLE TO THE DEATH. The remaining three bandits, thinking they had eluded their pursuers, have dismounted from their horses. After carefully surveying their surroundings, they begin to examine the contents of the mail bags. Deeply engaged in this work, they do not perceive the approach of the posse. The pursuers, having left their horses, steal noiselessly down upon them until they are completely surrounded. A desperate battle then takes place. After a brave stand, all of the robbers and several of the posse bite the dust.

SCENE 14.—REALISM. A life size picture of Barnes, leader of the outlaw band, taking aim and firing point blank at each individual in the audience. (This effect is gained by foreshortening in making the picture.) The resulting excitement is great. This section of the scene can be used either to begin the subject or to end it, as the operator may choose.

The End.

"ABOUT MOVING PICTURE FILMS"   1904

Excerpts from "About Moving Picture Films," *Complete Illustrated Catalog of Moving Picture Films, Stereopticons, Slides, Films,* Kleine Optical Company, Chicago, Illinois, October, 1904, pp. 30-31.

. . . The exhibitor who purchases a small quantity of films, say from 300 to 500 feet, is necessarily compelled to confine himself to short subjects. But if the purchase is 1000 feet, we advise one feature film of 400 to 500 feet, the balance from 50 to 100 feet each; if 2000 feet, there should be at least one long feature film, such as THE GREAT TRAIN ROBBERY, 740 feet, or CHRISTOPHER COLUMBUS, 850 feet. These long films admit of special advertising, that is to say, special emphasis on one subject, which is more effective than equal emphasis on a number of shorter films. The public has been educated to appreciate these long films which tell an interesting story, and need few words of explanation. . . .

Films may be divided into five classes according to the subject: 1, Story; 2, Comic; 3, Mysterious; 4, Scenic; 5, Personalities. The order indicates their popularity.

Under story films we include three sub-divisions: These may be (a) Historical; (b) Dramatic; (c) Narrative. The Comic may include the mysterious. Scenic films include such subjects as railway panoramas, rivers, water falls, cities, etc. Personalities include those whose chief attraction lies in the showing of some noted personage, like President McKinley, Kaiser Wilhelm, etc. . . .

Films made from actual events are not as popular as those which are photographed from a scene prepared for the camera.

The first requisite of a perfect film is photographic excellence. No matter how exciting the action, how thrilling a climax or how interesting a bit of scenery may be, it is undesirable if the photography is poor.

The next desideratum is continuous action. There should be no lagging in the story which it tells; every foot must be an essential part, whose loss would deprive the story of some merit; there should be sequence, each part leading to the next with increasing interest, reaching its most interesting point at the climax, which should end the film. A story which can be well told in 300 feet, loses force if stretched to 500 feet, and is correspondingly weakened.

The explanation of the success of THE GREAT TRAIN ROBBERY film lies in this; it follows accurately this analysis of what a perfect film should be. In photography it is beautiful, only one scene of the fourteen being somewhat dark: that where the passengers pile out of the coaches with "hands up." In the treatment of the story it is matchless. From the first appearance of the hold-up men in the railroad telegraph office, throughout the various chapters of the story, to the final killing of the bandits, the observer finds his interest rising, reaching its highest point at the end. He sees inexorable fate bearing down upon the malefactors, pursuing them with irresistible force, until with heavy hand it strikes them down. . . .

7. *The ancestor of all chase films? Britain's A DARING DAYLIGHT BURGLARY (1903): The flight across the brook, an episode which Porter could have copied in his subsequent film, THE GREAT TRAIN ROBBERY.*

CHAPTER **3**

"This Line is a Klondike":
The Nickelodeon

COMMENTARY

Between 1905 and 1908, nickelodeons sprang up like mushrooms, and motion pictures emerged as an industry; the old vaudeville theaters were therefore soon engulfed by competition, even though they had presented films as one unit of their programs from the moment they first became generally available.

"Motion Picture Films" (1905) recapitulates the history of the film since 1896, and reports further on "the evolution of public taste," now eager for "chase" films, all of which were supposed to have been derived from the British-made DAYLIGHT BURGLARY (or DARING DAYLIGHT BURGLARY). This prototype of dramatic "chase" films was produced by the Sheffield Photo Company, imported by Edison, and first advertised here in June of 1903. As an Edison import, it could have been studied by Edwin S. Porter who in several months would be filming his own "chase film," THE GREAT TRAIN ROBBERY.

The comic "chase" films reached their height in Biograph's PERSONAL. Like THE ESCAPED LUNATIC and THE LOST CHILD (all 1904), it was directed by Wallace Mc-Cutcheon, Senior, who was the Biograph director until Griffith came along in 1908.

1905   "MOTION PICTURE FILMS"

Introduction to the film section, *Complete Illustrated Catalog of Moving Picture Machines, Stereopticons, Slides, Films,* Kleine Optical Company, Chicago, Illinois, November, 1905, pp. 206-207.

The optical principle of the moving picture machine is practically the same as that of the magic lantern, the only difference being that the pictures appear on a flexible transparent film, passing the lenses in rapid succession, in place of a glass lantern slide at rest.

The films which carry the successive pictures consist of a long transparent celluloid tape, the length of which varies from 25 feet upwards, and contains a series of photographs taken at the rate of 15 to 25 feet (11a) per second. A film 1,000 feet in length contains about 16,000 individual photographs, taken in 18 minutes. The movement of the object photographed has been recorded in such rapid succession that when the films are moved past the lenses in the projecting machine, at the rate at which they were taken, the change from one picture to another is made so rapidly that the eye cannot detect it, and it seems to present on the screen a single picture with all the movements of life.

Moving picture films represent the very highest branch of photographic art—that of bringing before the eye lifesize reproductions of life motion with all its accompanying effects of light, shade and expression.

We believe that the following list of moving picture films is the first ever issued that is comprehensive. It includes the most desirable subjects of all makes, the selections having been based entirely upon merit, without prejudice or favoritism. The principal film manufacturers are most heavily represented, while those whose product is frequently open to criticism are represented by a few subjects of undoubted value.

The list embraces practically every popular subject now in use. A number of films have been omitted because the negatives are worn and good prints cannot be made. . . .

A critic may not approve of a film which is seen upon the curtain in our dark room, when the very same subject may have met with universal success before audiences. This is the final test, after all—whether a film "brings down the house." Films are bought to please audiences, and to increase the receipts, not to soothe the man who operates the machine.

Film manufacturers issue descriptive lists of their own product only, adding possibly films made by affiliated houses. Necessarily there will creep in an occasional subject, even in the most conscientious catalogue, which ought to be excluded. The father cannot use the knife on his own child. This list contains no cripples or imbeciles.

The investigator will occasionally find the same film in several manufacturers' lists, sometimes under different titles, each claiming it to be his own. There can be but one original; the others are copies. . . . Original films only will be delivered from the following list.

It is no longer customary to make films arbitrarily 50 feet in length, as in the early days of the art. Most of the present day subjects are longer, the duration upon the curtain depending upon the action.

There are three classes of motion picture exhibitions:

First: Those that are given in the same theater, week after week, necessitating frequent changes of program, usually weekly.

Second: Others that are given occasionally before practically the same audiences, as in churches, lecture rooms, lodge rooms and the like, which also require new subjects at every exhibition.

Third: Those given by traveling exhibitors, in different places, who may use the same subjects an indefinite length of time.

Exhibitors of the first class usually rent films 600 or 1,000 feet per week, new subjects being placed on exhibition every Sunday or Monday night. Sometimes a number of theaters join to form a circuit and purchase new films in place of renting them.

Exhibitors of the second class find the purchase of films too expensive for use but once, and can now rent films at the price of 1 cent per foot for one night's use; minimum quantity, 500 feet.

Exhibitors of the third class find it most economical to purchase films outright, as they are constantly exhibiting before new audiences.

The character of the moving picture exhibitions which are given for the entertainment of the public has undergone a very material evolution since the days of the first exhibitions in 1896. At that time all moving picture films varied very little in length and were approximately from 50 to 60 feet. The machines were so constructed that the films ran endlessly upon a rack and through the moving picture mechanism, the two ends of the film having been joined, and it was possible to project a 50-foot film for any length of time by repetition.

The number of subjects that were available was small and their variety limited: "Railroad Trains," "Cavalry Charges," THE MAY IRWIN KISS, "Serpentine Dances" and other subjects of a similar nature, which ended in no particular climax, made repetition possible.

As the art of making moving pictures developed, the number of subjects that were available increased, and there was a gradual development from the picturing of a limited number of sceneries into the invention of story films. The subjects gradually increased in length, and during 1897 the use of the rack for endless films was practically discontinued. During 1898 and 1899 a film 100 feet in length was considered a comparatively long film. There was considerable resistance on the part of exhibitors to the purchase of these films, as it was considered more desirable to have a greater number of subjects rather than fewer subjects of greater lengths.

The evolution of public taste, however, forced the exhibitor to recognize the availability of longer subjects and the average length of films sold became gradually greater, until at the present time the most popular films on the market are such subjects as THE LOST CHILD, 538 feet; THE GREAT TRAIN ROBBERY, 740 feet; PERSONAL, 371 feet; THE STRIKE, 440 feet. Unless a film has exceptional merit or some particular feature that attracts attention, 700 feet may be considered a limit as to length. There are a number of notable exceptions, such as A TRIP TO THE MOON, AN IMPOSSIBLE VOYAGE, LIFE OF NAPOLEON and ROBINSON CRUSOE. The popularity of the long subjects has become most marked within recent months. Those theaters which show moving pictures continually and which make weekly changes are constantly calling for single films from 400 to 700 feet in length and refusing to accept subjects from 50 to 150 feet on the ground that the public taste prefers the elaborate story that consumes from 8 to 18 minutes in the reproduction.

There has been also a marked change in the character of the subjects which are most popular. During the earlier years of the moving picture industry fire runs, railroad trains and panoramas taken from a moving train were among the most popular. These have lost their interest for the general public, and several of the most beautiful panoramas as well as scenes of travel that have been made recently are being rejected in favor of the story film which has been posed for the purpose of animated photography. It is interesting to note the development of a certain line of subjects after the original film was made that found favor with the public. What is known among moving picture exhibitors as "chase" films originated with the DAYLIGHT BURGLARY, an English film which showed an exciting chase after a burglar. This was followed by other "chase" films of greater or less interest. After this field had been fairly well exhausted there appeared a series of comic "chase" films, including THE ESCAPED LUNATIC, PERSONAL, THE LOST CHILD and THE SUBURBANITE. Of these, PERSONAL has been the most popular, and continues in active demand at the present time.

Progress in the manufacture of motion picture machines has been as radical as the evolution of the moving picture film.

The first machines that were used for public entertainment were very elaborate and heavy affairs, making it quite a serious matter to move them about. They weighed from 400 to 600 pounds each complete; a large part of the weight being due to a heavy iron pedestal which the makers considered necessary to minimize vibration on the curtain. It was soon discovered that this vibration was due to other causes than the instability of the machine, and the heavy supports were gradually discarded. The moving picture mechanisms also became much lighter in weight, and the most popular machines of the present day do not weigh more than one-tenth of those which were in use in 1896. The mechanism which gives motion to the film has also been simplified and its efficiency increased. The efforts of the inventors have been directed toward the manufacture of an ideal machine which would eliminate all apparent vibration and flicker from the picture projected upon the curtain; the ideal motion picture would be one with the absolute steadiness and even illumination of a good lantern slide projection. While it is probably impossible to obtain this ideal result, improvements have been made in motion picture machines, as well as in the manufacture of the films, which closely approach this condition. . . .

DAYLIGHT BURGLARY   **FILM 1903**

From *Edison Films,* Supplement No. 185, Edison Manufacturing Company, Orange, New Jersey, October Supplement, 1903, p. 11.
Code word *Utilidade*. Length 265 feet. Class B. $31.80

A burglar jumps a back fence and enters the rear of a house, by prying open one of the windows. It is evident that the people of the house discovered the thief and called the police (11b), for shortly after the robber enters the window, two policemen come along on a run and enter the place after him. Scene now changes to the roof. The burglar tries to escape, but is caught by one of the officers, and a fight ensues in which the officer gets the worst of it, and is thrown to the ground. The burglar escapes to the street through another house, closely followed by the second policeman. When the latter reaches the street and sees his comrade almost dead, he calls for the ambulance. This is seen rushing to the scene. The injured man is placed on a stretcher, carried to the ambulance, and then taken to the hospital. Calling for reinforcements, the second policeman continues to run after the thief. He chases him through the fields, over streams, etc. The thief finally reaches the railroad station just as a train is pulling out. He jumps on the train, and leaves the officers, who were close behind. The telegraph service is here brought into use, and when the train stops at the next station, a squad of police are there to meet it. The burglar alights and makes a break for liberty, but is soon caught and handcuffed, after a struggle. He is then taken to the lock-up to await trial. Exciting from start to finish.

PERSONAL   **FILM 1904**

From *Catalog,* Kleine Optical Company, November, 1905, p. 238.
Biograph. Length 371 feet. Class B. Code *Faa*. Price $44.52.

This is a comedy production founded on an advertisement in the New York "Herald," in which a Frenchman states that he would like to meet a handsome American girl with a view to matrimony. The rendezvous is at Grant's Tomb. When the hour for the appointment approaches and he sees the great crowd of girls waiting for him, he flees in dismay across the country, over bridges, through wheat fields, down embankments, over fences, the girls following close behind. He is finally captured at the point of a revolver and carried triumphantly to the nearest clergyman. This is in many respects the funniest chase film that has ever been made.

"GROWTH OF THE FILM BUSINESS"   **1906**

Editorial, *The Billboard,* Vol. 18, No. 37, Sept. 15, 1906, p. 16.

The invention of the moving picture machine inaugurated a new era of the amusement business. . . . The promoters of amusements were not slow in recognizing the merits of the invention, and the manufacture and jobbing of films rapidly grew to the proportions of a business involving the exchange of vast sums of money annually.
. . . In every town of sufficient size to support it there exists a theatre where moving picture shows are given exclusively. The admission is five or ten cents, and as many

shows are given every day as are warranted by the attendance. The larger towns support many institutions of this kind and dozens of new ones are being installed every week. Frequent changes of the picture bills are necessary, and this is where the film-renting establishments come in for their share in the business. They buy the films outright from the manufacturers and let them to the exhibitors.

Every up-to-date vaudeville theatre includes moving pictures as part of the performance. . . .

Then there are hundreds of traveling "shows" that set up in the halls or small opera houses and put on exhibitions of moving pictures. . . .

The picture theatre was a feature concession of the majority of the large parks last season. . . .

This evolution from the magic lantern is most remarkable, when considered from a scientific standpoint; but it is even more wonderful from a business point of view. It amounts practically to a revolution; and yet those who are conversant with the inside workings of the business maintain that it is still in its infancy.

What will it be in its prime?

1906   **The Jack-Rabbits of the Business**

From "Moving Pictures," *The Billboard,* Vol. 18, No. 41, October 13, 1906, p. 21.

Store shows and five-cent picture theatres might properly be called the jack-rabbits of the business of public entertaining—they multiply so rapidly. No one is in a position to even estimate the number of these exhibits which are now in operation; for an estimate covering today would be worthless tomorrow. In all the big cities they seem to be on every business block. In the middle-sized towns locations are being eagerly sought and no one can tell what the total will eventually be.

COMMENTARY

"The Nickelodeon" (1907) takes a very specific look at an operation still "multiplying faster than guinea pigs," and already, as the result of such films as THE GREAT TRAIN ROBBERY, involving their managers in "hot discussion with the uplifters of the public morals." It is interesting to compare "Trade Notes," from the same year, with the instructions for the de luxe presentation of THE FOUR HORSEMEN OF THE APOCALYPSE in 1921.

"The Nickelodeons" (1907) represents special consideration by Joseph Medill Patterson (a Chicago journalist who later became co-editor and publisher of *The Chicago Tribune*) of a phenomenon whose scope and power must have taken most readers of the article by surprise.

When he writes of motion pictures as "chasers" in vaudeville houses, he is not referring to "chase" films, but to the custom of placing films last on a program to indicate that the show was over. Patterson's date of 1888-1889 for the invention of the projector is misleading: in this period Edison and Dickson were moving toward experiments which led to the construction of the Kinetoscope, but it was not an accomplished fact until several years later. The Jeffries-Sharkey fight had been filmed by Biograph.

1907   "THE NICKELODEON"

From *The Moving Picture World and View Photographer,* Vol. 1, No. 9, May 4, 1907, p. 140.

There is a new thing under the sun—at least new within a short period of time—and entirely new in the sense that the public is waking up to what it means.

It is the 5-cent theater.

The nickel place of amusement made its appearance with no greater blare of trumpets than the noise of its phonograph horn and the throaty persuasions of its barker. It came unobtrusively, in the still of night. It is multiplying faster than guinea pigs, and within a few months has attained to that importance where we may no longer snub it as one of the catch-pennies of the street.

One day a Pittsburgh man hit on the 5-cent theater idea. He equipped a building at a cost of $40,000, bought a phonograph with a big horn, hired a leather-lunged barker and threw his doors open.

The theater was such an unqualified go in Pittsburgh that the men who started in competition with the originator of the scheme decided that a new popular chord had been struck in the amusement line. They hiked to Chicago and opened a theater near State and Van Buren streets. The theater prospered from the moment the barker first opened his mobile face to extol the wonders of the show "upon the inside." That was the beginning in Chicago.

Of course, they were opened in other cities, until now it is estimated there are from 2,500 to 3,000 5-cent theaters in the United States.

One of its chief attractions is the knowledge that if you are stung it is for "only a nickel, five pennies, a half a dime," as the barker says, and that if you don't like the show they can inflict only fifteen minutes of it on you.

Here are the ingredients of a 5-cent theater:

One storeroom, seating from 200 to 500 persons.

One phonograph with extra large horn.

One young woman cashier.

One electric sign.

One cinematograph, with operator.

One canvas on which to throw the pictures.

One piano.

One barker.

One manager.

As many chairs as the store will hold.

A few brains and a little tact. Mix pepper and salt to taste.

After that all you have to do is to open the doors, start the phonograph and carry the money to the bank. The public does the rest.

It makes little difference what time of day you go to a 5-cent theater. The doors are opened as early in the forenoon as there is a chance of gathering in a few nickels, the downtown theaters opening earlier than those in the outlying districts to accommodate the visitors. Each "performance" lasts fifteen minutes. At the end of each a sign is thrown from the cinematograph on the canvas announcing that those who came late may stay for the next "performance."

Often they stay for several. After they find out that nobody cares and that they can stay all day and far into the night and bring their lunch if they want to, they leave, disappointed because nobody tried to get the best of them.

They are great places for the foot-sore shopper, who is not used to cement sidewalks, to rest; and it took the aforesaid foot-sore shoppers about one minute to find this out. It is much more comfortable than to take street-car rides to rest, and they don't have to pay the return nickel.

The name of the play is flashed on the canvas, so that it may be identified if ever seen again. Understand that the young men who sing the "illustrated songs" are the only live performers in these theaters. The rest is moving pictures; and that is the startling part of the great favor with which these theaters have been received by the public.

44

The plays that are put on at the 5-cent theaters are for the most part manufactured abroad. Paris is a great producing center. London has numerous factories that grind them out. They are bought by the foot.

This system of buying drama and comedy by the foot has its distinct advantages. If the piece grows dull at any point the manager can take a pair of shears and cut out a few yards or rods, thereby enlivening the whole performance.

The worst charge that has been made against the 5-cent theaters is that some of them put on pieces of the blood-and-thunder type, depicting murders, hold-ups, train robberies and other crimes. This charge has led the managers of the new style theaters into a hot discussion with the uplifters of the public morals.

Few people realize the important part these theaters are beginning to play in city life. They have been looked upon largely as places of trivial amusement, not calling for any serious consideration. They seem, however, to be something that may become one of the greatest forces for good or for evil in the city.

On the other hand, in the congested districts the 5-cent theaters are proving a source of much innocent entertainment. The mothers do not have to "dress" to attend them, and they take the children and spend many restful hours in them at very small expense.

The possibilities of them in an educational way are unlimited. The tuberculosis society already has seen this and has under way a plan for having the cinematograph theaters show pictures which will instruct the public of the precautions to be taken against consumption. A great many educational lines might be developed among the people in this way.

1907   "TRADE NOTES"

From *The Moving Picture World and View Photographer*, Vol. 1, No. 19, July 13, 1907, p. 297.

In this day and age of moving picture popularity the manager of picture shows is kept busy thinking up some new and novel additions to his entertainment in order that he may prove a winner with the show-going public. One of these additions, and, in fact, the most pleasing one, is mechanical effects or sound effects as they are more commonly called. Quite a large percentage of those who attend moving picture entertainments where sound effects are successfully used, are kept guessing as to how they are produced.

For instance, the sound of horses' hooves upon a paved street is made very realistic by the use of a pair of cocoanut shells which are applied to a marble slab in a corresponding manner to the gait of the horse, changing from a walk to a trot or gallop as may be the speed of the horse in the picture. Sand paper blocks are another useful article and have a number of uses, the escape of steam from a locomotive, exhaust from an automobile, splash of water and a number of other effects are produced by this common article. A dozen whistles, bells, pieces of steel and broken glass are also brought into use.

To illustrate shots a pistol with blank cartridges is most commonly used; but as the nervous systems of most people, especially the ladies, are very much wrought upon by the loud report of a pistol, the use of a hollow block at the end of a stick when brought in contact with the marble slab, produces a good effect and does away with the harsh report of a gun. To enumerate all the different methods employed in the work of illustrating and to describe all the uses to which articles are put would require days and incidentally some columns of news space; suffice it to say that the successful man on mechanical effects has much to learn and is at least a busy man while the pictures are being shown.

Filming Out of Doors   1907

Excerpts from "How the Cinematographer Works," *The Moving Picture World and View Photographer*, Vol. 1, No. 19, July 13, 1907, p. 300.

. . . When the actors in moving picture dramas set forth from the factory to the nearby woods to be pictured for various scenes there is usually an accompanying string of small boys and curiosity seekers who follow in their train and sometimes interfere with the taking of the pictures. Sometimes the onlookers become so absorbed in the drama that is going on that they stray within the focus of the camera and mar the reality. Occasionally they add a note of naturalness to it, however. . . . Sometimes spontaneous, unrehearsed acts make a picture much more valuable. . . .

THE NICKELODEONS, The Poor Man's Elementary Course in the Drama   1907

By Joseph Medill Patterson, *The Saturday Evening Post*, Vol. 180, No. 21, November 23, 1907, pp. 10-11, 38.

Three years ago there was not a nickelodeon, or five-cent theater devoted to moving-picture shows, in America. Today there are between four and five thousand running and solvent, and the number is still increasing rapidly. This is the boom time in the moving-picture business. Everybody is making money—manufacturers, renters, jobbers, exhibitors. Overproduction looms up as a certainty of the near future; but now, as one press-agent said enthusiastically, "this line is a Klondike."

The nickelodeon is tapping an entirely new stratum of people, is developing into theatergoers a section of population that formerly knew and cared little about the drama as a fact in life. That is why "this line is a Klondike" just at present.

Incredible as it may seem, over two million people on the average attend the nickelodeons *every day of the year*, and a third of these are children.

Let us prove up this estimate. The agent for the biggest firm of film renters in the country told me that the average expense of running a nickelodeon was from $175 to $200 a week, divided as follows:

Wage of manager	$25
Wage of operator	20
Wage of doorman	15
Wage of porter or musician	12
Rent of films (two reels changed twice a week)	50
Rent of projecting machine	10
Rent of building	40
Music, printing, "campaign contributions," etc.	18
Total	$190

Merely to meet expenses, then, the average nickelodeon must have a weekly attendance of 4000. This gives all the nickelodeons 16,000,000 a week, or over 2,000,000 a day. Two million people a day are needed before profits can begin, and the two million are forthcoming. It is a big thing, this new enterprise.

The nickelodeon is usually a tiny theater, contining 199 seats, giving from twelve to eighteen performances a day, seven days a week. Its walls are painted red. The seats are ordinary kitchen chairs, not fastened. The only break in the red color scheme is made by

8. Biograph's PERSONAL (1904). *The next stage of the game was this: the comic chase film. Take-off point: Grant's Tomb in New York. Film-makers still find an exciting chase with eventual capture a very satisfying termination.*

half a dozen signs, in black and white, NO SMOKING, HATS OFF and sometimes, but not always, STAY AS LONG AS YOU LIKE.

The spectatorium is one story high, twenty-five feet wide and about seventy feet deep. Last year or the year before it was probably a second-hand clothier's, a pawn-shop or cigar store. Now, the counter has been ripped out, there is a ticket-seller's booth where the show-window was, an automatic musical barker somewhere up in the air thunders its noise down on the passersby, and the little store has been converted into a theatrelet. Not a theatre, mind you, for theatres must take out theatrical licenses at $500 a year. Theatres seat two hundred or more people. Nickelodeons seat 199, and take out amusement licenses. This is the general rule.

But sometimes nickelodeon proprietors in favorable locations take out theatrical licenses and put in 800 or 1,000 seats. In Philadelphia there is, perhaps, the largest nickelodeon in America. It is said to pay not only the theatrical license, but also $30,000 a year ground rent and a handsome profit.

Today there is cutthroat competition between the little nickelodeon owners, and they are beginning to compete each other out of existence. Already consolidation has set in. Film-renting firms are quietly beginning to pick up, here and there, a few nickelodeons of their own; presumably they will make better rates and give prompter service to their own theatrelets than to those belonging to outsiders. The tendency is clearly toward fewer, bigger, cleaner five-cent theatres and more expensive shows. Hard as this may be on the little showman who is forced out, it is good for the public, who will, in consequence, get more for their money.

Who the Patrons Are

The character of attendance varies with the locality, but, whatever the locality, children make up about thirty-three per cent of the crowds. For some reason, young women from sixteen to thirty years old are rarely in evidence, but many middle-aged and old women are steady patrons, who never, when a new film is to be shown, miss the opening.

In cosmopolitan city districts the foreigners attend in larger proportion than the English-speakers. This is doubtless because the foreigners, shut out as they are by their alien tongues from much of the life about them, can yet perfectly understand the pantomime of the moving pictures.

As might be expected, the Latin races patronize the shows more consistently than Jews, Irish or Americans. Sailors of all races are devotees.

Most of the shows have musical accompaniments. The enterprising manager usually engages a human pianist with instructions to play Eliza-crossing-the-ice when the scene is shuddery, and fast ragtime in a comic kid chase. Where there is little competition, however, the manager merely presses the button and starts the automatic going, which is as apt as not to bellow out, "I'd Rather Two-Step Than Waltz, Bill," just as the angel rises from the brave little hero-cripple's corpse.

The moving pictures were used as chasers in vaudeville houses for several years before the advent of the nickelodeon. The Cinematograph or Vitagraph or Biograph or [Projecting] Kinetoscope (there are seventy-odd names for the same machine) was invented in 1888-1889. Mr. Edison is said to have contributed most toward it, though several other inventors claim part of the credit.

The first very successful pictures were those of the Corbett-Fitzsimmons fight at Carson City, Nevada, in 1897. These films were shown all over the country to immense crowds and an enormous sum of money was made by the exhibitors.

The Jeffries-Sharkey fight of twenty-five rounds at Coney Island, in November, 1899, was another popular success. The contest being at night, artificial light was necessary, and 500 arc lamps were placed above the ring. Four cameras were used. While one was snapping the fighters, a second was being focused at them, a third was being reloaded, and a fourth was held in reserve in case of breakdown. Over seven miles of film were exposed and 198,000 pictures, each 2 by 3 inches, were taken. This fight was taken at the rate of thirty pictures to the second.

The 500 arc lamps above the ring generated a temperature of about 115 degrees for the gladiators to fight in. When the event was concluded, Mr. Jeffries was overheard to remark that for no amount of money would he ever again in his life fight in such heat, pictures or no pictures. And he never has.

Since that mighty fight, manufacturers have learned a good deal about cheapening their process. Pictures instead of being 2 by 3 inches are now 5/8 by 1 1/8 inches, and are taken sixteen insteady of thirty to the second, for the illusion to the eye of continuous motion is as perfect at one rate as the other.

By means of a ratchet each separate picture is made to pause a twentieth of a second before the magic-lantern lens, throwing an enlargement to life size upon the screen. Then, while the revolving shutter obscures the lens, one picture is dropped and another substituted, to make in turn its twentieth-of-a-second display.

The films are, as a rule, exhibited at the rate of which they are taken, though chase scenes are usually thrown faster, and horse races, fire-engines and fast-moving automobiles slower, than the life-speed.

How the Drama is Made

Within the past year an automatic process to color films has been discovered by a French firm. The pigments are applied by means of a four-color machine stencil. Beyond this bare fact, the process remains a secret of the inventors. The stencil must do its work with extraordinary accuracy, for any minute error in the application of color to outline made upon the 5/8 by 1 1/8 inches print is magnified 200 times when thrown upon the screen by the magnifying lens. The remarkable thing about this automatic colorer is that it applies the pigment in slightly different outline to each successive print of a film 700 feet long. Colored films sell for about fifty per cent more than black and whites. Tinted films—browns, blues, oranges, violets, greens and so forth—are made by washing, and sell at but one per cent over the straight price.

The films are obtained in various ways. "Straight" shows, where the interest depends on the dramatist's imagination and the setting, are merely playlets acted out before the rapid-fire camera. Each manufacturing firm owns a studio with property-room, dressing-rooms and a completely equipped stage. The actors are experienced professionals of just below the first rank, who are content to make from $18 to $25 a week. In France a class of moving-picture specialists has grown up who work only for the cameras, but in this country most of the artists who play in the film studios in the daytime play also behind the footlights at night.

The studio manager orders rehearsals continued until his people have their parts "face-perfect," then he gives the word, the lens is focused, the cast works rapidly for twenty minutes while the long strip of celluloid whirs through the camera, and the performance is preserved in living, dynamic embalmment (if the phrase may be permitted) for decades to come.

Eccentric scenes, such as a chalk marking the outlines of a coat upon a piece of cloth, the scissors cutting to the lines, the needle sewing, all automatically without human help, often require a week to take. The process is ingenious. First the scissors and chalk are laid upon the edge of the cloth. The picture is taken. The camera is stopped, the scissors are moved a quarter of an inch into the cloth, the chalk is drawn a quarter of an inch over the cloth. The camera is opened again and another picture is taken showing the quarter-inch cut and quarter-inch mark. The camera is closed, another quarter-inch is cut and chalked; another exposure is made. When these pictures so slowly obtained 49 are run off rapidly, the illusion of fast self-action on the part of the scissors, chalk and needle is produced.

Sometimes in a nickelodeon you can see on the screen a building completely wrecked in five minutes. Such a film was obtained by focusing a camera at the building, and taking every salient move of the wreckers for the space, perhaps, of a fortnight. When these separate prints, obtained at varying intervals, some of them perhaps a whole day apart, are run together continuously, the appearance is of a mighty stone building being pulled to pieces like a house of blocks.

Such eccentric pictures were in high demand a couple of years ago, but now the straight-story show is running them out. The plots are improving every year in dramatic technique. Manufacturing firms pay from $5 to $25 for good stories suitable for film presentation, and it is astonishing how many sound dramatic ideas are submitted by people of insufficient education to render their thoughts into English suitable for the legitimate stage.

The moving-picture actors are becoming excellent pantomimists, which is natural, for they cannot rely on the playwright's lines to make their meanings. I remember particularly a performance I saw near Spring Street on the Bowery, where the pantomime seemed to me in nowise inferior to that of Mademoiselle Pilar-Morin, the French pantomimist.

The nickelodeon spectators readily distinguish between good and bad acting, though they do not mark their pleasure or displeasure audibly, except very rarely, in a comedy scene, by a suppressed giggle. During the excellent show of which I have spoken, the men, women and children maintained a steady stare of fascination at the changing figures on the scene, and toward the climax, when forgiveness was cruelly denied, lips were parted and eyes filled with tears. It was as much a tribute to the actors as the loudest bravos ever shouted in the Metropolitan Opera House.

Today a consistent plot is demanded. There must be, as in the drama, exposition, development, climax and dénouement. The most popular films run from fifteen to twenty minutes and are from five hundred to eight hundred feet long. One studio manager said: "The people want a story. We run to comics generally; they seem to take best. So-and-so, however, lean more to melodrama. When we started we used to give just flashes—an engine chasing to a fire, a base-runner sliding home, a charge of cavalry. Now, for instance, if we want to work in a horse race it has to be as a scene in the life of the jockey, who is the hero of the piece—we've got to give them a story; they won't take anything else—a story with plenty of action. You can't show large conversation, you know, on the screen. More story, larger story, better story with plenty of action—that is our tendency."

. . . .

Civilization, all through the history of mankind, has been chiefly the property of the upper classes, but during the past century civilization has been permeating steadily downward. The leaders of this democratic movement have been general education, universal suffrage, cheap periodicals and cheap travel. Today the moving-picture machine cannot be overlooked as an effective protagonist of democracy. For through it the drama, always a big fact in the lives of the people at the top, is now becoming a big fact in the lives of the people at the bottom. Two million of them a day have so found a new interest in life.

The prosperous Westerners, who take their week or fortnight, fall and spring, in New York, pay two dollars and a half for a seat at a problem play, a melodrama, a comedy or a show-girl show in a Broadway theatre. The stokers who have driven the Deutschland or the Lusitania from Europe pay five cents for a seat at a problem play, a melodrama, a comedy or a show-girl show in a Bowery nickelodeon. What is the difference?

50   The stokers, sitting on the hard, wooden chairs of the nickelodeon, experience the

same emotional flux and counter-flux (more intense is their experience, for they are not as blasé) as the prosperous Westerners in their red plush orchestra chairs, uptown.

The sentient life of the half-civilized beings at the bottom has been enlarged and altered, by the introduction of the dramatic motif, to resemble more closely the sentient life of the civilized beings at the top.

Take an analogous case. Is aimless travel "beneficial" or not? It is amusing, certainly; and, therefore the artistocrats who could afford it have always traveled aimlessly. But now, says the Democratic Movement, the grand tour shall no longer be restricted to the aristocracy. Jump on the rural trolley-car, Mr. Workingman, and make a grand tour yourself. Don't care, Mr. Workingman, whether it is "beneficial" or not. Do it because it is amusing; just as the aristocrats do.

The film makers cover the whole gamut of dramatic attractions. The extremes in the film world are as far apart as the extremes in the theatrical world—as far apart, let us say, as *The Master Builder* and *The Gay White Way*.

If you look up the moving-picture advertisements in any vaudeville trade paper you cannot help being struck with this fact. For instance, in a current number, one firm offers the following variety of attractions:

ROMANY'S REVENGE (very dramatic) . . . . 300 feet
JOHNNY'S RUN (comic kid chase) . . . . 300 feet
ROOF TO CELLAR (absorbing comedy) . . . . 782 feet
WIZARD'S WORLD (fantastic comedy) . . . . 350 feet
SAILOR'S RETURN (highly dramatic) . . . . 535 feet
A MOTHER'S SIN (beautiful, dramatic and moral) . . . . 392 feet
KNIGHT ERRANT (old historical drama) . . . . 421 feet
VILLAGE FIRE BRIGADE (big laugh) . . . . 325 feet
CATCH THE KID (a scream) . . . . 270 feet
THE CORONER'S MISTAKE (comic ghost story) . . . . 430 feet
FATAL HAND (dramatic) . . . . 432 feet

Another firm advertises in huge type, in the trade papers:

LIFE AND PASSION OF CHRIST
Five Parts, Thirty-nine Pictures,
    3114 feet . . . . Price, $373.68
Extra for coloring 125.10

The presentation by the picture machines of the *Passion Play* in this country was undertaken with considerable hesitation. The films had been shown in France to huge crowds, but here, so little were even professional students of American lower-class taste able to gauge it in advance, that the presenters feared the *Passion Play* might be boycotted, if not, indeed, in some places, mobbed. On the contrary, it has been the biggest success ever known to the business.

Last year incidents leading up to the murder of Stanford White were shown, succeeded enormously for a very few weeks, then flattened out completely and were withdrawn. Film people are as much at sea about what their crowds will like as the managers in the "legitimate."

Although the gourdlike growth of the nickelodeon business as a factor in the conscious life of Americans is not yet appreciated, already a good many people are disturbed by what they do know of the thing.

Those who are "interested in the poor" are wondering whether the five-cent theatre is a good influence, and asking themselves gravely whether it should be encouraged or checked (with the help of the police).

51

Is the theatre a "good" or a "bad" influence? The adjectives don't fit the case. Neither do they fit the case of the nickelodeon, which is merely the theatre democratized.

Take the case of the *Passion Play,* for instance. Is it irreverent to portray the Passion, Crucifixion, Resurrection and Ascension in a vaudeville theatre over a darkened stage where half an hour before a couple of painted, short-skirted girls were doing a "sister-act"? What is the motive which draws crowds of poor people to nickelodeons to see the Birth in the Manger flashed magic-lanternwise upon a white cloth? Curiosity? Mere mocking curiosity, perhaps? I cannot answer.

Neither could I say what it is that, every fifth year, draws our plutocrats to Oberammergau, where at the cost, from first to last, of thousands of dollars and days of time, they view a similar spectacle presented in a sunny Bavarian setting.

It is reasonable, however, to believe that the same feelings, whatever they are, which drew our rich to Oberammergau draw our poor to the nickelodeons. Whether the powerful emotional reactions produced in the spectator by the *Passion Play* are "beneficial" or not is as far beyond decision as the question whether a man or an oyster is happier. The man is more, feels more, than the oyster. The beholder of the *Passion Play* is more, feels more, than the non-beholder.

Whether for weal or woe, humanity has ceaselessly striven to complicate life, to diversify and make subtle the emotions, to create and gratify the new and artificial spiritual wants, to know more and feel more both of good and evil, to attain a greater degree of self-consciousness; just as the one fundamental instinct of the youth, which most systems of education have been vainly organized to eradicate, is to find out what the man knows.

In this eternal struggle for more self-consciousness, the moving-picture machine, uncouth instrument though it be, has enlisted itself on especial behalf of the least enlightened, those who are below the reach even of the yellow journals. For although in the prosperous vaudeville houses the machine is but a toy, a "chaser," in the nickelodeons it is the central, absorbing fact, which strengthens, widens, vivifies subjective life; which teaches living other than living through the senses alone. Already, perhaps, touching him at the psychological moment, it has awakened to his first, groping, necessary discontent the spirit of an artist of the future, who otherwise would have remained mute and motionless.

The nickelodeons are merely an extension course in civilization, teaching both its "badness" and its "goodness." They have come in obedience to the law of supply and demand; and they will stay as long as the slums stay, for in the slums they are the fittest and must survive.

COMMENTARY

Certain exhibition problems were to plague theaters then, and for years to come; "Some Careless Operators" lists a few. This editorial is from The Moving Picture World, **a trade publication which first appeared March 9, 1907, and went on to exert considerable influence, always campaigning for sensible, conscientious projection, and for better film-making as well.**

The fall of a vaudeville theater and its replacement by motion pictures, chronicled here in the paragraphs about New York City's Bijou Dream, became a much more common incident in 1908. (Bijou Dream was a favorite name, to be found on motion picture houses in many cities and towns across the country.)

"SOME CARELESS OPERATORS"   1907

Excerpt from "Some Careless Operators," editorial, *The Moving Picture World,* Vol. 1, No. 41, December 14, 1907, p. 659.

We were paying a visit to one of our advertisers the other day, and he called our attention to a reel of film just returned from a nickelodeon. The film was absolutely new, never used before, and yet this film was useless for any further exhibition. It was scratched from beginning to finish in so disgraceful a manner that none but an arrant ignoramus of the value of film could have treated it so. A little time spent on wiping the machine, cleaning off all dust, and careful oiling, would obviate all scratches, or a good brush used on the velvet guides after each reel has been run through.

On another occasion we were shown a new film of which some three to four hundred feet had been broken all down the sprocket perforations. Film that breaks like this is shoddy, cheap and nasty. We have been trying to find out who manufactures this sort, but so far have failed. We have the assurance from Eastman Company that it does not emanate from them. Even in a case like this, when the operator sees the result he ought to at once stop and examine his sprocket, which may be out of gear and needs but the adjustment of a screw or two to again put it in order. Several exhibitions we have visited of late were very poor; one operator was working away at the crank and the machine was running heavily and groaning as if it was grinding corn, going off in leaps and bounds, giving a jerky, blurred picture on the screen, and what we were waiting for and expecting, soon came to pass—the film broke three times and there was a long, dreary wait after each break. The exhibition, which would ordinarily have taken fifteen minutes, occupied forty, and the audience went out with a sigh of relief. We spoke to the proprietor, and he said he had tried five operators and was giving this man a good salary, as he was supposed to be an expert. (He was, at carelessness.) Another exhibition was showing what was supposed to be a funeral procession, and the horses were walking at a sedate, stately pace, or ought to have been, but in this case they slid along the screen in a most ludicrous manner that brought a satirical laugh from the audience. The next picture was a hunting scene and here the operator reversed the whole performance. If operators will only bear in mind that the camera goes at one even rate of speed and fully catches all the action necessary, then if they will try and get this even rhythm of speed in their machines, they will secure the true life-like motion their pictures ought to depict.

Another defect very noticeable is the manner of operating the arc. We have seen rainbows in the sky, black patches in the center, and ghostly images galore. When we have spoken to the operator he has said: "Oh! It is the glasses that ain't just right." The condensors have nothing to do with the effect on the light. Each operator ought to know how to center his arc so that only a white light is seen on the screen; it is an easy matter to adjust the light to or from the condensor, up or down, right or left, until it is perfect. An operator does not know his business until all these little details are as simple as A B C to him. Another point we wish to touch upon is the fire risk. We were told about a fire that occurred in Pennsylvania in a complete fireproof box [booth]. No damage was done except to the film, the operator escaping with a few slight burns. His explanation of the fire was that the rapid friction in the takeup gear caused it to spark and set itself on fire. We told our informant to tell that story to the marines. The operator is known to be a most inveterate smoker—in fact, he often goes to bed with a cigarette—and our contention is that his cigarette is responsible for the damage and that he ought to seek occupation in another sphere, or give up smoking. . . .

1908   **New York Vaudeville Yields to Moving Pictures**

From *The Moving Picture World,* Vol. 2, No. 2, January 11, 1908, p. 22.

So great has been the growth of public interest in moving pictures within the last two years that one of the foremost vaudeville theaters in this city is to be devoted wholly to the new form of entertainment. The house is Keith and Proctor's Twenty-third street. Beginning on December 6 [1907] moving pictures, with descriptive songs, will form the shows there. Admittance will be five cents and ten cents. No seats will be reserved.

With the change in style of amusement, the theater's name also will be changed. Thenceforth it will be the Bijou Dream. It will be the largest and most perfectly appointed place in this country in which moving pictures are shown. The rapidity with which these pictures have developed into a popular amusement, especially for those who are unable to pay the price of admittance to the average show, is surprising. A few years ago, when the moving picture was introduced in connection with lectures, it was looked upon as an innovation that would be short-lived. But now millions of dollars are invested in such entertainments.

Arrangements have been made with American and foreign films to supply to the Bijou Dream the first sets of new pictures, so that in this theater the best scenes will be shown before they are seen anywhere else in this country. There will be three complete changes of pictures and songs every week.

CHAPTER 4

Griffith at Biograph (I): The Miraculous Year (1909)

COMMENTARY

Early film production centered in and around New York City where Biograph, Edison and Vitagraph maintained studios. (Exteriors for **THE GREAT TRAIN ROBBERY** were shot in New Jersey). Kalem studios were located at Stamford, Connecticut, but Essanay and Selig were as far away as Chicago, already indicating the westerly direction in which production was soon to travel.

David Wark Griffith (1875-1948), Kentucky born, had been fascinated by the theater but never became a major actor. Nevertheless, he played in stock, wrote a partially successful play for the vaudeville circuit (*In Washington's Time*) (**1901**), and travelled around the country in various theatrical ventures, notably with Nance O'Neil (**1906**), whose repertory that season included Thomas Bailey Aldrich's *Judith of Bethulia,* Sudermann's *Magda* and *The Fires of St. John,* and Ibsen's *Rosmersholm* and *Hedda Gabler.* His play *A Fool and a Girl* (**1907**) opened in Washington, but was discontinued in Baltimore as "too expensive" to perform.

Still hoping for success as a writer or actor, Griffith now turned to motion pictures, and applied to the New York studio of the Edison Company, where the script he offered was declined. Instead, he was given the leading role in a film, which in February, 1908 was reviewed as follows: "**RESCUED FROM AN EAGLE'S NEST** is a feeble attempt to secure a trick film of a fine subject. The boldness of the conception is marred by bad lighting and poor blending of outside photography with the studio work, which is too flat; and the trick of the eagle and its wire wings is too evident to the audience, while the fight between the man and eagle is poor and out of vision. The hill brow is not a precipice. We looked for better things." (12)

In other words, the film was old-fashioned even for its day. Griffith's salary for four days' work was $20.

In 1908 Griffith sold a few scenarios to the Biograph Company and acted in some of their films; meanwhile, an important weekly publication, *The New York Dramatic Mirror,* whose record of the American theater dated back to 1879, established a motion picture department (May 30, 1908) just in time to review the first films Griffith actually directed. He had been advanced by Biograph from actor to director, and his first Biograph, **THE ADVENTURES OF DOLLIE**, 713 feet long, was released July 14.

As director, he inherited the cameraman G. W. ("Billy") Bitzer, who had done various jobs at Biograph since 1896, and who continued to work with Griffith through the 1920's. Even if every Biograph film were missing, Griffith's extraordinary grasp of the medium would still be evident to us from Frank E. Woods' reviews in the *Dramatic Mirror*; Woods wrote general criticism under the signature "The Spectator," as well as unsigned comments on specific films.

THE REDMAN AND THE CHILD was apparently Griffith's Opus 3, and THE FATAL HOUR (August 18, 1908) appears to have been the first of his films to be edited into "alternate scenes" at the climax, inter-cutting between the progress of the rescuer and the dangers of the to-be-rescued. This technique, also called the switch-back or cut-back (because the action cuts back and forth between simultaneous happenings) should not be confused with the flash-back, in which from one point in time there is visual recall of the past. Those who wrote about Griffith and film-making slightly later considered the development of the switch-back to be his foremost contribution.

THE REDMAN AND THE CHILD   FILM 1908

From "Reviews of New Films," *The New York Dramatic Mirror*, Vol. 60, No. 1546, August 8, 1908, p. 7.

THE REDMAN AND THE CHILD (Biograph).—The best Indian film we have yet seen was produced last week by the Biograph Company. In many respects it is one of the best handled subjects ever produced by any company. The scenery is superb, the photography perfect, and the acting, especially of the Indian character, is of the highest class. But chiefly the story is original and consistent, and the scenes follow each other consecutively and naturally. Interest is aroused from the start, and is held with increasing power to the very end. An Indian has cached a bag of gold nuggets, which he shows to a little boy, to whom he has taken a fancy and to whom he presents two of the nuggets. Two outlaws rob the boy and brutally force him to reveal the Indian's treasure. They murder the boy's grandfather and escape in a canoe, taking the boy along. The Indian has taken a surveying party to a neighboring cliff, and through the telescope he sees the murder. He swears vengeance over the old man's dead body, and pursues the robbers in another canoe, overtaking them in the open water. Leaping from his canoe, he puts one to flight and kills the other by holding his head under the water. Then he swims after the first outlaw and overtakes him on land, where a knife duel ends in the Indian forcing his adversary's dagger to the heart. The last scene shows the Indian paddling home with the little boy who gently falls asleep in the canoe. The subject made such a hit at the Manhattan Theatre that it was held over two days by special request.

THE FATAL HOUR   FILM 1908

Excerpts from "THE FATAL HOUR," trade synopsis, *The Moving Picture World*, Vol. 3, No. 8, August 22, 1908, p. 142.

THE FATAL HOUR. A stirring incident of the Chinese White-Slave traffic (Biograph). . . . [In the course of this, the girl detective, who is trying to help break a white-slave ring, is seized by two of the villains, who, carrying her off to an old deserted house,] tie her to a post and arrange a large pistol on the face of a clock in such a way that when the hands point to twelve the gun is fired and the girl will receive the charge. Twenty minutes are allowed for them to get away, for the hands are now indicating 11:40. Certain death seems to be her fate, and would have been had not an accident disclosed her plight. [One of the villains] . . . after leaving the place is thrown by a street car, and this serves to discover his identity, so he is captured and a wild ride is made to the house in which the poor girl is incarcerated. This incident is shown in alternate scenes. There is the helpless girl, with the clock ticking its way towards her destruction, and out on the road is the carriage, tearing along at breakneck speed to the rescue, arriving just in time to get her safely out of range of the pistol as it goes off. In conclusion we can promise this to be an exceedingly thrilling film, of more than ordinary interest. . . .

Excerpt from "Reviews of New Films," *The New York Dramatic Mirror*, Vol. 60, No. 1549, August 29, 1908, p. 7.

THE FATAL HOUR (Biograph) . . . A wholly impossible story, with a series of inconsistent situations, and yet the wild drive to the rescue while the clock slowly approaches the hour of twelve, brings a thrill that redeems the picture.

COMMENTARY

1909 was the first of Griffith's two miraculous years, the other being 1914, when he finished the shooting of THE BIRTH OF A NATION and began INTOLERANCE.

At Biograph, with Bitzer, Griffith was anxious to improve the quality of motion pictures, pouring energy and imagination into the 1000-foot subject and two shorter films (or a total of approximately 2,000 feet) which, according to his usual schedule, he was required to direct and edit each week. The studio at 11 East 14th Street was cramped, but there was always painted perspective to give the illusion of space, and sometimes the company did venture out to perform against natural scenery in the surrounding territory.

A FOOL'S REVENGE and RESURRECTION were each advertised as a "Free Adaptation," since one compressed a full evening's opera, and the other a long novel, into one reel of film apiece.

FILM 1909   A FOOL'S REVENGE

"Reviews of New Films," *The New York Dramatic Mirror*, Vol. 61, No. 1577, March 13, 1909, p. 16.

A FOOL'S REVENGE (Biograph). This is the first American film that we have felt justified in pronouncing the equal in smoothness of construction and power of dramatic action of any of the Pathé "film d'art." The story is that of *Rigoletto*, adapted to motion picture requirements. The manner in which the court fool is acted reminds us strongly of Severin. The clear facial expressions as well as the natural but intensely suggestive gestures and poses of the character approach perfection in pantomimic art. The other characters are also acted with fine perception, especially the two cutthroats, and the production is mounted richly and in excellent taste, evincing throughout the most careful and intelligent stage direction. The Biograph Company is entitled to the warmest praise for its undoubted success in producing a work of moving picture art that must rank with the very best.

1909   **Beethoven in a Five-Cent Theater**

Excerpt from "Notes from Chicago," By Our Western Correspondent, *The Moving Picture World*, Vol. 4, No. 11, March 13, 1909, p. 300.

. . . We go down again and take a seat in the auditorium to see the latest Biograph—   57 "a grand film," we are told by Mr. Hines [manager of The Senate Theatre in Chicago]. A Pathé comic is on, with funny chases and crushed china, and the audience is shouting with delight. Here is the feature of the day, A FOOL'S REVENGE, by Biograph. A FOOL'S REVENGE is a highly dramatic subject on the theme of *Rigoletto*. A FOOL'S REVENGE is a film that keeps one in an intense suspense from beginning to end. The feature of the film is the beautiful girl that plays the fool's daughter in a way beyond criticism. The staging and acting in general are very good. The photography is superb. The film made a deep impression on the audience.

A pleasant variation from the eternal ragtime was a refined deliverance of classical music corresponding to the character of the picture, including Schumann's "Traumerei," and Beethoven's "Moonlight Sonata." The first time, indeed, we ever heard Beethoven in a five-cent theater. . . .

RESURRECTION   **FILM 1909**

Excerpts from "RESURRECTION." *The Moving Picture World,* Vol. 4, No. 22, May 29, 1909, p. 712.

Step by step the Biograph Company is making for itself a unique position among American film manufacturers. Within the last few months its reputation among exhibitors and the general public has increased by leaps and bounds. We doubt whether the exhibitors or the public could say off-hand exactly why they like Biograph pictures so much. It is sufficient for them that they like them and want more. The good photographic qualities of the pictures are now taken as a matter of course. But good photography alone will not make a successful moving picture film. There must be something more, and we think we know what that something more is.

It is the dramatic quality of the pictures that convincingly appeals to exhibitors and the public. The Biograph picture today tells a story and tells that story well. Moreover the Biograph film is one in which one is almost sure to see good acting. Unequivocally, therefore, we have no hesitation in saying that the Biograph picture of the moment is unexcelled for its dramatic and photographic qualities. . . . [The] former of these . . . is very evident in RESURRECTION, a recent release. We were curious to see how the Fourteenth Street Company interpreted Tolstoi's melancholy story. The public opinion on the film when we saw it echoed our own interest. As the picture started to move, there was a sudden hush in the theatre, which always indicates concentrated interest. And the hush continued right to the end of the film, when the afflicted girl kneels at the foot of the cross on the Siberian steppes. In these same scenes, where the fallen girl is on her way to Siberia in company with other unfortunates, and is knouted by Russian soldiers, there is an aspect of unreality, excessively sharp modeling and not particularly convincing snow, which we suppose could not be avoided owing to the exiguity of space at Fourteenth street. But in the preceding scenes . . . the Biograph staging is quite as convincing as that of an ordinary play. And then the acting of the leading woman and the prince—how fine and tragic the former is! how excellent the latter! We do not know the lady's name, but certainly she seems to us to have a very fine command of her emotions and to be able to express these emotions before such an unemotional thing as a camera. A very ordinary person indeed can act before a crowded house of interested men and women, but it takes a genius to do so with real feeling on a moving picture stage. For there is no eager, sympathetic audience of thousands before you there, but only the staff of the company or the matter-of-fact person who turns the handle and exposes so many feet of sensitized celluloid per minute on the players. . . .

FILM 1909   THE JILT

Excerpts from "Reviews of New Films," *The New York Dramatic Mirror*, Vol. 61, No. 1588, May 29, 1909, p. 15.

THE JILT (Biograph, May 17).—The first few scenes of this picture appear to be disconnected and drawn out to greater length than the nature of the scenes warrant. The affection of the two college boys could have been shown with less detail; their grief at parting is overdone, and a scene in which one of them saves the other from footpads appears wholly unnecessary. By economizing at the points noted there would have been room in the reel to introduce the woman who turns out to be "the jilt" with more clearness. It is some time before we find out who she is, after we see her courted by one of the college boys. She at first accepts his love and then jilts him, and he goes the downward path, which again is not clearly enough indicated, due to the absence of subtitles. . . . For the most part the acting is of the highest class and the photography is almost perfect. It is in the story itself that most cause for criticism is found.

COMMENTARY

It is apparent from the following three reviews that, unlike Griffith, Edwin S. Porter, who was responsible for production at the Edison Company, was having trouble introducing the switch-back to indicate concurrent action. Even if not actually directed by Porter, the films in question were supervised by him, or reflect his production methods.

FILM 1909   THE SALESLADY'S MATINEE IDOL

Excerpt from "Reviews of New Films," *The New York Dramatic Mirror*, Vol. 61, No. 1574, February 20, 1909, p. 16.

(Edison) . . . A New York melodrama manager . . . hires a champion pugilist to star in a new "thriller." . . . Later the saleslady reads the billing and determines to go. We see her seated in the balcony when the curtain goes up. Then we are shown a scene from the "thriller," but we do not know it is a scene from the play, as we see no sign of arch or footlights. Dastardly deeds are being performed but the pugilist hero smashes his way in and rescues the girl. Then we are shown the balcony, with the audience, including the girl, exhibiting by their faces and action their interest in the play. Another climax of the play follows, and this is a capital burlesque on the lurid melodrama. We recognize the stage this time, and see the "heavy" bind the heroine to the railroad track, but again the pugilist jumps in, scatters the scoundrels right and left and rescues the girl just as the "lightning express," a car and an engine made of scenery, bump their way across the stage. Another view of the balcony is now presented and to understand the conduct of the audience we are obliged to imagine that they are witnessing the railroad scene previously exhibited. Here is where skill in preparing the film for exhibition would have made this picture a model of its kind. If short scenes had alternated back and forth between the stage and the balcony, showing the progress on the stage and the effect on the balcony audience concurrently, the effect would have been greatly increased. . . .

FILM 1909   THE CURFEW BELL

Excerpt from "Reviews of New Films," *The New York Dramatic Mirror*, Vol. 61, No. 1590, June 12, 1909, p. 15.

(Edison, June 1) . . . In one respect only is there cause for serious criticism, and this is   59 in the order in which the scenes are arranged and connected. The scene showing Basil about to be shot should be cut into two or more scenes, the first one being inserted in the film immediately before or after the girl has grasped the tong of the bell to prevent the ringing of the curfew. As the picture now appears, the girl, Bess, climbs to the belfry and down again, preventing the ringing; runs some distance, secures a pardon from Cromwell and starts for the scene of the intended execution. It should now be nearly dark, but we are shown the troopers marching with the prisoner to the appointed place. He is stood up to be shot and the officer listens for the curfew bell, which should have rung some time before. We are obliged to conclude that somebody's watch was slow or they had all stopped on the way to take a parting drink.

LITTLE SISTER   **FILM 1909**

Excerpt from "Licensed Film Reviews," *The New York Dramatic Mirror*, Vol. 62, No. 1605, September 25, 1909, p. 16.

(Edison, Sept. 14) . . . The tenement roof scene is admirably handled, and the parlor scene would have been satisfactory also if a little ingenuity with a pair of scissors had been exercised by cutting the long parlor scene into short ones and alternating them with outside street scenes, so as to carry the two simultaneous actions along logically. The way it now appears in the film we see "little sister" entering the house through the window and then we see the interior with the youth being caught, the police being summoned and much time being taken in detail. All this while "little sister" is hanging to the outside of the window. When we see her coming in we are relieved, because we have commenced to wonder what has become of her. . . .

COMMENTARY

Frank Woods' praise of Biograph excellence might become almost monotonous were it not for his reports on Griffith's innovations, which sometimes consisted of placing a technical novelty from an earlier period of film production in a new and striking context. Also, Woods was not afraid to criticize when he felt something was unreal, or fell below the high standards Griffith had set for himself.

The scenario for THE LONELY VILLA was written by Mack Sennett, the Biograph actor who was to go on to create Keystone comedy and to discover Charlie Chaplin.

Griffith would probably have defended his jump cuts in A STRANGE MEETING and THE SEVENTH DAY as unavoidable because of the extreme compactness of the films.

Browning's PIPPA PASSES, mentioned in "The Importance of the Musical Accompaniment," seemed a triumph to reviewers, and *The New York Times*, in one of its rare glances at films, stated about the opening sequence that the sunlight wakes Pippa for her holiday "with light and shade effects like those obtained by the 'Secessionist' photographers." (13) This reference is to a group which centered around Alfred Stieglitz (1864-1946), the New York photographer who usually displayed the best of contemporary photographic work in his gallery at 291 Fifth Avenue. Many photographers of the time still leaned for inspiration on the Barbizon painters, or Rembrandt's deep shadows and to break that fascination, and shake photography out of its somnolence, Stieglitz had begun in 1909 also exhibiting drawings by Rodin, and the drawings, lithographs, water colors and etchings of Matisse. During the next few years he continued the same emphasis, with lithographs by Manet, Cezanne, Renoir and Toulouse-Lautrec, paintings and drawings by Henri Rousseau, drawings and etchings by Gordon Craig, drawings and water colors by Picasso, and water colors by Cezanne. It was at "291" that the work of some of these artists was literally seen for the first time in America.

FILM 1909   THE VIOLIN MAKER OF CREMONA

Excerpt from "Reviews of New Films," *The New York Dramatic Mirror,* Vol. 61, No. 1591, June 19, 1909, p. 16.

THE VIOLIN MAKER OF CREMONA (Biograph, June 7)—One grows so used to praising Biograph productions that it becomes difficult, at times, to find new words and phrases in which to describe the excellence of a film. In this subject the Biograph Company has repeated its previous best work in all respects and has left the reviewer no room for criticizing. The story is coherently arranged and intensely interesting, while the acting is almost perfect as to each character. The photography is particularly artistic — the closing scene in which the light is made to fade away on the figure of the sorrowful youth who has made the supreme sacrifice being art in its highest sense. . . .

FILM 1909   THE LONELY VILLA

Excerpt from "Reviews of New Films," *The New York Dramatic Mirror,* Vol. 61, No. 1591, June 19, 1909, p. 16.

THE LONELY VILLA (Biograph, June 10)—Possibly to show us that they have not forgotten how to do thrilling melodrama with intense interest, held in suspense till the final curtain, the Biograph producers have given us in this film a picture that will no doubt prove more popular than it deserves. For although the story is badly constructed, we are not inflicted with the grotesque style of acting that formerly distinguished this class of picture pantomime. The people move like real human beings and theatrical posing is entirely wanting. . . . Robbers lure a suburban citizen from his home by a fake message supposed to be from the man's mother. . . . *[The]* gentleman sets out in his automobile, which conveniently breaks down and he telephones his wife that he will be detained. He then learns, as we have already seen by the pictures, that . . . robbers have broken into the house. In alternate scenes we see the robbers laboriously breaking down one door after another as the wife and children bar the way with locks and light furniture, while the husband is making frantic efforts to secure a vehicle to come to the rescue. . . .

FILM 1909   THE LONELY VILLA

Excerpt from "Comments on the Week's Films," *The Moving Picture World,* Vol. 4, No. 25, June 19, 1909, p. 834.

(Biograph)—"Thank God, they're saved!" said a woman behind us at the conclusion of the Biograph film bearing the above title. Just like this woman, the entire audience was in a state of intense excitement as this picture was being shown. And no wonder, for it is one of the most adroitly managed bits of bloodless film drama that we have seen. From the moment the picture starts all is expectancy. . . . Indeed, when we saw the picture at Fourteenth street, the house literally "rose" at the story, it is so closely, effectively and convincingly told. . . .

FILM 1909   THE COUNTRY DOCTOR

Excerpt from "Reviews of New Films," *The New York Dramatic Mirror,* Vol. 62, No. 1595, July 17, 1909, p. 16.

THE COUNTRY DOCTOR (Biograph, July 7)— . . . There is also a touch of artistic sentiment in the opening and closing of the picture that should not go unnoticed—the panoramic view of the peaceful rural valley where the country doctor lives. At the opening of the story we see the valley bathed in sunshine. At the close we see it in the gloom of a darkening cloud. . . .

A STRANGE MEETING   FILM 1909

Excerpt from "Reviews of New Films," *The New York Dramatic Mirror,* Vol. 62, No. 1599, August 14, 1909, p. 15.

A STRANGE MEETING (Biograph, August 2)—There is a powerful moral in this film story and it is helped along wonderfully by the apt Biblical quotations which are interpolated as subtitles. Acted, as all Biograph pictures are, with intelligent feeling and produced with appropriate scenery, the film is one that will attract wide attention. There is, however, one fault to find with the picture—it lacks in smooth continuity. The story jumps from one scene to another, with lapses of intervening time without sufficient subtitles or connecting scenes to carry along the narrative. It is like a novel with different chapters omitted. . . .

THE INDIAN RUNNER'S ROMANCE   FILM 1909

Excerpts from "Reviews of New Films," *The New York Dramatic Mirror,* Vol. 62, No. 1602, September 4, 1909, p. 16.

THE INDIAN RUNNER'S ROMANCE (Biograph, August 23)— . . . *[Some early scenes]* are presented with such fidelity that we can believe we are witnessing the actual occurrences instead of mere acted moving pictures. . . . There is one circumstance that calls for criticism and it is an error that other film makers besides the Biograph frequently make. When the outlaws creep up behind the *[Indian]* girl to capture her she fails to hear them until they are close beside her. The thing looks unreal, more especially when we remember the sharp ears of the Indian race.

THE SEVENTH DAY   FILM 1909

Excerpt from "Reviews of New Films," *The New York Dramatic Mirror,* Vol. 62, No. 1602, September 4, 1909, p. 17.

THE SEVENTH DAY (Biograph, August 26)— . . . There is also another defect in the picture which has appeared in other Biograph subjects and which, it appears to the writer, could be corrected with advantage to these otherwise highly meritorious productions. Changes in scenes from one location to another are effected too suddenly. The characters leave the mother's parlor and immediately appear in the judge's chamber and vice versa, giving the impression that they are adjoining rooms, or at least in the same house. . . .

"1776": OR, THE HESSIAN RENEGADES   FILM 1909

Excerpt from "Reviews of New Films," *The New York Dramatic Mirror,* Vol. 62, No. 1604, September 18, 1909, p. 14.

"1776": or, THE HESSIAN RENEGADES (Biograph, September 6)— . . . Their escape from the house is not cleverly accomplished, as they go out of a window at the very elbows of two soldiers who are not even asleep; but once outside their actions are convincingly real. . . .

1909   **The Importance of the Musical Accompaniment**

Excerpt from "Spectator's Comments," *The New York Dramatic Mirror,* Vol 62, No. 1607, October 9, 1909, p. 16.

. . . Incidental music is claiming the intelligent attention of some of the picture manufacturers, notably the Edison and the Vitagraph. Some time ago the Edison Company commenced printing programmes of instrumental music suitable for Edison releases, and recently the Vitagraph Company announced that it would introduce properly arranged piano scores with each film of its manufacture. Now let some enterprising firm send along a prepared programme of sound effects to go with each subject, and another step upward will have been recorded.

The value of proper incidental music is well illustrated at the Keith and Proctor Union Square house, where the management pays particular attention to this feature. When the Biograph film IN OLD KENTUCKY was exhibited at that house the applause was more frequent throughout the reel than at other houses where the same subject was shown, and the difference is attributed to the excellent musical selections that were used.

Bad judgment in the selection of music may ruin an exhibition as much as a good programme may help it. Imagine a pathetic scene showing a husband mourning his dead wife accompanied by the strains of "No Wedding Bells for Me"! And yet this exact circumstance was noted by the writer recently. Not only in the matter of music is there room for incidental improvement in the management of picture houses, but also in many other respects. The use of posters in front of many houses betrays managerial ignorance that is sometimes appalling. Not long ago a Biograph Western dramatic subject called THE RED GIRL was advertised with a poster showing a soubrette dressed in red surrounded by a number of chorus girls and underneath were the words "Oh, fudge." The strong dramatic picture, IN OLD KENTUCKY, was billed with a lithograph showing a colored minstrel band, and as this is being written the writer hears that [Biograph's] PIPPA PASSES, adapted from Browning's beautiful poem, is billed at one house with a poster showing a man at a bar drinking a cocktail. . . .

COMMENTARY

The young unnamed actress who appears as Harum Scarum in THE MOUNTAINEER'S HONOR and in THE TEST is Mary Pickford, a debutante at Biograph that year. Someone immediately predicted: "she has a future if she doesn't permit her head to get swelled." (14) She did have a future: before many more years had passed she had become the top female star in America.

FILM 1909   THE MOUNTAINEER'S HONOR

Excerpts from "Review of Licensed Films," *The New York Dramatic Mirror,* Vol. 62, No. 1615, December 4, 1909, p. 17.

THE MOUNTAINEER'S HONOR (Biograph, November 25). — This is an exceedingly powerful and absorbing film tragedy amidst mountain scenes of marvelous beauty, which are presented to the best advantage by artistic photography. A phase of life peculiar to the mountain country of Kentucky is depicted, for the most part, with wonderful fidelity, and the characters are faithfully drawn with one exception, that of the young girl called Harum Scarum. This pretty miss, while altogether charming, is a bit too forward and kittenish in the presence of strangers to be accepted as a true type of that region, where unfamiliarity with the people of the world tends to make the inhabitants, especially the females, excessively shy and bashful until long acquaintance has won their confidence . . . . The mountaineer's home is also close by, as distances go in that region, as the pursuers run all the way up the rugged and picturesque hills to catch him. And yet at the opening of the story the young town man is so far away from home that he seeks shelter at the mountain cabin for the night . . . .

THE TRICK THAT FAILED   **FILM 1909**

Excerpt from "Reviews of Licensed Films," *The New York Dramatic Mirror*, Vol. 62, No. 1616, December 11, 1909, p. 15.

THE TRICK THAT FAILED (Biograph, November 29)—This clever farce comedy is so pleasing that we find ourselves wishing it were longer. It drags a little at first while working up to the real situation, but once the fun starts it moves spontaneously. Laughable as the comedy scenes are, however, it would appear that they would have been still funnier if they had not been cut short so frequently. It will be noted that this criticism is in reality the strongest kind of praise. . . .

THE TEST   **FILM 1909**

Excerpt from "Reviews of New Films," *The New York Dramatic Mirror*, Vol. 62, No. 1618, December 25, 1909, p. 16.

THE TEST (Biograph, December 16)—This is an amusing comedy of the young Wright couple of which we had several some months ago. Young Mrs. Wright is a charming little body and plays her part with delightful naturalness. Young Mr. Wright is also an effective comedian, but would he not be more so if he had not acquired the bad habit of telling his troubles to the camera? The appearance he gives of talking to the audience destroys the illusion of reality which is the strongest feature of good motion picture acting. A friend at the reviewer's elbow whispers that this is not a just criticism and that it is necessary to get the facial expressions over by looking squarely to the front, in order to make comedy situations effective. Perhaps he is right, but this reviewer will continue to maintain to the contrary. He can see no reason why humor will not gain the same strength from absolutely natural acting that is conceded to serious drama. . . .

COMMENTARY

At the very end of 1909, Griffith unexpectedly produced two "editorials" in film, the first being THE REDMAN'S VIEW: an indictment of white injustice to the American Indian.

THE RED MAN'S VIEW   **FILM 1909**

"Reviews of Licensed Films," *The New York Dramatic Mirror*, Vol. 62, No. 1617, December 18, 1909, pp. 15-16.

9. *D. W. Griffith's A FOOL'S REVENGE (1909). Biograph thought nothing of reducing the whole story of Rigoletto to a single reel, which was hailed as the first American film to equal French "smoothness of construction and power of dramatic action."*

THE REDMAN'S VIEW (Biograph, December 9)—This remarkable film is clearly intended to be symbolical of the fate of the helpless Indian race as it has been forced to recede before the advancing whites, and as such it is full of poetic sentiment and artistic beauty, and is at the same time an important step out of the beaten path. Whether the symbolism will be understood or not by the average spectator is another matter. However, even as a mere incident in Indian life it has deep interest, with a touching love story to give it color. An Indian camp is first seen with a young brave winning the love of a particularly pleasing little Indian maiden. The whites come and brutally drive the Indians away from their hunting grounds, and here the conduct of the red men will appear to some to be wanting in truth, either as a part of the symbolism or as a development in an Indian drama. Our Indians in this film make no real effort to resist or retaliate. They are not even armed with any sort of weapons and one wonders how they managed to exist. But on the other hand, viewed in an allegorical sense, it may be reasonably claimed that the feeble resistance of the red man against the white, taken as a whole, has really been of too little effect to be considered resistance at all. At any rate, in this picture they move on, leaving only the Indian maiden, whom the whites seize as their slave. Her lover has his aged father to help over the long and weary trail toward the setting sun. A subtitle in the film calls it the "long trek," but it may be doubted if this term is in harmony with the theme. When the Indians pause they are again forced on by the whites and when the maiden tries to escape she is dragged back. At last the old chief dies and his body is disposed of Indian fashion, elevated on poles. Now we see the young lover speeding back to the old camp to recover his sweetheart. She creeps out to meet him and they are about to escape when the whites swarm from the tent and hold them prisoners. The lover is told to release his hold of the girl or suffer death and he bravely defies them. It is the only bit of spirit accorded to the Indian character in the whole picture, and it gains its reward, for one of the whites interferes in the lover's behalf and they are allowed to go in peace, thus symbolizing the belated friendship we are showing for the red race. On the whole the film is another Indian classic to the Biograph's credit.

"SPECTATOR'S COMMENTS"   1909

Excerpt from "Spectator's Comments," *The New York Dramatic Mirror,* Vol. 62, No. 1618, December 25, 1909, p. 15.

The possibilities of motion picture literature continually increase in scope. First we had the scenic, topical and travel pictures, then the short comedies, next the dramas, and now the motion picture is used for a variety of educational and scientific purposes. But much as the cinematograph has encroached on the domains of the stage, the pulpit and the printing press, we had hardly expected it to enter the editorial field. We had thought that the editor in his sanctum would be exempt from this sort of rivalry. Vain hope. The Biograph Company in the past two weeks has shattered to smithereens the editor's fancied security by the production of two film subjects that are nothing if not editorials, and good ones at that. The two films referred to are THE REDMAN'S VIEW and A CORNER IN WHEAT.

The two films are such radical departures from the ordinary themes of current motion pictures that they merit comment. THE REDMAN'S VIEW, reviewed last week in *The Mirror,* is an appeal in pictures on behalf of the Indian. The Injustice that the red race has suffered at the hands of the white is held up to our eyes in convincing picture language, and the conclusion is conveyed that they are now receiving as wards of the nation only scant and belated recognition. . . .

1909   "ERROR IN A BIOGRAPH REVIEW"

From *The New York Dramatic Mirror,* Vol. 62, No. 1618, December 25, 1909, p. 15.

An error was made last week in *The Mirror's* review of the notable Biograph subject, THE REDMAN'S VIEW, the statement being made that the Indians were shown wholly unarmed. The alleged circumstance was made the basis for mild but unwarranted criticism, whereas additional praise would have been amply justified. *The Mirror,* therefore, hastens to make correction. THE REDMAN'S VIEW is an allegorical subject, showing in picture scenes the sad history of the red race, and opens with a scene showing the arrival of armed whites at an Indian village in the West. A short but ineffectual resistance is followed by the disarming of the Indians and their pathetic movement further west. The arms and the disarming escaped the eyes of the reviewer and occasioned the only adverse reflection that was directed against the picture, which was otherwise praised as a film of the highest class, conceived along original lines.

COMMENTARY

A CORNER IN WHEAT, Griffith's second "editorial," was subtitled "The Story of the Wheat in Symbolism." It draws ingeniously upon two works by the American realist Frank Norris (1870-1902): his short story, "A Deal in Wheat" (published posthumously, 1903) and his novel, *The Octopus* (1901). You will usually read that it is based upon Norris' novel, *The Pit,* which is the remark of someone who has never opened the book.

Reprinted here are "A Deal in Wheat" in its entirety, and two excerpts from *The Octopus.* In the first excerpt the "inter-cutting" in print reveals the origin, eight years earlier, of the inter-cutting for contrast in the film: the lavish banquet takes place at the home of the Railroad King (not the Wheat King), and is contrasted by the use of "alternate scenes," with the plight of Mrs. Hooven, who is starving with her child in the streets—a victim of the Railroad King's war on the farmers in the Valley. The second excerpt describes how the ambitious agent, S. Behrman, dies by falling unobserved into the hold of a ship while it is being loaded noisily with grain.

In August of 1910, another Griffith Biograph film, THE USURER, also attacked heedless diners: ". . . In contrasting scenes and with appropriate Biblical subtitles we see the usurer giving a luxurious wine dinner and an elaborate lunch while the collectors are out seizing the poor belongings of his victims who are unable to repay the money they have borrowed. . . ." (15)

FILM 1909   A CORNER IN WHEAT

"Reviews of Licensed Films," *The New York Dramatic Mirror,* Vol. 62, No. 1618, December 25, 1909, p. 15.

A CORNER IN WHEAT (Biograph, December 13).—This picture is not a picture drama, although it is presented with dramatic force. It is an argument, an editorial, an essay on a vital subject of deep interest to all. The theme is the rising cost of living, the inability of the masses to meet the increase and the part played by the speculator in bringing about this unfortunate condition. No orator, no editorial writer, no essayist could so strongly and effectively present the thoughts that are conveyed in this picture. It is another demonstration of the force and power of motion pictures as a means of conveying ideas. It was a daring step for the Biograph producers to take, to thus step out of the domain of picture drama as they have done in this film and in the one last week, THE REDMAN'S VIEW, but having taken the step and done so successfully, they are entitled to all the   67 praise they will undoubtedly receive for having opened up a new vein for motion picture subjects. The film opens with an artistic farm scene after the style of Millet, showing the sowers of wheat, hopeless and worn down by hard work. From these depressing scenes we turn to the affair of the speculator where the great corner is being arranged. The master mind issues his orders and the brokers appear in the wheat pit, where we see them struggling like ravenous wolves to control the wealth they did nothing to create. The corner wins and the defeated gamblers are brushed aside like the chaff of the grain for which they had fought. Another change and we see the city poor paying the increased price for bread or going hungry for want of enough money to buy. We get a glimpse of the dreadful breadline contrasted with the scenes of high life where the successful speculators are lavishing the money they have won. A sensational turn is given to the film when we see the speculator showing his friends through one of his elevators. He is handed a message telling him that he has cornered the world's supply and in the midst of his exultation he makes a misstep and falls to a terrible death in one of his own bins of wheat. We see him struggle and disappear from view in the dusty grain and we see again the breadline and the weary farmers. The film closes in the darkening night on the farm. The effectiveness of the subject is enhanced by the superb acting of the company. Every part is powerfully presented with telling truthfulness, except in one instance only, when we see the farmers sowing the wheat. No wheat would ever come up from the sort of sowing they do, but this slip is lost sight of in the artistic atmosphere of the scene and in the compelling pictures that follow.

Excerpt from " 'Spectator's' Comments," *The New York Dramatic Mirror,* Vol. 62, No. 1618, December 25, 1909, p. 15.

. . . We see contrasted in the pictures the struggling farmer who sows for small return, the scheming, gambling speculator who corners the wheat of the world, reaping more wealth than he can possibly use, and spending it in lavish opulence, and finally we see the suffering poor and the starving breadline, with bread doubled in price by the rise in wheat. These scenes are alternated with fine judgment, and the argument and lesson is too obvious to require explanation. . . .

"PICTURE HIT AT FIFTH AVENUE"   **1910**

From *The New York Dramatic Mirror,* Vol. 63, No. 1621, January 15, 1910, p. 13.

At Keith and Proctor's Fifth Avenue Theatre last week a notable exception was made to the manner of billing the moving picture with which the vaudeville bill was closed. Biograph's A CORNER IN WHEAT was the subject and it was specially featured in the billing and programme. . . .
The reception accorded the picture by the Fifth Avenue audiences during the week fully justified the billing and proves what *The Mirror* has claimed, that more attention should be paid by regular vaudeville houses to the pictures with which they close their performances.

A DEAL IN WHEAT   **1903**

From *A Deal in Wheat and Other Stories of the New and Old West,* Frank Norris, Doubleday, Page & Company, New York, 1903, pp. 3-26.

I. The Bear—Wheat At Sixty-Two

As Sam Lewiston backed the horse into the shafts of his buckboard and began hitching the tugs to the whiffle-tree, his wife came out from the kitchen door of the house and drew near, and stood for some time at the horse's head, her arms folded and her apron rolled around them. For a long moment neither spoke. They had talked over the situation so long and so comprehensively the night before that there seemed to be nothing more to say.

The time was late in the summer, the place a ranch in Southwestern Kansas, and Lewiston and his wife were two of a vast population of farmers, wheat growers, who at that moment were passing through a crisis—a crisis that at any moment might culminate in tragedy. Wheat was down to sixty-six.

At length Emma Lewiston spoke.

"Well," she hazarded, looking vaguely out across the ranch toward the horizon, leagues distant; "well, Sam, there's always that offer of brother Joe's. We can quit—and go to Chicago—if the worst comes."

"And give up!" exclaimed Lewiston, running the lines through the torets. "Leave the ranch! Give up! After all these years!"

His wife made no reply for the moment. Lewiston climbed into the buckboard and gathered up the lines. "Well, here goes for the last try, Emmie," he said. "Good-by, girl. Maybe things will look better in town today."

"Maybe," she said gravely. She kissed her husband good-by and stood for some time looking after the buckboard traveling toward the town in a moving pillar of dust.

"I don't know," she murmured at length; "I don't know just how we're going to make out."

When he reached town, Lewiston tied the horse to the iron railing in front of the Odd Fellows Hall, the ground floor of which was occupied by the post-office, and went across the street and up the stairway of a building of brick and granite—quite the most pretentious structure of the town—and knocked at a door upon the first landing. The door was furnished with a pane of frosted glass, on which, in gold letters, was inscribed, "Bridges & Co., Grain Dealers."

Bridges himself, a middle-aged man who wore a velvet skull-cap and who was smoking a Pittsburgh stogy, met the farmer at the counter and the two exchanged perfunctory greetings.

"Well," said Lewiston, tentatively, after a while.

"Well, Lewiston," said the other, "I can't take that wheat of yours at any better than sixty-two."

"Sixty-*two*!"

"It's the Chicago price that does it, Lewiston. Truslow is bearing the stuff for all he's worth. It's Truslow and the bear clique that stick the knife into us. The price broke again this morning. We've just got a wire."

"Good heavens," murmured Lewiston, looking vaguely from side to side. "That—that ruins me. I *can't* carry my grain any longer—what with storage charges and—and—Bridges, I don't see just how I'm going to make out. Sixty-two cents a bushel! Why, man, what with this and with that it's cost me nearly a dollar a bushel to raise that wheat, and now Truslow—"

He turned away abruptly with a quick gesture of infinite discouragement.

He went down the stairs, and making his way to where his buckboard was hitched, got in, and, with eyes vacant, the reins slipping and sliding in his limp, half-open hands, drove slowly back to the ranch. His wife had seen him coming, and met him as he drew up before the barn.

"Well?" she demanded.

69

"Emmie," he said as he got out of the buckboard, laying his arm across her shoulder, "Emmie, I guess we'll take up with Joe's offer. We'll go to Chicago. We're cleaned out!"

II. The Bull—Wheat At A Dollar-Ten

. . . . —and said Party of the Second Part further covenants and agrees to merchandise such wheat in foreign ports, it being understood and agreed between the Party of the First Part and the Party of the Second Part that the wheat hereinbefore mentioned is released and sold to the Party of the Second Part for export purposes only, and not for consumption or distribution within the boundaries of the United States of America or of Canada.

"Now, Mr. Gates, if you will sign for Mr. Truslow I guess that'll be all," remarked Hornung when he had finished reading.

Hornung affixed his signature to the two documents and passed them over to Gates, who signed for his principal and client, Truslow—or, as he has been called ever since he had gone into the fight against Hornung's corner—the Great Bear. Hornung's secretary was called in and witnessed the signatures, and Gates thrust the contract into his Gladstone bag and stood up, smoothing his hat.

"You will deliver the warehouse receipts for the grain," began Gates.

"I'll send a messenger to Truslow's office before noon," interrupted Hornung. "You can pay by certified check through the Illinois Trust people."

When the other had taken himself off, Hornung sat for some moments gazing abstractedly toward his office windows, thinking over the whole matter. He had just agreed to release to Truslow, at the rate of one dollar and ten cents per bushel, one hundred thousand out of the two million and odd bushels of wheat that he, Hornung, controlled, or actually owned. And for the moment he was wondering if, after all, he had done wisely in not goring the Great Bear to actual financial death. He had made him pay one hundred thousand dollars. Truslow was good for this amount. Would it not have been better to have put a prohibitive figure on the grain and forced the Bear into bankruptcy? True, Hornung would then be without his enemy's money, but Truslow would have been eliminated from the situation, and that—so Hornung told himself—was always a consummation most devoutly, strenuously and diligently to be striven for. Truslow once dead was dead, but the Bear was never more dangerous than when desperate.

"But so long as he can't get *wheat*," muttered Hornung at the end of his reflections, "he can't hurt me. And he can't get it. That I *know*."

For Hornung controlled the situation. So far back as the February of that year an "unknown bull" had been making his presence felt on the floor of the Board of Trade. By the middle of March the commercial reports of the daily press had begun to speak of "the powerful bull clique"; a few weeks later that legendary condition of affairs implied and epitomized in the magic words "Dollar Wheat" had been attained, and by the first of April, when the price had been boosted to one dollar and ten cents a bushel, Hornung had disclosed his hand, and in place of mere rumors, the definite and authoritative news that May wheat had been cornered in the Chicago pit went flashing around the world from Liverpool to Odessa and from Duluth to Buenos Aires.

It was—so the veteran operators were persuaded—Truslow himself who had made Hornung's corner possible. The Great Bear had for once overreached himself, and, believing himself all-powerful, had hammered the price just the fatal fraction too far down. Wheat had gone to sixty-two—for the time, and under the circumstances, an abnormal price. When the reaction came it was tremendous. Hornung saw his chance, seized it, and in a few months had turned the tables, had cornered the product, and virtually driven the bear clique out of the pit.

70

On the same day that the delivery of the hundred thousand bushels was made to Truslow, Hornung met his broker at his lunch club.

"Well," said the latter, "I see you let go that line of stuff to Truslow."

Hornung nodded; but the broker added:

"Remember, I was against it from the very beginning. I know we've cleared up over a hundred thou'. I would have fifty times preferred to have lost twice that and *smashed Truslow dead*. Bet you what you like he makes us pay for it somehow."

"Huh!" grunted his principal. "How about insurance, and warehouse charges, and carrying expenses on that lot? Guess we'd have had to pay those, too, if we'd held on."

But the other put up his chin, unwilling to be persuaded. "I won't sleep easy," he declared, "till Truslow is busted."

III. The Pit

Just as Going mounted the steps on the edge of the pit the great gong struck, a roar of a hundred voices developed with the swiftness of successive explosions, the rush of a hundred men surging downward to the center of the pit filled the air with the stamp and grind of feet, a hundred hands in eager, strenuous gestures tossed upward from out the brown of the crowd, the official reporter in his cage on the margin of the pit leaned far forward with straining ear to catch the opening bid, and another day of battle was begun.

Since the sale of the hundred thousand bushels of wheat to Truslow the "Hornung crowd" had steadily shouldered the price higher until on this particular morning it stood at one dollar and a half. That was Hornung's price. No one else had any grain to sell.

But not ten minutes after the opening, Going was surprised out of all countenance to hear shouted from the other side of the pit these words:

"Sell May at one-fifty."

Going was for the moment touching elbows with Kimbark on one side and with Merriam on the other, all three belonging to the "Hornung crowd." Their answering challenge of *"Sold"* was as the voice of one man. They did not pause to reflect upon the strangeness of the circumstance. (That was for afterward.) Their response to the offer was as unconscious as a reflex action and almost as rapid, and before the pit was well aware of what had happened the transaction of one thousand bushels was down upon Going's trading-card and fifteen hundred dollars had changed hands. But here was a marvel—the whole available supply of wheat cornered, Hornung master of the situation, invincible, unassailable; yet behold a man willing to sell, a Bear bold enough to raise his head.

"That was Kennedy, wasn't it, who made that offer?" asked Kimbark, as Going noted down the trade—"Kennedy, that new man?"

"Yes; who do you suppose he's selling for; who's willing to go short at this stage of the game?"

"Maybe he ain't short."

"Short! Great heavens, man; where'd he get the stuff?"

"Blamed if I know. We can account for every handful of May. Steady! Oh, there he goes again."

"Sell a thousand May at one-fifty," vociferated the bear-broker, throwing out his hand, one finger raised to indicate the number of "contracts" offered. This time it was evident that he was attacking the Hornung crowd deliberately, for, ignoring the jam of traders that swept toward him, he looked across the pit to where Going and Kimbark were shouting *"Sold! Sold!"* and nodded his head.

A second time Going made memoranda of the trade, and either the Hornung holdings were increased by two thousand bushels of May wheat or the Hornung bank account swelled by at least three thousand dollars of some unknown short's money.

Of late—so sure was the bull crowd of its position—no one had even thought of glancing at the inspection sheet on the bulletin board. But now one of Going's messengers hurried up to him with the announcement that this sheet showed receipts at Chicago for that morning of twenty-five thousand bushels, and not credited to Hornung. Some one had got hold of a line of wheat overlooked by the "clique" and was dumping it upon them.

"Wire the Chief," said Going over his shoulder to Merriam. This one struggled out of the crowd, and on a telegraph blank scribbled:

> "Strong bear movement—New man—Kennedy—Selling in lots of five contracts—Chicago receipts twenty-five thousand."

The message was despatched, and in a few moments the answer came back, laconic, of military terseness:

> "Support the market."

And Going obeyed, Merriam and Kimbark following, the new broker fairly throwing the wheat at them in thousand-bushel lots.

"Sell May at 'fifty; sell May; sell May."

A moment's indecision, an instant's hesitation, the first faint suggestion of weakness, and the market would have broken under them. But for the better part of four hours they stood their ground, taking all that was offered, in constant communication with the Chief, and from time to time stimulated and steadied by his brief, unvarying command:

"Support the market."

At the close of the session they had bought in the twenty-five thousand bushels of May. Hornung's position was as stable as a rock and the price closed even with the opening figure—one dollar and a half.

But the morning's work was the talk of all La Salle Street. Who was back of the raid? What was the meaning of this unexpected selling? For weeks the pit trading had been merely nominal. Truslow, the Great Bear, from whom the most serious attack might have been expected, had gone to his country seat at Geneva Lake, in Wisconsin, declaring himself to be out of the market entirely. He went bass-fishing every day.

IV. The Belt Line

On a certain day toward the middle of the month, at a time when the mysterious Bear had unloaded some eighty thousand bushels upon Hornung, a conference was held in the library of Hornung's home. His broker attended it, and also a clean-faced, bright-eyed individual whose name of Cyrus Ryder might have been found upon the payroll of a rather well-known detective agency. For upward of half an hour after the conference began the detective spoke, the other two listening attentively, gravely.

"Then, last of all," concluded Ryder, "I made out I was a hobo, and began stealing rides on the Belt Line Railroad. Know the road? It just circles Chicago. Truslow owns it. Yes? Well, then I began to catch on. I noticed that cars of certain numbers—thirty-one nought thirty-four, thirty-two one ninety—well, the numbers don't matter, but anyhow, these cars were always switched onto the sidings by Mr. Truslow's main elevator D soon as they came in. The wheat was shunted in, and they were pulled out again. Well, I spotted one car and stole a ride on her. Say, look here, *that car went right around the city on the Belt, and came back to D again, and the same wheat in her all the time.* The grain was reinspected—it was raw, I tell you—and the warehouse receipts made out just as though the stuff had come in from Kansas or Iowa."

72   "The same wheat all the time!" interrupted Hornung.

"The same wheat—your wheat, that you sold to Truslow."

"Great snakes!" ejaculated Hornung's broker. "Truslow never took it abroad at all."

"Took it abroad! Say, he's just been running it around Chicago, like the supers in 'Shenandoah,' round an' round, so you'd think it was a new lot, an' selling it back to you again."

"No wonder we couldn't account for so much wheat."

"Bought it from us at one-ten, and made us buy it back—our own wheat—at one-fifty."

Hornung and his broker looked at each other in silence for a moment. Then all at once Hornung struck the arm of his chair with his fist and exploded in a roar of laughter. The broker stared for one bewildered moment, then followed his example.

"Sold! Sold!" shouted Hornung almost gleefully. "Upon my soul it's as good as a Gilbert and Sullivan show. And we—Oh, Lord! Billy, shake on it, and hats off to my distinguished friend, Truslow. He'll be President some day. Hey! What? Prosecute him? Not I."

"He's done us out of a neat hatful of dollars for all that," observed the broker, suddenly grave.

"Billy, it's worth the price."

"We've got to make it up somehow."

"Well, tell you what. We were going to boost the price to one seventy-five next week, and make that our settlement figure."

"Can't do it now. Can't afford it."

"No. Here; we'll let out a big link; we'll put wheat at two dollars, and let it go at that."

"Two it is, then," said the broker.

V. The Bread Line

The street was very dark and absolutely deserted. It was a district on the "South Side," not far from the Chicago River, given up largely to wholesale stores, and after nightfall was empty of all life The echoes slept but lightly hereabouts, and the slightest footfall, the faintest noise, woke them upon the instant and sent them clamouring up and down the length of the pavement between the iron shuttered fronts. The only light visible came from the side door of a certain "Vienna" bakery, where at one o'clock in the morning loaves of bread were given away to any who should ask. Every evening about nine o'clock the outcasts began to gather about the side door. The stragglers came in rapidly, and the line—the "bread line," as it was called—began to form. By midnight it was usually some hundred yards in length, stretching almost the entire length of the block.

Toward ten in the evening, his coat collar turned up against the fine drizzle that pervaded the air, his hands in his pockets, his elbows gripping his sides, Sam Lewiston came up and silently took his place at the end of the line.

Unable to conduct his farm upon a paying basis at the time when Truslow, the "Great Bear," had sent the price of grain down to sixty-two cents a bushel, Lewiston had turned over his entire property to his creditors, and, leaving Kansas for good, had abandoned farming, and had left his wife at her sister's boarding-house in Topeka with the understanding that she was to join him in Chicago as soon as he had found a steady job. Then he had come to Chicago and had turned workman. His brother Joe conducted a small hat factory on Archer Avenue, and for a time he found there a meager employment. But difficulties had occurred, times were bad, the hat factory was involved in debts, the repealing of a certain import duty on manufactured felt overcrowded the home market with cheap Belgian and French products, and in the end his brother had assigned and gone to Milwaukee.

Thrown out of work, Lewiston drifted aimlessly about Chicago, from pillar to post,   73 working a little, earning here a dollar, there a dime, but always sinking, sinking, till at last the ooze of the lowest bottom dragged at his feet and the rush of the great ebb went over him and engulfed him and shut him out from the light, and a park bench became his home and the "bread line" his chief makeshift of subsistence.

He stood now in the enfolding drizzle, sodden, stupefied with fatigue. Before and behind stretched the line. There was no talking. There was no sound. The street was empty. It was so still that the passing of a cable-car in the adjoining thoroughfare grated like prolonged rolling explosions, beginning and ending at immeasurable distances. The drizzle descended incessantly. After a long time midnight struck.

There was something ominous and gravely impressive in this interminable line of dark figures, close pressed, soundless; a crowd, yet absolutely still; a close-packed, silent file, waiting, waiting in the vast deserted night-ridden street; waiting without a word, without a movement, there under the night and under the slow-moving mists of rain.

Few in the crowd were professional beggars. Most of them were workmen, long since out of work, forced into idleness by long-continued "hard times," by ill luck, by sickness. To them the "bread line" was a godsend. At least they could not starve. Between jobs here in the end was something to hold them up—a small platform, as it were, above the sweep of black water, where for a moment they might pause and take breath before the plunge.

The period of waiting on this night of rain seemed endless to those silent, hungry men; but at length there was a stir. The line moved. The side door opened. Ah, at last! They were going to hand out the bread.

But instead of the usual white-aproned undercook with his crowded hampers there now appeared in the doorway a new man—a young fellow who looked like a bookkeeper's assistant. He bore in his hand a placard, which he tacked to the outside of the door. Then he disappeared within the bakery, locking the door after him.

A shudder of poignant despair, an unformed, inarticulate sense of calamity, seemed to run from end to end of the line. What had happened? Those in the rear, unable to read the placard, surged forward, a sense of bitter disappointment clutching at their hearts.

The line broke up, disintegrated into a shapeless throng—a throng that crowded forward and collected in front of the shut door whereon the placard was affixed. Lewiston, with the others, pushed forward. On the placard he read these words:

> "Owing to the fact that the price of grain has been increased to two
> dollars a bushel, there will be no distribution of bread from this bakery
> until further notice."

Lewiston turned away, dumb, bewildered. Till morning he walked the streets, going on without purpose, without direction. But now at last his luck had turned. Overnight the wheel of his fortunes had creaked and swung upon its axis, and before noon he had found a job in the street-cleaning brigade. In the course of time he rose to be first shift-boss, then deputy inspector, then inspector, promoted to the dignity of driving in a red wagon with rubber tires and drawing a salary instead of mere wages. The wife was sent for and a new start was made.

But Lewiston never forgot. Dimly he began to see the significance of things. Caught once in the cogs and wheels of a great and terrible engine, he had seen—none better—its workings. Of all the men who had vainly stood in the "bread line" on that rainy night in early summer, he, perhaps, had been the only one who had struggled up to the surface again. How many others had gone down in the great ebb? Grim question; he dared not think how many.

He had seen the two ends of a great wheat operation—a battle between Bear and Bull. The stories (subsequently published in the city's press) of Truslow's countermove in selling Hornung his own wheat, supplied the unseen section. The farmer—he who raised

10. New at Biograph in 1909 was Mary Pickford (left, in black wig). With Billy Quirk (right), she appears here in Griffith's OH, UNCLE!, in which—as in THE TEST—they play the Wright couple. Center: James Kirkwood.

the wheat—was ruined upon one hand; the working-man—he who consumed it—was ruined upon the other. But between the two, the great operators, who never saw the wheat they traded in, bought and sold the world's food, gambled in the nourishment of entire nations, practised their tricks, their chicanery and oblique shifty "deals," were reconciled in their differences, and went on through their appointed way, jovial, contented, enthroned, and unassailable.

THE OCTOPUS: THE EPIC OF THE WHEAT—A STORY OF CALIFORNIA   **1901**

Excerpts from *The Octopus: The Epic of the Wheat—A Story of California,* Frank Norris, *The Complete Works of Frank Norris,* P. F. Collier and Son, N.Y., n.d. (copyright 1901 by Doubleday, Page and Company) pp. 438, 445, 468-469).

The Chariots of the Fog

. . . Presley assented in meaningless words. He sipped his wine mechanically, looking about that marvelous room, with its subdued saffron lights, its glitter of glass and silver, its beautiful women in their elaborate toilets, its deft, correct servants; its array of tableware—cut glass, chased silver, and Dresden crockery. It was Wealth, in all its outward and visible forms, the signs of an opulence so great that it need never be husbanded. It was the home of a railway "Magnate," a Railroad King. For this, then, the farmers paid. It was for this that S. Behrman turned the screw, tightened the vise. It was for this that Dyke had been driven to outlawry and a jail. It was for this that Lyman Derrick had been bought, the Governor ruined and broken, Annixter shot down, Hooven killed.

The soup, *purée à la Derby,* was served, and at the same time, as *hors d'oeuvres,* ortolan patties, together with a tiny sandwich made of browned toast and thin slices of ham, sprinkled over with Parmesan cheese. The wine, so Mrs. Gerard caused it to be understood, was Xeres, of the 1815 vintage.

———

Mrs. Hooven crossed the avenue. It was growing late. Without knowing it, she had come to a part of the city that experienced beggars shunned. There was nobody about. Block after block of residences stretched away on either hand, lighted, full of people. But the sidewalks were deserted.

"Mammy," whimpered Hilda, "I'm tired, carry me."

Using all her strength, Mrs. Hooven picked her up and moved on aimlessly.

Then again that terrible cry, the cry of the hungry child appealing to the helpless mother:

"Mammy, I'm hungry."

"Ach, Gott, leedle girl," exclaimed Mrs. Hooven, holding her close to her shoulder, the tears starting from her eyes. "Ach, leedle tochter. Doand, doand, doand. You praik my hairt. I cen't vind any subber. We got noddings to eat, noddings, noddings."

"When do we have those bread'n milk again, Mammy?"

"To-morrow—soon—py-and-py, Hilda. I doand know what pecome oaf us now, what pecome of my leedle babby."

She went on, holding Hilda against her shoulder with one arm as best she might, one hand steadying herself against the fence railings along the sidewalk. At last, a solitary pedestrian came into view, a young man in a top hat and overcoat, walking rapidly. Mrs. Hooven held out a quivering hand as he passed her.

"Say, say, den, Meest'r, blease hellup a boor womun."

The other hurried on.

———

The fish course was *grenadins* of bass and small salmon, the latter stuffed, and cooked in white wine and mushroom liquor.

"I have read your poem, of course, Mr. Presley," observed Mrs. Gerard. " 'The Toilers,' I mean. What a sermon you read us, you dreadful young man. I felt that I ought at once to 'sell all that I have and give to the poor.' Positively, it did stire me up. You may congratulate yourself upon making at least one convert. Just because of that poem Mrs. Cedarquist and I have started a movement to send a whole shipload of wheat to the starving people in India. Now, you horrid *réactionnaire,* are you satisfied?"

"I am very glad," murmured Presley.

"But I am afraid," observed Mrs. Cedarquist, "that we may be too late. They are dying so fast, those poor people. By the time our ship reaches India the famine may be all over."

"One need never be afraid of being 'too late' in the matter of helping the destitute," answered Presley. "Unfortunately, they are always a fixed quantity. 'The poor ye have always with you.' "

"How very clever that is," said Mrs. Gerard.

Mrs. Cedarquist tapped the table with her fan in mild applause.

"Brilliant, brilliant," she murmured, "epigrammatical."

"Honora," said Mrs. Gerard, turning to her daughter, at that moment in conversation with the languid Lambert, "Honora, *entends-tu, ma chérie, l'esprit de notre jeune Lamartine.*"

Mrs. Hooven went on, stumbling from street to street, holding Hilda to her breast. Famine gnawed incessantly at her stomach; walk though she might, turn upon her tracks up and down the streets, back to the avenue again, incessantly and relentlessly the torture dug into her vitals. She was hungry, hungry, and if the want of food harassed and rended her, full-grown woman that she was, what must it be in the poor, starved stomach of her little girl? Oh, for some helping hand now, oh, for one little mouthful, one little nibble! Food, food, all her wrecked body clamored for nourishment; anything to numb those gnawing teeth—an abandoned loaf, hard, mouldered; a half-eaten fruit, yes, even the refuse of the gutter, even the garbage of the ash heap. On she went, peering into dark corners, into the areaways, anywhere, everywhere, watching the silent prowling of cats, the intent rovings of stray dogs. But she was growing weaker, the pains and cramps in her stomach returned. Hilda's weight bore her to the pavement. More than once a great giddiness, a certain wheeling faintness, all but overcame her. Hilda, however, was asleep. To wake her would only mean to revive her to the consciousness of hunger; yet how to carry her further? Mrs. Hooven began to fear that she would fall with her child in her arms. The terror of a collapse upon those cold pavements glistening with fog-damp roused her; she must make an effort to get through the night. She rallied all her strength, and pausing a moment to shift the weight of her baby to the other arm, once more set off through the night. A little while later she found on the edge of the sidewalk the peeling of a banana. It had been trodden upon and it was muddy, but joyfully she caught it up.

"Hilda," she cried, "wake oop, leedle girl. See, loog den, dere's somedings to eat. Look den, hey? Dat's goot, ain't it? Zum bunaner."

But it could not be eaten. Decayed, dirty, all but rotting, the stomach turned from the refuse, nauseated.

"No, no," cried Hilda, "that's not good. I can't eat it. Oh, Mammy, please gif me those bread'n milk."

By now the guests of Mrs. Gerard had come to the entrees—Londonderry pheasants, escallops of duck, and *rissolettes à la pompadour.* The wine was Chateau Latour.

All around the table conversations were going forward gayly. The good wines had broken up the slight restraint of the early part of the evening and a spirit of good humor

77

and good fellowship prevailed. Young Lambert and Mr. Gerard were deep in reminiscences of certain mutual duck-shooting expeditions. Mrs. Gerard and Mrs. Cedarquist discussed a novel—a strange mingling of psychology, degeneracy, and analysis of erotic conditions—which had just been translated from the Italian. Stephen Lambert and Beatrice disputed over the merits of a Scotch collie just given to the young lady. The scene was gay, the electric bulbs sparkled, the wine flashing back the light. The entire table was a vague glow of white napery, delicate china, and glass as brilliant as crystal. Behind the guests the serving-men came and went, filling the glasses continually, changing the covers, serving the entrees, managing the dinner without interruption, confusion, or the slightest unnecessary noise.

But Presley could find no enjoyment in the occasion. From that picture of feasting, that scene of luxury, that atmosphere of decorous, well-bred refinement, his thoughts went back to Los Muertos and Quien Sabe and the irrigating ditch at Hooven's. He saw them fall, one by one, Harran, Annixter, Osterman, Broderson, Hooven. The clink of the wine glasses was drowned in the explosion of revolvers. The railroad might indeed by a force only, which no man could control and for which no man was responsible, but his friends had been killed, but years of extortion and oppression had wrung money from all the San Joaquin, money that had made possible this very scene in which he found himself. Because Magnus had been beggared, Gerard had become Railroad King; because the farmers of the valley were poor, these men were rich.

The fancy grew big in his mind, distorted, caricatured, terrible. Because the farmers had been killed at the irrigating ditch, these others, Gerard and his family, fed full. They fattened on the blood of the People, on the blood of the men who had been killed at the ditch. It was a half-ludicrous, half-horrible "dog eat dog," an unspeakable cannibalism. Harran, Annixter, and Hooven were being devoured there under his eyes. These dainty women, his cousin Beatrice and little Miss Gerard, frail, delicate; all these fine ladies with their small fingers and slender necks, suddenly were transfigured in his tortured mind into harpies tearing human flesh. His head swam with the horror of it, the terror of it. Yes, the People *would* turn some day, and turning, rend those who now preyed upon them. It would be "dog eat dog" again, with positions reversed, and he saw for one instant of time that splendid house sacked to its foundations, the tables overturned, the pictures torn, the hangings blazing, and Liberty, the red-handed Man in the Street, grimed with powder smoke, foul with the gutter, rush yelling, torch in hand, through every door.

———

At ten o'clock Mrs. Hooven fell.

Luckily she was leading Hilda by the hand at the time and the little girl was not hurt. In vain had Mrs. Hooven, hour after hour, walked the streets. After a while she no longer made any attempt to beg; nobody was stirring, nor did she even try to hunt for food with the stray dogs and cats. She had made up her mind to return to the park in order to sit upon the benches there, but she had mistaken the direction, and, following up Sacramento Street, had come out at length, not upon the park, but upon a great vacant lot at the very top of the Clay Street hill. The ground was unfenced and rose above her to form the cap of the hill, all overgrown with bushes and a few stunted live-oaks. It was in trying to cross this piece of ground that she fell. She got upon her feet again.

"Ach, mammy, did you hurt yourself?" asked Hilda.

"No, no."

"Is that house where we get those bread'n milk?"

Hilda pointed to a single rambling building just visible in the night that stood isolated upon the summit of the hill in a grove of trees.

"No, no, dere aindt no braid end miluk, leedle tochter."

Hilda once more began to sob.

"Ach, mammy, please, *please*, I want it. I'm hungry."

The jangled nerves snapped at last under the tension, and Mrs. Hooven, suddenly shaking Hilda roughly, cried out:

"Stop, Stop. Doand say ut egen, you. My Gott, you kill me yet."

But quick upon this came the reaction. The mother caught her little girl to her, sinking down upon her knees, putting her arms around her, holding her close.

"No, no, gry all so mudge es you want. Say dot you are hongry. Say ut egen, say ut all de dime, ofer end ofer egen. Say ut, poor, starfing, leedle babby. Oh, mein poor, leedle tochter. My Gott, oh, I go crazy bretty soon, I guess. I cen't hellup you. I cen't ged you noddings to eat, noddings, noddings. Hilda, we gowun to die togedder. Put der arms roundt me, soh, tighd, leedle babby. We gowun to die, we gowun to vind Popper. We aindt gowun to be hongry eny more."

"Vair we go now?" demanded Hilda.

"No places. Mommer's soh tiredt. We stop heir, leedle while, end rest."

Underneath a large bush that afforded a little shelter from the wind Mrs. Hooven lay down, taking Hilda in her arms and wrapping her shawl about her. The infinite, vast night expanded gigantic all around them. At this elevation they were far above the city. It was still. Close overhead whirled the chariots of the fog, galloping landward, smothering lights, blurring outlines. Soon all sight of the town was shut out; even the solitary house on the hilltop vanished. There was nothing left but gray, wheeling fog, and the mother and child, alone, shivering in a little strip of damp ground, an island drifting aimlessly in empty space.

Hilda's fingers touched a leaf from the bush and instinctively closed upon it and carried it to her mouth. "Mammy," she said, "I'm eating those leaf. Is those good?"

Her mother did not reply.

"You going to sleep, mammy?" inquired Hilda, touching her face.

Mrs. Hooven roused herself a little.

"Hey? Vat you say? Asleep? Yais, I guess I wass asleep."

Her voice trailed unintelligibly to silence again. She was not, however, asleep. Her eyes were open. A grateful numbness had begun to creep over her, a pleasing semi-insensibility. She no longer felt the pain and cramps of her stomach, even the hunger was ceasing to bite.

———

"These stuffed artichokes are delicious, Mrs. Gerard," murmured young Lambert, wiping his lips with a corner of his napkin. "Pardon me for mentioning it, but your dinner must be my excuse."

"And this asparagus—since Mr. Lambert has set the bad example," observed Mrs. Cedarquist, "so delicate, such an exquisite flavor. How *do* you manage?"

"We get all our asparagus from the southern part of the State, from one particular ranch," explained Mrs. Gerard. "We order it by wire and get it only twenty hours after cutting. My husband sees to it that it is put on a special train. It stops at this ranch just to take on our asparagus. Extravagant, isn't it, but I simply cannot eat asparagus that has been cut more than a day."

"Nor I," exclaimed Julian Lambert, who posed as an epicure. "I can tell to an hour just how long asparagus has been picked."

"Fancy eating ordinary market asparagus," said Mrs. Gerard, "that has been fingered by Heaven knows how many hands."

———

"Mammy, mammy, wake up," cried Hilda, trying to push open Mrs. Hooven's eyelids, at last closed. "Mammy, don't. You're just trying to frighten me."

Feebly Hilda shook her by the shoulder. At last Mrs. Hooven's lips stirred. Putting her head down, Hilda distinguished the whispered words:

"I'm sick. Go to schleep. . . . Sick. . . . Noddings to eat."

———

79

The desert was a wonderful preparation of alternate layers of biscuit, glaces, ice cream, and candied chestnuts.

"Delicious, is it not?" observed Julian Lambert, partly to himself, partly to Miss Cedarquist. "This *Moscovite fouetté*—upon my word, I have never tasted its equal."

"And you should know, shouldn't you?" returned the young lady.

———

"Mammy, mammy, wake up," cried Hilda. "Don't sleep so. I'm frightenedt."

Repeatedly she shook her; repeatedly she tried to raise the inert eyelids with the point of her finger. But her mother no longer stirred. The gaunt, lean body, with its bony face and sunken eyesockets, lay back, prone upon the ground, the feet upturned and showing the ragged, worn soles of the shoes, the forehead and gray hair beaded with fog, the poor, faded bonnet awry, the poor, faded dress soiled and torn.

Hilda drew close to her mother, kissing her face, twining her arms around her neck. For a long time she lay that way, alternately sobbing and sleeping. Then, after a long time, there was a stir. She woke from a doze to find a police officer and two or three other men bending over her. Some one carried a lantern. Terrified, smitten dumb, she was unable to answer the questions put to her. Then a woman, evidently the mistress of the house on the top of the hill, arrived and took Hilda in her arms and cried over her.

"I'll take the little girl," she said to the police officer. "But the mother, can you save her? Is she too far gone?"

"I've sent for a doctor," replied the other.

———

Just before the ladies left the table, young Lambert raised his glass of Madeira. Turning toward the wife of the Railroad King, he said:

"My best compliments for a delightful dinner."

———

The doctor, who had been bending over Mrs. Hooven, rose.

"It's no use," he said; "she has been dead some time—exhaustion from starvation."

In the Hold of the "Swanhilda"

. . . Once more the level of the wheat rose and the grains began piling deeper about him. Once more he retreated. Once more he crawled staggering to the foot of the cataract, screaming till his ears sang and his eyeballs strained in their sockets, and once more the relentless tide drove him back.

Then began that terrible dance of death; the man dodging, doubling, squirming, hunted from one corner to another, the wheat slowly, inexorably flowing, rising, spreading to every angle, to every nook and cranny. It reached his middle. Furious and with bleeding hands and broken nails, he dug his way out to fall backward, all but exhausted, gasping for breath in the dust-thickened air. Roused again by the slow advance of the tide, he leaped up and stumbled away, blinded with the agony in his eyes, only to crash against the metal hull of the vessel. He turned about, the blood streaming from his face, and paused to collect his senses, and with a rush another wave swirled about his ankles and knees. Exhaustion grew upon him. To stand still meant to sink; to lie or sit meant to be buried the quicker; and all this in the dark, all this in an air that could scarcely be breathed, all this while he fought an enemy that could not be gripped, toiling in a sea that could not be stayed.

Guided by the sound of the falling wheat, S. Behrman crawled on hands and knees toward the hatchway. Once more he raised his voice in a shout for help. His bleeding throat and raw, parched lips refused to utter but a wheezing moan. Once more he tried to look toward the one patch of faint light above him. His eyelids, clogged with chaff, could no longer open. The Wheat poured about his waist as he raised himself upon his knees.

Reason fled. Deafened with the roar of the grain, blinded and made dumb with its chaff, he threw himself forward with clutching fingers, rolling upon his back, and lay there, moving feebly, the head rolling from side to side. The Wheat, leaping continuously from the chute, poured around him. It filled the pockets of the coat, it crept up the sleeves and trouser legs, it covered the great, protuberant stomach, it ran at last in rivulets into the distended, gasping mouth. It covered the face.

Upon the surface of the Wheat, under the chute, nothing moved but the Wheat itself. There was no sign of life. Then, for an instant, the surface stirred. A hand, fat, with short fingers and swollen veins, reached up, clutching, then fell limp and prone. In another instant it was covered. In the hold of the "Swanhilda" there was no movement but the widening ripples that spread flowing from the ever-breaking, ever-reforming cone; no sound but the rushing of the Wheat that continued to plunge incessantly from the iron chute in a prolonged roar, persistent, steady, inevitable. . . .

11. Lillian Gish's first big chance at Biograph came in THE MOTHERING HEART (1913): rage, grief and frustration in the garden after the death of her baby. The principal scenes in this Griffith film are "done close up to the camera."

CHAPTER **5**

Griffith at Biograph (II): More Experiments

COMMENTARY

About 1910, Griffith delegated films to an assistant director, Frank Powell, and by 1911 he was tossing the Biograph comedies to Mack Sennett, who, with one eye on the master, worked out the style of comedy later called Keystone. Both of these men eventually left, but in 1913 Griffith still had two directors.

Most people associate Griffith with frantic climaxes, but he also introduced into his films a more deliberate tempo of acting—something Frank Woods termed "repose"— until his bosses began to wrangle with him about adopting a more sensational style. In January, 1910, he took the company on the first of their annual visits to California, following the lead of several companies which had already found California scenery and weather conditions profitable for Westerns. THE UNCHANGING SEA and RAMONA, in which the extreme long shot is noted by Woods, were filmed on the West Coast.

It is one of the great ironies of film history that Griffith, the director we wish to learn most about, was employed by a company which tried to keep his name, the names of their players, and most details of production, secret. In response to hard-breathing letters to fan magazines, other companies were loosening up with information about players, and when Biograph finally tipped its mitt, it was not until long after its rivals had been publishing names freely, as good business.

To compare Griffith, even anonymously, with the theatrical producer David Belasco, was a tremendous compliment. (**cf. p. 86, "The Spectator Calls Griffith a Genius."**)

FILM 1910   THE UNCHANGING SEA

Excerpts from "Reviews of Licensed Films," *The New York Dramatic Mirror*, vol. 63, No. 1638, May 14, 1910, p. 20.

THE UNCHANGING SEA (Biograph, May 5)—This subject may be properly classed with that other Biograph poetic masterpiece, PIPPA PASSES. The opening situation and the artistic atmosphere are suggested, as we are told in the film announcement, by the poet Kingsley's beautiful verses on "The Three Fishers," and to say that the film producer has caught with rare feeling the spirit of the poem is only to assert that which is obviously true. . . . The photography is superb, and the acting—well, it may be best described by stating that it conveys not one hint of acting at all. Every thought and feeling has been expressed with wonderful force, but with scarcely a gesture and with perfect naturalness.

Deliberation and Repose 1910

Excerpt from " 'Spectator's' Comments," *The New York Dramatic Mirror,* Vol. 63, No. 1641, June 4, 1910, p. 16.

   Probably the most marked change that has taken place in the style of picture acting in the last year or two has been in the matter of tempo. In the old days the pictures were literally "moving" pictures, and lively moving at that. Everything had to be on the jump. The more action that could be crowded into each foot of film the more perfect the picture was supposed to be. Some of this manner of picture acting still survives, usually when an old timer does the acting or directing, but, generally speaking, it has given place to more deliberation. People in the pictures now move about somewhat after the style of human beings, instead of jumping jacks. For all of which let us give due thanks to the special divinity that rules over motion picture affairs.
   One producing company, the Biograph, was a pioneer among American producers in this reform, and its films have long been distinguished by deliberation and repose, to such an extent that at one time it was a matter of much comment and criticism on the part of those who looked on the innovation as little short of sacrilege. Indeed, it may now be told, as a matter worthy of record, that the Biograph's first experiments along this line were undertaken with no little hesitation and fearsome doubt. Those having the responsibility for the change felt that they were treading on thin ice. So deeply rooted was the notion that speed was the thing, that the experimenters were fearful that their attempts to introduce real acting into the films would be met with derisive laughter. Possibly to their astonishment the change at once met with the approval of the public. The people who paid their money to look at the pictures applauded the new idea (new in American pictures), and from that moment the habit commenced to grow, and has kept on growing ever since. . . .

RAMONA **FILM 1910**

Excerpts from "Reviews of Licensed Films," *The New York Dramatic Mirror,* Vol. 63, No. 1641, June 4, 1910, p. 16.

RAMONA (Biograph, May 23)—When a motion picture producer undertakes to translate any standard literary or dramatic work into film language (if one may be permitted to thus designate this medium of transmitting thought), he owes it to his subject as well as to his own self-respect to give the translation or adaptation a tone and quality that at least approach that of the original. . . . This is what the Biograph producers have obviously attempted in their film rendition of Mrs. Jackson's novel, *Ramona,* and that they have succeeded to a marked degree cannot be doubted on witnessing the film in exhibition. . . . Attention should be called, however, to a few remarkable scenes—one of them the destruction of Alessandro's village, which we see with the poor Indian from a mountain top looking down into a valley a mile or more away. The burning huts, the hurrying people and the wagons of the whites are clearly visible, though they appear but as mere specks in the distance. . . .

On the Anonymity of the Biograph Players 1910

Excerpt from " 'Spectator's' Comments," *The New York Dramatic Mirror,* Vol. 64, No. 1647, July 16, 1910, p. 18.

. . . Recently *The Mirror* in this department contained a communication in which a reader asked the name of a certain picture player whose work he had noted in certain Biograph productions, among them LOVE AMONG THE ROSES and THE UNCHANGING SEA. In reply to this communication The Spectator stated that the Biograph Company does not make public the names of its players, holding that no good can come from it. Now comes a letter from a new independent company which is so amusingly and obviously an attempt to secure free advertising (rates on application) that it is reproduced here minus the name of the company and the player.

> *To The Spectator:*
>
> SIR.—We do not hold with others that no good can come with the policy of publishing the names of players in motion pictures.
>
> In answer to the letter of "Subscriber" in your column of July 2, we are glad to inform him that ——— is the man.
>
> ——— is the gardener in 'LOVE AMONG THE ROSES.
>
> ——— is the hero of THE UNCHANGING SEA.
>
> ———, with his "splendid work" and "attractive personality," has recently disappeared, it is true, but will shortly reappear, more splendid and attractive than ever, as leading man of the ——— films.
>
> Yours faithfully, ——— ———.

This incident affords a pretty good illustration of the reason why the Biograph Company objects to starring its players. The company holds, as The Spectator understands it, that it is not the personality of particular players that makes for success in picture production, and this without desiring to detract from the good work of the people who have appeared in Biograph films. The essential elements of successful film production are, the Biograph is believed to argue, first the story, second the direction and third competent people as a class and not as individuals. These views are not far different from those advanced by The Spectator in discussing motion picture producing, and they are certainly well borne out by the Biograph Company's experience. We have seen the personnel of its stock company changed from time to time until now scarcely one of the original faces is ever seen in its films and yet the Biograph standard continues steadily to advance. Players with little or no reputation and others with big reputations have appeared in Biograph pictures, some of them becoming favorites, but none of them individually essential to the advancement of Biograph reputation. Why then, it is asked, should a player who has been made, we might say, by the Biograph, seek to use for the benefit of another company that reputation which belongs mostly to the Biograph and not to him? It must be confessed that there appears to be considerable sense in this view of the matter.

Just how far an ex-employee may honorably go in coupling his name with that of his former employer or with the work of the former employer is a question in motion picture affairs that offers some complications. An author of a book may advertise himself as being the author of previous books notwithstanding that the publishers are not the same, but an author is not an employee and even with his independent standing in this respect he would hardly be justified in using his former publisher's trade name in giving competitive publicity to himself. On the stage there appears to be less recognized restriction. Players almost universally advertise themselves as having appeared in this or that play or for this or that big manager, and yet here too it would seem there should be a limit. Motion pictures, however, are like literature in one respect and the stage in another. They partake of the character of both. The actor in a picture, unless purposely starred by his employer, occupies a position at present not well defined, and he will no doubt remain in this uncertain position until time has developed his recognized standing.

The Spectator Calls Griffith a Genius   1910

Excerpt from " 'Spectator's' Comments," *The New York Dramatic Mirror,* Vol. 64, No. 1671, December 28, 1910, pp. 28-29.

. . . Before dismissing our friend the actor-exhibitor, one more paragraph of his letter should be considered. He has heard it rumored somewhere that David Belasco has been trying his hand at picture directing and that he "had a hand" in directing the production of THE BROKEN DOLL and some other superior Biograph productions. On this point The Spectator can set the inquirer right. Mr. Belasco has had nothing whatever to do with any production of the company named, although if he had been responsible for some of that company's best, it is the opinion of The Spectator that they would have reflected nothing but credit upon him.

This is not the first time The Spectator has known the Biograph producing director's work to be compared favorably with that of David Belasco. He has even been called the Belasco of motion pictures, which in the opinion of The Spectator scarcely does him full justice, for the reason that his talents have been displayed very often in motion pictures in ways not subject to comparison, since they are not possible to even approximate in theatrical stage direction. Not only has this director given evidence of creative and interpretive genius dramatically, but he has also evinced poetic sense and a fine appreciation of pictorial values. Furthermore, he has demonstrated a striking aptitude for taking raw acting material and molding it into finished and polished form. The number of motion picture favorites, both male and female, who have gained their schooling and reputations under his direction and are prominent elsewhere, is one of the recognized wonders of the motion picture business.

COMMENTARY

About this time Griffith began pressing for longer films, against the interests of the Biograph Company, who thought one-reelers were good forever. He finally compromised with a two-reel film, issued in two parts on successive release dates (HIS TRUST and HIS TRUST FULFILLED). Frank Woods celebrates the event in the following excerpt.

Perhaps Woods is correct in considering the Pathé L'ASSOMMOIR, of Zola (October, 1909), to be "the first double reel dramatic story," but a month earlier American Vitagraph had already begun the release of a four-reel version of *Les Misérables,* one reel at a time, over a three months' period (September-November, 1909). The three reels of UNCLE TOM'S CABIN appeared individually in July, 1910.

Biograph's WILFUL PEGGY (1910), with Mary Pickford, won the *Mirror* Merit List contest as "the best film ever produced."

Spectator on Longer Films   1911

Excerpt from " 'Spectator's' Comments," *The New York Dramatic Mirror,* Vol. 65, No. 1676, February 1, 1911, p. 29.

Picture stories requiring more than a reel of film for the telling are rare enough to make the recent Biograph releases, HIS TRUST and HIS TRUST FULFILLED, notable events, even if the pictures themselves did not stand out, as they do, as works of superior merit. Excluding from consideration religious and biographical subjects, the first double reel dramatic story was DRINK [L'ASSOMMOIR], produced by Pathé Frères, and it was not thought at the time to have been favorably received. Exchanges complained and exhibitors complained, although there is no good evidence that the public complained. On the contrary, it has since transpired that the exchanges and the exhibitors were wrong in this matter, as they have been in so many other matters—they didn't know their public nor did they have any idea how to handle a good thing when they got it. DRINK was a hit, as it now appears, having been voted for quite liberally in *The Mirror* Merit List contest [about outstanding motion pictures], notwithstanding the fact that it was issued as long ago as October 21 and 22, 1909, being voted for solely on memory. Handled in the manner that double or triple reel issues are now handled, being featured and exhibited complete at each performance, it should have had wide popularity.

It was not until UNCLE TOM'S CABIN was produced in three reels by the Vitagraph Company that exchanges and exhibitors realized the proper method to follow in cases of this kind. UNCLE TOM became at once a great favorite and still continues so, mainly because it is exhibited complete, all three reels at each exhibition. Here, then, we have a possible hint as to the real feature pictures of the future—the kind of pictures that the manufacturers have long been dreaming of—the kind that will live for return exhibition; that will be in such demand that reprints will be required. Does anyone imagine that UNCLE TOM'S CABIN in one reel would have occasioned any more demand than any other good, single reel subject? It is not probable. On the contrary, it is more than improbable. It is the fact that the exhibitor can advertise the film in advance as something extra and of more importance than the ordinary single reel subjects, and can then make good with a picture entertainment that fully satisfies and pleases his patrons, that makes UNCLE TOM'S CABIN a money making proposition for the theatres.

From this it follows that the two or three or four reel feature dramas must be intrinsically good or they will fail to fill the long-felt want. Mere length will not do. The subject must honestly warrant the length—in fact must demand the length, and this, it is most pleasing to state, the recent Biograph double reel does. HIS TRUST and HIS TRUST FULFILLED are among the very best things that the Biograph has ever produced, and that is saying a great deal, as any one will admit. While each reel is a completed story in itself, they go better together as one story, and wise exhibitors will show them in that way, advertising them in advance.

Both subjects, HIS TRUST and HIS TRUST FULFILLED, were reviewed in *The Mirror* last week, but it will not be out of place to call renewed attention to some of the particular points which distinguish this double subject. The battle scenes in HIS TRUST were managed with a skill that baffles criticism. Apparently an actual battle was in progress. There was no massing of participants with the obvious intention of crowding as many persons as possible within the field of the camera, and yet there was the evidence of numbers, apparently engaged in real fighting, but really forming a series of artificially arranged scenes, each of which might have been the subject of a painter's masterpiece. It was so, too, with the fire scene—it was genuine, the commodious structure erected for the purpose being burned to the ground and forming a picture never to be forgotten. Along with these elements of marvelous stage management and superior acting runs a story of strongly appealing character—an old negro servant faithful to the trust imposed upon him by his master, who has been killed in battle. Altogether HIS TRUST and HIS TRUST FULFILLED may be pronounced a Biograph masterpiece. . . .

COMMENTARY

HIS DAUGHTER provided examples of the technical tragedies which sometimes befell Griffith's assistants. The film was directed by Frank Powell.

The Biograph Company's second visit to Los Angeles in 1911 finds the West Coast already rivalling New York as the country's number one production center, and by the end of 1912, Southern California claimed to be the world's largest center of operations.

HIS DAUGHTER   **FILM 1911**

Excerpt from "Reviews of Licensed Films," *The New York Dramatic Mirror*, Vol. 65, No. 1680, March 1, 1911, p. 31.

HIS DAUGHTER (Biograph, February 23)—. . . The old father's fall was not convincing, and the girl's intention to leave the town was told only by the subtitle, as she ran out bareheaded and with no traveling equipment. There was also a technical error in the management of the scenes; exits from the interiors are to the right, but the immediate entrances to the exteriors are also from the right.

"LOS ANGELES AS A PRODUCING CENTER"   1911

By Richard V. Spencer, *The Moving Picture World*, Vol. 8, No. 14, April 8, 1911, p. 768.

Los Angeles within the short period of two years has reached a position in the moving picture manufacturing field where it is second only to New York. There are several good reasons for this remarkable growth, chief of which, of course, is the climatic advantage of Southern California. To understand the climate of this paradise of moving picture men, one must turn to the maps and notice the topographical features. Bordering Southern California on the north and east are two large mountain ranges. The first, or inner range, the Tehachipi's, with an average altitude of 6,000 feet, are only nine miles from the city limits at the closest place. Beyond them lie patches of desert and semi-arid lands with here and there a fertile farming valley. Fifty miles beyond the Tehachipi's lie the San Bernardino chain, the higher peaks of which exceed 11,000 feet and are snow-capped the year round. In the winter this high chain turns aside the blizzards that sweep down from the north and east, and in the summer they keep out the hot winds of the desert beyond.

The U.S. Weather Bureau reports show the following thirty-four-year average: Perfectly clear days, *one hundred and sixty four;* partly cloudy, *one hundred and fifty-six;* (coming under this heading are conditions preceding and following storms, which are less than 1/4, and the other 3/4 are days with early morning fogs, which, however, always clear away by noon, leaving the rest of the day cloudless). Cloudy and rain, *forty-six* (in which photography is impossible). In other words, the climate of Southern California provides 320 days for good photography, out of the 365.

Within a twenty-mile radius of Los Angeles may be found conditions suitable for exteriors from a tropic to a frigid background, and from desert to jungle. Twenty miles to the west lie the pleasure beaches with a score of high class beach resorts within a forty minutes' trolley ride to the city. In the summertime the beach attendance runs into the hundreds of thousands. There may be taken resort comedies with an Atlantic City or Coney Island background. Within the same radius on the same beach were taken the marine dramas made famous by the Selig and Biograph companies. Here were taken such pictures as: THE UNCHANGING SEA (Biograph); A TALE OF THE SEA (Selig); FISHER FOLKS (Biograph); THE BUCCANEERS (Selig); A MESSAGE OF THE SEA (Bison); the sea scenes from THE PADRE, a recent Selig release, and others. These pictures have been admired the world over for their beautiful scenic surroundings and perfect photography.

For scenes of city life there is no need to go beyond Los Angeles. The last Federal census in 1910 gave the city a population of 319,198. Various street scenes and scenes in the city parks have been pictured by the Selig, Biograph and Essanay companies. Those views taken ranged from comedy scenes to scenic. The winter population of the city approximates 500,000, which includes the tourists and wealthy guests that come to spend the winter months. As a theatrical center Los Angeles is known the world over for its splendid legitimate and moving picture palaces, and the immense number of them for a city of this size. The two local dramatic stock companies, the Belasco and the Burbank are known to be two of the best stock companies in the whole country. The Orpheum management in May will open their new theater. The building is one of the most costly and beautiful theater buildings west of New York. Of the moving picture theaters, Clune's Broadway, The Hyman, Tally's, the College and Clune's Main Street Theater cost close to $50,000 each to build, without the cost of the real estate or lease. It is needless to say that each is of excellent design and of excellent appointments throughout. With the growth of the city dramatically there came the booking agencies, the scene painting studios, theatrical costumers, and other supply companies. Los Angeles is famous for its beautiful parks and fine residence districts, exteriors of which occasionally creep into the films.

Within the same twenty-mile radius may be found some of the most beautiful country homes and gardens in the world. Several of these have been photographed by the Selig and Biograph companies, among which were the famous sunken gardens of the Busch estate in Pasadena, and the residence of Rudolph Schiffman of the same city. A scenic mountain railway offers the weary tourist an allurement in the shape of a trip from roses to the snow line in forty minutes.

Within the same radius and near Pasadena are two historic missions, San Gabriel and San Fernando. Here were photographed THE TWO BROTHERS (Biograph); THE PADRE (Selig), and other films, the story of which was written around the aged missions.

Los Angeles and vicinity have acquired their reputation in the production of Western and Indian pictures. Here, of all places, is the ideal location for the production of such films. Here is found the necessary rolling country cut up by foothills, treacherous canyons and lofty mountain ranges in the background. Within ten minutes' ride of Los Angeles is Griffith Park, the largest public park in the world. In this park have been produced nine-tenths of the Bison films of cowboy and Indian life. Here, too, the Selig, Kalem and Biograph companies have taken many pictures, most of them Westerns.

Each of the companies working here have their own ideas of location. The Selig Company chose Edendale, a city suburb, and have here erected a $75,000 plant. Within a block of them is the Pathé West Coast Studio, which, when completed, will probably represent a similar investment. A block below the Pathé Studio on the same side of the street is the Bison Studio. It is shortly to be enlarged and improved with new buildings. The Biograph Company last year occupied temporary quarters in Pasadena, but this year finds them at home in their new studio at Pico and Georgia streets in the heart of the city. The studio is to be permanent and will be occupied every winter by the company. Nine miles away, near Glendale, the Kalem Company have erected a studio in the foothills for the production of their Western and Indian films. Some sixty miles away, near Redlands, the Essanay Western Company are hard at work. At Long Beach, a local beach resort, a new Independent producing company is rushing operations to get into the market with their film. The company is known as The California Motion Picture Manufacturing Company. Another new Independent company of a similar name, known as The California Motion Picture Company, are also getting ready to enter the field. They will erect a local studio in the near future.

Many Eastern moving picture manufacturers have long had their eyes on Southern California as the *only* available locality in the United States possessing the necessary clear weather for perfect photography, nearness to market, scenery and other conditions necessary for moving picture production during the winter months. Transportation is another factor that must enter into the question. Los Angeles is the center of an interurban electric system whose many lines and divisions offer safe, rapid transportation to all parts of the country. Here, in a rapidly growing, modern big city, may be found every condition for films of city life. Here, too, is a surplus of high class theatrical talent

89

ready and willing to give their best efforts for the uplift of the pictures. The city has produced such moving picture stars as Hobart Bosworth, leading man for the Selig Company; Florence Barker (Biograph leads), Dorothy Bernard (ingenue leads for the Biograph Company), and other actors and actresses of equal talent. Every year finds Eastern winter conditions more unsatisfactory for motion picture work. Here weather conditions and climate permit work and photography the year around. The Selig forces lead the California rush, and thither they have lured the rest of the colony. More Eastern producers are known to be making preparations to come this year, and eventually Los Angeles, by reason of the few of the several advantages above set forth, will become known to the world, not as the second largest picture producing center, but the largest, bar none.

COMMENTARY

Woods finds A KNIGHT OF THE ROAD (1911) to be a milestone in the amplification of Griffith's editing technique. Still operating within the one-reel limit, he fragmented his sequence into more than fifty individual shots, "and maybe a hundred." (15a)

The embattled cabin of FIGHTING BLOOD constitutes an exciting Griffith motif which recurs even as late as AMERICA (1924). One of the three women in THE FEMALE OF THE SPECIES (1912) is Mary Pickford, back with Biograph after a year with two other film concerns. Before 1912 was over, she left the Biograph Company again, permanently, this time to return to the stage in a Belasco production.

Lillian Gish, whom Griffith had been featuring in films for less than a year, received her first big chance in THE MOTHERING HEART (1913). All the principal scenes in this film "are done close up to the camera," and it was one of the rare Biograph two-reelers.

A KNIGHT OF THE ROAD   **FILM 1911**

"Reviews of Licensed Films," *The New York Dramatic Mirror,* Vol. 65, No. 1688, April 26, 1911, p. 29.

A KNIGHT OF THE ROAD (Biograph, April 20)—This film is entirely out of the ordinary in the style of its production. One might think, on first thought, that it is a return to the old days of hurry-up in film acting, but it is hardly that, because it is acted so well and the flitting scenes join each other so logically. The average film drama may have from a dozen to twenty-five or thirty changes of scenes; this one has at least fifty, and maybe a hundred—the reviewer couldn't count them. It was all for the purpose of telling how a tramp saved a house from robbery by other tramps and was offered a home as a reward, but when he got up in the morning and heard the hustle and bustle of work in the household and looked outside to see the hands jumping into their labors, he escaped out of the window and went back to his buddy, who had boiled a few potatoes in a tomato can at a roadside fire. Toil was no part of this tramp's philosophy of life. As an experiment, just to show what the Biograph can do, the film is a success, but unless one watches sharp, not to miss a scene or a half dozen scenes, it may be hard for some to follow.

Griffith's Bounding Heroine   1911

Excerpt from "Seen on the Screen," by Freelance, *The Moving Picture World,* Vol. 8, No. 20, May 20, 1911, p. 1120.

You certainly have to hand it to Biograph for beautiful photography. Recently it was a Spanish gypsy thing—now it is IN THE DAYS OF '49, and if there is any concern making better pictures, from photographic standpoint, I wish some one would tell me where I can see them. Incidentally, there was a slight variation from a rather hackneyed theme in this love story, since the untrue wife, wishing to run away with a gambler, is rejected by the gambler after he has played cards for her with her drunken husband and lost, and the playlet ends happily. But the outdoor scenery is beautiful, the photography exquisite right straight along, and if the interiors are somewhat crowded and the action broken by too many changes of scene, the action itself is well done, and the acting first-class all the way through, albeit this leading lady, capable as she is, has still the absurd habit of jumping up and down to express delight as a child of ten might jump. Of course, the present scribe never saw the wife of a miner receive a letter saying her husband was doing well and asking her to join him, but his idea is that such news, while good, is not so frantically entrancing as to make the recipient behave like an inspired idiot. Perhaps the stage manager [director] cautioned her, for she then proceeded to give a convincing presentation of a dissatisfied wife who, later disillusioned, comes to her senses. . . .

FILM 1911   THE WHITE ROSE OF THE WILDS

Excerpt from "Reviews of Licensed Films," *The New York Dramatic Mirror*, Vol. 65, No. 1693, May 31, 1911, p. 31.

THE WHITE ROSE OF THE WILDS (Biograph, May 25)—This is melodrama with sentimental trimmings, all of which is exceedingly interesting because it is so capitally done. One of the most striking features of the production, to the experienced eye, is the almost perfect mechanical precision with which each scene is timed; it all goes like well oiled clockwork and there are no jarring moments. In several instances the joining of scenes, where an entrance is made through a door and we instantly see the act completed on the other side, the action is so carefully put together that it seems the same movement. This is closely approaching perfection in the technique of picture directing. . . .

FILM 1911   FIGHTING BLOOD

Excerpts from " 'FIGHTING BLOOD'—Biograph," *The Moving Picture World*, Vol. 8, No. 27, July 8, 1911, p. 1575.

(Biograph) . . . Riding about aimlessly through a most picturesque country-side, [the oldest son of the pioneer] . . . sees from afar an attack of Indians on the house of a white settler, and hastens back to warn his sweetheart and her family. And now events crowd each other with a rapidity that must even enthuse the most jaded. The struggle in the cabin furnishes all the suspense element one can possibly desire. After some minutes, which, of course, "seemed like days," the brave . . . lad finds soldiers and they are crack riders every one of them and not afraid to show it. The changes in the picture, showing the situation as it must have appeared to the combatants in the valley, and the situation as it really was, with the soldiers riding like demons down the mountain gorge toward the blazing cottage, produced a thrilling effect and lessened somewhat the suspense, which up to that moment, was well nigh unendurable. . . .

THE BATTLE   **FILM 1911**

Excerpt from "Modern Melodrama," by C. H. Claudy, *The Moving Picture World,* Vol. 11, No. 2, January 13, 1912, p. 112.

(Biograph, November 6) . . . In the first of the play we are shown a pre-battle [Civil War] dance. I take it the producer knew what he was about, yet it does seem as if there was a wee bit too much hoydenish action and undignified jumping around for the formal dances one associates with the days of '61. But there was nothing to criticise in the departure—the long, long lines of soldiers marching down the road, the waving cheering townspeople, the crowd of children, the cavalry coming after—indeed, the film was shut off and the scene changed while they were still coming. It may have been that the film was cut here, but its effect was most artistic. "We haven't time to show you the whole army," it seemed to say for the producer, "we have to get to business. But the army is there, as you will see."
And we did see. . . .

THROUGH DARKENED VALES   **FILM 1911**

Excerpt from "Reviews of Licensed Films," *The New York Dramatic Mirror,* Vol. 66, No. 1718, November 22, 1911, p. 26.

THROUGH DARKENED VALES (Biograph, November 16)— . . . A review of this film would not be complete without reference to the scenes in which the lonely, helpless condition of the blind peddler is emphasized by showing him at a distance, as he wanders alone, picking his way through the deserted streets. Here we have an effect gained by an extreme exactly opposite to the close, intimate point of view characteristic of Biographs since the very beginning.

THE FEMALE OF THE SPECIES   **FILM 1912**

"Reviews of Licensed Films," *The New York Dramatic Mirror,* Vol. 67, No. 1740, April 24, 1912, p. 28.

THE FEMALE OF THE SPECIES (Biograph, April 15)—The expressive title borrowed from literature has been used for the theme of a most remarkable drama, bringing out much depth and philosophy in depicting the fundamental motives in the life of womankind, and whether one agrees with the philosophy or not, it makes a most striking subject and one that has been handled with consummate art and understanding, remarkable for its originality, power of interpretation, and, above all, for the infinite power of conception and imagination which it reveals. The three leading roles are played by the three most distinguished leading women of this company, and their particular work in this film would be hard to excell—a fact particularly true of the woman playing the wife. Much praise is also due them because the scenes were apparently taken during a wind storm of sand, adding much realism and effectiveness to the picture. The picture opens, showing the utter desolation left in the minds of the survivors of a massacre. The wife and sister may still claim and share the support of a man in their respective husband and brother, but in the other part of the field rests a woman alone. The two surviving women bid her join them in their flight over the desert for water. Their distress and deprivation have brought all four to a state where all emotion is deadened to visible things, and the gross fundamental forces alone are left to be expressed. As they stop for water during the journey, the sister and wife leave the man alone with the woman, while they search for water. His intellect is now gone from weariness and hardship, and only his sense replies to the dominant, hidden power of her presence. His wife sees the response, and the man dies. The woman is blamed by the others, and a cry for vengeance stirs their minds against the other woman. At last against the struggle of her better nature the wife goes to kill the woman resting apart, but the blow of the ax is stayed by the cry of an infant wailing in the arms of a dead Indian woman, who had died from thirst on the desert. The common cry of motherhood unites them all, and they journey on in mutual forgiveness and love. As an artistic achievement it deserves a place among the classics, as there is a wealth of symbolism and significance in all the smallest details.

FILM 1913   THE MOTHERING HEART

"Feature Films on the Market: THE MOTHERING HEART," *The New York Dramatic Mirror,* Vol. 70, No. 1803, July 9, 1913, p. 28.

THE MOTHERING HEART (Biograph, June 21)—When it was announced some weeks ago that the Biograph Company would release a photodrama of two-reel length a considerable stir of pleasant anticipation was experienced among those interested in the Licensed pictures. The Biograph Company has long had the enviable reputation of doing things well, and it has, at least, lived up to the reputation with THE MOTHERING HEART. After due reflection we are convinced that it is one of the most notable productions, from an artistic standpoint, the Biograph Company has made. Lillian Gish, as the little mother, while showing extreme youth, interprets her part with pleasing taste and remarkable intelligence. There are moments when the pose which she is caused to assume seems to bear out too plainly a conscious purpose on her part. Some of her attitudes of a blank, unseeing nature when the heart is torn with grief, seem to be held a bit too long for the best effect. But she has sincerity and, altogether, she is charming. Walter Miller, in the role of the young husband who is led astray only to repent and return because of parenthood properly realized, exhibits a splendid personality all his own, which is saying much when we consider the present tendency among some picture players to copy one another. The basic theme is not wholly new to us: we have seen it handled before in divers ways, but in such a scene as we have at the close of this picture where the two estranged parents lean over the crib where lies the cold form of the baby, we have another evidence of the Biograph's ability to successfully manage a most delicate situation. For the girl to have accepted the man back on his first show of repentance would have been disastrous; but the need of him and his full regeneration are clearly shown in the final working out. It is noteworthy that all the principal scenes in the picture are done close up to the camera, and some of the photographic coloring is beautiful. Particularly is this true of the scene, "The New Light." One of the most remarkable scenes we have seen for atmosphere and completeness of detail is the cabaret cafe. It is a picture that grows upon one with reflection.

(Signed) G.

" RUDOLF SEEKING THE KING AT ZENDA"

THE PRISONER OF ZENDA

12. Edwin S. Porter: THE PRISONER OF ZENDA (1913). Renouncing the close-up as unnatural, he kept the figures always full-length on the screen and was proud of it. An audience unused to films clapped for all his outdoor scenes as if they were magic demonstrations.

CHAPTER 6

Thunder on the Right (1909-1913): Griffith Leaves Biograph

COMMENTARY

Griffith was proving "too expensive" for Biograph too; his bosses were constantly curbing and frustrating his desire to make longer, bigger pictures, and managed, for a time, to do so by merely suppressing the films: the two-reel THE MASSACRE (filmed in 1912), although released abroad, was held back from the domestic market until 1914. Also released, at last, in 1914 were three films from 1913: the two-reel THE BATTLE AT ELDERBUSH GULCH and BRUTE FORCE, and the four-reel JUDITH OF BETHULIA.

Yet other American companies were lengthening their films, and certain foreign imports, especially from Italy, had been exhibited in four and five reels as early as 1911.

Griffith's quarrel with his Biograph bosses seems to have been mainly a matter of differences over the scale and cost of the films. Probably not related to this, but rising simultaneously, were the attacks of the conservatives on him, as exemplified in the following articles: "The Factor of Uniformity" (1909), "Too Near the Camera" (1911) and "Cutting Off the Feet" (1912), in which the art the author wishes film directors to study is obviously not Degas'. The veteran Edwin S. Porter is applauded for model procedure in keeping his figures always full-length on the screen, and this first review of THE PRISONER OF ZENDA confirms that he was still doing so in 1913.

Even in the fall of 1908, the *Mirror* had remarked that Biograph films "are distinguished, like the Pathé, by their heroic size, enabling the actors to convey the ideas intended with the utmost clearness." (16) But the *Moving Picture World,* which did not care for that kind of thing, complained about the Biograph THE MILLS OF THE GODS (August, 1909) that some of the "figures tower almost up to the ceiling in their heroic size." (17) Then followed the period when screen people were "cut off at the tops of their heads and the bottoms of their waistcoats."

In spite of Griffith's reputation for the use of close-up, there is normally very little specific mention of this in early reviews. An exception occurs in a review of JUDITH OF BETHULIA which states: "One close-up view even shows Judith [Blanche Sweet] with the tears running down her cheeks . . . ." (17a)

1909   "THE FACTOR OF UNIFORMITY"

Excerpts from "The Factor of Uniformity," *The Moving Picture World,* Vol. 5, No. 4, July 24, 1909, pp. 115-116.

. . . *[The]* question of uniformity has come into our minds several times lately when we have formed members of the paying public at some of the theaters for the purpose of writing our criticisms. And it arose with the greatest possible prominence only last week, when, in company with a friend, we were examining some of the latest films. The figures in this picture arrested our attention. Or we should say a part of the picture. These figures were so large that they occupied the entire perpendicular dimension of the sheet, that is, the figures that were nearest to the camera. The consequence was that the people in the theater had the idea that the film showed a story that was being enacted . . . by a race of giants and giantesses. A little later on in the course of the picture the figures had been photographed at a greater distance from the camera and so were less monstrous to the eye; while, in even a third part of the picture, the figures were so far away from the camera that they appeared of their natural size—an effect which was more agreeable to the audience.

Now, here was a total lack of uniformity, due entirely to a want of intelligence on the part of the producer and the photographer, and the effect on the minds of the people who saw this picture was extreme dissatisfaction. There is only one other explanation for this apparent discrepancy in size of the various parts of this picture, and that is that the lens varied in focal length. Of course, this is absurd to suppose. Only one lens was used in taking the various parts of this picture. Where the fault lay was in the disregard of uniformity of conditions evinced either by the photographer or by the producer, or both. If these figures had been photographed at equal distances from the camera, then they would have appeared of equal sizes on the screen, instead of varying between the dimensions of a Brobdignagian monstrosity and Lilliputian pygmies.

It is curious to reflect that in an hour's entertainment of a moving picture theater, the visitor sees an infinite variation in the apparent sizes of things as shown by the moving picture. This is absurd. On the vaudeville or talking stage, figures of human beings do not expand or contract irrationally or eccentrically; they remain the same size. Not so on the moving picture stage, where, as we have said, one film shows us giants and another mannikins. Now this is eminently a case, we think, where some sort of attempt should be made by somebody to make things uniform. It is not our business, of course. We do not make the pictures. If we did, however, we should make them not on the mammoth scale, but more in accordance with the need of conveying the correct sensuous impression.

"TOO NEAR THE CAMERA"   1911

Excerpt from "Too Near the Camera," *The Moving Picture World,* Vol. 8, No. 12, March 25, 1911, pp. 633-634.

. . . There are very many moving pictures made nowadays, even by reputable makers, in which the figures are too near the camera: that is to say, they assume unnecessarily large and, therefore, grotesque proportions. The reason for this is manifold. Film-makers have the idea that the public want to see the faces of the figures large; consequently, the camera is placed too near the figures; or perhaps, it is an optical defect, the focus of the lens is too short.

Experienced photographers know that to get naturalness of effect in a picture a short focus lens should be avoided, otherwise you get distortion, that is, unnecessary enlargement in parts of the pictures. A great many of the moving pictures that are made, especially those produced in a studio, would be all the better if longer focus lenses were employed, or what amounts to the same sort of thing, if the figures were placed farther away from the camera. The Rex [Company] releases are examples, to our mind, of the proper thing to do. Here Mr. [Edwin S.] Porter works on a large stage, and places his camera at a considerable distance from his actors. The result is that he avoids abnormality of size, and when you see the pictures on the screen, they express the proper sensuous impression of size. . . .

1912   "CUTTING OFF THE FEET"

By H. F. Hoffman, *The Moving Picture World,* Vol. 12, No. 1, April 6, 1912, p. 53.

Some time ago in the columns of the *World* there was voiced a polite protest against the tendency of many motion picture makers to cut the feet of the actors out of the scene. There were fond hopes hereabouts that the morsel of suggestion thus cast upon the waters would some day come back twice blest, having blessed the sender as well as the giver. But the fond hope was not fulfilled; for, instead of following that bit of wise counsel, the film makers straightway began cutting off the figures at the *knees*. Nor did it end there. Things kept getting worse, until now it is a common sight to witness a photoplay the greater part of which is acted so close to the camera that the actors are seen only from the waist upwards.

Facial expression—that seems to be the dominating influence that brings this inartistic result. The American producers, after they learned the rudiments of their craft, uncovered an entirely new school of pantomime. In the heyday of the business, when exhibitors were making fortunes out of small investments, the European picture had the call. Pantomime to the old world was an exact science. Every known gesture and expression had for years been labeled and catalogued as definitely as the rows of bottles in a chemist's shop. With the play-going public of America, the European school of pantomime at one time found favor over our crude home-made productions. Exhibitors clamored at the exchanges for foreign films. This was disheartening because it really did seem that the American product would never catch up. But at last the American producer found himself. He evolved a school of pantomime that swept away the antiquated formulas and proved to be such a revelation as to eclipse the European school even with the Europeans themselves.

The difference between the two schools is broad and plain. The European school is based more upon bodily movements than upon the mobility of the face. The American school relies more upon the expression of the face and the suppression of bodily movement. It remained for the American to demonstrate that more dramatic emotion is to be expressed by keeping the body rigid than by violent gesticulation. Facial expression is the keynote of American pantomime. It has made American pictures popular all over the world. But now the question arises: Is facial expression being carried too far?

It appears that many of the factors that make for art are being ignored for the sake of getting facial expression. Artistic backgrounds are being sacrificed in the mad desire to catch the roll of the eye. Correct composition is being neglected for the same reason. Actors are sent to the tropics and to lands that are rugged in nature for the sake of their excellent backgrounds. When the pictures they make are thrown upon the screen, the actors so completely block out the scenery that they could as well have saved their car fare and done the work at home. If this tendency keeps up we shall soon be seeing nothing of the actor but his head and shoulders and those of "the girl," in which case a brick wall will be the only background necessary. It seems "everybody's doing it," except one—the Rex Company. Study their work for consistent and praiseworthy effort to keep the full figure on the screen. No lack of facial expression there.

When the average American producer is taxed with these shortcomings he will tell you that he is obliged to do as he does in order to get facial expression. According to his theory and practice an actor must be as close to the camera as possible so that the slightest movement of his countenance may be recorded. The only way to do this, he tells you, is to cut off the feet. What good are feet? No good at all—granted for the sake of argument, but not admitted. Now an example: A picture is made with all pedals amputated. The first print is projected for the inspection of the producer and the owner of the business. It is thrown upon the factory screen—a little 3 x 4 surface that renders the half-length figures no larger than the height of the frame, or about life size. The

97

owner will then complain that the facial expression is obscure, especially that of the actors further back. Later the same picture is shown in a theater and the foreground figures loom up like giants of old. The facial expression is then quite evident. The picture is *all* facial expression, and nothing else. Not in the film lies the fault, but in the small size of the factory screen. It may be contended that the question of size is only a relative matter, as the picture remains the same regardless of size. That is granted also for the sake of argument (with mental reservations).

Art is the element that suffers most by cutting off the feet. Moving picture making is going to be one of the fine arts, and the sooner that is understood by all hands the better. This brings us to the question of composition. Pictorial art is composition. A picture is a combination of several factors into a complete and harmonious whole. An arrangement with the feet cut off is not a complete and harmonious whole. There is something lacking. Most people cannot tell exactly what is wrong, but they feel it nevertheless. Neither can they analyze and tell why a composition is correct, but they realize it unconsciously because it satisfies. The French and Italian companies send us few pictures with the legs cut off, because most Latins have the artistic instinct and would consider such a composition as being defective.

Observations here and there, point to a little rule; that for every portion that is cut from an actor's lower extremities an equal measure of uninteresting ceiling or frieze must be added to the top. It will be left to the reader or the director as to whether a fine carpet pattern is or is not more pleasing to look at than an equal amount of gingerbread wall. Notice this sometime when you are at the movies.

A good training for directors is to visit art galleries. There one will see very few compositions with the feet cut off. The only paintings with the feet cut off are character studies and portraits, and those have no place as such in moving pictures.

A better training is to learn to paint. And after the director has learned to paint, let him illustrate a magazine story. Let him make pictures of the characters with their feet cut off. Then let him try to sell the stuff for a living and see how near he will come to starving to death.

"A NOTE ON IMPRESSIONIST PAINTING"   1887

Excerpts from "A Note on Impressionist Painting," by Theodore Child, *Harper's New Monthly Magazine*, Vol. 74, No. 440, January, 1887, pp. 314-315.

. . . Another marked peculiarity of the Impressionists is the truncated composition, the placing in the foreground of the picture of fragments of figures and objects, half a ballet-girl, for instance, or the hind-quarters of a dog sliced off from the rest of his body. The truncated composition was invented and perfected by M. Degas, the greatest of the Impressionists—an observer of great acuteness and a draughtsman of the first order. . . . And here we come to the explanation of the truncated composition: it is the artist's means of showing clearly what his intentions are. Thus, for instance, he wishes to show the different movements and various forms of the legs and feet of a troupe of ballerines, and so his picture contains simply the lower part of the stage and the top of the orchestra: we see the heads of the musicians and the legs of the dancers cut off at the level of the knees by the falling curtain. The composition is certainly strange, but it has a definite aim: it concentrates attention on the very parts where the painter wished it to fall. There is thought and purpose in all this apparent oddness, and in all the good work of M. Degas it will be found that the strangeness of the composition is invariably subordinated to some particular detail, some curious study of movement or pose where he brings into play his astonishing skill in drawing and his exact observation of attitude, pantomime, and light. For that matter, the truncated composition is no longer looked upon as a singularity. . . .

FILM 1913   THE PRISONER OF ZENDA

"Hackett on the Screen," *The New York Dramatic Mirror,* Vol. 69, No. 1784, February 26, 1913, p. 28.

All concerned with the Famous Players Film Company's four-reel production of THE PRISONER OF ZENDA, in which James K. Hackett plays the dual role of the King of Ruritania and Rudolf Rassendyll, may take pride in the completed product that was shown at the Lyceum Theater on the afternoon of February 18. From a seat in the last row of the orchestra Mr. Hackett watched his work on the screen, and scattered through the large audience were other members of the company that abandoned stage work long enough to act out the picture version of Anthony Hope's romance. Daniel Frohman, managing director of the Famous Players, appeared before the curtain to introduce the picture and give a brief history of the play. By means of motion pictures, he said, he hoped to see the art of great actors perpetuated and introduced to innumerable people in small towns who would not have an opportunity to see the players in person.

Unfortunately, owing to faulty projection, the picture was [not] seen at its best. Justice was not done the photography, that appeared uneven and at times blurred, through no fault in the film itself. This is only mentioned to correct a false impression that some of the audience, unaccustomed to motion pictures, may have gained.

The question of bringing the actors well to the foreground is open to debate, though it seems that in this instance a little closer camera work would have brought better results. Facial expressions, except in occasional instances, were sacrificed to an evident desire to get depth to scenes, necessary when many characters enter into the action, but of less obvious value when only two or three players are concerned in an incident where much may be communicated by varying expressions.

Beyond the advantages that might accrue from a closer view of the actors, points at which the picture could be improved do not suggest themselves. Edwin S. Porter, the director, has presented the story in a clear, interesting fashion, making the pictorial version adhere closely to the narrative as found in the book. The idea of showing each of the principal characters on the screen prior to the first reel, and giving a few words of explanation of the parts these characters are to play in the story, serves a good purpose in making identities clear. Even granting that the spectator is being introduced to THE PRISONER OF ZENDA for the first time, the plot development is easily followed. Studio settings, save in rare instances, suggest reality, and the outdoor scenes are pleasing. Particular praise is merited by the arrangement of settings in the last reel, where a drawbridge is lowered from the castle, and it is at this point that the picture excels in dramatic quality by reason of numerous rapidly changing scenes dovetailing into each other in a manner that excites the interest of the spectator.

The idea of the producers, and of Mr. Hackett himself, no doubt, was to make his performance as nearly as the requirements of pictures permitted, a duplicate of his stage appearance. To see Mr. Hackett in this film is to get considerable knowledge of his original playing of the role. The manly bearing, the expressiveness of forceful gestures and the play of his mobile features (when close enough to be observed) lose nothing by being transferred to the screen. Beatrice Beckley presents a charming figure as Princess Flavia, David Torrence makes a convincing "Black" Michael, whereas Frazer Coulter, C. R. Randall, Walter Hale and other members of the cast are uniformly capable. In the costuming and the directing of court scenes, in which many characters appear, the care that denotes a finished production is apparent.

(Signed) D.   **99**

THE PRISONER OF ZENDA   **FILM 1913**

Excerpt from "The Prisoner of Zenda," W. Stephen Bush, *The Moving Picture World,* Vol. 15, No. 9, March 1, 1913, p. 871.

. . . The direction of THE PRISONER OF ZENDA, I believe, was largely a work of intelligent and enthusiastic co-operation. The skill of a talented, experienced and ardent master of the silent drama is apparent at every turn. Mr. Porter knew the possibilities of his instrument and made the camera's conquest quite complete. He has disarmed and delighted the most captious of critics by the daring but entirely successful use of all those advantages which are peculiar to the motion picture and which the conventional stage can never hope to share. Take but one example. The judicious employment of outdoor scenes knitted the splendid story into a rapid and continuous whole, of which neither novel nor stage can give us even the shadow of a conception. The audience, mostly composed of theatrical people and perhaps somewhat inexpert in moving picture work, was quick to appreciate these advantages of the new invention and broke into applause whenever the action of the drama was carried on in the theater of Nature. To be sure all the outdoor settings were happily chosen, but the ordinary motion picture audience is well used to such settings and takes even the best of them as a matter of course. . . .

COMMENTARY

Griffith's single reel films, broken into an increasing number of shots and accelerating in pace, played directly on the nerves of the audience. Even the friendly Woods thinks he has gone too far (THE GODDESS OF SAGEBRUSH GULCH; FATE'S INTERCEPTION): the same director once praised for "repose" is now chided for lack of it. A less friendly critic, a certain ominous Dr. Stockton, sits down with stop watch and pocket counter to point angrily at Griffith for what he considers the excessive number of 68 scenes in the one-reel THE SANDS OF DEE (1912), with Mae Marsh.

Frank E. Woods left the *Mirror* in the summer of 1912 to write scenarios for films, became scenario editor for Biograph in Griffith's last months there in 1913, and then stayed with Griffith for four and a half years. At the premiere of THE CLANSMAN (THE BIRTH OF A NATION) in Los Angeles early in 1915, "The name of Frank E. Woods is shown upon the curtain . . . in recognition of the masterly work of 'Spectator' in connection with the massive script and intricate work of assembling in the cutting room. None but film people can realize the importance of Mr. Woods's work in such a titanic task." (18) (It was Woods who had suggested to Griffith that he film this work by Thomas Dixon, Jr.).

THE GODDESS OF SAGEBRUSH GULCH   **FILM 1912**

"Reviews of Licensed Films," *The New York Dramatic Mirror,* Vol. 67, No. 1737, April 3, 1912, p. 28.

THE GODDESS OF SAGEBRUSH GULCH (Biograph, March 25; Gane's Manhattan)—This is another Biograph melodramatic thriller, but while it has the undoubted Biograph strength as a tense, gripping production, it also calls for a word of warning. No matter how great and unapproachable a picture producer or any other kind of artist may be, he cannot afford to always strain after the sensational in an eternal endeavor to outdo himself, and that is what this picture appears to be. Life isn't one constant crescendo of strenuous rush and turmoil; and drama, to have its most commanding effect in representing life, must have its proper moments of repose. The soft pedal once in a while gives contrast even in the most robust music. It makes the crash sound louder when it does come. But with all crash and no soft pedal—all tense energy and no repose—one must get into a fever of hysterics to be in sympathy with the artist. Also this story, having no great underlying motive in it, fails to justify the strenuousity. The city sister came to visit the girl of the hills and stole her lover. The lover gave the city girl his gold, and robbers came to take it away from her. The hill girl looked on from concealment in the bushes and laughed at this, but changed her mind and ran for help. While the help was coming, the city girl, in the power of the robbers, recognized one of them, and he concluded that if he cut her throat she would tell no tales. But one of the other robbers had a better way. According to a caption of the film, he left a lighted cigarette and the house caught on fire. Now, this reviewer will bet a cookie, without knowing a thing about it, that this cigarette absurdity is a result of some restriction of the censorship half-wits. Probably the original story had the robbers set fire to the house, leaving the girl bound inside, but such an act in a picture, according to the infantile reasoning of the censorship sisters, would influence 20,000,000 picture spectators to hurry out and commit murder and arson. Hence the silly fiction of the cigarette, which excuses the producer for this discord, but it doesn't excuse him for what followed. The flames raged with tremendous fury—outside and in. According to all reason, the cabin should have been in ashes in a few minutes, and the girl nothing less than a cinder, and yet the lover rescued her and dragged her forth as clean as a whistle—free from the least trace of a scorching. It was rather an unproductive result after so much excitement.

FILM 1912   FATE'S INTERCEPTION

Excerpt from "Reviews of Licensed Films," *The New York Dramatic Mirror*, Vol. 67, No. 1739, April 17, 1912, p. 28.

FATE'S INTERCEPTION (Biograph, April 8)—While this story is not as deep and compelling as some of the Biograph themes, it is a gripping little tragedy, played and constructed after this producer's general vividness of action and notable power at sustaining suspense. In some instances, however, there seems to be too frequent a change of scene with a rapidity that destroys a full continuity of thought by too much change in action of scenes. . . .

1912   "THE PHOTOPLAYWRIGHT: SCENES AND LEADERS"

Excerpt from "The Photoplaywright: Scenes and Leaders," Epes Winthrop Sargent, *The Moving Picture World*, Vol. 13, No. 6, August 10, 1912, p. 542.

Recently we have been having a series of discussions with our Contributing Editor, the Rev. Dr. Stockton, as to the value of long and short scenes. It's been rather a one-sided discussion, for we think pretty much alike, but with a speculative interest in the subject, Dr. Stockton put in a day in the theaters recently and saw seventeen reels through twice each, counting scenes the first time and inserts the second. The day before he got only eight, but we submit that 50,000 feet of film in two days is going some. Dr. Stockton does not start out with a handful of ten-cent pieces and a desire to be amused. He carries a stop watch, a pocket counting machine, an electric flash lamp and a note book, and he does his work thoroughly. Here is his report on the two days work. The first column gives the number of scenes, the second the leaders, the third other inserts. The figures form an interesting study:

Lubin—"A New Beginning"	18	10	1
Lubin—"A Complicated Compaign"	11	11	7
Vita—"Sheriff Jim's Last Shot"	40	15	3
Cines—"Disowned"	18	7	3
Edison—"A Necklace of Crushed Rose Leaves"	22	14	0
Kalem—"A Prisoner of the Harem" (split reel)	15	15	3
Kalem—Educational subject, not tabulated			
Selig—"A Day Off"	24	5	1
Vita—"Wanted — A Sister"	32	10	0
Vita—"Adventure of the Thumb Print	46	11	0
Essanay—"The Understudy"	36	11	3
Biograph—"The Sands of Dee"	68	7	0
Lubin—"A Western Courtship"	41	7	3
Edison—"The Little Artist of the Market"	18	12	1
Selig—"The Hand of Fate"	35	19	0
Vita—"The Victoria Cross"	44	17	1
Lubin—"Becky Gets a Husband" (split reel)	28	11	0
Lubin—Industrial, not tabulated			
Cines—"A Daughter's Diplomacy"	25	11	0
Selig—"The Pennant Puzzle"	37	12	2
Edison—"Jim's Wife"	21	14	1
Lubin—"Just Pretending" (split reel)	24	2	5
Lubin—"A Pair of Boots"	14	0	0
Edison—"After Many Days"	26	14	0
Méliès—Run without title	21	10	1
Selig—"Dad's Girls"	31	15	2
Pathé—"On the Brink of the Chasm"	33	2	0

These figures are most decidedly interesting to the student of photoplay, and we believe that this is the first time this sort of table has been presented. We are frank to admit that we find some of the figures startling. Dr. Stockton comments:

> As to the stories: With the exception of the Edisons, the Cines and Selig's THE HAND OF FATE, the last a really big story, the stories of all the others, dramas and comedies alike, were as slim and attenuated as the Milky Way. It looks very much as if Edison and the foreigners were the only ones not bitten by the lightning bug, with the result that his releases are, to my mind, the only ones that are really drama. The others have lots of action, but no acting and no chance for any. I suppose if one wants to sell one's scripts one will have to conform to the prevailing jumping-jack tendencies, but Oh! for the time when a man who wants to see things done with at least some pretension to verisimilitude will have a show to getting something really worth while produced.

To this last we most heartily say Amen! A twenty scene drama is run up to fifty or sixty scenes, with an average time length of from fifteen to eighteen seconds each. Acting is not possible. Clarity of story is not possible. Unfolding of plot is not possible. There is a succession of eye-pleasing scenes, but no stories, and self-contented directors, with concrete crowded craniums, will presently be wondering why it is that the pictures are not as popular as they used to be; provided that they are capable of that much mental effort.

Apart from a slightly excessive use of leader, we agree with Dr. Stockton that the Edison stories are the most complete, simply because time is taken to act out the scenes instead of merely sketching them in, and while it may be evidence of our weak intellect and inability to appreciate art, we confess that we would go ten blocks to see an Edison where we would not cross the street for the average multiple-scened Biograph. Edisons have stories. Most Biographs are a succession of tableaux without plot.

Some years ago the Biograph introduced the idea of close-up pictures with the result that the picture world gradually became populated with a race of persons who were cut off at the tops of their heads and the bottoms of their waistcoats. Now that three times the proper number of scenes are used to cover up the thinness of Director Griffith's on-the-flap-of-an-envelope stories, everybody's doing it, and strong, vital, gripping plots are shelved in favor of the short story with numerous shifts. This may be heresy, but if it is, we are proud to call ourselves a heretic.

We do not quite agree with Dr. Stockton that it is necessary to write in forty or fifty scenes. Write twenty to thirty and let the director muss it up to suit himself. Write only enough leader to cover the unexplained points and let the rest be added in the cutting room by the man who wants them in. Just write a clean-cut script and let the faddists do their worst, but if you do write the forty scene stuff remember that you can only have sixteen minutes of action, no matter how many scenes you employ.

This list gives practically all of the Licensed manufacturers and is useful as a guide if you want to speed up.

1912   **A Record**

Excerpt from "The Photoplaywright," Epes Winthrop Sargent, *The Moving Picture World*, Vol. 13, No. 8, August 24, 1912, p. 764.

In the Stockton list the Biograph takes top notch with 68 scenes in THE SANDS OF DEE, but they are not quicksands alongside the same company's MAN'S LUST FOR GOLD. This contains 107 scenes, twelve leaders, the title and the censorship tag all on the thousand feet of film. There is one scene that runs four-fifths of one second according to three trials of a stop watch. We do not mention this as a pattern but as a horrible, a most horrible example.

Stick to your twenty or thirty scenes in writing your play and when some producers either get fired or restored to sanity you'll be in line again. Meantime let them take your proper script and fuss it up to suit themselves. About the time they speed up to 150 scenes in seventeen minutes and forty-five seconds something will drop with a crash that will wake the sleepers up.

1914   **"Biograph Whiskey"**

Excerpt from "Answers to Inquiries," *The Photoplay Author*, Vol. 3, No. 5, May, 1914. p. 157.

. . . We do not think it is necessary to actually write in as many flashes, or "cut-backs," as the finished pictures sometimes show. Use the cut-back judiciously, putting in as many of these "back and forth" scenes as may be really necessary to work up the interest and suspense. But don't overdo it—leave that to the producer. And that's not a joke or an error in writing on our part, for lots of producers do overdo it. It's an old story, 103 but did you ever see Biograph's MAN'S LUST FOR GOLD? The vaudeville comedian who said that "Biograph whiskey" was the kind that made you see moving pictures must have evolved the joke after trying to tell what this story was about. That photoplay was a case of "cut up," not "cut-back". . . .

A FEUD IN THE KENTUCKY HILLS   **FILM 1912**

"Comments on the Films," *The Moving Picture World*, Vol. 14, No. 3, October 19, 1912, p. 242.

A FEUD IN THE KENTUCKY HILLS (Biograph), October 3—An unusually tense picture, even for a Biograph. In it, after a few scenes that introduce excellently suggested types of mountaineers and give a few glimpses of mountain life, the action becomes like a whirlwind. It is a one-act picture of the almost complete annihilation of a mountain family. A love story softens it some; but it is a hard picture, almost brutal. It is for those who like their pictures fiery. It will surely please the gallery and also, we think, many who are not in the gallery; but, while we feel sure it will be a success, we cannot commend it wholly; it is likely to offend very sensitive minds, because it is a blood-thirsty picture.

COMMENTARY

Of these three Biograph films from 1913, only THE SHERIFF'S BABY was directed by Griffith, but the other two imitate the technique for which he was celebrated.

A GIRL'S STRATAGEM   **FILM 1913**

Excerpt from "Comments on the Films," *The Moving Picture World*, Vol. 15, No. 12, March 22, 1913, p. 1219.

A GIRL'S STRATAGEM (Biograph), March 10— . . . In the way the picture is written and in its general conduct it is a typical Biograph story. The action is held in pretty closely to its center of interest, and the scene-making searchlight snaps back and forth from one actor to another and seems to pick out the different elements of the situation almost simultaneously. This is a speedy method and makes the picture, as a whole, clear at the expense, now and then, of the acting. The scenes change so fast that the players now and then seem all arms and hands. . . .

THE SHERIFF'S BABY   **FILM 1913**

Excerpt from "Comments on the Films," *The Moving Picture World*, Vol. 16, No. 2, April 12, 1913, p. 164.

THE SHERIFF'S BABY (Biograph), March 29— . . . It gives a good picture of the desert and has speedy action. In places it is a bit awkward from slow turning on the part of the camera man. Those half-instant scenes, in which we catch a glimpse of quivering fingers and waving arms, but see nothing else, are not very effective.

FILM 1913   THE HERO OF LITTLE ITALY

Excerpt from "Comments on the Films," *The Moving Picture World,* Vol. 16, No. 3, April 19, 1913, p. 279.

THE HERO OF LITTLE ITALY (Biograph), April 3—There is a good story in this picture and the producer has made it exciting. As it approaches its climax, the scenes, flashed back and forth, keep the action concrete and almost breathless. But this playing for the thrill is not the best use of the motion picture camera; for in such there is almost no individual acting—everything goes to situation, nothing to character. It justifies itself at the box office; but so does the higher kind; the first has a more immediate, the second a more lasting effect. . . .

COMMENTARY

At last, in October of 1913, Griffith left Biograph and signed with Reliance-Majestic "at one of the largest salaries ever paid to a motion picture director." His farewell to Biograph moves Louis Reeves Harrison to tribute. The fact that Griffith directed all major Biograph films from 1908 until the summer of 1911 is unchallenged, but Frank Powell advertised that he "unassisted, made the FAMOUS BIOGRAPH COMEDIES from November, 1909, to May, 1911." (19)

Griffith now ran an advertisement in the *Mirror,* disclosing himself to the world outside the trade as "Producer of all great Biograph successes, revolutionizing Motion Picture drama and founding the modern technique of the art. Included in the innovations which he introduced and which are now generally followed by the most advanced producers are: The large or close-up figures, distant views as represented first in RAMONA, the 'switchback,' sustained suspense, the 'fade out,' and restraint in expression, raising motion picture acting to the higher plane which has won for it recognition as a genuine art." (20) He listed more than 150 films as his best, including the four which as yet were unreleased.

Biograph, which had never publicized him anyway, withheld his name as director when those four laggard films reached the market. A masterpiece of nervous cutting, and a glowing hit in Paris the autumn before, THE BATTLE AT ELDERBUSH GULCH was slipped into American theaters so unobtrusively that it does not appear even to have been reviewed. But after the success of THE BIRTH OF A NATION, when Biograph scrambled to re-issue earlier films and scrupulously identify them as being by Griffith, THE BATTLE AT ELDERBUSH GULCH was the only film granted the honor of re-release twice.

Griffith's bold juggling with, and breakneck pacing of film editing in 1912 and 1913—his use of motion continually intercepted, and continually resumed—exactly coincided with the American public's growing awareness in those years of a restless "crisis which threatens all the arts." (21) Reports from abroad described the "hysterical yelling" of the singer in Schönberg's revolutionary composition "Pierrot Lunaire," a work which seemed to be "strung together at random," and sounded "like madness." (22) In his quarterly, *Camera Work,* Stieglitz published the baffling Gertrude Stein on "Henri Matisse" and "Pablo Picasso," asserting that this was "the Post-Impressionist spirit . . . expressing itself in literary form." (23) Miss Stein herself, in later years, explained that in these two pieces she was "doing what the cinema was doing" (24): building up each portrait with statements superficially the same, but subtly different, like the successive frames of a strip of film, but to one enraged reader, she was inexcusably tearing words loose from their meanings, applying an egg-beater to the brain.

The extensive and notorious Armory Show, first startling New York in the spring of   105

1913, then going on to Chicago and Boston, publicly confronted American eyes for the first time with Brancusi, Braque, Derain, Gauguin, Nadelman, Picabia, Van Gogh, and for the first time with the paintings of Cézanne, Matisse, Picasso and Toulouse-Lautrec. Some of this new, foreign work seemed nothing more than "hysteria made visible." (25)

Griffith, who was in California during the first half of 1913, was occupied with THE MOTHERING HEART, THE BATTLE AT ELDERBUSH GULCH, and JUDITH OF BETHULIA at exactly the time when the Diaghilev Ballet in Paris was rehearsing and presenting first performances of Debussy's *Jeux*, and Stravinsky's *Le Sacre du Printemps*, both with choreography by the world's leading dancer, Nijinsky, and both failures with the public. The gestures of *Jeux*, which reveals three tennis players in a garden at dusk, were so split up into smaller movements that one critic called this a "ballet cinématographique," (26) and Stravinsky appears to have been uneasy over the choreography for both the premiere of *Le Sacre* and its revival in a recreated version seven years later. He charged that choreographers liked to break down the rhythmic episodes of the music into fragments, develop each fragment alone, and then splice them back together. A Parisian first-night audience rioted in protest over the music and dancing of *Le Sacre*; *Jeux* was found incomprehensible.

"DAVID W. GRIFFITH: THE ART DIRECTOR AND HIS WORK" 1913

By Louis Reeves Harrison, *The Moving Picture World,* Vol. 18, No. 8, November 22, 1913, pp. 847-848.

"Every important piece of literature, as every important work of plastic art, is the expression of a personality, and it is not the material of it but the mind behind it that invites critical interpretation."

"Lawrence" Griffith—such was his stage name—is one of those strange combinations, a realist in action and a mystic in temperament, who sees clearly the beauty about him and can transfer his artistic impressions to others because of that side of him which is eminently practical. He was a playwright by tendency, an actor from opportunity, a motion picture director by force of circumstances. He would have succeeded as a dramatist—he was working toward that end—but, while he was looking out of the front door for Histrionic Fame to drive up in a coach and four, there came a modest knock at the back door, and a poor little, ragged, half-starved New Art was there begging for a wee bit of stimulus and a spark of the fire of genius to keep from freezing to death.

This was only about five years ago. New Art was only a boy, but his haggard appearance and the exhausting life he had led made him appear older than he was. Larry became interested when the strange-looking boy produced a magic lantern and showed that he could throw an image on the wall that visualized motion. The playwright, by nature clairvoyant, by training accustomed to concentrate on a thousand and one problems of structure, form and treatment, saw instantly that New Art's magic lantern had possibilities undeveloped and not even dreamed of by the overpractical men who had been putting it to use.

They saw that it visualized motion, and that was the limitation of their vision. It was used to show moving trains and boats and horses and men. There were some primitive attempts at dramas, but they had no other name than "moving pictures," and this led to the profound conclusion, with few exceptions, that all the characters must be on the jump from the time they appeared until the hero died, or was embraced. Actors were told to lift their knees high in walking and be doing something every moment while the camera was recording the action. A performer was not earning his salary, he was not a moving picture, if he stood still for a few seconds.

In appreciation, not as a compliment, it may be safely said that Griffith started the young stranger on an entirely new road and contributed more than any other man of those days to the New Art's splendid progress. He had that faculty of mystics and dreamers that enables them to project their minds into futurity. The invisible world to come exists in definite form only for those who combine in their mental makeup three powers—those of keen observation, close reasoning, and illuminating imagination. Such men usually leave the world better off for their presence in it, especially when they are able to help themselves on to material success, such as Griffith has done, and to wider opportunity.

Probably others saw what Griffith saw in the future possibilities, but they lacked the outlet or the courage to break away from accepted ideas and introduce violent changes. There was need for courage. Nearly all "practical" men, those concerned with material rather than ideal considerations, opposed Griffith's work as wildly speculative and unsuited to what they honestly regarded as a commercial proposition rather than as an art. They still exist. There is still need for courage. But Griffith has blazed a path of glory for what is yet to become one of the mightiest instruments of thought transference, and the way is clear for men of creative genius to follow.

He started to depict emotion of the slow and intense kind. Just as a storm gathers, just as there are shimmerings of light and distant grumbling of thunder, before there is an outburst, he taught his interpreters to exhibit feeling. He dared try to show the subtle shades of thought, the deep-running undercurrents of passion, all the fascinating phases of human existence as we encounter them in real life. "But, Mr. Griffith," some practical gentleman would say, "you must keep in mind that this is strictly a commercial proposition. Give the people what they want."

A commercial proposition that depends for its very existence upon creative talent, whose structure is the work of selective taste, plastic imagination and power to formulate self-expression, ceases to be a good one from the moment it shrivels to a pulseless skeleton. All the traps to snare the unwary purchaser, all business schemes to market the mediocre, are short-lived. When there appears a man of fine artistic instincts, one inclined to give the best that is in him to the people—that is what they want—he is to be treasured. I know of no sounder common sense than to stimulate such men with encouragement—the very delicacy of their powers of discriminating makes them self-doubting.

I have sharply criticised several of the Griffith productions—he is in a state of evolution quite as much as the art itself—but there is a surprising charm in nearly everything he does when unhampered. His best interpreters give us the essence of this or that emotion instead of moving around like a lot of lay figures worked by invisible strings. He peels away the rind of human character; tears away the mask and bares the soul that has been hiding behind it. Motion often wearies the eye and confuses the understanding. He will fasten attention with immobility and suddenly transform silent mystery into tremendous revelation.

In a period of dull preparation, before the main action is under way, he will spread out before our eyes some beautiful or comprehensive tableau as compensation. Even when character and purpose begin to emerge from his visions of loveliness, when the architecture of the drama begins to assume importance, he plants a flower here or there, occasional tender notes in the large composition, like the man of dreams that he is. He is starting anew, and I hope his fondest dreams will be realized. I hope for the sake of the New Art that he has befriended that his finest conceptions will be materialized in grandeur or beauty on the screen.

Moving picture audiences are rapidly becoming critical, and men of discerning taste will be needed to respond, or even direct, this change. What has been said by a brilliant writer on dramatic subjects in general applies: "The decreasing insistence in plot, and a correspondingly stronger emphasis on character portrayal is one of the most hopeful signs of the times." With men of genius among writers and producers, the New Art will soon be a distinct one, unsurpassed by any other in its possibilities, ethical and artistic.

––––––––

Mr. Griffith was born in Louisville, Kentucky, the exact date of which event is not revealed by his biographer, but he was eighteen years of age when he first stepped upon the theatrical stage. A varied experience in stock companies, vaudeville and legitimate productions on the Pacific coast was his before he became known to the picture makers. One season he was leading man for Nance O'Neil, and this is believed to have marked his highest attainment in that line. About this time Mr. Griffith took to writing plays, some of which were produced in stock. It was in an effort to secure the production of a more pretentious effort in playwriting that he came east, and it was his failure in that effort that compelled him to seek employment with the most humble players in the picture studios. Engaged as an extra man at the Biograph Studio, he soon displayed such a marked talent in the art of picture production that he was given an opportunity to direct. At first his efforts along this line were hindered by the traditions of the studio, but the providential absence of the chief director for a few days gave him the opportunity he sought to stage a picture as he desired, and his reputation was made. This happened in the summer of 1908, and from that time until the summer of 1911 all Biograph productions—two each week—were made by Mr. Griffith. During that time the name of Biograph became famous the world over, and the art of staging pictures was revolutionized. From 1911 to the time of leaving the Biograph Mr. Griffith has had some assistance in the producing department, but he still turned out his quota of pictures, and can easily claim a total of five hundred productions during the five years he served as chief director of the Biograph.

While many of Mr. Griffith's ideas have been adopted by others to the general betterment of American pictures, probably the best service he performed for the art in America was the training he gave to the actors and actresses who worked with him and who now occupy lucrative positions by reason of that experience. Among those who acknowledge the benefit of the early instruction given by Mr. Griffith will be found these names: Mary Pickford, Harry Solter, Florence Lawrence, Arthur Johnson, Marion Leonard, Stanner E. V. Taylor, David Miles, Owen Moore, Thomas Ince, James Kirkwood, Henry Walthall, Flora Finch, Fred Mace, Frank Grandin, Frank Powell, George Nichols, Wilfred Lucas, Mack Sennett, William Cabanne, Mabel Normand, Dot Bernard, Bessie McCoy, Blanche Sweet, Billy Quirk, Charles Mailes, Claire McDowell, Tony O'Sullivan, Dell Henderson, Edward Dillon, Charles Murray, Lionel Barrymore, Vivian Prescott, Flo Labadie, Dorothy Davenport, Mae Marsh, Herbert Prior, Ashley Miller, Barney O'Neil, Courtenay Foote, Gertrude Prior, and many others who have since gained more or less applause from picture fans.

COMMENTARY

"At the Sign of the Flaming Arcs" documents Griffith at rehearsal in 1914. "David W. Griffith Speaks" conveys his thoughts about the close-up and the Dickensian switchback. Looking back at the Biographs, Griffith might well have written, as Dickens did in his prefatory note to the _Christmas Stories:_ "The narrow space within which it was necessary to confine these _Christmas Stories_ when they were originally published, rendered their construction a matter of some difficulty, and almost necessitated what is peculiar in their machinery. I could not attempt great elaboration of detail, in the working out of character within such limits. . . ." (27), yet no apology was needed.

"AT THE SIGN OF THE FLAMING ARCS"

Excerpt from "At the Sign of the Flaming Arcs," George Blaisdell, *The Moving Picture World,* Vol. 19, No. 1, January 3, 1914, p. 52.

It was a wise person who remarked that a really big man is never pompous. Which saying is recalled to mind by a mighty pleasant half hour's chat on an early Saturday afternoon with David W. Griffith. It is a remarkable fact that the most striking figure in the motion picture industry—the man who in whole truth may be said to have done more than any other to advance and bring us now to the day of the universal recognition of the greatness of the screen as a factor in the amusement world—it is, we repeat, a remarkable fact that for so many years the identity of this man should practically have been unknown outside of trade circles. The reason is simple. It was the policy of his employers that the public had no legitimate right to any knowledge of the personality of the men and women who made and appeared in their pictures. There was no belief in, there was utter repudiation of, the theory that the interest of the public was heightened in the productions of a company by a knowledge of the human elements entering into the construction of them—even if that information be restricted to the names of producer and players. In line with this business practice of the Biograph Company—it is now nearly a year since its abandonment, by the way—was the unusual disinclination of Mr. Griffith for publicity. He apparently cared little for it. This attribute was forcibly brought to the attention of the director's associates just after his recent alliance with the Mutual forces. They advised him to make public by means of an advertisement in the trade press a list of some of the successful pictures produced under his guidance. It was only after repeated urging that he consented.

The writer had gone to the Broadway studio of the Reliance Company to have a talk with Henry Walthall. He had met Philip Mindil, old-time newspaper man and all-around live wire, who is at the head of the Mutual's most efficient publicity bureau. Mr. Mindil is good to meet. When a man delays his departure for a half holiday on a sunny afternoon in the height of the Christmas shopping season just to entertain an intruding scribe and retains his affability you respect him.

Hopp Hadley, secretary of the Screeners and associated with Mr. Mindil, undertook to guide us about the studio. Near to the Broadway end of the building Jim Kirkwood was seated in a comfortable chair, his long frame sunk into its depths as he meditatively watched and guided the rehearsal of the players under him. We wandered to the Sixteenth Street part of the studio. Under lights fiercer than any that ever beat on a throne stood Blanche Sweet and Mae Marsh rehearsing a scene in the forthcoming feature production of Paul Armstrong's THE ESCAPE. In the play the two are sisters. Miss Sweet uttered no word. His lips did not move. She looked. You felt what she was thinking. Miss Marsh, a slip of a girl, looking even younger than she actually is—and she is in the teens—indulged in pantomime. Her lips moved, but she spoke not. A slight cough indicated the tuberculous taint of the character she was portraying. It was all very interesting.

For a quarter of an hour we stood by the camera just behind a tall man seated comfortably, a big brown fedora hat pulled over his eyes serving as a shade from the lights. He was talking into a megaphone. It was a mild, conversational tone. At times there would be a lull. Then again there would be advice, but the voice was not raised. So this was the man who so thoroughly inspires his players that they in turn may penetrate and stir the hearts of their audiences; who by his magnetism binds to him with hoops of steel these same players. It is a rare trait, this secret of commanding unbounded loyalty, an unusual equipment, especially in one of pronounced artistic temperament. It is a cordial handshake Mr. Griffith has for a stranger. It was early in the conversation that the writer referred to the Biograph picture, MAN'S GENESIS, released a year ago last July. The director said that within a few feet were two of the principals in the cast of that story. They were Miss Marsh and Robert Harron. It was the latter who had played Weakhands, but the writer had not recognized him. You are not long talking with Mr. Griffith before you realize that his chief aim is to reproduce life as it is—the avoidance of the stagey, the artificial, the affected. He said sometimes in a picture show, when a screen player was plainly overacting, he would be inclined to shudder at the remark of some enthusiast near by: "Isn't that splendid acting!" He said that successful stage artists were not necessarily good screen players. He instanced one well-known actor who had come to him for engagement, but who was only employed on an extra basis until the result of his work might be judged on the screen.

Asked as to the recent statement attributed to him about young players, Mr. Griffith smiled. "I was not quite accurately reported," he said. "What I meant was a youthful player for a youthful part. If the character calls for a girl of eighteen, I don't like to see it portrayed by a woman of thirty. When large figures are used the player is necessarily close to the camera. Then every line of the face is revealed." Mr. Griffith agreed that it is difficult if not practically impossible to fool the camera. He said that of course if a player has to indicate more than one age a resort to makeup is compulsory. Reference was made to some of the girls who have been so successful under Mr. Griffith's direction, included among others being Miss Pickford.

"Yes," said Mr. Griffith, "the public notes the successes, but it has no knowledge of the hundreds who are tried and fail to show the possession of that indefinite quality, that something in here"—as he tapped his temple—"which gives them the power to impart to others a clear realization of a given situation." Mr. Griffith told how for two years he had tried to secure a player in a certain branch of dramatics commonly supposed to be oversupplied, but had failed.

During the conversation Mr. Griffith made a statement than which none could more clearly reveal the size of the producer—his unstinted praise of work done in a studio other than his own. We had been talking of the great respect shown by experienced stage players for the remorseless camera. The writer had told how at the invitation of Producer [Edwin S.] Porter he was standing alongside the camera in the Famous Players studio when Mrs. Fiske was rehearsing a scene in TESS OF THE D'URBERVILLES. The great actress who in her long career had from the stage faced hundreds of thousands was, when she was preparing for the record of her work on the screen, perturbed by the interested scrutiny of but one. She intimated to Mr. Dawley her desire that there should be no audience. "By the way," we asked Mr. Griffith, "did you see the work of Mrs. Fiske in TESS?"

"I did," he replied. "I think it was the most wonderful performance I ever saw on the screen—surely one of the most wonderful. It moved me and it held me, for its art and for its life."

"DAVID W. GRIFFITH SPEAKS"   **1914**

Excerpt from "David W. Griffith Speaks," Robert E. Welsh, *The New York Dramatic Mirror*, Vol. 71, No. 1830, January 14, 1914, pp. 49, 54.

" . . . You say that some stage players look down on the motion picture. [D. W. Griffith is speaking.] I say that I would not have the average stage player in a picture of mine. Mrs. Fiske's work in TESS OF THE D'URBERVILLES was wonderful; Sir Johnston Forbes-Robertson being a great artist, I imagine should be able to do some good work in pictures, but we are speaking now of the average player. It would take them years to grasp one-tenth of the knowledge of the picture art that young members of our company already know. Aside from the value of a few big names I would much rather have real picture people in my plays. Where is the player that by a mere flash of the eyes, a passing of the hand over the forehead could convey half the emotion to the spectator that Blanche Sweet or Mary Pickford could give? Where is the stage player who studies real life and who duplicates real life as these players of the screen do?"

"Blanche Sweet. Mary Pickford." These names bring to mind another thought, and I ask Mr. Griffith for the secret by which he chooses and develops screen stars. Here we make another discovery. This man of the mind-stunning salary, this director with the power of a dictator, possesses the modesty of a hermit.

"There is no secret," he says. "I did not 'teach' the players with whom my name has been linked. We developed together, we found ourselves in a new art and as we discovered the possibilities of that art we learned together.

"It is this learning, step by step, that brought about the 'close-up.' We were striving for real acting. When you saw only the small full-length figures it was necessary to have exaggerated acting, what might be called 'physical' acting, the waving of the hands and so on. The close-up enabled us to reach real acting, restraint, acting that is a duplicate of real life. But the close-up was not accepted at once. It was called many names by men who now make use of it as a matter of course. 'Why,' said one man well known in the film world, 'that man Griffith is crazy, the characters come swimming in on the scene.' "

From talk of the close-up we come naturally to the switchback and the score of other innovations to the credit of this smiling, somewhat boyish, man in the chair before me. The evolution of the switchback as told by David Griffith proves the contention that the film is more akin to printed fiction than to the spoken drama.

"You remember," he continues, "in Dickens and other writers of his period the plan of saying, 'While all these dire happenings were occurring to our heroine, far away another scene fraught with interest was being enacted?' You remember how a chapter would end leaving you at the highest pitch of expectancy, while the author told of happenings somewhere else, but bearing on the main issue? This was the reason for the switchback, to draw the threads of the narrative together, to accelerate the action, to heighten the action. But the switchback can be abused, and is being abused. In many pictures I think the director used the switchback merely because he knew of nothing else to do at that particular moment, he used the switchback to hinder the action, to hold up the story, but that is all wrong. The switchback should be used only when absolutely necessary. It should be used to accelerate the action, to further the story, to help the spectator to a better understanding, and not to hold him back from the story. The switchback I use with fear. Each scene, even when only a snatch of a few feet of film, is carefully rehearsed time after time, and down to the finest details. The switchback must be as perfect as any portion of the story, and above all, it must give a very good, sound, reason for its existence before I will attempt to use it. . . ."

13. Max Linder, French comedian of international reputation, was admired by Bernard Shaw. At one time he was so prolific that three of his films were released here in five days. His style was said to have influenced Chaplin's.

CHAPTER 7

Foreign Invasion (I):
Films from France, Britain, Scandinavia, Austria, Germany, Italy, Russia

COMMENTARY

In the early years of the industry, films from France and Britain came to the United States in great quantities. France provided the sharpest competition for our domestic manufacturers. Hundreds of trick films, modern dramas, topicals, costume pieces and comedies from the studios of Pathé Frères, Gaumont and others, were shown on American screens; however, while French films were much admired technically, American audiences often balked at their story content. ("One wonders sometimes if there are no faithful ones in France.") (28) The Pathé Film d'Art series was a special undertaking; ASSASSINATION OF THE DUC DE GUISE circulated with a score composed for it by Camille Saint-Saëns. Max Linder, in his roles for Pathé Frères, was one of the first stars to become known around the world. In a letter dated August 19, 1912, Bernard Shaw wrote Mrs. Patrick Campbell, asking if she ever studied films, as he did, and telling her that Max Linder was the actor he knew best from observing him on the screen. The dapper Linder is supposed to have influenced Charlie Chaplin's style of acting, but he is not even mentioned in Chaplin's *My Autobiography* (**1964**).

When Bernhardt and Réjane appeared on the screen, the medium was sanctified for lesser actors. Several months after these films were shown in New York, Famous Players Film Company was launched in America (**1912**) with the four-part version, filmed in France, of Bernhardt's play *Queen Elizabeth*. Tinted and toned, the production was advertised as "a half mile of Rembrandt." (29) Famous Players now switched to domestic features with Porter's THE PRISONER OF ZENDA (**1913**), but many of the favorite stage actors they filmed looked somewhat elderly on the screen.

FILM 1909   INCRIMINATING EVIDENCE

"Many Notable Films," *The New York Dramatic Mirror*, Vol. 61, No. 1573, February 13, 1909, p. 12.

INCRIMINATING EVIDENCE (Pathé)—This is the first of the much talked of art films which Charles Pathé has been promising as a new departure and a revelation in the production of motion picture drama. It must be admitted that it more than meets every claim that has been made for it and sets a new mark in this class of film production.

This picture follows the story of M. Séverin's pantomime as now being presented in   113 the William Morris' vaudeville houses very closely. The title of the pantomime, which was reviewed at length in *The Mirror*, was Conscience, while this picture is called IN-CRIMINATING EVIDENCE. The figures are all of heroic size and the facial expression is shown off to remarkable advantage. The story opens in a Parisian cabaret, while in the pantomime it opens in a street. The other scenes are almost exactly like those of the pantomime. As a work of artistic photography the picture is noteworthy, and as a lasting memorial of the splendid acting of M. Séverin, it is invaluable.

ASSASSINATION OF THE DUC DE GUISE   **FILM 1909**

"Reviews of New Films," *The New York Dramatic Mirror*, Vol. 61, No. 1575, February 27, 1909, p. 13.

ASSASSINATION OF THE DUC DE GUISE (Pathé)—This is the second of the "film d'art" of the Pathé Company, and its superior quality in photographic excellence, superb acting, rich settings and costumes and skillful dramatic handling of a carefully constructed picture narrative distinguishes it as one of the few masterpieces of motion picture production. The story was written for Pathé Frères by M. Henri Lavedan, of the Academie Francaise, and the chief parts were played by Mlle. Robinne and Messrs. Lebargy and Albert Lambert of the Comedie Francaise. Warning is sent to the Duke de Guise at the house of the Marchioness de Noirmontiers that King Henry means to do him harm. The Duke laughs at the warning, telling the lady that the King dare not. In the picture this reply of the Duke is shown by having him write the words "he dare not" on a paper and handing it to her, which is the only discoverable inconsistency in the film. Spoken words could have been shown better in a subtitle, or their import could have been left to the imagination, as the Duke's conduct gives ample indication of his meaning. Heedless of the warning, the Duke goes to the Council meeting. We next see King Henry with ominous care arranging the plot for the murder with the men whom he has chosen for the purpose. He swears them on a crucifix, examines their swords, and concludes that daggers are better for the deed. Then he hides behind a tapestry, while one of the men is sent to summon the Duke. The Duke leaves the Council, undeterred by the objections of his friends, passes the King in hiding and enters amidst the group of conspirators. Not seeing the King, he turns, facing his enemies, who bow obsequiously as he confronts them individually. As he turns his back on them they start forward as if to strike, but he turns again, suddenly, and their menacing movements change to cringing attitudes—these eight or ten men seeking the life of one. Then, as he proudly walks away they rush upon him from behind. Fighting for his life, he struggles to the room where the King is in hiding, and here he falls pierced by the daggers and swords of the murderers. Now the King ventures out from concealment and they examine the dead man. The King himself lifts an eyelid and starts back in fright, thinking there is life, but they convince him otherwise and he recovers from his partial collapse. Searching the body they find a letter indicating that the Duke had been financing Spain in her war with France, and the King brutally kicks the head of his victim. A lock of hair is cut from the head and the King, placing it in a book, dismisses the conspirators and piously kneels to pray. Gruesome though the picture is, it is of such remarkable merit that we forget all but the artistic quality. The letters shown in the picture, especially the last one implicating the Duke with Spain, are not easily enough read and should have been written in clearer script.

ROMEO TURNS BANDIT   **FILM 1910**

"Reviews of Licensed Films," *The New York Dramatic Mirror*, Vol. 63, No. 1641, June 4, 1910, p. 16.

ROMEO TURNS BANDIT (Pathé, May 23)—Pathé Frères evidently realize the value of the excellent comedian, Max Linder, in picture farces, for they are using him frequently of late. In this story he appears again as an ardent suitor for a young lady's hand, the father being opposed to his pretensions. To convince him, the lover arranges with two of his friends to masquerade as bandits. They capture the father and leave him tied in a way that permits of his gaining his freedom in a short time. Then they pretend to kidnap the girl, and send word that they are holding her for ransom. Max now presents himself before the father and offers to rescue her, accomplishing the feat with a droll show of bravery and prowess that wins the old gentleman's gratitude and the hand of his daughter.

FILM 1910   MAX LEADS THEM A NOVEL CHASE

"Reviews of Licensed Films," *The New York Dramatic Mirror*, Vol. 63, No. 1641, June 4, 1910, p. 18.

MAX LEADS THEM A NOVEL CHASE (Pathé, May 25)—This is another Max Linder picture, with our friend in the character of a "Raffles" who gets safely away with the goods. This writer is not partial to stories of this character in motion pictures, although they should be no more harmful than when presented in type in newspapers and magazines. However, we all know Max isn't that kind of a chap, and we forgive him this time. He "swipes" a necklace from a lady's neck at a ball, and is pursued by the entire crowd, with a few Pathé policemen added. It is a chase picture, with a few new wrinkles, and ends with the escape of the culprit in a balloon.

FILM 1910   A PRINCE OF WORTH

"Reviews of Licensed Films," *The New York Dramatic Mirror*, Vol. 63, No. 1641, June 4, 1910, p. 18.

A PRINCE OF WORTH (Pathé, May 27)—This is the third film within the week in which Max Linder is introduced as the principal character. In this instance he appears in a new light, displaying an amusing versatility, even if he cannot be said to shine very brightly. He is supposed to be a prince in love with a strolling singer, whom he marries. His father and mother have picked another wife for him, and they are furious when he confesses the truth. But he is game and goes out with his young wife to earn his own living, becoming an acrobat. Some years later the pair have become headliners in vaudeville and we see Max doing a stunt on the stage. The exhibition is rather weak for a star act, though quite creditable for an amateur. His father sees it from a box and, his rage having passed away, he takes the son, wife and child home to the bosom of his family.

FILM 1912   BERNHARDT IN CAMILLE

Excerpts from "Reviews of Feature Subjects," *The New York Dramatic Mirror*, Vol. 67, No. 1738, April 10, 1912, pp. 26-27.

BERNHARDT IN CAMILLE (Produced by Film d'Art Society in France, controlled in America by the French-American Film Company)—Madame Bernhardt proves in this production, as had been anticipated, her wonderful adaptability to the peculiar forms of

115

expression required for finished picture acting. It is the mark of the great artist, demonstrated more vividly, if anything, than is possible on the theatre stage. With the art of which she is so much the master, she appears in the picture to be the living embodiment of Camille, unconscious of camera or of supposed spectators and conveying, not by pantomime, but by natural and significant actions and expression the progress of the story. The culmination comes in the death scene which Bernhardt's art renders in no way distressing, but tremendously impressive and convincing. She is standing in Armand's embrace with her face hidden from view. By her hand on Armand's shoulder we see the approach and victory of death—the hand drooping and falling like the flower from which Marguerite's sobriquet was derived. Fortunately the picture adaptation of Camille has been modeled with considerable success after the technique of the photoplay as developed by the experience and genius of those who have led in the growth in this new art. Had the adaptation been merely or even largely a reproduction of the action of the stage play minus the words it must have proved disappointing even with Mme. Bernhardt's great ability and prestige. But this pitfall has been avoided. The story is told by the photoplay method and told quite clearly, although it could have been more forceful perhaps and certainly more explicit in some of the scenes, as, for instance, the fragment of the duel scene, which, however, may have been cut down to a mere indefinite indication of the end of the duel, to avoid fancied interference of troublesome censors. In this, however, the producers were probably too cautious at the expense of the picture's art—a thing that was hardly necessary in a production of such distinction. In one other respect, also, the picture fails to realize the most advanced development of the photoplay. This is in the too numerous and too explanatory interscriptions [subtitles], many things being announced in words that are clearly understandable from the actions themselves. At times these advance explanations of what is to follow are annoying to the spectator and rob the picture story of its interest. All this, however, is no fault of Mme. Bernhardt, and will not prevent the motion picture record of her interpretation of Camille from being one of the masterpieces of the photoplay, destined to be preserved for posterity. The settings are magnificent and realistic and the support excellent. The photography also is of the best French quality. The photoplay is in two reels or parts.

REJANE IN MADAME SANS-GENE (Produced by the Film d'Art Society in France; controlled in America by the French-American Film Company)—Sardou's romantic play of the period of the first French Empire, adapted to photoplay form, becomes a delightful picture comedy, and, with Réjane herself as Madame Sans-Gêne, the production is lifted to the rank of a great feature. Madame Réjane's work in the picture play, while distinguished and displaying much art and insight, is not free from the sin, so often to be discovered in less distinguished actresses—the sin of playing direct to the front and for a supposed audience. This is the stage method—the inartistic stage method. To make her work even less satisfactory, she employs pantomime constantly, in a way that would never be done in actual life, thus detracting from the illusion of reality so necessary to the complete success of the motion picture form of expression. Nevertheless, the picture, which is in three reels or acts, is well constructed along photoplay lines, and all the players being finished and polished artists, the result is excellent. . . . The scenes where Sans-Gêne wins the friendship of Napoleon by presenting his old wash bill and also wins the pardon of Count Neipperg are the best. The interscriptions, however, are too numerous and long, as is the case with the Bernhardt picture.

COMMENTARY

The market for British films in America weakened after about 1907, and remained weak until the sound period. Foreign films—British, French, Italian—which were most popular

here before World War I, all lost their foothold, but staged a spectacular comeback later, on the far side of the sound barrier.

Dissolves were so old they were new in 1913 (DAVID COPPERFIELD).

FILM 1909   THE DRUNKARD'S SON

Excerpt from "Licensed Reviews," *The New York Dramatic Mirror,* Vol. 62, No. 1610, October 30, 1909, p. 15.

THE DRUNKARD'S SON (Hepworth, October 18)—This is a poor excuse for a dramatic subject. It is full of inconsistencies and the actors only walk through their parts, except when they are making vows to heaven or explaining things to the camera. One instance of impossible action will suffice: Three crooks are plotting to hold up a young fellow who is carrying money away from a bank. They stand outside the bank in the public street, in full view of those inside or of any chance pedestrian, waving their arms in wild gesticulations, telling each other how they are intending to rob their intended victim. And this is seriously offered as motion picture pantomime. . . .

1913   **A Scientific Explanation**

Excerpt from "Foreign Trade Notes: British Notes," "Our Own Correspondent," *The Moving Picture World,* Vol. 15, No. 1, January 4, 1913, p. 59.

The difficulty to produce in Britain films comparable to those from American or Continental studios is one of old standing and a continual sore spot to the home trade. The problem is neither financial nor experimental, but scientific. In brief, as soon as science makes the intensification of atmosphere possible, then can we hope to screen productions with the clarity and brilliance of those by foreign makers, but made in Britain. Personally I have both seen and heard of many untiring and admirable attempts by indefatigable workers to establish successful studios in various parts of the island. To designate one and all indiscriminately as being unsuccessful in their results would not only be unfair but untrue. Yet, on the other hand, none can really claim success as it is imported from the U.S.A., despite the praiseworthy attempts. In the months of June and July, when the light here is most actinic, a few very fair subjects, humorous and dramatic, have been filmed on the south coast, where the light is strongest. . . .

1913   **The Parsimonious British**

Excerpt from "Chicago Letter," James S. McQuade, *The Moving Picture World,* Vol. 16, No. 2, April 12, 1913, p. 149.

. . . The fact has long since sunk into the minds of British patrons of moving picture theaters that American films are the best in the market. American manufacturers, as a rule, do not figure up parsimoniously the pounds, shillings and pence that a film will cost before entering on its production. It is quality, not the cost, with all the best of our American manufacturers. When English manufacturers are ready to loosen their purse strings, and pay less attention to arithmetic, when considering the production of a film; when they are willing to pay the price to first-class actors and actresses to appear in their productions, they will have a market in America and we shall be delighted to see their product. Then, and not until then, will the British producer attain his proper position in the moving picture world. . . .

117

DAVID COPPERFIELD   **FILM 1913**

Excerpts from "David Copperfield," *The Moving Picture World,* Vol. 18, No. 1, October 4, 1913, p. 29.

Readers of Dickens and particularly those who love the great author's favorite book, *David Copperfield,* will be entertained and edified in seeing the pictured version of that story recently produced by the Hepworth Company of London, now being marketed in America by Albert Blinkhorn. American companies have given us, in a small way, some excellent motion pictures dealing with the life of David Copperfield, but these have been brief character studies in the main, not attempting to cover the entire story. The Hepworth picture is in six parts beginning with the childhood life of David at the Rookery, Blunderstone, and depicting the more important incidents up to the time of his marriage with Agnes, terminating with the Yuletide dinner.

. . . Rare discrimination has been exercised in the choice of events so that we have been given a story in pictures that holds together and does not tax the imagination of the observer or require a profound knowledge of the story itself in order to obtain the fullest enjoyment from the seeing of it.

. . . Considered from a purely mechanical point of view it would be difficult to find a flaw in the entire six reels. The photography is excellent and the settings reveal great care in arrangement. One noticeable innovation is the method of dissolving one scene into the next following and into the titles. There is none of that chopping off of scenes abruptly that is so destructive of illusion. The Hepworth idea is a great improvement and adds much to the pleasure of looking at motion pictures. American producers might adopt it to advantage.

COMMENTARY

A few Swedish films reached American shores before World War I checked imports from abroad: THE BACK MASKS, for example, directed by Mauritz Stiller and featuring Victor Sjöström, was released by Warner's early in 1913 as SAVED IN MID-AIR. Then between 1919 and 1924, imported feature-length films by both Stiller and Sjöström (who also became a director), caught the eye of the American film industry to the extent that both men were signed to direct in Hollywood. Stiller came over with Greta Garbo.

Danish films were also well received in the United States, and were praised for their acting, photography, and general attention to detail; TEMPTATIONS OF A GREAT CITY (1911) ran three reels. Asta Nielsen, by far the best-known Danish actress, made one film in Denmark and then, with her director, transferred her activities to Berlin. Reviewers in this country were disappointed that audiences here never gave her the adulation she received abroad, and her tragic failure with the American public was repeated in the 1920's. Most German films were unpopular in the United States; they were considered crude and clumsy, but "National Traits in Films" (1914) indicates that they were gaining in recognition just before the outbreak of World War I.

THE MIRACLE (1913) was filmed in Austria.

As I noted in my "Three Warnings" at the outset, foreign films are dated in this book according to the year of their American release, but in several instances they were produced a year or two before, and sometimes even considerably earlier than that.

TEMPTATIONS OF A GREAT CITY   **FILM 1911**

Excerpt from "Temptations of a Great City," *The Moving Picture World,* Vol. 8, No. 24, June 17, 1911, p. 1367.

. . . We noticed one thing very particularly in this European picture, and that is the fact that the Europeans are "stealing our stuff." Ordinarily in a Danish picture one would expect the foreign style of acting, such as the shrug of the shoulders and the drag of one foot after the other, and all the rest of the stereotyped styles of the European school. The Europeans are getting wise to facial expression. If it were not for a telephone that looked like a wedding cake and a policeman with a brass kettle on his head, no one would know that it is a foreign film. Not only that; if the Americans do not watch closely, the European actors are going to beat them at their own game of facial expression, because the four actors in this Danish film were certainly going some in the gentle art of suppressed emotion. It reminded the writer of the palmy days of the Biograph Company, when tense situations were worked up entirely with the eyes and slight movement. This film came as near to being one of the old Biograph masterpieces as anything that ever came from Europe, and it is good to observe that the Europeans are beginning to see some merit in the American school of acting. America is heartily sick of the shoulder-shakers, and it is quite possible that Europeans are getting sick of it themselves. . . .

FILM 1913   THE DEATH SONG

"Licensed Specials," *The Moving Picture World*, Vol. 18, No. 6, November 8, 1913, p. 612.

THE DEATH SONG (Pathéplay), October 23—This two-part offering deals with passions in a truthful, though not profound, way. There is nothing in it with which a moralist could find immediate and spontaneous fault; but the ground it grows in is not the best playground for children. It seems to have been made in Germany and the role of the heroine is played by Asta Nielsen, who is well known to picture fans. She plays the wife of a temporary invalid, is a good singer, and finding it necessary to make money, goes on the stage under the direction of a famous composer. She swears to be true to her husband; yet falls in love with her impresario; lets him fondle her for a moment and then repulses him until, at the end, he, getting too impetuous, she has to stab him to death to save her oath. Then she walks tragically out of the hotel in the care of the police. Miss Nielsen makes a striking figure with her black hair falling in masses around her ears and neck, and dressed in an extremely low-cut bodice of black silk made to fit as close as possible. Her acting is strong, but she plays in pantomime which (to American spectators) is not so effective as naturalness.

FILM 1914   THE DEVIL'S ASSISTANT

"Feature Films of the Week: THE DEVIL'S ASSISTANT," *The New York Dramatic Mirror*, Vol. 71, No. 1836, February 25, 1914, p. 36.

Two-Reel Pathé Film Featuring Asta Nielsen. To Be Released Feb. 26

Professor Harlow	Mr. Seldeneck
Marten, an artist	Mr. Wideman
Hans Braun	Mr. Worgitzsch
Karl Meyer	Mr. Albes
Hanna, his daughter	Asta Nielsen

More pictures of this caliber are needed to give Asta Nielsen a thoroughly favorable introduction to Americans. She is not known in the United States as she deserves to be; her name does not fall readily from the glib tongues of motion picture "fans," even her features on the screen may fail to evoke memories of previous photoplays, but all that will be remedied if the Pathé Company continues to exploit her in productions on a par with THE DEVIL'S ASSISTANT. No lover of good acting will watch a running of these two reels and promptly forget Asta Nielsen's irresistibly sympathetic portrayal of the unfortunate Hanna. In Germany she has a following that would make many American stars envious, and with a little judicious coaxing there is no reason why it should not be drawn across the sea. Her method is not typically German, or typically anything, except human. She does not depend upon a pretty face and figure and a few stock mannerisms; rather upon acting, and remarkably varied acting it is.

Enthusiasm over this particular film is aroused by the happy blending of a strong story, suggestive acting in the three dominant parts, and a fine regard for the details that give tone to an artistic production. There is a unity of effect in the staging and playing of each scene and a quite flawless photographic perpetuation of it all. The characters live and sin (some of them, at least) and are left at a climax of their suffering. Here is the skeleton on which the story is developed.

Hanna's father is a shiftless, impecunious drunkard; her lover is an honest gardener in the employ of Harlow, a prominent artist, who conducts an art school. He advertises for a model, and Hanna is engaged. Soon she falls in love with Marten, a promising painter. He leaves her in favor of Harlow's daughter, and Hanna, broken-hearted, following the example of her father, becomes a drunkard.

A year later, Marten, in search of a model to pose for a painting of hopeless despair, finds Hanna in a dive. She is the picture of hardened sin and misery. His offer to engage her as a model is accepted, and soon the portrait is progressing famously. The girl's father dies as a result of intemperance. Hanna is shocked into a determination to turn over a new leaf, and promises to marry her honest lover, Hans. She is happy, the expression of hopelessness leaves her face, and the artist is without a suitable model for his picture. He plies her with drink, makes violent love to her, and succeeds in arousing the evil nature which she had struggled to overcome. His masterpiece is completed, but the girl is lost; even the long-suffering Hans refuses to condone her downfall. Then the climax. Hanna tears the canvas to shreds and goes out into the street, back to the misery, the despair, the sins of her father.

Obviously, there is material here for a stirring drama, and not once is it slighted. Three times Miss Nielsen touches high points in emotional acting—when she meets her recreant lover in the dive, when she stands beside the lifeless body of her father, and in the studio temptation scene.

She is an actress who sheds real tears and can make an audience follow suit.

THE MIRACLE   **FILM 1913**

Excerpts from " 'THE MIRACLE' Is Splendid Pageant," *The New York Times*, February 18, 1913, p. 13.

'THE MIRACLE' Is Splendid Pageant
Wordless Mystery Play Shown in Moving Pictures, with Humperdinck's Music
RUSSIAN SYMPHONY PLAYS
Large Chorus of Singers Dressed as Nuns Pass Into Church, and German Legend is Disclosed

THE MIRACLE, a wordless mystery play produced abroad originally by Max Reinhardt, was presented last night at the Park Theatre in a moving picture version, with the aid of Modest Altschuler and the Russian Symphony Orchestra and a large mixed chorus. The book of the play was written by Karl Vollmoeller, and not the least important fact in connection with the production was that it served for the first hearing in this country of the music written for it by Engelbert Humperdinck, composer of *Koenigskinder* and *Haensel und Gretel.*

What was seen and heard last night went far to emphasize that the moving picture under certain conditions, conditions like those that prevailed last night, for instance, may be capable of providing entertainment to be taken seriously by audiences which have never seen the inside of a "movies" theater.

The arriving audience found an orchestra which overflowed the pit, crowded into the space formerly occupied by the first three rows of seats, and then put double basses and tympani, respectively, in the proscenium boxes at each side of the stage.

The rising curtain disclosed the front of a large church. Hardly had the gauze curtains in front of it risen to give a full view when chanting in female voices was heard at the rear of the house and a large chorus of singers dressed as nuns filed down each of the two center aisles and passed up on the stage, disappearing at the sides of the church. Its large center doors slid to each side and disclosed a screen, on which the pictures appeared.

The play, which was in two acts and an intermezzo, told a story derived from a German church legend. . . . *[Synopsis given.]*

There was a good deal of variety in the scenes of the play, which lent itself well to representation by moving picture, being rich in pageant effects and moving on broad lines. Careful staging was in evidence, and the backgrounds to the scenes were pictorially interesting. Humperdinck's music, which followed the events of the play, was an important part of the production. It was his usual crystalline score, several times employing folk-song foundations, and was well played. While not vociferous in applause, the audience seemed to like the entertainment.

1914   "NATIONAL TRAITS IN FILMS"

By W. Stephen Bush, *The Moving Picture World,* Vol. 20, No. 4, April 25, 1914, p. 488.

By this time we know our brothers across the big pond as well as our next-door neighbors. We know "English Traits" better than we could learn them from Emerson, we have become intimate with the countrymen of Hans Breitmann, we are most familiar with our friends in France and nothing is hidden from us in the character and the habits of our contemporaries in sunny Italy. It is all due to the motion picture. A boy or girl of fifteen, a regular patron of the motion picture theater, can today sit down and write a fair sort of essay on Europe and her nations.

We have all laughed at the follies and foibles of the transatlantic world so strikingly revealed on the screen.

I watched one Italian picture recently that was just one gorgeous dream of revenge. There is nothing more persistent than an Italian lady or gentleman in search of good dramatic revenge. In Naples and Sicily especially, children cry for it. It is offered as a wedding present to the bride and as a consolation to old age. There are intricacies of Italian revenge which we ruder children of the North are wholly unable to follow. I made an attempt to follow the course of revenge, or rather revenges, in the film I saw the other day. In the first reel, a brother revenged his sister, in the second reel there were two or three working revenges, while in the third everybody was revenging himself on general principles. The worst of it is there never seems to be any final revenge. Along toward the end of the second reel we heartily wish there might be some sort of a friendly settlement, but there never is. At the end the survivors are as thirsty for revenge as ever. It is a splendid thing for the Italian scenario writers. It simplifies their labors. Theirs is merely the task of finding the best and strongest kind of revenge, and the best and strongest revenge is always the oldest. Italians lay little store by a new, fresh revenge. A revenge which is not at least fifty years old might as well be left on the shelf or delivered

121

over to beginners to practice with. Next to its age, the greatest merit of the revenge is its complicatedness. If you want to write for the Italian market you might as well understand that a plain, simple or garden variety of revenge is an object of contempt among experienced writers. If you cannot involve everybody, from the babies in arms up, you might as well not try.

Next to revenge, and, indeed, its faithful concomitant in the Italian film, is the trap-door. A friend of mine with a statistical turn of mind, after carefully watching a large number of Italian films, figures that there is a well-sustained average of two trap-doors to a reel. In a weird film of probably Neopolitan origin, no less than eighteen trap-doors were counted in two reels, and in one phase of the development of the plot the heroine dropped through four trap-doors, consistently pursued by the villain.

In happy contrast to this feverish and insatiable desire for highclass and refined revenge is the German film, of which recently we see a good deal. The dominating desire of the German director is not to alarm his audience unduly. He may be the most daring and reckless fellow in the world, but he must stay within the speed limit. Heroes and heroines and villains are supposed to temper their rashness with care. They may step up to the edge of the precipice and (in the titles) threaten to jump down, but they must be careful at the same time. In accidents a desire for intense realism is always modified by a due regard for the personal comfort and safety of the performers. I have seen auto accidents in German films where everything went to smash and the hero and the heroine lay lifeless on the ground, but were unable to suppress a little smile of gratification at the perfect arrangements that had been made for their safety. I have seen another auto disaster in which it was thought sufficient to show a minor defect in the tire. The chauffeur repaired the defect smiling genially at the camera man, probably to reassure the director that he had not been hurt in the least. Even in the most horrible explosions and the most frightful collisions the principal performers make it clear to the audience that, however badly they may seem to have been injured for the sake of lending realism to the picture, they are in sober truth in the best of health and full of good humor and appetite.

The directors and actors in German films are not only required to refrain from alarming their audience, but they must be equally careful not to deceive their audiences too long. It is one of the cast-iron rules of the German film melodrama that the disguised detective must remove his disguise in full view of the audience as soon as he has done his trick. His failure to do so would leave a portion at least of the audience in doubt and confusion. The Germans love nothing better for a suitable background and atmosphere than a nice cemetery, the rural cemetery always preferred. They like to show well-kept graves and good, respectable tombstones. Next to these in degree of popularity are death scenes and nice, orderly funeral processions. These scenes are wholesome checks on any excess of swiftness in the action and a distinct rebuke to ultra-sensationalism in films. Action in some of these German-made films does not really begin until the start of the third reel, and by that time the audience which still holds out is generally asleep.

Have you ever known of a good, loyal, faithful, home-loving husband or wife in French films? Yes, there may be exceptions, but as a rule the damage to conjugal fidelity in the films of our Gallic brethren is out of all proportion. No doubt they have honeymoons there, but it is not long before the tie that binds begins to chafe and a perfect carnival of wickedness follows. They make light of these matrimonial *faux pas* in the French films and show a lack of irresponsibility [sic] which we Anglo-Saxons find it difficult to understand even in children. Except in rare cases the matter never gets serious enough for the invocation of the divorce courts; the weeping wife or husband either returns in repentance or both sides to the bargain laugh the incident out of their lives. They are, in the films at least, such light-hearted, unsophisticated creatures that it is hard to quarrel with them. They are not popular with censor boards. Another marked peculiarity of the French film is the detail of the meals at home. The family starting in on

14. Asta Nielsen in THE DEVIL'S ASSISTANT. This Danish dramatic actress was applauded by American critics in 1914, but audiences here—apparently missing "a pretty face and figure"—were slower to respond.

their soup is a familiar sight, and may be the prelude to anything—either a comedy or a tragedy or a fine hand-colored biblical story. Old-timers must remember the dear old French policemen in the early Pathé films, always traveling in pairs, always waxing their moustachios, always pompous and grave and always missing the man they were hunting for.

No doubt we appear quite peculiar from the European point of view, and I think we should thank some friendly critic for helping to see ourselves as others see us.

We suspect right now that they look upon us as a lot of money-kings with seared hearts and no ability to see anything but the different kinds of currency. Our tipping, let us hope, has made some impression upon its multitudinous beneficiaries, for in Europe they trail Americans by their ability to assuage the itch of the palm.

COMMENTARY

Italian films, long familiar in one-reel comedies and dramas, suddenly blossomed into spectacles in 1911 with THE FALL OF TROY (2 reels), THE CRUSADERS (4 reels), and DANTE'S INFERNO (5 reels). HOMER'S ODYSSEY (3 reels) seemed a miracle in 1912, but 1913 produced QUO VADIS in 8 reels ("2 hours and 15 minutes to project") (30), THE LAST DAYS OF POMPEII (6 parts) and ANTHONY AND CLEOPATRA (7 parts).

QUO VADIS played two performances a day for months in New York, at theater prices, with orchestral accompaniment and a success that encouraged the production of feature films the world over. The ancient kind of nickelodeon program composed of miscellaneous reels, was gradually beginning to die out; programs of the future would be built around a feature film, or, in the case of a very long one, devoted to that film alone. Furthermore, theaters were now erected specifically for the showing of films, not just converted from already extant buildings. The Strand, seating 2,900, opened in New York on April 11, 1914.

The climax of Italian importation came with CABIRIA, opening at the Knickerbocker Theater June 1, 1914, and later shown at the White House to President Wilson, his family, and members of the Cabinet. The tracking shots in this film are described below as "scenes . . . slowly brought to the foreground," whereas panning produced the effect of scenes "moved from side to side."

CABIRIA   **FILM 1914**

From "Feature Films of the Week: 'CABIRIA' *The Best Yet*," *The New York Dramatic Mirror*, Vol. 71, No. 1847, May 13, 1914, p. 40.

Itala Company's Production of D'Annunzio Story Magnificently
Spectacular
Ten-Reel Drama Written by Gabrielle D'Annunzio and Produced by the Itala Company. North American Rights Controlled by the Itala Film Company of America, Harry R. Raver, Director-General.

The last word in motion pictures has a way of changing almost before it has been pronounced, so it is well to be chary with prophecies. Under the influence of a freshly kindled enthusiasm, the temptation to point to the summit of photoplay art, and say "there stands CABIRIA" is strong. But the summit may still be hidden in the clouds. The climb upward during the last decade has been so persistent, who would venture to declare that the top has been reached? Only a bold prophet, surely. Therefore we remain on the conservative ground of film history and merely state that up to May, 1914, this Itala picture is the greatest photographic spectacle ever shown in America. Stupendous is the best adjective to suggest the impression it left on an audience in the grand ballroom of the Hotel Astor last Saturday afternoon.

Harry R. Raver was the host, and his guests, comprising most of the notables in filmdom, many of their half brothers of the stage and a decorative sprinkling from non-professional society, pretty nearly filled the large floor space and the mezzanine boxes encircling the room. For the most part, it was an assemblage intimately connected with the making of pictures and in consequence not over impressionable. No self-confident American producer is particularly anxious to award the banner of supremacy to Italian art, but this time, in common honesty, there was nothing else to do. Scene after scene presented spectacles of thrilling beauty that were a revelation, even to men acquainted with the camera and the tinting of film. Those who knew most about the difficulties to be overcome were the readiest to admit an unparalleled accomplishment. Only photographic art of the highest kind can imbue an audience with the awe that comes of seeing magnificent manifestations of turbulent nature and great world tragedies before which the petty worries of one life, of one age, even, seem of small moment. This work has the bigness, the epic quality that makes significant the life and death of civilizations long passed into history.

In print, unless he told it himself, the story of Gabrielle D'Annunzio would be involved and uninteresting. It is laid in the third century B.C., and deals with the fall of Carthage before the power of Rome. Cabiria, first as a child, about to be sacrificed as a burnt offering in the Temple of Molach and then as a young woman, for some time held as a slave, comes unharmed through numerous tragedies. And with her is the gallant Roman, Auxilla Fluvius, always accompanied by his giant slave, Maciste, who has the strength of Samson. We follow the rise and fall of kings and watch the ruthless tightening of the net around the doomed Carthagenians. Through all the varied action there runs a strong plot thread, not easily traced at times, to be sure, but always logical and leading to a definite and inevitable end.

The wonder of the film, however, is in the production, rather than in D'Annunzio's scenario. We are told that two years were spent in preparing the picture, and the statement is not hard to credit. To say that settings and photography are superb seems futile appreciation, for the same has too often been said of work elementary by comparison. There are not one or two big scenes to startle the attention, but a perfect succession of big scenes vying with each other in beauty, in immensity, or in excitement and not infrequently in all three. After a time the spectator almost loses his sense of surprise when he sees a new marvel. All things seem possible in CABIRIA, and anyway, it is not normal to retain a feeling of astonishment for three consecutive hours.

Right at the opening of the first reel, or episode, as it is called, is the mammoth Temple of Molach, whose cavernous entrance, approached by a broad flight of steps, is built to represent the open mouth of a great monster. Throngs of devout worshippers, with bowed heads, enter the temple to attend the sacrifice of infants. Inside, the effects of size and splendor and the horrible practices of heathen ritual, are yet more astounding. But soon the frailty of the strongest works of man, when pitted against the forces of nature, is shown. Mount Aetna is in eruption and from the yawning crater there pours a thick stream of lava. Flames shoot up into the air. The whole countryside is black, under the blanket of smoke, and along a roadway at the foot of the mountain, seemingly miles away, can be seen the doomed populace in panic-stricken flight—mere specks of humanity scarcely visible in the darkness, and above them the flaming crater. Rocks begin to crash through the roof of the temple, the supporting pillars loosen, the walls cave in, and from the wreckage of falling stone there is no escape, save for Cabiria and her nurse. These scenes are marvels of photography, lighting and staging.

Again, there has been nothing of its kind to approach Hannibal's crossing of the Alps, in which the impression of distance and a long line of soldiers, with their elephants, winding through the snow-capped mountains, is perfect. Then we have two wonderful

125

double exposure scenes. The Roman fleet is burning. One by one the ships are wrapped in flames. The night is made brilliant by the burning boats and hideous by the agony of helpless prisoners on board them. After close views of the flaming vessels, the scene shifts to show a broad sweep of ocean in the foreground, while the horizon is yellow with fire. Much the same effect is gained in the second double exposure scene, except that this time the fire is reflected across a desert instead of across the sea.

For sheer artistic beauty, there are scores of scenes demanding mention, such as that of the camels silhouetted against the sky as they move with graceful dignity over the crests of the hills. This is only one of many possessing the atmosphere of a painting. And in the way of a photoplay depiction of ancient warfare, the siege of Cerba stands supreme. Soldiers attempting to scale the battlements are hurled back on the heads of their companions, dropping some twenty-five or thirty feet, if one may believe his eyes. A veritable storm of missiles repels the advance, and where a dozen men fall, a dozen more press on to fill their places, until the people of Cerba are forced to yield. But descriptions of these magnificent scenes might be continued indefinitely without giving more than a faint suggestion of their power.

The cast is superb, and supporting the chief players are hundreds of "supers," whose efficiency may well make an American producer envious. Such material does not seem to be obtainable outside of Europe. Among the photographic novelties is one frequently used with fine effect. Scenes are slowly brought to the foreground or moved from side to side, quite as though they were being played on a movable stage. By this method full value is given to deep sets, and without any break the characters are brought close to the audience.

CABIRIA may be only a nine days' wonder in the film industry, but it is going to convince many doubtful people that high art and the motion picture are not incompatible.

(Signed) D.

COMMENTARY

Short Russian subjects had been included in the Pathé program and imported here as early as 1908. This review of "Russian Art Films" (1917) must have been written the very month of the Russian revolution. At least eight such features were released in America by Pathé, including THE QUEEN OF SPADES. Then, not until POTEMKIN arrived in New York in 1926 did most people become conscious that the Russians were filming again.

"RUSSIAN ART FILMS"   1917

Excerpt from "The Shadow Stage," Randolph Bartlett, *Photoplay Magazine*, Vol. 12, No. 6, November, 1917, p. 128.

By the time this signpost of cinema chronology reaches the reader, it is probable that the first of the Russian Art Films will have been presented publicly. Frankly, we are almost as interested as the importers of these phototragedies, in learning how they will be received by America. In those we have seen, A PAINTED DOLL and THY NEIGHBOR'S WIFE, there has been displayed such acting as seldom emanates from American studios. These Russians are serious artists. They do not employ the eyebrow and chest technique so popular among many exponents of American theatrical art. And the stories are free from heroes and heroines. Rather do they go too far in the opposite direction, the principle apparently being that there is a good deal of bad in the best little girl—and boy. The deluded maiden takes kindly to her luxurious downfall. The dying husband, so far from forgiving, devises a cunningly awful fate for his wife and false friend. The Slavic emotions, the world well knows, are terrific, and these Russians have written those emotions in letters of human fire.

CHAPTER 8

Films Fine and Foolish (1909-1918)

COMMENTARY

As at any other period in film-making, much was also being turned out which was routine, ridiculous or both. THE HEART OF A COWBOY, Essanay's Western drama with Broncho Billy Anderson, described here in progress in Denver in 1909, appears headed for the sort of foolishness which Louis Reeves Harrison satirizes in the classic first paragraph of his "Something New" (1912). Harrison's great expectations of feature films were answered before the end of the year by two American ventures of deeply serious intent: the Helen Gardner Company's CLEOPATRA, in six reels, and the Kalem Company's FROM THE MANGER TO THE CROSS, in five reels, filmed on location in Egypt and the Holy Land.

"The Social Uses of the Moving Picture" reviews the two-reel THE CRY OF THE CHILDREN, by the Thanhouser Company of New Rochelle, New York, a film expected to be a potent force in the fight for legislation against child labor. The father was enacted by James Cruze, who later directed THE COVERED WAGON (1923).

1909   "THE ESSANAY COMPANY OUT WEST"

From *The Denver Post*, reprinted in *The Moving Picture World*, Vol. 5, No. 23, December 4, 1909, pp. 801-802.

G. M. Anderson, secretary of the Essanay Film Company, of Chicago, has been in Denver for six weeks, "making pictures," and from here will take his little company to Las Vegas, then to Catalina Island.

"Our studio in Chicago," explains Mr. Anderson, "occupies a whole floor, and there we make all interior scenes, and maintain a picked permanent company of players. During the Summer we make outdoor pictures in and around Chicago, but when Fall comes, I take a photographer, property man and several principals, and follow the warm weather. Colorado is the finest place in the country for Wild West stuff. Some of the Eastern companies try to use the Adirondacks, but they don't get the effect that the Rockies give."

With Mr. Anderson, who acts the "heroes" himself, are J. J. Robbins, expert photographer; Jack O'Brien, a handsome young actor, who does the "heavies"; Arthur Smith, character actor, and W. K. Russell, property man and assistant hero and villain.

This is the traveling organization, leading ladies, soubrettes, ingenues, mobs, posses, etc., being secured from the stock companies and vaudeville houses of the various cities that serve as a base for operations. Some ten or twelve "Western dramas" have been staged and photographed by Mr. Anderson since his arrival, Golden and Mt. Morrison being the spots chosen for the purpose. Last Tuesday, for instance, THE HEART OF A COWBOY was put on at Mt. Morrison, and for the benefit of those who like color and charm, interest and new sensations, a day with a "moving picture" company is enthusiastically recommended. Leaving at 8 o'clock, the company reached Mt. Morrison at 9, where the train was met by a bunch of trained cow ponies and riders under command of the Morrison boys themselves. Up into the hotel flocked the company, the property man threw back trunk lids with a bang, and in a few minutes the principals were appareled and "made up," horses mounted, and away down the street, down by brawling Bear Creek, on to a little farm house, tucked away in a clump of lofty cottonwoods. Permission had already been obtained, and seated at ease on the grass, horses hitched, the company listened to this reading from Mr. Anderson:

Scene 1. Girl comes out of house, holding some kodak pictures of herself. Cowboy comes up, sees picture, and begs it from her. She refuses at first, but finally gives him one, writing "To Steve" on it. He asks her to walk with him, but she refuses and he departs.

Scene 2. As Steve goes out of the gate, he meets his partner, also named Steve, coming in. They shake hands and part.

Scene 3. Girl gives cry of joy as she sees newcomer. Throws herself into his arms. Playfully demands his pencil, and writes "To My Sweetheart, Steve" on the picture that she gives him.

Scene 4. As this Steve sits in front of his dug-out, looking at the picture of his sweetheart, the other Steve comes up. He demands to know what his partner is doing with the picture, and shows his own to prove that the girl is his sweetheart. Bad Steve sneeringly shows him his picture with "To my sweetheart" written on it. To settle the matter, however, they ride to the girl's house.

Scene 5. Call girl out. When an answer is demanded, she puts her arms around Bad Steve's neck, but holds the hand of friendship to Honest Steve. After a minute, he joins their hands and rides away.

Scene 6. Mexican rides up to Bad Steve's dug-out, and tells him of a chance to steal some cattle. Steve refuses at first, but finally consents, and they ride away.

Scene 7. Cutting a bunch of cattle out of the herd, and driving them away, Steve drops his picture.

Scene 8. Showing the thieves hurrying the stolen steers along. Steve goes to girl's house, and sends Mexican to sell cattle.

Scene 9. Rancher discovers his loss. Organization of the Vigilantes.

Scene 10. Ride of the Vigilantes.

Scene 11. Bad Steve visits the girl's house. As they sit on step, the Vigilantes ride up. They accuse Steve of stealing cattle, and when he denies, pull picture on him. The girl makes them stand back, and as she defends him, Honest Steve slips in beside his friend. Takes his picture out of his hat, and forces it into Bad Steve's hand. Bad Steve produces it as proof of his innocence, and Honest Steve steps forward and takes guilt upon himself. Vigilantes throw rope around his neck and lead him away. Girl throws arms about Bad Steve's neck.

Scene 12. Bad Steve comes to house and tells girl she must elope with him. She consents and hurries in to get her things. Mexican comes up and starts to divide money. Bad Steve stops him with curse, and leads him around to side of house.

Scene 13. Girl comes out and looks around. Hears voices and creeps around.

Scene 14. Steve and Mexican quarrel over division of money. As they wrangle, girl appears, learns the truth, and steps forward. Mexican starts to stab her, but she jerks revolver out of Steve's holster, and covers them both. Makes Steve hand her the money, write a confession, and then forces them to mount the same horse and jump the country.

Scene 15. Girl mounts horse and starts on her ride to save Honest Steve from lynching.

Scene 16. Girl riding.

Scene 17. Vigilantes riding with Honest Steve in their midst.

Scene 18. As they are about to hang Steve, girl rides up. Hands over money, shows confession and lifts the rope off his neck.

Scene 19. Girl gives Honest Steve another picture with "To my future husband" written on it.

Talk about the intelligence demanded by the theater. The company is supposed to grasp the entire idea at once, for Mr. Robbins mounts his machine and Mr. Anderson calls "First Scene." Miss Loma Besserer, the "girl" on the occasion, has played leads in many stock companies, but it was her first experience with "moving pictures," and started off with true "leading lady" refinement and reserve.

"No, no," cried Mr. Anderson. "Charming in a theater, Miss Besserer, and you certainly look like a picture. But you've got to ACT a picture! This is practically pantomime, you know. Turn loose!"

"Can I talk it?" she demanded.

"All you want. The machine doesn't take conversation."

And pretty Miss Besserer, giving a braver furl to her cowboy hat, did "turn loose," making up dialogue as she went along. All of them did, for that matter, and it was splendid dialogue, too, so good that the whole thing could have been put on a stage just as it was given. Once over a scene, Mr. Anderson calling corrections, Mr. Robbins putting down little stones to mark each position, and then the whirl of the machine. Scenes 1, 2, 3, 5, 11, 12, 13, 14, and 15 were taken one after another—all being house scenes—and by noon that part of the play was over. Not once was there a break made—scene succeeding scene with marvelous rapidity and telling effect—until the tableau, where the girl makes Bad Steve and the Mexican mount the same horse. Then the trouble began. Bad Steve would gain the saddle, but when the Mexican started to climb up behind him, off went the pony, and out of the picture. Pain on Mr. Anderson's face, anguish in the eyes of Mr. Robbins. Three times did this happen, and twice, too, did Miss Besserer's own horse bolt the picture when she came to mount for her own wild ride.

The jolliest sort of dinner in the little hotel, then remounting and the journey up into the hills, where the unsuspecting cattle grazed. Here Scenes 4, 6, 7, 8, 9, 10, 16, 17, 18 and 19 were taken, a deserted house being pre-empted for Bad Steve's home. Again Mr. Anderson's Gatling gun directions, and scene after scene without halt, until the cattle stealing. With infinite pains Mr. Robbins placed stones and bent bushes to show the exact radius in which the cattle must be stolen, but he forgot to tell the steers. Unaware of their responsibilities and new importance, the crazy beasts bolted the picture time and again, and by the time they did get bunched, stolen and photographed, both Bad Steve and the Mexican were sorry that they had ever quit the straight and narrow path. The Vigilantes made the flight across the front yard, Miss Besserer galloped madly up and down before the "machine," and just as the light was beginning to fail, the last picture was taken. A tired lot of players rode back to town, for every mind had been working at lightning speed, faces were weary from contortion, and all were hoarse from the rapid fire dialogue invented to help them out in their "pantomime." "Oh-h-h!" sighed Miss Besserer, "*Camille* is child's play to this."

These films will be sent to the head office in Chicago, and from there leased to "renters," as the jobbers of the "moving picture" industry are called. This lease calls for the return of the films after six months, for then they are worn out, and the company takes this means of protecting the people against spoiled pictures. The "renters" then lease them out to the "picture shows" at so much a day. The first run of the films, of course, are seen in the cities at the best shows, then they go to the next best shows, and on down the line until the expiration of six months finds them delighting the Podunk populace. Then they are sent back to Chicago, and "melted up," for there is a lot of silver in them. The Essanay Company, for instance, nets about $2,000 a year from this "melting up" process alone.

Money seems to be less an object with these "moving picture" people than with theatrical managers. The members of the company are better paid, for instance, and the "assisting talent" is handsomely recompensed. Leading ladies and leading men, according to their professional standing, are paid from $15 to $100 a day, and the Essanay Company even offered George and Josephine Cohan $2,000 for one dance. To show how great an inroad the "moving pictures" are making into theatrical receipts, and the closeness with which the syndicate watches such things, no actor or actress under control of Klaw & Erlanger is allowed to take part in any of the "plays," or even "do a turn." As for the "plays" themselves $100 is paid for a good one, and many of the country's famous authors are turning their attention to this new source of income.

"SOMETHING NEW"   1912

By Louis Reeves Harrison, *The Moving Picture World*, Vol. 12, No. 1, April 6, 1912, p. 23.

Mother is still unable to pay the rent in a large number of recent heartrending photo-sobs, and the promiscuous carrying off of little girls by the Indians is assuming the proportions of a national calamity, though a few thousands of them grow up with the tribes to fall-in-love-with and be-rescued by hatchet-faced cowboys with college-cut hair sapping their brows. The gun belonging to the fellow who didn't do it is still found near the corpse in lurid bloody-murder-dramas, and the cowboys led by the black-sombreroed sheriff with a tin star are, as usual, just about to hang the innocent hero when the cowgirl of ostentatious tootsies dashes to the rescue—suspense—with proof positive that murderers having an atom of common sense, to say nothing of careful training in their perilous vocation, are not in the habit of laying their weapons by the respective sides of their victims to insure their identification and subsequent capture—a fact which invariably escapes the attention of hasty hangmen all belted round with shooters, cartridges and lassos.

There are other themes. As this is an election year, "Terrible Teddy, the Trust Buster," or "Steam-Roller Bill, the Delegate's Dread," might do for a starter. The fact that twelve Supreme Court Judges, mere political appointees, have decided in a moment of aeroplane self-appreciation and overfed self-satisfaction that they outrank the elected President and Congress is rich with material for such a farce-comedy as delighted Gilbert and Sullivan. "The Modern Despot, or Thirty Years' Torture for Stealing Two Stickpins," is up to date, and almost anything new is preferable to the perennial presentations, whose stories are carefully foretold in the titles, through which we sit indulging in vain hopes for many lost hours.

Our ancestors of one or two centuries ago were restless people, fond of travel and discovery, and real Americans of to-day, whether newly-made or of Colonial families, have that progressive desire to see all there is to be seen of the world we live in, hence pictures of travel would be of live interest if selected by those who know how to *perceive* what is beautiful, novel or interesting as well as merely look at it, but few of this class of moving pictures are taken by men who grasp the continuity idea even if they select the best subjects. We are progressing in a lovely scene and just getting interested in its revelations when the film is cut and attention is sharply diverted to something unfit or lacking in harmony, and so we simply get a nibble of what we might fully enjoy otherwise, with thousand-foot reels devoted to a trip through the French Riviera, over the Maritime Alps, through the Italian Lakes, over the Swiss Alps, or through the canals of Venice, or up the ascent of Vesuvius, or through the streets of Paris, any trip that gives lovely scenery together with the characteristics of strange peoples, would serve to delight millions who cannot get away from home, and would prove educational to the little ones.

Do not forget those "little ones." Millions of parents are interested in them and in what they see at the "Movies." As I have already suggested and will point out more clearly in future issues the educational idea as applied to motion-pictures is getting a strong grip on the people, and anyone who disregards what the people want will go to the foot of the class and stay there until he gets into his marble head what the playwright means by action and reaction. Millions of children go to the picture shows and millions of parents follow them whose hearts and lives are bound up in the little ones. All that is low, vile and injurious will have to be eliminated from the small places of entertainment, and the sooner the better for the maintenance of interest among grown-up patrons. Every picture show in this country would be crowded to over-flowing if the screen program embraced what is new and attractive in science and travel as well as what is interesting and clean in history and the drama, for the American people are just what Lincoln said they were. As for the pictured stories, those well worth the telling will require two or more reels for their suitable presentation.

I am strongly in accord with Mr. Blackton's opinion—I do not pretend to say that he originated the idea, but it became the subject of more than one discussion between us— that the trend is towards grand musical drama. In another periodical (*The American Review of Reviews*) it is stated that the New York Philharmonic Society is to undertake the production of famous operas on the screen with his collaboration, but our conversation related to the production of original dramas devised for the screen on a grand scale with music composed especially for them. This not only *can* be done, but it *will* be done before another year passes by. The moment that producers realize that both playwright and composer must be given recognition and the regular percentage of box-office receipts accorded both, as in stage presentations, the *original* dramas, some of the finest the world has ever seen, will be forthcoming, and moving pictures will move up to a very high rank of artistic and profitable performance.

During the bicycle mania it was next to impossible to convince any manufacturer of the leg-propelled vehicle that it would be superseded by the autocar. He was too saturated with present success to care what happened in the long run, but the change came, and with the bigger appeal there was no decrease in the profits of either the makers or those who dealt directly with the public. Those who were progressive, who were men of broad scope and had a clear vision of future requirements of the people, went ahead on a larger scale than ever, while those who thought the ultimate had been reached either petered out in a small way, supplying a very limited demand, or lost all they had made in complete failure. I do not say that such will be the case in moving pictures, but the trend is unmistakeable.

As far as my own limited observation goes, feature plays are growing in strength as drawing attractions, and this tendency is confirmed by reports from many sources, but the movement is a cautious one except in a few instances, and the plays are either adaptations by hack writers or built on classic lines. These are doubly valuable when they are historically correct and entertaining, they are both instructive and interesting, but the big drawing cards are yet to come. They will be modern in motif, involve profound human interest of to-day, even if they are placed in historical or classic settings. I do not pretend to say what character of grand musical drama presented on the screen will sweep the country with overwhelming success, but it is safe to say that it will involve some masterly and convincing truth applying to our present or future condition or will present one or more principles that strum great chords of human sympathy.

Personally I will welcome the grand plays when they come, and I will especially enjoy the ones that help us to understand those problems of human nature which only Genius can purposely and patiently unravel, which tend to develop our ever-increasing capacity for knowledge and happiness.

"THE SOCIAL USES OF THE MOVING PICTURE"   1912

By W. Stephen Bush, *The Moving Picture World,* Vol. 12, No. 4, April 27, 1912, pp. 305-306.

The value of the moving picture as a means of agitating for the betterment of social conditions is self-evident. Nothing affects us more powerfully than the truth when it is preached in pictures. Less than a hundred years ago our social system was full of grave wrongs and abuses, which were eventually remedied and destroyed by pictures, cartoons and descriptions. The pen-picture, even when drawn by a masterhand, can never be as quickly and as universally convincing as the picture which derives its realism from the fact that it moves.

Abuses and wrongs cannot live except in darkness. The moment we throw a strong enough light on a real social wrong half the battle is won. A striking illustration of this fact was afforded recently during the last session of the New York Legislature. It appears that several efforts had been made to obtain an appropriation for shelter for poor blind children. The legislators who, no doubt, possessed the same sympathy for suffering that every human being feels, neglected to act in the matter; not out of callous indifference but because the rush of business and their own individual affairs claimed their attention. One day a little blind child suffering from the want of such a shelter was placed beside the presiding officer of the Senate. The sight so affected the legislators that the appropriation was voted at once without a dissenting voice.

Any motion picture portraying deplorable social conditions is therefore an agent for good. Some of the best known film makers of our country have given us pictures dealing with social evils and making a strong appeal for redress and reform. The Biograph, Selig, Vitagraph and notably the Edison studios deserve credit for their efforts along these lines.

The boldest, most timely and most effective appeal for the stamping out of the cruelest of all social abuses has been made in a two-reel production by the Thanhouser Company. The pictures are based on the touching poem of Elizabeth Barrett Browning entitled, "The Cry of the Children." More than two generations have passed away since the noble poetress told of the "children weeping ere the sorrow comes with years."

Since that time great efforts have been made by many good men and women to stop this evil. We are ashamed to say that the agitation against child labor has been far more successful in other civilized countries than in our own. For more than half a century all attempts to remedy the evil in the cotton mills of the South, where it appears in its most hideous shape, have been unavailing.

After an agitation lasting from the period of reconstruction to the present day, the best that has been accomplished was done by the present Congress. A law has now been passed, establishing a Federal Bureau, which, however, can do nothing but investigate conditions. It has no authority to change hours of labor or order any other restrictions. It cannot even recommend legislation, because Congress, under the Constitution, lacks authority to pass such laws. The best that can be hoped for is the creating of public sentiment through the publication of the results of its inquiries. There was evidence before Congress that boys and girls as young as six and seven years were put into the

15. G. M. ("Bronco Billy") Anderson, the first cowboy star, who survived THE GREAT TRAIN ROBBERY to make innumerable Westerns. The Denver Post reports on his filming of THE HEART OF A COWBOY in 1909.

mills and compelled to work ten and eleven hours a day. The results of such a state of affairs in degrading and debasing humanity, need not be described in detail here.

We are glad to say that the Thanhouser picture will accomplish the same results that are expected from the work of the Federal Bureau, to wit: the arousing of public indignation. The pictures are admirably conceived, do not at any time go beyond the line of probability and bring home their lesson in a forceful, but perfectly natural and convincing way. No dramatic derrick has been used to drag in a counterfeit love story. The makers of the film have kept before their eyes the one idea: the enlightening of the public as to the conditions and effects of child labor. While the picture skilfully paints the extremes of our modern social life, it has steered clear of the fatal error of the old time melodrama in which, instead of human beings, the spectator was compelled to see a set of angels and a set of devils. THE CRY OF THE CHILDREN as rendered by the Thanhouser Company, makes it plain that the mill-owner is as much a creature of circumstances and surroundings and economic conditions as the laborer. The picture shows the common bond of humanity between them and how the touch that makes all the world akin does not lose its magic in the wretched tenement of the laborer or in the mansion of the mill-owner or in the whirr of the factory.

A laborer and his family consisting of a wife and some half-grown children try to live in peace with the world and with themselves in spite of the awful conditions which surround them. They cannot, however, fight off the inevitable. The awful strain begins to tell on the mother who bears the heaviest burden. When she breaks down, the youngest child in the family who had been kept at home and treated as the favorite was compelled to go to work. She could not stand up to her cruel task and live. Nature had not made her little limbs for bearing the burdens of hard toil and the little girl dies a victim of overwork. The mill-owner's wife had offered to adopt the little child, but her offer had been rejected by the child herself. Later when the child began to realize the odds against the laborer in the struggle of life she went to the mill-owner's wife and asked to be adopted, thinking in that way to lighten the burdens of her parents and sisters. But the grime of toil had replaced the child-like grace and sacrifice of former days. The bitter hours in the factory had changed the happy laughing child into a haggard looking waif. In her altered appearance she found no longer favor in the eyes of her employer's wife and necessity drove her back into the house of torture. The end of the picture shows the grief of the parents and sisters of the dead child and the bitter and cutting remorse of the mill-owner and his wife. As we look at the latter we feel the awful weight of the poem's words:

> "But the child's sob in the silence curses deeper
> Than the strong man in his wrath."

Wherever these pictures are shown, converts to the necessity of thorough child labor reforms will be made by thousands. Owing to the determined opposition of Southern members of Congress the Federal Bureau entrusted with the investigation of child labor has had its powers narrowed and limited in many ways. In order to hamper the work of the Bureau as much as possible an amendment was tacked on to the law, which prohibits an investigator from entering the laborer's home, if the householder objects. This amendment was not dictated by any tender regard for the privacy of the home, but is to be a weapon in the hands of the mill-owner, who by threats and intimidation will seek to influence his employee against the investigators. Right here the power of the motion picture asserts itself. They may be able to bar the investigator, but they cannot bar the man with the camera. The camera must create the demand for remedial legislation and second the labors of the Federal Bureau.

The remedy, of course, lies entirely with the legislatures of the individual states. The report of the Federal Bureau will be read by hundreds at best, while the picture will be seen by millions. It seems to us that in the near future this fact will be recognized by the people most concerned in the matter, we mean organized labor. It was the labor element which forced the establishment of the Bureau from an unwilling Congress. The labor element ought to realize the advantages of the motion picture as a means of agitation and be swift in making use of them. The protection of the minors working in store and factory is one of the live issues of the coming campaign for the election of a president. The pictures here mentioned are therefore very timely and ought to be welcome to every intelligent and progressive exhibitor. We will confess ourselves much mistaken if THE CRY OF THE CHILDREN in motion pictures will not serve as a valuable campaign argument long before the votes will be counted in November.

1913   **Censorship in Ohio**

Excerpt from "Correspondence: Ohio," *The Moving Picture World,* Vol. 18, No. 11, December 13, 1913, p. 1292.

. . . In the first official report of Ohio's motion picture censors, at work in the Rose building, Columbus, it has been shown that 8,000 reels of film have been censored, increasing the state's exchequer just $8,000. Of these, 62 entire pictures were ordered cut out because of objectionable scenes, 800 were ordered modified, and 50,000 feet of film ordered eliminated from pictures which were proper enough except in parts. The censors have put the taboo on the turkey trot in film and among the other features the board objects to scenes showing a girl thief snatching a purse, thugs tying a victim to the railroad track, a crazy man clubbing an old man, men and women drinking from bottles, a woman putting poison into a decanter to poison her husband, placing a man in a dungeon and turning in water from the sewers upon him, striking a hunchback, putting rat poison on bread, an indiscreet dance done by a woman, crooks cracking a safe, and a muscle dance. . . .

COMMENTARY

It is customary to cite the popularity of the Pearl White serial, THE PERILS OF PAULINE, as evidence of the naïveté of movie audiences in 1914. On the contrary, Pearl's followers wanted their disbelief only lightly suspended (just like groups which today take delight in resurrected serials), and felt cheated when this was not possible.

Pearl (1889-1938) doesn't get included in the American poet Vachel Lindsay's sober study, *The Art of the Moving Picture,* which appeared at the end of 1915, and which he hoped would be a guide for classifying and judging current films. Lindsay's conviction that films were worth careful thought and analysis was still exceptional for that time, although THE BIRTH OF A NATION had by then begun to create a new public for motion pictures—a public which had never before paid any attention to them.

FILM 1914   THE PERILS OF PAULINE

"Independent Specials," *The Moving Picture World,* Vol. 20, No. 11, June 13, 1914, p. 1542.

THE PERILS OF PAULINE *[Sixth Episode]* (Eclectic). June 1—We can not truthfully say that this Pauline series is holding up very well. It started off finely, but is poor this week. This number carries the action on without getting it, in any true sense, along any. Rough incidents, in which the players are or seem to be in great peril, are not real action; they

135

are film users and need to be a bit better done than in this two-reel offering to be thrilling. The photography is poor.

THE PERILS OF PAULINE   **FILM 1914**

"Feature Films of the Week: THE PERILS OF PAULINE," *The New York Dramatic Mirror*, Vol. 72, No. 1862, August 26, 1914, p. 26.

Twelfth Episode in Series Produced by the Pathé Players for the Eclectic Company. L. J. Gasnier, Director.

Harry Marvin	Crane Wilbur
Pauline	Pearl White
Owen	Paul Panzer
The Gypsy Leader	Clifford Bruce

Near the opening of this picture, several ingeniously arranged dissolves show a peril that Pauline avoided in the previous installment. While she reads a newspaper account of the escape of lions at the wedding, which fate and Harry prevented her attending, the scene changed into the actual enactment of the startling events described in the paper. Of course, dissolves of this nature are not original with the Pathé director, but those used here seem particularly appropriate and well contrived.

The twelfth chapter of Pauline lacks the thrills of some of its predecessors, although there is a fair amount of melodrama introducing the usual characters, supplemented by a band of gypsies. Owen engages the leader of the band to kidnap Pauline and hold her prisoner in a sequestered camp. The plan works smoothly up to the point where the jealousy of a gypsy woman in love with the leader is aroused. As usual, Harry is scouring the country in search of his sweetheart. He meets the jealous woman, is advised of the whereabouts of Pauline, and downs her captor in a rough fight.

Then the gypsy woman seems to repent her kindness, for she finds a huge snake, conceals it in a basket of flowers, and sends the offering to the "pretty lady with the blond hair." Pauline buries her nose among the blossoms, and there the film ends, which is something like breaking off a story in the middle of a sentence.

Settings for the picture are all that the incidents require. Acting is kept in the key of exaggerated melodrama.

(Signed) D.

"THE POET AT THE MOVIES"   **1915**

"The Poet at the Movies," "F. H." [Francis Hackett], *The New Republic*, Vol. 5, No. 60, December 25, 1915, pp. 201-202.

The Art of the Moving Picture, by Vachel Lindsay. New York: The Macmillan Co. $1.25 net.

This is a joyous and wonderful performance. It is not a rhapsody or diatribe about the moving picture. It is not an autobiographical chronicle. It is an argument founded on plain facts and happy interpretations, rising to mysticism, a meeting place of the people capped in cloud. Only a corn-fed poet could have written it. It talks in terms of Mary Pickford, Blanche Sweet, Henry Walthall. It places John Bunny and Sidney Drew. It introduces CABIRIA, THE BIRTH OF A NATION, WHO'S WHO IN HOGG WALLOW [sic], THE BATTLE HYMN OF THE REPUBLIC, YOUR GIRL AND MINE, JUDITH OF BETHULIA. It is steeped in the present and the actual. But Vachel Lindsay has un-

16. *Pearl White in Episode 12 of THE PERILS OF PAULINE (1914), best-known of the early serials. Reviews were not kind to this serial as a whole, but the mid-air ending of this episode was intriguing: "something like breaking off a story in the middle of a sentence."*

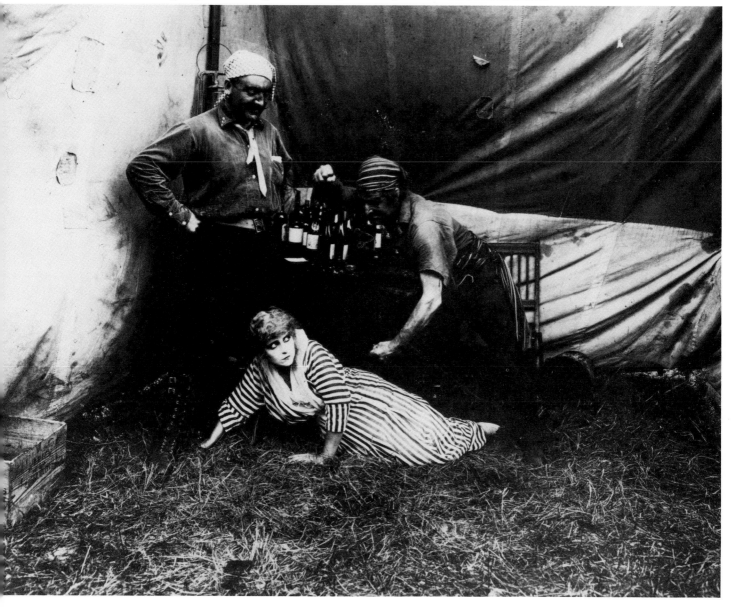

dertaken the fundamental brainwork necessary to an understanding of the moving picture art. He has done his heroic best to bring order out of aesthetic muddle and bewilderment. He has articulated a theory of beauty on the basis of the photoplay as we know it. Whether the theory stands or falls eventually, it is a bold and brilliant theory, really bold and really brilliant, and takes first place as an interpretation of the greatest popular aesthetic phenomenon in the world.

Mr. Lindsay is no worshipper of popular mechanics, no apostle of "a tin heaven and a tin earth." He is no demagogue. ("Our democratic dream has been a middle-class aspiration built on a bog of toil-soddened minds. The piles beneath the castle of our near-democratic arts were rotting for lack of folk-imagination.") Nor is he the kind of man who is dazzled by the plunderous profits and potentialities of photoplays. He respects the enterprise without adoring the exploitation. He respects the *vulgus* without adoring the vulgarity. He respects the mechanism without adoring the machine. He does not see "the redeemed United States running deftly in its jewelled sockets, ticking like a watch." He assents to America as it is, "the steam-engine, the skyscraper, the steam-heat, the flying machine, the elevated railroad, the apartment house, the newspaper, the breakfast food, the weapons of the army, the weapons of the navy." But his assent carries with it no subjection. "It is only in the hands of the prophetic photoplaywright and allied artists that the kinetoscope reels become as mysterious and dazzling to the thinking spirit as the wheels of Ezekiel in the first chapter of his prophecy. One can climb into the operator's box and watch the sword-like stream of light till he is as dazzled in flesh and spirit as the moth that burns its wings in the lamp. But this is while a glittering vision and not a mere invention is being thrown upon the screen."

But it is unfair to Mr. Lindsay to suggest his glittering vision at first. He himself does not come to it until he has written out with the extremest simplicity and clarity his own conception of the moving picture art, its classification and the basis for its criticism.

The art exhibition, plus action—that is his underlying conception. "Whatever the seeming emphasis on dramatic excitement, the tendency of the best motion pictures is to evolve quite a different thing; the mood of the standard art gallery." There are three kinds of pictures—action pictures, intimate pictures, splendor pictures. "Action pictures are sculpture-in-motion, intimate pictures are paintings-in-motion, splendor pictures are architecture-in-motion." A deaf and dumb art, its limit is the limit of the picture. "But the limit of pictorial beauty cannot be reached."

The action film is based, according to Mr. Lindsay, on the out-of-door chase. It gratifies incipient or rampant speed-mania. Its principal resource is inventiveness. It is falsely advertised as having heart-interest. "In the action picture there is no adequate means for the development of any full-grown personal passion." It provokes "the ingenuity of the audience, not their passionate sympathy." It is "impersonal and un-sympathetic." But its "endless combinations of masses and flowing surfaces" appeal to the sculptor. It can represent bronze elasticity, wave-beaten granite, living ebony and silver, the majesty of dancing, galloping or fighting figures. It is this artistic element that the producer has "allowed to go wild."

The intimate film, his next classification, "has its photographic basis in the fact that any photoplay interior has a very small ground plan, and the cosiest of enclosing walls." "It is generally keyed to the hearth-stone and keeps quite close to it." Intimate and friendly, the effect of this film should be delicate. And "it must first be good picture, then good motion." The pictures should "take on motion without losing their charm of low relief, or their serene composition." It should be possible to say: "This photoplay was painted by a pupil of Gilbert Stuart." ENOCH ARDEN, as Mr. Lindsay sees it, is the most successful drama of this kind. "Melodramatic interruptions or awful smashes" add nothing to such dramas. And it is the pictorial charm, the "fine and spiritual thing that Botticelli painted in the faces of his muses and heavenly creatures," which accounts for the popular love of Mary Pickford.

138

To photoplays of splendor, architecture-in-motion, Mr. Lindsay gives his greatest attention. The fairy splendor of non-human objects "is fundamental in the destinies of the art." It is to be found in "furniture, trappings, and inventions in motion." People become tired of mere contraptions. But they never grow weary of imagination. Crowd splendor, patriotic splendor, religious splendor, further entice him. "While the motion picture is shallow in showing private passion, it is powerful in conveying the passion of masses of men." He illustrates from THE BATTLE, an old Griffith Biograph. He analyzes the spectacular symbolism of CABIRIA. He conceives a motion picture akin to "By Blue Ontario's Shore." He imagines a photoplay of *Pericles*, of Jeanne d'Arc, and of his own Springfield in symbolism.

Assuming with Mr. Lindsay that "the keywords of the stage are passion and character; of the photoplay, splendor and speed," and accepting the wide suggestiveness of his classifications, the question remains whether he has been sound, in the first place, to minimize pantomime, and wise in the second to force so strongly the parallelism of the photoplay to sculpture, painting and architecture. In his chapter on hieroglyphics he certainly indicates his appreciation of pictures as a means of conveying ideas. But he does not dwell sufficiently anywhere on the possibilities of pantomime, and he strains his theory of photoplays as primarily plastic art. His terminology, moreover, is open to criticism. The word action is not in the same plane as the word splendor. And a word less loose than action could be found. But these objections are not meant to be inhospitable. No one could be inhospitable to a book so vigorous and creative and fertile. It goes, to my mind, to the root of the matter. It reveals vividly where the limitations and the opportunities of the moving pictures lie. There is nothing fanciful about it. There is nothing chimerical. It states and argues its position, and opens up the hope for beauty in a form of expression that has been enormously misunderstood.

In reporting this book it is impossible to preserve its savor. It is equally impossible to indicate its pregnant opinion on the many distinctions between plays and photoplays, between photoplays and motion pictures, on the censorship, the orchestra and conversation, on the plebiscite and criticism. The book itself must be read by all who are aware that "the photoplay cuts deeper into some stratifications of society than the newspaper or the book have ever gone," and who believe that "the destiny of America from many aspects may be bound up in what the prophet-wizards among her photoplaywrights and producers mark out for her." The mystic ecstasy of this belief will not be general. There will be many, even, to halt superciliously at the very conjunction of the moving picture and art. But Mr. Lindsay need not care. He has initiated photoplay criticism. That is a big thing to have done, and he has done it, to use his own style, with Action, Intimacy and Friendliness, and Splendor.

(Signed) F. H.

COMMENTARY

In Sousa-march prose, Julian Johnson conveys the essence of Douglas Fairbanks (1883-1939) bouncing through THE AMERICANO (1916), one of his satires compounded of calisthenics and optimism. Apparently this film is the take-off point for the counter-satire on Fairbanks that Sinclair Lewis wrote into Chapter 16 of his novel *Main Street* (1920), describing a feature which was supposed to be showing at the Rosebud Movie Palace in Gopher Prairie.

By 1917 Fairbanks had vaulted into the salary class of $1,000,000 a year, along with Charlie Chaplin and Mary Pickford. He was so much an idol, and the envied image of the American, that his films were used to open big New York theatres: the 2,200-seat Rivoli

in 1917 (**A MODERN MUSKETEER**), the 5,300-seat Capitol in 1919 (**HIS MAJESTY, THE AMERICAN**).

Anita Loos, the author of **THE AMERICANO**, and later, of the best-selling book *Gentlemen Prefer Blondes* (**1925**), **had been a youngster when she sold her first scenario to D. W. Griffith, who filmed it at Biograph (THE NEW YORK HAT, 1912).**

Fairbanks illustrates human speed. Mechanical speed is saluted in Aerial Views, descendant film of those early thrill shots where the camera had been placed in the front car of a swooping roller-coaster to give audiences near-heart-failure.

THE AMERICANO   **FILM 1916**

Excerpt from "The Shadow Stage," Julian Johnson, *Photoplay Magazine*, Vol. 11, No. 4, March, 1917, pp. 116-117.

. . . In writing about THE AMERICANO, the latest visual dynamite from the Fairbanks factory, we are considering Douglas rather than the doings.

In any expression about Douglas Fairbanks the temptation is to go far; the temptation is to say that he is *the* representative American actor for both ears and eyes.

If not, why not?

America is a large neighborhood of hustle and bustle, good nature and dogged persistence, fine animal spirits and outrageous optimism, much physical magnetism and few of the esoteric unguents. There are those among us who are cracked, crazy or strange, poets both ab and subnormal, dreamers for every hour in the day, melancholics, imaginaries, newthoughtists, revolutionaries, voluptuaries, hermits, heroes, cowards, saints, skunks. Of course. But they do not represent America.

The good-bad lovable chap Douglas Fairbanks always plays *does* represent America and the biff-bang Americanism for which we are justly and unjustly renowned.

The most interesting thing about Douglas Fairbanks is his future.

Here he is: a sane, commonplace, aggressive young fellow in his early thirties, getting a groundwork of combined experience and celebrity from which no middle-age triumph can jar him. He is devoted to the screen. Doesn't consider it a mere makeshift for the big money, but an absolute medium for the best that's in him. He is going to grow right along with camera-craft, and when, in a few years, we come to those absolutely certain sun-plays of serious life, let us hope that he will crown his career with a man of maturity who will be not only a triumph of acting but *a national expression.*

Anita Loos, the demi-tasse librettist, is a great help to our hero. Her frolicsome scenarios are not only immense entertainment, but they are satires more subtle than our contemporary vocal dramatists provide. Remember, in AMERICAN ARISTOCRACY, the distiller's wife who couldn't speak to the brewer's wife because she moved in a higher plane? This is scraping the paint right off the surface of society, and since the death of Clyde Fitch they're not doing it in the talkies.

Did we mention THE AMERICANO? Oh, yes! We have more story and less jumping than AMERICAN ARISTOCRACY vouchsafed. The chief concern is a Central American revolution, and the meddling therewith by a young New York assistant to a mining company. The inciter of his trip is Alma Reuben, whom we have previously noted as one of the most charming brunes in captivity. The buildings of the San Diego Exposition furnished fine, ready-made settings. Mr. Fairbanks literally falls on his enemies, in this picture, and the results in front of the projected fight are electric as an incandescent; whoops and howls from the audience spur the ghostly battlers to their set finish. After a great deal of pummeling Douglas really enfolds Alma, and in the midst of your surprise at this unexpected denouement the lights go up and your excited fair neighbor sticks her hatpin into the side of your head. . . .

1918   **Aerial Views**

Excerpt from "The Screen," *The New York Times,* December 30, 1918, p. 7.

. . . It is reported that Curtiss has built an airplane that can carry fifty passengers, but the hundreds of persons who filled the Rivoli [Theatre] yesterday afternoon were carried up and over the City of Washington by a single machine. They held to the arms of their chairs and dizzily watched the Monument revolve beneath them and the Capitol spin around like a top. They saw another plane whirl and dive above them and seem to go backward as their own shot by at greater speed.

These sentences do not exaggerate the sensations of the spectators of WASHINGTON'S SKY PATROL, which is the most thrilling airplane film exhibited here since FLYING WITH THE MARINES. The intermittent applause, quick exclamations, and nervous laughter that came from here, there, and everywhere in the house as the picture was shown were evidence of the sensations of its spectators. The film was made for the Rivoli by J. Thomas Baltzell. . . .

17. *An early photograph of Thomas H. Ince (left), with his cameraman, Ray Smallwood. Ince inherited the Western as a stale formula, but, addressing care to its production, gave it new logic, authenticity and vitality. The world has been responding ever since.*

CHAPTER 9

Thomas H. Ince

COMMENTARY

It speaks well for the sturdiness of the Western film that it survived the tradition of production in which Thomas Harper Ince (1880-1924) found it at the end of 1911. "The cowboys rode uphill on Tuesday, and downhill on Thursday," Ince used to say, (31) but even in those days, Westerns were being manufactured in overwhelming quantity. When Americans bewilderedly questioned this, they were told the supply was intended for the foreign market.

Ince, an actor like Griffith, was at first disdainful of the new art of films, because of their "low" origins; but in 1910, when a lull in his stage engagements found him "at leisure" in New York, he decided to try it, and acted in one film at $5 a day at the Imp studio. On the strength of this, he went to Biograph at an offered salary of $10 a day, which he boosted to $15 before he accepted it. Again, there was a single film, and then Ince returned to Imp with the promise of the first director's job that fell vacant. In December, 1910, he wrote and directed his first film for Imp.

The following month, Ince was assigned to direct Mary Pickford, who had just been lured from Griffith's Biograph Company at a weekly rate of $175, and his unit was sent to Cuba to film one-reelers. Having insisted on rapid advancement, he was forced to learn the rudiments of film directing and technique very quickly, and avoid mistakes which would be mercilessly revealed on the screen. It was not until he left Imp at the year's end, hired by the New York Motion Picture Company to make Westerns in California, that he firmly hit his stride. Then, with such films as the two-reel WAR ON THE PLAINS, and the three-reel CUSTER'S LAST FIGHT (both 1912), it seemed, as someone wrote, that the true history of early life in the Wild West was at last being written on the screen.

Self-trained as "an expert plot builder," Ince did "not fear to use numerous scenes to give clearness to his action," (32) and some of the photography which he encouraged for the heretofore lowly Western inspired comment on the "Corot mistiness" of its soft brown tones. (33) He wrote, directed, cut his own films, and met with widespread success. A work such as his two-reel THE BATTLE OF THE REDMEN (1912) was reviewed as "truly epical," and was compared with "the story of Samson and . . . the sack of Troy." (34)

Gradually, as production increased, he hired scenario writers and gathered directors around him, supervising their work by means of detailed shooting scripts at the primary stage, and later by control of the editing. "Tom Ince, of Inceville" gives us a look at his accomplishments at the end of 1913, the year which, along with the production of

shorter films, had seen the release of his special 5-reel THE BATTLE OF GETTYSBURG. Inceville, by the way, was closer to 20,000 than to 2,000 acres.

"TOM INCE, OF INCEVILLE"   **1913**

By W. E. Wing, *The New York Dramatic Mirror*, Vol. 70, No. 1827, December 24, 1913, p. 34.

The Wonderland Which Began with One Stage and Now Covers an Investment of $35,000—A Complete Municipality.

———

"For the love of Mike, boys, take a look and tell me if I have gone crazy!" cried Bob, who, in advance of the hunting party stood on an abrupt wall of a canyon and gazed into the depths with protruding eyes.

We hastened forward and gazed upon an unusual scene. For three days we had fought our way over that uncouth and unlovely range, missing out on two bucks and a beautiful doe in our efforts in deer hunting, side-stepping numerous bobcats and other playful denizens of the heights. Then, without warning, we brushed through the underbrush and looked down upon a Japanese village, beautiful in its planning and artistic in its dress. We assured Bob that we saw everything that his excited vision perceived, but he still was suspicious that the stuff he carried in his bottle was not treating him right.

We had to make a wide detour to reach the bottom of the mountain and encountered another shock. It was an Irish settlement, true to life. In our retreat down the gulch we ran the gamut of erratic emotions. For a bit of Switzerland, a peaceful Puritan settlement, and substantial colonies of various nations hastened our delusion that the Santa Ynez range had suddenly gone mad. Upon arriving at the peaceful Pacific we found the finishing touch. Weighed at anchor beyond the breakers we observed an ancient brigantine of grandfather's time, with cutlass-armed men swarming over the sides. To complete this mad-house medley a bunch of incoherent cowboys wrangled on the sands of the beach.

For fear that the gentle reader will believe this introduction written from a padded cell, I will explain that our hunting party merely had blundered upon Inceville the remarkable mountain and seashore home of the Broncho and Kay Bee companies. The locations in the fastness of the wilds make a more fantastic appeal than is written here for each village is a permanent affair, the result of long and careful development on the part of Thomas H. Ince, Vice-President and Manager of the New York Motion Picture Company. Nor did the wonders cease in the canyons as we saw them that day. In that two thousand acres of location Ince is raising stock galore as well as feed and garden truck on a wholesale scale.

Selecting this uncouth but striking coast range which lies above the city of Santa Monica, Ince established his first studio less than two years ago. He began with one little stage. Since that time he has extended construction throughout the mountains, each colony laid in its suitable and logical location. With more than seven hundred people on hand and an investment of $35,000 in buildings, Ince now is the proud manager of an organization as complete as a municipality. His shops construct everything from uniforms and furniture to houses. His cultivated lands feed the multitude. His range of locations travels in leaps and bounds from naval battles on the broad Pacific to the wild West, mountain life, Ireland and the Orient and in fact to every country save the extremely tropical. His first brigantine was the Fremont, a noted vessel in the days of the gold rush. A sister ship, almost a replica of the Fremont, has been secured and pirates once again ride the raging main.

To the writer the most striking feature of Inceville, aside from its wondrous array of foreign colonies, was its system. Although housing an army of actors, directors and subordinates, there is not a working hour lapses in which all the various companies are not at work producing results. We failed to see actors made up and dressed for their various roles, loafing about the stages or on locations; perturbed directors running here and there attempting to bring order out of the chaos, while locations waited and camera men idly smoked their cigarettes, waiting for the "next scene."

System with every-minute efficiency. "It can't be done," declare studio managers. "It is the character of the business that these rules cannot be applied strictly. There are delays; there always will be delays. They are unavoidable in picture making." These declarations I have heard, in reply to queries, in many studios. Therefore it would be advisable for Mr. Ince to patent his system and put it on the market.

With preparations laid out in detail from finished photoplays to the last prop, superintended by Mr. Ince himself, far in advance of action, each of the numerous directors on the job at Santa Ynez canyon is given his working script three weeks ahead of time. When the time arrives for putting on a picture, the costumes are on the hooks of the tailor shop; locations are ready, props are on hand and the producer has had much time in which to familiarize himself with the script. Filled with the theme and action, he goes out and, with the cogs of the big Ince machine oiled to the smallest gear and the entire plant running as smoothly as an automobile in the hands of a salesman, the picture travels from beginning to end without delays. To my mind this is the modern miracle.

Yet the work of the tireless Ince is not completed. More villages and ships are in store for the studio. More companies are being planned for the big things which the future holds. A fine club house, with billiards, pool, various other games and a dance hall, is coming soon. A motion-picture house for the further entertainment of employees' evenings, is to be erected, while other free amusements are included in the plans. Ince is looking after the comfort of his employees with the same infinite care as that summoned to construct wonderful Inceville, where even the electricity for lights and machinery is generated from a private plant—remarkable Inceville of the Santa Ynez.

Tom Ince himself is a marvelous machine. A human dynamo, he travels a pace which few care to follow. From early morning until 1 or 2 o'clock the following morning are his usual hours. Not only does he personally superintend the manufacturing, building and production of his mammoth studio, but he sits with Scenario Editor Richard Spencer many hours each week, hammering ideas into shape or building up chosen photoplays to the Broncho and Kay Bee standard. He also cuts the film turned out in the canyon to the tune of about 8,000 feet a week. The initiated will read these statements with doubting eyes, but they must stand as facts.

Ince is the "White Hope" of filmdom so far as physical and mental toil is concerned. He is built on the same plan physically. With a large head, shrewd countenance, stocky frame and muscled like the statue of an ancient gladiator, his physique has been able to withstand the terrible strain of the years. Despite the warning of fearful friends, he continues to grind on, his health seemingly unimpaired by his titanic task, which is measured largely by his remarkable success.

Out at Santa Ynez canyon there are hundreds of employees. Loyalty to their chief is their first and foremost thought, for he is a worthy leader who always is in his place at the fore of the workers. They love the master architect of this great studio, to the most humble soul and to such loyalty must be charged much of the efficiency which produces result upon result.

COMMENTARY

William S. Hart (1870-1946), a combination of Uncle Sam, Indian scout, and every boy's

grandfather when young, was Ince's biggest star. Ince brought Hart to films in 1914 to play in two-reelers, but also featured him in THE BARGAIN, one of the first full-length Westerns written directly for the screen, not adapted from a novel or a play. Later, however, Hart and Ince quarreled, and Hart broke away from Ince's supervision.

In 1914, Ince produced two special features, THE WRATH OF THE GODS and THE TYPHOON, both with the Japanese actor, Sessue Hayakawa.

THE BARGAIN   **FILM 1914**

"Feature Films of the Week: THE BARGAIN," *The New York Dramatic Mirror,* Vol. 72, No. 1874, November 18, 1914, p. 32.

Five-Part Western Drama, Produced by Thomas H. Ince and William H. Clifford for the Paramount Programme.

Jim Stokes . . . . William S. Hart
The Sheriff . . . . J. Frank Burke
Phil Brent . . . . Barney Sherry
Nell Brent . . . . Clara Williams
The Minister . . . . James Dowling

Evidently Thomas H. Ince and William H. Clifford, whose names are frequently bracketed under the titles of two-reel Western pictures, determined to give themselves a free rein in producing a typical Western subject on an extraordinarily large scale. It is as if they took the photoplay recipe that has been found adequate for shorter films and doubled, or tripled, all of the ingredients to make the biggest picture of its kind on record. The similarities and differences between this production and less pretentious Westerns, suggest the comparison of a circus in Madison Square Garden and one in a country village. Each adopts practically the same means to catch the public fancy, and the difference lies in the degrees to which the means have been perfected. Instead of one ring, there are three rings; the menagerie is larger, the clowns and acrobats more proficient; still, a circus is a circus, and likewise a Western melodrama is just that.

But before considering the story that makes the classification so unmistakable, it is best to avoid the danger of seeming to dismiss THE BARGAIN as a picture of small moment. On the contrary, it may be pointed to as a model of what can be accomplished in a popular field of photoplay work. The exteriors, photographed in the Arizona canyon, offer a sequence of glorious views in which the rugged wildness of a virgin country predominates. There is variety and a keen regard for a wise placing of the camera in gaining picturesque effects. Probably no preceding film has done such full justice to the scenic wonders of Arizona, which in itself is sufficient to give the picture a high recommendation.

In the matter of locations, then, audiences will find a stunning array of backgrounds containing the virtues they have learned to admire in Western films. The differences, of course, are all in favor of THE BARGAIN, for it is much more massive and in consequence more impressive. And to keep pace with the magnitude of the production in its physical aspects, the producers constructed a combination saloon, dance hall and gambling house that quite does away with the notion that the Western underworld drinks and gambles and fights in cramped quarters. This remarkable set seems large enough to accommodate a townful of cowboys and desperadoes, without hampering the movements of the dancing girls in soiled finery.

146   Returning to the story, we find these classic standbys of Western melodrama—Jim

Stokes, a bandit, who is doubly dangerous because he uses two guns where lesser men use one; Nell, the innocent girl he loves and marries under false pretenses; the minister who happens along in time to unite them; Nell's rough but honest father, and the inevitable sheriff. All of these people are true to type, which is equivalent to stating that there is little individual characterization in putting them through the series of carefully planned situations. Just as surely as two and two make four, a bandit hero will wish to reform when he falls in love with the right girl, and providing the marriage is performed early in the story, as it is here, the young wife is doomed to many hours of watchful waiting while her husband is paying the penalty of past misdeeds.

But to compensate for somewhat elementary character drawing, the picture contains what many people prefer—a story replete with action and the suspense which an expert plot builder, such as Mr. Ince, seldom fails to create. The scenes in which the sheriff captures Stokes, loses the stolen money at the gambling table, and regains it through the boldness of the "two-gun man," are continually exciting, and nothing short of thrilling is the sensational fall of a horse and rider down a steep embankment. They roll over and over, yet miraculously enough are spared to continue in the picture.

William S. Hart gives a virile, convincing performance in the part of Stokes; the sheriff is well presented by J. Frank Burke, and Clara Williams is sufficiently appealing in the role of Nell. Altogether there need be no question about the wide popularity of this production.

(Signed) D.

COMMENTARY

Ince's production of two-reelers continued into 1915, with feature-length films appearing more frequently now in his schedule. He was releasing through Mutual, which also handled the Majestic-Reliance product supervised by Griffith, and the Keystone comedies of Mack Sennett

SATAN McALLISTER'S HEIR, a two-reeler shot in one week in 1914 and released March 11, 1915, is typical. The complete shooting script follows. In the original manuscript, filmed scenes are pencilled "O.K.," extraneous scenes pencilled "Out." The cost sheet testifies to Ince's economical business sense.

Ince's method was diametrically opposed to Griffith's. If Griffith relied on a scenario at all (some said he never did), he would begin "by tearing the scenario to pieces." (35)

FILM 1915   Scenario for SATAN McALLISTER'S HEIR,

By C. Gardner Sullivan and Thomas H. Ince, No. 352

Produced by Walter Edwards

SATAN McALLISTER'S HEIR
CAST OF CHARACTERS

SATAN McALLISTER	WALTER EDWARDS
DOLLY ELLIS	THELMA SALTER
BOB ELLIS	THOMAS CHATTERTON
HATTIE ELLIS	MARGARET THOMPSON
COWBOYS—15	INDIANS—9

147

LOCATIONS

INTERIORS

INTERIOR WESTERN SALOON 1-3-5-6-7-8-9-10
SHACK KITCHEN 61-64-66-77-79
INTERIOR CAVE 122-124-125-126-128-130-132-135-137-143-152-154

EXTERIORS

EXTERIOR WESTERN SALOON 2-4-17
PRAIRIE 11-12-13-14-15-19-21-22-23-25-27-29-30-31
GRASSY VALLEY 16
HILL SKYLINE 18-20-32-34
BANK OF SMALL CREEK 24-26-28
EXTERIOR ROUGH SHACK 33-36-38-40-42-44-45-46-47-48-49-50-51-56-
57-58-60-63-65-67-76-78-80-82
REAR OF SHACK 35-37-39-41-43
ANOTHER PRAIRIE SET 52-62
LITTLE CREEK 53
SANDY BASIN 54-74
ROCKY HILLSIDE 55
ROCKY RAVINE 59-70
ANOTHER PRAIRIE SET 68
CACTUS IN SAND 69-71
SAND 72-73-75-81-83-90-97
RANCH YARD 85-87-88-89-91
GATE OF RANCH YARD 86
ROCKY GULLY 92-99-101-108-109-110
PRAIRIE 93-95-107-112
BIG ROCK 94-96-98-100-102-103-105
HILLSIDE 104-106
ROCKY RAVINE 111
NARROW PASSAGE IN ROCKS 113-115-117
ANOTHER ROCKY PASS 114-116-146-148-150
RAVINE 118
ROCKY RIDGE 119
ROCKY SLOPE 120
MOUTH OF ROCKY CAVE 121-147-149-151-153
ROCKY LEDGE 123
SIDE OF ROCKY CAVE 125-127-129-131-133-134-136
ANOTHER PRAIRIE SET 138-140-142
ANOTHER PRAIRIE SET 139-141-144-145

COST SHEET

Director: Edwards   Camera: Gove

Commenced Dec. 22nd.   Completed Dec. 28th.

Stock   276.27
Labor & Operation, Property Man   19.04

Ranch R. & M., Salaries	56.57
Laboratory Operation	74.73
Payroll, Undist.	182.55
Total Payroll	609.16
Picture Expense, Direct	20.15
Laboratory, Material	40.26
Kitchen R. & M., Add. R. R. & M.	31.90
General Picture Expense	113.62
Total California Picture Expense	815.09
Negative Film Used	3,579 ft.
Positive Film Used	3,960 ft.
Cost Per Reel (2 Reels)	407.55
Cost Per Reel Foot	.41
Total California Picture Expense	815.09
3,579 Ft. Negative Stock at .03	107.37
3,960 Ft. Positive Stock at .0265	104.94
Grand Total Picture Expense	1027.40
Grand Total Cost Per Reel (2 Reels)	513.70
Grand Total Cost Per Reel Foot	.51

SCENARIO: SATAN McALLISTER'S HEIR

SCENE 1. CLOSE UP ON BAR IN WESTERN SALOON

A group of good Western types of the early period are drinking at the bar and talking idly—much good fellowship prevails and every man feels at ease with his neighbor—one of them glances off the picture and the smile fades from his face to be replaced by a strained look of worry—the others notice the change and follow his gaze—their faces reflect his own emotions—be sure to get over a sharp contrast between the easy good nature that had prevailed and the unnatural, strained silence that follows—as they look, cut—

SCENE 2. CLOSE UP ON SATAN AT HITCHING RAIL BEFORE WESTERN SALOON

TITLE: "SATAN" McALLISTER, THE RICHEST, MEANEST AND MOST HATED RANCHER IN THE WYOMING VALLEY

Satan is tieing his horse to the rail— he finishes and looks brazenly about him— Satan is all that his name implies—he is a sinister gun-fighter, a man-killer and despite the fact that he is without fear, a bully of the worst type—he delights in hurting and abusing people and dogs, and the more forlorn appearing they are, the greater his delight in tormenting them—everybody is afraid of him and hates him—he knows this and revels in it—he exits, looking for trouble at every step—

149

SCENE 3. CLOSE UP ON BAR: SAME AS 1.

Flash back to the men at the bar—they show Satan is coming and wait uneasily, none of them knowing but that he will be singled out for Satan's abuse—

SCENE 4. EXTERIOR SALOON: WESTERN

Satan comes on from the sideline with a sneer—have a lonesome looking dog sitting before the saloon door—Satan boots him off the picture and smiles cruelly as he hears the dog yelp—he looks about for something else to abuse but finding nothing, exits into the saloon—

SCENE 5. CLOSE UP ON BAR

Cut back to the men waiting—they force smiles now and say with an effort at cordiality: "hello Satan"—Satan comes on—he takes them all in, in a contemptuous glance and ignoring their greeting, demands that the bartender wait on him—the latter hastens to comply—Satan dislodges a half soused cow puncher from the bar with a heavy blow on the head and throws him out of the picture—the others show how they hate him and would like to get him but he has them completely cowed—Satan drinks off a glass of whiskey and sets it down—he gazes about him to see if he can catch anyone staring at him and then centers his gaze off one sideline with an air of interest—PANORAM TO A TABLE IN THE CORNER OF THE SALOON WHERE A BEARDED DRUNK IS SLEEPING PEACEFULLY, THE DRUNK IS ON THE HOBO TYPE—

SCENE 6. CLOSE UP ON BAR

Cut back to Satan watching— he sees the drunk and a cruel smile comes over his face—the others watch him silently—Satan orders the bartender to draw him a huge and heavy glass schooner of beer—the bartender obeys—Satan takes it in his hand and again looks off the picture—

SCENE 7. CLOSE UP ON TABLE: SALOON CORNER

Flash of drunk asleep—

SCENE 8. CLOSE UP ON BAR

Cut back to Satan—he takes a deliberate aim and hurls the schooner of beer off the picture in the direction he is gazing, with all the force he can muster—

SCENE 9. CLOSE UP ON TABLE: SALOON CORNER

Cut back to the drunk asleep—have someone throw a schooner of beer so that it hits the wall directly over his head and splatters all over him—get over the idea of the glass landing with awful force—if it will break without damaging anyone, so

150

18. The vast set for Ince's super-Western, THE BARGAIN (1914), one of the first full-length
Westerns written directly for the screen. Although the reviewer notes a certain reversion to
pattern, he admits it is "the biggest picture of its kind on record."

much the better—the drunk awakens with a frightened start, the beer streaming over him, he gazes off the picture and then seeing who it is, forces a sickly smile—

SCENE 10. CLOSE UP ON BAR

Cut back to Satan—he is a little disappointed that he missed the drunk but the sight of the latter covered with beer compensates him for this—he turns and orders himself another drink, utterly ignoring the others who stand eyeing him furtively—if one of them would take the lead they would murder him on the spot but no one is willing to take the chance—

SCENE 11. CLOSE UP ON FRONT SEAT OF MOVING PRAIRIE SCHOONER

TITLE: FROM EAST OF THE MISSOURI, BOB ELLIS AND HIS WIFE, HATTIE.

Bob Ellis and his wife, Hattie, are seated together, gazing about them eagerly and talking as Bob drives—they are not of the far West types but farmers from the middle West—Bob is a good looking, hard working young chap and his wife is a pretty farmer's daughter—they are very happy with each other and are full of enthusiasm and hope over settling in the new country—

SCENE 12. PRAIRIE

The schooner driven by Bob comes on past the camera and starts into the background—two horses are hitched to the schooner and a third is tied behind—a string of cattle, roped together by the horns are also tied to the back of the wagon—show seven or eight steers if we have them—use whatever cattle there are at the camp—as the wagon works along into the background sideline, it stops—

SCENE 13. CLOSE UP ON DOLLY IN PRAIRIE SCHOONER

TITLE: THEIR SIX-YEAR-OLD DAUGHTER, DOLLY

Dolly, about six years old and a bright pretty little girl, is sitting near the end opening of the wagon, gazing straight ahead of her at something in the wagon—her eyes are sparkling with gaiety and she is pursing her lips as she whistles and calls: "come on Rags. Come on"—she whistles again and snaps her fingers—

SCENE 14. CLOSE UP ON PILE OF BLANKETS ON FLOOR OF SCHOONER

TITLE: "RAGS"

There is nothing to be seen but the blankets at first and then a puppy shoves his way from beneath them—this puppy ought to be a wonder—get the most disreputable looking little dog you can find—in his way, he should be a character—he comes out from among the blankets whisking his tail and yelping excitedly and runs to Dolly—PANORAM TO DOLLY AS RAGS RUNS TO HER—she seizes him and squeezes him to her—she worships the dog—register this clearly—as she plays with him get over the idea of the wagon starting again—

SCENE 15. CLOSE UP ON SCHOONER IN PRAIRIE

It is moving off the sideline and into the background followed by the horse and cattle—

SCENE 16. GRASSY VALLEY OR PRAIRIE

TITLE: UNAWARE OF McALLISTER'S DEEP HATRED OF "NESTERS," ELLIS DECIDES TO LOCATE IN THE VALLEY ADJOINING THE McALLISTER RANCH

The schooner has been driven into the foreground as the picture goes on—Bob and his wife have jumped off the seat and are standing gazing about in delight at the country—Dolly comes on frisking with Rags from the back of the schooner—she runs about them playfully and they smile at her and stop a moment to play tag with her—register the idea of a peaceful, simple little family—Bob and Hattie get over the idea of the sub-title and he turns to unhitch his horses—show the cattle still tied to the end of the schooner.—

SCENE 17. EXTERIOR SALOON: SAME AS 4

Satan comes on from the door—a couple Indians who are standing before the saloon, exit quietly off the sideline—he gazes after them with a bitter smile and then, going to the hitching rail, mounts his horse and rides off the picture—

SCENE 18. HILL SKYLINE: PRETTY SHOT

TITLE: AN HOUR LATER

Shooting along the skyline—McAllister rides on into the camera—he is coming at a trot but halts as he nears the camera and turning in the saddle, gazes with angry surprise off the picture—

SCENE 19. PRAIRIE

Flash of Bob's cattle grazing about the schooner—the horses are also picketed out and cropping the grass contentedly—a fire is burning before the schooner and Hattie is preparing a meal—Bob is constructing a lean-to nearby out of canvas and sticks—Dolly is playing with Rags—

SCENE 20. CLOSE UP ON SATAN: HILL SKYLINE

Satan is staring off the sideline in deep anger—he says savagely "another one of them damn nesters. I'll get rid of him quick"—he wheels his horse and rides quickly off the sideline—

SCENE 21. CLOSE UP ON SCHOONER AND FIRE

Cut back to Hattie getting the meal—Dolly comes on and stands watching her—Hattie picks up a canteen and starts for water but Dolly begs to go and her mother yields—Dolly exits with the canteen and Rags—

SCENE 22. PRAIRIE

Bob's camp shows in the background—Satan rides on aggressively past the camera and starts into the background—show Dolly in the background beyond the camp with the dog and heading away from the camera—

SCENE 23. CLOSE UP ON SCHOONER: ALLOW FOR ACTION

Cut back to Hattie getting the meal—Bob comes on and sniffs at the fire hungrily—he says "I'm starved"—they both turn quickly and look off the picture—Bob's face expands into a smile and he says with the air of a man who is glad to see another of his kind "Howdy mister. How are you"—he and Hattie look up in friendly greeting as Satan rides on but their faces change as he makes no response but scowls at them fiercely—he dismounts with deliberation and comes up to them, eyeing them both with an evil sneer—he says: "who invited you to make yourself so much to home?"—Bob says uneasily: "why nobody, we thought we'd——"—Satan interrupts him savagely—he says "never mind what you thought. Shut up and listen to me"—

SCENE 24. BANK OF SMALL CREEK

Dolly comes on romping with Rags and starts to fill the canteen—

SCENE 25. CLOSE UP ON SATAN, BOB AND HATTIE AT SCHOONER

Satan is coldly telling them they will have to get out—they look at him and at each other apprehensively—he speaks—INSERT TITLE—

"I AIN'T WHAT YOU MIGHT CALL A SOCIABLE CUSS AND I AIN'T ENCOURAGIN' NEIGHBORS."

BACK TO ACTION—Satan continues to gaze at Bob with a deadly contempt—the latter looks at him but says nothing—

SCENE 26. CLOSE UP ON DOLLY AT CREEK BANK

She has filled her canteen and is leaning over drinking from the creek—Rags is fussing about her and she cups her hands and fills them with water that he may drink—see if he won't drink—make a cute scene of it—

SCENE 27. CLOSE UP ON SATAN, BOB AND HATTIE AT SCHOONER

Cut back to Satan ordering them to leave—Bob starts to speak but Satan interrupts him and says—INSERT TITLE—

"WHEN THEY DON'T TAKE THE HINT AND MOVE ON, I ANNOY THEM PLUM SCANDALOUS"

BACK TO ACTION—he drops his hands suggestively on the handles of his pistols and holds the pose for the moral effect on them—they stare at him and show they are frightened and discouraged by his attitude—

SCENE 28. BANK OF SMALL CREEK

154   Flash of Dolly leaving with Rags and the filled canteen—

SCENE 29. CLOSE UP ON SCHOONER. ALLOW FOR ACTION

Satan, having delivered his speech is now ready to leave—he turns calmly and mounts his horse, ignoring Bob and Hattie as though they were a couple of sticks—he rides off the picture and they stand looking after him in dejected silence as Hattie clings to Bob's arm—Bob slowly recovers from the shock—his eyes flash and his face hardens—he thrusts out his chin and says "I'm damned if I'm going to let that man drive me out of here like that. He doesn't own this land any more than I do"—she is frightened and says "But he is such a terrible man"—

SCENE 30. CLOSE UP ON OTHER SIDE OF SCHOONER

Dolly comes on gaily with the canteen and followed by Rags—

SCENE 31. CLOSE UP ON SCHOONER

Cut back to Bob and Hattie—he says "He may be a terrible man but he don't own the earth and I'm going to stay for a while any way"—he talks on angrily when, Hattie, showing she hears Dolly, puts her finger to her lips in caution—he stops talking and Dolly comes around the end of the schooner with the canteen—her parents conceal their worry from her—

SCENE 32. CLOSE UP ON SATAN ON HORSE ON HILLTOP

TITLE: LATER. McALLISTER FINDS HIS WARNING HAS BEEN IGNORED.

Satan is sitting tensely in his saddle [looking] off the picture—

SCENE 33. EXTERIOR ROUGH SHACK IN PRAIRIE

REGISTER THE IDEA OF THE SHACK HAVING BEEN JUST BUILT—Bob is just finishing nailing on the hinges of the door—Hattie comes on from the inside, her apron filled with shavings—she dumps them in a pile near the house and she and Bob stand back and look it over—they are very proud of their new home—

SCENE 34. CLOSE UP ON SATAN ON HORSE ON HILLTOP

Cut back to Satan watching—he turns slowly in the saddle and facing the camera, says, "His ideas of movin' and mine aint exactly alike, but I aim to teach him my way"—he carefully inspects his pistols and rides out of the scene down over the top of the hill—

SCENE 35. CLOSE UP ON REAR OF SHACK

Dolly is seated on the ground leaning against the shack and seeking to fit an old waist of her mother's upon Rags—she is extremely busy—

SCENE 36. EXTERIOR SHACK

Cut back to Bob and Hattie—she is suggesting some little change as to the door and he is listening to her—she looks up quickly with a suppressed shriek and Satan rides on—Bob, who is unarmed, turns and stares at him—Satan, keeping his eyes on both of them, dismounts and strides up to Bob—his manner is slow and 155 sinister—Bob and Hattie wait for him to speak—he looks them both over and grins sarcastically—nobody says a word but they stand staring at each other—

SCENE 37. CLOSE UP ON REAR OF SHACK

Flash back to Dolly trying to get the waist on Rags—

SCENE 38. CLOSE UP ON SATAN, BOB AND HATTIE AT SHACK

Bob and Hattie, standing close together, are still gazing at Satan who is enjoying their evident fear of him—he speaks—INSERT TITLE—

"SEEMS TO ME YOU ARE HANDLIN' YOUR LIFE MIGHTY CARELESSLIKE."

Back to action—Satan addresses this remark with deadly insult to Bob—Bob flushes and stiffens but his gaze falls on Satan's guns and he subsides—he says "It aint no crime to try to make an honest livin' "—Satan says "Mebbe not, but it IS a crime to get gay with me"—

SCENE 39. CLOSE UP ON DOLLY. REAR OF SHACK

She has tied the waist about Rags after a fashion and is surveying him with admiration when she shows she hears voices—she knows some one is talking to her father and rises with interest and exits, followed by Rags—

SCENE 40. EXTERIOR SHACK

Cut back to Satan abusing Bob and Hattie and telling them to get out at once—Bob, pale but determined, does not reply but looks at Satan, half fearfully, half defiantly—Dolly followed by Rags, comes on from around the corner of the shack—she sees Satan, hears him cursing and reviling her father and stops in surprise and looks at him carefully—

SCENE 41. CLOSE UP ON DOLLY AT SHACK

She is gazing off the picture with a wondering expression which gradually changes to sympathy for her father—she is deeply hurt that he should be abused—Rags, who is standing at her feet, sees a stranger and exits, wagging his tail in welcome—be sure he wags his tail as he leaves this scene—Dolly doesn't notice he is gone as she gazes at the strange man who is so mean—

SCENE 42. CLOSE UP ON SATAN, BOB AND HATTIE AT SHACK. ALLOW FOR ACTION

Cut back to Satan giving Bob his last warning "I ain't caring about repeatin' myself and I'm givin' you the last line of talk I intend to"—he says—as he talks, Rags comes on wagging his tail and runs up to Satan in boisterous puppy welcome—Satan sees him and taking a step forward kicks him off the picture—have him get his foot under Rags and lift him up into the air—

SCENE 43. CLOSE UP ON DOLLY AT SHACK

Cut back to Dolly listening in sorrow—she suddenly starts and then her eyes flame with anger—she shows she sees Satan kick Rags—Rags comes on, his tail between his legs and whining for sympathy—Dolly is enraged beyond measure—that her puppy should be kicked inflames her against Satan and she reaches down and picks up a rock—she takes a quick careful aim and throws it off the picture with all her might—

SCENE 44. CLOSE UP ON SATAN, BOB AND HATTIE

Cut back to Satan repeating his threats—he suddenly claps his hands over one eye and staggers back with a cry of pain—have him have the rock in his hands and as he puts them over his eye, show it fall to the ground—he is blinded by the pain for the second and reels—Bob and Hattie are stricken with terror—

SCENE 45. CLOSE UP ON DOLLY

She is standing, her eyes flashing as she watches off the picture—she says, "There you nasty man, how do you like to be hurt?"—still fighting mad, she walks up to Satan—PANORAM TO SATAN AND BOB AND HATTIE AS DOLLY WALKS—Satan has by this time recovered himself somewhat and turns and glares about him like a wild man as he bellows "Who did that?" Dolly steps squarely in front of him and her chin thrust out says "I did, you bad, bad man"—her temper is fully aroused and she confronts him fearlessly and ready to go on with the battle—he glares at her as she answers him and then rubbing his injured eye, bends down slightly and takes a better look at her—

SCENE 46. CLOSE UP ON SATAN

He is staring off the picture as though he couldn't believe his own senses—his eye hurts him deeply and his temper is flaring but in spite of this, gradual look of wonder comes over him and this slowly gives way to a reluctant admiration—INSERT TITLE—

THE FIRST PERSON HE EVER MET WHO WASN'T AFRAID OF HIM.

BACK TO ACTION—Satan registers this idea and tries to hide a grim smile—he advances slowly off the picture—

SCENE 47. CLOSE UP ON DOLLY

She is waiting defiantly—her eyes blaze anew and Satan comes on slowly—he stoops down and stares into her face with a strange expression—she returns the look and they gaze straight into each other's eyes—her hands clench at her side as she looks at Satan and he notices this—

SCENE 48. CLOSE UP ON BOB AND HATTIE

They are both staring off the picture in fear and waiting to see what will happen—Bob, half fearing that Satan will punish Dolly, seeks to free himself from Hattie, and attack the bully but Hattie holds onto him—she has great faith in Dolly's years being a protection—

SCENE 49. CLOSE UP ON SATAN AND DOLLY

Cut back to them staring into each other's eyes—Dolly does not yield an inch and   157 so bitter a look of hate flashes over her that Satan smiles—gazing at her—he puts up one hand and ruefully rubs his damaged eye—the other eye he slowly winks at her—she tosses up her head disdainfully—

SCENE 50. CLOSE UP ON BOB AND HATTIE

Cut back to them watching—they both smile in a relieved way—Bob thinks that Dolly has softened Satan and feels much relieved—

SCENE 51. EXTERIOR SHACK

Bob and Hattie, smiling, are watching as he straightens up from over Dolly who continues to regard him with unabated hostility—Satan gazes about him and sees Bob and Hattie smiling at him—His face settles into a hard expression and turning his back on them he walks slowly to his horse—on his way he passes Rags—he lifts his foot to kick the puppy and then turns and looks at Dolly who is still eyeing him threateningly—he rubs his eye again and with a grim smile mounts his horse and rides off—Bob and Hattie and Dolly all stand silently watching him, the little girl still nursing her wrath and her parents wondering what to expect now—register the fact that Satan's friendship does not extend beyond Dolly—

SCENE 52. CLOSE UP ON SATAN ON HORSE. PRAIRIE

He is riding slowly along thinking—he frowns deeply and then in spite of himself a broad grin crosses his face as he says "The little fire eater, damned if she didn't near bust open my eye"—

SCENE 53. CLOSE UP ON LITTLE CREEK

TITLE: THE DRY SPELL

Pick out a location as much like SCENE 24 as possible but register the idea of the title—just a little muddy water should show here and there—Bob's cattle are wandering up and down this creek—Bob rides on and drives them off past the camera—he follows despondently—have some one on the sidelines do a lot of shouting at the cattle so that they appear very nervous—BE SURE TO REGISTER THE FACT THAT THEY HAVE DRAINED THE CREEK ABOUT DRY—

SCENE 54. SANDY BASIN

TITLE: CRAZED BY THIRST, THE CATTLE WANDER AFAR, AND THE EFFORTS OF BOTH ELLIS AND HIS WIFE ARE REQUIRED TO TRACE THEM.

Show two or three steers moving rapidly along—chase them into the picture and get over the idea of their being wild from thirst and in search of water—

SCENE 55. ROCKY HILLSIDE

Flash of a few more steers or cows—same idea as in previous scene—

SCENE 56. EXTERIOR SHACK

Hattie is ready to mount her pony—Bob, tightening the saddle girth on his horse, is about ready to join her—both are pale worn out and utterly discouraged although they try to keep up—Dolly, wearing a long apron that comes down to the floor, comes on in the doorway to wave them goodbye—her sleeves are rolled up and she has a dish rag in her hand—both Bob and Hattie go to the door—

SCENE 57. CLOSE UP ON SHACK DOORWAY

Dolly is standing in the doorway—Bob and Hattie come on and kiss her goodbye—they are heartbroken at being obliged to leave her alone but she takes it bravely and tells them not to worry—they show they must leave and kissing her again, exit—

SCENE 58. EXTERIOR SHACK

Dolly is standing in the doorway as Bob and Hattie come down to their horses in the foreground—they mount—as they do, Rags rushes on from the doorway and starts to follow them—Dolly calls and Bob orders him back but he is minded to go along. Bob dismounts and calling Rags to him, picks him up and carries him to the doorway—he reaches inside the doorway and takes down a coil of rope—

SCENE 59. ROCKY RAVINE

Flash of two or three steers trotting along—

SCENE 60. EXTERIOR SHACK

Cut back to Bob and the rest—Bob is finishing tieing Rags to the cabin, he leaves him quite a little rope—Bob mounts again and he and Hattie ride off waving back at Dolly—she turns rather forlornly as they exit and then consoling Rags over his fate, exits back into the doorway—

SCENE 61. SHACK KITCHEN

IDEA OF NEWNESS AND ROUGHNESS—nothing but boards—a bench has been built against one wall and is used as a table—it is covered with tin dishes—Dolly comes on and resumes washing these dishes—show quite a pile of them—a small window shows and a fireplace—pegs are about the walls with various articles and pieces of clothing hanging from them—Dolly is very lonesome and down cast but forces herself to cheer up and starts to whistle—

SCENE 62. PRAIRIE

Bob and Hattie ride on past the camera and then separate—he instructs her as she rides away from him and they exit off opposite sidelines—

SCENE 63. CLOSE UP ON RAGS AT SIDE OF SHACK

He has the rope in his mouth and is chewing on it vigorously —

SCENE 64. SHACK KITCHEN

Cut back to Dolly—she has finished washing the dishes and is arranging them in a neat pile on the bench—

159

SCENE 65. CLOSE UP ON RAGS AT SIDE OF SHACK

Cut back to Rags chewing on the rope—cut it so that only a thin strand holds it—have some one call him so that he bounds forward and breaks this strand—cut the picture before he gets out of the scene—

SCENE 66. SHACK KITCHEN

Cut back to Dolly—she is wiping off the bench with her dish rag—she is through now and takes off her apron and exits gladly—

SCENE 67. EXTERIOR SHACK

Have Rags with a piece of rope hanging about his neck waiting before the door—Dolly comes on from the door—she sees he is free and says "you naughty dog. How did you do that?"—she seeks to grab him but he frisks about her and runs off the picture—get him excited in this scene so that he jumps about and does a lot of barking—she follows him off calling to him to stop—

SCENE 68. PRAIRIE

Rags runs on followed by Dolly—he will not let her catch him and they both exit—

SCENE 69. CLOSE UP ON CACTUS IN SAND

TITLE: AN HOUR LATER
THE SURRENDER

Rags comes on and stops—he looks off the picture and wags his tail—if possible have him tired out from playing when you take this scene—Dolly comes on slowly—she is tired out from the long chase and sinks in the sand—beside Rags and putting her arm about his neck scolds him solemnly for running away—she is so tired she leans against him as she talks to him—

SCENE 70. ROCKY RAVINE

Flash of Bob driving a few cattle ahead of him as he rides into the camera—

SCENE 71. CLOSE UP ON CACTUS IN SAND

Cut back to Dolly and Rags—she realizes she must be starting back and although she is far from rested, gets up—she exits holding onto the piece of rope which is tied about Rags' neck—

SCENE 72. SAND

Dolly and Rags come on uncertainly—they wander aimlessly across the sand and finally exit—

SCENE 73. SAND

TITLE: LOST

160   Dolly and Rags come on slowly into the camera—they stop close to it and Dolly

19. *William S. Hart (center), with J. Frank Burke and Clara Williams, in* THE BARGAIN: *"Just as surely as two and two make four, a bandit hero will wish to reform when he falls in love with the right girl." Being a* Good-Bad Man *helps.*

gets over the idea of the title—she does not know which way to turn and her eyes fill with tears—if you can make him do it, have Rags sit down and look up at her—she turns to him and says: "Oh, you needn't look at me. It's all your fault. Come on now and help me"—she tugs on his rope and they exit past the camera—

SCENE 74. SANDY BASIN

Flash of Hattie rounding up a couple steers—have them running rapidly as she chases them and seeks to turn them back—

SCENE 75. SAND

Dolly and Rags come on, trudging wearily—they cross the picture and exit as Dolly seeks in vain to sight some familiar mark—

SCENE 76. EXTERIOR SHACK

TITLE: LATE THAT AFTERNOON

Hattie, covered with dust and exhausted, rides on—she dismounts stiffly and goes up to the door calling to Dolly—there is no answer and she exits into the house—

SCENE 77. SHACK KITCHEN

It is as Dolly left it—Hattie comes on and calls: "Dolly, where are you?"—there is no answer and she begins to grow alarmed—she calls again loudly—

SCENE 78. PRAIRIE: SHACK IN BACKGROUND

Bob rides on driving most of his cattle ahead of him—he leaves them and rides into the background for the shack—

SCENE 79. SHACK KITCHEN

Cut back to Hattie calling Dolly—she is extremely frightened now—she opens a sideline door and looks in, but showing Dolly is not there, exits in a panic—

SCENE 80. EXTERIOR SHACK

Bob rides on and dismounts—as he does, Hattie rushes from the shack, wild-eyed and hysterical—she runs to Bob crying: "Dolly is gone"—he cries: "What?"—she says: "Yes, she is nowhere to be found. I've searched the house"—he says: "She must be about somewhere"—he is badly frightened but tries to be calm—he goes up to the shack and then notices Rags is missing—he picks up the piece of rope and looks at it—

INSERT END OF CHEWED ROPE

BACK TO ACTION—the rope enlightens Bob as to why Dolly is not there—he says excitedly: "Rags got away and she followed him, God knows where"—Hattie starts to cry but he rallies her saying: "She is simply wandering on the prairie somewhere. We'll find her"—

SCENE 81. SAND

Flash of Dolly, all in and hardly able to walk, slowly dragging herself along and pulling Rags after her—

SCENE 82. EXTERIOR SHACK

TITLE: FRANTIC, ELLIS DETERMINES TO APPEAL TO McALLISTER TO AID IN THE SEARCH FOR DOLLY.

FOREGROUND ACTION—cut back to Bob seeking to rally Hattie but he himself is crazed with fear and grief—he registers the idea of the title and telling her to search the adjacent prairie, helps her into the saddle—he jumps onto his horse and they both ride off rapidly—

SCENE 83. SAND

Dolly and Rags come on past the camera—both are exhausted—if you can do it, have Rags lie down in the sand—Dolly seeks to arouse him and then, refusing to desert him picks him up and carries him off the scene—if he is too heavy, have her drag him off the sideline close to the camera—get a pathetic little scene here—

SCENE 84. PRAIRIE

Hattie rides on looking about her in all directions and calling continually for Dolly—

SCENE 85. RANCH YARD

TITLE: THE McALLISTER RANCH

SHOW A COUPLE LONG WATERING TROUGHS—have as many cattle as is possible crowded about these troughs and drinking—McAllister is standing by a trough in the foreground watching his men water the cattle—show several cowboys among whom are quite a sprinkling of Mexicans—McAllister is the same as ever and his men are all afraid of him—suggest a fence about the yard—there is a stir among the men and McAllister looks up and off the picture—

SCENE 86. GATE OF RANCH YARD

Bob rides on up to the gate and through it at a wild pace—

SCENE 87. CLOSE UP WATERING TROUGH. RANCH YARD. ALLOW FOR ACTION

McAllister is waiting in anger and wonder—he steps back slightly, his hands on the handles of his guns—Bob rides on and wheels up his horse in a cloud of dust—McAllister says "What the hell do you mean by comin' over here? Why you damned—" Bob interrupts him and says—INSERT TITLE—

"MY BABY IS LOST. WILL YOU HELP ME FIND HER?"

BACK TO ACTION—Bob leans from his horse and watches Satan desperately—Satan starts and says "The little girl?" "Lost?" Bob says "Yes, she wandered away   163 with her dog"—Satan stands there hating to aid his enemy and seeking to make up his mind—

SCENE 88. CLOSE UP ON SATAN

His natural mercilessness and cruelty and the chance to get back at Bob are strongly urging him to have nothing to do with the search for Dolly but the memory of the little girl comes back to him and he cannot fight it off—as he stands there DISSOLVE BACK TO SCENE 49 WHERE DOLLY DEFIES SATAN AND HE WINKS AT HER—DISSOLVE BACK TO SATAN AT THE WATERING TROUGH—the recollection of the only being he ever felt a spark of feeling for, softens his face—he seeks to hide it but a fear for the little girl has come over him—he straightens up and looks off the picture—

SCENE 89. CLOSE UP ON WATERING TROUGH

Cut back to Bob in an agony of suspense awaiting Satan's answer—Satan looks at him and says—INSERT TITLE

"NOT FOR YOUR SAKE, BUT FOR HERS, I'LL HELP YOU."

BACK TO ACTION—Bob starts to thank him but Satan turns and yells off the picture—a couple cowboys run on and he orders them to turn out everybody on the ranch—he runs off the picture after them—

SCENE 90. SAND

Flash of Dolly staggering along carrying Rags in her arms—

SCENE 91. RANCH YARD

Satan, Bob and a bunch of cowboys are riding out through the gate—lots of action, speed and dust—

SCENE 92. ROCKY GULLY

FOREGROUND ACTION—Dolly comes on carrying Rags—she sinks down helplessly and then feeling she must go on, gets a new hold on Rags and exits with him, carrying him—

SCENE 93. PRAIRIE. LONG SHOT

Satan and Bob and the others ride on in the middle background—where they separate on both sides into a huge fan and ride on widening out as they go—Satan on the extreme left end of the fan, passes close to the camera, his face showing his great anxiety—it is the first time he has felt a worry over any human being and it hits him hard—

SCENE 94. CLOSE UP ON BIG ROCK

Dolly reels on with Rags in her arms and plumps down by the rock—she simply cannot go any further—she hugs Rags tightly to her and buries her face against him as she sobs and tells him they are lost—she is so tired that even her fear and sorrow cannot keep her awake, and she leans heavily against him in her drowsiness—

SCENE 95. DISTANCE SHOT OF PRAIRIE AND BACKGROUND HILLS

Flash of the cowboys, Bob and Satan riding away from the camera in a wide half circle—get over the idea of great distance here—

SCENE 96. CLOSE UP ON DOLLY AND RAGS AT BIG ROCK

TAKE LOTS OF PAINS HERE AND GET A PRETTY PICTURE—Dolly, her arms about Rags and her head nestled on him, is sound asleep—Rags should also be asleep or pretending to be—have them both covered with dirt and sand—

SCENE 97. SAND. DAWN

TITLE: THE DAWN FINDS McALLISTER WIDELY SEPARATED FROM THE REST OF THE SEARCHING PARTY.

McAllister, tired and heavy-eyed, rides on looking about him and calling loudly "Dolly, are you here?"—he exits past the camera—

SCENE 98. CLOSE UP ON DOLLY AND RAGS AT BIG ROCK. DAWN

Flash of them sleeping together—

SCENE 99. ROCKY GULLY

McAllister rides on into the background, looking about him on all sides—he rides into the foreground and stops, about discouraged—he takes off his hat and runs his hand over his forehead wearily—he is about to turn and ride back when something ahead of him catches his eye and he bends forward with a start—

SCENE 100. CLOSE UP ON DOLLY AND RAGS AT BIG ROCK

Flash back to them asleep—

SCENE 101. CLOSE UP ON SATAN ON HORSE IN GULLY

He is staring off the picture and he utters a whoop of delight which he quickly suppresses as he says "Shut up you damn fool, do you want to scare her to death"—he rides forward slowly—

SCENE 102. CLOSE UP ON BIG ROCK. ALLOW FOR ACTION

Cut back to Dolly asleep with Rags—Satan rides on and dismounts—he goes softly to Dolly and bends down over her—just the head of the horse should show in the picture—

SCENE 103. CLOSE UP ON SATAN. DOLLY AND RAGS AT ROCK

Satan is bending down over Dolly and he touches her tangled hair reverently—this arouses Rags and he sits up and looks at Satan—Dolly, feeling Rags move, also awakens, she reaches out sleepily and then sits up—as she does she sees Satan gazing at her—she remembers him and her old feeling of enmity for him comes back—she grabs Rags as though to protect him and regards Satan with flashing eyes—he smiles rather wistfully and then speaks insert title—

165

"DON'T BE MAD AT ME. I'VE COME TO TAKE YOU HOME."

Back to action—Satan says this so gently that it surprises himself—Dolly sees that she has not to deal with a different person [sic]—she looks at him a moment and then believing him implicitly, throws her arms about his neck and kisses him in her great relief and gratitude—he returns the kiss awkwardly and nervously pats her head—all past strife is forgotten by her and she now gravely presents Rags to be kissed—Satan hesitates a second and then yields—he is kneeling beside her and drawing her to him, he asks her to tell him how she wandered so far—she starts to talk—get a fine heart interest scene here—

SCENE 104. HILLSIDE

TITLE: A WANDERING BAND OF CHEYENNES, AFTER AN ALL-NIGHT CAROUSAL OVER A STOLEN BARREL OF WHISKEY, START AN INCIPIENT UPRISING.

A bunch of drunken Indians are whooping and dancing around a barrel, the top of which has been broken in—it is empty and they kick it disgustedly down the hill—their ponies show in the background—the Indians are all crazed with booze and are brandishing their weapons and telling what great men they are—

SCENE 105. CLOSE UP ON BIG ROCK

Cut back to Satan with Dolly and Rags—he tells her they must be starting back—he leads the horse fully into the picture and lifts her on—she starts to mount behind but she looks at Rags who is watching the proceedings and holds out her arms appealingly—he chuckles and hands Rags to her—he mounts and they ride off—

SCENE 106. HILLSIDE. SHOOT THE OTHER WAY

Cut back to the Indians in their frenzy—they begin to mount and ride off the picture down the hill, shooting their rifles and yelling—have them do some good riding here—

SCENE 107. PRAIRIE

Bob exhausted and torn with grief, is sitting on his horse near the camera and waiting—Hattie, about to collapse from her saddle, rides on—as she asks him if there is any news she sways weakly—he leaps from his horse and runs to her just in time to catch her as she faints—he lays her on the ground and fans her with his hat—

SCENE 108. ROCKY GULLY. SHARP BEND IN FOREGROUND.

Satan, with Dolly and Rags, rides on and heads for the bend—as he does, he stops his horse abruptly and listens with a look of surprise and deep fear—

SCENE 109. ANOTHER ANGLE OF GULLY

Flash of the Indians riding into the camera shooting and whooping.

SCENE 110. ROCKY GULLY. SAME AS 108

Cut back to Satan with Dolly and Rags—he says "Indians or I'm a fool"—he listens again and then wheels and rides rapidly back into the gully—before he can exit, the Indians ride on around the bend—they sight him and with wild whoops of joy start in pursuit.

SCENE 111. ROCKY RAVINE. LONG SHOT

Satan, with Dolly and Rags, rides on from the background hotly chased by the Indians—he is going faster than they are and gains on them before he passes the camera—get a good exciting chase scene here with lots of speed—TURN CAMERA SLOWLY—as the Indians begin to ride past the camera—CUT—

SCENE 112. PRAIRIE

Flash of cowboys assembling in the foreground from all directions and reporting no success—

SCENE 113. NARROW PASSAGE IN ROCKS

Satan rides on with Dolly and Rags—he stops the horse and leaps from it—grabbing a lariat from the saddle horn he rapidly starts to uncoil it, listening all the while tensely—Dolly, frightened, but having great confidence in Satan, watches him silently as she clings to Rags—

SCENE 114. ANY ROCKY PASS

Flash of Indians riding in hot pursuit—

SCENE 115. CLOSE UP ON SATAN'S HORSE. NARROW PASSAGE IN ROCKS

TITLE: THE SACRIFICE FOR THE BABY WHO STONED HIM.

Satan, working deftly and with great speed, is binding Dolly and Rags securely into the saddle—Dolly realizes that he intends to remain behind and objects hotly—she holds out her arms to him and begs to stay with him—he seeks to quiet her and completes tieing her to the saddle—

SCENE 116. ANOTHER ANGLE OF ROCKY PASS

Flash of Indians riding rapidly across the picture—

SCENE 117. CLOSE UP ON SATAN'S HORSE. SAME AS 115

Cut back to Satan and Dolly and Rags—she begs him not to stay behind but he tells her he will be all right—he bids her goodbye with a smile and she leans forward to kiss him—he kisses her tenderly, grips her convulsively by the shoulder in farewell and then strikes the horse a sharp blow on the flank—the horse dashes off—Satan stands a moment with dimmed eyes gazing after it and then whipping out both his pistols, runs off the scene in the opposite direction—get an affecting scene where Dolly and Satan bid each other goodbye.

SCENE 118. RAVINE

The horse bearing Dolly and Rags gallops on—TURN CAMERA SLOWLY—and exits—

SCENE 119. CLOSE UP ON ROCKY RIDGE

Satan is standing back of the rocks firing with both pistols off the scene—he retreats slowly past the camera, firing and re-loading—

SCENE 120. ROCKY SLOPE

The Indians, some of them dismounting, others already on foot, are firing hotly up the slope and slowly making their way up it—show puffs of smoke coming from the background—use plenty of smoke and make the picture look businesslike—show a couple Indians killed—

SCENE 121. MOUTH OF ROCKY CAVE

TITLE: AN HOUR LATER, HIS LAST CARTRIDGE

Satan, torn and disheveled and bleeding from a wound across his forehead, runs on—he has but one pistol now—he shows he has eluded the Indians for the moment—he stops at the mouth of the cave and listening tensely, takes out his last cartridge and puts it in the pistol—still listening, he exits cautiously into the mouth of the cave—

SCENE 122. INTERIOR CAVE

GET A GOOD LIGHT EFFECT HERE—IDEA OF SUNLIGHT STRIKING AN ANGLE OF THE INTERIOR FROM THE OUTSIDE—Satan comes on and leans against the wall of the cave weakly—

SCENE 123. ROCKY LEDGE

Flash of Indians scattered out and searching for Satan—they have lost him and are yelling with rage and disappointment—

SCENE 124. CLOSE UP ON SATAN IN CAVE

SAME LIGHT IDEA AS IN SCENE 122—Satan is standing breathing heavily as he clutches his pistol—he shows he hears the Indians searching and a grim smile flickers over his face—have his face bloody and smeared with dust—

SCENE 125. SIDE OF ROCKY CAVE

BE SURE THIS IS READILY IDENTIFIED AS THE SAME CAVE IN WHICH SATAN IS HIDING—an armed Indian comes on—he listens and then starts to climb up the rocks to the roof of the cave—PANORAM AS HE GOES—on the roof of the cave, the Indian bends down—he then drops on his knees and flattens his face against a chink in the rock—

20. *Blanche Sweet as Anna Christie (1923) in the first Eugene O'Neill play to reach the screen. Ince surprised the skeptics who thought he would never — in his last years — depart from sure-fire box-office films.*

SCENE 126. CLOSE UP ON SATAN IN CAVE AS SEEN THROUGH HOLE IN ROOF

GET OVER THE EFFECT OF THE SHAFT OF LIGHT FROM THE ROOF STRIKING SATAN AND BRINGING HIM OUT IN BOLD RELIEF—he is still standing, pressed against the wall of the cave and facing the mouth as he listens—

SCENE 127. CLOSE UP ON INDIAN ON ROOF OF CAVE

The Indian is peering through the opening—he shows he sees Satan and smiles in cruel triumph—he aims his rifle carefully through the opening and fires—

SCENE 128. CLOSE UP ON SATAN IN CAVE

Cut back to Satan hiding—he hears the pursuit still going on and again smiles grimly as he thinks that after all he may get away with his life—show a puff of smoke spurt into the picture from the top—Satan spins about violently shot in the back—he staggers and then collapses in a heap—

SCENE 129. CLOSE UP ON INDIAN ON ROOF OF CAVE

Cut back to the Indian—he is holding his rifle and listening intently—he feels sure his shot went home—

SCENE 130. CLOSE UP ON SATAN ON FLOOR OF CAVE

GOOD LIGHT OVER HIM—Satan is lying face downward—he slowly and painfully rises on his hands and looks up at the roof—he realizes how he was shot—the old devilish spirit comes over him and he snarls like a wolf as he stares at the roof—he has but one idea, to get the Indian who shot him—he picks up his pistol from the floor and gripping it with difficulty, waits, his eyes fixed on the roof—

SCENE 131. CLOSE UP ON INDIAN ON ROOF OF CAVE

Cut back to the Indian listening—he hears nothing and, clutching his rifle in one hand, leans over the opening and peers through—

SCENE 132. CLOSE UP ON SATAN ON FLOOR OF CAVE

GOOD LIGHT OVER HIM—cut back to Satan watching the roof—he suddenly whips his pistol over his head and with a wild yell of hate and revenge fires upward—

SCENE 133. CLOSE UP ON INDIAN ON TOP OF CAVE

Cut back to Indian peering through the opening—he jumps backward wildly, regains his feet then reeling drops his rifle and flattens out across the rocks dead—

SCENE 134. ANOTHER ANGLE OF ROCKY LEDGE OR ROCKS

The rest of the Indians are still searching for Satan—they stop and all show they hear the shots in the distance—they begin to whoop afresh and start to exit on the run—

SCENE 135. CLOSE UP ON SATAN ON FLOOR OF CAVE

TITLE: HIS LAST WISH.

SAME GOOD LIGHT EFFECT—cut back to Satan—he is dying fast and can hardly muster enough strength to hold on—he registers the idea of having a last wish to record—he picks up a piece of pointed rock with which the floor of the cave is littered and crawls painfully to the wall of the cave—PANORAM AS HE GOES—he only goes a few feet as he was supposed to be close to the wall when shot—have this wall a very smooth piece of stone—Satan crawls to it and propping himself up starts to scratch a message on it with the pointed stone—his hand drops a couple of times but he forces it back and continues to write—

SCENE 136. ROOF OF CAVE

The Indians come on over the roof from the back—they find the dead body of their comrade and with many yells of hate and vengeance begin to exit down the side—

SCENE 137. CLOSE UP ON SATAN AT WALL OF CAVE

BEAUTIFUL LIGHT EFFECT—Cut back to Satan writing—he finishes and his arm drops limply—he has completed his task and is ready for the end—he succeeds in forcing himself up so he can read what he has written—a tender sad smile comes over his face and he sinks gently back onto the floor, his head pillowed on one arm, and passes out—an Indian's head comes on and regards him intently—as the Indian stares at him, close slowly with an iris lens—

SCENE 138. PRAIRIE

OPEN SLOWLY WITH IRIS LENS—the horse bearing Dolly and Rags comes on from the far background as the picture begins to open—show him come in all the way to the foreground and exit past the camera—TURN CAMERA SLOWLY AND REGISTER SPEED—

SCENE 139. PRAIRIE

Bob is standing in the foreground supporting Hattie who is leaning against her horse and weeping bitterly—the cowboys are clustered about, sympathetic, and not knowing what to say—one of them glances off the picture and then turns to the rest excitedly as he says "Looka over there"—they all look—

SCENE 140. PRAIRIE

Cut back to the horse galloping along with Dolly and Rags—

SCENE 141. PRAIRIE

Cut back to Bob, Hattie and the cowboys—they all see the horse—it revives them like a flash—the cowboys, with yells of joy, gallop off—Bob helps Hattie on her horse and they both ride off after the rest—

SCENE 142. PRAIRIE

The horse bearing Dolly and Rags comes on from the background pursued by Bob, his wife and the cowboys—as they near the foreground the horse is overtaken and caught by cowboys who ride in on either side of his head—they halt in the foreground and Hattie and Bob leap from their horses and rush to Dolly's side, hysterically embracing her and trying to untie her and Rags—

SCENE 143. INTERIOR CAVE

GREAT LIGHT EFFECT—flash of the Indians inspecting Satan and the interior of the cave—they grunt to each other and begin to exit—

SCENE 144. CLOSE UP ON DOLLY, BOB, HATTIE AND GROUP OF COWBOYS: ALLOW FOR ACTION

Dolly, covered with dust and tear-stained, has one arm about her mother's neck and the other about her father's—she is sobbing and says "My big, good man stayed up there to fight the Indians"—her words electrify the rest—they cry: "Indians"—she says: "yes, lots of them, too"—they start to rush off the scene—Bob turns Dolly over to her mother and rushes with them—PANORAM TO THE HORSES—Bob and the cowboys rush on, mount and ride off like the wind—

SCENE 145. CLOSE UP ON DOLLY AND HER MOTHER

Hattie, kneeling by her horse, has her arms about Dolly and is holding her tightly and seeking to console her—Rags is hanging around anxiously—Hattie picks Dolly up and helps her onto the horse—she leads it off the picture in the opposite direction taken by the cowboys—Rags follows her off—

SCENE 146. ROCKY PASS SAME AS 114

TITLE: THE RECKONING

Bob and the cowboys ride into the picture—they halt abruptly in the foreground and point off past the camera excitedly—

SCENE 147. MOUTH OF CAVE

Flash of Indians dancing about and celebrating their victory over Satan—

SCENE 148. ROCKY PASS

Cut back to Bob and the cowboys—they pull out their guns and opening fire at a lively rate, dash off past the camera—

SCENE 149. MOUTH OF CAVE

Cut back to the Indians dancing—get over the idea of a sudden hail of shot—several of the Indians fall—the others make a rush to escape, shooting back as they go—FAST ACTION—the cowboys rush on, some afoot, the others mounted—a hot skirmish follows in which the Indians flee, leaving most of their number dead or wounded—the cowboys chase them—

SCENE 150. ROCKY PASS

The Indians, only a few of them, run on past the camera, closely pursued by the cowboys who are shooting them down—show enough of this to register the idea of a slaughter and then cut—

SCENE 151. MOUTH OF CAVE

Bob and one of the cowboys are standing looking into the mouth of the cave—they get over the idea of blood stains on the rocks and exit into the cave as they trace them—

SCENE 152. CLOSE UP ON SATAN AT WALL OF CAVE

BEAUTIFUL LIGHT EFFECT—Satan is lying dead close to the wall—Bob and the cowboy come on—they discover him and bend down over him—they see he is dead—Bob rises sadly and is about to direct the cowboy to help him remove the body when the cowboy notices the writing on the wall—he points to it in wonder and he and Bob bend over it to get a better view—INSERT CLOSE UP OF WRITING SCRATCHED IN WHITE AGAINST A BLACK BACKGROUND, WITH THE IDEA OF THE BACKGROUND BEING A ROCK—THE WRITING SHOULD BE SCRAWLY BUT PLAIN, IT READS:

I, SATAN McALLISTER, DYING AND KNOWING WHAT I AM DOING, HEREBY WILL MY RANCH AND EVERYTHING I OWN TO THE BEST ENEMY AND TRUEST FRIEND I EVER HAD, DOLLY ELLIS, SIX YEARS OLD. THIS GOES.

BACK TO ACTION—Cut back to Bob and the cowboy reading the writing—they turn silently and gaze at each other—Bob chokes and bows his head and the cowboy, after looking at him a moment, exits softly—

SCENE 153. MOUTH OF CAVE

Other cowboys are coming into the picture and clustering about the cave—the cowboy who was with Bob comes on from the cave—they see him and start forward but he gently pushes them back as he says "Not yet, boys, wait a minute, wait a minute"—they stop and look at him for an explanation—

SCENE 154. CLOSE UP ON BOB AND SATAN AT WALL OF CAVE

BEAUTIFUL LIGHT EFFECT—Bob is standing gazing down at the body of Satan—his features are rigid—he slowly drops to one knee beside the body and reaching for one of Satan's hands, takes it in his own—he grips it tightly as he looks into Satan's face—then he says brokenly: "Old man, forgive me. I had you all wrong"—as he holds the pose, CLOSE THE PICTURE VERY SLOWLY WITH AN IRIS LENS—

THE END

COMMENTARY

In 1915, Ince joined with Griffith and Sennett to furnish releases for the weekly program of the Triangle Film Corporation; Ince and Griffith were responsible for the features, 173

Sennett for the short comedies. Lauded in America as a "Rodin of Shadows" (36), Ince was also praised in France, where his films were admired by general audiences, as well as by Jean Cocteau, and members of the Dada group.

After Triangle, he went on to release films through other companies, but his reputation as a producer suffered some decline in the 1920's, at which point he must have constantly been reminded of a statement he had made several years earlier: "The most accurate barometer of public opinion is the box-office." (37) A year before his untimely death in 1924, Ince rallied valiantly against the charge of being solely a maker of "box-office" films, by purchasing the rights to *Anna Christie*, bringing Eugene O'Neill to the screen for the first time (1923), in a much-praised transcription.

ANNA CHRISTIE   **FILM 1923**

"The Screen: Life, Love and the Sea," *The New York Times,* December 10, 1923, p. 20.

> With Blanche Sweet, George Marion, William Russell, Eugenie Besserer and others; adapted from Eugene O'Neill's play of the same name; directed by John Griffith Wray; "Minature Review." At the Strand.

Seldom is the task of writing about a picture approached with the keen enthusiasm we feel for the film version of Eugene O'Neill's play, *Anna Christie,* which happens to be one of those isolated instances that causes you to forget almost that the story is being told in nothing more tangible than lights and shadows flung upon a screen. Abundant credit is due the producer and the director for the skillful, impressive and artistic handling of this production, and also for the restraint concerning motion picture license. This photodrama, now at the Strand, is an example of progress in film history, and let us hope, one which will help to deter some producers from putting forth money and effort into nonsensical contraptions. It sheds light on the way directors can strengthen their productions.

John Griffith Wray directed this photodrama under the supervision of Thomas H. Ince. They have enlisted the services of excellent players, which makes it quite obvious that good acting is half the battle in getting the desired results from a story, especially when you are dealing with a grim and gripping theme. Blanche Sweet, as Anna Christie, makes the shadow impersonation live. In fact it would be difficult to imagine any actress doing better in this exacting role. She is ably supported by the genius of George Marion who appears as Chris, Anna's father. Carelessness, ignorance and average playing might have knocked this story higher than Gilderoy's kite.

The old sea is blamed for everything that happens, for the mariner has a job that takes him from home and flings temptation constantly in his path. Chris damns the sea, but in the end he and the stoker, Matt Burke, take to it again.

Miss Sweet does some marvelous acting through this story, and she seems to glow with the idea of a newly discovered life in her love for Burke, to whom she confessed her unwilling fall. Chris is equally capable, never failing to get the utmost out of his bent back, his forelocked, thick hair, his broad nostrils, capacious mouth with a thick under-lip, and his dog-like expressive eyes. There he is, garbed in his rough double-breasted suit, clumsy shoes, the picture of a seafaring man, trying to make the most of being skipper of a barge.

The sequence wherein his paramour, Martha—she of the slovenly skirts whom drink has claimed with clenched fingers—awaits Anna, is admirable. Chris is seen imbibing to his heart's content, but is suddenly sobered by a letter from Anna, then living on a farm in Minnesota, who announces her intention of coming to New York at once. The letter has been delayed, being delivered to a saloon, usually patronized by Chris and Martha, well portrayed by Eugenie Besserer. With a grin on his ignorant countenance, Chris hastens away to put on a clean collar and freshen up his appearance. Anna enters the saloon. It is Martha's first intention to steer the girl away from her father, but eventually she relents and urges the girl to toss away the cigarette she is smoking and not let her father know that she drinks. Anna is the picture of a wayward lass, with pretty eyes and mouth, but one accustomed to swallowing whiskey and knocking the ashes off cigarettes. Old Chris comes in, when Anna, at Martha's behest, has chucked her cigarette away. To Chris, Anna is the personification of all that a daughter should be, and also a newly acquired pleasurable possession. He does not know that Anna only a few moments before had told Martha: "You're me, forty years from now."

One of the minor weaknesses of this picture is the presenting of a miniature steamship at sea, wrecked through a collision with a helpless barge. Matt Burke is shown in the stokehole, then escaping with his colleagues, and finally being pulled aboard Chris' barge. Hatred of one of his own kind strikes from his eyes when Chris discovers Anna caring for Burke, whose head has been cut. Burke, played by William Russell, is splendid as a tower of strength, which serves him well in a tussle with Chris, when the old Swede plucks forth his knife. Burke's corded muscles stand out, his build being further accentuated by his height and expansive chest.

Anna's frequent utterance had been: "Gawd, how I hate men—every mother's son of 'em!" But she succumbs to the stoker's glare. Chris is as jealous of Burke as he was of the sea fog, which Anna declared made her feel clean.

Anybody who sees this picture will remember Chris' great face when he describes to his daughter in his abbreviated vocabulary the pleasure of a trip on a coal barge, and his subsequent delight when his daughter agrees to accompany him. There is splendid suspense in this story, especially where the girl leaves the saloon and contemplates throwing herself into the water. Chris rushes at her and adjures her to come with him, Burke having quit, following her confession of wrong. Anna's hat, her glass bracelets and earrings, her shabby blue suit make her seem so real. Love, pleasure, anxiety, sorrow, regret and remorse are constantly rising in her attractive face. One of the closing titles, after the grunting visage of Chris is shown, runs: "Fog, yust all the time, you can't see where you go—but she, old davil sea, she know."

Here is a picture with wonderful characterization that tells a moving and compelling story—a film that is intensely dramatic, and one that will win new audiences for the screen.

21. Chaplin in SHOULDER ARMS (1918): "the glory-dream of a recruit." However, "Being completely funny on a background of completely terrible war is not only difficult, but dangerous." Verdict: "a perfect handling of a delicate subject."

CHAPTER 10

Mack Sennett and Charlie Chaplin

COMMENTARY

Mack Sennett (1880-1960), who described himself as "a flop in musical comedy," took the plunge into films in 1908 at the Biograph studio in New York. THE CURTAIN POLE (1909) was a Biograph, directed by D. W. Griffith and featuring Sennett.

In 1911 Griffith let Sennett direct the Biograph comedies, and Sennett developed the type of fast-moving burlesque of melodrama that he later (1912) called Keystone, when he set up his own comedy company. COHEN COLLECTS A DEBT, his first Keystone release, shows that he was editing in the very manner which had caused Griffith's critics to cry out in protest, and AT TWELVE O'CLOCK shows him parodying an old Biograph (THE FATAL HOUR, 1908).

Charlie Chaplin (1889-) was signed for Keystones late in 1913; TILLIE'S PUNCTURED ROMANCE (1914), one of Sennett's infrequent features, ran six reels, setting a new record in length for screen slapstick; and A VILLAGE VAMPIRE (1916) appeared as a Triangle-Keystone, made for the company in which Sennett was associated with Griffith and Ince.

FILM 1909 THE CURTAIN POLE

"Reviews of New Films," *The New York Dramatic Mirror,* Vol. 61, No. 1575, February 27, 1909, p. 13.

THE CURTAIN POLE (Biograph)—It has been so long since we have seen a "chase" picture from the Biograph people that we had commenced thinking they had forgotten how to make one. Generally speaking, this would not be a matter for regret, for the chase has been done so much and often so badly that it has grown into disrepute, except when produced with exceptional originality. In THE CURTAIN POLE, however, we have a "chase" carried out with plausible consistency and fairly seething with surprising and laughable collisions and situations. A polite Frenchman calling on friends finds them trying to hang a curtain on a curtain pole. He volunteers to do it for them and breaks the pole, after which he insists on going out and buying a new pole. Unfortunately he meets a friend and imbibes too freely. Then the fun commences, showing Gaston trying to get back with the pole. It is quite impossible to adequately describe.

COHEN COLLECTS A DEBT   **FILM 1912**

Excerpt from "Reviews of Supply Company Films," *The New York Dramatic Mirror,* Vol. 68, No. 1762, September 25, 1912, p. 29.

COHEN COLLECTS A DEBT (Keystone, September 23)—As one sits through this eight or ten minutes of senseless, idiotic horseplay he wonders what it is all about. Never once is the spectator allowed to grasp the thread of the story, if there is a thread, and all he is treated to is a continuous show of waving arms and prancing feet. . . .

AT TWELVE O'CLOCK   **FILM 1913**

"Independent Film Stories: Mutual Film Corporation: AT TWELVE O'CLOCK," *The Moving Picture World,* Vol. 15, No. 13, March 29, 1913, p. 1364.

AT TWELVE O'CLOCK (Keystone, March 27)—An Italian makes love to a girl and is repulsed. She favors another man, and the Italian uses drastic measures to rid himself of his rival. He finally becomes angered at the girl and kidnaps her. He ties her to a post and arranges an infernal machine, attached to a clock, which will shoot off a revolver at 12 o'clock. The weapon is pointed at the girl, who makes frantic efforts to escape as the hands creep toward the fatal hour. The lover makes frantic efforts to rescue his sweetheart, but is driven away by the burly villain. The police are notified, and have all manner of mishaps in reaching the scene. The lover finally secures a big magnet, which he sticks through the barred window at one minute of twelve, and it pulls the hands back. The villain listening, with watch in hand, for the sound of the shot, is nonplussed when 12 o'clock passes without a report, and he enters. He readjusts the device, and again the lover keeps the hands from recording 12 o'clock. After many amusing incidents the police finally break into the house and snatch the girl away "in the nick of time," as the pistol is fired, shooting the villain in the leg.

TILLIE'S PUNCTURED ROMANCE   **FILM 1914**

"Other Feature Films: TILLIE'S PUNCTURED ROMANCE," *The New York Dramatic Mirror,* Vol. 72, No. 1872, November 4, 1914, p. 36.

Mack Sennett Produces a Six Part Comedy Featuring Marie Dressler. . .

Keystone Comedy in Six Reels. Written and Produced by Mack Sennett

The Country Girl . . . . .Marie Dressler
The Stranger . . . . .Charles Chaplin
The Other Woman . . . . .Mabel Normand

Mack Sennett has produced a much enlarged, a de luxe edition of Keystone burlesque, plus the inimitable Marie Dressler. It is difficult to keep an audience in continuous laughter through six reels of film; facial muscles rebel and demand a rest. If they did not, if it were natural for people to maintain the same mirthful pitch for one hour and a half at a stretch, TILLIE'S PUNCTURED ROMANCE would provide sufficient provocation. The picture is an experiment that must show whether rapid, farcical action is wanted in large doses. The great popularity of Keystone one and two-reel subjects is a matter of

Mack Sennett
Keystone Film Co.

22. *The youthful Mack Sennett, creator of Keystone comedy. Sennett watching one of his films being run off in a pre-release state: "There's a slow spot. Cut it. Let him get his surprise over, then flash back to the wife. . . . Put back a few feet more of the dancing. . . ."*

common knowledge. If by any chance these six reels are less in demand, it will be merely because they are too much of a muchness. Their like is not recorded in the annals of the past, nor are they likely to be bettered tomorrow, or the next day, or even the day after that.

Charles Chaplin, the idol of the hour among film comedians, and Mabel Normand, with her pretty eyes and her nice gift for humorous expression, need no introduction. They are as entertaining as ever, which is equivalent to stating that they are exceedingly entertaining. Chaplin personifies more eccentricities than one expects to find in the make-up of a dozen ordinary men. He does the oddest things in the most natural way, altogether more effective than doing odd things in an obviously odd way. One brings spontaneous laughter, the other a consciousness that we should laugh, but don't feel like it. However, the worth of these players is a familiar story, whereas Marie Dressler is a brand new and extraordinary treat for film audiences.

In the part of Tillie—reminiscent of *Tillie's Nightmare,* seen on the stage a few years ago—she is a leader in the fun-making and fully as good in her way as Chaplin is in his. She does not balk at a little rough handling now and then—no Keystone player ever does—but there is much more than mere horseplay in Miss Dressler's performance. Her expressions are all that is needed to convey to an audience the state of Tillie's emotions during the course of her fluctuating romance. Were it necessary to pick out the cleverest bit of acting in the production, one might select the scenes in which Miss Dressler simulates a spirit released from all bothersome worldly cares and a body that moves with fluent irregularity. One drink or two drinks did it, but Tillie may be excused, for she was fresh from the farm and knew no better.

Of course the picture has much to offer besides the three players mentioned. Director Sennett utilizes most of the actors connected with the Keystone aggregation, and in matters of staging he has outdone himself. The ballroom in which Tillie makes her first plunge—plunge is right—into society, is approached by an impressive stairway, just made for sensational entrances, and is large enough for everybody to dance the fox trot at the same time. It is an ideal location for a rough-house on a very large and very destructive scale. When the walls no longer can contain the stampeding guests; when, in other words, a typical Keystone whirlwind finish is under way, the riot extends to the waterfront, an automobile is run off the end of a dock, the police dart recklessly here, there and everywhere in motor-boats, Tillie is nearly drowned; there is, in fact, nothing to mar the effect of complete pandemonium.

Director Sennett set a fast pace for a six-reel journey and ended with a sprint. Audiences will laugh all right enough, there is no doubt about that, but they may be short of breath before the finish.

(Signed) D.

"MACK SENNETT PREMIER CREATOR OF LAUGHS"   1915

From *The Triangle,* Vol. 1, No. 3., November 6, 1915, p. 6.

Keeps Fit by Hard Athletic Training—Producing Two Keystones A Week
Office Resembles Big Gymnasium

Los Angeles. —Mack Sennett, whose genius for packing five laughs into a comedy situation where only one laugh grew, put Keystone on the motion picture map and made it almost cover the map, is one of the busiest men in a busy game.

Since he undertook the seemingly impossible task of completing two double-reel Keystone comedies for the Triangle program each week and of keeping it up indefinitely, he has been a life-size personification of one of his own 500-revolutions-a-minute comedies.

Many men have been called human dynamos and with fair excuse. But Sennett probably develops the highest voltage of any man in this, the highest pressure business on earth. He not only works under forced draught all day for seven days a week—he does very little else, night or day, but think, talk, direct and act photoplays.

How this man keeps up the pace is a mystery to most even of the men directly associated with him. There is a solution to the mystery and it is partly revealed by a glance into the actor-director-manager's dressing room at the Keystone studios in Los Angeles.

It is a small room almost as bare as the cell of an ascetic. But its contents tell a story. In the centre is a narrow bunk, rather high set, beside [which] are scales such as you see in a Turkish bath or a doctor's office. In one corner is a huge stack of rough towels and here and there are dumb bells and lifting weights.

Now you have it, this is an athlete's room rather than an actor's or a business man's.

Mr. Sennett is in hard physical training all the time. Early in the morning before most of the rest of the world is up he is off for a cross country run. Five miles is his usual distance. The other training work is sandwiched in between hours of picture-making.

"Where is Mr. Sennett's office?" asked a visitor the other day to a group of his assistants. Some looked blank and the others grinned.

"He hasn't any," was the answer. "If you can't find him on any of the stages, in the projection room or any of the work shops or the lunch room or anyone else's office, look in that dressing room of his. But he's sure to be around somewhere."

And that bare little dressing room with nothing but a wooden bunk to sit on is a good place to try first, for it's the quietest place in several acres of ceaseless activity.

The director of Keystone's destinies looks the trained athlete he is, but he knows also how to save his vitality. In the projection room where he watches the daily progress of each play, he is a good deal like a bored and sleepy lion as long as things on the screen are going exactly right. But a Keystone comedy is never good enough to suit Sennett for more than a few seconds at a time and at least three assistants are standing on mental tiptoes to catch his volley of quick orders.

"Ah! There's a slow spot. Cut it. Let him get his surprise over, then flash back to the wife. . . Sub-title that just before the Doctor enters. . . Put back a few feet more of the dancing and set the insert back four scenes. . .Ford doesn't register dismay quick enough—You'd better do that over again. . . ." And so forth for an hour until the mind of the rare visitor from outside is in a dizzy whirl.

The art of cutting a film into presentation shape is almost as important as the art of making the picture. And it is part of the secret of Keystone effectiveness. A photoplay at the start is seldom less than three times its final length. Directors not infrequently will expose 20,000 feet of film to get a two-reel play of 2000 foot length. The effective elimination of from four to nine feet of film for every single foot saved is what makes a master-director of photoplays, for that one foot must be chosen to tell all that was in the original five or ten and tell it better than it was told originally.

Mr. Sennett's genius for packing a story into a few feet of film with the aid of this process of elimination is stamped all over Keystone work and picture men recognize it instantly. They would imitate it if they could, many of them. That they have failed is evidenced by the recognized premiership of the Keystone product and its inclusion in the distinguished Triangle program.

But cutting a picture is only the final process. Long before that must come the ideas— dramatic, photographic and mechanical—that together make a Keystone comedy the fastest fun on earth.

"How do they ever think up such extraordinary things to do?" is a question asked by about a million motion picture fans a day.

181

It is a difficult question to answer but it is done almost entirely at the Keystone studios where a corps of "ideas" men, working in collaboration, feed suggestions to the ingenious and alert directors. Mr. Sennett, who is "into everything" himself provides the largest share. He finds ways to carry out seemingly wild and impossible plans and, toiling with the dogged persistence and the inexhaustible energy that his physical preparedness provides, he creates undoubtedly more hearty laughter than any other human being.

A VILLAGE VAMPIRE   **FILM 1916**

Excerpt from "Reviews of Feature Films: A VILLAGE VAMPIRE," *The New York Dramatic Mirror*, Vol. 75, No. 1946, April 8, 1916, p. 30.

. . . A VILLAGE VAMPIRE is a sensational, burlesque, melodramatic comedy of the type that the Keystone Company has been doing so well recently. It is designed along the regular Keystone lines, starting with a slow tempo and gradually increasing its speed until it arrives at one of those side-splitting, hair-raising climaxes. Anna Luther makes a good jump with a horse off a cliff about thirty or forty feet high into a river below. Also a couple of bridges are blown up, a stamping mill set on fire, and other features too numerous to mention. Fred Mace is his usual funny self.

COMMENTARY

In this interview by Theodore Dreiser, author of *Sister Carrie, Jennie Gerhardt* **and** *An American Tragedy*, **Mack Sennett traces the first twenty years of his screen career, from 1908 to 1928. Oddly enough, he does not mention Griffith, from whom he learned so much through observation and conversation, and to whom he later gratefully acknowledged his debt in print. Dreiser mistakes Fort Lee, New Jersey, for "Fort George."**

When Sennett speaks of such players as Harry Langdon, Eddie Quillan and Madeline Hurlock, he is referring to the period of the 1920's.

Dreiser had already made public his enthusiasm for certain films; in particular, the German-made THE CABINET OF DR. CALIGARI, (shown in New York in 1921 and revived five years later), von Stroheim's GREED (1924), and some of the works of Charlie Chaplin.

"THE BEST MOTION PICTURE INTERVIEW EVER WRITTEN"   1928

By Theodore Dreiser, *Photoplay Magazine*, Vol. 34, No. 3, August, 1928, pp. 32-35, 124-129.

The Great American Master of Tragedy brilliantly interviews the Great American Master of Comedy

My admiration for Mack Sennett is temperamental and chronic. I think it dates from that long ago when he played the moony, semi-conscious farm hand, forsaken by the sweetly pretty little milkmaid for some burlesque city slicker, with oiled hair and a bushy mustache. And it endures today when he is a multi-millionaire, the owner of a moving picture studio with some twenty-two or twenty-four stages, and an established reputation as the producer of comedy of a burlesque type. For to me he is a real creative force in the cinema world—a master at interpreting the crude primary impulses of the dub, the numbskull, the weakling, failure, clown, boor, coward, bully. The interpretive burlesque he achieves is no different from that of Shakespeare, Voltaire, Shaw or

Dickens, when they are out to achieve humorous effects by burlesquing humanity. To be sure, these others move away from burlesque to greater ends. It is merely an incident in a great canvas. With Sennett it is quite the whole canvas. But within his range, what a master! He is Rabelaisian, he is Voltairish. He has characteristics in common with Sterne, Swift, Shaw, Dickens—where they seek to catch the very thing which he catches. Positively, if any writer of this age had brought together in literary form—and in readable English—instead of upon the screen as has Sennett—the pie-throwers, soup-spillers, bomb-tossers, hot-stove-stealers, and what not else of Mr. Sennett's grotesqueries—what a reputation! The respect! The acclaim! As it is, there exists today among the most knowing of those who seek a picture of life as it is—or might be were it not for these inherent human buffooneries which Mr. Sennett so clearly recognizes and captures—a happy and sane tendency to evaluate him properly.

And so, for the past fifteen or eighteen years—whenever and wherever I have seen the name of Mack Sennett posted above a movie, I have been tempted and all too frequently possibly have succumbed to an incurable desire to witness his latest antic waggeries. The bridges, fences, floors, sidewalks, walls, that give way under the most unbelievable and impossible circumstances. The shirt-collars that, too tightly drawn, in attempts to button them, take flight like birds—the shacks (like the one in Chaplin's GOLD RUSH) which spin before the wind, only to pause, with a form of comic terror for all, at the edge of a precipice, there to teeter and torture all within—trains or street cars or automobiles that collide with trucks and by sheer impact transfer whole groups of passengers to new routes and new directions! Positively, as I have often told myself at such times and countless others, are not these nonsensicalities but variations of that age-old formula that underlies all humor—the inordinate inflation of fancy to heights where reason can only laughingly follow; the filliping of the normal fancy with the abnormal? I think so. And Mr. Sennett has been for these past twenty years or more—and still remains—the master of that.

Thus when the opportunity came to interview him I seized upon it with avidity. And in the Ambassador Hotel in New York, after many cautious preliminaries on the part of a representative, there he stood in perhaps his workaday, official mood. It was arranged that I was to meet him for luncheon and so he came—a somewhat stocky and yet well-knit, gray person, with a touch of the careless in his appearance and an eye gray and soft, yet suggesting a forceful, searching intellect behind it and one that might on occasion have a granitic quality; yet with a sagging, half-lackadaisical manner, which, none-the-less, as one might well know, could be a manner only. And guarded by a business manager—shrewd, pleasant, friendly sort of person, watchful of his employer's interests on this occasion, yet helpful to both of us in a genial way. This is the individual, as I understood it afterward, who writes most of those startling captions that help to edge the whirligig humor of Sennett's productions.

"Just a canceled stamp in the post-office of life."

"—and as hungry as a sparrow at a Scotch picnic."

"—so stupid he thought pickled herring ought to be reported to the dry squad."

"He believed that woman's place was in the home and not in the English channel."

"Call for my laundry at my apartment—it's just a little step-in."

"—and so dumb she thought a meadow lark was a picnic."

"—and so stupid he thought an oyster bed was where fish slept."

Boldly and courageously I started the ball rolling by asking: "Just what excuse have you to offer, Mr. Sennett, for one more of your comedies?"

And then, to my real amusement and astonishment, I saw a faint flush steal over his face—the face of the, to me, greatest creator of joyful burlesque the world has ever known. Instantly I was moved to abandon the pose back of the question, but was forestalled by the Irish adequateness to resist any blow, which is his to a terrifying degree.

183

"Well, now, that reminds me of a row I once saw in one of the streets up here in Harlem. Two men were fighting. An Irish policeman came up to stop it, but couldn't get the hang of it by watching. So finally he grabbed the nearest one by the neck and shook him until he was dizzy. Then, as soon as he let him go, he said: 'Now, what's all this about?' And that's how I feel now."

"But there's still the question," I persisted teasingly.

"Well, you can't tell," he said. "It may be that I think that stuff's funny."

"Acquitted on the grounds of delusion," I said. "But there's still something worse. You're here to give a complete reason for your being—the artistic faith that is in you. You're to tell me what you think the intrinsic nature of comedy is—why, for instance, you prefer it to drama or melodrama—and—"

"We made a melodrama once," he interrupted, smiling, "or started to. I don't know whether I ought to confess that, though," he added, a boyish and naive smile playing over his face.

"And what happened to it?"

"Well, I don't know exactly," he went on, an infectious chuckle emanating from his throat. "We kind of got lost. We had a plot, we thought, but when we got it worked out, people laughed when we thought they ought to cry or shiver."

"Yes, that might have been a little disconcerting," I agreed.

"It was," he said—and in that same, dry, dubious tone that characterizes so much of his best manner. "We tried to fix it up, make it more sad or something. But we had to turn it into a comedy."

"What a tragedy!" I ventured.

"Yes, sir, a comic tragedy—that's what came of it at last, I think. I scarcely remember what happened to it."

But anyone taking Mack Sennett's genial, easy manner for anything but a front or mask behind which lurks a terrifying wisdom and executive ability would be most easily deceived. For, looking at him as he sat there—the bulk and girth of him—I could see the constructive energy and will, the absolute instinct and force, which has led and permitted him to do so ably all that he has done. It was interesting just to feel the force and the intelligence of him, his willingness and determination to give a satisfactory account of himself—his mental, if not emotional, satisfaction with himself—his dry, convincing sanity that assures him to this hour—and rightly so, I think—that his view is as good as any other.

I had read an article by one writer who said, quoting Sennett: "You have to put in some rough stuff if you want to make them laugh. Only exaggeration up to the *nth* power gets the real shout." And another quoting this same Sennett said: "You have to spill soup on dignity to get a real burlesque laugh." And I agree, whether Sennett said these things or not. In the world of the commonplace, only the extraordinary, the unbelievable almost, is truly amusing or interesting.

But let that be as it will. Here was Mr. Sennett, and most agreeably, seeking to interpret himself. So I said, after a time:

"When you first started out years ago—but exactly when was that, if you don't mind?"

"Oh, back in 1908 with the Old Biograph."

"And how did you come to get into that work, if it isn't too much trouble to you?"

"Well, I was a flop in musical comedy—used to sing pretty well, but I never could get the fancy stepping of the chorus man. So I went to work in the Biograph pictures. They didn't make comedies then, just sentimental romances and very meller melodramas and tragedies—what tragedies! These were awfully funny to me; I couldn't take them seriously. I often thought how easy it would be, with the least bit more exaggeration—and they were exaggerated plenty as it was—to turn those old dramas into pure farce."

184   "I couldn't get the comedy idea out of my head and finally persuaded two other

fellows to go into partnership with me on producing comedies. We didn't have any money, but at the time this didn't impress us as being important."

"And so, the Keystone Comedy Company came into being, didn't it?"

"Yes. We hired a camera man and started out. That camera man—he was the most impressive-looking camera man in the world. He looked like a Russian grand duke and had the lofty manners of an Oriental prince. We didn't stop to inquire whether he knew anything about cameras; we hired him on the strength of his grand ducal whiskers."

"And how about your first studio?"

"We didn't have any studio. We just carried the cameras and props on our shoulders and started off somewhere on a street car. Usually we hung around near Fort George."

"My God," I exclaimed sadly, "of all places."

"Yes," went on Sennett solemnly, "and we had so little money that we had to make three comedies before we had the film of the first one developed; we could get it done cheaper that way, you see. And I remember how proudly we went into the projecting room to see our maiden effort; and how we came out staggering with dismay. The grand ducal camera man hadn't turned the crank fast enough, and consequently the picture didn't move—it leaped in wild and fantastic kangaroo bounds!"

"Like some of your best comedians since?"

"Yes, like some of my best ones since. But to go on. There was nothing to do but throw the stuff away and start all over again. By this time we were flat broke. We made a pool of all our watches and stickpins and got together enough money to go to California. I brought two actors West with me, the two business partners remaining in New York.

"When we arrived in Los Angeles, I wandered out to an unfrequented part of town where the families kept goats in their back yards. I rented a vacant lot and had a little shanty put up. This was my first studio and the little shack is still standing there in the middle of our twenty-two acres of studios in Edendale. I guess I'll never tear that shanty down.

"It took a lot of physical endurance to get through the work I undertook in those days," he went on reminiscently. "Every morning when the bricklayers were going to work I went out to the 'studio' and got the props ready for the day's work. We made new sets by pasting some wall paper over the old ones.

"All day I acted in my pictures myself and directed, too. At night when the other actors had gone home, I stuck around late cutting the film shot the previous day. I was telephone operator, bookkeeper, actor, director, publicity man and film cutter. It was a job.

"Finally I shipped the first comedy to my partners in the East. Their verdict was prompt. 'Terrible,' they wired me. I took a cinch in my belt and started another comedy, which was eventually shipped. The answer was just as prompt: 'Worse,'

"I wonder now that I didn't lose heart entirely, especially with money by this time being as scarce as hen's teeth. Then I got a 'break,' as we now call it. It happened that the G. A. R. was holding a convention in Los Angeles and there was a great parade. As a last desperate chance I photographed this parade; took some comic scenes to fill in and made a war comedy. This time the message that came back from New York was: 'Great.'

"It was easy from then on."

And it was pleasing to see him sit and cogitate in a pleasant April manner in regard to his own past. And none of the hardened granite that one suspects in his nature from time to time showing in his words or eyes. Instead, nothing but Rabelaisian gaiety and vitality.

"But to return to my first question—your artistic excuse for being—the animating faith that is in you?" I said, after he had finished all this.

He stared unblinkingly, the blue-grey of his Irish eyes fronting me like two milky, unrevealing crystals.

"My artistic reason for being! The faith that is in me! I guess I never thought of those things when I started out, but I can give a fair answer now, I think. Everyone wants to laugh at something. Mostly at other people's troubles, if they're not too rough."

"But you never thought of that when you started, you say?"

"Oh, I must have—as a comedy idea—but not as a philosophy," was his prompt reply.

"And you still adhere to it?"

"Something uncomfortable happening to the other fellow, but not too uncomfortable? Yes. Things must go wrong, but not too wrong. And to some fellow that you feel reasonably sure can't be too much injured by it—just enough to make you laugh—not enough to make you feel sad or cry. And always in some kind of a story that could be told very differently if one wanted to be serious, but that you don't want to be serious about, see?"

"I see. But years ago, when you started, the type of comedy you produced was decidedly crude, wasn't it? I recall the hot stoves on which people fell, the hot soup that steamed down their backs, the vats of plaster, or tar, or soap, that they fell into; the furniture, walls, ceilings, even houses, that fell on them; the horses, wagons, trains that ran over them. Any change in that respect?"

"Well, no. I don't know that there is any actual change in the kind of burlesque that makes people laugh, although there is some, I guess, in the way it's presented. For instance, ten or fifteen or twenty years ago, a man might sit on a hot stove longer than he would today and without the audience stopping laughing. Or, maybe, more trains could hit him and all in the same picture. Fifteen years ago the settings could be cruder than they are today, and a waiter in shirt sleeves and no collar could spill soup down the shirt front of a laborer and get a laugh, and that in some ordinary one-armed place not very nice to look at. Today an American comedy audience seems to want better surroundings or settings. And if the waiter is of the Ritz or Ambassador type, the customer a gentleman in evening clothes—or a lord—so much the better! But the spilling of the soup remains the same. It has to be sort of rough trouble for the other fellow in burlesque, or no laugh."

And here Mr. Sennett interpolated a bit of reminiscence out of his old Biograph days. It appears that when he first began to make comedies in opposition to the melodramas of the hour, the Biograph chiefs looked on them with doubt and at times disfavor. "They're too rough," they said. "Too many people fall downstairs or out of windows, or get shot or run over. Can't you be funny without being so rough?" "No," I told them, "I can't. You've got to get the laughs, haven't you? And then I'd show them that you couldn't reach the crowd by refined comedy. If you wanted the big crowds and the big laughs, you had to have the stuff a little rough. And, as I say, except for dressing the actors and the scenes a little better today, there isn't so much change."

One of the things I was moved to ask at this point was, slapstick being what it is, was there any limit to the forms or manifestations of this humor? And to my surprise, yes, there was, and is.

"No joke about a mother ever gets a laugh," he insisted most dogmatically. "We've tried that, and we know. You can't joke about a mother in even the lightest, mildest way. If you do, the audience sits there cold, and you get no hand. It may not be angry—we wouldn't put in stuff about a mother that an audience could take offense at—but, on the other hand, it is not moved to laugh—doesn't want to—and no laughs, no money. So mothers in that sense are out. You have to use them for sentiment or atmosphere in burlesque."

"In other words, hats off to the American mother," I said, thinking of that sterling epitome of America—*Processional*. "But not so with fathers," I added, after a time.

"Oh, fathers," he said dryly. "No. You can do anything you want to with them. Father's one of the best butts we have. You can do anything but kill him on the stage."

186   "And as for the dear mother-in-law," I interjected.

23. The Mack Sennett Bathing Beauties in SHE LOVED HIM PLENTY (1918). Theodore Dreiser: "And now what about your bathing beauties, Mr. Sennett? What have you to say for that as an idea—artistic or otherwise?" Sennett: "Well, what's wrong with it?"

"Better yet. Best of all, unless it is an old maid."

"No quarter for old maids, eh?"

"Not a cent. A free field and no favors where they're concerned. You can do anything this side of torture and get a laugh."

In silence I began to brood over the human or inhuman psychology of that, but got nowhere for want of time. After all, Mr. Sennett was being interviewed, and I had to go on.

"Tell me one thing," I asked. "You used to act most amusingly. Do you ever act nowadays in your comedies?"

"No."

"Any reason?"

"Well, acting isn't my business any more. You can't direct the activities of a big motion picture studio and wear grease paint at the same time. Oh, once in a while I go out on the stage and show someone how to work out a bit of business, but never anything more than that. Most of my time is spent on the stories and gags."

At this point Mr. Sennett's manager contributed the information that the rest of his employer's time was spent supervising the direction, editing and titling of the comedies that bear his name.

"But years ago, as I understand it, you wrote nearly all your own slapstick. Is that right?"

"Well, pretty nearly, at first."

"But not any more?"

"Not so much. Oh, once in a while I get an idea or so—the same as anyone else—and, when I do, I call a stenographer and dictate it roughly. We have a lot of stages out there to keep going. But I don't know that I can say that anybody writes 'em. We have a board of scenario writers now—twelve or fifteen all the time—and they all work together more or less.

"Whenever anyone has a real idea in the rough, it goes before that board, and they thrash it out among themselves. Of course, everyone sits in on that—myself and everyone else who wants to. Everyone is absolutely free to say what he thinks is wrong and without prejudice on anybody's part. In fact, everybody is encouraged to do that. But once in a while, even when one of us gets a plot we think is all right to start with, we can't make it work. No one can, at times. We have had plots on which we all worked, for a week or ten days, without being able to solve some problem which, if we didn't solve it, ruined the whole thing. And then, finally, we had to give it up because it just couldn't be solved.

"Some of these things are more difficult than you think, and sometimes we even get superstitious about them and change the spot on which we are trying to work so as to change our luck. In fact, it's come to this—that we have spots, or rooms, or places, which we consider lucky or unlucky. I remember one time, we had one of these tough problems and we had moved around from one place to another on the lot for days, trying to work it out. And finally I bundled the whole crowd in a car and took 'em away from the lot entirely and out to a new place on a hill, or rather a mountain top, in Griffith Park. We had our lunch and our cigars, but we no sooner got out and settled than one fellow jumped up, smacked his hands together and said: 'It's a letter.' What he meant was that the problem could be solved with a letter. For weeks after that we went out on that hill in the hope of getting results in other cases, but we finally gave it up because it was kind of far and the results didn't always warrant the trips."

And now I recalled that Mr. Sennett has always been very much interested in personality—that fascinating something which makes celebrities out of unknowns. The list of the subsequently-to-be-famous stars from Chaplin to Langdon, who, unheralded and unknown, were first fostered and trained by him, is long. And so I said:

"You have detected and trained a number of film geniuses. How do you define that 'something' that sets a certain-to-be-star apart from those who do not happen to possess it?"

"I wouldn't know how to define it exactly," he replied.

"Then there's no one characteristic that is common to all beginners who finally reach a high place and great fame?"

"Well, maybe one, yes," he returned, after pausing and drumming on the table, "though some people who don't become stars have that, too."

"And that is?"

"A tireless desire to work."

"Is that all?"

"No, not all. There's something else. An intense interest in their own future or success. They all have that—if they get over."

"Anything else?"

"Well, I'll tell you. They have a phrase in pictures now which everybody uses when they want to describe the thing you're talking about—the something that makes a star, as opposed, say, to the absence of it in someone who can never hope to be one. They say, 'He's got It,' or 'She's got It.' And the way they emphasize the word 'It' tells you what they mean. But if you tried to make them say what they mean by It, they couldn't tell you. And I couldn't either, because the style or expression of that It is so different in different people. Take Douglas Fairbanks now. His It, as I see it, is a wonderful athletic skill and that laughing, defiant smile he has, together with the power to strike an effective and interesting pose. On the other hand, Chaplin has a nervous, frightened look when he wants to use it and the gift of making you feel that he is trying to get away with something that he shouldn't and yet making you sympathize with him. Then Harry Langdon, who I consider the greatest of them all."

"Greater than Chaplin?" I interpolated.

"Yes, greater than Chaplin," he replied. "Well, Langdon suggests a kind of baby weakness that causes everybody to feel sorry for him and want to help him out. He's terribly funny to me. On the other hand, Langdon knows less about stories and motion picture technique than perhaps any other screen star. If he isn't a big success on the screen, it will not be because he isn't funny, but because he doesn't understand the many sides to picture production. He wants to do a monologue all the time; he wants to be the leading lady, cameraman, heavy and director all in one. So far in my experience that attitude has never proved successful."

Our conversation here drifted toward the finding of the most celebrated of these funny people. It is thought by some that Sennett could not have helped Chaplin to fame and fortune. But to me, the reverse seems true. He could, or should have been able to. He is the strong, wise, elemental director and master, really. There is an impressive and, for some I am sure, a terrifying force to him. I can easily see how he could manage fourteen lots and a hundred comedy stages, if he chose. He has convictions and the poise that is born of them. And convictions spring from innate perception.

But to return. As Mr. Sennett told it, he had in his Keystone Comedy Company, in New York, at that time a comedian, Ford Sterling. This Sterling was going to quit him because, as he expressed it, "he could get more money than I could pay him."

"I tried to coax him to stay but there was nothing doing. Then I remembered a little Englishman I'd seen one night at Morris' three-a-day on the American roof. And I sent around and hired him."

"Charlie Chaplin, you mean?"

"Yes."

"And what about Chaplin? Was he anything like what he is today?"

"Not so different. Of course, we've all had a lot of experience since then. Chaplin didn't have that make-up he uses now. That costume was assembled on my lot out there in Los Angeles." (By then the Keystone Company had removed to Los Angeles.) "He tried out several different make-ups before he found that one. The first he used was that of a drunk—a man in evening clothes, with a red nose—the old stuff, you see. It didn't go very well, in fact wasn't different enough to give it originality. Then he tried other things—I forget just what. In those days we used to get on new make-ups and run around the stage to see if we could get a laugh from the rest of the gang. One day Chaplin took a pair of Chester Conklin's baggy trousers, the small derby that Roscoe Arbuckle always wore, and the big shoes which were a part of Ford Sterling's old makeup. The cane was one of Chaplin's own props—he always used a cane. Well, as soon as I saw the get-up, I knew that was *it*.

"I remember one thing about Chaplin. He was the most interested person where he himself, his future, the kind of thing he was trying to do, was concerned, that I ever knew. He wanted to work—and nearly all the time. We went to work at eight o'clock and he was there at seven. We quit at five, say, or later, but he'd still be around at six, and wanting to talk about his work to me all the time. The average actor, as maybe you know, is just an actor. When it's quitting time, he's through. His job is done. He's thinking of something else—maybe even when he's working—and he wants to get away so he can attend to it. But these personality people are different.

"Why, this fellow Chaplin used to fairly sweat if he thought he hadn't done a thing as well as he should have. And he was always complaining of this, that, and the other—the kind of director he had, the kind of actors that worked with him, that his part wasn't big enough, that he ought to have more stage room to do the thing the way he wanted to do it. And when the time came that he could see the film of the day's work, he was always there, whereas, most of the others in the picture would never come around. And if anything in the run didn't please him, he'd click his tongue or snap his fingers and twist and squirm. 'Now, why did I do that that way? What was the matter with me, anyhow? So and so (the director) should have caught that. Heavens, it's terrible. There's always something wrong.'

"Chaplin's one fellow who has to work alone, and alone he works."

"And," he went on, "Harry Langdon is another of the same sort. He came to me four or five years ago and I picked him for a sure thing. About the same case as Chaplin—same temperament—only I think him the greater artist."

"Why?"

"A wider range of emotions and so a wider appeal."

I took the matter under silent critical examination.

"And in Langdon the same restless energy and criticism of everything. Why, nothing was ever right, because, like Chaplin, he had his own ideas, exactly, of how everything should be done. And he didn't want to be interfered with, although, of course, he was there under contract and had to take direction from others."

"Are women stars more or less difficult than men to handle—artistically or commercially?" I here interpolated.

"Less so, for me, I think. I can't speak for anyone else. They may be more temperamental at times in regard to this point and that—things of no great consequence artistically or practically—but they're not so eager to run things all alone. They 'troop' better. Most often you can hold them by showing them that you're trying to do the best you can under the circumstances.

"Gloria Swanson had one of the most delightful personalities of any girl on our lot when she played in our comedies. Besides being sincere and conscientious and a hard worker, she had charm that attracted the admiration of everyone who came in contact with her."

It must have been twenty minutes of, or after, for here we both paused and rested. And then, after a time, we came back to the matter of humor in connection with women—whether they had it to the same degree as men—whether there were as many humorous or witty or waggish women as men. Decidedly not, thought Mr. Sennett, and some difference in the sexes must account for it. Yet now and then, as he explained, there appeared the real woman wag or wit, and how excellent she was. Instantly he cited Mabel Normand, and after her Louise Fazenda, and then Polly Moran. Distinctly they had humor. And, in the case of Mabel Normand, it was so elusive and yet so real that while you knew it was there, yet you could scarcely say where it was. Why, that girl could walk down the aisle of a church, in the midst of services, and without offense to anybody, and without any outward sign of any kind that you could definitely point to, could get a laugh, or at least a smile, and from everybody.

"I don't know what it is," he interjected here. "For the life of me I couldn't tell you how or why. But she can do it. And Louise Fazenda can almost do it. As for all the other women I know, mostly you have to create humor for them. It isn't inside. They can get it over if you drill them, but unless you do they haven't so much to offer—and that goes for some who are pretty fair in pictures." (He declined to say who.)

"I was just thinking of a nice woman we had out there at the studio." He laughed at this point. "Good actress, too. Played crazy parts that we created for her, but did it under protest sometimes because she didn't always like it." (And all this in connection with what I was just saying.) "Well, we got up a part in which she had to wear a big red wig and a cauliflower ear." And here he went off into another low chuckle that would bring anyone to laughing.

"What a shame!" I said, thinking of the hard-working, self-respecting actress.

"I know," he replied. "It was sort of rough." And he laughed again. "But we couldn't let her off." And into that line I read the very base and cornerstone of that ribald Rabelaisian gusto and gaiety that has kept a substantial part of America laughing with him all of these years. Slapstick vigor—the burlesque counterpart of sentiment—the grotesquely comic mask set over against the tragic.

Sennett is obviously the artist who takes delight in developing latent possibilities in screen aspirants. For he now began to tell me of others in this grotesque field in whose future he had the greatest faith. One of these is a youth by the name of Eddie Quillan, now working for him, of whom he said: "Now, there's a boy who would make good." (That unquenchable enthusiasm for developing talent.)

"What makes you think so?" I said.

"Well, he has talent. He is enthusiastic, and he has a line of his own. Just like every other fellow that gets over, he likes to work and he criticizes himself. The more I see of his work, the more sure I am he is going to be a success."

He then spoke of a girl, Madeline Hurlock, who gave no particular promise of stardom at first.

"I tried her out," he said, "and most of us were puzzled at first because we put her in one thing and another and she didn't seem to do anything. Just stood around, as far as we could see. And we thought she was a total loss, or I did. But after a while we began to hear from exhibitors. They showed interest in her—liked her personality—asked who she was. Then I began to understand that there was something about the way she did stand around, perhaps, that was interesting to the public—her poise. So I began to surround her with the kind of material that would bring her out. And she herself, the more she becomes used to this work, is developing characteristics and stunts which are certain to make her into a sure-fire personality if she keeps on."

"Another star?" I said.

"I think so," he replied. "And then," he went on, that same light of the creator as well as discoverer in his eye, "we have a kid—a baby girl—whose mother brought her in to me—Mary Ann Jackson. Hundreds and hundreds of babies are brought in to be tried out, but it's just like it is in everything else—one stands out and another doesn't and we were lucky enough in her case to find a baby we think is going to develop into a national

191

celebrity. I am not saying that because these people are connected with me, because new personalities are coming up everywhere. I always notice that as one personality passes into oblivion, there's always another comes along somewhere."

"And you think you have three of 'em?" I asked.

"Well, yes, that's what I think," he replied.

But there still remained the Mack Sennett of the bathing beauty fame to interpret and I wanted to talk of that, to say nothing of the beauty herself, as a national and even international feature—the only successful rival, as I see it, to Mr. Ziegfeld and his Follies Girls that has ever appeared in America or elsewhere. And so I said: "And now what about your bathing beauties, Mr. Sennett? What have you to say for that as an idea—artistic or otherwise?"

"Well, what's wrong with it?" he countered. And one could see the ancient "Irish" in him simmer.

"Nothing wrong with it," I replied. "Didn't I pay a special admission price the time you sent your group around the country? But was it your idea or someone else's—that of organizing and sending such a group around? And was she a purely commercial proposition, likely to bring in hard cash, as someone has charged, or an artistic idea to you?"

He paused to think and finally replied: "Nothing so definite as either. Everyone likes to look at a beautiful girl. It sort of helps out the days, doesn't it? Besides, in the kind of burlesque comedy I was doing, there had to be a relief in the form of beauty of some sort. There's no chance for sentiment in the kind of thing we do—or very little. You can't have a girl stick her toe in a brook and make moon eyes at a boy across the way in a burlesque. Mostly—especially in the old days—it was sorta rough, and we had to have something or someone as a contrast, so I thought of sticking in a pretty girl or two—the prettier the better."

"And that's all there was to it?"

"Well, nearly all. Of course, then the business grew and we had a lot of them around, somehow the idea of bathing pictures came up. I suppose we did a lot of those comedies by the sea, with bathing girls in them, because they made a pretty picture. And then I suppose someone on a newspaper first called them 'Bathing Beauties.' But pretty soon, just the same, there she was, labeled. And pretty soon after that, it became 'Mack Sennett's Bathing Beauties' because I was almost the only comedy producer in the field who used them. And I had the most of them. Well, when an idea like that catches on, and you see that the general public is interested, you'd be dumb if you didn't see what to do about it. I don't know now whether I or someone else suggested getting the girls together and sending them around one season—I think it was one of the first distributing agents here in New York that first thought of it—but anyhow, it finally looked to be the thing to do and we did it."

"You did it, you mean."

"Well, I agreed to let it be done."

"And created a more striking thing than the Follies."

"You think so?"

"I do."

"Thanks. Of course, there was criticism. There always is where a lot of pretty girls are used in a public way like that. Besides, human beings will be human beings and in the old days when the business was new there wasn't as much restraint as there is now. Couldn't be. Things were too disorganized—too many things to do and think of. And, of course, there was talk whenever a girl cut up a little, or ran away and got married. And there always will be undesirables show up in every line of work, even among girls. But today we don't stand for them. We want nice girls—the kind of girls who live at home. And what's more, " and here he grew quite emphatic, "we give them every chance of leading just the sort of life that the public respects. And I guess the public knows it, for

192

there's very little criticism of any kind any more. Mostly we're looking for the girl of ambition and with talent, especially where she's pretty—the one who wants to get somewhere—and when you get that kind you find girls who can look out for themselves, and want to—they don't need watching."

His manner indicated that he had said all he could think of in regard to the bathing beauty and I could think of no further phase of her to discuss. However, there was another thing that interested me—a comment he had made on the everyday actor as such—the one without much talent or ambition, yet whom he uses in numbers, and so I said: "What about the average actor—you who love the potential star so much?"

"Oh, him," he said reminiscently. "Well, he's all right. I shouldn't really say anything about him, for, after all, he is what he is, and he can't help it, and what's more, he's useful—very. The only trouble with him as far as his own future is concerned is that he's lazy—or if not that, then he feels no call or inspiration to do anything more than just the thing he's told to do or is shown how to do.

"I've employed a lot of them in my time, and there's no essential difference in the temperament of any of them.

"Sometimes I have to laugh when I think of these people, and sometimes I'm sorry for them, for here they are, with the same opportunities as Chaplin, Langdon, Harold Lloyd, Fairbanks, Pickford, Swanson—anybody—and they do just what they have to do and no more. They are easily satisfied. They do not know the restlessness and discontent that is forever eating at the heart of a real artist. Nor do they ever experience the bubbling enthusiasm and burning ambition and unshakable optimism of the fellow who gets there. The difference between the ordinary actor and the artist might be compared to the difference between an adult and a child; the adult, prosaic, practical, working from necessity, and rather disillusioned.

"The artist—the child—a gypsy, curious, impractical, enthusiastic, a tireless worker at the work he loves, idealistic, never knowing quiet and contentment.

"Well, I guess the average actor is just a tradesman, working at his trade; he might as well punch a clock with the carpenters and mechanics.

"You say to one of them, 'Well, you have to be a fireman today. Here's the part.' And they'll take it and get instructions as to about what's wanted. Then they'll dress it and put in the usual funny stuff about a fireman—the stuff they know or thought of years before. But anything new? No! Or very little—so little that it doesn't make any real difference in their standing from year to year. Yet you know always that whatever you give them to do they'll do well enough, but that's all. Just so they get by. And after that, well, they're thinking just like any clerk—or nearly so—of what time it is. Maybe they have a wife and kids, as most of them have—and they live in some neighborhood where they know everybody and go to parties or dinner, or to church, or to lodge-meeting at night. Or maybe it's some real estate deal they're interested in and thinking of at the very time they're working, playing those crazy roles. Yet any one of them with a spark of fire could step out of the ranks and begin to attract general attention. But they haven't got it.

"And it isn't their fault. They can't get it. They weren't born with that urge that makes the artist work his head off all day, then think and talk and play his work the rest of the time."

And here he went off into one of those still, contemplative moods, laying his chin in one of his interesting, forceful hands, and thinking, as well he might.

And lastly there was the matter of Mr. Sennett himself—his present "right now" mood in regard to himself and his work. For back of this gray, somewhat carlessly dressed man, as I could feel, and even see by his manner, was his fortune of at least fifteen millions. And world-wide fame for his name. And his big studio in Los Angeles, with its many big stages; to say nothing of companies. And on a mountain, which he is having cut off at the very top in order to give himself sky space and field breadth, a great house. And his old Irish-Canadian mother, as I understand, is to have a special entrance in this grand house, so that she won't be compelled to come in contact with the crowd he must ever meet.

A charming, sensitive touch, that. And so I said:

"And now, what of the future, Mr. Sennett? Any special developments?"

"No, none in particular that I see at the moment. Of course business conditions are changing. We produce more and more films. The public taste is changing.

"They want better dressed comedians—fewer axes and the like of that, maybe. But apart from that. . ."

"Are you as much interested in comedy as ever?"

"Just as much—yes—maybe more so."

"Never get weary of it all?"

"Oh, I won't say that. For a few minutes, maybe, at times. Not so much longer."

"Haven't ever a desire to get away for a long time and rest?"

"Well, sometimes I think I have. But I soon get over it. If anything, the game gets more interesting to me. I can scarcely stay away from the studio. Take this particular trip. I did think I'd like to come here and stay three months or so for a rest or change somehow.

"But here I am—only here three or four weeks and anxious to get back. Habit, maybe.

"You might call it a bad one—my ruling weakness or sin. Well, that's the way it is." He smiled amusedly and I could see so clearly in his face his love for his work. He will die making comedies.

But here I added by way of finis:

"You don't intend to try any more melodrama, I suppose?"

"Oh, I don't know. I may. . ." he laughed.

"Or dramas? Or tragedies?"

"No tragedies. That's your game. You can have it."

"And as for bathing beauties"

"Well, when the public gets tired of looking at attractive women. . ."

He stirred, and I rose.

Together we strolled out into the lobby of the Ambassador.

Already a telegram or two for him—a boy with a letter.

"If you want to, and will, come out and stay around the lot for three weeks or a month, and see for yourself. I'll throw everything open to you. You can look around the stages and make friends with the actors and directors, sit in on the comedy-building conferences, interview anybody you like—even me—go out to the homes of those who work for me and see how they live.

"It's an interesting world, and it might make a book. . ."

"Or a Mack Sennett comedy," I replied.

"Or a Mack Sennett comedy," he repeated.

The interview was over.

COMMENTARY

Charlie Chaplin's first film, MAKING A LIVING, a Keystone for Sennett, was released February 2, 1914, and instantly he claimed the attention of both reviewers and the public. HIS FAVORITE PASTIME was the seventh of his 35 Keystone films. He was presently to begin writing and directing his own films.

After a year with Sennett, Chaplin was signed by Essanay at $1250 a week; at Keystone he had made $150. "The Funniest Man on the Screen" describes his first day at the Essanay studio in Chicago, where he made only HIS NEW JOB (1915) before moving out to California. He would not long continue before the camera "without the slightest notion" of what he intended to do; one of the undiscouraged perfectionists of film-making, he was eventually to spend as much as several years planning and polishing a single feature film.

FILM 1914   MAKING A LIVING

"Independent [Films]: MAKING A LIVING," *The Moving Picture World*, Vol. 19, No. 6, February 7, 1914, p. 678.

MAKING A LIVING (Keystone), February 2. —The clever player who takes the role of nervy and very nifty sharper in this picture is a comedian of the first water, who acts like one of Nature's own naturals. It is so full of action that is is indescribable, but so much of it is fresh and unexpected fun that a laugh will be going all the time almost. It is foolish-funny stuff that will make even the sober minded laugh, but people out for an evening's good time will howl.

FILM 1914   HIS FAVORITE PASTIME

"Independent [Films]: HIS FAVORITE PASTIME," *The Moving Picture World*, Vol. 19, No. 12, March 21, 1914, p. 1526.

HIS FAVORITE PASTIME (Keystone), March 16.—One of the few farcical comedies in photoplays that gets continous laughter. The comedian, whose favorite pastime is drinking highballs [Chaplin], is clever, in fact, the best one Mack Sennett has sprung on the public. He is a new one and deserves mention. The situations in this offering are finely handled. This is a real comedy.

1915   "THE FUNNIEST MAN ON THE SCREEN"

By Victor Eubank, *Motion Picture Magazine*, Vol. 9, No. 2, March, 1915, pp. 75-77.

Mr. Chaplin threw up his hands. "I have been in the Essanay studio just fifteen minutes," he said, "and I don't know anything about anything."

I had heard of Charles Chaplin joining the Essanay Company and hurried to the Essanay studios at Chicago to get an interview on the new comedies I understood he was to put out.

I met a rather handsome man with almost jet-black hair and brown eyes which looked at me with a seriousness I should scarcely connect with a comedian. In fact, altho I have seen him in comedies many times on the screen, I should not have known him.

I imagined I would see a man about forty years old, tall and with a comical expression. He is short, and he hardly smiled at all during the half-hour I talked with him. He takes his work as seriously as ever a "heavy man" is supposed to do.

He wore not a jewel: no stick-pin, no ring, no watch, nothing in the line of or-namentation. I think he paid at least $15 for his suit, tho I did not have the nerve to ask him. But he told me himself, with just a trace of a twinkle in his eye, that he had been grossly insulted by a newsboy, who recognized him, the first minute he landed in Chicago.

"I don't care anything about dress," he said. "As I got off the train a newsie spotted me. 'What do you think of that hamfat?' he yelled to his companion. 'One hundred thousand bucks a year, and he looks like a tramp.' "

When I asked Mr. Chaplin for a history of his life, he came nearest to grinning of any time I was talking with him.

"There is little to tell," he said. "I was born in a suburb of London twenty-five years ago. I went on the stage because there seemed nothing else to do. In fact, I don't know

195

anything else. Both my father and mother are on the stage, and so were all my ancestors as far back as I can trace the family tree. I was practically born on the stage.

"I started my stage career at the age of seven, when I did some clog-dancing in a London theater. Then I appeared in *Rags to Riches*, an Anglicized American production. Later I left the stage to attend the Hern Boys' College, near London, where I stayed two years before the lure of the footlights took me back to the stage again.

"I was with the Charles Frohman Company in London for three years, with William Gillette, and I played Billy in *Sherlock Holmes*. I came to America first when playing the lead comedy part with Fred Karno's *A Night in an English Music-hall*.

"It was only a year and a day ago that some one got the hunch that I could make good in Motion Pictures, and here I am. Yes, I am going to start immediatley on a new line of comedies, and I believe they will beat everything else I have ever put out.

"The first time I looked at myself on the screen, however, I was ready to resign. That can't be I, I thought. Then when I realized it was, I said 'Good-night.' Strange enough, I was told that the picture was a scream. I had always been ambitious to work in drama, and it certainly was the surprise of my life when I got away with the comedy stuff.

"I know now why my comedy is good, if you will pardon me for saying that (and I found he did when he began to talk on comedy), but I didn't when I first started. I was on a train from San Francisco to Los Angeles. I picked up a train acquaintance. He said, when we got off, 'I want to take you to a Motion Picture show and show you a nut.' When I saw the screen, there was I. He said, 'The man is clear crazy, but he certainly can put across the comedy stuff.' He didn't know me at all. I thought, 'Crazy as a fox,' as you Americans say it, but I'm willing to be it as long as I can keep out of the asylum and on the screen."

When I asked Mr. Chaplin about comedy, he pulled a long, long face.

"It really is a serious study," he said, "altho it must not be taken seriously. That sounds like a paradox, but it is not. It is a serious study to learn characters; it is a hard study. But to make comedy a success there must be an ease, a spontaneity in the acting that cannot be associated with seriousness.

"I lay out my plot and study my character thoroly. I even follow the character I am to represent for miles or sit and watch him at his work before I attempt to portray him. For instance, I recently took the part of a barber. I even went and got my hair cut, which is my pet aversion. In fact, I never get it cut until the boys along the street yell at me. Then I know it must be done, and I submit to the slaughter.

"But I picked out a particularly busy barber shop, so that I could sit there a long time before my turn came. I watched all the barber's ways. I studied out exactly what he did, and what he might be expected to do in my photoplay. Then I followed him home that night. He was some walker, and it was three miles to his home, but I wanted to know all his little idiosyncrasies.

"With the plot in my mind, I go before the camera without the slightest notion of what I am going to do. I try to lose myself. I am the character I am representing, and I try to act just as I have previously thought the character would act under the same circumstances.

"You can understand that while the camera is working there is not much time to think. You must act on the spur of the moment. In one hundred or less feet of film there is no time to hesitate.

"In this way I think you can get more spontaneity into the action than trying to study out all the detail beforehand. That, in my opinion, is fatal. It makes the film look stilted and unnatural.

"In fact, naturalness is the greatest requisite of comedy. It must be real and true to life. I believe in realism absolutely. Real things appeal to the people far quicker than the grotesque. My comedy is actual life, with the slightest twist or exaggeration, you might say, to bring out what it might be under certain circumstances.

24. "The road smiles like an old friend" when Chaplin approaches at the beginning of THE TRAMP (1915). But when at film's end he retreats, minus the girl, Chaplin permits a moment of pathos.

"People want the truth. In the human heart, for some reason or other, there is a love of truth. You must give them the truth in comedy. Spontaneous acting hits the truth nine times out of ten, where studied work misses it just as often.

"But there is a time and place for everything. Even in slapstick comedy there is an art. If one man hits another in a certain way at exactly the right psychological moment, it is funny. If he does it a moment too early or too late, it misses the mark. And there must be a reason to produce a laugh. To pull off an enexpected trick, which the audience sees is a logical sequence, brings down the house.

"It is always the little things that bring the laughs. It is the peculiar capers, the little actions suited to the situation, that make the hit.

"Motion Picture comedy is still in its infancy. In the next few years I expect to see so many improvements that you could then scarcely recognize the comedy of the present day."

COMMENTARY

The intensely favorable reaction of intellectuals to Chaplin was evident relatively early, but not early enough to antedate his discovery by the vast movie-going general public. "The Mob-God" (1915) appeared in the avant-garde American magazine *The Little Review,* **which was later to serialize Joyce's** *Ulysses.*

In THE TRAMP (1915), Chaplin experimented with an ending which shows him trudging off alone up the road. Two reviewers are of different minds about its success.

Once again, in 1916, Chaplin changed companies, going to Mutual at $10,000 a week. It was for Mutual that THE IMMIGRANT was filmed, and "A Day with Charlie Chaplin on Location" chronicles one day's filming for the two-reeler released as THE ADVENTURER, which completed his Mutual contract.

In 1917, Chaplin signed with First National at a salary which placed him in the $1,000,000 class, with Douglas Fairbanks and Mary Pickford. Henceforth, of each film Chaplin made, 155 prints were distributed and sold at the same time.

Specialists who make lists of Chaplin masterpieces usually include near the top the three-reel SHOULDER ARMS (1918), which appeared just shortly before World War I ended.

"THE MOB-GOD" 1915

By "The Scavenger," *The Little Review,* Vol. 2, No. 3, May, 1915, pp. 45-46.

The seats creak expectantly. The white whirr of the movie machine takes on a special significance. In the murky gloom of the theater you can watch row on row of backs becoming suddenly enthusiastic, necks growing suddenly alive, heads rising to a fresh angle. Turning around you can see the stupid masks falling, vacant eyes lighting up, lips parting and waiting the smile, mouths opening waiting to laugh. A miracle is transpiring. A sodden mass inclined toward protoplasmic atavism, a smear of dead nerves, dead skin, fiberless flesh is beginning to quiver with an emotion. Laughter is about to be born. The lights dance on the screen in front. Letters appear in two short words *[THE TRAMP]* and a gasp sweeps from mouth to mouth.

The name of a Mob-God flashes before the eyes. Suddenly the screen in front vanishes. In its place appears a road stretching away to the sky and lined with trees. The sky is clear. The scene is cool and healthy. The leaves of the trees flutter familiarly. The road smiles like an old friend. And far in the distance a speck appears and moves slowly and jerkily. Wide open mouths and freshened eyes watch the speck grow larger. It takes the form of a man, a little man with a thin cane. At last his baggy trousers and his slovenly shoes are visible. His thick curly hair under the battered derby becomes clear. He walks along carelessly, quietly, with an infinite philosophy. He walks with an indescribable step, kicking up one of his feet, shuffling along.

Laughter is born. The vapid faces respond magically to His presence. Pure, childish delight sounds. The faces are bathed in a human light. A noisy, wholesome din fills the theater. And the little man comes down the road with his calm and solemn face, his sad eyes, his impossible mustache, his ridiculous trousers, and his nervous, spasmodic gait amid the roars and wild elation of idiots, prostitutes, crass, common churls, and empty souls converted suddenly into a natural and mutual simplicity. The stuffy, maddening "bathoes" that clings to the mob like a stink is dispelled, wiped out of the air. Laughter, laughter, shrieks and peals, chuckles and smiles, the broad permeating warmth of the simplest, deepest joy is everywhere.

Charlie Chaplin is before them, Charles Chaplin with the wit of a vulgar buffoon and the soul of a world artist. He walks, he stumbles, he dances, he falls. His inimitable gyrations release torrents of mirth clean as spring freshets. He is cruel. He is absurd; unmanly; tawdy; cheap; artificial. And yet behind his crudities, his obscenities, his inartistic and outrageous contortions, his "divinity" shines. He is the Mob-God. He is a child and a clown. He is a gutter snipe and an artist. He is the incarnation of the latent, inperfect, and childlike genius that lies under the fiberless flesh of the worshippers. They have created Him in their image. He is the Mob on two legs. They love him and laugh.

"Fruits to Om."

"Glory to Zeus."

"Mercy, Jesus."

"Praised be Allah."

"Hats off to Charlie Chaplin."

FILM 1915   THE TRAMP

"Review of Feature Films," *The New York Dramatic Mirror*, Vol. 73, No. 1897, April 28, 1915, p. 39.

THE TRAMP (Essanay, April 12). —You would really be surprised to see how much fun Charles Chaplin gets out of a brick, or a pitchfork, or whatever he takes up. And later, when he is sent out to milk the cow and, by mistake, meets the bull, as in the old yarn, the house rocks with laughter. Certainly the work of Charles Chaplin has never been any funnier than here, and that is saying as much as is, within the circumstances, possible. Pity that he must carry the whole film himself. One laughs at the other characters, but only when they are being knocked down, or when he plays some trick on them. He is represented as a tramp, and in helping save the farmer's daughter earns the gratitude of the farmer who puts him to work. This allows of the whole range of fun he may create in trying to reconcile himself to his new and distasteful environment. The very end is rather dramatic, in comparison, and falls flat by reason of its contrast, with the tempo of what had preceded. Also the photography at times might have been clearer, and there were instances where working a little closer to the camera would have brought the comedy of his expressions out better.

1915   "CHARLIE"

Excerpt from "Greenroom Chitchat," Arthur Swan, *The New York Dramatic Mirror*, Vol. 74, No. 1907, July 7, 1915, p. 8.

. . . Mr. Charles Chaplin is that very rare, well-nigh unique, person among film farceurs, an artist. Many of his antics belong to buffoonery of the commonplace brand, and

199

most of his pictures are bad enough, surely. But Mr. Chaplin comprehends pantomimic expression (most of his clown confreres do not) which gives a certain value to whatever he does.

It is in the little touches that this performer shows at his best. Take, for illustration, the opening of THE CHAMPION, where Charlie sits eating his grub and confabulating with his faithful dog. There is no acceleration of action here; it is almost wholly a matter of physiognomy. This is Mr. Chaplin and movie farce at their best. So also, the finale of THE TRAMP, than which, as a whole, a more fatuously sentimental farce-melodrama can hardly be imagined: here Charlie is shown wearily trudging away from us up a long hilly dusty road; he has been disappointed in love, poor chap and his every step speaks of the bitterness of his sorrow. Then, suddenly, there is a care-free shrug of the shoulders, and the old familiar gait is once again his own. But a "moving" episode like this must be seen to be appreciated. . . .

THE IMMIGRANT   **FILM 1917**

Excerpt from "The Shadow Stage," Julian Johnson, *Photoplay Magazine*, Vol. 12, No. 4, September, 1917, pp. 99-100.

. . In a shrapnel-smashed world, Mr. Chaplin is today the greatest single lightener of the iron burden. This statement is made in solemnity, with discretion and during sobriety. If there is any other device or being which has so successfully chased the imps of pain with lashes of laughter, chroniclers of current events are uninformed of his or its whereabouts. From the desert places of Mongolia to the Himalayas; from Petrograd to Gibraltar; from Rio to the villages of the Andes, Mr. Chaplin's smile and cornerings are almost as well known as they are in America, or France, or Japan—which enterprising country, indeed, has not a few slant-eyed imitators who are professional Charlies for the Nipponese.

The preceding paragraph is not an attempt to rattle anything out of a husk of perfectly-shucked news, but by way of introduction to a very live topic: Mr. Chaplin's growing and very genuine artistry; an artistry I dare say comparable to Mr. David Warfield's, or to Mr. Lew Fields' when that variable gentleman is hitting on all cylinders.

Did you see THE IMMIGRANT? I not only saw THE IMMIGRANT, but I saw some light, disparaging reviews of it—one or two by metropolitan critics. Henceforth, these persons can never make me believe anything they write, for the subject of their malministrations is a transparent intermezzo well repaying the closest analysis. In its roughness and apparent simplicity it is as much a jewel as a story by O. Henry, and no full-time farce seen on our stages in years has been more adroitly, more perfectly worked out.

It has, to an extraordinary degree, those elements of surprise which are necessary in every play and which put the capstone of humor on comedy, because they add to the ludicrous the deliciousness of the unexpected. Examine, for instance, the passages in which our shabby-genteel finds a half-dollar, and, slipping it as he thinks into his pocket, but really through a hole in his trousers, enters the palace of tough service and orders with the independence of a capitalist. How cunningly these sequences are bound together! Our gourmet-hero has no sooner destroyed a half-dozen orders than he discovers himself decidedly not in funds. Then the grim procession of waiters, headed by the vast Eric Campbell, to destroy a recreant customer and oust his remains. The plot fairly curdles when, in answer to Mr. Chaplin's gasping query as to the cause of the trouble, the giant replies ominously: "He was ten cents short."

In dizzying succession come the waiter's loss of a fifty, Mr. Chaplin's screaming salvage of the piece, his return to calm—and the waiter's discovery that the half is pewter! Probability on a single incident would now be quite exhausted under ordinary circumstances, but Mr. Chaplin brings to his table a friendly artist. There is some polite fumbling for the check—and the knight of the rattan cane is out-fumbled! His payment of the waiter with his friend's change concludes what is without any doubt at all the longest version on a single comedy incident ever put on the screen—a variation worked out with such patience and skill that every sequence of action seems entirely natural and spontaneous.

There is one flash of Chaplin's inimitable pathos in this picture: that rollicking moment in which, lifting the petite hand of la Purviance, he discovers clutched within it the black-bordered handkerchief which tells the story of her mother's death. Simply, sincerely, and with a look of infinite pity he lowers her hand. The moment, genuinely affecting though sandwiched in boisterousness, is a little flash of genius.

THE IMMIGRANT is singularly free from vulgarity. . . .

1917   "A DAY WITH CHARLIE CHAPLIN ON LOCATION"

By James E. Hilbert, *Motion Picture Magazine*, Vol. 14, No. 10, November, 1917, pp. 59-61.

In balmy (?) July I spent my vacation in the Santa Monica Mountains, near Los Angeles, at a place called Los Flores Canon. It is a summer camp, and is situated between the rugged mountains and the great Pacific Ocean. Los Flores is the only thing that is not as nature made it. For twenty miles around it is the narrow road, with its still narrower bridges that span the smaller canons, that leads to the camp.

It is here that our famous Charlie is doing his latest stunt, entitled THE ESCAPED CONVICT [THE ADVENTURER].

There was some excitement in the camp the morning he arrived; tents were deserted, and the little store at the camp did more business in ten minutes than it usually does in a week. We all gathered around, and Charlie treated the bunch to ice-cream and soda-water; and then he promptly offered $5 for a cup of English-breakfast tea, which the storekeeper could not provide. One of the campers came across with the tea and hot water, and Charlie made the tea himself, using three handfuls for the cup. He had on a convict suit used thruout the picture, and while drinking his tea he posed gracefully for our cameras, poising his cup and saucer in an I-don't-care-if-you-do-fall fashion.

Having duly paid for the tea and posed for several more private cameras, Charlie and his company started for the "location," where the first scene was to be taken, with us campers bringing up the rear. It was quite a procession. Charlie, in his jail suit, took the lead; then came the jail guards carrying their rifles, and the camera-men with the cameras over their shoulders, and an actress in a fancy bathing-suit was next in line. The rear guard was composed of some extras in their diverse make-ups, and the campers, some in bathing-suits, some wearing bathrobes, and bewhiskered fishermen with their oilskins and rubber boots. Ladies wearing pantalets and in riding-habits; and others too numerous to mention, made up the second section of the parade. It would have made quite a sensation if it had marched down Broadway.

But, anyway, the scene was to be taken on the side of a mountain. The guide climbed up first; then he threw a rope down, and Charlie tied it about his waist. The guide started to pull on the rope, and, believe me, it was a whole comedy in itself to see Charlie climb that mountainside. He had on those long shoes about ten times too large for him, and every time he took a step up he slid down two. When he was about half-way up he lost his hat and it started to roll down the mountainside, and Charlie, in his haste to recover it, nearly pulled the guide down with him, burning the guide's hands with the swiftly moving rope as it pulled thru his hands.

Finally Charlie got mad at the preposterous shoes and yanked them off. He tied them together, threw them over his shoulders, and made a new start in his stocking-feet, much

201

to the amusement of the campers, who were taking in every agonized look Charlie made as he stepped on the sharp stones.

At last, when he reached the location, nearly four hundred feet from the road, he wasn't satisfied with it at all, and he returned to the road, still in his stocking-feet. Then the motors started to purr, and they, camp-followers and all, were off to find a new location.

After a suitable location had been found and Charlie had viewed it from every angle, with his hands over his eyes, sailor fashion, he breathed a sigh of relief and smiled blandly at the crowd below.

He ordered the cameras up and prodeeded to take the picture. A dummy dressed as a prison guard was to be rolled down the mountainside, and when everything was ready it was started on its way. It did not reach the much-desired bottom; instead it dangled by its coat-tail in midair from a shrub on the mountainside. Thereupon Charlie complimented it for its foresight in stopping short of its destination and for wasting several feet of good film. With much difficulty the dummy was recovered, and once more started on its way down, with better results this time.

The next scene was one which must be taken on the narrow road, and a director's "imp" was sent out on a motorcycle in the direction which the camera faced, in order to stop the traffic coming that way. In his haste to get away, the "imp" upset a nice young lady and her camera, who was trying to get a snap of Charlie. With much gusto and gallantry, Charlie assisted the young lady to her feet. He posed specially for the dear girl.

Action was soon on again. As if lightning had struck him, Charlie bit the dust, for the special purpose of tripping a guard who was hot after him; then, jumping up, he ran a few feet, then dropped again, the guard turning a somersault as he tripped over him the second time; then Charlie got away; the guard, lying where he fell, slowly recovered himself, only to be knocked down again by two more guards who came running pell-mell down a trail on the mountainside.

I am sorry to say that Charlie got real mad. A flivver that refused to stop for the "imp" was in the picture, and it had to be done all over again. Charlie wished "Henry much peace!"

The scene was taken again, but just as Charlie made his get-away and the guards were starting down, a lovely big rattlesnake loomed up on the trail and stopped the whole proceedings.

The two guards stopped short, and a long pole was procured, and Mr. Snake was promptly executed. Charlie tried again, and to make sure everything was right, he went thru his dialog:

"No more flivvers coming? No. No more snakes in sight? No. Are you ready up there, you bum guards? Yes. Are the caps off the cameras? Yes. Remember, Joe, I will trip you right here; fall heavy and get up quick. Then you know the rest. All ready! Camera!"

At this point some one mentioned that it was "Friday, July 13th," and, with an exclamation of annoyance, Charlie said with the tones and air of finality:

"We shall all go home at once. This is my Jonah day, and I *absolutely* refuse to work any more today."

"Absolutely?"

"Absolutely!"

SHOULDER ARMS

FILM 1918

Excerpts from "The Shadow Stage," Julian Johnson, *Photoplay Magazine*, Vol. 15, No. 2, January, 1919, pp. 67-68.

. . . Mr. Chaplin shares Mr. Griffith's situation as the most eagerly awaited producer in motion pictures. Why? Because every audience has come to know that his successive entertainments, like those of Mr. Griffith, are the fruition of long days and weary nights of intense study and experiment, heroic cutting, endless rejection, continuous retake and infinite patience. When you see a new Chaplin picture your ticket does not insure you a laugh every two seconds, but it does entitle you to witness the untimate endeavor of an artist who has completely mastered his business. Do you have this same assurance when you face the transparencies of most of the famous dramatic stars? Write your own answer. . . .

In SHOULDER ARMS Charlie Chaplin so easily and perfectly gets away from the bewildering trousers, the rattan cane and the immortal derby that his escape, at last, is scarcely the matter of a moment's thought.

Here he is in khaki, canvas leggings and army hat—yet how many of us have insisted that the gentlemanly essentials named in the preceding paragraph were an absolutely necessary part of his success?

SHOULDER ARMS is the glory-dream of a recruit. It is a perfect handling of a delicate subject, and in its treatment the comedian has shown, more completely than ever before, his faculty for getting inside a character, and grasping, as if by intuition (but really by hard work) all that character's salient points. The best thing about this film is that the rookie sees his own little weaknesses, his hardships, his hopes, his glories, his quaint vanities and small fears—he sees himself. If this film is not 100 per cent triumph in our army camps in Europe all bets and guesses fail.

Right in the midst of a guffaw one stops to admire a skilful mastery of even the new technique of war. Camouflaged as a tree, and motionless in a grove, he is absolutely undiscoverable until he moves. What a chilling satire of Flanders rain, too, is that scene of sweet slumber in the inundated dugout! Daintily shaking out his submarine pillows the comedian tucks the watery blanket about his shoulders—and sinks beneath the black flood with only the phonograph horn to give him air. Looking at this passage is enough to give one pneumonia by suggestion. The customary hint of breezy amour is lightly, deftly touched in a momentary scene with the cynical and evil-thinking crown prince.

Being completely funny on a background of completely terrible war is not only difficult, but dangerous. As far as we can see, only Chaplin and Bairnsfather have been wholly successful and wholly apropos.

COMMENTARY

Although many early Chaplin films seem to have enjoyed perpetual circulation since their initial release, they began in 1919 to appear among the larger New York houses, and, after re-exhibition in these, became almost staple shorts in the small art theatres during the latter half of the 1920's.

1919   "IN THE NEWS NET"

Excerpt from "In the News Net," *The New York Times*, February 23, 1919, Section 4, p. 6.

Hugo Riesenfeld will institute a "Chaplin Revival" at the Rialto Theatre, beginning today with A NIGHT IN THE SHOW [1915]. Other productions which have established themselves by their quality will be revived, all of the re-issues being exhibited under the general head "Rialto Comedy Classics."

Concerning his venture, Dr. Riesenfeld writes:

"We are conducting what I consider a most interesting experiment on behalf of the art of the motion picture. We are endeavoring to demonstrate the permanent value of good pictures. No one questions the permanent and lasting value of good music, good books, good painting. But the young art of the motion picture has not yet sufficiently asserted itself. Still we have some pictures good enough and old enough to warrant their representation under metropolitan auspices as old masters or true classics of the screen.". . .

25. D. W. Griffith: THE BIRTH OF A NATION (1915): "The war scenes present the Griffith technique on a broader scale than it has ever been seen. . . . Awe-inspiring panoramas are followed by nerve-gripping close-up views of hand-to-hand fighting."

CHAPTER 11

Outposts of the Cinema's Advance:
THE BIRTH OF A NATION (1915)
and INTOLERANCE (1916)

COMMENTARY

After leaving Biograph in 1913, D. W. Griffith supervised the releases of Reliance-Majestic, for whom he personally directed four features, all released in 1914: THE BATTLE OF THE SEXES and HOME, SWEET HOME; THE ESCAPE and THE AVENGING CONSCIENCE. Then, in July of that year, with independent financing, the project closest to his heart got under way "boiling and sizzling": the filming of THE CLANSMAN, with loyal Bitzer behind the camera.

Under this title, it was shown at Los Angeles February 8, 1915. On March 3, it opened at the Liberty Theatre in New York as THE BIRTH OF A NATION, and closed its first New York run after an advertised 620 consecutive performances.

This 12-reel masterwork, an almost incredible demonstration of Griffith's powers, attracted a whirling controversy over his treatment of the Reconstruction period in the South, and remains controversial to this day. The subtitle about impartial presentation quoted in *The Mirror* review, no longer appeared in the prints which Griffith later authorized as being complete. As these prints now stand, the film is composed of 1,374 separate shots, exclusive of subtitles.

In an article unsigned, but most certainly by Alexander Woollcott, who invented the "Second Thoughts on First Nights" department in *The New York Times,* objections to Griffith's use of the cut-back are advanced.

The film's revival at the Capitol Theatre in New York, for a two-week run in May, 1921, provoked a reassessment in *The Times*, which now measured it against developments in motion pictures since 1914, including imported German spectacle films, and Griffith's own current manner. Still considered "one of the pre-eminent works of today," THE BIRTH OF A NATION continued to accumulate both the prestige and invective which were to make it the most famous of all American silent films.

FILM 1915   THE BIRTH OF A NATION

" 'THE BIRTH OF A NATION' Summit of Picture Art", *The New York Dramatic Mirror,* Vol. 73, No. 1890, March 10, 1915, p. 28.

Griffith Blends Spectacle, History and Drama with Hand of a Master in His Latest Screen Production

Presented by David W. Griffith at the Liberty Theatre March 3. Twelve-Reel Historical Drama Founded on Thomas Dixon's Story, *The Clansman*. Adaptation Prepared by D. W. Griffith and Frank E. Woods. Produced Under the Direction of D. W. Griffith. Photography by G. W. Bitzer.

Colonel Ben Cameron	Henry Walthall
Margaret Cameron, the elder sister	Miriam Cooper
Flora, the pet sister	Mae Marsh
Mrs. Cameron	Josephine Crowell
Dr. Cameron	Spottiswoode Aitken
Wade Cameron, the second son	J. A. Beringer
Duke Cameron, the youngest son	John French
Mammy, their faithful old servant	Jennie Lee
Hon. Austin Stoneman, Leader of the House	Ralph Lewis
Elsie, his daughter	Lillian Gish
Phil, his elder son	Elmer Clifton
Tod, the younger son	Robert Harron
Jeff, the blacksmith	Wallace Reid
Lydia Brown, Stoneman's mulatto housekeeper	Mary Alden
Silas Lynch, mulatto Lieutenant-Governor	George Siegmann
Gus, a renegade negro	Walter Long
Abraham Lincoln	Joseph Henabery
John Wilkes Booth	Raoul Walsh
General U. S. Grant	Donald Crisp
General Robert E. Lee	Howard Gaye

The scoffers came to see CABIRIA, and left overwhelmed with admiration, but only half-converted. "It is a triumph of pictorial art," they said, "but its appeal is solely to the eye, and we have long granted that province to the motion picture."

They came again to see THE BIRTH OF A NATION. But this time found tongues stilled, minds stunned, as the last scene faded from the screen. Here was drama that wrung tears from a far-from-impressionable audience, spectacle worthy of panegyrics, a treatment of human problems that has furnished seed for endless discussion. And it is a *motion picture*.

One is sorely tempted to seek safety in bromides when setting out to review THE BIRTH OF A NATION. The pen falters in vain search for means of expression, and collapses with "The greatest picture ever produced." But this bromidic truth tells only half of the story; it means comparison, and Griffith's greatest triumph in THE BIRTH OF A NATION is in a field in which he is a pioneer. We may compare the stupendous battle scenes with the spectacular CABIRIA, the intense dramatic passages with moments in a half-score of productions, but with its selection and treatment of a vital theme the past offers nothing for comparison.

This is the summit of Griffith's achievement—he has created thought and discussion. Perhaps he may not have moulded that thought to his own ideas, the discussion may more often be disagreement, but that is the penalty of grappling with throbbing themes. You may not approve of the reopening of old sores to furnish a present-day thesis, but Griffith has presented his justification, for you to accept or reject, in the introductory sub-title, "The viewpoint of the South on the great events of the Civil War and the Reconstruction period has never been impartially presented in the pages of history."

That presentment Griffith sets out to give. He chose *The Clansman* for his text, but dug deeper for his foundation. The Stonemans of the North, and the Camerons of Piedmont, N. C., furnish the personal element. Austin Stoneman is a "power in Washington"; his children, Phil, Tod and Elsie, are friendly with the Camerons. The sons' visit to Piedmont

206

serves to introduce us to the placid beauties of the South of 1860. A few deft touches paint it a contented and carefree South. Then we are whirled into the vortex of the Civil War, and from here on Griffith mingles spectacle and story with the hand of a genius, his eyes set always on the creation of a single impression—that of sympathy, bordering on admiration, for the South of the Reconstruction period, the South of the Ku Klux Klan. His means to the end are twofold, firstly, a portrayal of the bitterness engendered by the Civil War and the heavy hand of desolation it laid upon the South; second, the painting, in broad, scarlet strokes, of the negro granted equality, and the attempt of the radicals of the North to "crush the White South under the heels of the Black South."

The war scenes present the Griffith technique on a broader scale than it has ever been seen. In that showing the burning of Atlanta we look from an eminence across a plain dotted with the figures of the fleeing populace and harassing troops. Tearful women, clinging to their helpless children, and wounded, stumbling soldiers in gray pass before us. The high note is sounded with a masterpiece of double exposure when the flaming city is shown above the panic-stricken flight.

It is difficult to hope that any war scenes will soon surpass those showing the Petersburg battle. For miles away the perspective disclosed twisting lines of opposing trenches. Cannon and rifle belch, and now and again serried lines of blue or gray surge forth to the charge. Awe-inspiring panoramas are followed by nerve-gripping close-up views of hand-to-hand fighting. The bombardment by night and Sherman's march to the sea are only two of the many other war views that deserve more lengthy mention than is possible here.

But Griffith has his purpose in view, and lest you be carried away by the martial aspect of the conflict, he craftily interposes views of the real sufferers, the "folks at home." From a pulse-quickening charge you are transported to a heart-torn mother learning of the death of her sons. This portrayal of war is undoubtedly one of the strongest of arguments for universal peace, though that is a by-product of the picture, and not its underlying motive.

The close of the war finds Ben Cameron returning to a Piedmont that is in ruins. But the South is indomitable and sets out hopefully to rebuild a shattered empire. Then the fanatical mind of Booth removes the South's greatest friend. The scene showing the assassination of Lincoln is a masterpiece of screen technique and historical accuracy. It is real enough to shock.

The showing of events up to this tragedy has taken close to six thousand feet of film. As presented at the Liberty Theatre this forms the first act. The second half deals more particularly with *The Clansman* and its terrible story of the suffering of the Reconstruction. Carpetbaggers flood the South, and under the leadership of Stoneman they plan political domination through the control of the enfranchised negro. Little instances of negro agression, mounting in importance, lead up to the producer's commanding justification for the Ku Klux. Flora, Ben's younger sister, is forced to suicide by jumping from a cliff to escape the attack of a crazed negro. The Ku Klux, organized by Ben Cameron, as the result of an inspiration most cleverly shown, avenges her. A night is chosen to disarm the negroes.

We are now approaching scenes that, in their swift onrush of action, surcharged with excitement, reach the pinnacle of intensity. The blacks' answer to the Ku Klux is a night of terror for Piedmont. While they overrun the stricken town, terrorizing the white populace, the Ku Klux members are gathering at a distant point for the supreme effort. Dr. Cameron and his family have been forced to flee, pursued by a hounding pack of negroes. Elsie Stoneman seeks aid from Silas Lynch, a mulatto leader of the blacks. His reply is a proposal of marriage; her indignant rejection is met with violence and she is imprisoned, while preparations are made for an enforced wedding. Flashes take us from this scene to various other parts of the hell-ridden town, then to the Camerons besieged in a cabin surrounded by armed negroes, and finally to the Ku Klux Klan, silent, spectral

207

figures, gathering in the shadowed woods. Word is brought of Elsie's peril and the mad race to the rescue is begun. There seem to be hundreds upon hundreds of the white-clad figures, as they stretch out in pale relief against the night's darkness.

The pitch is heightened by every device of the Griffithian art until the climax, with the conflict in the streets of Piedmont, the rescue of Elsie and later of the Camerons, and the day dawns with a Ku Klux triumphal parade.

The love story of the main characters is settled, and here the picture could well end. But "even Homer nods," and trite allegorical passages are dragged in to preach a universal peace moral. They seem weak in comparison with the wonders that have preceded, lame in their application to a story that in every other respect is developed with the hand of a master craftsman.

The acting is such as only Griffith can command. Henry Walthall's work is at all times impressive. His moment of agony on realizing that his pet sister is dead is a bit of histrionic art that will not be easily erased from the memory. Mae Marsh surpasses the fondest prophecies of her admirers as Flora Cameron. Her every move is carefully planned acting, yet so clever is the art that it is not acting. But why attempt to give due credit to such a cast? Lillian Gish, George Siegmann, Ralph Lewis, Josephine Crowell, Spottiswoode Aitken, Mary Alden, Jennie Lee, one and all, principals and minor characters, down even to the extras, seem to be players of ability. Miriam Cooper's work causes surprising disagreement. There are those who praise her repression, others who criticize the over-stress of placidity.

But the hand of Griffith overshadows all. Telling his story fearlessly and masterfully, at times he cuts deep beneath the skin, till one must question the brutality while praising the art. Times are when he seems more the skillful lawyer than the impartial historian, but never is he a boresome pleader. If there is to be a greater picture than THE BIRTH OF A NATION, may we live to see it.

(Signed) W.

THE BIRTH OF A NATION

FILM 1915

Excerpt from "Second Thoughts on First Nights," *The New York Times*, April 18, 1915, Section 7, p. 6.

. . . So remarkable and elaborate a photoplay as THE BIRTH OF A NATION, which is now drawing crowded houses in half a dozen cities, is familiarly used to instance how far motion pictures have gone, but it might be quite as aptly used to suggest how far they still have to go. For all its enormous cost and care, for all its impressive pageantry of arms and men, it is, we may hope, not the last word in motion pictures. It is simply the latest word. The photoplay, if not in its infancy, gives evidence of being still in its callow youth.

There are certain tricks of the trade the movie will outgrow. It will surely outgrow, for instance, that trick technically known as the "cut back," which shifts the scenes back and forth in the irresponsible and mischievous manner of the dancing spot of light reflected from the mirror in a small boy's hand. The film director, flushed with the realization that he could move about with a freedom unknown to the stage, has been so delighted with this liberty that he has indulged himself incontinently, without pausing to consider that he might be playing havoc with that precious element called tension. It is easy to predict that the cut back, and similar evidences of restlessness, will fade gradually from the screens, to be used only on special occasions to follow, say, such converging lines as Dickens traced so effectively when the three men gathered in Jasper's rooms on the night of Edwin Drood's disappearance, or as Barrie traced when, in the book, he followed through the thunderstorm the separate paths leading up the hill where the Lady Babbie and Gavin Dishart were being married.

But these are rather lofty comparisons, and a recent visit to several films shown hereabouts suggests forcibly that the analogies might be sought more properly in literature of another plane. For observe the tone that is given to THE BIRTH OF A NATION by the captions, or "flashes", that tell of the "poor bruised heart of the South," that speak of "the opal gates of death," and make such utterances as this:

"The Love strain is heard by fond hearts above the land's miserere."

They sound as if they had been written by Harold Bell Wright in an off moment and been revised by Florence Barclay.

You might make a dozen predictions as to the work of the film director of the future. You may be sure, for example, that he will not jostle so many people into a scene that the thread of the story is lost in the crowd, nor will he, in preparing an old stage favorite for the screen, toil dutifully to get so much into the scenario that the result is such mystifying confusion as afflicted the early part of THE HEART OF MARYLAND. He will go on developing the resources that are not open to the stage, such vistas of Rome as enrich the background of THE ETERNAL CITY, which has come to the Astor, and such glimpses of great armies on the march and in the field as reward a visit to THE BIRTH OF A NATION.

1909   **Establishing the Dramatic Focus**

Excerpt from "Reviews of New Films," *The New York Dramatic Mirror*, Vol 62, No. 1604, September 18, 1909, p. 14.

. . . The last scene [in "1776": or, THE HESSIAN RENEGADES] in particular is stage managed with a skill that is peculiar to the Biograph director [D. W. Griffith]. In a small room crowded full of people the two chief characters, most admirably played, the old man and the Hessian officer, stand out in definite relief, without rendering the scene in any way unnatural. . . .

FILM 1921   THE BIRTH OF A NATION (Revival)

From *The New York Times*, May 2, 1921, p. 12.

D. W. Griffith's motion picture classic, THE BIRTH OF A NATION, has been revived for a week at the Capitol Theatre. A good many photoplays have been made and the dramatic screen has progressed importantly in a number of directions since this picture opened at the Liberty Theatre on March 3, 1915, six whole years ago—only six years ago, but the production that was sensationally pre-eminent then remains one of the pre-eminent works of today.

It has rivals now, and in some things they surpass it. Several of them have photographic subtleties and other cinematographic qualities that it does not possess. It lacks the unity and coherence of later motion picture masterpieces, and free imitation of its melodramatic devices has weakened their effectiveness. But when all of this is admitted, THE BIRTH OF A NATION still needs no apology. It stands today a truimphant achievement of the screen.

As melodrama, it is one of the most genuine thrillers ever made, and it shows some of the best acting, some of the most vivid, if sketchy, characterization, to be found on the screen. As a spectacle it still has power to stir the imagination notwithstanding the fact

209

that there are other pictures built on a larger scale and more finished in detail. If it seems crude in places, and is in the last analysis chiefly a glorified melodrama, it has, nevertheless, a glory of its own.

Considered as a historical work, THE BIRTH OF A NATION is a thing of contradictions. Some of its scenes are truly flash-backs to the period of civil war and reconstruction in America. Sometimes it is almost epic in quality. But in many scenes it is falsely romantic and as blindly partisan as the most violent sectional tradition. It may be said that, as a rule, it comes closest to historical truth when it is furthest from Thomas Dixon. It has always been a great pity that, in undertaking to build a photoplay on the struggle between the North and South, Mr. Griffith went for material to so garbled and prejudice-feeding an account as *The Clansman*. He permanently impaired his work by doing so.

THE BIRTH OF A NATION takes on a new interest in comparison with Mr. Griffith's later productions. It gives evidence that its maker has advanced in some ways since 1914-15, while retrograding in others. Apparently, for example, he has become more sure in putting character on the screen and has developed a more competent idea of dramatic unity, but he seems, on the other hand, to have lost something of the sense of restraint in telling a story and to be more addicted to shallow and platitudinous preaching. There are actually cinematographic bits in THE BIRTH OF A NATION which are not shouted down by subtitles, and there are intense scenes cut quickly, when they should be cut, and many illuminating flashes on details of action and character that leave them bright in the imagination, not dulled by overemphasis. One cannot suppress the hope that, in some respects, Mr. Griffith will soon return to his earlier style.

It is a pleasure of course to renew acquaintance with the now prominent players in THE BIRTH OF A NATION, Henry Walthall, Mae Marsh, Miriam Cooper, Lillian Gish, Mary Alden, George Siegmann and the others in the cast have seldom been better, and often much worse, than they were six years ago. And the brief but clear-cut performance of Robert Harron reminds the spectator afresh that the screen suffered a real loss in his death.

The picture has a new musical accompaniment at the Capitol, adapted by S. L. Rothafel and arranged by Erno Rapée, William Axt and Hermann Hand, which, though effective now and then, is much too noisy most of the time.

COMMENTARY

In 1914, when THE BIRTH OF A NATION was completed but not yet released, Griffith, at the peak of his creativity, launched on a modern drama to be called THE MOTHER AND THE LAW. He soon realized that unless he enlarged this in some way, it would come as a severe anti-climax after his Civil War film, so he added three stories from three different centuries to the original narrative, and instead of handling each as a separate unit, he intercut them.

In 1915, Griffith joined Triangle, with Ince and Sennett, to supervise features, but continued to work independently on this great film, eventually to be known as IN-TOLERANCE. By June it was "more than one-half finished," (38) and it was shown in New York on September 5, 1916, but in spite of its dynamic verve and originality, IN-TOLERANCE ended up as probably the greatest financial disaster films have ever known.

"Comment and Suggestion" in *The New York Dramatic Mirror*, remarks on Alexander Woollcott's criticisms of INTOLERANCE, mentions Münsterberg's book, *The Photoplay: A Psychological Study*, and quotes the perceptive realizations of the Boston *Transcript* reviewer that Griffith's early Biographs predict both THE BIRTH OF A NATION and INTOLERANCE. It is unusual to find an observer of these two feature films who was also acquainted with Griffith's shorter works.

210   Julian Johnson's review suggests that the failure of INTOLERANCE was a result of its

26. *D. W. Griffith: THE BIRTH OF A NATION: "The second half deals more particularly with* The Clansman *and its terrible story of the suffering of the reconstruction. . . . We are now approaching scenes that, in their swift onrush of action . . . reach the pinnacle of intensity."*

limping score. As recommended, Griffith did later work out "a whole evening" of the Babylonian story, calling it **THE FALL OF BABYLON (1919)**, and in 1919 he also released **THE MOTHER AND THE LAW**, reclaimed from **INTOLERANCE**, as a separate feature. Johnson was right: Griffith never again told a story on the screen in the manner of **INTOLERANCE**.

INTOLERANCE   **FILM 1916**

" 'INTOLERANCE' In Review," Frederick James Smith, *The New York Dramatic Mirror*, Vol. 76, No. 1969, September 16, 1916, p. 22.

David Wark Griffith's screen spectacle presented at the Liberty Theater on September 5. "A sun play of the ages" in a prologue and two acts. Entire production under the personal direction of Mr. Griffith. Musical arrangement by Joseph Carl Breil. Photographic chief, G. W. Bitzer. Principals of the cast:

The Woman Who Rocks the Cradle	Lillian Gish
Miss Mary Jenkins	Vera Lewis
Jenkins, Industrial Magnate	Sam de Grasse
The Girl of the Modern Story	Mae Marsh
The Girl's Father	Fred Turner
The Boy of the Modern Story	Robert Harron
Mary Magdelene	Olga Grey
Catherine de Medici	Josephine Crowell
Charles IX	Frank Bennett
Henry of Navarre	W. E. Lawrence
Duc d'Anjou	Maxfield Stanley
Admiral Coligny	Joseph Henabery
Brown Eyes	Marjorie Wilson
The Father of Brown Eyes	Spottiswoode Aitken
The Lover of Brown Eyes	Eugene Palette
The Foreign Mercenary Soldier	A. D. Sears
The High Priest of Bel	Tully Marshall
The Mountain Girl	Constance Talmadge
The Rhapsode	Elmer Clifton
Prince Belshazzar	Alfred Paget
Nabonidus, King of Babylonia	Carl Stockdale
Attarea, favorite of Belshazzar	Seena Owen
A Friendless One	Miriam Cooper
The Musketeer of the Slums	Walter Long
The Bride of Cana	Bessie Love
The Kindly Policeman	Tom Wilson
The Governor	Ralph Lewis
Cyrus	George Siegmann
The Mighty Man of Valor	Elmo Lincoln
Chief detective	Edward Dillon
Catholic Priest	Louis Romaine
Judge of the Court	Lloyd Ingraham
Warden	W. H. Brown
Kindly neighbor	Max Davidson
The wife	Miss Lee
Babylonian mother	Kate Bruce
Auctioneer	Martin Landry

Brother of the girl . . . . Arthur Meyer
Attorney for the Boy . . . . Barney Bernard
Babylonian Judge . . . . Lawrence Lawlor
Society social worker . . . . Mary Alden
Duc de Guise . . . . Morris Levy
Mary the mother . . . . Lillian Langdon
Gobryas, Lieutenant of Cyrus . . . . Charles Van Cortland
Chief Eunuch . . . . Jack Cosgrove
Marguerite de Valois . . . . Georgia Pearce
Cardinal Lorraine . . . . Howard Gaye
Bridegroom of Cana . . . . George Walsh

It is easy enough, as you catch your breath at the conclusion of INTOLERANCE, to indulge in trite superlatives. Film reviewing has been over superlatived. But this new Griffith spectacle marks a milepost in the progress of the film. It reveals something of the future of the spectacle, something of its power to create pictures of tremendous and sweeping beauty, drama, and imagination. The future will come when the great writer unites with the great producer.

INTOLERANCE, of course, instantly challenges comparison, by reason of its creator, with THE BIRTH OF A NATION. One is the dramatization of a novel, a gripping, even thrilling visualization of a story dealing with a theme of national interest—our own Civil War. On the other hand, INTOLERANCE is the screening of an idea. That alone places it as an advance.

THE SCREENING OF AN IDEA

Mr. Griffith sought a theme which has traced itself through history. He advances the proposition that humanity's lack of tolerance of opinion and speech has brought about the world's woes. Taking four periods of history, he traces the working out of this idea. We have, perhaps, come to assume that our own age is one of singular meddling and busy-bodyism. But Mr. Griffith points out that the thing has been the same through the ages.

Briefly, the periods depicted revolve around the fall of Babylon in 538 B. C., the coming of the Nazarene and the birth of the Christian era, the massacre of St. Bartholomew's day in France during the reign of Charles IX, and the present day. Mr. Griffith, of course, handles his four plots at one time. The threads are interwoven. The moments dealing with the life of Christ, it may be noted here, are brief, being in reality rich tableaux of the persecution of the Savior. Griffith has endeavored to humanize Christ. These moments are handled with reverence, dignity, and beauty of picture. Indeed, there are moments worthy of Tissot. Once, oddly, the director attains a singular effect of a shadow cross upon the figure of Christ.

The modern theme of INTOLERANCE has a Western town as its locale. The owner of a factory reduces wages that he may make extended—and widely heralded—contributions to charity. A strike devastates the town and the workers are forced to move away. The boy and the girl of the story, now married in the city, still remain the playthings of intolerance. The boy is sent to prison for a crime he never committed. In his absence the baby is taken away from the mother by a charitable society. The boy, on returning, becomes innocently involved in a murder and, through his criminal record, is convicted. The story finally races to a climax when, as the execution is about to take place, the wife, aided by a kindly policeman, hurries to the governor with the confession of the real murderer. They miss the executive, who has taken a train. The policeman commandeers a racing car and they speed after the express. The execution is stopped just as the death trap is to be sprung.

213

SPECTACLE'S APPEAL LIES IN BABYLONIAN STORY

The principal appeal of INTOLERANCE, however, lies in the Babylonian story. Here we see Belshazzar ruling Babylon with his father, Nabonidus. He is a kindly, generous monarch—as kings in those days went—but the high priest of Bel resents his religious tolerance. So, when Cyrus, king of the Medes and Persians, attacks the walled city, the priest betrays Babylon. So the city falls, after a mighty battle such as never before had been conceived in mimicry.

Mr. Griffith has reconstructed the city of Babylon—according to authentic records and researches, we are told by the programme and we may well believe. The city, with its great walls, three hundred feet high and big enough on top for two war chariots to pass, its temples, its lofty halls, its slave marts, and its streets, lives again, seething with life. The attack upon Babylon is handled on a tremendous scale. We are shown Cyrus's camp in the desert sands. Then we see his cohorts, his barbarians from distand lands, his war chariots, his elephants, his great moving towers, advance upon Babylon. Great catapults hurl rocks upon the defenders. Moulten lead is thrown from the walls. Showers of arrows fall. One great siege tower, black with fighting men, is toppled over and goes crashing to the ground. Ladders, manned by warriors, are flung down. So the battle goes a day and a night. Treason finally gives over Babylon, in the midst of a great bacchanial feast of victory.

This theme is unfolded with Mr. Griffith's fine skill in handling hundreds and thousands of men. There is a certain personal note in the spectacle. Belshazzar, his favorite, Attarea, the boisterous little mountain girl who loves the king from afar, and the crafty priest of Bel are finely humanized. The tremendous applause at INTOLERANCE'S premiere, occasioned when Babylon first fought off the invaders, was a vital compliment to the skill of the producer. One forgot that, with the fall of the city, fell the Semitic race, and that ever afterwards the Aryan people controlled the affairs of civilization.

HUGUENOT THEME LEAST COMPELLING

The final, and least compelling, theme deals with Catherine de Medici and her instigation of the massacre of the Huguenots in Paris in 1572 under the cloak of religion. The personal side of the story deals with two Huguenot lovers, victims of the cruel religious persecution. This theme has been carefully staged, in the bigness of its court interiors, the depth of its street scenes, and its handling of the ruthless massacre.

The defense of Babylon brings the first half of INTOLERANCE to a big climax, while the last portion is largely given over to the climax of the modern plot thread. Finally, we are shown the idealistic future, with two armies racing to meet each other, only to throw down their arms and clasp hands. This is banal, of course, but Mr. Griffith intends it to weave the themes together and point to the future, when tolerance will make war and all evils impossible.

A certain symbolical note is touched by frequent, half shadowy, glimpses of a woman rocking a cradle. Mr. Griffith gives programme explanation of the symbolism: "Through all these ages Time brings forth the same passions, the same joys and sorrows, the same hopes and anxieties—symbolized by the cradle 'endlessly rocking.'"

THE CONSTRUCTION OF THE FOUR PLOT THREADS

INTOLERANCE, let us sum up once more, stands at the outpost of the cinema's advance. It has an idea. It has a purpose. From a structural standpoint, the handling and weaving of four plots are revolutionary. There is never a moment's lack of clarity. Each story sweeps to its climax. Since the interest is divided, it would be reasonable to assume that the dramatic interest might, too, be divided. But the grip of INTOLERANCE, to our

214

way of thinking, surpasses THE BIRTH OF A NATION. Power, punch, and real thrills are there—thrills to equal the preceding Griffith spectacle. Its themes are overtopped by spectacular trappings, dwarfing them in a measure. The modern story, in its melodramatic present dayedness, seems a bit below the key of the historical divisions. It is lurid, even conventional, in its final working out. But, in its early moments, it points a caustic finger upon certain phases of modern charity, particularly upon the salaried up-lifter. And it is the one vigorous story of the spectacle.

Griffith makes his point in INTOLERANCE. There are obvious moments, moments a bit overdone, lapses to banality, but, on the whole, INTOLERANCE is a mighty thing. Its spectacular appeal is certain.

The musical arrangement of Joseph Carl Breil has impressive moments. There is no strain, however, to equal the barbaric African theme, which ran through THE BIRTH OF A NATION.

The production has been awaited for new methods of plot handling and production. The mingling of four themes of different periods, told in parallel form, has not been tried before. It was a daring experiment. The method of blending the plots, switching from one to the other, is adroitly done. It will have its effect upon coming productions.

THE PRODUCTION

The spectacle, a number of times reveals close-ups of characters' faces which occupy the whole screen. Sometimes these advance in the camera eye to full screen size. It is an effective way of driving home the dramatic mood of the scene.

We find Griffith making his usual frequent and effective use of detail, as in the flashes of the doves in the shadows of the house as Christ passes, the close-ups of the Hebrews in the Judean streets, the page boy half asleep in French court, and the modern girl tending her pitiful little geranium in her tenement room.

Skillful use is made of camera tricks in handling the seeming hurling of soldiers from the Babylonian walls. We apparently see them strike the ground in front of the camera.

Care has been taken with the sub-titles. The bombastic captions of THE BIRTH OF A NATION are absent. Some humor and much historical information are to be found in the sub-captions of INTOLERANCE.

The camera work everywhere is beautifully artistic. We recall, for instance, nothing in screen production more striking than the episode of Christ and the woman taken in adultery.

CAST OF INTOLERANCE LONG AND ABLE

The cast of principals is long and able. Mae Marsh stands pre-eminent for her touching playing of the girl of the modern story. Seena Owen makes a striking and unforgettable figure as Attarea, the favorite of Belshazzar. She lends genuine appeal to the picturesque role. Constance Talmadge gives buoyancy and spirit to the mountain girl. Miriam Cooper sounds a certain poignant note as a modern girl wrecked on the wheel of sorid city life. Marjorie Wilson has opportunity to reveal little more than prettiness as the Huguenot heroine.

Robert Harron makes the most of his role of the boy of the modern story, almost a victim on the altar of modern intolerance. Alfred Paget's playing of Belshazzar has nobility and humanness. Tully Marshall makes the High Priest of Bel sinister and clean cut.

There are scores of slender roles well done. Prominent among these is the huge faithful warrior of Elmo Lincoln, who dies fighting for his king against hopeless odds. The kindly policeman of the modern story, done by Tom Wilson, stands out. Louis Romaine gives realism to the prison chaplain.

215

All in all, INTOLERANCE is a stupendous production. It has the romance of four civilizations.

Frederick James Smith

INTOLERANCE   **FILM 1916**

Excerpt from "Second Thoughts on First Nights," Alexander Woollcott, *The New York Times*, September 10, 1916, Section 2, p. 5.

Unprecedented and indescribable splendor of pageantry is combined with grotesque incoherence of design and utter fatuity of thought to make the long-awaited new Griffith picture at the Liberty an extraordinary mixture of good and bad—of wonderful and bad. Ever since he unfolded THE BIRTH OF A NATION to an astonished world, there have been sundry efforts—all of them painfully unsuccessful—to rival or even approach it. And, although as a fulfillment of the promise of his first big picture, INTOLERANCE is a severe disappointment, Mr. Griffith has always seemed, and still seems, the one most likely to give us the great motion picture of this generation.

To those watching with curiosity, if not with warm interest, the tumultuous development of the movies, Griffith alone has seemed to hold their secret. It is a little as though a piano had been left as a new, mysterious and potentially glorious instrument on the shore of an unexplored South Sea island. Many natives approach it tentatively until one strikes a key by accident. Then they all swarm forward and bang away with enormous complacency. Perhaps they can play one note as well as Paderewski but their compositions are apalling. This until—wonder of wonders—one among them goes to the instrument and, being something of a genius, strikes from it chords of beautiful harmony. How still more wonderful would it be if only he had a great composition to play!

For, in his more ambitious projects, Mr. Griffith has had strange inspirations. It has been as though a Wagner were asked to weave a great music drama from a novel by Harold Bell Wright, as though Maeterlinck were called upon to dramatize Marie Corelli. His BIRTH OF A NATION was discolored from its source in the most paltry Dixonese, and his present composition is derived from the cloudiest thought imaginable.

For his new picture, Mr. Griffith has taken two stories and woven them together as two separate threads are woven in a skein. The first is a striking melodrama of the slums, differing from the ordinary movie thriller only by the cunning of the photography, the thin veneer of sociological import and the enchanting play of expression on that most exquisitely sensitive face the screen has found—Mae Marsh's. The second is a historical pageant of the fall of Babylon. Interwoven with them are the more slender and more intermittent threads which trace the massacre of St. Bartholomew's Eve and follow Christ from the first miracle to the Cross. And Mr. Griffith calls it all INTOLERANCE.

This scheme of interweaving stories is promising, but of a value as yet undemonstrated, so complete, in this instance, is the confusion of the skein in which are tangled such utterly unrelated threads. The two minor currents of narrative and suggestion are sufficiently illustrative of intolerance, but not so the major episodes. They have no bearing on the idea whatsoever. As a high-handed philosopher of history Mr. Griffith outdoes all others. The best of them is a bit devious, straining a point here and there, perhaps, to prove history by the food-supply theory, say, or the climate theory or what not. But it has remained for Mr. Griffith to achieve a philosophy of history by a bland misuse of words and their meanings. The method is simple. You take any historical fact, from a Persian siege to a modern prison, and call it an example of intolerance. It may not be an example of intolerance, but never mind. Call it that, and there you are. By this method has Mr. Griffith brought an extraordinary jumble under

27. D. W. Griffith: the multi-storied INTOLERANCE (1916): "The principal appeal of IN-
TOLERANCE, however, lies in the Babylonian Story." Constance Talmadge, as "the boisterous
little mountain girl who loves the king from afar," amuses herself with a lesser personage: Elmer
Clifton as The Rhapsode.

one magic name. In puzzling over this incoherence, you are inclined to guess, and indeed it is only fair to assume that he started with one idea and finished with another, that the entire Babylonian episode was devised and possibly completed before the intolerance idea ever entered his head. So what he proffers as a spectacular "lay-over for meddlers" is really nothing of the sort. It is a pity this huge effort of the pre-eminent director should have in it so much to provoke the patronizing smile. And incidentally Mr. Griffith was scarcely entitled to berate *intolerance,* even in this confused manner, after the offensively bigoted Simon Legreeism of his own BIRTH OF A NATION.

The parts of INTOLERANCE that defy criticism are the beautiful vistas in old Jerusalem and the entire reconstruction of ancient Babylon. Griffith waves his wand, and, after many centuries, the ancient city rises from its ashes. The imagination and personal force represented in such an achievement suggest a man of stature. Really, Mr. Griffith ranks with Cyrus. They both have taken Babylon. And the Babylonian picture would in itself be worth going miles to see. Here are splendors for you—scenes of wonder that richly reward a visit to the Liberty. . . .

INTOLERANCE   **FILM 1916**

Excerpt from "Comment and Suggestion," "Motion Pictures," Frederick James Smith, *The New York Dramatic Mirror,* Vol. 76, No. 1970, September 23, 1916, p. 19.

GRIFFITH FINDS A NEW PHOTOPLAY FORM

Let us, once for all, consider the argument, advanced by a number of theatrical reviewers, that INTOLERANCE is incoherent. These critics, knowing little or nothing of the screen drama, are puzzled by the film spectacle's lack of so-called dramatic technique. Indeed, the screen authorities seem puzzled by its variance with accepted script standards.

Mr. Griffith himself explains this point. "Events are not set forth in their historical sequence, or according to accepted forms of dramatic construction, but *as they might flash across a mind seeking to parallel the life of the different ages.*"

The spectacle is developing a new technique. INTOLERANCE is a first step. Other producers will follow.

The Griffith spectacle is not incoherent. It is told by a new means. It is not confused. It builds its structure securely. But it builds in a new fashion.

* * *

A few of the commentors have noted in INTOLERANCE the dawning of a new photoplay form. The parallel stories of the spectacle are told in a multitude of interlarded flashes, being—as Mr. Griffith explains—a visualized mental process.

What effect will this have upon the future development of the screen? Let us approve of the Boston *Transcript's* hope that "American producers take the technical freedom of INTOLERANCE to heart and get away from many of the stiff conventions of the present-day method of telling a story on the screen."

THE BUILDING OF INTOLERANCE

Missing this vital point of the spectacle, Alexander Woollcott, the critic of the New York *Times,* advances the theory that Griffith started with one idea and finished with another—that the entire Babylonian episode "was devised and possibly completed before the intolerance idea ever entered his head." This argument Mr. Woollcott advances to explain what he terms the spectacle's "grotesque incoherence of design and utter fatuity of thought."

Griffith, we understand, conceived and created the modern portion of INTOLERANCE first, terming it THE MOTHER AND THE LAW. Then the intolerance idea grew in his mind, and he built the Babylonian, Judean and Medici themes to present that ethical propaganda. Thus grew INTOLERANCE.

***

Just how the dawn of a new photoplay form—an outgrowth of the flashback—came to the director we cannot judge. Professor Hugo Münsterberg has delved into the photodrama from this angle. Possibly Griffith started out to startle by his virtuosity in handling four themes—and hit upon the new film empire. We doubt this, however. It seems legitimately conceived by a man well able to conceive it.

* * *

THE EVOLUTION OF GRIFFITH

"The [general] effect is naturally a stunning departure from the customary moving picture, developed though it is from Mr. Griffith's own invention, the 'flash back,' " says the Boston *Transcript* in commenting upon INTOLERANCE. "But it is not so much of a departure from Mr. Griffith's past as many may think. Just as the two distinct stories told, one following another, in the two halves of THE BIRTH, may be traced technically to his earlier Biograph films, THE BATTLE and THE BATTLE AT ELDERBUSH GULCH, so you may find 'studies' for the various parts of INTOLERANCE in other films made in those almost prehistoric but immortal days when the future of the photoplay and of Mr. Griffith was being made at the old Biograph studios. The slum life of the modern story in INTOLERANCE was handled in half a dozen films like THE MUSKETEERS OF PIG ALLEY, blending the romance of the 'gun man' with an intimate realism of treatment. The fall of Babylon had its prototype in JUDITH OF BETHULIA. The Christ story has figured in a dozen bits of allegory in photoplays of other periods. The Renaissance of Charles IX is almost wholly novel to the screen, but Griffith has handled Italian costume of that period in THE PERFIDY OF MARY and THE BLIND PRINCESS AND THE POET. There is even a bit of Mr. Griffith's old 'Pickford stuff'—as the 'trade' calls the impetuous precocities of that 'favorite'—in the girl from the mountains who descends upon Babylon, displays her tempestuous talents in the marriage market, and ends by driving a rocking chariot to the relief of the city."

* * *

"The element of propaganda was just as evident in the old Biograph days," continues the *Transcript*. "Mr. Griffith has always been fascinated by the ability of the films to show, both in action and in printed 'leaders,' an ethical point of view. He taught a sort of cave-man pathology in MAN'S GENESIS, wherein Weak Hands defeated Brute Force by wit in battle for Lily White; he showed the eternal struggle of the scholar-husband and the light-minded dancer-wife in OIL AND WATER; he made a sort of 'Everywoman' of the films in THE BLIND PRINCESS AND THE POET; and the list might be continued almost indefinitely.

"The final parallel in Mr. Griffith's past is HOME SWEET HOME, a film from which one might draw up the whole structure of INTOLERANCE, with one technical exception. In that film, he showed us first John Howard Payne writing his famous song in the midst of a riotous life, to which death brought no atonement. Then came three separate stories, 219 one of a small town, one of the sea coast and one of society, in which the moral effect of that song was demonstrated. Then he saw, as a final allegory, Payne in hell and progressing to heaven by virtue of the power of his song. The comparison is clear in all but one regard. The parallel stories of INTOLERANCE are developed in a hundred interlarded flashes, whereas those of HOME SWEET HOME came one after another, each complete and consecutive.

"As to Mr. Griffith's success with his strange mixture of his own and the world's past and his strange excursion into a new photoplay form, there may be, of course, a dozen different opinions.". . .

INTOLERANCE   **FILM 1916**

Excerpts from "The Shadow Stage," Julian Johnson, *Photoplay Magazine*, Vol. 11, No. 1, December, 1916, pp. 77-81.

The metropolitan critics who preceded me in learned discourse upon Mr. Griffith's sun-play, INTOLERANCE, shot away all the superlatives which were our common property. Thus deprived of the communal ammunition I must lay about me with a week-day set of words and present facts garnished neither with rhapsody nor raillery.

INTOLERANCE is a collective story of the penalites paid through the centuries to those "who do not believe as we believe." It occupied its maker's attention for at least a year and a half. Both the notion and the generalship are his. INTOLERANCE is more than the world's biggest photoplay. In size and scope it is the biggest art-work of any description in a decade.

Here is a joy-ride through history; a Cook's tour of the ages; a college education crammed into a night. It is the most incredible experiment in story-telling that has ever been tried. Its uniqueness lies not in a single yarn, but in the way its whole skein of yarns is plaited.

Its distinct periods are four: Babylon, at the end of the regency of Prince Belshazzar; Judea, in the time of Christ; France under the inquisitorial high tide of St. Bartholomew's; and the American Now, with the intolerances of capital, labor, and the courts. None of these tales runs straightaway. You stand in medieval France and slip on the banana-peel of retrogression to Chaldea. You are sure America has you—a wink has aviated you back to Palestine. It is much like listening to a quartette of excellent elecutionists simultaneously reading novels by Arnold Bennett, Victor Hugo, Nathaniel Hawthorne and Elinor Glyn. . . .

There has never been such scenery, anywhere, as the edifices reared for the Babylonian episode.

Pictorially, the greatest filmings are the Judean scenes, perfect in composition, ideal in lighting, every one in effect a Tissot painting of the time of Christ.

The Chaldean visions will teach history to college professors.

Altogether, the accuracy and authority of INTOLERANCE's historic information is stupendous.

The finest individual acting accomplishments are Mae Marsh's. The unique figure is Constance Talmadge, as The Mountain Girl; the most poignantly beautiful, Seena Owen, as Attarea, favorite of Belshazzar. But there are no male assumptions even approaching the chief portrayals in THE BIRTH OF A NATION.

Mr. Bitzer's photography, devoid of anything sensational, flows like the transparent, limpid style of a finished writer. It is without tricks, and without imperfections.

An attempt to assimilate the mountainous lore of this sun-play at a sitting results in positive mental exhaustion. The universally-heard comment from the highbrow or nobrow who has tried to get it all in an evening: "I am so tired!"

Profoundest of symbols is the Rocking Cradle—"uniter of here and hereafter"—which joins the episodes. This mysterious ark of life, the stuff of a dream in the dimness of its great shadowed room, almost belongs to infinity. Lillian Gish is the brooding mother.

The music is sadly inefficient—the most inefficient music a big picture ever had.

Thousands upon thousands of feet of this photoplay never will be seen by the public. In the taking, this story rambled in every direction, and D. W. G. relentlessly and recklessly pursued each ramble to its end. At least half a dozen complete minor stories were cut off before the picture was shown at all.

In all probability, INTOLERANCE will never attain the popularity of THE BIRTH OF A NATION. It has not that drama's single, sweeping story. It appeals more to the head, less to the heart.

Babylon is the foundation-stone, and seems to have been the original inspiration, of this visual Babel. Its mighty walls, its crowds, its army, have won many long-drawn "Ahs!" of sky-rocket admiration. But these were not essentially Griffith—anyone with money can pile up mobs and scenery. Mr. Griffith's original talent appears in re-creating the passions, the ambitions, the veritable daily life of a great people so remote that their every monument is dust, their every art-work lost, their very language forgotten. This is more than talent; it is genius.

You were taught that the Jewish Jehovah traced destruction's warning in letters of fire on the wall of Belshazzar's palace; and that Cyrus, to get in, drained the Euphrates river and walked on its bed under Babylon's gates. See this picture and get the facts. Babylon was peacefully betrayed by the priests of Marduk long after it had successfully withstood as frenzied a siege as the Persian conqueror could bring.

Not content with rearing the vast barriers and marvellous gates you have seen illustratively reproduced in these pages, the California necromancer showed life as it ran its slender course among the poor more than twenty-five centuries ago. Always of this undercurrent is The Mountain Girl, a wild, wonderful little creature, to be followed from semi-slavery through the civic courts to the marriage market, where she is released by an impress from the roll-seal Belshazzar has strapped upon his wrist. Thereafter she is, to the death, a sweet Amazon in the service of her great *Sar*. The camp of Cyrus, with the "Institution" of the Medes and Persians, is as instructive as a West-Asiatic history. The attack upon Babylon, with its terrible towers, its demoniac "tank" of Greek fire—flaming prophecy of the Somme juggernauts!—its ferocious personal encounters, is unparalleled in battle spectacles. Behold the vivid though perhaps dubious realism of gushy close-ups of sword-thrusts. Heads literally fly off above shearing swords, hot lead sears, rocks crush, arrows pierce horridly—and withal there is the unconquerable animation and fury of ultimate conflict.

Otherwheres, the sensuous glory of the Chaldean court. No brush-master has painted more Oriental splendors than those boasted by the golden bungalow of Nabonidus, quaint father of the virile voluptuary, Belshazzar. Beauty blooms in wildest luxuriance in this New York of the Euphrates. The dances of Tammuz, god of springtime, flash forth in breath-taking nudity and rhythm as frank as meaningful. They are flashes, only; that is why they remain in the picture. One cannot imagine a more beautiful thing than Seena Owen as Attarea—a veritable star of the East. The tiny battle-chariot with its cargo of a great white rose, drawn down the table to Attarea's Belshazzar by two white doves, chances to remain the only untouched thing in the palace of death which Cyrus enters. There is pathos! Tully Marshall as the High Priest of Bel, Elmer Clifton as the Rhapsode, George Siegmann as Cyrus—three players who are especially redoubtable.

The magical David [Griffith] pounds his points home by contrast. From the solemn grandeur of Ishtar's high altar, with its costly burnt offering of propitiation, he flashes to an aged widow offering her all to the same deity—three turnips and a carrot, covered with a little oil.

221

The France which our film-etcher rears for the massacre of St. Bartholomew is as fine a France as Stanley Weyman pictured in words. Griffith spares neither exactness nor feeling. With delicate touches he builds up keen interest in the home of Brown Eyes—then slaughters the whole family. Wonderful characters here are Josephine Crowell's Catherine de Medici; and Charles IX, as played by Frank Bennett.

Much has been taken from the Judean scenes, but so much remains to hail as optic poetry that the loss is negligible. I can think of nothing finer in the handling of light, nor in the massing and moving of figures, than the "marriage in Cana." More education! The complete wedding rite, with its odd observances according to Hebrew tradition, is a transcription from Minor Asia such as one cannot find outside the pages of Josephus. Stirringly dramatic, yet faithful to the letter of the gospels, is the scene in which Jesus faces those who would stone the woman taken in adultery. There is a scene of The Christ laughing, conversing, supping, interchanging views—a man among men. And there is the *Via Dolorosa*.

The modern story is, among other things and preachments, an attack upon the arrogance of "Foundations," and that tyranny of some organized charities which makes their favored more victims than beneficiaries. In its essence, the modern tale seems to me a dull, commonplace movie melodrama. In it Mr. Griffith seems to lose his perspective of character. He makes commonplace types and personifications, not his usual creatures: thinking, feeling men and women.

Mae Marsh and Robert Harron portray victims of poverty, lack of education and evil surrounding. Both are driven from the home town by strike participation. The boy turns *cadet*—eventually reforms to marry Mae. His underworld master, "The Musketeer of the Slums," frames him criminally for this desertion, and, in the language of the caption, he is "intolerated away for awhile." In the interim, the Musketeer endeavors to "make" the boy's wife, who has lost her baby to intolerant uplifters. In the grand encounter of Musketeer, Musketeer's girl, boy and wife, the monster is shot, the boy is blamed though the mistress did it, and the capital sentence is carried out—nearly, but not quite—in the perfect gallows-technique of San Quentin penitentiary.

Best in the modern spectacle are not the dull details of things that happen, but the lifelike performances of those to whom they happen. Mae Marsh's flirtation in court with her husband as the jury deliberates his life away—she a scared, drab little figure of piteous noncomprehension—here is a twittering smile more tragic than the orotund despairs of Bernhardt. Miriam Cooper, as the Musketeer's mistress, gives an overwhelming pastel of jealousy and remorse. All actresses who honestly provide for home and baby by the business of vamping and gunning, would do well to observe Miss Cooper's expressions and gestures. Miss Cooper is police dock—she is blotter transcript. Her face is what you *really* see some nights under the green lamps. Harron is ideal as the boy, and Walter Long, as the Musketeer, approaches but does not equal his performance of Gus, in THE BIRTH OF A NATION.

Spades are not once termed garden implements in this sector, nor are the kisses paternal or platonic.

In this stupendous chaos of history and romance the lack of a virile musical score is the chief tragedy. Proper melody would have bound the far provinces of this loose empire of mighty imagination into a strong, central kingdom.

I wish Mr. Griffith had worked out a whole evening of his great Babylonian story. Sticking to this alone, he would have added an art-product to literature as enduring as Flaubert's *Salammbo*.

If I may predict: he will never again tell a story in this manner. Nor will anyone else. The blue sea is pretty much where it was when the sails of the Argonauts bellied tight in the winds of a morning world, and so are the people who live in the world. Still we wish to follow, undisturbed, the adventures of a single set of characters, or to thrill with a

28. *D. W. Griffith: INTOLERANCE: "the sensuous glory of the Chaldean court. . . . Beauty blooms in wildest luxuriance in this New York of the Euphrates." The tremendous set for the great hall.*

single pair of lovers. Verily, when the game is hearts, two's company, and the lovers of four ages an awful crowd. . . .

Vachel Lindsay's review of Hugo Münsterberg's book serves as an introduction to his comments on INTOLERANCE, and also as an obituary of Münsterberg himself, a Harvard professor whose field was experimental psychology and who died on the verge of writing a new series of articles about films.

The Diaghilev Russian Ballet, with Nijinsky, had been seen in America for the first time in 1916, and was engaged in its second American tour when Lindsay's review appeared.

"PHOTOPLAY PROGRESS" 1917

By Vachel Lindsay, *The New Republic*, Vol. 10, No. 120, February 17, 1917, pp. 76-77.

The Photoplay, a Psychological Study, by Hugo Münsterberg. New York: D. Appleton and Company. $1.00

Saturday afternoon, December sixteenth, here in my home town, I happened to be talking to the woman's club on the motion picture. I took the opportunity to speak of our particular debt to Professor Münsterberg's little book, *The Photoplay*. So it was with the feeling of the sudden loss of a comrade in a new quest that I read of his death in the bulletins in the State Register window that very evening.

Like most readers of *The New Republic* I could not have conversed with him long at a time on international matters. But I had had a most gratifying correspondence with the professor about the films. I had anticipated a glorious evening with him in some photoplay theatre this spring, where we would have been absolutely at one in our joy in the hopeful young art.

The Moving Picture World, the thunderer of the screen journals, says in large print, in the number for January 6th, 1917: "In the death of Professor Hugo Münsterberg, the motion pictures loses a firm friend and advocate. He was a close student of the possibilities of the pictures along educational and test lines, and had he lived it is very probable that pictures would have been liberally used in the universities within a short time."

Münsterberg shows in his book that the most routine motion picture has in all its apparently mechanical circumstances the beginnings of art. The book builds up out of these intrinsic qualities the higher photoplay as it is and may be.

The professor writes a noble declaration of independence for the photoplay artist. He gives him a charter of freedom, based on these intrinsic qualities, a charter of freedom that in many ways resembles that of the musical composer, and in others that of the philosopher.

First for practical reasons, then for theoretical, I have opposed music while the film is running. But so many of my friends have condemned my anti-musical position as the weakest place in my armor, that I have told them to read Münsterberg, and work out the faith that is in them. Possibly because philosophy is close to music, and music is the most mathematical and scientific of the arts, the book offers a basis on which such a faith can be founded, though it is not explicit in the book. But to this end I further recommend an article in a recent number of *Reedy's Mirror* (St. Louis), entitled The Movies and Music. It is by Richard L. Stokes, and well done, nine generous columns. Beginning with Münsterberg, he theorizes into hypothetical existence a photoplay

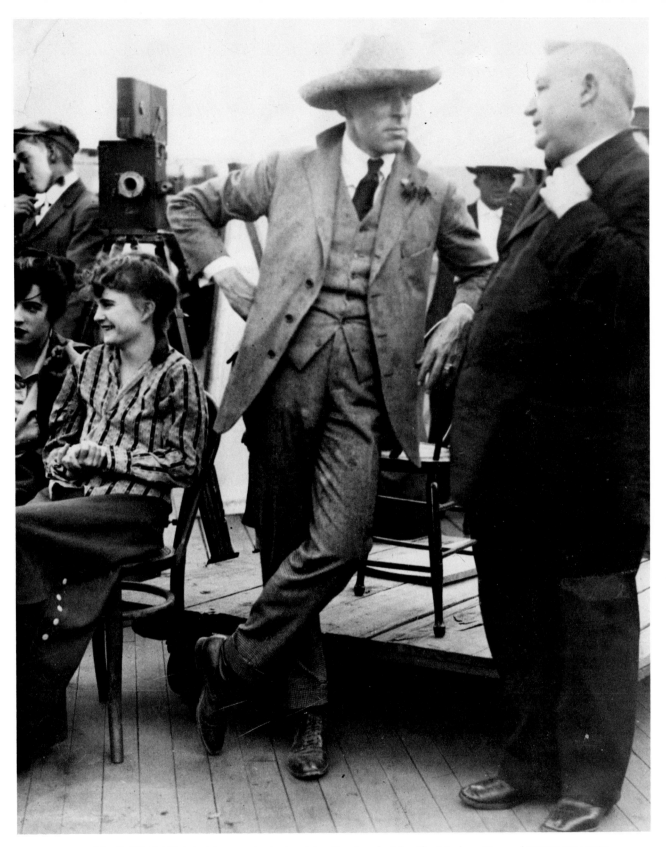

29. *D. W. Griffith (with straw hat) about to direct a shot for the Modern Story of INTOLERANCE. Below his right elbow: Mae Marsh, sitting with Miriam Cooper. Vachel Lindsay was to write of the film: "The ages make a resonance behind . . .simple plans and terrible perplexities."*

cousin of Wagner Opera and Russian Ballet. But at present music and the motion picture are not often speaking acquaintances, no matter though they be stretched upon the same gilded procrustean bed.

While Münsterberg does not utterly neglect the pictorial side of the films, he dwells more upon the motion qualities. Certainly a just balance of these elements, and a study of previous arts that include them must go into the theory of criticism. By dwelling upon the motion in its deeper meaning our psychologist, in his most notable declaration, shows how the films have set us free. He says, page 173: *"The photoplay tells us the human story by overcoming the forms of the outer world; namely, space, time and causality, and by adjusting the events to the forms of the inner world: namely, attention, memory, imagination and emotion."*

And he italicizes a little later: *"While the moving pictures are lifted above the world of space and time and causality, and are freed from its bonds, they are certainly not without law."* This law, stated a little later, is: *"The perfect unity of plot and pictorial appearance."*

Münsterberg, in these declarations, and others, unintentionally wrote the guide-book to the newest photoplay experiment, INTOLERANCE.

People have spoken of Griffith's alleged "sheer sensationalism" in his plot in which he shows four periods of time conversing with one another. But jumping back and forth over barriers of time is the most accepted thing in the photoplay hurdle-race. You have seen films where the hero has visions of his childhood to urge him on to doughty deeds. Three scenes of the past alternate with three scenes of to-day in his thoughts, that the comparison may be rousing. The heroine has visions of her two possible futures if she chooses the prunes on the one hand or the peaches on the other. And as to jumping over geographical spaces, the photoplay dialogue that technically replaces the old stage interchange of words is a conversation between places, not individuals. In a moonshiner drama that I saw last week the director alternated the cabin in the field, the revenue detectives on the road and the still on the hillside. We were given a conversation between these units. One picture, guns, horses, detectives and all seemed to be calling, "We are coming." Another picture, the still, the bushes and the hillside seemed to be answering: "We are hiding yet." The picture of the cabin, the field and the young moonshiners seemed to say: "We suspect nothing, but are on guard on general principles." Round and round this conversation progresses as the pictures alternate, till the still is finally destroyed, and the cabin besieged and taken.

The principle holds good, no matter how lofty the theme, or how far apart the places in the dialogue may be in time or geographical distance. In Griffith's INTOLERANCE, Babylon is shown signalling across the ages to Judea, and there is many a message that is not printed out on the films or put into the apparently explicit publicity matter. And in like manner the days of St. Bartholomew and of the crucifixion signal back to Babylon sharp or vague or subtle messages. The little factory couple in the modern street scene called The Dear One and The Boy, seem to wave their hands back to Babylon amid the orchestration of ancient memories. The ages make a resonance behind their simple plans and terrible perplexities. The usual shallowness of appeal of private griefs and loves as shown in the most painstaking intimate films, their inability to arouse complete responding passion in the audience, is thus remedied. The modern story is made vibrant by the power of whirling crowds from the streets of Time. The key hieroglyphic is the cradle of humanity, eternally rocking. This photoplay is given power not by straining for depth of passion, but depth of what might be called tableau-emotion, a much more elusive thing.

But we have applied only one of Münsterberg's conclusions to the film. I would advise the reader to go rapidly through the book, find the drift of the italicized passages, go to INTOLERANCE, then re-read the book carefully, then go to INTOLERANCE again. For the most part neither the book nor the film have been estimated in any but a nickelodeon way. Their profound relation has not been noted, when it is to the credit of both Münsterberg and Griffith, and should contribute to the progress of aesthetics in America, before film or book are old. What appears to be the high austere opposite of this film may be born by the study of it. But blind condemnation or blind submission gets us nowhere. And the same may be said of the book, that has been elaborately praised, but completely ignored, by the professional photoplay critics of the big newspapers.

Vachel Lindsay

30. Mary Pickford, "America's Sweetheart." "Any Pickford picture is an event in film circles, and . . . it is standing-room-only time as well." "Little Mary" was earning $1,000,000 a year in 1917 and charming such a critic as Vachel Lindsay into seeing one of her films six times.

CHAPTER **12**

A Good Girl and a Bad One: Mary Pickford and Theda Bara

COMMENTARY

Third of the stars cited by The Times **as earning $1,000,000 a year in 1917 was Mary Pickford (1893-), "America's Sweetheart," who first entered films at Biograph in 1909. The three features reviewed here were all made between 1915 and 1917. Perhaps Vachel Lindsay brings us closest to her in his observations about A ROMANCE OF THE REDWOODS, directed by the fast-risen Cecil B. DeMille. Lindsay saw the film six times.**

Lindsay confuses Mary Pickford's stage appearance in Belasco's A Good Little Devil **(1912) with her film of IN THE BISHOP'S CARRIAGE; she returned to films after her Belasco success. Annette Kellermann was a swimmer and diver whose one-piece bathing suit was very daring for the time.**

Miss Pickford's curls and coaxing manner, so indispensable to the movie audience in the first and second decades of this century, were wholesome entertainment in the Jazz Age of the Twenties. The screen conundrum for Mary Pickford to solve was: how to win attention as a good girl in the age of flappers.

In 1919 she, Charlie Chaplin, Douglas Fairbanks, and D. W. Griffith formed their own company: United Artists.

FILM 1915   ESMERALDA

Excerpt from "Feature Films of the Week: ESMERALDA," The New York Dramatic Mirror, Vol. 74, No. 1917, September 15, 1915, pp. 32-33.

. . . Any Pickford picture is an event in film circles, and take it from the Strand audience, it is standing-room only time as well. For "Little Mary" packs the aisles and throws the announcer into hoarse despair, a most remarkable performance on a hot Summer's night. But it was in no way more remarkable than the offering which the sweltering patrons of pictures' most popular actress had paid and suffered to see, for while Pickford pictures are always worth while, this chances to be one of the Pickford photopeaks, that, ranking with HEARTS ADRIFT and TESS OF THE STORM COUNTRY, may look down upon anything as presumptuous as a mere feature picture.

Pickford pictures also differ in another way, this having to deal with a matter of script treatment, a bit of foresight that aims to give photo-fans every bit of pleasure they may derive from the treasured features and looks of its diminutive favorite. Not even the least important scene may be omitted. "Little Mary" must enter a door, must close it from the inside, mount the stairs, and repeat the performance with her access to her own room. And did Mr. Kirkwood [the director] fail to allow her to pause on the stairs or to show her in at least one close-up every hundred feet, every fondly critical standee would be able to tell at once where her director had made his vital error. It is, moreover, an old-fashioned Pickford that greets her audiences, one with little bonnet, treasured muff, and sleeves puffed at the shoulders that wins the instant approval in another get-up. And it is the kind of a character that allows her to move the assembled devotees to tears and smiles in alternate waves of perfect understanding at the trials of a young country girl whose love affair runs very far from smooth. The audience laughed at the little feminine frills and the spasmodic movements of the girl just as they tried not to let the rest of the celluloid cohort know that "Little Mary's" tears awakened a similar response in front of the screen. Take it all-in-all, it was as fine an opportunity as this charmer has ever had. . . .

POOR LITTLE PEPPINA   FILM 1916

Excerpt from "Feature Films of the Week: POOR LITTLE PEPPINA," *The New York Dramatic Mirror,* Vol. 75, No. 1941, March 4, 1916, p. 28.

. . . To analyze the acting of Mary Pickford is about as satisfactory as trying to draw a definite conclusion from a metaphysical premise. After much circumlocution, after the use of many words and the expenditure of much gray matter one is forced to the inevitable conclusion that Mary Pickford is Mary Pickford. She has a charm, a manner, an expression that is all her own. She seems to have the happy faculty of becoming for the time being the character which she is portraying. At no time does one ever gather the impression that Mary Pickford is acting. She is the epitome of naturalness. But why go on? The sum and substance of it all is that Mary Pickford is unique, and irrespective of the strength or weakness of any picture in which she appears the fact that Mary Pickford appears in it makes it a good picture. . . .

A ROMANCE OF THE REDWOODS   FILM 1917

"Queen of My People," by Vachel Lindsay, *The New Republic,* Vol. 11, No. 140, July 7 1917, pp. 280-281.
> Mary Pickford in A ROMANCE OF THE REDWOODS. Scenario by Cecil
> B. DeMille and Jeanie Macpherson. Produced under the direction of
> Cecil B. DeMille. Presented by the Artcraft Pictures Corporation.

This is a Lasky production, by the same group that gave JOAN THE WOMAN. For star we have Mary Pickford instead of Geraldine Farrar. Jeanie Macpherson and DeMille give us, in the scenario, an American heroine they can understand. Our photoplays depend for their final advancement upon good scenario writers. The scenario carries everything upon its back like a camel. Most scenarios have exceedingly weak backs. *Wid's* "The Bradstreets of Filmdom" says the plot is *The Girl of the Golden West,* plus *Salomy Jane.* But it carries its load fairly well, I think, and *Wid's* thinks so too.

The production might be called The Doll, the Derringer and the Mask, and into it steps the queen of my people, Mary Pickford. There is an old vaudeville song, Every American Girl is a Queen. O. Henry believed that, and we have his shop-girl stories. Democracy crowns those it loves. Mary is a queen in especial, born from an all-conquering machine. The story of her rise is so romantic the fans have almost forgiven her fish-eyed exploiters.

230   When the nickelodeon was a black and stinking conspiracy, with a sagging sheet for a

screen, with few lights but the lantern itself, the films were scratched till they looked like a rainstorm of pitchforks and hay wagons. They were hurried through for the sake of blurring the storm. Some one dashed past the pitchforks to our hearts. There she stayed. The would-be Bowery tough who took the tickets wrote to a similar person higher up. A portrait was put in front of the cave, when all other actors were anonymous. "Little Mary." Not the full name. Just "Little Mary."

After reigning alone a long time in her cave of Adullam, suddenly the child was gone. She was a Broadway star, the first one made by the outlawed films. She had the leading part in Belasco's production of *In the Bishop's Carriage*. We found her full name was Mary Pickford. In due season Mary came back to her people, and such a shout went up from the backwoods that all Broadway was moved with envy. A hundred queens plunged into the films, disputing the first, but we remembered Mary from the days of old. Stupid directors now conventionalized her first aspect among the pitchforks, no matter how she begged to break away. Her Frohman, Artcraft and other productions were department store wares. Her direst slums were stagy. TESS OF THE STORM COUNTRY, HEARTS ADRIFT, SUCH A LITTLE QUEEN, RAGS, HULDA FROM HOLLAND, LESS THAN THE DUST, THE PRIDE OF THE CLAN, etc., were winsome monkeyshines, varied with strained melodramas—of late stretched to seven reels. Her directors did their best to make her personal appearance like that of the young female on the cover of the *Cosmopolitan Magazine*. In some ways she was the little Eva of this generation. A POOR LITTLE RICH GIRL is her most successful rollick in her baby manner. Sometimes in that film she is innocent eight, sometimes dangerous sixteen, with no notice given of change of time.

In the audience last night were at least seven maidens wearing the Mary Pickford curls that mix up eight and sixteen. Girls wear them to the age of twenty-two. They wear them to the university classes, unless spoken to by the dean of women. Walk three blocks and note how, though no fashion magazines have endorsed it, Mary Pickford is imitated as was Queen Victoria in her youth. You say other stars have this fortune. Not to the Pickford excesses.

In the ROMANCE OF THE REDWOODS she hides her curls. She is Jennie Lawrence, a New England girl. The refinement of the type is emphasized by the delicacy of the lighting, etc. Art gallery qualities are imparted to her and her eloquent trappings by art director Wilfred Buckland and cameraman Alvin Wycoff. The film is eighty-eight minutes long, seven reels. It should be five reels, with more sorting of the chief properties.

Yet they are significant, and good to look upon. It is the year '49. We have a conversation between the playing-card target in the west, and the piano in New England. Then in the New England parlor, the orphan Jennie Lawrence accepts her mother's last request. It is that she be sent to her uncle, who left for California, two months ago. We are west again. We see a handsome Indian Chief and his braves. The uncle is cut off from the rear of a wagon train. Behind his dead horse he barricades himself, and sells his life dearly. Then the east puts in its word. We see the heroine packing those old fashioned trunks. We see the tiny derringer hidden in the shoe. It is the hieroglyphic symbol of the spirit of Jennie.

In the west, Black Brown, the fugitive, exchanges name, clothing and papers with Jennie's dead uncle, whose body he finds on the road. Thus he turns back a posse. Now the east goes west. We see Jennie landed on the California coast, and starting for Strawberry Flats, which is in classic Calaveras county. We see her fare, two gold slugs, in her mitten. Now bags of dust taken from the Sacramento stage act out two sharp episodes in the cabin of the fake John Lawrence. Then he parades Strawberry Flats with good citizen airs. The home mail is distributed. He is made an uncle, for there is a letter announcing Jennie. Now the redwoods show us the tiny queen at their feet, with her guide and her much loaded burros.

231

Now Jennie is alone in the Lawrence cabin. Black Brown comes. She rows with him with great spirit. Finally he takes her to the gambling hell, with chivalrous permission to tell on him. They are all too wild to listen. He saves her from the grip of Dick Roland, who is drunk enough to think her a barroom hanger-on. At length by her own choice she tells the crowd Brown is her uncle. Now note the hieroglyphics. The arrow hole in the uncle's bloody papers, a black-snake whip, Jennie's little derringer, Brown's six-shooter, the gambling paraphernalia, the silk hat of the boss gambler, the dancing shadows on the doorways, all enable these episodes to be vividly given with few printed words on the screen. Then comes the wolf in the moonlight. He scares Jennie into the cabin. But she will not sleep under that roof. Hence the lantern moving to the stable, the buffalo robe becoming a couch. Later comes the blaze of sunrise in the face of the sleeper. At breakfast everything from griddle cakes to an apron is picture-writing to tell the finely graded progress of Jennie's conquest of the tough.

Later comes the delicate nonsense of the call from lonely hearted Jim Lyn. In a dizzy flirtation the Sacramento paper, the daisy and the skein of yarn are used against both gentlemen. The yarn is Lyn's web of fate. The good-bye bow to Lyn is Mary Pickford, grown up.

Later, doing Brown's mending, the lady finds a handkerchief mask, with eyeholes complete. This mask is as much the headline hieroglyphic of Brown as the derringer is of Jennie. Thus, later, we have a conversation between the girl's hands. She holds the mask in one, in the other a torn letter. It is a letter to Dick Roland from his mother. Dick has been quite gentlemanly and apologetic to our girl. But as a mere adjunct of the day's work the outlaw has just robbed Dick and driven him to a reckless death. Meanwhile Black Brown with this wicked gold buys her a doll, in humorous allusion to her size, but actually the symbol of his tenderness for her, the third outstanding hieroglyphic of the piece.

In the cabin she and Brown have it out in a sign conversation in which the doll is played against the mask and the letter, and later the revelation of Roland's sack of dust. The repentant robber promises to send the gold to the boy's mother, as the letter shows it has been promised. Brown says to Jennie: "I love you, do you understand? Promise me you'll help me, and I'll play straight." It is really what the American people say to their good queen.

The penitent has no luck washing gold. Jennie in his absence begins washing clothes. Bundles of laundry are hieroglyphics for loyalty, taunting, embarrassment. The bandit, wishing to be a generous provider, relapses. He holds up a stage, in which, unknown to him, Jennie and Jim Lyn are going to a picnic. Jennie's little derringer wounds him in the hand. It had missed him back there, when she first met him in the cabin. Mary Pickford is equal to the tragedy of secret recognition as she is equal to several trials of her tragic quality through the story.

Back in the cabin, Jennie has another show-down with her man. The little derringer testifies against a toy pick, a pan of gold-dust, and a wounded hand. Brown vainly tries to introduce a pile of laundry in rebuttal.

Lyn has his suspicions. He precedes the vigilance committee to the cabin. He looks for and finds a derringer-wounded hand. A long rifle-barrel comes through the window. The whole committee enters with guns and *the rope*. Jennie with difficulty wins clemency for Brown. She confesses she is not his niece but his sweetheart. This is without result. Finally she takes the clothes from her doll on the sly. She shows them as baby clothes, implying she is a prospective mother. They grant a grudging parole to Brown. Then a member of the party in a Tippecanoe Benjamin Harrison gray stovepipe hat says: "As justice of the peace of Calaveras County I pronounce you man and wife." The two are allowed to go. Under the redwoods the goddess from the machine takes her dubious hero to her heart, with the face of a mother of men.

232   Last year, in the Chicago Little Theatre, in a talk on the new Irish poetry Padraic

31. Theda Bara as the appraising vampire in GOLD AND THE WOMAN (1916). One of her 39 films for the Fox Film Corporation, it was attacked as usual by the censors: "eliminate two murder scenes . . . all love scenes between vampire and guardian. . . ."

Colum quoted an excellent saying by William Butler Yeats. "Rhetoric is heard, poetry overheard." For the first time in my knowledge, the acting of Mary Pickford is permitted by her directors to have divine accident in it, poetry overheard. Setting and support might be called a high type of rhetoric. We glimpse the make-up boxes of both Belasco and Bret Harte, and later boxes.

The redwoods are a mere backdrop. Redwoods might count as much in a great film as the epic Mississippi does in *Huckleberry Finn*, or the ocean in Pierre Loti's *Iceland Fisherman*. The DeMille aggregation has the intelligence and refinement to produce such a result if they can find genius somewhere. Let them go forward. Let them give us short-story films. Let them leave behind the make-up boxes and the dramas. Let them look more toward the Pacific, and more deeply into the redwoods. Let them rehabilitate people like Annette Kellermann or Henry Walthall. Walthall has been spoiled of late by bad photography, scenarios and directing. Annette Kellermann has always had bad photography, scenarios and directing. These two have been more unfortunate than Mary.

Mae Marsh is a finer actress and artist than Mary Pickford. She has had better directing. Mary Pickford has the advantage of a unique and lonely start. Naturally the first-born of the films has been given the crown. It is also a great deal in a time of sorrow to be the incarnation of the Happy Ending.

In the ROMANCE OF THE REDWOODS it begins to appear that the higher the imagination of Mary Pickford's scenario writer and director, the more sensitive her response. If there is anything in a film at all it is worth seeing three times. I went to this one six times because I was glad Mary was beginning to emerge. I have found her portrait among Botticelli's muses in the Chicago Art Institute. Botticelli is classed as a sophisticated person. To repudiate this girl in haste is high treason to the national heart. America says to her silly little saint: "I love you. Do you understand? Promise me you'll help me, and I'll play straight."

Vachel Lindsay.

COMMENTARY

Although it was rumored that Theda Bara (1890-1955) was far from the million dollar bracket in salary, she had nevertheless embarked on her career with a vampire film, A FOOL THERE WAS (1915), which was reputed to have brought the Fox Film Corporation a profit of exactly that amount.

Fox rushed her through 38 more features in the next five years; in some of them, as a Vampire, she committed ever more monstrous crimes against domesticity, and in others, as a non-Vampire, she drew yawns at the box office. She saw herself as demure, but there was no escaping the Carmens, the Cleopatras, and the Salomes for Theda Bara.

One fatal day, quite early in the flash of her brief reign, audiences began to laugh at the excesses of her scenarios, and by 1919 her career was virtually over.

Finally, as the century neared its third decade, she fell victim to the emergent Flapper, who stripped her of her most valuable properties: allure, aggression, and impatience at the sight of marriage.

The Kansas Board of Censors, perpetually gunning for her films, rejected the first four *in toto*. What it did to others is indicated below.

Her reputation now rests almost entirely on missing films.

A FOOL THERE WAS
FILM 1915

"Reviews of Feature Films," *The New York Dramatic Mirror*, Vol. 73, No. 1883, January 20, 1915, p. 31.

Adaptation of Porter Emerson Browne's Play of the Same Name. Produced in Six Parts by William Fox for the Box Office Attraction Company. Directed by Frank Powell.

John Schuyler	Edward Jose
His Wife	Mabel Frenyear
Their Child	Runa Hodges
The Vampire	Theda Bara
The Doctor	Frank Powell
The Doctor's Fiancee	Minna Gale

When shown before an invited audience at the Strand Theater this picture was preceded by a recitation of Kipling's poem, "The Vampire," the inspiration for Porter Emerson Browne's drama, and, in turn, for Frank Powell's photoplay. Exhibitors using this film might well adopt the idea, for the tragic verses place an audience in the mood for what is to follow:

> A fool there was and he made his prayer
> (Even as you and I!)
> To a rag and a bone and a hank of hair
> (We called her the woman who did not care)
> But the fool he called her his lady fair
> (Even as you and I!)

After hearing the poem recited to the bitter end, one is rather anxious to know more about this Fool and his "rag and a bone and a hank of hair." They suggest an interesting couple. We would like to see just what sort of a mess they made out of life and the picture is here to show us—to show us, in fact, quite graphically.

It is bold and relentless; it is filled with passion and tragedy; it is right in harmony with the poem. For a few moments during the last reel we had fearful premonitions of the approach of a happy ending—the Fool turned into a repentant wise man—but fortunately there is no such inartistic claptrap. He is a wreck, he dies and the Vampire continues on her path, red with the blood of men. The film, then, remains true to its theme, for which the producers are to be thanked.

The people are of to-day, with the interests of modern business and social life; but the veneer amounts to nothing when shot through by the lightning bolt of sex. The Vampire is a neurotic woman gone mad. She has enough sex attraction to supply a town full of normally pleasing women, and she uses it with prodigal freedom. To come in contact with her is like touching the third rail, and all along the track we see, or hear about her victims. Some are dead, others are beggars tramping the streets, still others complete her work with a bullet through the brain. Such is the end of the youth who is deserted in favor of John Schuyler.

The affair with Schuyler starts on an ocean liner, and is continued abroad under the warm sun of Italy. Alternating with langorous tableaux and intense kisses, with which the Vampire holds her latest Fool, are scenes showing Schuyler's wife and child at home in America, the simple pathos and comedy relief in the picture being supplied by the little girl. In passing, it may be remarked that the scenes introducing the child are human and appealing; but the appeal is overworked and one incident, at least, that of the child, her doll and the butler might better be omitted.

Completely dominated by the woman, Schuyler returns with her to New York, where his physical and moral degeneration continue, despite efforts of his wife and friends to drag him out of the quicksand of the Vampire's lips. "So some of him lived, but the most of him died (Even as you and I)."

Director Powell has used enough secondary characters to fill out an adequate plot, and they are well played; but the real acting in the picture, the kind of acting that is interesting every moment, is supplied by Edward Jose as the Fool and Theda Bara as the Vampire. During his decline from a strong, self-reliant man of affairs to a spineless weakling, fit only for the alcoholic ward of a hospital, Mr. Jose undergoes a remarkable change that affects every expression of his personality. Miss Bara misses no chance for sensuous appeal in her portrayal of the Vampire, a horribly fascinating woman, vicious to the core and cruel. When she says, "Kiss me, my fool," the Fool is generally ready to obey and enjoy a prolonged moment, irrespective of the less enjoyable ones to follow.

The physical side of the production has been well looked after, with many attractive settings and clear photography that includes several pleasing light effects.

(Signed) D.

DESTRUCTION   **FILM 1916**

"Reviews of Current Productions: DESTRUCTION," Lynde Denig, *The Moving Picture World,* Vol. 27, No. 2, January 8, 1916, pp. 255-256.

Theda Bara Plays the Most Wicked of Evil Women in the Latest Fox Melodrama. Reviewed by Lynde Denig.

The horrors in this five-part melodrama are piled on so heavily, and the woman played by Theda Bara is so outrageously evil that an audience finds several of the scenes rather amusing. Here is an instance where the attempt to startle and terrify, because it is overdone, fails to carry conviction and the response of the spectator is far from that expected by the producer. At the New York Academy of Music, where DESTRUCTION was shown, the audience followed the first two reels patiently and after that revealed its good sense by laughing at the preposterous wickedness of the character portrayed by Miss Bara in her most forceful manner. For a time it appeared as if the melodrama were destined to become a farce.

There could be no better indication that the Fox Company has about reached the limit in the production of abnormal photoplays, likewise that Miss Bara is ceasing to touch the emotions by depictions of erotic women. Having provided a diet of horrors for many months, the Fox producers evidently thought the time had come to increase the dose and present in DESTRUCTION something more horrible than usual. But the public, instead of being stimulated, refused to swallow the new concoction of sensationalism and merely laughed.

Technically, William S. Davis has provided a first rate production, terminating with a fire scene of the most spectacular quality, and there is some praiseworthy acting, especially by the player in the role of the drink-crazed factory worker, who abuses his wife and eventually shares the fate of the impossible Ferdinande in the burning house. The gorilla-like ferocity of this actor is impressive. Miss Bara is not to be blamed for the picture's failure as an emotional melodrama, for she acts precisely [as] in the past and that, no doubt, is what the Fox company wishes.

GOLD AND THE WOMAN   **FILM 1915**

(Fox, 6 reels)
(Rejected by censors; passed by Appeal Board, subject to the following eliminations: Reel 1, eliminate two murder scenes; shorten one to a flash; reels 2, 3 and 4, shorten all persuasive scenes between guardian and vampire; reel 4, eliminate all love scenes between vampire and guardian except one, which is reduced to a flash; eliminate all

cigarette scenes; reel 5, eliminate all scenes of vampire and shorten drinking scene of guardian to a flash.)

"Gold and the Woman," *Complete List of Motion Picture Films Presented to the Kansas State Censors for Action from January 1 to April 1, 1916*, Crane and Company, Printers, Topeka, Kansas, 1916, p. 8.

FILM 1917   CLEOPATRA

(Fox Film Corporation)
  Eliminate: Reel 1, Suggestive advances of Cleopatra on Caesar; all close-ups of Cleopatra in the arms of Caesar; close-ups of exposed limbs, and breasts, and abdomen; all close-ups of Cleopatra luring Sharon and lying on couch and in arms of Sharon; close-up of Cleopatra and Anthony in embracing scene on couch, where Cleopatra's body is exposed.

"Cleopatra," *Complete List of Motion Picture Films Presented to the Kansas State Board of Review for Action from October 1, 1918, to December 30, 1918*, Kansas State Printing Plant, Imri Zumwalt, State Printer, Topeka, 1919, p. 4.

FILM 1918   WHEN MEN DESIRE

WHEN MEN DESIRE—Standard Pictures (Theda Bara). Fox Film Corporation. Eliminate title, "I admit it, Dearest Elsie, I intend to keep you here for myself"; title, "This couldn't be better. It isn't Strassburg, where, like a fool, I thought I'd have to marry you to possess you"; title, "Marry you—marry you."

"When Men Desire," *Complete List of Motion Picture Films Presented to the Kansas State Board of Review for Action from January 1, 1919 to March 31, 1919*, Kansas State Printing Plant, Imri Zumwalt, State Printer, Topeka, 1919, p. 17.

FILM 1918   THE SHE DEVIL

THE SHE DEVIL—Standard Pictures (Theda Bara). Fox Film Corp. Approved as rebuilt. Eliminate girl smoking.

"The She Devil," *Complete List of Motion Picture Films Presented to the Kansas State Board of Review for Action from April 1, 1919, to June 30, 1919*, Kansas State Printing Plant, Imri Zumwalt, State Printer, Topeka, 1919, p. 29.

FILM 1918   SALOME: Approved as Revised

SALOME (Theda Bara), Fox Film Corp.
  Eliminate close-up of Salome in opening bathing scene. Shorten scenes and titles of Salome with John in cell, so as to eliminate her sensual advances to him. Shorten to flash Salome stretched on floor with head on platter.
  The above picture was presented to the Board and rejected, and again presented as revised by the manufacturer and approved with eliminations.

"Salome," *Complete List of Motion Picture Films Presented to the Kansas State Board of Review for Action from July 1, 1919, to September 30, 1919*, Kansas State Printing Plant, Imri Zumwalt, State Printer, Topeka, 1919, p. 17.

237

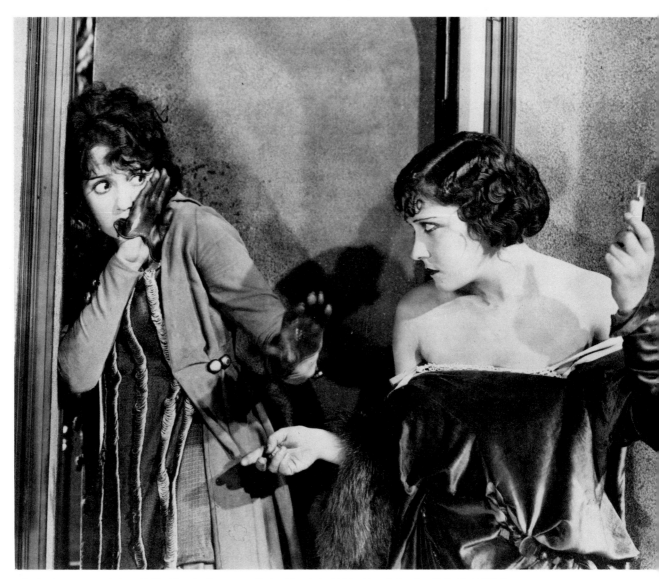

32. Gloria Swanson (right), Wife No. 1, threatens Bebe Daniels, Wife No. 2, in Cecil B. DeMille's
WHY CHANGE YOUR WIFE? (1920). Would club women of the middle west protest this "society
sex film"?

CHAPTER 13

Cecil B. DeMille

COMMENTARY

There has been a tendency to write off the films of Cecil B. DeMille (1881-1959) that appeared in the 1920's as cleverly constructed to prolong the dreams of the mob pushing in past the box-office, and, on the basis of this, to write off his entire directorial career (1913-1956)—not from a financial, but from a critical, point of view.

A corrective view of the DeMille capacities is at last possible as some of his pre-1921 films are being restored to view, including THE CHEAT (1915), with Fannie Ward and Sessue Hayakawa, which, not only in the savage branding scene, startled America and France into applause.

Mr. DeMille's notions about spectacle, he has written, derived from Italian importations, especially CABIRIA and THE LAST DAYS OF POMPEII. His own first venture into the field of historical spectacle came with JOAN THE WOMAN (1916), starring Geraldine Farrar, world famous soprano and energetic member of the Metropolitan Opera Company in New York. This was her fourth film for DeMille; he had already filmed her stormy CARMEN (1915).

Julian Johnson finds he must reach back to THE BIRTH OF A NATION for a comparison, by-passing Ince's atypical CIVILIZATION (1916), a war-time legend about peace.

WHY CHANGE YOUR WIFE? (1920), sparkling and wise, is not what we would today call a "sex" drama, but Burns Mantle, much as he enjoyed it, worried about the film's reception in middle America, and about the survival of its type altogether in view of Theda Bara's fate.

THE TEN COMMANDMENTS (1923) seemed to *The New York Times* to be two films of sharply varying quality hitched together. Not again until THE KING OF KINGS (1927) would a DeMille film be so well reviewed in the Twenties.

FILM 1916   JOAN THE WOMAN

Excerpts from "The Shadow Stage," Julian Johnson, *Photoplay Magazine*, Vol. 11, No. 4, March, 1917, pp. 113-116.

. . . Though it is not faultless, JOAN THE WOMAN is the best sun-spectacle since THE BIRTH OF A NATION, and in the opinion of the writer only that sweeping review of arms and hearts has excelled it. THE BIRTH OF A NATION trumps all the picture spectacles yet made for its insistent humanity; its irresistible combination of power and simplicity, tempest and tenderness. Mechanically as well as photographically JOAN equals but does not surpass [Thomas H. Ince's] CIVILIZATION, that photographic and mechanic milestone of flivver story; in legend and development of dramatic interest it would be absurd to mention CIVILIZATION in this connection. Mr. Griffith's radiant crazy-quilt, INTOLERANCE, is also put by.

Miss Jeanie Macpherson is credited with the book of this opera for the eyes. She begins with Eric Trent, of the English expeditionary force in Northern France. Trent is in a trench at night, and, finding a projecting bit of rusty iron, pulls and digs until he has extracted the remnant of a sword of the period of Charles VII. In his vision, as he sleeps, Joan appears. The story of the shepherdess begins. . . .

In the welter of magnificent impersonations let us seize upon the Charles VII of Raymond Hatton as a sterling example. Here is a screen-made actor whose study possesses the finest subtleties, the most adroit effects, absolute verity to human nature. It is an old saying that great parts make great actors, but of all flip quips, this is the most histrionically unjust. Charles VII *is* a great part, but in all the range of photographic and speaking performances I can think of no one who would—to me, at least—put this characterization across so thoroughly. The petulance and the weakness and the vanity of Charles, Hatton manages to express without a single bodily movement. His face is at once a drama and a novel. He has such fine bits of business; for instance, the scene after the palace revel in which he thrusts merely the tips of his fingers, absent-mindedly, down the back of a drunken woman's dress to caress her shoulder. Here, without lewdness, is the complete expression of an orgy!

Those who object to Miss Farrar's Joan because she is rising to battle-cruiser weight had best turn to their histories. Joan is described as broad, short, heavy. But Joan had a peasant's face, placid except for wonderful eyes. One of Farrar's eyes reflects Riverside Drive, the other, Fifth Avenue, and her mouth seems to be saying "Broadway." This is perhaps quibbling, but the prima-donna's Joan is a bit too sophisticated in appearance. In CARMEN she *was* Carmen; in JOAN THE WOMAN, she is an accomplished and clever actress, possessed of enormous physical valor, dramatic resource in gesture which is at moments thrilling, and great personal appeal. Her appetite for punishment and abuse has been paralleled only by the heroisms of Mabel Normand when Keystone prolapsed to dress suits and stellar names. . . .

To me, the great moment of JOAN THE WOMAN was the episode in Charles' shabby court where Joan pleads for soldiers to save France. As she talks the dim and shadowy figures of great knights in armor, on battle-chargers which would have upborne the Norse gods, plunge over them all, through the hall. This is more than double photography; it is handling a camera as Michelangelo handled his chisel—it is Michelangeloing the sunshine. This is the first time that the psychic force of active photography has been turned on an audience along lines fully demonstrated by the late Hugo Münsterberg—and completely neglected by all directors.

The material side of the picture is splendidly taken care of. The reduction of a feudal fortress, the sweep of a great field of knights to the charge are big incidents. The flash to mouth of a hundred brass trumpets, the glitter of five times as many pennanted lances, the arching of what seem a thousand great swords demonstrate overwhelmingly the drama of arms in the mailed centuries.

William Furst's musical score is a pleasant one, and while it rises to no particular merit, it never angers by its complete inefficiency—as does the INTOLERANCE orchestration. Those who criticize Mr. Furst for his large use of the "Marseillaise" on the

ground that it was not composed until hundreds of years after the winds had scattered Joan's ashes, have no imagination. The "Marseillaise" is not a localized tune; it is a melodic expression of the spirit of France.

Mr. DeMille has not Mr. Griffith's almost demoniac faculty of making even an extra do in a picture just what he would do in life. JOAN THE WOMAN could stand a bit more humanity here and there. Nevertheless, it is a big and splendid thing. . . .

FILM 1916   JOAN THE WOMAN

"Joan the Prima Donna," excerpt from "Second Thoughts on First Nights," Alexander Woollcott, *The New York Times*, February 25, 1917, Section 3, p. 2.

In JOAN THE WOMAN there is so much that is stirring and beautiful that it ranks among the finest things the motion picture has achieved thus far. The beautiful and exalted pageantry of the coronation is the sort of spectacle that takes the breath away and lingers always in the memory. Among the many beauties in this sumptuous photo-pageant, however, it is impossible to include the rampageous Geraldine Farrar. Her conception of the matchless Maid of Donremy is not sufficiently different from her notion of Carmen to satisfy quite the spectator's mind and heart. One shudders to think what impression of Jeanne d'Arc is thus being imparted to this generation by the picture on the Forty-fourth Street screen. Thousands will come to think of her as a buxom and somewhat amatory lady with an extraordinarily knowing eye—mature, sophisticated, and theatrical to the last. Something of the valiant frailty of the idealized, canonized Joan (far more important, of course, than the authentic Joan), something of the spiritual beauty, something of the ecstasy of the maid who heard the voices in her father's garden and was moved by them to take up the sword for her King—all this we might have had if some one else, Mae Marsh, perhaps, had been chosen for the Joan of the screen. . . .

FILM 1920   WHY CHANGE YOUR WIFE?

"The Shadow Stage," Burns Mantle, *Photoplay Magazine*, Vol. 17, No. 6, May, 1920, pp. 64-65.

There is nothing more certain; nothing, at least, of which we feel more certain than that

(1) Cecil DeMille's WHY CHANGE YOUR WIFE? will prove one of the sex best sellers of the month;

(2) That somewhere out in the middle west, where the clean prairie winds blow across the brows of a native Anglo-Saxon multitude, a woman's club or two or four or six will meet, and in the course of meeting, adopt resolutions condemning the present tendencies of the screen as they relate to the sensual and the fleshly feature;

And (3) that later certain financial interests in conference assembled in richly paneled New York offices will give the resolutions the cursory glance, familiarly known as the once over, and proceed to a re-reading of night letters received from the same locality relating the experience of Hiram Bezitz, the local exhibitor, who was forced to call out the fire department to help him shoo an overflow mob away from his theater after it had been packed to the rafters with those eager to see Cecil DeMille's WHY CHANGE YOUR WIFE?

241

History repeats itself in the cinema theater as surely as it does in the legitimate theater, and as often. The sex drama is dead; long live the sex drama! The vamp is a goner; here comes the vamp! The producer of sex plays, or sex literature, is like a chef with a favorite delicacy. He serves it as long as there is any call for it. As the sale grows he tries to still further improve it by adding new seasoning to his confection. And in the course of time he invariably over-seasons the dish and the public turns against it. If you don't believe that possible, ask Mr. Fox and Theda Bara! Or the gentlemen who fattened off the white slave crusade a few seasons ago, both in the pictures and the drama.

Just now Director DeMille is at the extra-seasoning stage. Having achieved a reputation as the great modern concocter of the sex stew by adding a piquant dash here and there to DON'T CHANGE YOUR HUSBAND, and a little something more to MALE AND FEMALE, he spills the spice box into WHY CHANGE YOUR WIFE? and the result is a rare concoction—the most gorgeously sensual film of the month; in decoration the most costly; in physical allure the most fascinating; in effect the most immoral.

Some day, so sure as we both shall live, and sooner than we now surmise, I'm thinking, we shall see a reaction against the society sex film. Largely because the more highly seasoned it becomes the more untrue it is and the more insidiously dangerous to a public that has a quietly effective way of protecting itself.

Mr. DeMille and his studio associates know that the "moral" they have tacked on to this picture—that, in effect, every married man prefers an extravagant playmate-wife, dressed like a harlot, to a fussy little home body who has achieved horn-rimmed spectacles and a reading lamp—is not true of normal husbands anywhere in the world, however true it may be of motion picture directors. But there is enough hidden truth contained in it to make a lot of husbands and wives unhappy, and a lot of fathers and mothers uneasy. From which centers of observation the return kick is likely to start, and gather such momentum as it proceeds that when it lands the recipient will be surprised.

Just as a picture, however, this screened yarn of a rich young husband, who, objecting to his wife's plainness and her thrift, thought to buy a few thin, lacy things for her to wear, and then fell in love with the model who showed them to him, is effectively told and pictured. It has the fault of all artificial stories, but its characters are interesting. Divorcing the wife and marrying the lingerie model, young husband discovers his mistake about the same time his first wife decides to do a little wild dressing on her own account.

As a result of her exhibition, beginning at the ankles and the shoulders and extending thence north and south to the belt line, husband decides he has made a great mistake. And after he slips on a banana peel and chips a sliver or two of bone out of his poor old head, and his first wife nurses him with the left hand while she beats up the interfering second wife with the right, he knows he is wrong. So he changes back.

The settings and the costumes of the actors are, as previously noted, gorgeous. Thomas Meighan as *le pauvre poisson* who was taught to prefer the simple virtues of the home-broken wife, and to know that horn-rimmed spectacles are aces when worn for virtue's sake, frowned and suffered and looked handsome in every scene. He is making sure-footed progress toward stardom. Gloria Swanson and Bebe Daniels, besides being histrionically competent, were glorious camera subjects, wrapped and unwrapped in a million dollars' worth of lace and lingerie. The Sennetts and the Sunshine boys may outdo Mr. DeMille as masters of the lower limb displays, but he completely distances them in the technique of the torso. William DeMille furnished the text for WHY CHANGE YOUR WIFE?

THE TEN COMMANDMENTS   **FILM 1923**

"The Screen: Remarkable Spectacle: THE TEN COMMANDMENTS," *The New York Times,* December 22, 1923, p. 8.

33. *Theodore Roberts as Moses urges on the Israelites in DeMille's THE TEN COMMANDMENTS (first version; 1923). This striking Biblical section is linked to a Modern Story which* The New York Times *found by comparison an "ordinary and certainly uninspired movie."*

With Theodore Roberts, Charles de Roche, Estelle Taylor, Julia Faye, Terrence Moore, James Neill, Lawson Butt, Clarence Burton, Noble Johnson, in the great spectacle; in the modern story are Edyth Chapman, Richard Dix, Rod La Rocque, Leatrice Joy, Nita Naldi, Robert Edeson, Charles Ogle and Agnes Ayres.

It is probable that no more wonderful spectacle has ever been put before the public in shadow-form than the greatly heralded prelude to Cecil B. DeMille's costly film, which opened last night to a brilliant and eager gathering in the George M. Cohan Theatre. It is called, and it hardly seems necessary to mention the title, THE TEN COMMANDMENTS. It is built in two sections, the spectacle and the melodrama. Two men might have directed this feature, as it goes from the sublime to the out-and-out movie. Not that the latter part is bad, but that almost any melodramatic picture would have fitted into the second section of this photodrama.

But the sight of the Israelites in bondage in Egypt, their slaving before the chariots, their treatment by the despots of the day, the swiftly drawn chariots and their steeds, and the great bas-reliefs of figures whose shin-bones would have made two big men. All this was obviously directed by a genius who held in his hand the cost. There are many impressive colorful scenes of the Israelites in the desert, some of them appearing better and more natural than other such effects we have witnessed on the screen.

Charles de Roche, whom we first met in a minor part of THE SPANISH JADE, who recently was seen as a Hindu with Pola Negri in THE CHEAT, impersonates the terrible Rameses. He was impressive, and like all the other players in this section of this picture, wore his raiment of cloth and metal as if it were comfortable.

There was the death of all the first born of the Egyptians, and the great and so-called magnificent Rameses praying to his god throughout the night to put life into his boy's body, and no life came. His god had no power like the God of the Israelites.

Coupled with the orchestration there has been nothing on the film so utterly impressive as the thundering and belching forth of one commandment after another, and the titling and photography of this particular effect was remarkable. It was the quivering, crashing, resounding blare from the string and wind instruments that did much to assist in the desired effect. The sky clouds, and then seems to burst, and from the ball of smoke appears golden lettering with one or another of the commandments, stress being laid upon those that are considered the most important, if one may say such a thing.

The costumes in this million dollars' worth of prelude are splendidly created, and not in a single instance is there a jarring note in this regard. Theodore Roberts, who recently was seen in the character of a businessman with a cigar in his mouth, gave an excellent portrayal of Moses, the Lawgiver. His make-up was faultless, and the sincerity with which he acted this part made the whole affair doubly effective. Undoubtedly it was a series of sequences that made one think, that carried a message, that was done with meticulous precision, and boomed forth so well that it would have needed an unusually perfect modern drama to stand up in comparison with it. In this spectacle, with a good photographic and scenic effect, the crossing through a water-flanked path of the Red Sea was shown, and it drew applause from the packed theater. Prior to that there was the Pillar of Fire which confused and halted the Egyptians hastening after the slaves they had released through fear of the God of the Israelites.

But—and unfortunately we have to say but—the strain on Mr. DeMille told, and as soon as he swept on to his modern drama he was back to the ordinary and certainly uninspired movie, one in which the direction at times had "business" apparently intended to appeal to the very young. Too many "inserts" were shown. In one case there was a letter which was put on the screen three different times, and from what we now remember once would have been sufficient. The cracking walls of a cathedral being constructed by the hapless man in this portion of the film are brought out so many times that it is extremely tedious, and we would also like to say that if an old mother reads her Bible it is no reason why a motion picture director should have her carrying around a volume that weighs about a hundred-weight. Also, why have her pictured after death with the same huge Bible? This is a story of two sons, one bad and the other good, a woman from a leper island, and the breaking of all the Commandments by the conscienceless love-making, unfaithful and plotting weakling.

At the same time it must be admitted that in this melodrama there are also some excellent and well thought-out ideas, and some eye-smiting shots. There is considerable suspense where the wife of the wicked brother ascends to the top of the scaffolding of the rickety structure, constructed with rotten cement. It is the catching of her heel on a corner that uncovers the cheap and rotten concrete, as she nearly falls. And Mr. DeMille has not forgotten to give his spectators an impression of height in the full sequence. You see the woman ascending, you see her looking down, and although a car appears insignificantly small upon the roadway, this young lady can detect her husband out with another woman in an automobile.

Whatever has been done in the second installment of this picture—which in all is said to have cost a million and one-half dollars and classed by Mr. DeMille as "the cheapest picture ever made," because of the reward in sheckels it will reap—one must say that great heights of costuming and direction have been attained in the prelude.

The actors are capable throughout, and the performance in the modern portion of Rod La Rocque, as the wicked son, was particularly commendable. Richard Dix was good as the faithful and law-abiding son.

1925   **Cecil B. DeMille at Work**

Excerpt from "How the Great Directors Work," Harry Carr, *Motion Picture Magazine*, Vol. 29, No. 4, May 1925, pp. 117, 128.

. . . Cecil B. DeMille always wears puttees and riding clothes on the sets. Attached to his belt he has a little case in which he carries pencils, pens and other tools. A DeMille set is like a royal court. Honestly, this is not of his doing; rather it is a sincere tribute of admiration from his helpers. But anyhow, if he asks for a megaphone, a dozen people leap for it. Actors, assistant directors and writers. Along in the middle of every big scene, his necktie always gets irksome. He tears it off and throws it aside. Someone is always there to catch it. It is amusing to see them waiting for it—with jealous eyes upon each other.

No director has more difficult tasks to accomplish, more tense and nerve-wracking scenes. I can always tell when he is laboring under the strain of one of them. His eyes begin to twinkle and snap and he becomes dangerously and elaborately polite.

When he was taking the big scene in THE TEN COMMANDMENTS, where Moses looked down upon the children of Israel worshipping the golden calf, there were several hundred people on the set. Each one of those hundreds had a definite, fixed thing to do. It was very trying. DeMille stood upon a high platform and talked to them through a magni-box. This electric telephone arrangement is so wonderfully tuned that it was as though he were whispering in an extra's ear. Only he wasn't whispering.

The great difficulty was to keep them from laughing. Not that they felt funny. But they were all half hysterical.

Mr. DeMille's icy, clear-cut voice cut the aïr like slashes of a sword.

"I would like to remark," he said, "that if any one of you feels humorous, laugh now. If any one of you laughs after I say 'Camera,' I will do my best to extract the humor from the situation. Also I will see to it, in this and in all future pictures that I may make, that you have abundant leisure to devote your whole attention to your sense of humor."

It was a threat that made them shudder. It was the click of the lock that would forever banish them to the outer edges of the land of oblivion—somewhere out back of beyond. Nobody laughed, although several fainted.

Nevertheless, the actors adore DeMille. He is a considerate, courteous gentleman. Also he "knows how." No director who is not an expert is ever popular with his people. It is the dubs who are hated.

CHAPTER 14

BROKEN BLOSSOMS, and Some Griffith Films of the Twenties

COMMENTARY

D. W. Griffith's HEARTS OF THE WORLD (1918), which followed INTOLERANCE, and was a big film about World War I, seemed to throw his future into question. Some of the program features he then made for Paramount-Artcraft were very disappointing, and he definitely lost ground.

His fondness for soft focus photography, forecast in several earlier films, reaches its climax in BROKEN BLOSSOMS (1919), however, his first release for the new United Artists Corporation, and this work as a whole restores him to the top of the heap. *The Times* **remarks on his masterly handling of slow tempo, a renewed manifestation of the "repose" of the old Biograph days.**

FILM 1918 THE GREATEST THING IN LIFE

Excerpt from "The Screen," *The New York Times,* December 23, 1918, p. 9.

. . . Mr. Griffith has introduced into the photoplay some remarkable photographic effects. A number of his pictures have a soft portrait-like tone that seems to have been produced by some novel process and is used to refine the poetic quality of the photoplay. . . .

1919 THE GREATEST THING IN LIFE

Excerpt from "Across the Silversheet," Hazel Simpson Naylor, *Motion Picture Magazine,* Vol. 16, No. 2, March, 1919, p. 73.

The punch of this latest David Griffith picture seems to be in his ability to have Germans break down doors effectively, instead of using situations that break down the door of a person's heart. In producing another war picture Griffith does nothing big or unusual to justify our confidence in his being the greatest director. The most daring moment of this new production is when the white soldier and the negro soldier seek refuge in the same shell hole, showing the kindness of the negro and the breaking down of the white's prejudice. Little Lillian Gish is shown to beautiful advantage in three or four close-ups of a new type which idealize her expression. The rest of the time she jumps "ingenuishly" all over the place. The charm of Lillian is a very poignant thing and should not be tampered with in this manner, no matter how great the director. Fortunately we still have memories of her sanity and dignity in THE LILY AND THE ROSE. . . .

THE GIRL WHO STAYED AT HOME   **FILM 1919**

Excerpt from "The Screen," *The New York Times,* March 24, 1919, p. 11.

D. W. Griffith never produces what, judged against the field of photoplays, could be called a poor work. His power of making pictures is too great and by now too instinctively self-assertive to permit his falling below the average of others. But he is sometimes disappointing, because the public has come to expect so much of him and he cannot always live up to expectations. In one or two of his recent pictures, especially in A ROMANCE OF HAPPY VALLEY, he was disappointing, at least to some. It is a pleasure, therefore, to record that his latest work, THE GIRL WHO STAYED AT HOME, at the Strand this week, satisfies every expectation. Judged by the Griffith standard, it is good. In some ways it even adds to its producer's long list of achievements.

For one thing, Mr. Griffith does in it what he usually requires a longer photoplay for. He weaves several stories together in the same plot and preserves unity, at the same time using one story to heighten the suspense of another or ease its tension, and finally bringing all of his narrative threads to an even end. Mr. Griffith has been noted for his ability to handle plots of varied and extensive range, but he has never done it so well before in a photoplay designed for routine exhibition. THE GIRL WHO STAYED AT HOME is not what is called in the trade a "super-production," it is a regular Artcraft release; yet it has all of the scope and wealth of treatment that might be put into a "super" film.

Another characteristic that THE GIRL WHO STAYED AT HOME shares with the greater Griffith productions is its blending of melodrama, delineation of character and humor. The melodrama seems an integral part of the play's action; the characters, although a bit heroically drawn, impress themselves upon the mind as individuals, and the humor, instead of being forcibly inserted as undisguised "comedy relief," comes spontaneously as the three-fold story progresses.

And, of course, Mr. Griffith's subtlety and strength in making pictures, scenes of pure beauty and scenes of dramatic meaning, has not failed him. He is not only an artist in pictorial composition, but, by technical skill, often along original lines, he produces effects that others in time learn to imitate. No pictures seem to have the perspective of his. Some of them are practically stereoscopic. Also, in some way which has not yet become general, he dramatically emphasizes the central figures of a scene by throwing all its other objects so out of focus that they remain to provide suitable background and environment for the action without competing with it for the interest of the spectators. This is an artistic development of the close-up. In certain scenes it has all of the psychological effect of the close-up and something else. It makes the action more eloquent by keeping it in its environment, it preserves the continuity of the story, and it adds smoothness and beauty to the picture as a whole. And when Griffith does make a close-up, it is a soft, delicately shaded portrait.

These remarks, while general, are pertinent here because they appertain particularly to THE GIRL WHO STAYED AT HOME. . . .

34. *Richard Barthelmess and Lillian Gish in Griffith's BROKEN BLOSSOMS (1919), "the first genuine tragedy of the movies." Not content with the tints in the film itself, Griffith arranged for a glow of Chinese blue to be thrown from the projection booth onto the screen while the film was in progress.*

THE GIRL WHO STAYED AT HOME FILM 1919

Excerpt from "Across the Silversheet," Hazel Simpson Naylor, *Motion Picture Magazine*, Vol. 17, No. 5, June, 1919, p. 67.

. . . In my opinion, Mr. Griffith slightly overuses the close-up. However, these new misty effects of his are artistic enough to bear watching. Considering Griffith's success in handling war subjects and his recent lack of impressiveness in [A ROMANCE OF] HAPPY VALLEY, I am wondering if our supposedly greatest director is limited, or is his failing a persistent refusal to recognize a worth-while story. . . .

BROKEN BLOSSOMS FILM 1919

Excerpts from "The Shadow Stage," Julian Johnson, *Photoplay Magazine*, Vol. 16, No. 3, August, 1919, pp. 55-56.

If the celluloid prints of our day were destroyed by some strange lover of gelatine among the moths and larvae there would remain for the researchers of the next generation only the play-bills and the press-notices. And on viewing these I imagine they would say, "This man Griffith certainly had the world by the tail—year after year these laudations! How tiresome! Was there no one else deserving the top of the column?"

But at the risk of being called a mere D. Wark sycophant by those that follow me, I must continue praising David W. The immediate object of today's anthem is, as you probably surmise, BROKEN BLOSSOMS, a great photoplay of insignificant title.

Let me say that Mr. Griffith's distinction lies not in the fact that he writes fine narratives on the screen. Other men do that. The extraordinary part of Griffith is that he has never ceased to be a pioneer. He continues to advance. He dares to present novelties of form and novelties of material. He does not always get away with it, but he keeps right on pioneering. He is a long ways from dead, and already the Shakespeare-Bacon controversy has crawled out of its narrow cell and taken a new form in the hexagonal debate as to who invented the close-up. People keep on appropriating his notions and he keeps on putting forth new notions. He is like a doctor who seldom troubles to make his nostrums proprietary—a year or two after some Griffith knick-knack has been generally adopted almost anybody can tell you that Griffith didn't invent it at all—Harold Mike Biggs did it first, in A SIGHT FOR THE GODS.

To come to a more intimate consideration of BROKEN BLOSSOMS: it is the first genuine tragedy of the movies. An unhappy ending doesn't constitute tragedy: tragedy seems foreordained; the drums of doom are sounding from the first steps of the pageant. So they are for Lucy, the forlorn little thing without a last name, unwelcome child of a Limehouse bruiser, idol of a half-crazy Oriental idealist. Mr. Griffith's adaptation of Thomas Burke's grotesque red story, "The Chink and the Child," is extraordinarily clever. There the Celestial was little more than a coolie—an old beast of the East in whom, somehow, the forlorn little girl lit a queer late lambent spark of immortality. It would have been hard to make an Occidental audience accept Burke's slant on this dirty, dried old citron; sounds well enough in a book that you don't have to read aloud, maybe, but in a show it would almost certainly be disgusting. Especially to men, who sometimes reverence women more than women reverence themselves. So in making the Chinaman a splendid but embittered and fallen young Buddhist, D. W. rose authorially in that moment right alongside Mr. Burke.

For the rest, the tale runs as written except for the very finish, with Lucy dragging out her cowering little life by the London waterside, beaten into semi-imbecility by her accidental father, picked up, reverenced, honored and enthroned by the lonely opium-eater, and at length slain in a monstrous moment of mock-virtue by the insensate chunk that caused her to come into the world. Then the beast dies before the Chinaman's gun, the Chinaman dies upon his own knife, and the cycle is finished. There is a satisfaction in the death of all three that is an unconscious verification of both its art and its truth. Burrows the battler should not survive the weak little thing he made and slew, and for the yellow man to go on living would have been a hideous hell.

The visualizing of this bitter-sweet story is, I have no hesitancy in saying, the very finest expression of the screen so far. There seems to be no setting or accessory which is not correct in its finest details. The composition is a painter's. The photography is not only perfect, but, with caution, is innovational, and approximates, in its larger lights and softnesses of close view, the details of bright and dark upon the finest canvases in the Louvres of the world. . . .

Mr. Griffith has added a revolutionary color touch by the use of a Chinese blue, thrown, not by the projector or out of the film, but independently, from the projection booth. This is not a tint and it does not give the impression of colored film. It has a dramatic value which can only be compared to the vital, living blue of the incomparable scene-painter Urban.

Photographer Bitzer has done the best work of his career in this picture.

The fated trio is played by Lillian Gish, as Lucy; Donald Crisp, as Battling Burrows, and Richard Barthelmess, as the Yellow Man. The piece is high tide for all of them.

Miss Gish has been allied with the delicate flowers upon Griffith's tapestries for a long, long time, but here she is called upon to play more than a delicate flower. She must, and does, characterize a little creature of infinite pathos. She has to be both Lillian Gish and Mae Marsh of old rolled into one sorrowful little being, and her success in this strange combination of motives and beings is absolute. Mr. Crisp as the ferocious Battler is more than physically violent; he has, by many little side touches given intriguing, even humorous little glimpses into the bovine mental processes, the vast self-satisfactions of an ox such as Burrows would be. Mr. Barthelmess as the Chinaman is lofty, exalted, immeasurably removed from a sordid world and its sordid passions, and a calm, implacable dispenser of fate in the last phase. Edward Piel, George Beranger and that delightful pugilistic thespian, Mr. Kid McCoy Selby, perform small parts with admirable finish.

Only one part of this splendid essay is open to real criticism. Mr. Griffith is not a title writer and his words most inadequately garb his visions. The spoken titles are not so bad, but the descriptive phrases lean lamely upon crutches of sentimentality.

FILM 1919   BROKEN BLOSSOMS

Excerpt from "Griffith's Art," *The New York Times*, May 25, 1919, Section 4, p. 3.

. . . Another element of BROKEN BLOSSOMS that accounts for the effect of the whole is its tempo. Mr. Griffith, conscious at all times that he was composing a tragedy, regulated the action to tragic time. Spectators are impressed from the beginning with the dignity and solemnity of the story. It is not only that the action is slow—it is—it takes a man longer to walk across the street in BROKEN BLOSSOMS than in other photoplays—but that the whole movement of the successive scenes is in harmony with the spirit of tragedy. In this connection it seems appropriate to refer to the classic Greek tragedies, which achieve much of their power by the manner in which the catastrophe comes inexorably from the steady march of inevitable events. BROKEN BLOSSOMS is strongly suggestive of the classic model. . . .

"Out-of-Focus" Close-ups   1920

Excerpt from "Plays and Players," *Photoplay Magazine, Vol. 17, No. 4, March, 1920, p. 104.*

. . . The other picture men who have been hoping and praying that they might achieve the same shadowy, impressionistic effects as in BROKEN BLOSSOMS will be surprised and comforted to hear this. A certain producer was talking to the manager of a New Jersey film theater. "I always heard that Griffith was so much," said the manager. "Well, isn't he?" asked the producer. "Say," said the manager, "those close-ups in BROKEN BLOSSOMS were so out-of-focus when I started to run that there print that I had to cut out most of them!".

COMMENTARY

WAY DOWN EAST (1920) and ORPHANS OF THE STORM (1922), both filmed on the East coast, still find D. W. Griffith holding the scales of his fame pretty steady. *The Times* **compares the latter film with the German-made ALL FOR A WOMAN (DANTON), shown about a month earlier at the Strand. AMERICA (1924) was Griffith's last big spectacle.**

After AMERICA came ISN'T LIFE WONDERFUL? (1924), a moving work about the German food shortage, which Griffith had filmed on location near Berlin. It was not a financial success, and in the works that followed it during the last half of the Twenties, most people felt that Griffith had sunk into a tide of routine commercial productions. In all, in this decade, he directed fifteen films.

WAY DOWN EAST   **FILM 1920**

Alexander Woollcott is the author of this unsigned review from "The Screen," *The New York Times*, September 4, 1920, p. 7.

Anna Moore, the wronged heroine of WAY DOWN EAST, was turned out into the snowstorm again last evening, but it was such a blizzard as she had never been turned out into in all the days since Lottie Blair Parker first told her woes nearly twenty-five years ago. For this was the screen version of that prime old New England romance, and the audience that sat in rapture at the Forty-fourth Street Theatre to watch its first unfolding here realized finally why it was that D. W. Griffith has selected it for a picture. It was not for its fame. Nor for its heroine. Not for the wrong done her. It was for the snowstorm.

And not the snowstorm alone, but the peril-fraught river with its rush of swirling ice cakes. For in the WAY DOWN EAST of the movies Anna Moore goes not merely forth into the snowy night. She also takes a leaf from the book called *Uncle Tom's Cabin* and is borne down the river as the ice jam breaks, borne swiftly toward the falls where she will be dashed to pieces unless the gallant Dave, who is making an Eliza-like pursuit, can get to her in time. It is at once an exciting race and an amazing spectacle, Griffith at his best in the climax of a picture which set its first New York audience whistling and stamping with unfeigned approval.

True, here and there comes a suggestion of papier-mâché danger, of studio ice, of dummy figures and all that, but for the most part it is uncommonly well done, and the effect is breath-taking. No doubt a large part of last night's audience was made up of intimate well-wishers of the parties concerned, spectators who would have died gladly rather than find a single fault in the new Griffith picture. But no such explanation is needed of the hubbub which followed the ice-jam scene at the end. Any audience would have cheered it, and all audiences will.

35. *D. W. Griffith (right) and his cameraman, G. W. ("Billy") Bitzer, during the shooting of WAY DOWN EAST (1920). Bitzer had been with Griffith since the early days at Biograph. For this film, the great snowstorm and blind whipping wind were real, but certain of the ice-cake shots were faked.*

For the rest, the old Fireside Companion tale is worked out with that same story-telling art, that imagination, sense of beauty and ingenuity of craftsmanship which, with the additional aid of a considerable propaganda, have made Griffith's name a great one in motion pictures. To be sure he has used only the familiar tricks and puppets of rural life as it is understood by our theater, but then he was not making a screen version of New England life. He was making a screen version of a New England play.

Then think what a menagerie of innocent little animals such a play permits him to have, what close-ups of birds and apple-blossoms, what fadeaways of chickens, what cut-backs of heifers—all running along to an orchestral accompaniment that includes every old tune from "Little Brown Jug" to "Jingle Bells."

Anna is played by Lillian Gish, whose exceptional mobility of countenance makes her an interesting being to watch in the throes of such emotion, even when her face, all dissolved and rearranged with woe, is put close to the camera and held there interminably. As usual, this delicate and lovely face of hers goes so far in expressing that she knows no wrong that sometimes it conveys the suggestion that she knows nothing at all. David is capitally played by Richard Barthelmess, the extraordinary player of BROKEN BLOSSOMS, and "that city chap" is done by one of our best stage villains, Lowell Sherman.

After all, the best possible description of WAY DOWN EAST was furnished by Mr. Griffith himself in his advance notice to the public, the one in which he let it be known that this was just "a plain, old-fashioned story for plain, every day human beings," but "most expensive." He could have added that the snowstorm and the scenes on the ice-jammed river would appeal also to fancy, every-other-day human beings—to every one in fact.

WAY DOWN EAST   **FILM 1920**

Excerpt from "Drama," Robert C. Benchley, *Life*, Vol. 76, No. 1977, September 23, 1920, p. 542.

. . . Speaking of wronging women, WAY DOWN EAST has been put into the movies by the prodigal Mr. Griffith, and now may be seen reeling its way through several hundred thousand dollars at the Forty-fourth Street Theatre. It seems hardly fair to Anna to revive the old scandal just as it was beginning to be forgotten, and it certainly is not fair to the public to revive the old comedy scenes just as we were congratulating ourselves that a few slight scars were all that were left on our memory. The whole picture, captions and all ("There stands the man who deceived me!"), might very well serve as a delightful burlesque just as it stands, were it not for the fact that Nature, who is reputed to be even more prodigal than Mr. Griffith, has furnished some remarkably beautiful scenery and snow effects which make the whole picture worth sitting through. Especially well have "the Master" and Nature worked together in a tremendous ice-floe scene, which was not, owing to the limited facilities on William A. Brady's stage, in the original production. In this scene, the young hero, wearing a long fur overcoat which he certainly does not need, and carrying an extra wrap over his arm in case it should turn colder by night, leaps from floe to floe down what seems to be the entire length of the Connecticut River in order to save Anna, the gel who had been done wrong and who is riding, peacefully and unconsciously, down stream toward the falls on a cake of ice.

The whole problem of the drama, after all, is whether or not Anna was worth it. A straw vote taken in this department shows an overwhelming sentiment in the negative. Number of votes cast, one; number in favor of saving Anna, none. Number in favor of letting her ride over the falls, one. . . .

FILM 1922   ORPHANS OF THE STORM

"The Screen: ORPHANS OF THE STORM," *The New York Times*, January 4, 1922, p. 11.

> Produced by D. W. Griffith, with Lillian and Dorothy Gish, Joseph Schildkraut, Frank Losee, Catherine Emmett, Morgan Wallace, Lucille La Verne, Sheldon Lewis, Frank Puglia, Creighton Hale, Leslie King, Monte Blue, Sidney Herbert, Leo Kolmer, Adolphe Lestina and Kate Bruce in the cast. Based on D'Ennery's *The Two Orphans*. At the Apollo.

One of the most enthusiastic crowds that ever filled a theater for a motion picture packed the Apollo Theatre last night for the opening of D. W. Griffith's latest film spectacle, ORPHANS OF THE STORM. As the vivid scenes of the historically colored melodrama flashed one after another on the screen every one surely felt that Griffith was himself again. All of his old power to make moving pictures with life in them, to put the point of meaning into them and the fire of continuous action was evident once more. His mastery over mobs and sweeping panoramic scenes, and his definiteness in the use of expressive details, were demonstrated again.

ORPHANS OF THE STORM is a stirring, gripping picture, chiefly because of its pictorial range. Nothing is too large and nothing too small for Mr. Griffith's use. The mob storming the Bastille, a five-mile cavalry race to the rescue of the heroine, a tumult in an extensive open square, these show Griffith, the maker of spectacles. But these big scenes are illuminated and intensified by shots of details of the action, two men meeting in a hand-to-hand encounter, the horses' hoofs as they tear along, one man falling with a bayonet in his side. And the richness and waste of a feast is emphasized by a slice of cake and the thin cut of a juicy roast. So, first of all and above everything else, OR-PHANS OF THE STORM is a motion picture. That is its triumphant distinction.

Secondly, however, or, moreover—according to your taste—it is a melodrama. Mr. Griffith has taken the old stage thriller, *The Two Orphans,* and thrown it into the midst of the French Revolution. The revolution is not merely suggested, as, according to report, it was in the play. It is around and in and sometimes above the action of the story of the two sisters-by-adoption who are caught in its whirlpool. And thus the photoplay becomes historic. It is staged and costumed to represent the day, and historic characters of the revolution. Danton, Robespierre and others appear prominently in the story of the two sisters. And, although it takes chronological and other liberties with history, its atmosphere and general appearance are authentic, according to testimony which Mr. Griffith has taken the trouble to provide and also according to the spectator's impression.

But it remains a melodrama, nevertheless, for the historic characters become figures of the story rather than men of their times. Danton, for example, is used as the rescuing agent when the heroine is about to be guillotined, and Robespierre seeks to send her to her death because she once saved Danton and he also doubts her moral character. And the final act is a restaging, with embellishments, of the rescue scene of INTOLERANCE, or as it was later shown in THE MOTHER AND THE LAW. There's no doubt of the passing effectiveness of this scene; it is done with the utmost skill, but its outcome is never for a moment in doubt. The seasoned spectator, no matter how he may let himself go, knows that every delay is a device to heighten the suspense and every advantage given the rescuers is calculated to evoke his cheers. He may feel the suspense and he may cheer— then, again, he may not—he may simply admire the execution of the incident—but, whatever he does, he is not surprised when the girl is saved.

Thus, ORPHANS OF THE STORM is a thrilling melodrama, but a melodrama throughout.

And as a melodrama, its fictional characters, or its historical characters in fictional   255 actions, are conspicuous. Of these the Misses Gish, Lillian as Henriette Girard, and Dorothy as her blind sister, head the cast in fact as well as name. Each gives a telling performance. Joseph Schildkraut, as the aristocratic Chevalier de Vaudrey, looks the part, which, more than in most cases, is important for his role, and in many scenes he acts with an easy sureness that opens the screen to him (if he chooses to continue in motion pictures). The Danton of Monte Blue is earnest and sometimes effective, though it must be admitted that his performance often lacks the spontaneous vitality expected of the great orator, and suffers from comparison with the recent Danton of Emil Jannings. Sidney Herbert's Robespierre is adequate, if, for some, not as convincing as the Robespierre of Werner Krauss in ALL FOR A WOMAN. Especially vivid performances are given by Lucille La Verne as Mother Frochard, the old hag; Frank Puglia as Pierre, her son, and Leslie King as Jacques-Forget-Not of the Revolutionary Tribunal.

Post-Premiere Revisions

1922

Excerpt from "Screen, Current Pictures," *The New York Times,* January 29, 1922, Section 6, p. 2.

. . . Incidentally, ORPHANS OF THE STORM affords an interesting illustration of how a photoplay, commonly supposed to be much less fluid than a stage production, may be revised after its formal presentation. It is well known, of course, that film may be cut and pasted almost indefinitely, so that scenes shown originally may be eliminated, and others at first held out inserted wherever an exhibitor chooses, but Mr. Griffith has gone further than this. Since the opening of ORPHANS OF THE STORM at the Apollo he has himself observed, and has engaged others to observe, the reaction of spectators, and as a result he has not only deleted certain scenes, but has made others at his studio in Mamaroneck and put them into the photoplay. Frank Puglia as Pierre, for instance, has been brought to life and kept alive for the happy ending; Creighton Hale has been given additional space as the amusing Picard; the Carmagnole dancers now have more to do, and the scene at the guillotine has been made less horrifically detailed, according to reports from the front of the house. . . .

NURSING A VIPER

FILM 1909

Excerpt from "Licensed Reviews," *The New York Dramatic Mirror,* Vol. 62, No. 1612, November 13, 1909, p. 16.

NURSING A VIPER (Biograph, Nov. 4).—The astonishing strength and power of this subject makes it one of the most notable ever produced by any company, American or foreign, although there are those who may hold that it is too powerful in some of its most gruesome details. Certain it is that a few feet of film at different points in the action might have been omitted without injury to the story, thus escaping possible complaint. The time of the story is placed at the opening of the first French revolution, when the half-starved peasantry broke out in indescribable savagery against the hated aristocrats. A nobleman fleeing from the mob seeks refuge with a Republican, who is protected by the rabble. The nobleman assumes the disguise of the Republican's servant and takes the opportunity of insulting the Republican's wife, whereupon that gentleman throws the viper to the human wolves outside the house. In order to account for the groveling terror of the nobleman when he finds that he must face the mob, we are shown various scenes outside the house with the mob in action, slaughtering and throttling their helpless captives, women as well as men, and the thing is so well done that the chills fairly chase each other up and down the spine of the most hardened spectator. Evidently the producer [D. W. Griffith] was fearful that he might not get his atmosphere of horror strong enough without showing many of the most brutal details, but in this he was mistaken. The actual murders and the carrying of a woman's head about on a pike pole might have been cut out and there would still have been ample atmosphere left for all necessary purposes. The dividing line where brutal details in a picture should cease is a difficult one to determine. A number of great pictures, such as Pathé's LA TOSCA, have depicted scenes of horror with dangerous fidelity and have escaped without much, if any, complaint, it being held that the nature of the subjects warranted the extremity of realism. In the present subject it must be admitted that there is ample basis in history for all the details shown and much more, but at the same time it is *The Mirror's* opinion that for general circulation in picture houses films depicting scenes of this character should be managed with careful discretion.

1922   ORPHANS: **Urban and Suburban**

Excerpt from "Plays and Players," Cal York, *Photoplay Magazine*, Vol. 22, No. 2, July, 1922, p. 93.

. . . What a difference music makes.

The finished orchestral accompaniment to Griffith's ORPHANS OF THE STORM, at the Apollo Theater, off Broadway; and the haphazard score which attended the picture in its various suburban settings provided a contrast.

Somehow the touching scenes didn't impress, or the ride-to-the-rescue thrill, nearly as much in New Jersey as they did in Manhattan. . . .

1922   **Griffith Prepares a Film**

Excerpts from "Griffith: Maker of Pictures," Harry Carr, *Motion Picture Magazine*, Vol. 24, No. 7, August, 1922, pp. 88-89.

. . . To see a Griffith rehearsal is a marvelous experience. It is to sound the most subtle depths of acting. Griffith goes over the play—over and over, until the actors are ready to commit suicide—but each time it grows a little under his hands. The gorgeous little touches of art which have been planned there in the old dining-room [of some hotel] with a couple of kitchen chairs for stagecoaches and a chalk-line for a mountain chasm, are among the masterpieces of American drama.

Every once in a while, D. W. will leave his chair by the little kitchen table and act one of the scenes himself. Sometimes he is a little sixteen-year-old girl, screaming with fright; and again a maiden, fancy-free, flirting with her lover. But somehow it never seems grotesque or funny. That's how good an actor he is.

At last, one morning you go out and D. W. is walking in front of a new set, with Huck Wortmann. Huck is the man who built Babylon in INTOLERANCE, and all the other marvels of Griffith pictures. Huck is a stocky, steel-eyed old stage carpenter. If you asked him to build an exact reproduction of heaven, he would merely take another chew of tobacco and say, "All right; it'll be ready a week from Monday." Nobody would ever know how he found out; but the set would look just like the place.

And so the picture begins. . . .

It gives you a thrill to see him directing Lillian Gish in her big scenes—as, for instance, the baptism of the [dying] baby in WAY DOWN EAST.

Dear, patient Lillian. I can see her now, waiting quietly for the lights while the   257 cameramen are nervously fussing with the lenses. There is a tense feeling in the air, like waiting for a battle to begin.

"Are you ready?" says Griffith.

"Yes, sir," says the cameraman.

"Camera," says Griffith.

And Lillian begins. Scarcely a word is spoken. Once in a while Griffith speaks a word of caution in a low voice. "Slower, slower." Then he will speak the lines for her—"My God, he is dead." She is like some wonderful sensitized instrument, vibrating to a master impulse.

"Cease," says D. W., at last, to the cameras. And he nearly always at such moments turns to the group around him with his eyes filled with tears. He is very easily affected, very easily driven to tears by art such as hers. It is only Lillian Gish who stands there, quietly waiting to do it again. Even the stage carpenters are frequently in tears. . . .

Every night we all went to the projecting-room to see miles of film run off. Every scene for a Griffith picture is taken three or four times by three or four cameras. The consequence is, we would absolutely go to sleep from exhaustion looking at these "takes." Even now I can hear Griffith's voice coming to me across a chasm of sleep; I can drowsily make out that he is asking, "Do you like the second shot or the fifth shot best?"

Griffith shot over eighty thousand feet of that ice scene in WAY DOWN EAST, and used only twelve hundred feet.

Finally the picture comes to an end; then we write the sub-titles. Griffith has the strength and endurance of a prize-fight champion. And, by the way, he is a very fine boxer and all-around athlete. In these terrible days, at the end of a picture he will shoot close-ups all morning, arrange music with a professional conductor all afternoon, have financial conferences all the early part of the evening, and write sub-titles all the rest of the night. These sub-title conferences take place over the length of a big table, formerly used by the directors of the Standard Oil Company when they used to foregather at Flagler's.

D. W. smokes interminable cigarettes—that is to say, he lights millions of them, takes a puff and lights another one. At the end of a title conference the place looks like a jury room.

He never gets through writing titles. I have seen him dictating them, sitting in the dark theater, two hours before the first performance was to begin.

The try-out of a Griffith picture is great fun. He gets his staff into a flock of automobiles and we go trundling upstate to some queer country town, where we fill the hotel. Wondering crowds stand around the street corners to see him pass. You scatter around through the audience and hear what the people say. Then the local manager comes up full of mysterious importance and we are all invited up to the Elks' Club to a midnight supper of lobster à la Newburgh—and other things. . . .

Coming back from the try-out, Griffith always proceeds to tear the picture all to pieces. He never gets through taking a picture. Sometimes, months after it has appeared on Broadway, he is still taking new shots, to be cut-in.

At last the big night—the Broadway opening—dress suits—critics—actors in boxes—personal appearances—a speech before the curtain—D. W. in a darkened box with a little row of electric buttons where he can signal to the orchestra leader or the stage hands.

Then, at last, at three or four o'clock in the morning—the society people and critics gone—D. W. and his "little gang," as he called us, with the morning papers still damp from the press, somewhere in a little soiled restaurant, eating scrambled eggs—talking it over.

"MR. GRIFFITH AT WORK"   **1924**

Excerpt from "Mr. Griffith at Work," *The New York Times*, January 13, 1924, Section 7, p. 5.

36. Griffith's ORPHANS OF THE STORM (1922): The last-minute rescue, "done with the utmost skill," but its outcome is never for a moment in doubt, even though the cavalry has to travel five miles. The frail figure in white, near collapse on the platform, is Lillian Gish.

The sun sent a bar of gold across the glistening waters of the Sound as we approached the old Flagler home at Mamaroneck in which David Wark Griffith makes his studio, and where he is now directing stray scenes of AMERICA, the picture of the American Revolution, on which he has been working for the last eight months. Our car was driven by a capable Japanese chauffeur, who took the turns in the road at splendid speed.

In a few moments we were inside the old mansion watching Mr. Griffith at work. He was standing in a prison dungeon with a cobble-stoned flooring, discoursing in low tones with Lionel Barrymore, who was sitting on the jail cot. Mr. Barrymore plays the role of Walter Butler, a character without a single redeeming attribute. Griffith was in modern clothes, and Barrymore in boots and breeches and shirt of gloomy hue.

Holding his cigarette between his fingers, Griffith stepped back to the firing line of the three cameras, and then called out "Lafayette," just loud enough to be heard in this unusually quiet studio. The Marquis de Lafayette, with his aide, stepped through the oaken door into the dingy-looking cell, his sword clanging, his tri-cornered hat set off by a red ribbon, and cream-colored lace protruding through the gap left by his graceful cape that hung in folds down to the calves of his high boots.

"So—sen-timen-tal," prompted Mr. Griffith, after the brilliantly attired aid had introduced the great Frenchman. "You—look—charming—just—now," continued Griffith, weighing the cigarette between his long fingers. "You—think—it might be possible to get him out of there, Barrymore—Ah, that would be—wonderful!"

Reflects Moods.

As he uttered the different sentences with pauses, Mr. Griffith appeared to act the different parts himself. He put himself with swift transition into the moods he wanted the players to feel. The overhead Cooper-Hewitts vied with the fading daylight visible through the upper windows.

They had a second rehearsal. "Allow me to present the Marquis de Lafayette," came from Griffith. "Now the sympathy, Lafayette," instructed Griffith, who calls his characters according to the name in the story. "This place is bad for—you," urged Griffith. "That is enough."

Even the electricians were interested in the scene, a minor one in this production, regarding which Lionel Barrymore is extremely enthusiastic. It seemed strange that this actor, then seated on the cot in a cell, would be seen that night in the stage success, *Laugh, Clown, Laugh.*

"Your lights," ordered Mr. Griffith, and there was silence—only broken by the words from the director and the buzz of the winding of the cameras. After that was finished Griffith suggested trying the scene once more, and while preparations were being made Mr. Griffith told us that he would soon have to take a test of a George III, then sitting on a red plush chair, evidently hoping his build and physiognomy would be acceptable.

The cameras ceased to grind and Mr. Griffith approached Barrymore. "I don't think he would kiss your hand—no, I'm sure he wouldn't." Barrymore agreed with the director.

Looking around one saw actors yawning, others reading, and some listening in a distant section to one man relating a story. They were all made up and clad, ready to be called. As the scene was enacted once more, Griffith's voice was heard: "You hear them coming—the key. Open—" And once more the Marquis was introduced by the aide and once more he retired. But this time, Barrymore's face had to change, after Lafayette left him, from a smile to a sneer, and the words from Griffith for Butler's mouth were, "Well, you French frog-eater." Then Barrymore banged his fist in the palm of his hand. . . .

ISN'T LIFE WONDERFUL?   **FILM 1924**

"The Screen: Mr. Griffith's New Picture," Mordaunt Hall, *The New York Times,* December 1, 1924, p. 17.

ISN'T LIFE WONDERFUL?, with Carol Dempster, Neil Hamilton, Helen Lowell, Erville Anderson, Frank Puglia, Marcia Harris, Lupino Lane, Paul Rhekopf, Count von Schacht and Robert Scholz, adapted from a story by Major Geoffrey C. G. Moss, directed by David Wark Griffith; "On the Wings of Song," with Miriam Lax, soprano; Inga Wank, contralto; Beatrice Wichtwick, mezzo soprano, and others; THE CURE, an "Out-of-the-Inkwell" cartoon. At the Rivoli.

The struggle of Germany's poor for food in 1923 is the theme of David Wark Griffith's remarkable new film offering, ISN'T LIFE WONDERFUL?, which is the principal attraction at the Rivoli this week. It was translated to the screen from a story written by Major Geoffrey C. G. Moss, formerly a brother officer of the Prince of Wales in the Grenadier Guards. Major Moss had said that incidents arising from the occupation of the Ruhr Valley made him bitterly antagonistic to the French.

Mr. Griffith, however, disregards the inspiration for this literary effort and contents himself with a fling at the Kaiser and those responsible for war, without any reference to France. Through countless deft and effective touches in this simple yet deeply stirring narrative Mr. Griffith again proves himself a brilliant director. He depicts the listlessness and dulled eyes in individuals resulting from an ill-nourished condition, the apathy to meals consisting of little more than horse turnips, morning, noon and night; the disappointment in the scramble for a bit of meat, the exhilaration of a family over the hardly believable sight of a bowl of steaming potatoes, the arousing of exuberant spirits in half a dozen persons through the possession of a single egg and the boundless joy caused by a feast with liverwurst.

The exteriors of this photoplay were made in Copenick, near Berlin, which is the actual background of the author's story. The interiors were produced in Mr. Griffith's Mamaroneck studio. The principal players, Carol Dempster and Neil Hamilton, are ably supported by others in the cast.

The love story of Inga (Miss Dempster) and Hans (Mr. Hamilton) is unfolded with charming simplicity, there being only a few instances in which Mr. Griffith's direction is theatric. He propounds the idea that although scenic beauty loses its attraction to famished persons, love is paramount. Inga and Hans diffidently inform the family that they wish to get married, which elicits the apathetic inquiry: "On what—turnips?"

Theodore, a student son, works in a night club, where, to prevent the stealing of food the waiters are searched as they leave. One is delighted when two Americans buy all the liverwurst in the night club for Theodore. One billion marks worth of liverwurst! It wasn't a very big piece after all, but when Theodore encounters Hans and Inga, who have dug up plenty of potatoes on their allotment, the three dance arm in arm through the middle of the narrow road, their faces lighted up with delirious joy. This scene will surely bring applause every time it is shown.

On the same day as Theodore received his magnificent gift, one of the two hens lays an egg. Inga holds the precious egg in her two hands as she shows it to her grandmother.

Inga supplements her daily toil by working at night mending cane-seated chairs in an antique shop, being paid in secondhand furniture. She deprives herself of her quota of potatoes so as to give food to Hans when he is ill, and to impress him as being well nourished, she pads her cheeks with paper.

In a moment of affluence the sons send Inga to buy three pounds of meat. A long line is seen outside the butcher's shop, the door of which is guarded by armed soldiers. An hour passes, two hours, three hours, and still Inga has not gained the threshold of the shop. Meanwhile the price of meat has nearly doubled, which she learns as she watches the man continually changing the chalk figures on a slate. In the end she has insufficient money to buy enough meat, so invests it in bread. Another scene shows a line waiting

261

outside a horsemeat shop, and dejection darkens the faces of men and women when they are told there is no more.

Poverty stamps its mark even in the pathetic cabaret show, in which the dancers wear paper costumes which rip and tear when slightly strained. Toward the end of this picture Hans and Inga are seen as victims of lazy marauders who steal all their cartload of potatoes. Hans is beaten until he is unconscious, but when he opens his eyes and learns from Inga that all the potatoes are gone, he looks at her and as he kisses her says [to console her and restore her spirits, that even so]: "Isn't life wonderful?"

Erville Anderson impersonates an absentminded professor. He gives a splendid performance in which delicate comedy touches are most appealing. Lupino Lane plays the part of one of the boys, and he also cheers up the story, which after all is so well told that it is rarely depressing. Miss Dempster is excellent in her exacting role. She looks delicate, wistful and natural without any exaggerated make-up. Mr. Hamilton is capable as Hans, but he hardly impresses one as being in want of food. Helen Lowell does very well as the grandmother.

Possibly this story would be even stronger if the sequence with which it is ended were put back [earlier in the film] and replaced by the dinner chapter, which would make a powerful climax.

Dr. Hugo Riesenfeld introduces this picture with a beautiful prologue with twinkling sapphire stars embedded in a midnight-blue background, enhanced by the colorful costumes of the singers.

Max Fleischer's cartoon, THE CURE, is unusually clever.

CHAPTER 15

Chaplin in the Twenties

COMMENTARY

Charlie Chaplin was the first of three major comedians of the American silent period to step up from shorter films to starring features—the other two, of course, being Harold Lloyd and Buster Keaton. This review of THE KID (1921), Chaplin's second feature, echoes some of the objections to his "vulgarity." Also on the program at this benefit showing was the German film PASSION (MADAME DUBARRY), directed by Ernst Lubitsch, which a month before had made Pola Negri a star literally over-night on Broadway.

In "Dear Mr. Chaplin," Stark Young of *The New Republic* urges Chaplin toward drama. The "last picture" in which Chaplin had appeared was PAY DAY (April, 1922), but it did not, as Young thought, complete his First National contract; this did not happen until THE PILGRIM (February, 1923).

The film which left Chaplin free to do what he liked was A WOMAN OF PARIS (October, 1923); he wrote and directed it, and in it he featured Edna Purviance (who had appeared in so many earlier comedies with him) and Adolphe Menjou. Chaplin himself played only a minor bit as a railroad porter. Considered extremely subtle, sophisticated and original, A WOMAN OF PARIS, although certainly not a runaway hit, nevertheless exerted so much influence on future production that it is described as having "changed the entire motion picture business." It is one of the key films of the time, but un- fortunately it has never been made generally available for study.

FILM 1921   THE KID

"The Screen," *The New York Times*, January 22, 1921, p. 9.

Charlie Chaplin is himself again—at his best, in some ways better than his previous best, and also, it is to be regretted, at his worst, only not with so much of his worst as has spoiled some of his earlier pictures. His return to the screen after more than a year's absence is in THE KID, which was shown last night at Carnegie Hall as the feature of an entertainment for the benefit of the Children's Fund of the National Board of Review of Motion Pictures. In the near future the picture will come to the Strand Theatre for its regular Broadway run.

THE KID is not only the longest comedy in which Chaplin has appeared since becoming the best-known figure of the film world, but it is real comedy. That is, it has something of a plot, its people are characters, and the fun of it is balanced with sadness. And Chaplin is more of a comedian than a clown. It is the comedy that has been foreshadowed by the former shorter Chaplin works.

Also, although the screen's unequaled comedian is in no danger of losing his laurels to any one, haste must be made to mention a new individual in his company, as much of an individual as Chaplin himself, and a source of immense delight. This person is a wonderful youngster by the name of Jack Coogan, surely not more than 6 or 7 years old, and as finished, even if unconscious, an actor as the whole screen aggregation of players is likely to show. He is The Kid, and he will be remembered in the same image with Chaplin. They have many scenes together, and every one of them belongs to both of them. Come on, Jack Coogan, there must be more of you.

The blemish on THE KID is the same that has marred many of Chaplin's other pictures—vulgarity, or coarseness. There is only a little of it in the present work, just two scenes that will be found particularly offensive by some. They are funny. That cannot be denied. One laughs at them, but many try not to, and are provoked with themselves and Chaplin for their laughing. This is not good. The laugh that offends good taste doesn't win. And these scenes would never be missed from THE KID. It has plenty of unadulterated fun to go far and long without them. Why can't Chaplin leave out such stuff? Why don't the exhibitors delete it?

There is less pure horse-play in THE KID than in the other Chaplins. The comedian depends chiefly upon his inimitable pantomime, and it scores every time. He also gets many laughs from the ludicrous situations which he concocts. There's nothing clumsy about the picture's continuity. Its "comedy relief" actually comes as a well-timed relief.

The story is simply about a curious derelict who has an abandoned baby thrust upon him. His life with the child fills most of the six reels, and comes to happy issue after a dream of heaven, which for burlesque stands alone.

The competent cast also includes Edna Purviance and Tom Wilson, Chaplin's reliable leading woman and favorite policeman.

Also on the program was the German picture, PASSION, with Pola Negri, which rang as true as ever, especially for those who delight in the purity of its acting.

Between the pictures Michio Itow danced, and was well received.

"DEAR MR. CHAPLIN"   1922

By Stark Young, *The New Republic*, Vol. 31, No. 403, August 23, 1922, pp. 358-359.

Dear Mr. Chaplin: You get hundreds of letters every week no doubt, but I have seen your last picture—which they say completes your contract and leaves you free to do what you like—and I must write to say that I hope this will indeed be the last of its kind and that now you will go on to a larger field. How many people have said this to you I have no way of knowing. But your friends, I am sure, insofar as they are able to see, must have said it often.

This is how it stands. You have created one of the great clowns of all time. This Charlie of yours needs no portrait anywhere: he is foolish, pathetic, irrepressible, flickering, comical, lovable beyond all words; he is light as air; he is a blunderer with a heart not solid but worn like a flower on a child's sleeve; a sexless gallantry; he is a tireless curiosity drawn to things as a monkey to a peephole or a moth to a flame; a gentle blithe dreamer and acrobat; a mask; he is a little, grotesque music; a dear laughter carried lightly in everybody's breast; a gay, shy classic; a world figment.

But you have finished your creation. It was perfect long ago. Already it begins to slow down. It shows a falling off in invention and zest; it shows a kind of boredom in you

37. The Eternal Cop, observed with caution by Charlie Chaplin, as The Tramp, and Jackie Coogan in the title role of THE KID (1921). This was Chaplin's second feature-length film, which set up another outcry from viewers who wanted to enjoy his slapstick without being subjected to his "vulgarity."

despite the great art with which you sustain the flow of it, the lightness, the airy intensity. Better still it is than all the clowns in the world put together could do, or comic artists anywhere; but it is yet not quite its own best; it is a little weak judged by itself. You have the achievement of it, however, to rest on, whatever happens, whatever you turn to. And you have your own genius and accomplishments to go forward on. The greatest actor in English you are very easily. You have a technique completely finished for your needs so far; an absolute accuracy of the body and the idea, a perfect identification of gesture and intention. You have the musical quality without which no acting is consummate; it appears in your incomparable fluidity of action and in your beautiful, unbroken continuity of style. You have precision and extraordinary economy. You have invention. And—what is the last test—you have been able to give to all this craft and abundance of technical resource that final genius of vitality that makes it really universal, of the people, who long before the critics ever knew of you recognized your credit though your craft was hid from them.

But with all this you have done only one thing. Why not go on? There are so many things that you could do. There is *Liliom* for example. What could you not do with that part where Mr. Schildkraut made it a role that was expert only, always crowded in motif and business and nearly always touched with vulgarity and insistence? You could do *He Who Gets Slapped*. Or with study you could do *Peer Gynt*, and many other parts. But better than all of these, you could do new things written by you or for you, things in which you would use your full endowment, comic and otherwise. And finally you might do the one most important of all things so far as moving pictures go, and that is to develop things calculated strictly for it and for no other art, made up out of its essential quality, which is visual motion and not mere stage drama photographed. In sum, you might really create in terms of the moving picture as you have already created in terms of character.

But all this will have to be a real change, Mr. Chaplin, or at least a real and definite openness to change and to new embarkations. It cannot be done by writing Charles instead of Charlie on the billboards, or altering the makeup of your eyes and mustache or shortening your riotous shoes. Such ventures in change amount to nothing and get nowhere. Go in at your full tilt. Go in for what you yourself like, for what satisfies you completely. And say that if the taste of the public does not like your work the taste of the public will have to change.

I think we can all understand some of the difficulties you have to struggle with when you think of taking such a step. There is first of all the natural desire to hold on to what you have won for yourself, to your enormous following. And always, of course, there are people around you who at the very mention of it will tell you that you will lose your place in the sun; who will try to hold you back, out of ignorance or kind solicitude or avarice or jealousy or general timidity. And there is the dread that you might feel of having your serious efforts laughed at, though you can master that if you choose, and can even use it to great ends, use superbly this tension and confusion of laughter and tears together. And not least in your way there is the peculiar money standard in our theatre, not the love of money exactly but its acceptance as a gauge of success, a measure of an actor's height; and you, naturally, may be human enough to compete with the others on their own grounds, however little they can compete with you on what is really yours. But all this is obvious: you know your own dream.

The truth is, you—like many an artist and many men not artists in America just now—are at the crossroads. You have got to choose. It grows clearer and clearer to us all that we are like children getting what we want, but what we want only in competition with each other, not profoundly, not out of ourselves. As time goes on and our relative values get more and more defined, we observe that much of the kind of success we see means only more gasoline, more food, more Victrola records made by other people, more

266

motion. It is forced on us that if we want more life we must look ahead to get it, and must choose what after all we will go after if we are not to be lost. We can see at any artists' club, the crowd of such as have taken for their art the watchword of business success, poor wise arrivals who knew how to play the game, knew what the public wanted and put it over as soap and collars and varnishes are put over with us, and who are now empty-faced, gregarious, unsubtle, unoriginal, bored, vivacious and stale. The necessity for a choice has grown very clear. These last few years especially for many an artist and many another man have been a comment on that experience that Francis Thompson wrote of, that divine pursuit, that flight down the nights and days and arches of the years, and the labyrinthine ways of one's own mind, and in the midst of tears, and under running laughter, from those strong feet that followed, followed after. The folly of that flight is one of those spiritual practicalities we cannot dodge, the common sense of the soul.

And whatever you may think, the cold facts remain, the truth in plainsong. Your public has had an instinct. It has liked the right thing, the best to be had. But the large public is like the natural world: it uses up for its own ends what it finds and then throws it aside. For a while, then, your great public will like, as it has liked, your best art as it comes along. Then later you will have the humiliation and the disillusionment of seeing them applaud equally or even more loudly—partly as the fruit of long habit—your less good things, applaud the bad more than the good was applauded. And this is the bitter last scene of all for a great artist, who can only sustain it easily by increased vanity and egotism. The public's way—which is nature's—of using and throwing aside is right almost, however cruel; for otherwise we should have in the end a survival of what is worse than dead. And yet there is a degree of devotion and survival that is a good thing. There is a degree of permanence of interest and of ideal relationship to art, among cultured men, that is good for art and its complete unfolding; just as there is a degree—though strictly limited and easily carried to unhealthy excess—of sublimation of the natural body into something of more ideality and a more permanent essence. And this you would find among a more cultured audience, of the judicious, as Hamlet would say, however few they might be at first compared to your old millions. And then, too, there is the hard biological fact not to be blinked, of your going off, the sheer physical decline from perfection. And, whether that descent has already begun or not, it is certain at least that this particular thing that you have done is possible physically only a few years more. The spring will go out of it.

And, in conclusion, dear Mr. Chaplin, the main thing is that you be happy as an artist in your own living. And that one can see from your pictures you are not. You have your dreams, we can see that, a passionate and delicate insurgence within you, a poetry and a music and a poignancy that eats into you. One feels that this man we see there on the screen knows very well that most of the people around him know little about him; knows that he has accepted too much cheap praise already and inferior court. He knows that he, like any creative artist, must always be alone and strange, as the mystery of creation is always alone in the material world; he must always be alone exactly as that little figure of his Charlie always stands out from any scene around him by its wistful luster and pathetic vividness. And this pathos, but half expressed, is what gives you now a good part of your appeal—for even little boys want to take you in their arms as they do their teddybears. It is like the pathos of life itself, which arises from our sense in life of the half-expressed, the passionate and tender and violent pushing against the dumb obstacles of fact and matter. If in your work this pathos goes no further than it does now, it will in time be lessened and gradually become a gap, a lack, or a mere pitifulness and half-defeat. But if you carry what is yourself further toward its full expression in a more complete art you will express more life, something more beautiful, comic, tragic, and profoundly characteristic of you. That of course is what you want, one sees it behind that mask of yours. And it seems only fair to tell you that there are those among your admirers who want you to have it, and believe that you need not fail except as every artist must fail, by comparison, as Leopardi said, with your own dream.

Stark Young.

A WOMAN OF PARIS   **FILM 1923**

Excerpt from "Pictures of the Past Week," *The New York Times,* October 7, 1923, Section 9, p. 4.

The greatest comedian of the silent drama, in a single production which he directed, has demonstrated vividly that most of the motion picture experts are working in a rut, and that new photoplay dramatics are necessary to increase interest in new results thrown upon the screen. He shows that keen attention and study of the smallest details are worth more than all the big sets and gigantic spectacles to which so many directors have been devoted for the last two years.

Charles Chaplin had an idea for a story and a different way of producing it—an idea he wanted to get off his mind. He was quite willing to take the risk of failure, so soon after he had finished the last picture in which he appeared—THE PILGRIM—he settled down to producing an unpretentious story, part of which he evidently mapped out in his mind while stopping at the pretentious Claridge's Hotel in Paris.

He was in an enviable position, it is true, for, unlike many directors, his word was law and he was absolute master of the situation when directing his players. Moreover, they had great faith in his ability and his judgment. Other men with the megaphone frequently discover that they have not the co-operation of the players. A star often insists upon his or her own way in doing something, no matter what may be the desires of the director; and on the other hand, when the player offers suggestions to this same director they are in return spurned by the man supposed to be in charge of the picture.

Chaplin the Czar.

Chaplin has had none of this friction with which to contend. If the new way of producing a picture had been unsuccessful, nobody could have been blamed but himself. He was responsible not only for the direction of the photoplay but also for the authorship of the story. The players he cast in the different roles of A WOMAN IN PARIS obviously realized that they had a marvelous opportunity, having implicit faith in his direction. Chaplin was also the financier, or angel, of his own production, which is said to have cost him $400,000, besides the sacrifice in time in not working all those months on one of his comedies, which always bring home the bacon.

Sooner or later it will be learned that Chaplin's conception of direction not only compels more serious consideration of photoplays, but that his ideas of handling a story are just what the public wants. Hitherto too much attention has been paid to the players in their desire for close-ups, and also to exasperating flashbacks, so often bewildering to those who see pictures, and a trick which frequently suspends the interest in the narrative.

In his A WOMAN OF PARIS, Chaplin has handled the different scenes so that the production gathers in interest with sustained suspense. The comedian shows his genius as a director in studying out new "business" in what another man might have set down as unimportant scenes. And instead of indulging in long-winded descriptive subtitles filled with absurd similes, this bold producer has insisted upon brevity, from which he obtains telling effects. "Idiot!" and "Liar!" are two of the spoken titles in this picture, and it chances that "Idiot!" is just what a French girl would have said in the circumstances. Chaplin's whimsicality is manifest when, after the girl has called the wealthy man a liar, they kiss. Even this kiss is portrayed in a way different from that in which it has always been done. It is a petulant kiss and not one of affection, for the woman still sulks. No cuddling accompanies this pecking of the lips, something altogether unusual in cinema work.

Some Clever Touches.

In another sequence, Pierre, following a spat with Marie, enters his home and immediately decides to call her up. At precisely the same moment, while her old sweetheart is pacing in front of the building in which she lives, Marie is seized with the same idea, so that the two calls come as one, and both ask: "Did you call?"

There are many other similar human touches, and one we must not omit is when the luxury-loving Marie suddenly declares her desire for a home and children. Pierre goes over to the window and then beckons to Marie. Below on the pavement one sees three children following their parents, one being slapped by the poor mother, while the father is bent under a burden he is carrying.

Stealth seems to mark the opening of this picture, as Marie is seen going quietly to her room in the little cottage in an obscure French village. Then the unsympathetic father appears and quietly turns the key in the lock of the girl's room. The sweetheart next is seen waiting for the girl, who comes to the window and announces that she is locked in. The young man climbs up and helps the girl down from the easily accessible window. They go for a walk and on returning find the window locked, and the father refuses to permit his daughter to enter the house, whereupon they retreat to Jean's abode, where his angry father refuses to permit the girl to stay. All this is done with the tersest titles, with most effective acting and photography.

Jean accompanies Marie to the little railway station, giving her money with which to buy the tickets for Paris, and he returns to his home to get his bag, to discover that his father has been taken ill, due to his great rage with his son. After waiting until it is nearly time for the train to arrive, Marie rings up Jean on the telephone, and through a misunderstanding as to the delay, she decides to go to Paris alone. Instead of seeing a train enter the station, one merely receives an impression that the train has arrived, through shadows and lights from the windows shed upon the platform. This is extremely cleverly done.

Studious Detail.

A year later, Marie has made a financial success through her beauty. Everything she wants is furnished by Pierre Revel, known as the wealthiest bachelor in Paris. There are some splendid scenes in an expensive French restaurant. The acting of the headwaiter lends bright comedy to the sequences in which he appears. Marie's luxurious existence is studiously shown, and her fast young friends are fine characterizations. The bickering she has with Pierre, after having found her old sweetheart, is pictured with realistic nicety. In fact there isn't a single scene in this production that is not just a little different from any other photoplay with which it might possibly be compared. Mostly it is the detail, to which much studious thought and attention has been given, that is responsible for the great charm of this unusually fine production.

Now that Mr. Chaplin has taken the initial risk, and the assured success of the new methods proved, let us hope that other producers and directors will learn all they can from the little man who has for the time being shed his funny clothes and make-up. Then the public can go to see cinema productions knowing that whatever confronts them, certain old tricks have been tossed into the discard and they are spared the agony of seeing them. . . .

1923   **An Acid Test for A WOMAN OF PARIS**

Excerpts from "Will Charlie Kick Off His Old Shoes?," Harry Carr, *Motion Picture Magazine*, Vol. 26, No. 5, December, 1923, p. 86.

. . . Directors have always protested that you couldn't convey the impression of real life by having the actors act in the way people really do.

In A WOMAN OF PARIS Charlie Chaplin has given a terrific answer to that doubt.

When her son is brought home dead—a suicide for love of a prostitute, all the mother does is to go on giving the facts about him to an interviewer. She does not move or make a gesture. She does not even go through the series of gulps and lip-biting that is supposed to go with the school of "repressed acting." She does literally nothing except stand still; yet the tragedy is there, stark and terrible. . . .

Charlie told me that his principal worry about the picture was the attitude of the less educated patrons. Like most real artists, he despises the work of art made for the so-called intellectual few.

He tried it out at the Beverly Hills Hotel at a party given to the youthful Cornelius Vanderbilt and it got over there; but that didn't mean much to him. He tried it on Doug [Fairbanks] and Mary [Pickford] at their home and that meant more; they having the expert angle. Finally he took the picture out to a neighborhood theater frequented by steel-workers and waited while it got the acid test. He says the finest triumph of his whole life came when a baby began to cry and the wife handed the infant over to her husband, "Hey," she said, "you take him home, I'm going to see the rest of the picture.". . .

"HOW THE GREAT DIRECTORS WORK"   1925

Excerpt from "How the Great Directors Work," Harry Carr, *Motion Picture Magazine*, Vol. 29, No. 4, May, 1925, p. 52.

Almost every one who visits a motion picture studio is surprised to find the directors more interesting than the stars they are directing.

Charlie Chaplin is an amazing sight. In the first place, he will not work at all unless—or until—he feels like it. Sometimes he will spend days on end just sitting around the sets talking himself and his actors into the right mood. The camera never starts until that right mood arrives. When the camera begins shooting, Charlie goes through many emotions—and motions. Sometimes he will throw himself flat on his stomach with his chin propped up on his hands. At other times he sits all hunched up in a chair.

I remember one day while they were taking A WOMAN OF PARIS, that one of the actresses did not please him. In the middle of her emotion, she stopped and looked around: the director had disappeared. He was back in a corner of the set. He was sitting down, bowed with grief. His hands covered his face. It had been too much. He peeked at her through his fingers like a little boy. At length he raised his head and said to her with bitter reproach, "Trying to make you act is like writing love-letters on butcher paper." Charlie is even more particular than [Ernst] Lubitsch. The scene in A WOMAN OF PARIS where the old mother saw the body of her son brought home, was taken eighty-two times before Charlie got it to suit him. . . .

COMMENTARY

Chaplin completed only two more films in the silent period: THE GOLD RUSH (1925) and THE CIRCUS (1928), but his silent releases continued into the sound period (CITY LIGHTS, 1931; MODERN TIMES, 1936). It was not until 1940 that he released a dialogue film: THE GREAT DICTATOR.

In "Chaplin Explains Chaplin," the actor refers to Josef von Sternberg's THE SALVATION HUNTERS (1925), which had greatly impressed Chaplin and Fairbanks, and

38. *A wistful host awaits the dance-hall girls who have forgotten his invitation: Chaplin in* THE GOLD RUSH *(1925). He had travelled before into this area of pathos in* THE KID *(1921)* and A WOMAN OF PARIS *(1923), and would again in* CITY LIGHTS *(1928-31).*

which they had secured for distribution through United Artists. Its bad critical reception, however, led to a rumor that their own belief in the film had been shaken.

During the first Los Angeles run of THE BIRTH OF A NATION, Chaplin went to see it on an average of once a week.

Stark Young, in "Charlot in Rome," sends in a foreign report on THE GOLD RUSH. Tom Mix had become not only the number one cowboy star of the United States, but one of the favorites of Europe as well. "Perla Bianca" is Pearl White. Valentino had died in New York that summer, which explains the revival of such a cluster of his films, including LO SCEICO (The Sheik).

"CHAPLIN EXPLAINS CHAPLIN"   1925

By Harry Carr, *Motion Picture Magazine*, Vol. 30, No. 4, November, 1925, pp. 31, 88.

> And he also confesses why his great ambition is to film the life of Christ. Says Charlie: *"Christ had charm, and a sense of humor. . . . He was what we call a mixer; yet He was always alone. . . . Nobody understood Him. . . . That is the supreme tragedy. . . ."*

A little shrinking self-conscious figure slipped into the almost empty dining-room where Hollywood had been at luncheon. Two or three of us still lingered—to the obvious disgust of the waiters.

It was Charlie Chaplin. He nodded to us shyly—then slipped in at the end of the seat. It was somehow a time for confidences. Next to a moonlight night, there is nothing like a half empty café.

Somebody congratulated him on THE GOLD RUSH; and Charlie nodded at me. "You said some hard things—and some good things about my picture," he said; and added with a shadow of a smile: "You were exactly right—both times."

And then he had an afterthought. "Except that place where you said I was getting sophisticated."

"Well, aren't you?"

Charlie shook his head. "Never sophisticated," he said. "I am not sophisticated at all. I read in the papers where I have this and that large motive for doing things; but they are wrong. It is pure instinct with me—dramatic instinct. I don't figure it out: I just know it is right or wrong."

"But you were so sophisticated in A WOMAN OF PARIS that the picture failed."

"Oh, it wasn't such a failure. It has made $100,000."

"Which side of the argument are you on? It was the picture that changed the entire motion picture business; and yet it didn't get up much excitement at the box office."

"It wasn't because it was too sophisticated; it was because it held out no hope. It was just like life. The people wanted to see the boy saved from suicide; and have the girl go back to him, and have them live happily forever after."

"In other words, it was tragedy."

"Yes, it was tragedy." Charlie hesitated; then he went on: "I like tragedy. I don't like comedy."

"You what! You don't like comedy?"

"No. I like tragedy; it is beautiful. The only comedy that is worthwhile is when it has beauty. That is all there is in life—beauty. You find that and you have found everything. Only it is hard to find."

Somebody asked him if his plays did not go better in Europe—plays like A WOMAN

OF PARIS.

Charlie suddenly grew interested. "Now, I like to talk about this—the way my plays go in different parts of Europe. I suppose it is so with all stars; I happen to know best about mine.

"In Russia, for instance, my plays go better than almost anywhere; yet they do not think I am funny at all. People have written me that the audience came out of THE PILGRIM in tears. They think of me over there as an interpreter of life. In Germany, they are only interested in my plays from the intellectual standpoint. In England, they like them for the clowning—the funny feet."

Charlie did not say so; but I am told that in Russia they have put up statues of him in the niches where the figures of saints and czars used to be. He is regarded as so profound a student of life that a Russian writer has written a book comparing him with the ponderous German philosophers.

Suddenly the talk flopped back to movies.

"Charlie," asked one of us, "what's the matter with the movies anyhow? The pictures are all getting bad."

"They aren't," said Charlie. "There is nothing much the matter with the movies except in this: all the situations possible in drama have been worn threadbare by pictures. They have been done a million times."

"What's the way out; what can be done about it?"

"The next course that pictures will take is narrative: the very episodic plays that have been avoided. Plays like THE GOLD RUSH, which is just a little story about a poor little 'cove' up there all alone in Alaska trying to do the best he could. Plays will be character studies like that."

"Why aren't there any great actors appearing on the scene; why are all the great ones old-timers?"

"Because they all copy each other. The new ones who could strike out for themselves imitate some star upon whom their admiration has been fixed."

Charlie gazed dreamily away, then he added: "One of these days a new screen genius will suddenly bob up and turn the world around. I don't know who he will be, but I am willing to gamble he will be a roughneck."

I asked Charlie what he considered the best thing in THE GOLD RUSH. He replied, after a moment's pause, that it was the scene where the girl in the music hall was looking discontentedly out over the throng—looking for a real man in the ruck. And the little "cove" thought she was looking straight at him; then, when he realized she was looking over his head that was the best moment, he said.

I asked him what he considered his best play; and without hesitation, he replied that it was EASY STREET.

"And the best single scene?"

"Well . . ." he hesitated and looked unhappy. "I don't know, but I guess it was one of the scenes in THE KID."

I asked him what he considered the best pictures ever made, and this was the list he gave: (Cheers from Griffith.)

    THE BIRTH OF A NATION
    INTOLERANCE
    HEARTS OF THE WORLD.

Chaplin looked at us defensively, as though prepared to resist to the last, and said he still considered von Sternberg's SALVATION HUNTERS to be one of the best pictures ever made. "They objected to it because the people were not real; but of course that was the greatness of the picture. They weren't supposed to be real. They were symbols—thoughts."

We talked of Charlie's future. He said that as soon as he gets enough money to risk it, he intends to make his long deferred picture on the sad life of a clown. He knows people will not like it; but he is going to make it anyhow.

And Charlie has one other great ambition. It is an open secret that the unpleasant publicity attending his marriage stopped a plan of his to film Papini's *Life of Christ*. There was even some thought of his lending his own marvelous actor's art to the leading role.

Charlie talked of the character of Jesus Christ. No adequate performance—no representation either in literature or on the stage has ever been given of Christ.

"To me," said Charlie, "the most profoundly tragic and interesting thing ever written was the work of Sadikichi Hartmann—half German, half Japanese. His book, *The Last Thirty Days*, was the finest thing ever written of Jesus Christ."

Charlie said that his conception of Christ is different from the usual pious, solemn, sad-eyed figure seen on the stage.

"Christ was evidently a man of the utmost social charm, with humor. You read of Him in the Bible as a dinner guest at the houses of the rich and poor—and an honored guest. He was what we call a mixer; yet He was always alone. He tried to give His message to the world, and nobody understood Him. That is the supreme tragedy."

"Charlie," I asked, "is life worth while?"

"At times," he answered.

"For instance?"

"For instance, I lie down on the beach on my back and look up at the sky and stop thinking, in a sort of empty bliss. Then my tummy tells me it is time to eat—and I eat. Then I lie down again in the sand. And life is worth while."

Harry Carr

"CHARLOT IN ROME" 1926

By Stark Young, *The New Republic*, Vol. 48, No. 619, October 13, 1926, pp. 217-218.

On my right sit a young American painter, all talent and florid industry, and a friend of his, a Genoese lady of a great family; the three of us have come from our hotel in Rome to see LA FEBBRE DEL'ORO, which is going at two theaters simultaneously, after having been already shown in Rome, and which I have seen in other cities posted as LA STRADA VERSO L'ORO, THE GOLD FEVER and THE STREET TO GOLD.

Before the lights go off we speak of the movies, the cinema.

For his part, the painter says, he adores Italian movies, when he gets back to New York or goes to an American film in Italy he finds it very flat and mild, after the heaving and panting, the fire and eye-rolling of the Italian film stars. He never tires of seeing their bosoms heave with great sighs of love and despair; he delights in their rich clothes and lavish chambers, those beds swathed in lace, billowing with satin, wreathed with damask hangings, he delights in their whiskered princes and tragic young men; and most of all he is happy when the pinnacle is reached and they chew rose leaves.

He thinks the Italian cinema artists have talent then? the Signora asks. At crises, the painter says, they have, their fire comes through. But the cinema method, where the director is everything, the actors mere machines, told to smile, swallow, weep, as the director decides, such a method is beastly. Ah, yes, she has seen plays being produced, the lady says, such a method can never make a great art. She returns the compliment by telling us something of the American movies that she likes.

Tome Meeks, this descendant of the great duke and admiral declares, she likes ah very much! He is so beeg and he does such things, and you cannot but like his smile, ah, that is a smile indeed! Yes, apart perhaps from Charlie Chaplin, who is of course unique, her favorite protagonista is Tom Mix. I recall the many posters for Tom Mix that I have seen over Italy, in famous old theaters, in slums. He is a favorite, and there are, too, the posters for Constance Talmadge, Ricardo Cortez, Perla Bianca. A Roman prince, the next head of a great house, has told me that his favorite artist is Mary Pickford. And plastered over Rome now are the announcements of Fatty Arbuckle, his play is called FATTY E L'AMORE INFRANTO. On every postcard stand are photographs of these players and many another, very few of them Italian, most of them from Hollywood.

Three pictures of Valentino's are in Rome this week, THE FOUR HORSEMEN, LO SCEICO and THE YOUNG RAJAH, and more to follow. Valentino came from the region near Bari on the eastern coast of Italy. But here his pictures have been under a cloud. It was partly because his quality was not very Italian, more Spanish indeed, with that static method and grave emphasis. But the direct reason for this unpopularity has been due to Valentino's changing his citizenship. With this new spirit working in Italy, with a growing national sense and tightening racial nerves and consciousness, Valentino's giving up his country was deeply resented. Our Marconi, they said, look at him, he lives in England, he is more English than Italian, but he is still an Italian citizen. A boycott arose against the Valentino films. In Sicily a hall was wrecked by the mob for daring to show this actor. Valentino, himself, it is said, at length wrote a letter to Mussolini, giving the arguments for such a change, and Mussolini is said to have sent out an order that the boycott should cease. Now that Valentino is dead the theaters and newspapers are full of him.

The lights are off, the film begins. Toward those snowy high passes press the line of adventurers, in their worn clothes, their backs bent, their frying pans, picks, ropes and so on very much to the fore. Some of the details are difficult for this audience, the frying pans and the general conditions of the event. But presently Charlie Chaplin enters and a gale of happy laughter runs over the house, followed by an attention very marked. Indeed as the picture goes on the silence is much greater than it is at the opera in Italy and as still as a mass compared to Italian theaters. The place is packed to the doors.

Then almost at once begins the practice common in all Italian cinemas. THE GOLD RUSH has not been on two minutes before something is left out, you remember that Charlie Chaplin stood before you much longer, gave you a fuller statement of that first moment. This cutting will shorten the time necessary to run off the film and thus allow for more repetitions in an evening and so more spectators and more tickets. As the picture proceeds, the hunt for gold, the dinner on the shoe, the Christmas dream and finally that last act—which drops so under the level of Charlie Chaplin and of the picture—the cutting appears frequently enough, half a minute less of this, half a minute less of that, two minutes pared off a scene, now and then a whole scene taken out. We see nothing of the bear that in those first moments comes sniffing round the cliff and later appears when the men are starving in the hut, which last without the first loses its point. Even the serving and eating of the shoe is shortened, though you might think every second of it precious and immortal and though the Italian audience gave it an ovation.

Seeing that cutting you wonder how much the Italian understands the Chaplin quality. On various billboards there have been posters of some actor applauded in vaudeville who impersonates Charlie Chaplin, and the impersonation lacks every inner quality and almost every likeness save the obvious properties. At THE GOLD RUSH this Roman audience does not laugh very much, and yet they seem not to feel the pathos of him. The cutting would seem to imply no perception of his method. Perhaps the quick Italian eye sees the whole of a stage idea faster and wants a speedier exhibition and winding up. But the very essence of this Chaplin art lies in its beautiful unbroken rhythm; you can see him establish a motive, it begins, it finds one or two actions that will reveal it, it comes to the end and waits a moment like a phrase in music echoing itself, it is finished. The Italian method on the other hand is in general more impromptu; it is apt to be redundant if not casual or worse, where Charlie Chaplin's is economical, pure and poignant.

The harlequinade of this art, they know, the lustre of its spirit and movement, you cannot doubt that. And they perceive, out of the long tradition that lies in the Italian past, the whole commedia that exists within this one mind. They know how many of the antique characters live in this one figure, and how much of the spirit of all the commedia dell'arte Charlie Chaplin embodies. In him its many persons and aspects are constantly implied, his brain and his poetry has for Italians a familiar dexterity and whim and invention. What they make of this figure of Charlie, their Charlot, of his defeat, his pure abstraction and poignancy I do not know, nor how much they translate all this into their own or universal terms. I do know that everywhere in Italy you see posters of Charlot and his pictures, and that the Genoese lady, as the lights come on, says to us, quite forgetting her compliments to the size and feats of Tom Mix, that Charlie Chaplin is unique in his art, the greatest artist of them all.

Stark Young.

CHAPTER 16

The American Film, 1919-1924

COMMENTARY

In 1916 the critic James Huneker wrote: ". . . the 'movies' have killed the drama. No doubt, when we all own a motor-car, the 'movies,' too, will go out of business." (39) This was the same year in which Douglas Fairbanks drove a Stutz Bear Cat in REGGIE MIXES IN, but he was never associated as closely with cars on the screen as Wallace Reid.

THE ROARING ROAD (1919) opened the way for more Wallace Reid (1890-1923) films built around cars (DOUBLE SPEED, EXCUSE MY DUST). This star, a clean-cut, collar-ad type who seemed the personification of the All-American Boy, later died of dope addiction. James Cruze directed THE ROARING ROAD, but left the car-and-train race as a virtuoso set piece to Frank Urson (just as Fred Niblo left the chariot race in the 1925 BEN-HUR to other hands); the other two films were directed by Sam Wood.

Lon Chaney (1883-1930) was already well-established in films as a skillful make-up artist before he made THE PENALTY (1920), which contained one of those specialty roles of his, involving the subtraction of expressive parts of the body. (He had achieved wide public notice only the year before, playing a fake cripple in THE MIRACLE MAN.) Wallace Worsley was to direct him again in THE HUNCHBACK OF NOTRE DAME.

FILM 1919   THE ROARING ROAD

Excerpt from "The Screen," *The New York Times*, April 14, 1919, p. 11.

THE ROARING ROAD, at the Strand this week, comes to an exciting finish with a race between an automobile and a train. It is exciting, as the involuntary exclamations and applause of the spectators yesterday afternoon testified. The spectators seemed to feel themselves on the train when the passengers were seen scampering from one side of the car to the other or crowding eagerly at windows to watch the tearing automobile. The people in the theater seats shared their sensations. And a noticeable feeling of pleasant relief after high tension calmed the house when the race was over, with the automobile a winner.

Frank Urson is reported to have directed the reproduction of the race [although James Cruze directed the film as a whole]. To him, therefore, must go credit for a masterpiece of picture-making. He knew just when and where and how to use the camera, when to

277

show a flash of the car, when to cut in with the train, when to give a glimpse of the excited passengers, where to throw highlights, and how to use darkness to intensify the suspense. Just jumping from the train to the automobile and back would never have made the race real. But by showing now a glint of the smooth tracks ahead of the train, now the beam of the automobile's headlights, now the expressions on the faces of the passengers, now the engineer and fireman at work in their cab, first one almost instantaneous picture and then another, the director succeeded in giving the spectators such a comprehensive view of all the action that they felt themselves a part of all of it. The race is one of the distinct triumphs of the moving picture. . . .

THE ROARING ROAD   **FILM 1919**

"THE ROARING ROAD," excerpt from "Across the Silversheet," Hazel Simpson Naylor, *Motion Picture Magazine*, Vol. 17, No. 6, July, 1919, p. 62.

(Paramount) This picture is supposed to star Wallace Reid, but according to the number of close-ups of Theodore Roberts smoking a cigar, I should say it was starring a new brand of tobacco. Although I quarrel with the infrequency with which the handsome Wally is allowed to come within camera range, I cannot but admit that the production as a whole is a mighty interesting piece of work. The story also was recounted in last month's *[Motion Picture] Magazine*, so you know it concerns a peppery young auto salesman, his red-peppery employer, his daughter and an auto race. The race between the machine and a train has been well handled by Director *[James]* Cruze. Every ounce of suspense, interest and thrill is maintained until the very end, while all the comedy possible is extracted from the conflict of the two men's hot tempers. Some of the photography is unnecessarily harsh on Ann Little, and Wally Reid is conspicuous because of the distance they keep him from the camera, otherwise THE ROARING ROAD is satisfactory. . . .

DOUBLE SPEED   **FILM 1920**

"DOUBLE SPEED," excerpt from "Across the Silversheet," Hazel Simpson Naylor, *Motion Picture Magazine*, Vol. 19, No. 5, June, 1920, p. 110.

(Paramount) This is my idea of a truly original, peppy, entertaining and wholesome movie. Wallace Reid is in great danger of becoming more popular than ever if he continues to decorate such comedies as these and little Wanda Hawley is intensely likable. The tale concerns the adventures of a rich young chap who starts West in his deluxe motor car, camping on the way. While he sleeps one night, tramps rob him of the car and everything he possesses excepting a blanket and his watch. A kindly, poor family in a Ford, carry him the rest of the way, but when he arrives in Los Angeles in his borrowed clothes his bankers won't recognize him and he is forced to pawn his watch, which he does under an alias. Shortly after his purchase of a suit of good clothes he bumps into a girl driving his car. She mistakes him for a chauffeur and engages him on the spot. From that time on the fun and complications wax greater and greater until the mystery of his identity is successfully cleared up after their elopement. Theodore Roberts and Tully Marshall aid in some of the finest comedy moments. . . .

EXCUSE MY DUST   **FILM 1920**

"EXCUSE MY DUST," excerpt from "The Shadow Stage," Burns Mantle, *Photoplay Magazine*, Vol. 18, No. 1, June, 1920, p. 68.

39. Rudolph Valentino and Alice Terry in Rex Ingram's THE FOUR HORSEMEN OF THE APOCALYPSE (1921). An impassioned exposure of the waste and futility of war, the film revealed the star potential of Valentino, and it was revived five years later, after his death.

(Paramount-Artcraft) I liked Wallace Reid's EXCUSE MY DUST, first, because it is a good short story, attractively screened, and second, because its creators have not tried to make it anything more than that. One of the eleven or fourteen things we all find to object to in pictures is the obvious effort of scenaroist and director, the one usually abetting the other, to build a mansion out of the material laid down for a bungalow. When the thing is finished the foundation is fairly solid, but the superstructure is so very wobbly and thin you can plainly see through it.

EXCUSE MY DUST relates a plausible and interesting incident in the life of "Toddles" Walden, erstwhile demon driver of the good old Darco bus that won the Los Angeles-San Francisco race in "Speed Up."

No sex stuff here, and no suave young villain. Just a good, interesting, at times exciting, and always well told short story. The ingratiating Reid is as cheering a screen hero as usual, Theodore Roberts is excellent as the blustering "J. D.," and Ann Little is a lovable wife. . . .

THE PENALTY   **FILM 1920**

"THE PENALTY," excerpt from "The Shadow Stage," Burns Mantle, *Photoplay Magazine*, Vol. 19, No. 3, February, 1921, p. 66.

(Goldwyn) Here is a picture that is about as cheerful as a hanging—and as interesting. You can't, being an average human and normal as to your emotional reactions, really like THE PENALTY, any more than you could enjoy a hanging. But for all its gruesome detail you are quite certain to be interested in it. It at least offers an original story, and heaven and all the angel fans know how scarce they are. Also it has been screened by that crafty Goldwyn crew with a good sense of the dramatic episode and a free employment of theatrical tricks. Chief of these is the trick of making Lon Chaney "what he ain't"—a perfectly good legless wonder—by bending his legs back at the knees and strapping them against his thighs. You can see the strap arrangement, and you know the long coat conceals the feet, but you are extremely interested in watching him try to fool you. Then there are several sets of trick scenery—a practical fireplace that slides up into the chimney and reveals a secret cavern below, flaring, as it were, with the white hot flames of hell; rope ladders hung below peek-hole windows that the legless one may climb up like a misbegotten spider to take a look around; trap doors through which the investigating youth in search of the heroine is shot down to the villain-infested depths below. Chaney's role is that of a man who has sworn to be revenged upon society in general, and one man in particular, because, as a boy, he was crushed in a traffic jam and had both legs amputated above the knee by a careless surgeon who might have saved him. Legless, but bitter, he becomes one of those "rulers of the underworld" who have only to push a white button to summon an army of cutthroats, dope fiends and fancy lady-friends. But after getting all his enemies in his power the wicked one is restored to the world of decent men by an operation which removes a blood clot from his brain, and while he is later killed by one of his old pals the happy ending is provided by the appearance of Mr. Chaney with legs attached. It is a remarkably good performance this actor gives, and he is capably assisted by Ethel Grey Terry, Kenneth Harlan, Claire Adams and Charles Clary. Wallace Worsley's direction helps the picture a lot. Charles Kenyon and Phillip Lonergon wrote the scenario, from a Gouverneur Morris story. . . .

COMMENTARY

280   **THE LAST OF THE MOHICANS (1921) by Maurice Tourneur (1876-1961) was largely**

made by Tourneur's protégé, Clarence Brown (1890-   ), after an accident to the director. In discussing it, Burns Mantle anticipates by 14 years the movement to preserve films which got under way in 1935 with the founding of the Museum of Modern Art Film Library in New York, and, the same year, with the Cinemathèque Française in Paris and the National Film Archive in London. The Motion Picture Department of The George Eastman House in Rochester, New York, was founded in 1948, with James Card as curator.

Charles Ray, a star developed by Ince, specialized in bucolic roles. His subtitleless film, THE OLD SWIMMIN' HOLE, preceded several celebrated German imports, also without subtitles.

THE FOUR HORSEMEN OF THE APOCALYPSE revealed the star potential of Rudolph Valentino (1895-1926) in a romantic recollection of World War I. It was revived five years later, after Valentino's death, with a success that was only partly due to the memorial factor. Rex Ingram (1892-1950) continued to direct through the Twenties, and in 1921, again with Alice Terry (who was to become his wife) and Valentino, he also filmed THE CONQUERING POWER, based on Balzac's *Eugénie Grandet*. In THE PRISONER OF ZENDA (1922) and SCARAMOUCHE (1923), Ingram featured Miss Terry and Ramon Novarro (1899-1968), Ingram's discovery after differences of opinion estranged him from Valentino.

FILM 1921   THE LAST OF THE MOHICANS

"THE LAST OF THE MOHICANS," excerpt from "The Shadow Stage," Burns Mantle, *Photoplay Magazine,* Vol. 19, No. 5, April, 1921, p. 78.

If we had a National Cinematographic library, as we should have, into the archives of which each year were placed the best pictures and finest examples of the cinematographic art achieved during that year, and I were on the board that voted upon the admission or rejection of submitted films, I certainly should include THE LAST OF THE MOHICANS in my list of eligible exhibits. There is, to me, an impressive effort made in this fine picture of Maurice Tourneur's to treat a big subject with dignity and a certain reverence to which its traditions entitle it, and yet to do so without losing sight for an instant of its picture possibilities. Uncas, the Indian, is neither a handsome thing to look upon, nor yet a romantically fascinating hero. But Uncas is real, and the adventures through which he leads the trusting Munros are thrillingly true to the spirit of the story. Tourneur differs from most of the directors in his class in that he can achieve great beauty of background without sacrifice of story value, and while he does permit a certain repetition of his favorite shots, the views from a darkened cave through to the blazing firelight or sunlight or moonlight beyond, for example, with silhouetted figures against the light, they seldom interfere with the spectator's interest in the tale. There is more good melodrama in THE LAST OF THE MOHICANS than in a half dozen crook plays; more fine, hair-raising fights, and one supreme climax in the leap from the cliff that has not been equalled for several seasons. There is a nice sense of delicacy in the treatment of the romance, and there is as fine an effect in the panoramic close-up of the escaping villagers as I ever have seen screened. The cast, headed by Albert Roscoe, as Uncas, Wallace Beery as the wicked Magua, Barbara Bedford as Cora Munro, is well chosen, Roscoe and Beery giving especially good performances. . . .

FILM 1921   THE OLD SWIMMIN' HOLE

Excerpts from "The Shadow Stage," Burns Mantle, *Photoplay Magazine,* Vol. 19, No. 6, May, 1921, p. 51.

Eventually, the perfect picture, my friends tell me, and write me, will be the picture without a single subtitle. A picture so simply, so logically and so forcefully told on the screen that printed captions will not only be unnecessary to its understanding, but in which their intrusion would prove a distinct irritation to its audiences. And I half suspect they are right.

But it happens that I have been waiting for some years now to see what equally enthusiastic friends have told me, and written me, will be the perfect play on the speaking stage—a play that shall preserve absolutely the unities as laid down by the esteemed Dr. Aristotle some hundreds of years ago; the unity of time, necessitating that it shall cover in action only such time as is consumed in its playing; the unity of place, which demands that it shall require only the most logical changes of scene, and the unity of action which prohibits those arbitrary lapses of time between acts that span either a day or a generation, or the curtain lowered momentarily, as the witty George [Jean] Nathan once remarked, "to indicate a lapse of morals."

One or two plays have achieved the perfect form within the last twenty-five years. But the perfect form has generally been the most openly and frequently violated of all the accepted guides to structural perfection.

So it will be, I fear, with the perfect and titleless picture. Heaven knows there are whole volumes of wordy and meaningless titles that we could now do without. They have ruined as many pictures as they have saved, and cluttered and hampered and handicapped many a story that might have offered good entertainment, if left to tell itself. But to do the picture editors justice, there also have been pictures that have been vastly helped by their titles, and many a light comedy has had its quota of laughs doubled and tripled by the cleverness of its captioning. . . . As a matter of fact, the titling question resolves itself to this: When they're good they help; and when they're poor they're awful.

THE OLD SWIMMIN' HOLE

(First National) There have been two samples of titleless pictures recently that have lent strength to the arguments of those opposed to them. One was THE KID, in which Charles Chaplin found it practically unnecessary to explain in print either the intentions of his characters or the lapses in his story. The other, Charles Ray's THE OLD SWIMMIN' HOLE, goes even farther and has not so much as a single subtitle throughout its six reels of length. Of course, it is not a story that demands titles. No one in it could possibly have anything worth titling to say, and there is no story at all in the plot sense. It is a day in the life of a small-town boy, a rather overgrown and clumsy small-town boy, necessarily, as Ray plays him, but a lovable, human, untheatrical type. It could go on and on for sixteen as well as for six reels and, so long as it was kept as human and as true to the general acceptance of a small-town boy's life, as Ray and his director, Joseph De Grasse, keep this much of it, it would be an interesting and enjoyable picture. . . .

THE FOUR HORSEMEN OF THE APOCALYPSE   **FILM 1921**

Excerpt from "The Screen," *The New York Times*, March 7, 1921, p. 8.

The motion-picture version of Vicente Blasco Ibañez's impassioned novel of the war, *The Four Horsemen of the Apocalypse*, was presented for an indefinite run, under the direction of Dr. Hugo Riesenfeld, at the Lyric Theatre last night. A large number of spectators, many of them invited for the occasion, gave it hearty approval.

It is as a work in kinetic photography that the screened FOUR HORSEMEN should first be considered, because its standing as a photoplay depends upon its pictorial properties and not upon its relation to a widely read novel. The most important fact about the production, then, is that, although it has a good deal of the wordiness, erratic tempo and illogical emphasis common to screen adaptations of printed stories, it is nevertheless distinguished from many other works of its kind by genuine cinematographic qualities. It is made, if not entirely, at least in large part, of telling moving pictures. Many of its scenes are the result of fine photography, and, better still, fine cinematography. Rex Ingram, the director of the production, is among those who believe that principles of painting and sculpture should be applied to motion pictures, and scenes in THE FOUR HORSEMEN are concrete illustrations of what the application of these principles means. Evidently Mr. Ingram's expressed ideas are not merely subjects of idle conversation with him. He tries to do what he says ought to be done. His pictures, for examples, are smooth and soft, and yet as distinct as the sharpest photography could make them; they are effectively lighted; and their dramatic, as well as purely pictorial, value has been moving and still objects. Mr. Ingram must have devoted much time and thought to composition, and in a number of instances he has achieved something different and better than materials at the disposal of other directors and frequently used by them in the last few years. For example, there is a scene of troops marching through a French village, which is scarcely a new subject at this post-war date, yet Mr. Ingram has presented it with new effectiveness by breaking the main line of march of the troops and occasionally diverting from it companies and squads of men. Thus he has given fluidity and unity to his whole scene instead of dividing it into two still pictures as a continuous column of men moving in a straight line or simple curve would do—and often has done in other photoplays.

Mr. Ingram has made many eloquent motion pictures. This means that, although the spectator now and then has the impression that the photoplay is simply the novel splendidly illustrated, this impression is dissipated as often as it is formed by scenes and successions of scenes which speak for themselves, tell their part of the narrative in their own language without the aid of words. The execution of the citizens of Villeblanche, for example, is done in pure cinematography, and is one of the most impressive incidents of the story. In bringing the symbolic Four Horsemen into the photoplay Mr. Ingram again has done his work cinematographically, and with such a discerning sense of the unreal in reality that what might easily have been banal or incongruous has become a pervading and leavening part of the picture.

The photoplay has been cast with a clear eye for types and casting ability. The characters used primarily to give color to the picture—South American natives, Spanish, French, and German specimens—are all strikingly individualized, and those who have the more extensive roles not only look their parts but act them intelligibly, especially Rudolph Valentino as the young Julio, Joseph Swickard as old Don Marcelo, Alice Terry as Marguerite, Alan Hale as Karl von Hartrott, and Nigel De Brulier as Tchernoff, the Russian mystic.

Many will want to know, of course, how closely the photoplay resembles the book, and they may be assured that it is, on the whole, a faithful and appreciative translation of what Blasco Ibañez wrote. There have been changes, some necessary or wise, others capricious, but June Mathis, who made the scenario, has followed the main trend and thought of the novel. All things considered, she has done a difficult job well. There have been omissions, of course, as all of the book could not be put into a film of reasonable length, but the part of the story that is its reason for existence, the latter section dealing with the war, has been treated adequately and in the intense spirit of the original. The section dealing with South American life has been only sketched, though vividly in spots, and its chief character, the old centaur, Madariaga, has just been mentioned in passing, so to speak. The love affair between Julio and Marguerite and the character of Tchernoff have been considerably idealized, and the death of Julio has been made more

283

melodramatic than it was in the novel. Also the spiritistic element, absent from the book, has been introduced into the photoplay, and another innovation, much less justifiable, is the bringing in of a pet monkey which has been made to act as if he definitely understands and sympathizes with the moods and situations of the human beings around him. Of course, trained animals do not do this, and the tricks of the monkey are simply broad comedy, entirely out of harmony with the rest of the story. It was felt, no doubt, that "comic relief" was desirable in so serious a work, and accordingly the incongruous animal was dragged in to supply the missing ingredient, but the added stuff does not accomplish the first business of an ingredient, which is to mix with the other ingredients of a compound. It is too bad that the adapters felt called upon to monkey with their material.

When all is said about THE FOUR HORSEMEN, however, the central fact remains that it is an exceptionally well done adaptation of a novel, and an extraordinary motion picture to boot. . . .

THE FOUR HORSEMEN OF THE APOCALYPSE (Revival)   **FILM 1926**

Excerpt from " 'FOUR HORSEMEN' Still Better Than Most Films," Mourdaunt Hall, *The New York Times,* October 3, 1926, Section 8, p. 5.

Whatever Rex Ingram's production of THE FOUR HORSEMEN OF THE APOCALYPSE may lack in up-to-date lighting and photography, there is no doubt it outshines most of the pictorial offerings in the splendid clarity of its story. The continuity of this feature, produced more than five years ago, is amazingly fine, which is no small achievement, considering the number of characters that Mr. Ingram had to handle. Never for an instant is the spectator confused regarding the identity of the different individuals flashed on the screen.

The strong point about this stirring entertainment often is the weak point in current productions, which proves that the film producer still is far too fond of pandering to some popular thrill or featured episode irrespective of whether it deserves being stressed. The picture-going public is tiring of lofty halls and sunken bathtubs, preferring a coherent story, with accurate dramatic emphasis. The conventional situations that run through so many pictures ought to have been discarded long ago for the reproduction of the simplicity of everyday life or naturalness, combined with a sound idea of human psychology.

Another creditable point in THE FOUR HORSEMEN is the careful selection of the players for the respective types. One does not find a man of Teutonic features thrown into a French role just because he is a good actor, and the make-up of the players is far more natural than in many pictures released this year. Then, too, the figurantes in Mr. Ingram's film have a pleasing ease in their acting, whether in uniforms or civilian clothes. There are none of those old-fashioned poses and gestures, and the whole tempo of the photoplay flows with admirable evenness.

There have been a number of war pictures since THE FOUR HORSEMEN; but, aside from King Vidor's masterpiece, THE BIG PARADE, and George Fitzmaurice's THE DARK ANGEL, there is in few of them any scene comparable with that in which the German officers are making merry in the Desnoyers' Marne chateau. It is just as one would picture it mentally, and there is in it a glimpse that reminds one of Guy de Maupassant's "Fifi." The Prussians in 1914 did very much the same thing as they did in 1870. The officers were overbearing fighters, making the most of every luxury they could find, being careful even to spare a fine chateau so that if they managed to forge ahead to where the structure was they would be sure of a comfortable billet. In picturing this scene, with all its greed and cruelty, Mr. Ingram has stayed within bounds. One can

284

readily imagine what such a sequence might have been had it been handled by a director who visualized greater things than the truth for every incident as it marched along. . . .

1921   "FROM CAMERA TO SCREEN"

From *The New York Times*, August 7, 1921, Section 6, p. 2.

Most people, and especially those who have had to wait until Monday for the kodak prints which the corner drug store man promised them on Saturday, know that when the cameraman turns the crank of his machine in the studio he exposes negative films from which positive prints have to be made before any pictures can be seen in a theater, but there are few who have any more than a vague idea of how the thousands of feet of positive film in a photoplay are obtained from the milky-white negative that comes out of the camera. The negative is developed, of course, and then printed, but a good deal more than the little black trays, tin tanks and wooden frames familiar to amateur photographers is involved in the process. And the present laboratory machines and methods by which duplicate positives often more than a mile in length and divided into hundreds of scenes are obtained have not been spontaneously arrived at. They are the result of as much invention, adaptation and industry on the part of the laboratory men as have contributed to the perfection of the camera itself and the dramatic development of photoplays.

Lewis E. Physioc, Superintendent of the Goldwyn Laboratory in Culver City, Cal., has supplied this department with an account of how the laboratory began and how it has grown to meet the demands of the studio and the theater. He says that in recent years the laboratory has developed more than the camera, the present machines for taking pictures being only improvements of the earlier ones, whereas the laboratories are radically different in many particulars.

"In the early days," says Mr. Physioc, "films were printed on primitive machines operated by hand, of the stop or intermittent type, exposing a single frame at a time at the rate of about eight frames a second. Their capacity under the best conditions was 4,000 or 5,000 feet of film a day, and after a negative had been run through one of them to make a few positive copies it was hardly fit for further use.

"When the method of cutting scenes into reels was changed more speed was necessary, and motors were attached to the printers. This change led to other improvements, which made their own difficulties.

"At first each scene was printed separately as many times as it was required for the duplicate copies of the photoplay to be exhibited, but splicing the scenes in their proper order necessitated so many joints in each positive that it frequently came apart as it was running through the projection machine. The introduction of the cut-back and other short scenes, some of them only two or three feet in length, aggravated this trouble, and finally led to the joining of the negative into 200-foot rolls, with all scenes assembled as they were to be shown. In this way, the splices in the positive were reduced from 100 or more to five or six, but as the scenes in the negative were of varying density, an uneven positive resulted when the printing was done with an unvarying light.

"It was therefore found necessary to devise some means of changing the intensity of the light as the scenes changed, and this was accomplished by recording degrees of light intensity at certain relative positions of light to negative, and later by means of the rheostat. A notch in the side of the negative warned the operator when a new scene was approaching the printing aperture, and he changed the light to suit it. As crude as this method was it was a great improvement, but it was trying on the operator.

"Nowadays we have magnificent printing machines, with automatic light changes,   285 silently turning out 15,000 feet of film a day. No part of the negative's surface is touched in the process, so scratches are avoided. Conditioned air service and thermostat systems that maintain perfect drying conditions in all temperatures and conditions of the weather are also used."

Mr. Physioc adds that chemical evolution has kept pace with that of laboratory equipment. He says:

"Films were first developed on great drums that required large, open, shallow tanks which exposed so great an area of the developing fluid to the air that it was constantly undergoing rapid oxidation. Its power and quality differed for each drum put into it, and uniformity in developing was therefore impossible. Now, however, we have machines protected against dust and air, through which the film passes automatically without being touched by hands.

"Also, in the beginning the developers were compounded in ignorance, the operators naturally using the same formulae for the large quantities required that they had been accustomed to use for smaller quantities in still photography. Foggy, grainy and contrasting negatives were the result, until it was learned that new formulae had to be worked out for the larger quantities. Manufacturers of chemicals have also learned to maintain a standard of purity in their products hitherto unknown.

"The quantities of these chemicals used can hardly be appreciated by the outsider. For example, as much as 2,400 pounds of hyposulphite of soda is sometimes used in one bath, and from $200 to $600 worth of silver is reclaimed from this after it has been exhausted."

A developing bath, Mr. Physioc adds, often contains as much as 250 gallons of fluid, the chemicals in which must be the same today and tomorrow and every day it is used.

"IMPROVED TECHNIQUE"   **1921**

From *The New York Times*, September 4, 1921, Section 6, p. 3.

What has been generally regarded as the motion picture slump of the last few months has not been altogether a bad thing for the screen, in the opinion of those veteran scenarists, John Emerson and Anita Loos. The desire of producers to reduce expenses by eliminating scenes and saving film, they say, has resulted in progressive changes in scenario technique which might have waited years for adoption otherwise.

Mr. Emerson and Miss Loos write their scenarios together and their opinions, at least those publicly expressed, about motion pictures invariably coincide, but when quotation marks are used it gives the impression of a Montgomery and Stone song if the words are attributed to both of them. So let Mr. Emerson speak:

"There is a great deal of talk about developments in technique," he says, "but one seldom finds any specific statement as to just what these changes are. It is rather difficult to be specific in such matters, but Miss Loos and myself can number off a few of them, at least.

"First comes the diminution of the number of sequences—that is, episodes—in each picture. Formerly there were literally dozens of sequences, which tended to give the picture a choppy, jumpy effect, with a most syncopated tempo. These sequences are like the acts or scenes of a play, and, just as the play has gradually reduced the number of acts and scenes, so the movies are reducing the number of sequences.

"Secondly, there has been a move toward the elimination of what are known as 'narrative' sub-titles—those deadly inserts which read, 'Little Mary comes home and tells father that mother has gone away forever,' thereby ruining all the action which follows. Of course, in most cases these titles have been used to cover places where several

hundred feet of film have been cut out in order to shorten the photoplay, but that is no

40. *Douglas Fairbanks in the title role of* THE THIEF OF BAGDAD *(1924), forcing his way to the sleeping princess in a room that for spaciousness "looks like one of the* ROBIN HOOD *sets." Like Chaplin, Fairbanks inclined toward the heroic, but constantly broke the mood with satire.*

excuse so far as the audience is concerned. Today writers and directors have come to appreciate the undramatic quality of these inserts, and are striving to eliminate everything but the essential lapse-of-time and change-of-locale titles by trying to write continuities which will not necessitate big cuts after the picture is made.

"Thirdly, one of the most important developments is a standard scenario form which makes possible a rough estimate of the number of feet of film which a photoplay will consume in the making. It is an odd fact that no man or woman living can really estimate lengths from reading scripts. That is why pictures are always too long and have to be cut down before release, a most destructive process. And because in the 'old days' no two scenarios were alike the problem was still harder. One man would abbreviate his English, so that 500 feet of action was told in 100 words, the next man would elaborate, so that whole pages went to describing a single close-up; some wrote their scripts like novels, some like plays, others like business letters, each changing the form to suit his own likes and dislikes. There were writers who left out nearly all of their titles, planning to put them in after the picture had been filmed, and there were others who wrote almost nothing but titles."

COMMENTARY

Max Linder, who had been so popular in imported French comedies around 1910, came over in 1917 to make three short comedies for Essanay (a projected series of 12 was cut short by illness), but this now Chaplin-mad country was not very attentive. He came for the second time to America in the early Twenties, making as his third and final feature here, THE THREE MUST-GET-THERES (1922), a good-humored burlesque of Fairbanks' THE THREE MUSKETEERS, of the year before.

ROBIN HOOD (1922), directed by Allan Dwan (1885-   ), is a monumental example of the Fairbanks trick of remaining a twentieth-century American even in the context of another century. The opening reference in the review is to Fairbanks' THE MARK OF ZORRO (1920).

With the 5-reel GRANDMA'S BOY (1922), Harold Lloyd (1894-1971) definitely said goodbye to the short comedies he had been making since 1915. Briefly in the employ of Mack Sennett, he developed, under other direction (Hal Roach), a complete slapstick character—Lonesome Luke—before changing into the bespectacled idealist of his comedies of the Twenties. Box-office returns of that decade indicate that Lloyd's popularity sometimes surpassed Chaplin's.

Robert E. Sherwood, who wrote film criticism for *The New York Herald* and for the old *Life* magazine (of which he became editor), included this discussion of GRANDMA'S BOY in a volume intended to be the first of a series of annual publications about films, but there was insufficient audience for the project, and the volume stood alone, never followed by its intended sequels.

The hidden villain of the year was radio, soon to become a much greater threat to the welfare of the film. *The New York Times* headlined on May 21, 1922: "RADIO GETTING RESULTS FROM HOME SETS," adding that "Radio receiving has passed the experimental stage and reached the point where it is a source of amusement, pleasure and instruction to the average person. . . ." (40)

THE THREE MUST-GET-THERES   **FILM 1922**

"THE THREE MUST-GET-THERES," excerpt from "The Shadow Stage," *Photoplay Magazine*, Vol. 22, No. 6, November, 1922, pp. 90-91.

288   (Allied Artists) Closely following the Fairbanks version this burlesque reaches the

extreme height of comic artistry. It would make Dumas turn in his grave—and chuckle. With Max Linder in the part of *Dart-in-again* and Bull Montana as the aesthetic *Cardinal*, the interest is never allowed to lag.

Beautifully mimicking the tricks of Doug—and yet never losing his own identity—Max Linder tells the famous story of heroism and daring. His duels are riots of laughter, and some of the business employed to get effects falls little short of inspiration. Use is made of the slow motion camera—notably on the wild return trip to Paris. The episode of the queen's token is rendered absurd—and yet there are times when a real thrill of excitement is felt. The subtitles are not the work of a genius—but they're funny enough!

Everyone who has viewed THE THREE MUSKETEERS should see this. It will be enjoyed just as much—but in a different way. . . .

FILM 1922   GRANDMA'S BOY

"GRANDMA'S BOY," *The Best Moving Pictures of 1922-23*, Edited by Robert E. Sherwood, Small, Maynard and Company, Boston, 1923, pp. 9-13.

Directed by Fred Newmeyer. Written by Harold Lloyd, Sam Taylor and Jean Havez. Produced by Hal Roach. Distributed by Pathé. Released September 3, 1922.

Cast of Characters

The Boy	Harold Lloyd
The Girl	Mildred Davis
Grandma	Anna Townsend
The Rolling Stone	Dick Sutherland
The Sheriff	Noah Young

The success of Harold Lloyd during the past two years has been phenomenal, but not incomprehensible. This buoyant, bespectacled young comedian is an apostle of the American faith: he represents the personification of pep, spontaneity and determination. He is a natural-born world beater. He delights in building apparently insurmountable obstacles and then, with a sunny smile, surmounting them.

Moreover, Lloyd's humor is as native to these United States as George Ade's. Charlie Chaplin is distinctly continental in style, and Buster Keaton's comedy smacks of the London 'alls; but Lloyd, clad in a pinch-back suit, a straw hat and a pair of horn-rimmed spectacles, is at least one hundred per cent American. He is clean and wholesome, but not to an offensive degree (like Chaplin, he knows the most vulnerable and laughable portion of a policeman's anatomy, and is not afraid to exploit it); he is as fresh as an Oregon breeze and he is willing to play the goat as long as it is profitable. Indeed, his shyness, and his excessive timidity, serve to heighten the effect of his ultimate triumph.

Harold Lloyd has rushed forward lately at an increasing rate of speed. Always popular, since the days when he appeared as "Lonesome Luke," he has now established himself ahead of all the other stars as a box-office attraction. Within two years he has produced five pictures, A SAILOR MADE MAN, GRANDMA'S BOY, DR. JACK, SAFETY LAST and WHY WORRY? all of which have achieved astounding success. No actor or producer in movie history has ever made such a record—or so much money; no star at the present time is so much in demand as Harold Lloyd. Douglas Fairbanks, Mary Pickford, D. W. Griffith and Charlie Chaplin may absorb all the prestige, but it is Harold Lloyd who ranks at the top in the vital statistics.

Although the remarkably high standard that he has maintained throughout all his   289 recent comedies makes it difficult for me to indicate any decided preference, I place GRANDMA'S BOY in this book because it happened to be his most original effort of the year, and also the greatest departure from his usual form. It was his first five-reel venture and his first attempt at anything approaching serious drama.

Lloyd started out to make a two-reel comedy of GRANDMA'S BOY, but his first idea grew as the production progressed, and he worked over the picture for six months before he was satisfied that it was ready for release. He had a theme in mind—that cowardice is a complex which can be cured by psychoanalytical treatment—and this presented so many possibilities that Lloyd simply could not restrain himself. He ran wild.

His hero was a hesitant youth ("the boldest thing he ever did was to sing out loud in church," to quote a subtitle). Whenever this boy scented danger he would seek refuge behind the frail person of his aged grandmother, who, for all her years, knew something of the teachings of the ultra-modern Dr. Freud.

The boy loved a girl—as boys frequently do—but his painful timidity restrained his amorous impulses and prevented him from pressing his suit with any degree of success. The situation seemed hopeless.

Then, one dark night, a ferocious tramp visited the quiet community in which the boy lived, and terrorized the local citizenry. The sheriff decided that a state of military law must be declared, and appointed his fellow townsmen deputies to find and apprehend the unwelcome guest. Among the motley mob thus armed with authority was the boy, and it was he of course who first encountered the tramp. As usual, he fled for protection to his mild little grandmother. She seized a broom and chased the tramp away.

At this point the sweet old lady realized that violent curative measures were essential, and she decided to subject her grandson to the power of suggestion. Removing the small ivory figure from the head of her umbrella, she told the boy that it was a charm, given to his grandfather during the Civil War by a witch. Grandpa, she explained, had been timorous himself—until he came into possession of this talisman; then he stepped out and, single-handed, subdued a large portion of the Federal Army.

This fantastic tale was visualized on the screen, and formed one of the most hilariously funny episodes in the picture. Harold Lloyd, wearing square-lensed spectacles, whiskers and a Confederate uniform, impersonated his grandfather.

When the boy had absorbed this story from his grandmother, he grasped the confidence-giving charm and started after the tramp. After a chase as thrilling and as broadly comic as any in the literature of slap-stick, Lloyd captured the brute and dragged him home by the heels. His final conquest, of course, was the girl.

Lloyd constructed each scene of GRANDMA'S BOY as carefully as though it were the mainspring of a watch. He is always a conscientious craftsman, and his work is a subject of tremendously serious importance to him. There is nothing haphazard about his methods; he puzzles over every episode and situation, working it out first in his mind and then in the action itself. He has a remarkably clear vision and an acute sense of risibility; he knows instinctively what will be naturally funny, and what will merely be forced.

Together with his principal gag-men, Jean Havez and Sam Taylor, his producer, Hal Roach, and his director, Fred Newmeyer, Lloyd practically resolved GRANDMA'S BOY to blue-prints. Although the foremost quality of the finished product was its spontaneity, it was actually a well-calculated, studied piece of work.

Long after the picture had been completed and shown to audiences at various theaters in and about Los Angeles, Lloyd continued to pore over it—cutting, editing, revising, polishing and retaking scenes that didn't obtain sufficiently stentorian laughs. I accompanied Lloyd on one of his pre-view expeditions (it was at Hoyt's Theatre, in Long Beach, California), and I had an opportunity to observe how keenly and intelligently he can criticize his own work. GRANDMA'S BOY was run for the assembled audience with no previous announcement, and without musical accompaniment. "I want it to be cold turkey," said Lloyd to Mr. Hoyt, the exhibitor. "If they like it this way, I'll know it's pretty near right."

Needless to say, they liked it, but Lloyd himself found a few flaws, which he proceeded to remedy when he took the film back to his studio.

The girl in GRANDMA'S BOY was played by Mildred Davis, who has since become Mrs. Harold Lloyd. Dick Sutherland was sufficiently formidable as the burly tramp, and Mrs. Anna Townsend made a charming, appealing figure of the grandmother. Mrs. Townsend lived for seventy-nine years before she made her debut on the screen; a year later she died. But she will be remembered by everyone who was privileged to see her in GRANDMA'S BOY.

There is no one in the movies whose success has been as gratifyingly legitimate as Harold Lloyd's. He has worked hard and intelligently for his laurels, and he has earned every scrap of recognition that he has received. Fame and fortune often descend upon the most unworthy objects, but in the case of Harold Lloyd, you may rest assured that full justice has been done.

FILM 1922   ROBIN HOOD

"The Screen: ROBIN HOOD a Great Spectacle," *The New York Times*, October 31, 1922, p. 15.

> *With Douglas Fairbanks, Wallace Beery, Sam de Grasse, Enid Bennett, Paul Dickey, Billie Bennett, Willard Louis, Alan Hale, and others; directed by Allan Dwan, from a story by Elton Thomas, photography by Arthur Edeson. At the Lyric.*

To Zorro and D'Artagnan, Douglas Fairbanks has added Robin Hood, and Robin Hood is the greatest of the three.

In the motion picture that opened at the Lyric last night, Douglas Fairbanks has gone beyond anything he has ever done before. He has made a picture which, for magnificence of setting, richness of pageantry, beauty and eloquence of photography and impressiveness of action has probably never been equalled before, surely not surpassed. And it is also a lively, loping story, a tale of Merrie England, true, it seems, in its picture of the day, even of the crudity as well as of the romance, and teeming with action which, if not historic, yet happens before your eyes on the screen of the Lyric and convinces you to your unbridled delight.

The story divides itself effectively into two parts. In the first part there is no Robin Hood, but the Earl of Huntingdon instead, a favorite of King Richard, a champion of the tournament, and second in command on the King's Crusade. He is a sturdy, prepossessing Knight, but not the bounding Fairbanks you know, and he moves amid stupendous castles, in great throngs, robed and splendid in his cloak and coat-of-mail. But it is the magnificence of the settings that are most impressive here. Such towering halls, high battlements and far-reaching halls and courts have never been seen before in this age, and they have been so comprehensively photographed that no effect of size with grace is lost. The thing is a tremendous spectacle.

And then the story changes. Richard goes on the Crusade, Prince John becomes the tyrant of England and the Earl of Huntingdon returns to take to the forest as Robin Hood. Then the personal story, which has been held in the background, though never lost in all the magnitude and pageantry of the first part, breaks out and takes complete possession of the picture. Robin Hood, Little John, Friar Tuck and the others of the forest against Prince John and his canned constabulary—it's a battle, a quick succession of starts and skirmishes and escapes, with Robin Hood darting and sending darts everywhere, appearing unexpectedly, disappearing to defeat expectation and always the terror of the

291

rich and powerful and the bright benefactor of the poor and weak. It is in this part of the picture that Douglas Fairbanks had his fun. And how those in the theater last night enjoyed him.

In the end, of course, Richard returns, Robin Hood is restored and he and Maid Marian, after separations and dangers, are re-united. The story ends with Richard pounding on a thick door and calling "Huntingdon," while Earl Robin and the Maid are on the other side uninterested, for the moment, in him and the festivities in their honor.

Credit for the production must be delivered in bulk. All of those responsible cannot be named. First among them, of course, is Mr. Fairbanks, and then, perhaps, Allan Dwan, the director, who managed his scenes amazingly well; Arthur Edeson, the photographer, who was essential and never failed, and Elton Thomas, who provided the workable story. The cast is strikingly good, especially Wallace Beery as Richard I, Sam de Grasse as Prince John, Paul Dickey as Sir Guy of Gisbourne, Alan Hale as Little John and the lovely Enid Bennett as Lady Marian Fitzwalter.

COMMENTARY

William S. Hart and the old-style Western had become sadly obsolete by 1923, superseded by the snappy new-style cowboy, Tom Mix (1880-1940) and by such Western "specials" as THE COVERED WAGON, directed by James Cruze (1884-1942).

THE HUNCHBACK OF NOTRE DAME gave Lon Chaney his most famous role as the hunchbacked Quasimodo. According to F. Scott Fitzgerald, novelist-historian of the times, FLAMING YOUTH, the Colleen Moore (1902-   ) flapper film, marked the industry's first recognition of the Jazz Age, although, as he noted, the Jazz Age was scarcely news by 1923. In the days of Prohibition, liquor was not allowed within a three-mile offshore limit. (41)

During the Twenties, popular jazz bands like Waring's Pennsylvanians and Ben Bernie's Orchestra were often booked in at theaters to bolster a bill when the feature had only mild drawing power, or they were retained as house bands, like Paul Ash's. This was the decade of dances like the Charleston (1923) and the Black Bottom (1926) and a local dance contest could help to break house records.

THE COVERED WAGON   **FILM 1923**

"The Screen: A Movie of the Prairies," *The New York Times*, March 17, 1923, p. 9.

> Directed by James Cruze, adapted by Jack Cunningham from the story of the same name by Emerson Hough, with J. Warren Kerrigan, Lois Wilson, Alan Hale, Charles Ogle, Ethel Wales, Ernest Torrence, Tully Marshall, Guy Oliver and John Fox. At the Criterion.

The years 1848-49 are as deeply stamped in American history, perhaps, as any other period, even including that of 1776. The story of the sweep across the continent, for the opening of Oregon and the wresting of gold from California, is one of the high romantic chapters of Western chronicle to which every human being of the iron-railed, and paved-street age responds. The men, women and children of 1848-49 lived an epic—and it is the spirit of this epic, the magnitude and meaning and vivid reality of it, that James Cruze and his associates have caught and preserved in THE COVERED WAGON, which opened at the Criterion Theater last night. It is a tremendous picture.

Emerson Hough wrote a story. Presumably he wrote the story—the story of the pioneers who set out in the long wagon trains across the unknown prairies, mountains and streams that separated them from the promised land of Oregon, the story of their dangers and struggles and perserverance, the story of their failures, too, and the story of their division when news of the discovery of gold in California lured many from the Oregon goal to the glittering land of quicker wealth.

This is the story that Emerson Hough wrote, and so to him must go first credit for what the screen now possesses. But when James Cruze undertook to put this story into motion pictures his task was only begun. He had to comprehend the epic, he had to visualize it in its vastness and its vivifying details, and he had to translate what was expressed in words into living, speaking motion pictures. And this is what he has done. When you see the scenes of THE COVERED WAGON, you may think, at first, that such pictures make themselves. A long train of prairie schooners streaming across the open landscape, the wagons floating on a broad river through which the horses and oxen pulling them swim, prairie fires, fights with Indians, a buffalo hunt—these things compose themselves into stirring scenes—or so you think.

But the very size of it all, the necessity for coherence and individuality in the story and all the parts of it, make the job exceedingly difficult. Any one might have gotten pictures, perhaps, no one could have failed to get something with such material, but if Mr. Cruze had not mastered his subject, if he had not managed and handled it at every point, the result would have been a hopeless jumble, an amorphous mass of big scenes and trivial details, meaning nothing and tiresome to the most faithful spectator. That he was able to take such a big subject, and, while keeping it big, yet control it and vitalize it with separate people, little incidents and connected events, entitle him, the director, to unstinted credit. He made a motion picture. He didn't just muddle through one.

He didn't do the job alone, of course. His scenarist, Jack Cunningham, and the cameramen can take all the credit they desire, for they deserve it, and the cast, the people who characterized pioneers of the story, became in reality the people of a real adventure, and, being necessary to the life of the thing, made it live.

It is impossible to deal in full with the acting. Standing out in the excellent field is Ernest Torrence, as a true old Western scout. He is the Torrence of TOL'ABLE DAVID and other works, but not a villain this time. He is hard and rough and raw, but right. And how Torrence does do him. There's Tully Marshall, too, as an eccentric trader of the plains. With Torrence he takes much of the picture and makes it go.

Alan Hale as the villain of the plot is effective, so is Charles Ogle as the captain of the train, Ethel Wales as his wife and John Fox as the irrepressible kid. Lois Wilson, the heroine, is more than acceptable. You take her gladly as the girl the hero must love, and J. Warren Kerrigan meets the requirements of the hero's part.

Thus, you see, there is a story. It's nothing amazing, but it isn't cheap. It's interesting, it gives you something detailed and definite for your interest to center upon, and it never gets in the way of the bigger story of "Westward Ho," of the push of Americans across the continent.

And the best part about the photoplay is that it is a motion picture. Its scenes speak to you. Many of them have the quality of greatness. Minor faults might be found with the production, but it would be quibbling to introduce them here. THE COVERED WAGON is a big picture done, as is not often the case, in a big way.

FILM 1923   THE HUNCHBACK OF NOTRE DAME

"The Screen: The Hideous Bell-Ringer," *The New York Times*, September 3, 1923, p. 9.

With Lon Chaney, Ernest Torrence, Tully Marshall, Patsy Ruth Miller, Norman Kerry, Nigel de Brulier, Raymond Hatton, John Cossar, Harry von Meter, Roy Laidlaw, Albert McQuarrie, Jay Hunt, Harry Devere,

293

Eulalie Jensen, Gladys Brockwell, Winifred Bryson, Pearl Tupper, Eva Lewis, Jane Sherman, Helen Brunneau, Gladys Johnston and others. At the Astor Theater.

As the central figure in the film conception of Victor Hugo's *The Hunchback of Notre Dame*, Lon Chaney portrays Quasimodo, the ape-like bellringer of the famed cathedral, as a fearsome, frightful, crooked creature, one eye bulging but blind, knees that interfere, sharp, saw-edged protruding teeth, high, swollen cheek bones and a dented and twisted nose—a "monstrous joke of nature." He gives an unrestrained but remarkable performance in this production, which opened last night at the Astor Theater, where there gathered familiar faces of the stage and screen, literary lights and men-about-town.

Naturally there is much in this picture which is not pleasant any more than the works of Poe, some of Eugene O'Neill's strokes of genius, the stories of Thomas Burke, Stacey Aumonier and many of the masters of the pen in the olden days. It is, however, a strong production, on which no pains or money have been spared to depict the seamy side of old Paris. The "set" of the cathedral is really marvelous, having the appearance of stolidity and massiveness, and in sequences looking down from it to the streets below give one a dizzy idea of height. If there were nothing else to see in this film it would be worth while to gaze upon the faithful copy of Notre Dame.

The streets of Paris of yesteryear are also well constructed, but if they were not so mudless and dustless they would be more real and less like stage settings.

Chaney throws his whole soul into making Quasimodo as repugnant as anything human could very well be, even to decorating his breast and back with hair. He is remarkably agile and impressive when showing his fearlessness for a great height, and the strength of his awful hands by climbing down the facade of the cathedral, and on one occasion down a rope, looking like a mammoth monkey on a stick. And yet in this distorted body there was gratitude, for Esmeralda is carried to sanctuary from the gibbet by this muscular ogre.

Undoubtedly the most picturesque person in this photodrama is Clopin, the king of beggars and assassins, a character that Ernest Torrence plays and appears to enjoy. He is introduced several times in the so-called court of miracles, where the halt become nimble and the blind see. Torrence is a commanding figure, seated on a block-like throne, handing down his laws to his hordes.

The highest dramatic sequence in this film is where Clopin calls upon his filthy crew to storm the cathedral, and the director, Wallace Worsley, has made this a most telling, inspiring incident. The ragged, half-starved mob comes forth at Clopin's behest, from the sewers, the alleys, the underground muck-pots and the hovels in which many of them dwell, and, with gathered numbers as they rush along, they charge upon the church with torches, sticks and knives. Quasimodo strains himself lifting heavy granite blocks, which he drops over on the advancing mendicants and murderers, finally hurling a heavy teak beam on the frenzied lot. It pinions four under it when it falls, but unfortunately they seem to be too neat in their fall to be realistic.

Eventually this beam is used as a battering ram, and one sees, as if from the cathedral towers, the diligent ant-like mortals banging the ram on the oaken portals of the cathedral.

Patsy Ruth Miller has the part of Esmeralda, a truly pretty, chubby girl, whose only fault is the over-decorating of her upper lip, which was too perfectly "bowed." However, her acting is unusually good in the many difficult scenes in which she has to appear. Her paramour, Captain Phoebus, is capably portrayed by Norman Kerry.

Louis XI is played by the careful Tully Marshall, who makes every scene in which he appears count for something.

294   Throughout this drama there is one humorous sequence—one which is pictured in an

interesting manner. It is where Quasimodo appears before the court for kidnapping Esmeralda. The Judge is deaf, but is too proud to admit it. The hunchback doesn't care a rap about his similar affliction and admits it. The prisoner says one thing, and the Judge, not understanding a single word, pretends to have heard, forthwith ordering Quasimodo to be flogged with twenty lashes.

There are a number of changes, obviously necessary, which have been made in this adaptation. The story is subservient to the atmosphere and the acting. It is merely that a girl befriended Quasimodo when he was arrested for a nocturnal attack, inspired by the wicked brother of the Archdeacon. She is arrested finally herself, accused of having stabbed Captain Phoebus, with whom she was in love, and is saved by the hideous bellringer. However, the film holds the interest because of the excellent acting and "sets" and the splendid atmosphere throughout the drama. True, the cast has certain weaknesses, but they are not obtrusive. It is a drama which will appeal to all those who are interested in fine screen acting, artistic settings and a remarkable handling of crowds, who don't mind a grotesque figure and a grim atmosphere.

FILM 1923   FLAMING YOUTH

"The Screen: Marble Hearts and Halls," *The New York Times,* November 26, 1923, p. 15.

> With Colleen Moore, Milton Sills, Elliott Dexter, Sylvia Breamer, Myrtle Stedman, Betty Francisco, Phillips Smalley, Walter McGrail, Ben Lyon, George Barraud, John Patrick, Geno Carrado, Gertrude Astor, Michael Dark and others, adapted from the novel by Warner Fabian, directed by John Francis Dillon; potpourri of light music. At the Strand.

The beguiling and resourceful tactics of a flapper, from her plebe days to her graduation as a bachelor of hearts, are engrossingly portrayed in FLAMING YOUTH, the new picture which is adorning the Strand screen this week. The censor, possibly with an eye on the artistic photography and settings, appears to have exercised unusual leniency with this photoplay, which was adapted from the novel of the same name published under the pseudonym of Warner Fabian.

One bedroom in this picture is shielded from the gaze of the curious by filmy lace portieres, and of course no production of this sort would be complete without its swimming bath sequence, which happens to be done in a different way in this film. The order for lights on and swimming is followed by the guests being shown in a semi-silhouette, disrobing, revealing their undergarments, the men being in knee-length summer attire and the women in the usual lace decorated affairs. Undoubtedly the director has observed box-office regulations in making this rather risqué entertainment, which it is safe to prognosticate, will be more than moderately successful, as the heart affairs, the dancing scenes, and the characterization of the saucy flapper who becomes infatuated with her late mother's erstwhile devoted admirer, will prove quite entertaining to both sexes.

Colleen Moore gives a vivid performance of the jazz-devoted novice once she gets her hold of the theme. There are moments in the beginning when her rendition is a little artificial. But after her awkward trip downstairs in exotic pajamas—which are not really graceful—she lives the part of a pert young thing, whose hair is cut with a bang on the forehead, whose eyes are full of mischief and whose arms are long and slender. She is Patricia Fentriss, known as Pat, whose eyelids are touched up a shade lighter than elephant's breath, with eyebrows which in their neatness and abrupt finish are similar to those on a wax doll. She is a busy little bee, ready with her sting, or to give a "white kiss,"   295 but who becomes inflamed with rage when a "red" or real kiss is forced upon her lips Her profound study seems to consist of Gertrude Atherton's *Black Oxen.*

At the outset Pat from the balcony observes the gay party going on in her home, and she decides to wear one of her sister's evening gowns and join in the gaiety. She sees her mother, Mrs. Fentriss (Myrtle Stedman), in the arms of a man, and soon is discovered herself in a similar pose, and instantly ordered off to bed.

"Baby must go back to her cradle," taunts the young man.

The mother finds herself a victim to the giddy life, and after asking another admirer to write her a letter every day regarding Pat's conduct, she says that she feels that her time has come "to face the great Dim Guess." She dies, and Dr. Bobs faithfully writes the letters about Pat, placing them in a small safe, to which the mother before breathing her last, has given Pat the combination. Cary Scott, impersonated by Milton Sills, who has been in Paris, appears at the Fentriss home, and is shocked to hear of his old friend's death. He instantly takes a great interest in the flapper daughter, but soon has to go abroad again. In the meantime the effervescent Pat becomes enamored of a wet-lipped violinist, Leo Stenak, and she forms one of a party aboard a yacht.

The musician insults the girl, who locks herself in a cabin, the door of which is broken open by the passionate and infuriated violinist. Pat eventually escapes by flinging herself into the sea, and is rescued by a sailor. There is a shot of a big liner entering New York Harbor, passing the little yacht. On the ocean greyhound Cary Scott is seen. He concludes the yacht is carrying a three-mile limit party.

Milton Sills is sympathetic as the hero, and Myrtle Stedman is charming as the mother. Other performers give a splendid impersonation of their respective parts. The moral of this picture is to show the emptiness of the pace-killing life.

COMMENTARY

THE THIEF OF BAGDAD (1924), long in preparation, was one of the most eagerly awaited of the Fairbanks films. When it finally appeared, it raised a distinct question as to whether or not this athletic man alone could animate such a mighty pageant, but Sherwood praised it, and thought it represented "the farthest and most sudden advance that the movie has ever made."

1924 would always be a brilliant year if only because of Buster Keaton's SHERLOCK JR. and THE NAVIGATOR. With Harold Lloyd, Keaton (1895-1966) stood as one of Chaplin's two imposing rivals of the decade. He had started in films with Fatty Arbuckle, a Mack Sennett graduate, and until 1923, with one minor exception, he made only short comedies. Both the films reviewed here begin quietly, for comedians had learned to "glide into" their work, avoiding an early major climax with which it would be inconvenient to compete as the film progressed.

THE IRON HORSE, a "sort of sequel" to THE COVERED WAGON, was the first great success of John Ford (1895-   ). He had been directing since 1917, but emerged more clearly in the 1930's as one of the foremost American directors. HE WHO GETS SLAP-PED, with Lon Chaney, was the second American film by Victor Seastrom (1879-1960), who was seen on the screen here in 1913 and ten years later came in person from Sweden to Hollywood. ("Seastrom" is an Anglicization of Sjöström.) To later generations, he is best known as the old professor in Ingmar Bergman's WILD STRAWBERRIES (1959).

THE THIEF OF BAGDAD   **FILM 1924**

"The Screen: Arabian Nights Satire," *The New York Times,* March 19, 1924, p. 19.

With Douglas Fairbanks, Snitz Edwards, Charles Belcher, Julanne Johnston, Anna May Wong, Winter Blossom, Etta Lee, Brandon Hurst, Tote Du Crow, So-Jin, K. Nambu, Sadakichi Hartmann and Noble Johnson; written for the screen by Elton Thomas, directed by Raoul Walsh, photographed by Arthur Edeson, presented by Comstock and Gest. At the Liberty.

Imagine a clever satire on the *Arabian Nights* with marvelous photography and you have an inkling of Douglas Fairbanks' new picture, THE THIEF OF BAGDAD, which was presented last night in the Liberty Theater to an audience which one might see at the opening of a favorite opera with a great tenor and a famous prima donna. Seeing that this film (the word hardly seems to fit such a wonderful picture) treated of scenes in Bagdad, Morris Gest, that Prince of Miracles in O. Henry's "Bagdad on the Subway," saw fit to give the audience a thoroughly Oriental atmosphere, with drums, ululating vocal offerings, odiferous incense, perfume from Bagdad, magic carpets and ushers in Arabian attire, who during the intermission made a brave effort to bear cups of Turkish coffee to the women in the audience.

It is a picture which reminds one of Barrie, of Kipling, of Hans Andersen, and for the time that one is beholding the miraculous feats of the photographer, the remarkable sets and costumes that are a feast for the eye, one forgets all about the humming, buzzing, brilliantly lighted Broadway, and for the time being, if you will, becomes a child again.

Douglas Fairbanks is his happy-go-lucky self throughout the picture, in which he shows his dexterity and agility, but not to an extent to destroy any illusion the photoplay sheds on the audience. In most of the production Fairbanks is bronzed and naked to his waist line, showing a fine depth of chest and impressively muscular arms.

There are mammoth scenes in this effort, which add to the splendidly told story with a remarkably perfect atmosphere of *The Thousand and One Arabian Nights*. One sees the City of Bagdad, with polished paving lending a reflection that causes one to look upon it as a city suspended in mid-air. There are desert scenes, and a wonderful Crystal City, supposed to be under the sea, which was actually built out of glass.

To reach the Crystal City, Fairbanks has to dive to a great depth into the sea, and this effect is obtained through the aid of the slow motion camera and glass. The Thief, who is enamored of a fascinating Princess whose errand he is attempting to accomplish, is attacked by a brontosaurus of the seas, and with a sharp knife the tiny man—as he seems on the screen—like St. George of old, slays the monster.

He has numerous other escapades with dreadful-looking beasts, and then he goes through the Cavern of Fire, and in course of time discovers the famed Flying Horse. This white steed with wings was the cause of uproarious laughter as, with Fairbanks on its back, it sped across the screen.

He is actually a young man in search of his birthright—true manhood and power over men—who has discovered that happiness cannot be stolen. Once he has found his quest he is able to give birth to armies, and to use a cloth that makes him disappear, leaving only triangular reflection showing where he is. The trick photography is in no place better than where the magic carpet is introduced. It was discovered by a plethoric Prince, eager for the Princess's hand. This carpet is seen flying from the floor of the palace, up stairways, through doorways and out into the skies. It is wonderfully effective and inspiring.

There are Buddhas that have fingers about twelve feet long, doors with teeth that open from the sides, top and bottom and close in the middle, that look as if they were thirty feet high, great gates that dwarf dozens of men, and a magic rope, which the thief steals, and on which he is able to climb at will. You see him sling this rope into the air and in a second the agile star of this picture is clambering up it.

Julanne Johnston makes a stunning Princess, lethargic but beautiful. Her bed is in the midst of a room that looks like one of the ROBIN HOOD sets. Anna May Wong impersonates the Mongol slave and So-Jin enacts the Mongol Prince. So-Jin is remarkable for his undemonstrative countenance, cruel and comfortable, with just a scintillation of a smile when dirty work is to be done. Snitz Edwards, with an excellent make-up, has the role of the Thief's Evil Associate. Noble Johnson figures as the Indian Prince. He is effective and true to type, with a splendid imitation of an Indian beard.

The Thief only has to toss powder to the floor to make an army. No sooner has the powder turned to smoke than up come a dozen men, and soon one sees what looks like an army of more than a thousand aiding the one-time Thief of Bagdad. Never has an audience shown its appreciation of such an entertainment as the one in the Liberty did last night. This film is filled with brilliant ideas that caught the sympathy of the audience, so that they were actually thrilled when the Thief arrived in time to aid the Princess.

There are some wonderfully well-worked-out double exposure photographic effects, and even to an experienced eye the illusion is in nearly every instance kept up to a state of perfection. It is something that could only be accomplished by means of the camera and the screen, something that one could never see upon a stage.

It is such an entrancing picture, wholesome and beautiful, deliberate but compelling, a feat of motion picture art which has never been equaled and one which itself will enthrall persons time and again. You can see this film and look forward to seeing it a second time.

THE THIEF OF BAGDAD   **FILM 1924**

"The Silent Drama," by Robert E. Sherwood, *Life,* Vol. 83, No. 2161, April 3, 1924, p. 32.

After seeing THE THIEF OF BAGDAD, I am more competent to understand the motives which inspired the sturdy Britons who have been struggling for years to reach the peak of Mt. Everest. I now know what it means to be able to say, "Well, I've been to the top."

Standing at the point marked by this Arabian Nights' entertainment which Douglas Fairbanks has fashioned, I can look down to the lesser summits of ROBIN HOOD, BROKEN BLOSSOMS, PASSION and the rest; several miles below, and barely discernible from this dizzy altitude, lie WHERE IS MY WANDERING BOY TONIGHT?, RAGS TO RICHES and THE OLD NEST.

There may well be higher peaks than that achieved by THE THIEF OF BAGDAD—but if there are, they have not as yet been charted on any of the existent contour maps.

THE THIEF OF BAGDAD is the farthest and most sudden advance that the movie has ever made and, at the same time, it is a return to the form of the earliest presentable films. I remember that the first picture I ever saw was a ferociously fast French comedy, in which one of the characters was dressed by magic. His clothes leaped at him from the closet and fitted themselves about his passive form, his boots scurried across the floor and slid onto his feet, and his shoe laces wiggled into place like twin serpents.

That was, technically, "trick stuff"—and it is now sneered at by the hyper-realists of Hollywood, who refuse to admit that a scene is ever faked.

It is trick stuff of this same sort that makes THE THIEF OF BAGDAD extraordinarily fascinating. Fairbanks has not been afraid to resort to magic of the most flagrant variety. He has used ropes which, when thrown into the air, will become rigid and scalable, golden apples which will restore life to the dead, idols' eyes of crystal in which the future is revealed, magic carpets which fly through the heavens, winged horses, star-shaped keys to open the Palace of the Moon, and golden chests from which vast armies

41. Buster Keaton as the projectionist in SHERLOCK JR. (1924). This same year he also appeared in THE NAVIGATOR, in which "his wildest emotions are reflected by an occasional upward turn of his right eyebrow."

may be conjured with the flick of a finger. There is also a supply of genii, djinns, talismans and fire-breathing dragons.

Of course this wizardry is possible on the screen; the first French comedy proved that. But Fairbanks has gone far beyond the mere bounds of possibility; he has performed the superhuman feat of making his magic seem probable.

When, in THE TEN COMMANDMENTS, Cecil B. DeMille caused the Red Sea to part, every one remarked, "That's a great trick. How did he do it?" There are no such mental interruptions for the spectator in THE THIEF OF BAGDAD. He watches Fairbanks' phenomenal stunts without stopping to think of them as tricks. He accepts them as facts.

THE THIEF OF BAGDAD has a marvelous fairy tale quality—a romantic sweep which lifts the audience and vaporizes it into pink, fluffy clouds. It also has much beauty and much solidity of dramatic construction.

Fairbanks and Raoul Walsh, the director, have devised scenes of overwhelming magnitude and grandeur; but in doing so, they have not neglected the details. They have built, with incredible magnificence, the City of Bagdad—and they have also built a story which is sound and workable, and which proceeds rhythmically and gracefully at a steadily increasing rate of speed.

One derives from THE THIEF OF BAGDAD the same childish thrill that is furnished by a first perusal of Hans Andersen's stories. It is enthrallingly romantic, inspiringly unreal.

If any one can see this marvelous picture and still choose to sneer at the movies, I shall be glad to escort him to Hollywood and feed him to the largest dragon in the Fairbanks menagerie.

SHERLOCK JR.   **FILM 1924**

"The Screen: A Lively Comedy," *The New York Times*, May 26, 1924, p. 21.

> With Buster Keaton, Kathryn McGuire, Ward Crane, Joseph Keaton, Horace Morgan, Jane Connelly, Irvin Connelly, Ford West, George Davis, John Patrick and Ruth Holley, written by Jean Havez, Joseph Mitchell and Clyde Bruckman, directed by Mr. Keaton; overture, "La Tosca"; Riesenfeld "Classical Jazz," "Covered Wagon Days." At the Rialto.

As one watches SHERLOCK JR. being unfurled on the Rialto screen, one might observe with a sigh after 500 feet have passed that it is about time the comical Buster Keaton skipped into action. Just about then you realize that something has happened—one of the best screen tricks ever incorporated in a comedy—the laughter starts, and for the balance of the picture you smile, snigger, chuckle, grin and guffaw.

As the embryo sleuth whose actual occupation is that of a projection machine operator in a nondescript motion picture theater, Keaton finds the tables turned on him when the pawn ticket for a stolen watch is discovered in his own pocket. He returns to work, dejected at the thought of losing his girl, and falls asleep in the operator's booth as a picture is being screened. What one sees is his dream, which in a measure is something like the dream sequence in HOLLYWOOD [directed by James Cruze the year before].

One views Mr. Keaton seeing his girl on the screen with the villain, he who had really stolen the watch. You see Keaton join the characters in the picture he is projecting, and then he is kicked out of the picture by the villain. He is about to sit on a doorstep when the scene changes and he discovers that he is at the foot of a garden wall. The scene switches again and he narrowly escapes being run down by a train. He does get out of its way, and is then seen peering over a high cliff, which scene changes into the sight of Buster on a rock in midocean. He is pondering in thought, listening to the wild waves, when in comes a scene of Broadway or some traffic-congested thoroughfare. For the most part of this production our hero is endeavoring to get out of the picture he is projecting, or at least out of the swiftly changing sequences into which he has penetrated in his desire to throttle the villain, played by the sinister-appearing Ward Crane.

After viewing the antics of the hero on the screen of his own theater, the director, none other than Buster himself, has seen to it that the whole affair is brought closer so that one witnesses the full size result. Of course the first part of this long sequence is boisterously funny, and nary the flicker of expression crosses the Keaton countenance, except through the eyes. His face might be made of stone for all the resiliency there is in it.

This is an extremely good comedy which will give you plenty of amusement so long as you permit Mr. Keaton to glide into his work with his usual deliberation.

FILM 1924   THE IRON HORSE

"The Screen: The Railroad Pioneers," *The New York Times,* August 29, 1924, p. 6.

> With Winston Miller, Peggy Cartwright, Charles Edward Bull, James Gordon, Will Walling, George O'Brien, Madge Bellamy, Fred Kohler, Cyril Chadwick, Gladys Hulette, James Marcus, Francis Powers, J. Farrell MacDonald, James Welch, Colin Chase, Jack O'Brien, Walter Rogers, George Wagner, John Padjan, Charles O'Malley, Delbert Mann, Jack Ganzhorn, Chief Big Tree, Chief White Spear, Frances Teague, Stanhope Wheatcroft and Edward Piel, written by Charles Kenyon and John Russell, directed by John Ford. Special music score by Erno Rapee. At the Lyric.

Another stirring chapter in American history was told last night when a picture entitled THE IRON HORSE was presented at the Lyric Theatre by William Fox, before a gathering that included persons prominent in the film firmament and men who are powers in the railroad world. This ambitious production dwelt trenchantly upon the indomitable energy, resourcefulness and courage of those who spanned the continent with steel. Little does one realize in these days of modern comforts, the tirelessness of those Americans who shed their life's blood with a smile in the race to get first to the goal with rails and ties.

Gray-haired men, whose fathers had constructed railroads in the pioneer days, were much moved by the spectacle in shadows that passed before their eyes. And some of them wept, not so much at the story interspersing this gigantic accomplishment of the '60's as the sight of the men working with sledge hammers on the spike nails, as tie after tie and rail after rail were laid down. They wept also when they saw the slow moving old engine with its ungainly funnel, which to the folk of the olden days ran so smoothly on its quickly constructed path of iron.

As one watches this film one is impressed by the fact that Americans have had more to battle against than any other nation. In the first place they had miles by the thousand to conquer, then they had the difficulties of the terrain, and finally they had literally to fight their way along as they were working, for they were attacked night and day by hostile Indians who could not and would not understand the white man's ways. Their arrows pierced the hearts of those who carried on in their almost impossible task, and knowing the limited numbers of the invaders of their soil, the redmen charged and charged again and again in an effort to weaken the energy of the railroad pioneers.

In this picture is shown with true dramatic emphasis the welding together of two great points with steel. One sees the Indians bearing down on those working at a job, which in   **301** all conscience is bad enough even in these days, without having to believe that their lives are in danger from an energetic enemy. One might just as well imagine men constructing a steel skyscraper being shot at when they have just about finished the framework of their great structure.

Yet with all their discomforts amid the great risk, it is shown, and truthfully in this picture that these pioneers had a keen sense of humor. They were sports, and as sports they had to settle disputes even among themselves. For no chapter of history in a film can be told without a heroine, a hero and a villain, and the chances are that this is a more or less accurate description.

As scene after scene passes in shadows and lights upon the screen one cannot help thinking of that remarkable production, THE COVERED WAGON, to which THE IRON HORSE is a sort of sequel. Sometimes people in the audience wondered why cattle figured so often in the picture, forgetting that these railroad builders had to eat. One is also impressed by the fact that in every halt of any consequence, they founded towns as they went along, and usually the first sign painted was that for a saloon.

There are herds of buffalo, with that famous old scout, Buffalo Bill, firing into the animals to kill to feed those who must live. It was incidentally through the efficiency with which he accomplished this work that Colonel William Frederick Cody derived his nickname of Buffalo Bill.

The outstanding actor in this production is not the good-looking hero, nor even the comely girl, but the man who officiates in the comedy character, that of Sergeant Slattery. Francis Powers plays this part beautifully, making one think of many characters in American history, of Kipling's *Soldiers Three*, and also of Marryat's *Masterman Ready*. When things are dull and men are gloomy it is Sergeant Slattery who takes upon himself to lighten up matters with a joke or a laugh, and even when he is gripping his gun against the Indians there is a twinkle in his eye.

Of the many scenes which drew applause last night were those on the desert, where hosts of men were scampering along with a will in laying their ties, while others equally handy wielded their sledge hammers and riveted the rails to the wood. It looked like a slow job even if it were merely a score of miles, but to realize the immense distance that had to be covered almost made one cover one's eyes with one's hands.

John Ford, the director of this film, has done his share of the work with thoroughness and with pleasing imagination. There are certain stretches in the production that are long and at times tedious, but this is due to the cutting and is a fault which can be remedied. While George O'Brien, who impersonates the heroic Davy Brandon, is quite good in most of his acting, the producers have permitted him to have too much of the show at certain junctures, especially where he heaves his manly chest. In the fights with Cyril Chadwick, who plays Peter Jesson, he is capable, although at times too theatric. He seems to remember that he is a fine young specimen of manhood. His shirt sleeves are tucked up high enough to give one a good view of his biceps, which appear to be frequently strained for effect.

The climax to this production is where the Union Pacific and the Central Pacific engines touch headlights at Promontory Point, Utah—which happened on May 10, 1869. After this happens the stalwart Davy Brandon is seen standing with a foot on each rail, surveying the accomplishment started by his father.

Madge Bellamy is seen as Miriam Marsh, the sweet young heroine, who is really very pretty and sympathetic. Charles Edward Bull has the role of Abraham Lincoln, and his make-up as the martyred President is so good that the mere sight of him brought volleys of applause from the spectators. Chadwick is splendid as the despicable Jesson, making the most of every situation, but nevertheless leaving one with the impression that his mustache and collar are rather up to date.

302   The real villain, the man with two fingers off his right hand who is always concealing

this fact by keeping his hand in his coat pocket, is Deroux, who slew Brandon's father. Fred Kohler handles this role with restraint and full effect.

This is an instructive and inspiring film, one which should make every American proud of the manner of men who were responsible for great achievements in the face of danger, sickness and fatigue. They were, as we said, true sports, who worked with a vim and got satisfaction and even fun out of the hazardous labors.

FILM 1924   THE NAVIGATOR

"The Screen: On a Drifting Vessel," Mordaunt Hall, *The New York Times,* October 13, 1924, p. 21.

> With Buster Keaton, Kathryn McGuire, Frederick Vroom, Noble Johnson, Clarence Burton and H. M. Clugston, written by Jean Havez, Clyde Bruckman and Joe Mitchell, directed by Mr. Keaton and Donald Crisp; overture, "Orpheus"; "Bohemia," a camera tour; "In a Song Shop"; special prologue. At the Capitol.

Buster Keaton's sphynx-like face is to be seen at the Capitol this week in a nautical film-farce, called THE NAVIGATOR, wherein his wildest emotions are reflected by an occasional upward turn of his right eyebrow. Now and again the Keaton eyes evince a suggestion of life, but his lips barely bulge. To have a contrast to this comedian's placidity of countenance, we had only to look at those watching this picture. Mouths were wide open in explosions of laughter and eyes sparkled with merriment.

THE NAVIGATOR is an excellent panacea for melancholia or lethargy, as it is filled with ludicrous and intensely humorous situations. It even strikes one as being astonishing that this comedian can keep such perfect control over his physiognomy during the action of this parcel of mirth. While it took three writers to pen the narrative and two directors to produce it, the actual players are limited to Mr. Keaton and Kathryn McGuire.

It is funny enough to see this indefatigable stoic as a pampered young man in a wonderful mansion, but, as might be gathered, it is even more absurd to view his actions when he and the heroine are alone aboard a drifting steamship.

This time Mr. Keaton is seen as Rollo Treadway, a young man who is helpless without servants and who even rides in his expensive automobile to cross the street. Being bored, he announces to his butler that he thinks that it is a good thing to be married. Without further ado he goes over to Betsy O'Brien and proposes. Betsy, who never pictured herself as Rollo's wife, promptly spurns his offer of marriage. Anticipating his honeymoon, Rollo had bought two steamship tickets for Honolulu, to which spot he decides to travel alone. As early rising is distasteful to him he decides to board the vessel that night, and while doing so his tickets are blown away by a sudden strong gust of wind. He gets on the wrong ship, but goes to bed in one of the staterooms. Betsy, in seeking her father, who had been held up and gagged by spies, rushes aboard the same steamship, not knowing that the hawsers have been cut.

Far out at sea next morning Rollo discovers there is nobody at the helm or in the engine room and, what is more important to him, not a steward to serve him breakfast. Suddenly he hears gentle footfalls, and there is an amusing chase around the decks of the vessel. Betsy runs away from the sound of Rollo, and Rollo is keenly anxious to get away from what he imagines to be some terrible ghost. Their subsequent meeting is the cause of much hilarity, especially when Rollo makes coffee with sea water.

Later he is seen as a diver, the vessel having gone ashore off an island inhabited by

303

countless cannibals. Under water he is prodded by a swordfish and caught by the arm of a ravenous octopus. Above, the cannibals have boarded the vessel and captured Betsy, to whom Rollo tries to signal that he wants to come to the surface. Finally he frightens the savages by strolling out of the water onto the beach.

While there is no denying the jocular and farcical action of this picture, there are stretches which should be cut, as some of the humor is just a bit overdone. Nevertheless, Mr. Keaton deserves untold credit for his originality in thinking up most of the funny scenes.

HE WHO GETS SLAPPED   **FILM 1924**

"The Screen: The Clown's Revenge," Mordaunt Hall, *The New York Times,* November 10, 1924, p. 20.

> With Lon Chaney, Norma Shearer, John Gilbert, Tully Marshall, Marc McDermott, Ford Sterling, Clyde Cook, Harvey Clarke, Paulette Duval, Ruth King, Brandon Hurst and George Davis, adapted from Leonid Andreyev's play, directed by Victor Seastrom; overture, "1812," Tchaikovsky; "Fifth Anniversary of the Capitol"; ballet corps, "Dance of the Hours"; "There is No Death," Geoffrey O'Hara. At the Capitol.

At the Capitol this week there is a picture which defies one to write about it without indulging in superlatives. It is a shadow drama so beautifully told, so flawlessly directed that we imagine that it will be held up as a model by all producers. Throughout its length there is not an instant of ennui, not a second one wants to lose; it held the spectators spellbound yesterday afternoon, the last fade-out being the signal for a hearty round of applause. This celluloid masterpiece is Victor Seastrom's picturization of Leonid Andreyev's play, *He Who Gets Slapped,* which was presented before the footlights in January, 1922, with Richard Bennett in the principal role.

The more enlightened producers were enthusiastic over Mr. Seastrom's THE STROKE OF MIDNIGHT, which was at the same time considered too depressing to be a financial success over here. Nevertheless, this and other productions caused the management of Goldwyn Pictures, Ltd., to engage this director to make pictures in California. Mr. Seastrom left his native heath, Sweden, and his first American-made production was Sir Hall Caine's NAME THE MAN, a lugubrious story filled with anachronisms. A friend of the director predicted at the time that, although he did not like NAME THE MAN, Mr. Seastrom eventually would turn out a production which would startle the film world.

Undoubtedly the story is half the battle with an accomplished director, and in HE WHO GETS SLAPPED Mr. Seastrom obviously realized that he had his great opportunity. He selected his cast with punctiliousness, choosing Lon Chaney, who will be remembered for his work in THE HUNCHBACK OF NOTRE DAME and other films, to play the part of the heart-broken scientist who became a clown. Never in his efforts before the camera has Mr. Chaney delivered such a marvelous performance as he does in this character. He is restrained in his acting, never overdoing the sentimental situations, and is guarded in his make-up.

The first flash on the screen shows a clown twisting a colored ball, which gradually fades out into the figure of Beaumont, the scientist, gazing upon a revolving globe. There are many such clever touches in different chapters of this absorbing narrative which deals with the ultimate revenge of the scientist-clown, merely known as "He Who Gets Slapped," on the man who stole the glory for his work and also his wife. You see the student arguing with Baron Regnard before a gallery of aged notables, and suddenly the nobleman slaps the scientist's face. The old men rock in their mirth, and this, coupled with the loss of his wife, spurs the student to become a clown with a small traveling French circus. As the principal fun-maker, with a score of other painted-face clowns, he is seen making audiences roar with laughter by being slapped. At the time he had no thought of revenge, but one day he sees the Baron in a seat. The sight of what happened to him in front of the scientists comes before his eyes. One sees the clown fading into the gallery of wise old men, and then again the clowns are shown.

There is the dressing room of the circus, and the pretty daughter of an impecunious Count. The girl (Norma Shearer) soon falls in love with her partner in her riding act, Bezano (John Gilbert). The Count wants her to wed the Baron, and the scheming is discovered by He, the clown. He is weak in fistic encounters, so cooly arranges for a terrible death for the Count and the Baron. He loves the girl, Consuelo, too. She had stitched on his dummy heart night after night of the show. You see him move the lion's cage up to the door of the little ante-room, which is all ready for a wine supper. Then he enters himself by another door, and in an encounter with the girl's father he is stabbed by the Count's sword-stick. He grips his breast tightly to stay the flow of blood, and gradually crawls toward the door, which has only to be opened to release the wild beast. There is wonderful suspense in this stretch, and one is stirred when one sees the startled lion spring through the open door.

Mr. Seastrom has directed this dramatic story with all the genius of a Chaplin or a Lubitsch, and he has accomplished more than they have in their respective works, A WOMAN OF PARIS and THE MARRIAGE CIRCLE, as he had, what they did not have, a stirring, dramatic story to put into pictures.

Miss Shearer is charming as Consuelo, and Mr. Gilbert, who gave such an excellent account of himself in HIS HOUR, is a sympathetic sweetheart. But the person who is entitled to honors only second to Mr. Chaney is Marc McDermott, who takes full advantage of the strength of his role. Tully Marshall is splendid as the scapegrace Count.

For dramatic value and a faultless adaptation of the play, this is the finest production we have yet seen.

305

42. *Pola Negri as Madame du Barry pleads for her life in the final sequence of Ernst Lubitsch's German film, called PASSION in its American release. To avoid angry resentment in the wake of World War I, the film was billed first as an "Italian," then as a "European," spectacle.*

CHAPTER **17**

Foreign Invasion (II):
Ernst Lubitsch

COMMENTARY

Ernst Lubitsch (1892-1947) was born in Berlin, acted on the stage under Max Reinhardt, and entered films as an actor in Germany in 1913. He soon became a director, and, after a series of shorter films, finally directed his first feature: THE EYES OF THE MUMMY, in 1918, with the Polish actress Pola Negri and the great German character actor Emil Jannings. In the same year he also made a CARMEN, starring Negri.

A big-scale and more important film, MADAME DUBARRY, with Negri as the DuBarry and Jannings as Louis XV, followed in 1919. Several films later, Lubitsch again directed Negri in SUMURUN (1920), from the Reinhardt stage pantomime; he himself played the screen role of the hunchbacked clown, having previously performed it in the theater. Negri had also played in *Sumurun* on the stage.

At this point, after some deliberation, Associated First National Pictures, an American firm, purchased the American rights to MADAME DUBARRY, renamed it PASSION, and, with a sense of gamble, as there was some doubt as to how New York would accept a film of German origin (the Metropolitan Opera had still not restored the performance of works in German, a language dropped there since 1917), exhibited it at the big Capitol Theatre on Dec. 12, 1920. It was a sensation, and that dream of every aspiring actress shaped into a fact: Pola Negri, hitherto unknown here, "disarrayed hair—the wrong profile to the camera" and all, awoke next morning (in Berlin) a star in America.

PASSION was first advertised as an "Italian" film, then as a "European" one. To further disguise its German origin, only the Polish Negri's name was given. The eventual American fame and prestige of Emil Jannings, who appears as the King in PASSION, began with his advertised appearance as Henry VIII in DECEPTION, the title under which Lubitsch's film ANNA BOLEYN was exhibited in New York in 1921 for an applauded four-week run at the Rivoli Theatre.

The Lubitsch-Negri CARMEN, retitled GYPSY BLOOD, was shown in New York shortly after. SUMURUN (ONE ARABIAN NIGHT) followed in October, and before 1921 was out, Lubitsch had darted over on an American visit, attending the première of Griffith's ORPHANS OF THE STORM. Both Lubitsch and Negri were engaged for Hollywood.

307

PASSION (MADAME DU BARRY)   **FILM 1920**

From *The New York Times*, December 13, 1920, p. 19.

One of the pre-eminent motion pictures of the present cinematographic age is at the Capitol this week. It is most inappropriately entitled PASSION, and has been imported from Europe, having originated in Northern Germany, by Associated First National Pictures, Inc. The Polish actress, Pola Negri, plays its leading role, and its director was Ernst Lubitsch, who is said to have a reputation as a cinematician of the first rank abroad.

According to report, the Continental name of the picture was DU BARRY, and this title might well have been retained, for it comes as close to giving a key to the story as any that comes to mind. The story is that of Louis XV's mistress in her environment, and this environment, the life of the day, with its individual figures and its human masses, at least as they are popularly imagined, is the real material of the narrative. Du Barry herself is only a part of it all, and so are the others, especially the King and Armand de Foix, who, with the woman between them, form the three principals of the plot. It is about these three, the toy of erratic destiny, the mad King, and the humble first love of the du Barry when she was only Jeanne, the milliner's apprentice, that the action centers, but they are merely the centre of action that radiates in all directions and reaches through the Court of Louis and the seething life of Paris, from the omnipotence of the fat Bourbon tyrant to the overwhelming might of the frenzied revolutionary mob.

It is in building this story of pre-revolutionary France, reaching its peak in the revolution, that Mr. Lubitsch has done something notable. The affairs of Mme. du Barry, Louis and Armand by themselves are simply sordid, with Armand's part in them dignified somewhat by a touch of tragedy, and any director who let them stand out from their background would have had merely a sordid tale to tell. But Mr. Lubitsch has had the skill to weave them into their setting, make them a part of all that is going on, and, while keeping them in the centre as objects of focused interest, he has never permitted them to hold the interest exclusively. So his picture has dramatic sweep as well as localized intensity; it lives as a human document; and it satisfies historic curiosity. How far it departs from actual history is immaterial. So far as the present writer is able to judge it has caught the atmosphere and meaning of its time, and historical fiction has accomplished its object when it does this.

It is also as a cinematician that Mr. Lubitsch and whoever may have been responsible with him have won distinction. The settings seem truly of the Paris of the latter eighteenth century, and the costuming and habits of the people portrayed are harmonious with them. And few spectacles, if any, have surpassed the scenes of the street crowds and revolutionary mobs, which increase in number and importance as the story hurries to its final scene—du Barry at the guillotine. The French Revolution has never been so vividly pictured, probably, as in this photoplay. What it was, as ugly as it was, and as human, is forcefully presented, which means dramatically.

But all that Mr. Lubitsch and his associates behind the camera did could not have made PASSION the living thing it is without its cast. Seldom has a photoplay been as excellently acted. First among the players is Pola Negri. Here is one of those rare persons with screen personality. Her moving photograph is stamped with individuality. And largely because of her definite pantomimic ability, or whatever distinctive motion picture acting may be called. It is not physical beauty that wins for her. She is lovely in many scenes, it is true, but some of her features are not beautiful, and she makes no apparent effort to pose becomingly without regard to the meaning of her performance. She is expressive. That is her charm. She makes du Barry real, as fascinating as she has to be, with as much of the appearance of dignity as she must have on occasion, and as contemptible and cowardly as she was. She actually wins sympathy for a woman who cannot at any time be admired. This is an accomplishment.

The other players in the cast are not named but whoever they are they play right up to Pola Negri, especially those who impersonate Louis XV [Emil Jannings], Armand de Foix, the Duc de Choiseul, the Comte Jean du Barry, and Paillet the cobbler. Also many in the large assemblage of people brought into the picture contribute importantly to its success.

PASSION, therefore, may be written down as one of the pre-eminent pictures of the day. Its shortcomings are the shortcomings of the photoplay of the current period, with its lack of color, its subjection to the literal rather than the imaginative camera, and its dependence upon "words, words, words." In PASSION the photoplay about reaches its limit of excellence, and reveals its limitations. And the excellence and the limitations are together a guarantee of something greater than the photoplay to come. Meanwhile, let DU BARRY, as it must be thought of, be enjoyed.

1920   "NEW FILM RECORD SET BY PASSION"

From *The New York Times*, December 23, 1920, p. 28.

German-Made du Barry Picture,
Sold Here for $40,000,
Worth $500,000

U.S. RIGHTS WENT BEGGING

106,000 Saw Photoplay in First Week—
$10,000 Estimated Daily
Receipts

PASSION, the first important film of foreign origin to achieve success in this country since the war, is a production of the Germans, now being shown at the Capitol Theatre, where crowds have witnessed the screen version of Mme. du Barry's rise to power with none of the hostility that has greeted attempts to revive German opera and drama. So doubtful were the chances of this production's success in America that it is said to have been offered for a song in Berlin to American producers.

At the time that the production was finished in Berlin, the latter part of last year, the German producers would have been glad to take $10,000 for the American rights, which finally were sold for $40,000 to the Associated First National Pictures, Inc., of 6 West Forty-eighth Street. Conservative estimates place the value of the American rights today in excess of $500,000.

The first engagement of PASSION was opened at the Capitol Theatre on Sunday, Dec. 12. This house, with a capacity of 5,500 seats, is reputed to be the largest cinema theater in the world. There have been five performances a day since the first engagement, and the attendance during the first week is said to have been 106,000. Although the gross receipts could not be ascertained from the theatre, they are estimated by motion picture trade journals at $10,000 a day, which would have represented exceedingly gratifying receipts for a whole week six years ago.

Last Sunday the crowd was so great that extra policemen had to maintain order and clear traffic. Those who either gained admittance or sought it were estimated at 40,000. The result was a record week's showing.

The American rights for the German film production were procured last September by David P. Howells, who acted as broker for the Associated First National Pictures, Inc. He saw the picture in Berlin soon after its production. Mr. Howells last night told a reporter for *The Times* that there were representatives of other American distributors in Berlin at the same time, but they refused to buy the film even at its lowest figure.

309

The producer was the Universam Film Aktiengesellschaft of Berlin, and it found setting for the French historical picture in and around Berlin. The principal role was taken by Pola Negri, who, in a cable dispatch from Berlin to *The Times*, recently was described as "Frau Pola Negri, one of Germany's most famous film stars," at the time that she was robbed of valuable jewelry. This cable was followed by a statement from the distributers that Pola Negri was a Pole and a friend of Paderewski.

COMMENTARY

Lubitsch returned to Germany to direct Negri in DIE FLAMME (MONTMARTRE), and it was during its production in Berlin that he had this interview with *Photoplay's* **representative. Then Lubitsch came permanently to America; he first directed Mary Pickford in ROSITA, momentarily putting aside a plan "to do modern stories of American life as a relief from the long series of historical dramas and as proof of his versatility."**

"THE FILM WIZARD OF EUROPE"   1922

Excerpts from "The Film Wizard of Europe," Herbert Howe, *Photoplay Magazine*, Vol. 23, No. 1, December 1922, pp. 28-29, 98-99.

First View of Ernst Lubitsch in Action

The man who gave fame to Pola Negri, to Louis XV of France and to Henry VIII of England—
The German film wizard, master of tragedy, and the man who makes history live—
"The Griffith of Europe," sometimes called, because of the genius with which he made PASSION, DECEPTION, and THE LOVES OF PHARAOH—
Ernst Lubitsch, star-maker and king-maker, sat opposite me in the lunch room of his Berlin studio, his face beaming like a harvest moon over a platter of *kalbschnitzel*.
The broad smile broadened—
"My hobbies—hobbies," he lingered over the unfamiliar English word, "Ya, my hobbies is d'piano, d'cello and d'shimmie.
"Good dancer," he blinked, his little black eyes crinkling out of sight. "Every night I dance in New York.
"Pretty girls in America. Ya, Ziegfeld Follies. Um!"—many ecstatic blinks—"Ya, I vill like to work in America."
He was beaming from every pore. His secretary, a German boy whose English still has the flavor of German idiom, suddenly asked me if I had any chewing gum for Mr. Lubitsch.
"He is a great friend of the chewing gum," said the secretary.
Lubitsch demanded to know what was being said and then endorsed with, "Ya— California Fruit." Emphatic nods and blinks.
"It is very difficult getting him this California Fruit," sighed the secretary. "It is not much in Berlin. Sometimes I must go all over town looking. And it is all my fault. It is not allowed to smoke on the 'set,' and Mr. Lubitsch did not know what to do without his cigar. So I say, 'You must chew.' He say, 'Ya, but what I chew?' I say, 'chewing gum.' And now I spend all my time looking down this California Fruit."
Such is the master of tragedy. "The man who never stops smiling" is what they call him around the studio. A plump, alert, restless little fellow of thirty with a broad

humorous mouth, a hooked Semitic nose, crinkling bead eyes and a lock of ink hair sprawling Napoleonically over a high forehead.

As he wheels restlessly to and fro on the "set," one arm behind him, his head cocked on the side, his eyes on the floor, he looks like a Dutch comedian doing a burlesque of Napoleon.

Over a neat business suit he wears a loose linen duster, the sort his carpenters wear. He seems to have no particular place or significance on the stage. He has no puttees, no megaphone, no director's chair with his name emblazoned across the back. In fact, he might be called a director without a country.

No sooner do you get him focused in the crowd of players and workingmen than—poof!—he has vanished like a genie. Ah, there he is!—popping up like a jumping jack beside Pola Negri. He whispers a suggestion. You wonder how she could have caught it, he is gone again so quickly.

The extras have crowded around to see the great Negri do her scene. From somewhere Lubitsch has let out a terrific bellow—"*Drehen!*" meaning "Camera!" The players are in action. Extras and workmen crowd closer to watch. Pretty soon you notice a little man darting around like a terrier on the outskirts of the crowd trying to get a peek. He can't see a thing on account of the extras, so he jumps upon a chair and looks over their heads. It's the director, the great Lubitsch. In a second he's off the chair and diving between the legs of the camera. He lets out another horrifying whoop. Something is wrong. He contorts his brows at fearful angles, making a diabolical face which is funnier than the smiling one of the minute before. Then he grins—as though amused by his fearful countenance, which has had no effect upon anyone but himself. He bounds among the players to act a "bit" for a little girl playing a *cocotte*. He is a very funny coquette, but he knows the business, every glance, every wink, every instinctive gesture of the flirt. . . . Then off again on a feverish pace as if he had lost all interest in the affair.

I pinioned him behind the piano upon one of these excursions—he always has music with his scenes. Seeing me, he plopped down on the stool and commenced playing very sour snatches from *The Music Box*.

"You know the *Moosic Box* sonks?" he asked, grinning. "Und *Sally*"—more soggy notes, with Lubitsch beaming over them as if to coax them into melody by the sunshine of his smile.

We talked of American films. I asked him which of our stars he considered best.

"The best of all—the greatest actor in the world—*le plus grand*," he emphasized in three languages, "is—Ch'pln. Great tragedy actor—Ch'pln."

"Chaplin a great tragedy actor?"

"Ya—Ch'pln greatest actor of everything."

If Chaplin is the great tragedian, Lubitsch, the tragedy-maker, is the great comedian. But he is entirely serious in his appraisal of our films and players.

"Harold Lloyd—," he blinked his pleasure. "I saw him in New York—good—*good*—*very* good!"

Of the women—

"Ah, Pickford," he nodded.

"And Miss Lillian Gish, Mr. Lubitsch," interposed the secretary.

"Ah—Lillian Gish—ORPHANS OF THE STORM—Lillian Gish—ah, ah, ah," he teetered on his heels and went into a veritable paroxysm of blinks. . . .

It was noon and everyone was awaiting the arrival of Pola Negri. She usually makes her entrance at about twelve o'clock. Someone came in and told Lubitsch that she was actually in her dressing room employed in making up. He celebrated the fact by taking another drink of strawberry water and bursting into song.

Things grew a little more tense in expectancy. Lights were adjusted. Players began to take their places in the "set," which was an exact reproduction of a famous Parisian café of 1860. A huge bar maid in *décolleté* took her place behind the glasses and bottles, her

311

shoulders looming over the bar like a range of the snow-capped Alps. The camera men began to jimmy with their instruments, as camera men always do. And then—somehow—you felt La Negri had arrived.

I couldn't see her, but the presence was conveyed, psychically and by murmurs. The secretary scurried past me whispering, "She's here—back there by the door to the café." I kept my position, however. It was peaceful and secure, and I'd been told that Pola was not feeling very well.

After the usual interminable wait, while lights and cameras and extras were changed all around again, Lubitsch came clambering into view. He took a place behind the cameras. Gave a quick squint and then—"Nay-gree!"

Swish, whish of silken skirts. A voice, somehow suggesting Camille, called tremulously, " 'Allo! 'Allo!" And Negri came strolling flirtatiously into view, casting mesmeric eyes to right and left, tapping an old gentleman on the ear with her pert green parasol, finally pausing at the steps to greet a gallant who rushed forward to kiss her hand. Then she rolled her great black eyes and winked—the wickedest wink a woman ever wunk.

The scene was enacted as though it were entirely impromptu. Unless you hear the camera click or observe very closely you never realize Negri is acting; her naturalness is perfection. She requires no direction.

"All she needs to know is the story," observed the secretary. "She does not need to study or think about it. It is instinct with her."

The same appears true of Lubitsch. He directs by instinct.

The part Pola was playing was that of a Parisian demi-mondaine who falls in love after a life of amorous adventure. Her lover, whom she inspires to success, is about to put her aside because she is a handicap to his position. When she realizes the insincerity of his love she throws herself from a balcony onto the pavement below and is killed.

But here comes the good old Americanizing touch.

There will be two endings, one happy and one sad.

I don't know exactly how the tragedy will be turned into a happy-ever-after comedy. Perhaps there will be a shot showing Pola falling onto the studio mattress instead of the supposed paving blocks.

The American public—the American public with the mind of a twelve-year-old child, you know—it must have life as it ain't. Yet that public swept PASSION into one of the greatest successes of film times. And PASSION ended with the lovely Negri head beneath the blade of the guillotine—and no pardon on horseback to save her.

However, there are two endings. It's entirely up to you. Drama is supposed to be Life. Unfortunately we have no choice as to our endings in Life.

As a director Lubitsch is a dervish. He can whirl through more work in a day than most directors can get past in a week. The most spectacular scene of THE LOVES OF PHARAOH was shot in three days. He doesn't rehearse his players before starting a picture, as Griffith does. And he does not rehearse very much during actual filming.

Before he turns a camera upon the production, however, every detail of the story has been charted and all the research work has been completed by the art director. In collaboration with Lubitsch the scenarioist has turned the story into continuity. I saw the bulky script lying in state on a table some distance from the "set." Lubitsch never went near it. It was like a lovely white corpse awaiting final disposition. Yet every detail of that scenario was being observed as scrupulously as the last wishes of the dead. Lubitsch does not improvise as many directors do. Chaplin, for instance, starts with a seed which gradually germinates. Lubitsch has written the story in carbon on his mind; every phase is indelible.

He has an uncanny memory. I will never forget the awe-stricken look upon the face of

Frederick James Smith, *Photoplay*'s managing editor, when Lubitsch recognized him in the crowd at the premiere of ORPHANS OF THE STORM. The astounded Frederick swore it was the first time a director had ever recognized him. The little film wizard had met hundreds of interviewers and film people during his few weeks in America yet he could remember a face and a name in an instant. His secretary told me that he could call any extra man by name who had worked for him years ago.

If Lubitsch is a fast stepper on the "set" he certainly is a shimmie dancer in the cutting room. You would imagine that he was mad at the film. He tears at it until you almost think you hear him growl. Now and then he holds it up to the light and gives it a blink— swish, crackle, zipp—and another five hundred feet goes a-reeling. THE FLAME OF LOVE, the Negri picture he just finished, required about three days to cut and assemble. Any other director I've ever observed would take two weeks for an ordinary program feature. THE LOVES OF PHARAOH, originally in ten or twelve reels, required less than a week.

This faculty for rapid cutting must be attributed to a supernatural memory, one which carries the story so perfectly that lightning decisions are possible. Some directors spend as much time on assembling a picture as upon photographing it, for it is generally conceded that this part of the production is of vital importance.

Lubitsch cannot work slowly. He must work while his enthusiasm is ablaze. Ask him which he considers his best pictures and he will always reply that it is the one he is working on. That is his real conviction; if it weren't he couldn't keep at it.

I choose a happy time to visit Ernst Lubitsch, and perhaps a little of his exuberance was due to his approaching marriage to Irni Kraus, a Berlin girl who has played small parts in several German pictures but who has yet to make her debut in a Lubitsch film.

Very few people around the studio knew of the dramatic moment approaching in the life of the little director. No one had been informed officially. I did not learn of it until the day before. Then I accounted for the puzzling scene between Negri and Lubitsch on the first day I called. I had told Lubitsch that we had heard he was married to Pola. All brimming over with glee, and afraid lest he would burst before he told her, Ernst scampered off to where his gorgeous Nay-gree was sitting. He blurted out what I had said, and chuckled as Pola tossed back her head, her hand on her breast, in a typical gesture of laughter. He also looked very pleased when she quickly leaned forward and patted him affectionately on the cheek.

"A wonderful, wonderful woman," is the expression Lubitsch uses again and again about Negri. There is no one in the world like her—no one. He thinks DECEPTION his best directorial effort—next to THE FLAME OF LOVE—but I objected that Negri was not in it to raise it to the stellar heights.

"Of course Henny Porten is good," I added, "But—"

"Pola is better!" shot Lubitsch, triumphantly. "No one like Pola—no one."

They have had their temperamental skirmishes. I wish I might have witnessed one. As a battler Lubitsch must be as funny as Chaplin, Pola as divine as Duse. These tilts always have the same ending, I'm told, Pola awarding a pat or a kiss upon the again-happy countenance of Ernst . . . Catherine the Great and her prime minister.

While Lubitsch was shy about confiding the joyful news of his marriage he was outspoken in his delight over the possibility of coming to America to work. "America by Christmas" is his banner cry. He may arrive for Thanksgiving, as Paramount is planning to grant his wish and allot him a few acres of floor in the Long Island studio. He wants to do modern stories of American life as a relief from the long series of historical dramas and as proof of his versatility. His ability doubtlessly can make the transfer, but I wonder if he will be as pre-eminent in the modern field as in the period. Still, what man wants to be without a rival?

It's a little bit mean of him, though, just when we were progressing so well in our history to drop us back into kindergarten. I never realized what a good teacher Prof.

Ernst was until I visited Versailles. If it hadn't been for PASSION I would have had no appreciation for the bedroom of Louis XV. I might have thought that the little secret door by the bed was to the closet where the king kept his Sunday crown. But having seen PASSION I knew that it was the door through which Madame Du Barry came each evening at bedtime to shake hands with the king and wish him goodnight.

Perhaps the fact that Mr. Lubitsch has become a staid married man also has something to do with his desire to abandon the life of kings. Kings are bad company for married men.

I inquired of the secretary if Mr. Lubitsch had ever contemplated doing the rather exciting life of ex-Kaiser Wilhelm.

"Better you should not ask him that," advised the secretary. "The Kaiser is Mr. Lubitsch's pet dislike."

Before coming to America he will do one picture based on the life of Johann Strauss, the waltz king.

No honeymoon interrupted production activities at the Lubitsch plant. Indeed, Albert E. Kaufmann, Paramount's general manager of foreign productions, was wondering whether at last Lubitsch would stop work for an entire day. The secretary was of the doleful opinion that there would be only the usual half hour for lunch, Lubitsch muttering the nuptial vows between helpings of *kalbschnitzel*.

Perhaps you remember seeing Lubitsch as the hunchback in his production of ONE ARABIAN NIGHT. But he made his fame as an actor by playing comedy roles, on both stage and screen. He's a natural comedian and has that constitutional shyness and modesty for which Harold Lloyd, as well as Chaplin, is distinguished among the tribe histrionique.

His friendliness is real and eager—"Be sure you come and see me when I come to America," he urged, as though he expected to have a rather lonely time of it.

Ernst Lubitsch, a Napoleonic little gnome, a Dutch comedian who can make the whole world weep, a little man with a big smiling heart. If he isn't a genius he's what a genius ought to be.

And if you don't think he's a hundred per cent American just bring on the jazz, the chewing gum and the shimmie.

ROSITA   **FILM 1923**

"The Screen: The Girl and the Guitar," *The New York Times*, September 4, 1923, p. 14.

> With Mary Pickford, Holbrook Blinn, Irene Rich, George Walsh, Charles Belcher, Frank Leigh, Mme. Mathilde Comont, George Periolat, Bert Sprotte, Snitz Edwards, Mme. de Bodamere, Donald McAlpin and Doreen Turner, adapted by Edward Knoblock, directed by Ernst Lubitsch. At the Lyric Theatre.

Nothing more delightfully charming than Mary Pickford's new picture, ROSITA, has been seen on the screen for some time. The combination of Edward Knoblock, Ernst Lubitsch and Mary Pickford is a difficult one to equal. One could almost say that the titles of this picture, which was presented last night at the Lyric Theatre, where society, stage and screen were represented, equal the acting, and in mentioning names one ought to include Holbrook Blinn, who gives such an excellent performance as Carlos of Spain.

The photography is as perfect as the acting of the principals, and the sight of the interiors and exteriors elicits murmurs of admiration. Exquisite is an adjective that fits this film as well as any, and it would be a quibbler indeed who could find much fault with it. One might say that Mary Pickford is not dark and, therefore, palpably not indigenous of Spain. As one gazes at the swiftly flowing narrative one does not care whether her hair is red. For the time being she is to Seville an exotic blonde, full of vivacity and as saucy as you please.

Her introduction is well heralded. The jolly inhabitants of Seville see her coming before she is pictured on the screen. Their faces light up, beaming with pleasure at the presence of the saucy girl with the guitar. No wonder a king fell in love with her. As she portrays Rosita before the camera all in the audience last night seemed to feel their hearts go out to her. And as for Mr. Blinn, the more he is seen in pictures, the better we shall like it, for here is a man who can act, a man who overdoes nothing and who does not plaster his face with obnoxious make-up.

He sets the pace in this film, with his leering eyes, his passionate mouth, his boyish shame before his consort, and—well, there is not a dull moment from beginning to end. In fact, one would like to see the production again, and it seems like a good book, a pity when it's ended.

The King is first introduced, with the announcement that his affairs are heavy on his hands. One sees three fair women playing a stupid game of smacking each other's hands, and the frivolous monarch obviously is enjoying every smack and he receives every instant the fullsome flattery rung into his ears by the bewitching females.

Rosita and her guitar spin a song of "I know a King." She goes on to sing that he is a "royal rake, who rakes in all his subjects make." As the film unfolds, the song becomes more bitter. Rosita dazzles Carlos, and he gives her jewels, a palace, and all the time the girl is in love with young Don Diego, who has been flung into prison for fighting a duel in the streets.

Rosita's mother is decidedly plethoric, a home-loving creature, accustomed to doing her own washing—something she still clings to after moving into the palace. One sees the sniffing menials in livery highly disgusted at the clothesline in the room.

When Rosita is called upon to see the King, she espies on the table a tempting dish of bon-bons, which finally vanquishes her, and which she attacks with energy—the rapacious appetite of a healthy beauty, unafraid of the results upon her figure. The King thinks that he will kiss this minx. But the minx declines the royal lips. There are the jealous eyes of the Queen ever on the alert.

One of the fetching scenes in this picture is where Carlos is dallying with two beauties in the Madrid gardens, where there is a pleasant see-saw. The Queen arrives and both beauties are shot to the ground, the King forgetting that he must hold down his end. This film is filled with such amusing pictures skillfully directed and beautifully photographed.

Both Mr. Blinn and Mary Pickford are impressive in the sequences where the King has decided to dine tête-à-tête with Rosita, who has in store for the monarch a gruesome surprise. But it turns out, after all, that her lover whom she imagined was dead, is only shamming because he has been told to do so to save his life.

There is a touch of *If I Were King* in this plot, with Rosita as a female Francois Villon. The agile Rosita flings herself on tables, and this reminds us that this production is most aptly cut. There are no scenes opening up without action, something is happening all the time, and suspense runs from sequence to sequence. Rosita is known as the fair Spaniard, but her eyes are flashing and dark, without any distasteful crude make-up— such as blue eye-lids.

The crowd scenes are pleasingly pictured, as also are the witty sequences inside Rosita's home. This is one of the most charming productions in which Miss Pickford has appeared.

COMMENTARY

Lubitsch's THE MARRIAGE CIRCLE (1924), apparently influenced by Chaplin's A　　315

WOMAN OF PARIS, inaugurated the cycle of his social satires. Iris Barry, writing in the London *Spectator*, reviews the film. She was a co-founder of the London Film Society the following year, and, ten years later in New York, became the curator of the Museum of Modern Art Film Library when it was established.

Of Miss Barry's seven producers of genius, Lubitsch is the subject of the present chapter; Chaplin, Griffith and Seastrom have already been discussed; and Fritz Lang and Robert Wiene are covered in Chapter 19. The best-known film of the German director Karl Grune, THE STREET, was shown here in 1927. Other Grune films to reach America were: TWO BROTHERS and JEALOUSY (1928), WATERLOO and AT THE EDGE OF THE WORLD (1929). His ARABELLA, filmed in Germany with Mae Marsh, was reviewed here in 1928 as RACING THROUGH.

More contemporary foibles came under scrutiny from Lubitsch in THREE WOMEN and FORBIDDEN PARADISE (1924), KISS ME AGAIN and LADY WINDERMERE'S FAN (1925), and SO THIS IS PARIS (1926).

THE MARRIAGE CIRCLE   **FILM 1924**

"The Cinema: Hope Fulfilled," Iris Barry, *The Spectator* (London), Vol. 132, No. 5003, May 17, 1924, p. 788.

A really efficient comedy—in which there is perception behind the wit and a perfect rounding of the action so that nothing irrelevant or forced mars the bright sparkle—is a rare thing. The very word recalls so pat our appreciation of writers like Sheridan, Molière or Congreve that it comes as a surprise to find in THE MARRIAGE CIRCLE . . . something on the screen in their tradition; a surprise even though one had held that the cinema *was* capable of delineating pictorially comedies as witty as anything in the theatre's repertory. Hitherto the cinema has shown us, in Harold Lloyd, Larry Semon and the late John Bunny, for example, only the succulent fun of the music-hall and the circus, not the dry wit of true comedy; it has provoked laughter by physical peculiarities, acrobacy, clowning. Even Chaplin as an actor is hardly an exception: his mixture of farce and pathos has always been conceived too emotionally, too little cerebrally, to be right comedy. It was, however, Chaplin, the producer of A WOMAN OF PARIS, who opened the way for what has now been done.

THE MARRIAGE CIRCLE may well silence those who claim that the film cannot compare as a dramatic form with the stageplay. For this is at once perfect cinematography and perfect conventional drama. Lubitsch, the producer of this delicious piece, has shown, not told, the story. Everything is visualized, all the comedy is in what the characters are seen or imagined to be thinking or feeling, in the interplay, never expressed in words, of wills and personalities. There is a minimum of subtitling, and the progress of the plot is not dependent on the letterpress. Gestures and situations, so lucidly presented that one is perfectly aware from the "pictures" alone of what is happening, give rise to other gestures and other situations which—because of the permanence of visual memory—one recognizes as the logical result of what has occurred before. There is a peculiar mental delight in watching a plot develop so. And with curious boldness Lubitsch has drawn on the minimum of the cinema's technical resources. Here are no magnificent halls, no costly crowds, no multiplicity of scene, no great bridgings of time or space. This deliberate limitation gives the film perfect unity. Lubitsch uses only one focus, brings the five characters up to us a little magnified and intimate, and, keeping them at that constant range, sets the action going simply, precisely, without hesitation.

The story is unassuming. Dr. Braun and his wife are perfectly happy. Professor Stock and his wife live in a strained atmosphere of *laissez faire* which threatens to explode in divorce at the least pretext. Mrs. Stock, with a determination proper to the nasty carnal little creature she is, sets her cap at the amiable and helpless Dr. Braun. And Braun's partner, Dr. Mueller, sees fit to declare his passion for Mrs. Braun. An intricacy of situation develops between these five people. The solution of the plot is an exquisite misunderstanding which is a triumph of comedy. Of course, the story is not very edifying. But then neither *The Importance of Being Earnest* or *The Way of the World* is exactly a Sunday School narrative. And it is witty. It is also marvelously well acted, by film-stars whom one has seen often before and never remarked (except Adolphe Menjou when Chaplin made him act in A WOMAN OF PARIS). But Lubitsch is a genius of a producer, and Monte Blue and Florence Vidor as Dr. and Mrs. Braun are transfigured, from the charming but passionless stars of yesterday, into real people, living characters, not those meaningless types so frequent, chiefly because of the paucity of the acting, on the screen. Menjou as Professor Stock, a little older than his Pierre of A WOMAN OF PARIS, a little dryer, is *impayable*.

Now, while the scheme of this film is simple, the psychology of motive in it is enchantingly complex, and any attempt at a verbal description at once demonstrates the superiority of the pictorial over the verbal method of telling such a story. Henry James could, in a light mood, have told it as minutely as Lubitsch has in pictures: but at what a length. I do not believe that any dramatist living or dead could relate it in dialogue quite so delicately, so intuitively or so effortlessly as this unpretentious film does. Therefore, I cannot understand why not one of our playwrights or novelists has yet been attracted to this new subtle method of dramatic expression and of story telling. Certainly, they allow themselves profitably to be "adapted" to the cinema, but their artistic satisfaction must usually be about as great as would be that of Matisse were he to allow, say, Mr. J. D. Beresford to write a novel on the subject of one of his paintings. Possibly some of our writers will see THE MARRIAGE CIRCLE and be convinced at last that there really is an unequalled opportunity for self-expression in the medium of a film. I even hope that subsequently a few of them will unite in presenting a humble petition to one of the seven producers of genius there are (the names are Lang, Grune, Wiene, Lubitsch, Chaplin, Griffith and Seastrom) to be allowed to go to school under them in their studios and learn the business of writing for the screen. The great and lonely seven might well admit reinforcements.

Iris Barry

1923   "LUBITSCH ON DIRECTING"

From *The New York Times*, December 16, 1923, Section 9, p. 5.

Ernst Lubitsch, the man who made Pola Negri famous, who directed PASSION, DECEPTION and latterly ROSITA with Mary Pickford, has been squandering a few days in New York searching for a story. He wants something dramatic, virile, containing picturesque atmosphere without being a costume film. He pricks up his ears at the suspicion of a good yarn, and wherever he wanders, at luncheons, at dinners, in the homes of friends, in the subway crush-hour, he is looking for something or somebody to bring the idea of a story to him, so that he can say he wants such and such a play or some particular book.

Lubitsch is a small man physically, slightly given to promising plumpness. His dark eyes are keen and smiling. He is very earnest, but like the angels, treads lightly when it comes to criticism. He prognosticated titleless pictures for the future, which may mean from two to twenty years, qualifying this utterance with the conclusion that these pictures without words will be utterly different from any being made now. Paintings of great masters, he argues, speak for themselves, and therefore a motion picture should tell its story. He raised his eyebrows when we suggested that pictures without titles   317 would be like a wordless stage production. He also ignored the brief, yet interesting, title of an oil painting in his conjectures.

Modest and Quiet.

This great director's English is restricted and hesitating, and he is modest and quiet. One of the most interesting statements he made concerned the players when shooting a scene. He said he aimed to obtain action that spoke, and found that too many rehearsals of a scene often tired the players, who toward the end went through the performance correctly, but without the spark with which their portrayal was endowed at the outset.

In beginning the interview Mr. Lubitsch said:

"It is my idea to work with the scenario writer from the very beginning, and as I do so I build up in my mind exactly how I am going to direct the picture. When the scenario is finished I know just what I want. It is important that a scenario should be a good manuscript, as it is essential in the directing of a picture. You have to know before you start 'shooting' what to do in every scene. Some scenes are taken according to necessity and not according to their continuity. You may begin work on the last scene and then skip to the middle of the production. Therefore, how can one start at the end without having mapped out carefully beforehand every detail of direction of the production?

"Then, I try to exclude titles wherever possible. I want all action, where it is feasible, to explain itself without titles to interrupt the suspense, which is so often killed by the insertion of words. For a modern realistic drama, we must have spoken titles, but even these should be made to read just as one speaks in real life, and not according to the stiff conversation of books. The ideal manuscript is one without titles, but it is not for today or tomorrow, but in a couple of years or infinitely longer. This has nothing to do with pictures as they are produced nowadays. In our titles we borrow from the stage or the novel. Later we will have discovered the motion picture style.

An Intimate Drama.

"It is very interesting to have every scene speak for itself and what I talk about in this regard may not happen for fifty years. In the painting you understand what it means without titles. All the great masters explain themselves. In my last picture I experienced a great change in my career, as it is the first time I have made an important modern drama. I have gotten away from spectacles, as there are only five characters in this film, which is called THE MARRIAGE CIRCLE. It is a very intimate drama. Even the script of the story was different, and I never got so close to real life as I have in this picture. It is a narrative of a serious marriage problem—light, if you like, but very real, and not overdone. Some people are given to being too heavy on the screen. We want realism, and the players should act as they would in the same circumstances in real life. You don't act heavily in real life. I have attempted to exclude this in my last picture.

"My chief worry now is looking for a story. It is always a worry, and far harder to decide on a story than to direct. The American pictures are fine—there are no pictures that speak as well as the American productions. It is difficult to say which is the best picture I have seen here. How can one say whether Molière or Shakespeare is the cleverer, or compare Bernard Shaw and Gerhart Hauptmann? I think that A WOMAN OF PARIS is a marvelous production. I like it because I feel that an intelligent man speaks to me, and nobody's intelligence is insulted in that picture, the treatment and atmosphere in it being wonderful.

"I had a wonderful actress in Mary Pickford [in ROSITA] and the same adjective applies to Holbrook Blinn. In my latest effort the five players are Marie Prevost, Florence Vidor, Monte Blue, Adolphe Menjou and Creighton Hale. None of them is overdressed. I wanted to have them attired just as they ought to be for such a story. So there are no million dollar jewels and no gorgeous clothes. There is no sweet, nice acting, which is unreal. We want to touch the emotions of the people who see this picture. The players have on as little make-up as possible—only that which is necessary for the lights.

The Spark in Acting.

"Yes—yes—I do believe that some time in the future stories will be written direct for the screen. I prefer a manuscript written for the screen by somebody familiar with the dramatic construction of a picture.

"As far as I can, I try to keep the action going without tiring the players, I think over my medium shot when I am making my long shot, and I am ready for what I want when it comes to a close-up. I don't want to get the actors fatigued, and only when it appears absolutely necessary do I insist upon going over the scene three or four times. You lose the feeling when you do. A player may have just the expression you want, but on the fourth or fifth attempt he is too sure of himself."

FILM 1924   THREE WOMEN

"Mr. Lubitsch's Direction Outshines His Narrative," by Mordaunt Hall, *The New York Times,* October 12, 1924, Section 8, p. 5.

From the viewpoint of direction Ernst Lubitsch's recent production, THREE WOMEN, is one of the most brilliant achievements ever thrown upon a screen, something to be classed with the same director's THE MARRIAGE CIRCLE and with Chaplin's notable effort, A WOMAN OF PARIS. Although we cannot disregard the great value of a satisfying story with plausible incidents and contrasts in characterizations, it is nevertheless true that we would sooner view a poor story well directed than a good story handled in an indifferent way. Whatever is thought of the narrative of THREE WOMEN, it must be admitted that in spite of the excellent performances of the players, especially Pauline Frederick's impersonation, the story suffers in comparison with the direction.

Mr. Lubitsch's picture is produced with a minumum of subtitles, and yet one is never left in doubt as to the action of this photoplay, as not only is the acting thoroughly comprehensible, but in some cases the utterances of the players can be readily understood through the movements of their lips. The average number of captions in the ordinary feature-length picture runs from about 100 to 150, and there have been instances where the title writers have put in as many as 250 subtitles. In THREE WOMEN Lubitsch uses 42 titles, and about 90 per cent of these are spoken titles, the other 10 per cent being descriptive matter to cover the passage of time, which would take too much footage in the film to explain in action or allegory. Mr. Lubitsch had about 54 titles in THE MARRIAGE CIRCLE, it being ever his desire to substitute action for captions.

The settings of this picture, while ambitious in some scenes, are never so extravagant that they detract from the expression and actions of the players. The simple manner in which Mr. Lubitsch opens up this latest effort kindles immediate interest in the narrative, as we see first nothing but the registering arm of a weighing machine. Then Mrs. Mabel Wilton is introduced with a wry look on her face, caused by disappointment at her weight and the fact that she is consuming part of a lemon. Mrs. Wilton's chief annoyance is the fact that her daughter is 18 years old and very pretty. The mother, however, is a fortunate widow with $3,000,000, and therefore she is not neglected by a certain coterie of men because she is a trifle passé.

Age and Amusements.

There is a lively scene of a charity fête, in which children are seen sliding down a   319 chute. Mrs. Wilton is not too old, she thinks, for such amusement, and she too indulges in the joys of the young, of which she quickly tires in her enthusiasm for dancing. Edmund Lamont (Lew Cody), a reckless scamp, who ostentatiously throws his money away, is a worry to his creditors. Lamont approaches several women, among whom is Mrs. Wilton. Before asking one of them to dance, Lamont calculates which one of them is the wealthiest. His method of doing this is to take mental stock of their gems. Mrs. Wilton's diamonds easily bring about a decision in her favor, and Lamont is soon seen cavorting about the waxed floor with the wealthy widow in his arms. Mr. Lubitsch gives close-ups of the pearls of some of the women and the striking adornments worn by Mrs. Wilton. One also sees intermittently the expression on Lamont's face as he gazes from one to the other. Here it strikes one that Mrs. Wilton is too attractive to feel bound to accept the attentions from such a scoundrel as Lamont. So one can't help thinking she is very foolish when she succumbs to his flattery.

The love affair progresses, and Jeanne Wilton, the daughter, disappointed with the scant correspondence she receives from her mother, decides to leave California and go to New York. She suddenly appears before Mrs. Wilton, who finds the girl an inconvenience on account of her age. Jeanne was in love with Fred Armstrong (Pierre Gendron), but soon after her arrival in the East she forgets about him and accepts Lamont's attention, this unscrupulous flirt having learned that when Jeanne marries she will inherit half the Wilton wealth. Apparently Jeanne is most susceptible to admiration, and just because her mother leaves her alone so often she unconsciously steals Lamont. It is only natural to conclude that her mentality must have been affected by journeying East, as there does not appear any real subtle attraction about Lamont for a girl who has been brought up in a sane and sensible university. So one begins to think that both mother and daughter are weaklings.

Black-Hearted Lamont.

Lamont is a bit worse than most villains of his type. He does not seem to know on which side his bread is buttered. One would imagine that after he had married the pretty Jeanne and made himself comfortable with her million and one-half dollars he would have sobered down to a decent life. Such is not the case, and he immediately becomes insanely infatuated with Harriet, a bedizened creature to whom gold is everything. Harriet is the one of the three women who, for the brief time she is seen on the screen, is really natural. She is bad and scheming and therefore one does not expect any virtues in her conduct.

In the course of viewing this photodrama we came to the conclusion that film actresses ought to be careful what they put on their finger nails. Miss Frederick uses some red stuff which results in her nails appearing very dark on the screen.

There are certain melodramatic effects in this production which do not help the story any more than the scrap Lamont has with a tipsy, belligerent patron in a cabaret. Lamont is struck with a champagne bottle and his death is foreseen. Soon he recovers to continue his villainy.

Harriet has exotic tastes at home. She has black sheets and pillow covers on her bed, and wears a black nightgown and a black negligee.

When Mrs. Wilton sees the silhouettes of Lamont and her daughter in a struggle, she rushes to their room and in a tussle with Lamont shoots him. Apparently Mr. Lubitsch does not favor lengthy court scenes, as he disposes of this murder trial with more speed then Jersey justice. The jury comes in with the verdict and the foreman, when addressing the Judge, shakes his head, thus saving Mr. Lubitsch a subtitle.

Mr. Lubitsch's next picture [FORBIDDEN PARADISE] is soon to be released. In it Pola Negri, whom he directed in PASSION, has the leading role.

1925   **Lubitsch on the Set**

Excerpts from "How the Great Directors Work," Harry Carr, *Motion Picture Magazine,* Vol. 19, No. 4, May, 1925, pp. 52-53.

. . . No one who sees Ernst Lubitsch at work will ever forget him.

He is as eager as a bull-terrier trying to break loose to run after a tom cat. He has black eyes that glitter like wet anthracite coal. You can always tell how things are going by the sparkle. When the star is inspired to great artistry, it seems as though Lubitsch's eyes shoot sparks.

I am always expecting to see him fly into a terrific passion and tear the scenery to rags. But he never does. I have never seen him lose his temper. He has the patience of Job. The nearest approach to temperament I have seen in him is when the carpenters on an adjoining set make too much noise. He demands the stillness of the tomb.

The other day I saw him trying to make an actor execute a formal bow after the manner of Continental army officers. That was all he had to do: come to the door and bow. Click his heels: bend the stiff back-bone; straighten the stiff back-bone. One—two—three!

Time after time Lubitsch would stand in the doorway and do it for him.

"Oh yes, I see," the actor would say. And then he would proceed to do it just exactly wrong. If Lubitsch had seized an ax and had chopped him into a fricassee, I would have gone into court and testified that it was justifiable homicide. And thereafter would have sought to induce Congress to vote him a medal on the ground that he was a public benefactor. But Lubitsch never lost his patience or courtesy.

There is only one way you can ever tell that Lubitsch is working under a severe nervous strain. While they are changing the position of the lights for the next "shot," he paces up and down—usually behind a piece of scenery—like a caged tiger.

You realize it also when he makes the close-ups. He usually sits on a little camp chair, and you can see his face going through the emotions with the actors. In his intensity, he leans forward from his chair, often with his hands gripped on the arms. The more intense the scene, the more pronounced his "lean."

Lubitsch is, himself, a finished actor. Before the camera starts shooting he nearly always acts each scene for the actors. Sometimes with an effect startling for the spectators to behold. As, for instance, when I saw Pauline Starke, watching him studiously, while he turned himself into a shy young girl for her instruction [in FORBIDDEN PARADISE].

Even Pola Negri does not escape being shown. Although she has been under his direction for so many years that she senses his wishes from a word or a gesture.

Oddly enough, Lubitsch is the most popular director of the screen—both with stage hands and actors. Yet he is the most exacting and most difficult to please.

When they were making THE MARRIAGE CIRCLE, I saw Florence Vidor unlock the drawer of a bureau sixteen times before she satisfied him. She and Creighton Hale had a famous kiss in that same play. They had to do it thirty-nine times before Lubitsch said "Goot!" And afterward he told me that he liked to work with them: they caught the idea so easily!

Between whiles, Lubitsch is a wild, rollicking blade. He will go over to the piano and hammer out American jazz until every one starts dancing. While he was making ROSITA with Mary Pickford, he spent his spare time trying to make a cello play "Yes, We Have No Bananas.". . .

FILM 1925   LADY WINDERMERE'S FAN

"Exceptional Photoplays: LADY WINDERMERE'S FAN," *National Board of Review*

Magazine, Vol. 1, No. 1, March-April, 1926, pp. 11-12. (With the permission of the National Board of Review of Motion Pictures.)

Directed by . . . . .Ernst Lubitsch
Photographed by . . . . .Charles van Enger

CAST

Lord Darlington . . . . .Ronald Colman
Mrs. Erlynne . . . . .Irene Rich
Lady Windermere . . . . .May McAvoy
Lord Windermere . . . . .Bert Lytell
Lord Augustus . . . . .Edward Martindel
Duchess . . . . .Helen Dunbar
Duchess . . . . .Carrie Daumery
Duchess . . . . .Billie Bennett

In LADY WINDERMERE'S FAN Ernst Lubitsch has given us another of his finished and technically surprising photoplays—masterpieces of their kind and cream, surely, of polite drama, in one direction, and polite satire, in the other, in motion pictures. Going back to Wilde's play, he has built upon its skeleton a graceful, smoothly muscled form of cinematic adaption which, while it has no Titan power, is interesting in every movement and in every gesture of its intelligent action. Adhering closely to the structure of the original, this picturization of LADY WINDERMERE'S FAN avoids the Wildian cleverness, supplanting it with the Lubitsch ingenuity, at once recognizable from its manner of glowing narrative, rich, imaginative and perfectly translated in the language of the screen. In place of thrills of situation, thrills of spectacular sets, thrills of mobs and masses and what-not, a keener thrill—one always to be experienced before this sort of motion picture entertainment by intelligent patrons of the cinema (for Lubitsch is always of the cinema in contrast to those directors who are always, and merely, of the movie)—is awakened by the inner fabric of the picture lying there like a taut warp for the sure and shimmering pattern on the shifting screen, a pattern changing in rhythm, yet its color never varying in good taste and the design ever more clearly established and defined from scene to scene, through embellishment on embellishment, until the full, ordered plan is executed. How many directors of motion pictures today can give you that accomplishment?

The story of how Mrs. Erlynee, beautiful, witty, determined—and *déclassé*—came back to London and, unrecognized by her daughter, the bride of Lord Windermere, saved that young lady's reputation from scandal by claiming her fan in the lodgings of Lord Darlington where she had fled after a misunderstanding with her husband who she believed was having an affair with the notorious Mrs. Erlynne, is perhaps too well known to repeat further. It is a good story and has bequeathed a situation to innumerable progeny reared by other writers after, and doubtless before, Wilde. But it is no better a story than Mr. Lubitsch's film, and the film has the advantage since it is in the medium of today. The important thing to see is that a good story can be made a better picture— when a Lubitsch handles it—sheerly through cinematic qualities developed through thorough understanding of what the screen should and can do as distinguished from what it should not and cannot do. And for the additional reason that when it does this, it is doing what is beyond the power of the written word in books and the spoken word on the stage. Such uses of the medium in LADY WINDERMERE'S FAN are too many to enumerate. They consist of such little, all-important matters as matchless cutting, unique camera angles, precisely natural movements of the actors, backgrounds that are like depths in paintings, and finger-touches of control of the mass that keeps it fluid yet

322

never allows it to become muddy. What a clear screen, indeed, is that of Mr. Ernst Lubitsch, and what a frame of delightful proportion is set around it by his quiet and choice imagination.

To pause at the film's technical quality for a moment and offer an illustration: Lord Darlington and Lady Windermere have gone out into the garden in the rear of the stately London house in which the great party is being held. He is imploring her to leave her husband and come with him. Mrs. Erlynne appears, coming out of the house, on the balustrade overlooking the garden. She sees the man and her daughter behind a box hedge quite far off. Now, the camera is never brought near to Lady Windermere and Lord Darlington. Their heads bob back and forth across the distant box hedge. You see them about as Mrs. Erlynne sees them. The effect is perfect, the drama of the scene behind the hedge is precisely, vividly, and how uniquely told, and the air of the clandestine that awakens Mrs. Erlynne to the potential danger of the situation to her daughter is created so as to make the audience see what Mrs. Erlynne sees, and feel as she does, without bringing directly to our gaze Lady Windermere in flight before an impassioned man in a dark garden, a touch of artistry which a messy, man-handling close-up would almost certainly have spoiled by coarsening the visual image. Mr. Lubitsch has not forgotten that his characters are well-bred.

The cast throughout is capable, as the Lubitsch casts invariably are. That loveliest actress of our screen, Irene Rich, contributes a Mrs. Erlynne that makes us feel at every turn what a fine lady is this, and how unconscionable was the smugness of the British society that tried to throw her out. If Mr. Lubitsch was interested in the Wildian attack on the snobbery of the swells, he has pointed it mainly through Miss Rich's Mrs. Erlynne and the connotations to be drawn from the attitude of the characters as they are reflected from her, and at all times cinegraphically, for the Wildian dialogue of the play is avoided in the titles, which are scant and to the point, and not fillips to, but accessories of, the action.

FILM 1926   SO THIS IS PARIS

Excerpt from "The Screen: Lubitsch Rings the Bell Again," Mordaunt Hall, *The New York Times,* August 16, 1926, p. 10.

. . . . No matter how brilliant may be the picture Mr. Lubitsch produces, he succeeds invariably in inserting a transcendental stroke. Few will forget the brilliant scene in which a fish rippled through the reflection of the lovers about to embrace in FORBIDDEN PARADISE. In KISS ME AGAIN Mr. Lubitsch portrayed a rain shower without calling for a flood of water *[*in the usual cliché style*]*, and in the film translation of LADY WINDERMERE'S FAN he denoted haste in writing a note by having a wet blot of ink on the paper. In SO THIS IS PARIS his tour de force is an extraordinarily brilliant conception of an eye full of a Charleston contest, with vibrant kaleidoscopic changes from feet and figures to the omnipotent saxophones. This dazzling episode is like the dream of a man after drinking more than his share of wine at such an event. The comedy in this film had, up to that time, kept the audience in constant explosions of laughter, but the startling dissolving scenic effects and varied "shots" elicited a hearty round of applause. . . .

FILM 1926   SO THIS IS PARIS

Excerpt from "Lubitsch's New Comedy Sparkles With Keen Wit," Mordaunt Hall, *The New York Times,* August 22, 1926, Section 7, p. 2.

323

. . . The movement of this scintillating farce-comedy is artfully carried out, first with a keen and clever portrayal of the characteristics of three of the persons involved and a few words to give one a quick flash of the fourth character. The speed of the action accelerates until the high spot is reached by a fascinating series of scenes of a Charleston contest. This portion of the film, despite the subject with which it deals, has been produced with no little artistry. In fact its vibrant scenes depict such a wealth of imagination that the ordinary dance sequence, so frequently introduced in films, flops into mediocrity before it. Mr. Lubitsch obtains a remarkable effect through varied "shots" and quick dissolves, and when the full aggregation of excited dancers is shown, it gives one a capital conception of a high pitch of enthusiasm. Then again one perceives the busy feet of the dancers, then their figures and then the tireless musicians, in "long shots" and "medium shots," the fade-outs or dissolves taking but a fraction of a second. This thrilling scene is infectious, one that seemed to exact applause from all. . . .

COMMENTARY

Lubitsch's THE PATRIOT (1928), which represents the first and only time he directed Emil Jannings in Hollywood, was a return to the more ponderous European manner. Set at the court of Russia's mad Czar Paul, it brought cries of anguish from the hinterlands of the U.S.A., where the box-office took a nose-dive when the film went into general release.

THE PATRIOT   FILM 1928-1929

"THE PATRIOT," "Box Office Record," *The Motion Picture Almanac—1929*, The Quigley Publishing Company, Chicago, Illinois, 1929, p. 204.

(Paramount) Emil Jannings, Florence Vidor, Lewis Stone, Vera Voronina, Neil Hamilton, Harry Cording, 10 [reels]. *November 19-20-21.* Played this three days to an empty house, but it was no fault of the picture. A great picture and should make the big boys in the big towns dust off the S. R. O. sign. Print good and best photography ever seen on our screen. (Midway theatre, Martinsville, Va.—Small town patronage.) A wonderfully made picture, but it did not draw. I believe this picture the most suggestive picture we ever ran. Just another reason why we need censorship. The small town exhibitors need clean pictures. (Lyric theatre, Wooster, Ohio—General patronage.) *December 26.* Wonderful picture, but too long. No doubt Jannings is a wonderful actor and we expect great things from him here a this is our first picture of his. Lewis Stone almost steals the picture from Jannings. (LaCrosse theatre, LaCrosse, Kansas—General patronage.) *January 1-2-3.* Wonderful picture as far as acting is concerned, but a big flop at the box office. It has no drawing power. The title kills the drawing power of the picture. (Strand theatre, Griswold, Ia.—General patronage.) *January 1-3.* An excellent picture that was a complete flop for us. We lost money, and although the flu and bad weather had something to do with it, can't lay all of it to that alone. (Legion theatre, Holyrood, Kan.—Small town patronage.)

CHAPTER 18

Two Rebels: Erich von Stroheim and Robert J. Flaherty

COMMENTARY

Two rebels who bucked the Hollywood system, especially in terms of the length of time necessary to complete films, were Erich von Stroheim (1885-1957) and Robert J. Flaherty (1884-1951), one of whom worked in the midst of things, and the other well away from them.

The Vienna-born von Stroheim started as an extra in Hollywood in 1914, played several minor parts in THE BIRTH OF A NATION, and became one of Griffith's assistant directors for INTOLERANCE. The Mordaunt Hall article which follows was printed in 1924, after GREED, probably von Stroheim's most important film, was released in New York. It seems to have been written after a conversation with Carl Laemmle, president of Universal Pictures and von Stroheim's former boss, who had attended this film première. To the relief of Universal, GREED was made for Metro-Goldwyn Pictures.

1924   "PERSISTENT VON STROHEIM CONQUERED FILM MAGNATE"

By Mordaunt Hall, *The New York Times*, December 14, 1924, Section 8, p. 7.

One is bound to be interested in a man who in 1908 was a gay Austrian officer, who afterward became a fly-paper salesman in New York, and then capped the climax by being the first motion picture director to make a production that cost more than $1,000,000. This man is Erich von Stroheim, whose latest pictorial effort, GREED, an adaptation from Frank Norris's *McTeague*, is now running at the Cosmopolitan.

Money and time are said to mean nothing to Mr. von Stroheim, who on more than one occasion has taken more than a year to produce a story and then wanted to see it shown in a length that would take more than eight hours. He cut GREED down to a length that took six hours to view, and is quoted as saying that any audience would be glad to sit through it. It was finally shortened to a reasonable footage.

Mr. von Stroheim's impersonation of an autocratic Prussian officer in D. W. Griffith's HEARTS OF THE WORLD is said to have been one of his first screen performances. Soon after that he portrayed a German officer in other pictures, until such a character became too unpopular even in the roles of villains. So, Mr. von Stroheim found himself an able one-part actor whose services were not wanted.

Nothing daunted, he suddenly decided that he ought to be a director, and forthwith wrote a scenario, which he desired to bring to the attention of Carl Laemmle, President of Universal Pictures Corporation.

So in a new suit of clothes he went to see Mr. Laemmle. He was told that Mr. Laemmle was out, at which he took a seat and declared he would wait. He recognized Mr. Laemmle when that man appeared and with military precision he saluted the wealthy producer. In his office Mr. Laemmle asked who was the man waiting outside, and when he was informed that it was Mr. von Stroheim he told his secretary to say that he was too busy to see him.

His Persistence.

For two weeks Mr. von Stroheim turned up every morning to see Mr. Laemmle until the latter decided to end the Austrian's visits by seeing him. When he was closeted with Mr. Laemmle, Mr. von Stroheim said that he had written a great scenario, which would make the finest picture ever made. He amplified this by asserting that his literary effort was a supreme one, and whetted Mr. Laemmle's interest by adding that it would cost only $25,000 to produce. Mr. von Stroheim further stated that, besides directing the picture, he would play the heavy role himself, which would save money.

This figure, the man's persistence and his enthusiasm he had for the story made a deep impression on Mr. Laemmle, who finally decided to see what the man could do. The narrative had merit, and it would surely be worth $25,000, thought Mr. Laemmle.

THE PINNACLE, as the story was then known, took six months to produce, and it cost $85,000. Gibson Gowland, who plays the leading part in GREED, was cast in this production. It was a new type of picture, and the head of Universal decided that it would be wise to change the title, even without the acquiescence of the director and author. Hence it was called BLIND HUSBANDS [1919].

As this picture was successful, Mr. Laemmle decided to give Mr. von Stroheim another opportunity, and he asked him to direct THE DEVIL'S PASSKEY. The film magnate told the Austrian that he liked his direction and also his acting but he said that he had decided to deprive himself of the pleasure of seeing von Stroheim on the screen, as it caused the production to take too long and consequently increased the cost. THE DEVIL'S PASSKEY was to cost not a penny more than $75,000.

Mr. von Stroheim was the personification of self-satisfaction when he terminated work on the new picture. He had cunningly made the American officer in half of the picture seem like a scoundrel and then in the latter portions had turned him into a gallant gentleman. Instead of spending only $75,000 on this photoplay, von Stroheim spent $185,000, and he took nine months to produce it. No wonder that Mr. Laemmle threatened to have no more dealings with this calm, clever but costly director!

FOOLISH WIVES

The direction of THE DEVIL'S PASSKEY [1920] attracted attention in producing circles and Mr. von Stroheim came on to New York and eventually sought Mr. Laemmle. Again Mr. von Stroheim prevailed upon Mr. Laemmle to let him direct another picture for his concern. Curiously enough, it ended with an arrangement being made between the two men which amazed persons inside and outside the Universal organization. There was talk that a man who could sell fly-paper could sell anything.

It is said that Mr. Laemmle agreed to permit von Stroheim to produce FOOLISH WIVES and that the picture was to be made at a cost not to exceed $250,000. In the midst of production one of the principal players, Rudolph Christians, died. He played the part of the American ambassador. Nearly two months were taken up in finding a man who could make up so well that he could duplicate Mr. Christians' appearance in the latter part of the picture. Finally Robert Edeson was chosen for this difficult task.

43. *Retribution in Death Valley: the close of Erich von Stroheim's GREED (1924), with Gibson Gowland (left) as McTeague overtaken by Jean Hersholt as Marcus. This great long film, ruthlessly cut before release, impressed some as the peak of production in America. Others found it a farce and an insult.*

Scenes were taken, and the production went on and on, and it seemed to the players, the camera man and assistant directors that von Stroheim did not know how to end the picture.

Mr. Laemmle was desperate, and the film was finally brought to an end with a subtitle. Then Mr. von Stroheim went to some scheduled spot with a few of his staff to cut and assemble the production. He reported, in course of time, to Mr. Laemmle, saying that he had the picture complete in thirty-two reels. He said that such a length of film had been shown in different theatres in Germany. One saw the first chapters in one theatre one night and the following chapters in other theatres on different nights. The idea did not appeal to Mr. Laemmle, and he set his foot down and called in Arthur Ripley to cut the production to a possible length. It was then shortened to ten reels [1922], while some say that it might have been a better story if it had been held to fourteen or fifteen reels. Incidentally, each reel is 1,000 feet, which takes from twelve to fifteen minutes to screen.

Took Cutting Calmly

It was anticipated that von Stroheim would rage when he saw what had been done to his pet picture. But the director took the cutting very calmly. The release date of this production was already a year old. It is said that he had actually shot 200,000 feet of action without duplication. When von Stroheim cut this effort to thirty-two reels he said that he could never take another foot out of it. This production cost $1,110,000.

When von Stroheim saw the picture he admitted that Mr. Ripley had done a good job. At the present moment it is said that Universal is within $50,000 of being even on this photoplay. The publicity and talk that this production caused heartened Mr. Laemmle, it is said, but his friends still did not expect that he would engage Mr. von Stroheim again. However, Mr. Laemmle looked upon the director as a genius and hoped that he could get him to make a picture in a reasonable time at a moderate cost.

So to the intense surprise of Universal officials, Mr. Laemmle gave von Stroheim another opportunity. MERRY-GO-ROUND was to be produced and von Stroheim was engaged to make it. The production was to cost $100,000. The director went about making this picture in his usual leisurely way, and Mr. Laemmle discovered that in two months Mr. von Stroheim had made about one reel. Laemmle then called in Rupert Julian and gave him the script for MERRY-GO-ROUND, asking him how long it would take him to make the picture. The reply was that it would be done in eight weeks. Hence Mr. Julian assumed the directorship of the picture. [1923.]

Mr. von Stroheim did not hasten in making GREED, and he inculcated into that effort some rather obnoxious action, dwelling with crafty emphasis on the dramatic portions. It is a picture in which crude vulgarity is set forth upon the screen in a fashion never attempted before.

THE MERRY WIDOW His Next

Now possibly Mr. von Stroheim is making a picture more suited to his natural bent. It is the picturization of THE MERRY WIDOW, with Mae Murray. His experience in the Austrian Army and knowledge of Vienna will serve him as a director of this film.

Friends of von Stroheim declare that he is a clever director without any regard for money or time, and in the producing of pictures, as in any other business, time is money.

When Mr. Laemmle came out of the Cosmopolitan after the presentation of GREED, he was quoted as saying that he thought Mr. von Stroheim was a great director. Somehow or other he did not appear envious or enthusiastic regarding the new production.

COMMENTARY

Photoplay's **review of FOOLISH WIVES (1922) is typical of the ambivalent attitude toward von Stroheim in America: he was felt to be a genius, but also a dangerous spendthrift, who might ruin the industry financially and the nation morally. Kansas, of course, was lying in wait for FOOLISH WIVES.**

FILM 1922   FOOLISH WIVES

"FOOLISH WIVES," *Photoplay Magazine*, Vol. 21, No. 4, March, 1922, p. 70.

A review of a picture that is an insult to every American.

So much publicity has been given this picture, which was released too late to be included among the Shadow Stage reviews, that we feel our readers would like to know what it is all about.

This—the much-heralded million-dollar production—has been shown at last, in fourteen reels *[sic]*. It is the most eccentric film ever put together. At times startlingly beautiful, at other times repulsively ugly, it is an amazing hodge-podge.

The American public cannot be expected to pay the million dollars that Universal, and Erich von Stroheim, have wasted, not spent.

An unworthy theme, the ugly amours of a pseudo-count from Russia, it has been produced with consummate care and unceasing imagination.

There is no doubt that Mr. von Stroheim probably spent almost the press-agented million on his sets and other effects; if he had spent as much time on his story—if he had had a tale worth telling—he would have earned the applause of that Broadway firstnight audience and every other audience in the world.

As it is, he has made a photoplay that is unfit for the family to see; that is an insult to American ideals and womanhood.

To point a doubtful moral, von Stroheim has adorned a gruesome, morbid, unhealthy tale. That he could give to it his admitted genius for detail and artistic talents is nothing short of incredible.

Portraits such as Griffith himself never dreamed of. Beautiful bits of acting. Monte Carlo, as real as itself. Photography and decoration of unsurpassed appeal. And an insight into continental morals and manners such as only, so far, we have been able to get from certain books and paintings.

All wasted, on a story you could never permit children or even adolescents to see. A story that sickens before you have seen it half told. Your verdict is ready before the end.

Absurdities and atrocious melodrama; astounding subtleties and keen beauty—a beautiful waste.

Von Stroheim wrote the story. It is, as we have said, morbid; more, it is unreal. He has lifted one of his most effective episodes right out of Frank Norris' masterpiece, *Mc-Teague*. At other times, he is almost original. He never knows when to let a scene alone; he whips it into insensibility before he lets it go. Consequently, every sequence is twice too long.

This picture, which has been advertised, actually, as "a one hundred per cent American" enterprise, is an insult to every American in the audience. Consider: an American, of sufficient prestige and importance to be selected by the President of the United States as a special envoy in charge of a vitally important mission to the Prince of Monaco, is depicted as a man who does not know how to enter a room or wear formal dress!

His wife is represented as the type of woman who strikes up a terrace flirtation with a   329

Russian count who accepts money from a serving maid! To say nothing of the continual innuendoes to American ideals; the little sly thrusts at our traditions and our sentiments.

The actors are all good. Rudolph Christians is excellent; Miss Du Pont pretty and perfumed and exceedingly commonplace as the Foolish Wife—there is only one of them. Mae Busch is sparkling and would have been more if she had had an opportunity; Maude George makes the most of her role; she has it—the talent and the temperament; Dale Fuller is exceedingly good. Von Stroheim, who is a competent actor at all times, projects himself into too many scenes.

He has abused his directorial privileges.

This film may make money. That is a question. It is not a picture that will do you any good. It is not good, wholesome entertainment.

It is not artistically great.

It is really nothing.

FOOLISH WIVES Censored   1922

FOOLISH WIVES," *Complete List of Motion Picture Films Presented to the Kansas State Board of Review for Action July 1 to September 30, 1922, pp. 6-7.*

(Universal) Reel 1—Eliminate Count Sergius looking up and down simple girl. Close-up of camera rising from feet to head of girl. Count looking around to see if he was observed. Reel 2—Eliminate Vera smoking. Eliminate title, "You know, Cousin, I have always had a weakness for American women." Close-up of Count looking at wife's stocking and close-up of wife pulling down dress. Also Count smiling at action. Reel 3—Eliminate action of ambassador's evident confusion and removing of gloves. Reel 5—In hut scene, eliminate scene of Sergius putting on stocking, wife's look of horror and action of pulling down cover. Eliminate mirror episode. Close-up of Count looking in .mirror. Count removing belt. Shorten to brief flashes scene of Count at bedside of sleeping wife. Reel 6—Eliminate Count kissing Maude George in the carriage. Reel 7—Eliminate all of maid's action in falling by bedside—her tearful face and Count's conversation with her. Cut out close-up of Count looking at child, licking lips and scene by bedside lifting cover. This occurs in the counterfeiter's home. Reel 8—Eliminate title, "Preparing to stalk the white doe. Brass buttons are strong magic." Reel 11—Eliminate title, "Three hours after midnight. The Villa Amorosa in darkness." Insert the title, "Beaten and broken, without money he goes to rob the counterfeiter." All views of child in fear and Count cautioning her. All scenes of child after father hears falling flower pot. Eliminate women smoking throughout.

COMMENTARY

As early as 1920, von Stroheim had announced his intention of filming Norris's novel, *McTeague*. When he finally set about production of the film, which became GREED, he left out the passages in the book describing a vaudeville show to which McTeague takes his girl, Trina Sieppe, and her family, and which features the Projecting Kinetoscope in San Francisco. *Photoplay's* editor, James R. Quirk, published a dramatic about-face editorial praising von Stroheim, even before seeing GREED.

Stroheim Plans to Film *McTeague*   1920

Excerpt from "Picture Plays and People," *The New York Times,* January 25, 1920, Section 8, p. 6.

. . . Erich von Stroheim, in whose name the 'von' now reappears after a complete, if temporary, eclipse, is to direct a screen version of Frank Norris' *McTeague* for Universal. H. Gibson-Gowland, who played Sepp, the Alpine guide, in Stroheim's first and notable picture, BLIND HUSBANDS, will probably be the leading man in the production. . . .

1899   **McTeague and the Sieppe Family at the Vaudeville Theatre in San Francisco**

Excerpts from *McTeague: A Story of San Francisco,* Frank Norris, P. F. Collier & Son, N.Y., no date *[copyright, 1899, by Doubleday & McClure Co.],* pp. 63, 68-69.

. . . And after this came a great array of other "artists" and "specialty performers" . . . and last of all," The feature of the evening, the crowning scientific achievement of the nineteenth century, the *[projecting]* kinetoscope.". . .

The kinetoscope fairly took their breaths away.
"What will they do next?" observed Trina, in amazement. "Ain't that wonderful, Mac?"
McTeague was awe-struck.
"Look at that horse move his head," he cried excitedly, quite carried away. "Look at that cable-car coming—and the man going across the street. See, here comes a truck. Well, I never in all my life! What would Marcus say to this?"
"It's all a drick!" exclaimed Mrs. Sieppe, with sudden conviction. "I ain't no fool; dot's nothun but a drick."
"Well, of course, mamma," exclaimed Trina, "it's—"
But Mrs. Sieppe put her head in the air.
"I'm too old to be fooled," she persisted. "It's a drick." Nothing more could be got out of her than this.
The party stayed to the very end of the show, though the kinetoscope was the last number but one on the programme, and fully half the audience left immediately afterward. . . .
On their way home, they discussed the performance.
"I—I like best der yodlers."
"Ah, the soloist was the best—the lady who sang those sad songs."
"Wasn't—wasn't that magic lantern wonderful, where the figures moved? Wonderful—ah wonderful! . . .". . .

1923   **Stroheim Among the Bowies**

Excerpt from "On the Camera Coast," Harry Carr, *Motion Picture Magazine,* Vol. 26, No. 1, August, 1923, pp. 69-70.

. . . The other day I went to San Francisco to see Erich von Stroheim filming the gruesome Frank Norris story, *McTeague,* which has been re-named GREED.
Von Stroheim has rented an entire neighborhood out in the very streets where the scenes of the story were laid.
He raked San Francisco with a fine tooth comb to get the exact pictures and furniture that the author describes.
In one instance, he bought everything in a San Francisco residence. Strange to say, his greatest difficulty was to get permission from the Prohibition enforcement officials to put up an old-fashioned saloon sign.
When I got there, von Stroheim was low in spirit. He was trying, without success, to

331

get Mr. Gibson Gowland, the actor who takes the part of McTeague, to allow a professional knife-thrower to send a bowie whizzing by his nose to stick quivering in the board wall.

"You know I sent all the way to London for you to play this part. Is this the way to treat me?" pleaded von Stroheim.

"Yeh," said the actor. "But you didn't say anything about throwing knives at me."

"But I can't get the right feel of the scene if we've got to fake it," implored von Stroheim.

"Yeh, but I don't want to get the feel of those knives going through me," said Gowland firmly.

Von Stroheim, to encourage him, stood up and let the knife thrower fill the air with bowies. "All right for anybody who wants to do it but not for me," said Gowland with finality. . . .

GREED **Unslaughtered** 1924

Excerpt from "On the Camera Coast with Harry Carr," *Motion Picture Magazine*, Vol. 27, No. 3, April, 1924, p. 76.

. . . I saw a wonderful picture the other day—that no one else will ever see. It was the unslaughtered version of Erich von Stroheim's GREED. It was a magnificent piece of work, but it was forty-five reels long. We went into the projecting-room at 10:30 in the morning; we staggered out at 8:00 that night. I can't imagine what they are going to do with it. It is like *Les Misérables*. Episodes come along that you think have no bearing on the story, then twelve or fourteen reels later, it hits you with a crash. For stark, terrible realism and marvelous artistry, it is the greatest picture I have ever seen. But I don't know what it will be like when it shrinks from forty-five to eight reels. Von Stroheim is imploring the Goldwyn people to make two installments of it and run it on two different nights.

Could any other director in the world have gotten away with this? One of the best love scenes in the picture is played with the lovers sitting on an outfall sewer pipe down which the body of a dead cat has just drifted. And I give you my word, it is a tender, beautiful and romantic love scene. . . .

GREED **FILM 1924**

"The Screen: Frank Norris's *McTeague*," Mordaunt Hall, *The New York Times*, December 5, 1924, p. 28.

> With Gibson Gowland, Jean Hersholt, Chester Conklin, Sylvia Ashton, ZaSu Pitts, Austin Jewell, Oscar and Otto Gottel, Jan Standing, Max Tyron, Frank Hayes, Fanny Midgley, Dale Fuller, Cesare Gravina, Hughie Mack, Tiny Jones, J. Aldrich Libbey, Rita Revela, Lon Poff, William Barlow, Edward Gaffney, S. S. Simonx, and others; adapted from Frank Norris's *McTeague*, directed by Erich von Stroheim. At the Cosmopolitan.

The sour crème de la sour crème de la bourgeoisie, and what might be its utterly ultra habits, were set forth last night before an expectant gathering in the Cosmopolitan Theatre in the fleeting shadows of the picturized version of Frank Norris's *McTeague*, which emphasized its film title of GREED. The spectators laughed, and laughed heartily,

44. *Stroheim's THE WEDDING MARCH (1928): Fay Wray as the Viennese heroine kneels in the cathedral set in Hollywood. The cameraman noted Stroheim's attention to "Every little thing, no matter how tiny, even to the number of candles and their length, that were used in the cathedral." Small town exhibitors groaned.*

at the audacity of the director, Erich von Stroheim, the producer of FOOLISH WIVES, and the director who was responsible for part of MERRY-GO-ROUND. Last January this picture was thought by its director to be perfect in forty-two reels, which took nine hours to view. He capitulated to its being cut down to about 30,000 feet, and is said to have declared that any audience would be content to sit through six hours of this picture. However, it was cut to less than half that length.

It is undeniably a dramatic story, filled with the spirit of its film title, without a hero or a heroine. The three principals, however, deliver splendid performances in their respective roles. Gibson Gowland is unusually fine as McTeague; but from beginning to end this affair is sordid, and deals only with the excrescences of life such as would flabbergast even those dwelling in lodging houses on the waterfront.

Mr. von Stroheim has not missed a vulgar point, but on the other hand his direction of the effort is cunningly dramatic. There is McTeague, who graduated from a worker in the Big Dipper Gold Mine to being a dentist without a diploma. He hails his new work with silent satisfaction, and when Trina Sieppe, Marcus Schouler's sweetheart, comes to his "painless parlors," he examines her teeth, informing her in due time that she must have three of them extracted and a bridge. The cost immediately enters her mind, but finally there is acquiescence, and she succumbs to the ether. McTeague gazes upon her quiescent countenance, and then, after fighting against his desire, he kisses her.

Sometime afterward he tells Marcus that he is in love with Trina, and the latter surrenders his sweetheart, who on the morning she went to McTeague's parlors had bought a chance in a lottery, the high prize of which was $5,000.

Soon after this one hears that Trina has won the $5,000, and Marcus's countenace is black and ominous. Then follows an obnoxious wedding scene with grotesque comedy. Hans Sieppe, the bride's father, insisting on drilling the figurantes, even to chalking marks on spots for them to stand on. Mr. von Stroheim outdoes himself in the wedding breakfast sequence, as the participants at the meal all attack the edibles in a most ravenous manner, the male element being protected from their ignorance of etiquette by napkins tucked around their necks.

In the struggle for existence Mrs. McTeague clings to her $5,000 even after McTeague is forbidden to practice dentistry and is forced to seek his livelihood as best he can. She gradually becomes a miser, counting her gold on her bed and concealing it in her trunk as fast as she can when she hears her husband's heavy tread. Then she grows eager for every penny she can extort from him, going through his pockets when she knows by his breathing that he is asleep.

It all ends as might be anticipated—in the murder of the woman by McTeague, who escapes to Death Valley with the sack of golden coins, which his wife had polished with such meticulous care night after night.

Marcus, who, in spite of protestations of friendship, had never forgiven McTeague for depriving him of the $5,000, is one of the first to read of the reward offered for the murderer. It is not long before he and a posse are plunging forth into the sun-scorched desert in search of their quarry. The Death Valley scenes are stark reflections of what happens in such circumstances and true to Frank Norris's story. Mr. Gowland gives a realistic portrayal of a man struggling along on the hot sands with the blazing sun overhead. He has the gold. He has killed his wife. And Marcus is after him! The climax is not only mindful of Frank Norris's story, but also of Jack London's "Love of Life." Mr. von Stroheim has introduced situations which make the fight for existence still stronger in its appeal than one would have imagined. Fancy two men struggling in the desert suddenly seeing the only possible chance of life—water—being carried away by a frightened mule!

Irving Thalberg and Harry Rapf, two expert producers, clipped the production as much as they dared and still have a dramatic story. They are to be congratulated on their efforts, and the only pity is that they did not use the scissors more generously in the beginning.

Mr. Gowland slides into the character and stays with it, and in spite of McTeague's aggressiveness and obvious hot temper, he and his wife are the only characters with whom one really would care to shake hands. Mr. Gowland is clever in his exhibition of temper and wonderfully effective in the desert scenes with his sweaty arms and bleary eyes.

Marcus Schouler is impersonated by Jean Hersholt, an efficient screen actor, but in this film he is occasionally overdressed for such a part. His role also calls for demonstrations which are not always pleasant. ZaSu Pitts portrays the role of Trina, into which she throws herself with vehemence. She is natural as the woman counting her golden hoard, and makes the character live when she robs her husband of trifling amounts. The other members of the cast are capable.

| 1925 | "MY ESTIMATE OF ERICH VON STROHEIM" |

"My Estimate of Erich von Stroheim," James R. Quirk, *Photoplay Magazine*, Vol. 27, No. 2, January, 1925, p. 27.

Frankly, I used to consider Erich von Stroheim a foreign upstart, who when he had pleaded with Carl Laemmle for an opportunity and was given it, rewarded his benefactor with ingratitude. I resented his FOOLISH WIVES, and still do. I resented his insistence on giving us his continental viewpoint of the sex relationships. I resented the stark brutality of his screen treatments. I thought he was trying to glorify himself at the expense of the producers who entrusted him with their money. I considered him a *poseur* of the first water, a forty-five calibre egotist. But I have changed my opinion of the man. I must give the von Stroheim his due.

Now I see that through it all the man has been fighting the whole motion picture business in an effort to express himself. His severest critic, and I have been called that, could never accuse him of any ambition to make himself solid with the producers as a good "commercial director." He wanted to make pictures for the sake of making them— "art for art's sake" in the finest sense of the word.

An egotist, yes, I haven't changed my opinion on that, for egotism in one form or another is the driving impulse of every great accomplishment. But I think I have misjudged von Stroheim's motives. Certainly his motive was not the accumulation of money, for today he is flat broke, without a swimming pool or a silver-plated megaphone to his name, living from picture to picture, without a studio to lay his head. He is the artist, living in the garret of the motion picture Latin quarter.

Only a man of this type would have essayed the translation of *McTeague* to the screen, and if the producers who financed him have any complaint because of the length of time he took to make the picture, or the expense, they should realize that unwittingly they have become patrons of the arts. Much as it may hurt they will probably accept with motion picture modesty whatever praise is forthcoming on that score.

I have not had the opportunity to see his GREED, made from Frank Norris's great novel, *McTeague*, because Metro-Goldwyn are trying frantically to cut it from thirty miles of film down to an evening's entertainment of ten miles or less, but those who have seen it proclaim it a masterpiece. Rex Ingram, in whose judgment I place confidence, tells me it is the greatest translation of life to the screen ever produced.

McTeague is a great novel though never a best seller. It is a gruesome story of life in one square block of tenements in the poorer sections of San Francisco. It is a large   335 painting of drab color in which there are few spots of the sunlight of human kindness. Von Stroheim has chosen his screen title well, for it is a sermon on the futility of the lives of little people who spend their whole existence in a miserly anticipation of the "rainy day," shutting out every human emotion but greed.

I am awaiting his GREED with more anticipation than is compatible with one who has seen almost every motion picture of consequence ever made, and who by this time should view "masterpieces" with the blasé air of a *boulevardier* surveying the ankles of a pretty shop girl.

Von Stroheim will probably shock us again with the brutality of his picturizations. He will probably attempt to show us in detail the throat-cutting episode in which the money-mad Polish junkman kills his demented wife. I will not see it anticipating a delightful evening's entertainment. I will go prepared. But after all I do not have to see it unless I want to, do I?

. . . Stroheim's Grim Shadows   1926

Excerpt from "Masters of the Motion Picture," Matthew Josephson, *Motion Picture Classic*, Vol. 23, No. 6, August, 1926, p. 66.

Those deeply moving experiences which I demand of a great art that almost leaves wounds and scars in the memory, come in fragments of GREED, Erich von Stroheim's great picture. To see this is like living through the night of one of those big storms on the Atlantic.

There were striking differences in method from Lubitsch. First, there is nearly as much shadow in Stroheim's work as there is light in Lubitsch's. Instead of trying for an effect of lightness, he wants to be ponderous and tragic.

McTeague is an uncouth and simple being of the lower classes with a tragic life-story which Stroheim sought to represent, episode after episode. It was not a picture for tenderfeet, for the film in its unflinching realism goes down to the very dregs of life.

In my memory the picture divides itself into two parts: the action in the city up to the murder and the flight of McTeague in the desert. The early scenes were infused with an atmosphere of drab horror and piled up incitements to crime. Stroheim used "camera angles" and light to get the most impressive lines and shadows he could. Above all, he wanted to make each set fairly drip with feeling. A master of atmosphere, he composes each scene with the idea of driving home an emotional effect rather than a picture of action. He focuses his camera from many different angles; he creeps upon things and surprises them; now he lingers over them and seems to wonder about them.

Camera Angles

I don't know who first invented these "camera angles." At any rate, Stroheim uses them with telling effect. Finding that you can get startling results by suddenly devoting the whole spread of the screen to a few small things, or even part of one thing, they let it sweep about their material like a huge, superhuman eye, now looking at something from close by, now from below, now from twenty stories above. And these queer "angles," when used with artistry, helped to emphasize some things above others, to fix, in short, certain impressions in your head. It gives the camera an amazing grip on you.

In the early scenes of GREED there is a shot of the wedding group advancing up the narrow stairway of McTeague's house, seen from the top of the hallway. From the point at which you see them, they all look peculiarly distorted, flattened. There is something uncanny about this effect, and it gives you a nameless fear, which is just one of the moods Stroheim wants to evoke.

It was these new and terrible sensations of deep shadows and masses, of heavy tragic movements that I got from GREED.

For cinema compositions that aim at atmosphere, the early scenes of GREED have not yet been excelled by American work. . . .

COMMENTARY

After THE MERRY WIDOW (1925), a success both financially and critically, von Stroheim left M.G.M. and went to work for Famous Players. In 1926 he started on THE WEDDING MARCH, the first half of which reached the American public in the fall of 1928, but the rest of it was never shown publicly in this country. Before THE WEDDING MARCH was released, von Stroheim had already launched on plans for a new production with Gloria Swanson, first to be called THE SWAMP, then QUEEN KELLY. It was supposed to take only ten weeks of shooting, but was finally abandoned, when, by 1929, it had gone on too long, had eaten up too much money, and the end still was not in sight.

FILM 1925   THE MERRY WIDOW

"THE MERRY WIDOW," excerpt from "The Silent Drama," R. E. Sherwood, *Life*, Vol. 86, No. 2239, October 1, 1925, p. 24.

Allusion has already been made on this page to Erich von Stroheim [as, with Lubitsch and Seastrom, one of the leading directors of Hollywood], the extravagant, inconsistent, unreliable genius whose name in Hollywood is mud. It is a pleasure to record that he has at last triumphed over his oppressors; in THE MERRY WIDOW he has produced not only a fine picture but one that will actually make money in the box office.

THE MERRY WIDOW is a free translation into pictorial terms of the libretto on which was once draped Franz Lehar's lovely melodies and those hideous monstrosities known as "Merry Widow hats." It is at best a silly, artificial story, but that is of no importance. The main things are von Stroheim's direction, von Stroheim's profound knowledge of composition and scenic effect, and John Gilbert's magnificent performance as Prince Danilo. Gilbert gives an eloquent, vibrant, keenly tempered interpretation of what might have been a trite romantic character. At every point he sparkles with brilliance; and at times he bursts into flame.

In what we radical journalists call "the title role," Mae Murray is far, far above her usual form. She fails to fidget or frolic or romp; she is actually subdued. This must be more of von Stroheim's dirty work.

Possibly my intense delight in THE MERRY WIDOW was influenced by the fact that Lehar's music accompanies the film. These soft, soothing strains from the violins of Vienna create a sentimental glow which reduces the hard critical faculty to a quivering pulp. . . .

1927   "AN UNRETOUCHED CLOSE-UP OF 'VON' "

By his Cameraman, B. Sorenson, *Motion Picture Magazine*, Vol. 33, No. 6, July, 1927, pp. 39, 88-89.

I can name dozens of people who have threatened to resign their positions rather than work with employers that have the reputation of being slave-drivers. It has been my good fortune to spend several months with a man with a name such as this. To me, the ones who shirk from such an experience are missing the opportunity that comes but once. The first two weeks with this particular individual certainly were an ordeal. Previous experience had spoiled me. I thought that over eight hours a day was criminal, and to work nights was beyond my comprehension. The first day we started at nine in the morning, at ten-thirty that night we were still going strong with no prospect of quitting, so absorbed had this man become with his work that time meant nothing. Next morning seven of us tried to quit, but the office made a very good excuse and we hung on. The funny thing is we are still with the crew and couldn't be driven away. Stroheim's overwhelming personality and ability create respect that is impossible to describe. There isn't a person working with him (in his company you work with him, not for him) that isn't willing to devote his or her entire time, because it's like being in school, every minute new situations and obstacles arise, and we learn new ways from him to overcome them. Ways that in future years, if we are still in the same business, will be beneficial to us.

During the shooting and rehearsing of a scene, that after the picture is released will create wide-spread comment as to the ability of the actors, a visitor made this remark, "That man is impossible. If I were in Miss ——'s place I would walk right off the set and tell him to go to Hell." The truth is that we had been on that particular close-up since two that morning and it was daylight then. And every minute of that time was spent in abuse to Miss—— to break a haughty, stubborn, know-it-all spirit and opinion of herself. To get this result it took just such abusive treatment. To print what he said and how he said it would be embarrassing; as a matter of fact, you would say, "I don't believe that man would talk to a lady like that." Had we not known him, we would all have harbored the same thoughts. But after each severe lashing he would look at us and wink. Even Miss——knew why he talked the way he did. Because of such peculiar ways of working, such as this, visitors are few; they start untrue rumors as to his character. There has not been a day during the picture that some individual has not wanted to thrash him, but thirty seconds later Von apologizes whole-heartedly for his hasty remarks.

We had one very noted visitor that said, "When I came here I expected to see a Prussian military organization, instead it was a bunch of boys at school, the most congenial troop I have ever seen." To explain more clearly this free yet respectful attitude we have toward him, one of his most earnest workers said the other day, "If Mr. Von was not so familiar with his help, he could accomplish more." She is dead wrong. Were it not for the personal feeling, his crew wouldn't stay a day.

There is a great deal of talk about his slow way of working. Have you ever really compared a picture of his with that of any other director? If you have, haven't you found why he takes so much time? He has spent hours on scenes, but when he finished them—well, you can read on the actors' faces just what that particular part of the story is to express. Every scene is a builder toward the end. They are like the cogs in a wheel, each one seems indispensable.

The most admirable thing about him is, he is not stuck on himself. Starting as a prop man, he has grown with his success. No matter if it is the cheapest laborer on the job that makes a suggestion, if it is good, it is used, and the laborer gets the credit for it. Stroheim is very liberal with his praise and just as free with his criticism. So long as one is capable and productive, he will be with him. In one particular department he has changed heads five times because of incapability.

To the whole picture industry von Stroheim is years ahead of all. As an example of his ability, one of the highest paid directors, who has an enviable reputation, offered to work for nothing just to be on the set, if Von would permit it. Not as an executive, but as a laborer. To command such respect must be backed by ability.

45. *THE WEDDING MARCH: Stroheim directs himself and Maude George. He was not fully sure of himself as an actor, and suffered agonies of self-consciousness when noted actors visited the set: "my knees quiver and I shake all over. . . ."*

Von has a sense of perspective that is so keen it creates amazement in our minds. Every little thing, no matter how tiny, even to the number of candles and their length, that were used in the cathedral. When a man's mind observes minute detail such as that, larger things are like mountains to him. Everything with him has to be right, not mediocre. It seems uncanny, when he has a dozen people working in one scene, that their every little movement would be observed.

As an actor, Mr. Von thinks himself of the worst. I can point out a dozen instances to prove this firm belief. On several separate occasions Stroheim was just getting ready to work when actors of noted ability and fame were shown on the set. They were asked to leave because of the embarrassment caused to Mr. Von by his attitude of self-condemnation and self-consciousness. His own way of expressing this is, "I am scared silly, my knees quiver and I shake all over the minute I step in front of a camera with the lights on, and I know I have to do something. I am like a kid—I forget everything—my mind becomes a perfect blank." At present he is working in scenes surrounded by capable people, and this disbelief in his ability is so pronounced that it is embarrassing to all of us. This concerns his acting only. He has a sneaking belief that his directing ability is on a par with anyone else's, and it is only through this weak belief in himself that he keeps on making pictures. If he should ever take the same attitude toward his directing, I am afraid we would likely find him with his son in the fire department some place. It seems to be his and his son's one hobby. Erich Jr. and Sr. have every known apparatus for fire fighting in miniature form and use them, both being accomplished firemen.

One of his greatest assets is his adherence to realism. To get realism in his pictures I have heard him abuse everyone *often*. Some shots of himself have been postponed for days, because as he expresses it, "I don't feel the thing, and unless I do, I know the audience won't grasp it." Many actors have come to him with marvelous opinions of themselves and their ability. All have had these opinions quickly changed because of their lack of realism, caused by too much acting. I have heard him plead for hours, "Please be yourself; don't act, just be natural, that's all I want. The instant you start acting, it shows. Now, try it again, please, and be your natural self." And unless they are natural, after many, many trials, he shouts, "Look out; don't get me sore again. If you can't be natural, say so; if not, we will get someone else. I am not running any school for actors. Try it again and do it as you would in real life." With his determination to have things right, he keeps rehearsing until they are. Coupled with this determination for realism is the good fault of being too analytical. Everything that is done is very carefully thought out. Many times we are asked what we would do if we were placed in the same place and under the same conditions. From Harry Carr I learned that during the writing of the script every scene had to have dozens of reasons before they would either be used or left out of the script. Every little detail was acted out, even to how a man should stand inside a room. All this, months before actual shooting began. Do you wonder why everything is so technically correct. Stroheim's pictures are so true to life that all the superstitions that we all have are used when there is the slightest excuse for one. The funny thing being that he is superstitious himself. Along with this he likes to make his audience think, and instead of telling you a thing directly, he uses with great success symbolical signs.

His biggest asset is his versatility. A capable writer (he has always written and titled his own scripts), good musician, severe dramatic critic, marvelous comedian. Could fill any position with a picture company from grip to cameraman and be perfect in it. A most marvelous host.

THE WEDDING MARCH   **FILM 1928**

Excerpts from "Key City Reports," *Motion Picture News*, Vol. 38, No. 16, October 20, 1928, pp. 1221-1222.

. . . Cleveland

The downtown first run houses here continue to draw capacity attendance. Interest in the new sound pictures grows keener each week. All of the houses are advertising extensively, and some of them are exploiting as well. But the effort is showing the desired results, and even a spell of the hottest October weather on record has failed to lessen public interest in the new screen productions. . . .

THE WEDDING MARCH opened up very big at the Allen. Every local critic gave it a big boost, some saying it ranks among the best pictures ever made. Although no records were broken, it showed a good record at the end of the week. . . . *[THE WEDDING MARCH was released with a synchronized score.]*

New Orleans

With downtown first run theatres playing outstanding film productions during the past week and summerlike weather prevailing, business reached record-breaking proportions. . . .

Erich von Stroheim's masterpiece, THE WEDDING MARCH, did the second best business of the week, being shown at Loew's State Theatre. The film, long awaited by movie lovers of New Orleans, was highly praised by critics and patrons alike. . . .

FILM 1928   THE WEDDING MARCH

"THE WEDDING MARCH," "Box Office Record," *The Motion Picture Almanac — 1929,* The Quigley Publishing Company, Chicago, Illinois, 1929, pp. 208-209.

(Paramount) Erich von Stroheim, Fay Wray, Matthew Betz, Dale Fuller, George Fawcett, Maude George, George Nichols, Hughie Mack, Cesare Gravina, 14 *[reels].—December 12-13.* Well, the agony is over. I am a glutton for punishment, but this picture sure made me run up the white flag as the people came out. I thought perhaps I might be mistaken, so I asked numerous ones what they thought of the picture and two of them said they guessed it was all right (notice they just guessed) and what some of the others said you would not print so I won't tell you. (Perkins theatre, Holton, Kan.—Small town patronage.) It's a 14-reel messed-up picture. We had it booked for three nights, but we didn't have the nerve to offer to show it the second night. In London or in some foreign country, in a big city where are all classes of nationalities, it might be understood and called a big picture. I tell you, in my opinion pictures like this one will sure cause your patrons to almost get mad at you and say things to you that are not pleasant to take. You see, this picture was sold to us as a special and we had to advance the price of admission for them to come out on it. Even if it had gone over big, our loss on it would have been heavy, but my three sons have all kinds of confidence in Paramount and they feel confident that this company will make it satisfactory. (Dixie theatre, Durant, Miss.—General patronage.) *November 28-29.* The poorest Paramount picture I have played this year, not much of a story and has the poorest photography imaginable. There is about 200 feet of technicolor that is very foggy, makes you think your projectors are out of focus. I advertised this very highly and raised the price of admission. Only a few came and I was glad of it. Any program picture that I have run this year is better entertainment. (Cozy theatre, Duchesne, Utah—General patronage.) Fourteen reels of wasted film. Too bad the exhibitors are compelled to show those high priced flops. (Harvard theatre, Harvard, Nebraska—General patronage.)

1928   "QUEEN KELLY GOES INTO ACTUAL PRODUCTION"

Hollywood, Oct. 30—Contradicting published reports that Gloria Swanson and Erich von Stroheim have split and following many postponed starting dates, QUEEN KELLY went into actual production Thursday morning on location at the old Lasky ranch.

The present schedule calls for completion of the picture by the end of January. Gloria's next picture, CLOTHES, is now being written by Harvey Thew.

COMMENTARY

Robert J. Flaherty's two feature-length films of the Twenties, NANOOK OF THE NORTH (1922) and MOANA (1926), reflect his integrity, his invention, and his sense of poetry, as well as, in their choice of locale, his desire to work by himself beyond the reach of editorial influences which he must have felt would be detrimental to his purpose. Both films, in themselves a grand counterpoint to the busy life and increasing sophistication of the times, were released, in a gesture of minor inspiration, as emphatic contrasts to the prevailing New York weather: the Eskimo film in June, the Samoan film in February!

Frances Taylor Patterson, in writing of NANOOK, uses the words "information" and "beauty," but the term which Mrs. Flaherty uses in "The Camera's Eye" is "documentary," an adjective which passed into the language as a noun for indicating just such films as she and her husband made. The unnamed Russian film she mentions was Eisenstein's POTEMKIN, seen in New York the same year as MOANA.

NANOOK OF THE NORTH   **FILM 1922**

"NANOOK OF THE NORTH," Frances Taylor Patterson, *The New Republic,* Vol. 26, No. 401, August 9, 1922, pp. 306-307.

In a day of emotional and artistic deliquescence on the screen, a picture with the fresh strength and pictorial promise of NANOOK OF THE NORTH is in the nature of Revelation. It may be said to be the first photoplay of the natural school of cinematography. Here are natural scenery, natural actors, the unembellished conte of a portion of life in Ungava. The "stars" are the native esquimaux. The "extras" are the polar bear, the seals and the walrus that wander about the ice country. The "sets" are the frozen fastnesses of the North. For drama there is the struggle of Nanook, the hunter, to wrest sustenance from barren wastes of snow. For the note of heroism there is the seemingly hopeless battle he wages against the elements. There is no conventional plot fabric. There are no fictionized situations. Yet the picture is dramatic in the highest sense of the word. There is suspense in the huntsman's combat with his quarry. The outcome is as sustained as it is doubtful. There is a vicarious satisfaction for the spectator in his final triumph. The film is a story of a people transcribed through the experiences of the hunter Nanook. The photoplay may be said to have its analogue in contemporary literature in *Maria Chapdelaine.* As Louis Hemon has set down in memorable words the simple traditions of Lake St. John and Peribonka, so Robert Flaherty has set down in memorable pictures the primitive gropings of these esquimaux of the far North toward the light of science and civilization.

But all this, it may be argued, is not entirely new in the history of the screen. There have already been filmed exquisite scenics. The camera has long ago imprisoned bits of beauty in distant corners of the earth. It has brought home to us glimpses of strange peoples and strange customs. There have been Martin Johnson's CANNIBALS OF THE SOUTH SEA ISLANDS, Vandenburgh's PIGMIES OF CENTRAL AFRICA, Burton Holmes' Travelogues, Bruce's WILDERNESS TALES. But NANOOK OF THE NORTH is different from all these. It has, as I have said, a strikingly dramatic quality. And in addition it has a continuity which these forerunners lack. There is unity—there is singleness of impression in NANOOK. The film marks a transition from the so-called educational film and the formal photoplay. It bridges a lacuna which has long cried aloud to be bridged. The narrative unwinds absorbingly. It flows smoothly and naturally to completion.

Anthropologically the esquimaux are a remarkable people. Their minds are singularly keen and alert. Certainly it is amazing to see the vast amount of scientific information these unlettered huntsmen have acquired through empirical methods. The building of the igloo—a feat which can be accomplished in the short space of an hour—is at a glance akin to wizardry, but in reality shows a mastery of the laws of equilibrium and gravitation. A knowledge of light, of reflection and refraction, is exhibited by Nanook's method of fitting a window into the igloo. Naturally enough the light of Heaven cannot penetrate the opaque snow blocks which form the walls of the hut. So, from a neighboring stream, Nanook cuts a clear square of ice. This he fits into the top of the igloo. Still the light through the "glass" is dim. Nanook intensifies it, however, by placing a great block of white snow vertically above the window, thus reflecting light into the inner recesses. The constant problem of these people is to outwit nature. They must use the cunning of their eyes and their hands to convert animal life into the coin of the realm—food and fuel. The process makes them uncannily inventive. Out of apparent nothingness they create the necessities of life and a few luxuries. Light and heat they gain from soaking moss—the only vegetation which survives the bitter cold of that country—in walrus oil. This they burn on the outer rim of a stone vessel hollowed shallowly. The moss is the wick, of course, and forms a ring of flame on the edge of the vessel instead of burning in the centre as our wicks do. Knives, harpoons, sea gaffs they make from the ivories of the walrus tusks. Metal is unknown to them. Boats are fashioned from skins and ribbed with odd bits of driftwood. Nanook's wife has a complete sewing kit, needles of sharp ivory, thread from the sinews of animals. With these she makes trousers of bear skin and coats of reindeer fur.

But although the picture is full of information which steals into the mental content of the spectator ere he is aware, the greatest appeal of NANOOK OF THE NORTH is its pictorial beauty. Harbors locked fast to the sea. Ice-floes moving with solemn force. Imperishable snow "five thousand summers old." Low banks of clouds with "the copper ball of the sun a mockery in the sky." Impenetrable silences. Infinite solitude. The picture has managed even to imprison the elemental forces of wind and cold. In this sense the picture is creative art: it projects and sustains a mood. In another sense it is reproductive art in that it captures natural beauty. With the exception perhaps of the Swedish picture, SIR ARNE'S TREASURE, which utilizes the splendor of a Scandinavian winter, there has never been a more graphic representation of hibernating nature. If for no other reason than the portrayal of the snow storm, the film must rank as a thing of beauty. The composition is masterly. The director felt that the things which best epitomize the spirit of loneliness and desolation in the North are the howling of the dog teams, the eerie lament of the wind and the swirling of blown snows. Yet these are sound impressions. All three nevertheless had to be caught within the picture if the regional atmosphere of grim infinitude was to be created. This Mr. Flaherty managed admirably to do by a graphic representation almost equivalent to literary onomatopeia. Instead of having a word, he had a picture represent sound. The result is winter visualized. The picture calls up Grieg's music and the Aurora Borealis.

We have said that the film marks the beginning of the naturalistic school of cinematography. Yet all this naturalness has been achieved through the purely artificial means of the camera. And it is precisely here that the picture manages to turn craftsmanship into artistry. The director has used his mechanical device to gain the highest quotient of dramatic efficiency. The camera is subordinated to, and in fact almost eliminated from, the final effect. It is an invisible magician. There is no internal evidence that a camera was used. The story is the story of the esquimaux. Therefore, 343 with the single exception of the white trader at the lonely trading post, not a white man obtrudes himself upon their territory.

That the picture exists at all is due to the possession of remarkable qualities by the director, who is a fellow of the Royal Geographical Society, an engineer by profession and an explorer by preference. To produce such a picture required skill of no mean order. There was need for thorough photographic knowledge to record the thin blue light of the North, that "unwarming light which only seemed where'er it fell, to make the coldness visible." There was need for an artist's eye to select the stretches of white wastelands and to compose them into cinematic beauty. There was need for persevering patience to secure any sort of photographic effects in the short spaces of Northern sunlight which is not kindly to actinic processes at best. The obstacles offered by nature to the taking of her own picture in some of her fiercest manifestations were almost insuperable.

One other thing about NANOOK OF THE NORTH. It is composed and expressed in terms of the motion picture. We are excessively weary of adaptations from the other arts, the art of the stage and the art of the printed word. Here at last begins our native screen language, as original in concept as THE CABINET OF DR. CALIGARI, yet as natural as that is fantastic. It reproduces actual beauty as CALIGARI reproduces expressionistic beauty.

Frances Taylor Patterson

"THE CAMERA'S EYE" 1927

By Mrs. Robert J. Flaherty, *National Board of Review Magazine*, Vol. 2, No. 4, April, 1927, pp. 4-5. (With the permission of the National Board of Review of Motion Pictures.)

> Mrs. Flaherty assisted her husband in the production of the films NANOOK OF THE NORTH and MOANA—Editor's Note.

The suggestion I have to make with regard to the motion picture is that great dramatic films in the future will be made without story, stage or star—will be made from life. The basis for this suggestion is a mechanical fact. Suppose, for instance, an actor were to simulate the peculiar gait of a sailor, and a real sailor were to walk down the street beside him, the human eye might not be able to distinguish between them. Take a motion picture of them, however, and there would be no doubt as to which was the acted and which was the real. The reason for this is that the camera's eye is penetrating to a degree far greater than the human eye. Its mechanical genius is its capacity for infinite detail. In the motion picture camera this capacity for detail becomes infinite subtlety in the rendering of motion. Motion becomes infinitely revealing—so much so that when it is the unconscious, spontaneous motion of nature, we see, far beyond the capacity of our own eyes to see, to the pulse and rhythm of life.

Mr. Flaherty and I have experimented in this truth-telling of the camera with races of people. Think of the world as a mosaic of different peoples, each with its own way of life which it has built up through centuries into a definite, distinct pattern. Each pattern is an ideal. To each people this ideal, its life, is dramatic.

Experiments were begun by Mr. Flaherty in Baffin Land, in a little one-roomed shack with the snow houses of the Eskimos poking up out of the snow wastes around it.

The ideal man of the Eskimos is the great hunter. It is he who with his bravery and skill keeps his race from starvation. The story of this people is the story of the hunter with his spear, his dogs, his sledge, his kayak, on the ice floes, in the mountains and valleys of ice, winning his life-giving kill, through the drift of snow and the lash of wind, winning his shelter, his house of snow, block by block.

46. *NANOOK OF THE NORTH* (1922). *Robert Flaherty's film, shot in the Hudson Bay area, seemed not only "full of information," but of "pictorial beauty" as well. It established the documentary movement by creating the form.*

To take this man, the dog, the seal, the barren ice, the barren snow, the sunlessness and bitter wind, and pile these up in your consciousness, incident by incident, scene by scene, starker and ever more stark—can you see how in this way might come out of it all for you a story overwhelming in its reality?

From this Northern life we went south to Samoa to make a picture there of the Samoans. In the North we knew the life of the people, knew it well. Mr. Flaherty had explored there for years. He knew the pulse and rhythm of that life and the camera was his willing tool. But here in Samoa we did not know the life of Samoans; we had it all to learn; and at first we didn't think of learning it. We thought we knew all about how to make our film. Just as in the North the Eskimos hunt animals, so here we would have the Samoans hunting creatures of the sea. We went all over everywhere hunting up tiger sharks and giant octopi that these gentle people might do battle with them. We worked hard for months, with utter discouragement. We got nothing for our pains. There were pictures we got, but there was nothing in them. Our camera had lost its cunning. It no longer gave us the feeling of looking into life. It balked, baffled us. It simply wouldn't work. We packed our cameras away and sat down to think. Hunting really had nothing to do with the life of these people. Their life is as different as possible from the life of the Eskimo. Their ideal is an invention. They have invented their great man, their chief, and then out of singing and dancing and feasting and the art of fine speech they have made elaborate ceremony and ritual, and it is this that is the drama of their life, expressed in beautiful movements of the body. "Are the movements of these people really so beautiful?" we are asked. Yes. Because, for so many generations have they been practising these beautiful movements that beauty has entered into even the commonest things they do; whether they sit or stand or walk or swim, there is that beauty of movement, rhythm, the philosophy, the story of their life. So that simply in the beautiful movement of a hand the whole story of the race may be revealed. Now we had the secret. Here was the matter for our philosophical camera's eye. We unpacked our cameras again.

There is a fascination in making a picture of this kind. For this second sight, this truth-telling of the camera, is a will-o'-the-wisp. I saw pictures of elephants taken for the screen—elephants, elephants, nothing but elephants, six reels, an hour of elephants on the screen. They were beautifully photographed, wonderful pictures. Shot after shot passed and I was filled with admiration. But suddenly I gave a gasp. My heart missed a beat. The hair almost stood up on my head. Only for a flash—a second on the screen, and it was gone. But in that shot, in that second, had come to me the very breath of the jungle and its beasts—the terror, the alarm, the dread, the essence of that strange jungle life. Out of all these pictures, in this one shot alone was there that second sight, that penetrating to the heart of things, of the camera.

And what we had to do in that Samoan picture was through all the scenes of the everyday life of the people to find and use this second sight of the camera to reveal that beauty of movement which is the lyric soul of the people, to reveal it until it would flood through and saturate the picture, like a perfume, never to be forgotten.

Leave strange races and come nearer home to our own people. Suppose we wished to make the picture of a settler in Rhodesia with his ox-train trekking into the heart of the veldt and carving a home for himself amidst savage nature, black men and wild beasts—a theme like that of THE COVERED WAGON.

We might draft out a story for this picture, with a hero, a villain and a girl, choose the actors for our characters, plan out each scene, arrange each set, choose our locations, and with our cameras and carpenters and electricians and megaphones and makeup boxes and wagons and painted savages, make the picture. Or, we might simply pack our cameras on our backs and go to Rhodesia, find there characters whom the drama of their life and their struggle have moulded in expression of face and body, who are feeling the thing they are doing, so that every movement they make tells the story; watch them doing and living and fighting their fight, with its tears and laughter, its comedies and tragedies, its quiet and its sudden alarm, its heat and its cold, its hunger and its fear; live there until the drought and flood, the tall grass, the ambush of the wild beasts, and the timidity or boldness, the love or fear of the black brother, are made plain; and over all this let the camera roam and win from it bit by bit the story that it can tell by that genius it has of second sight.

There has recently been exhibited a Russian film that uses the camera in this way. An historical incident has been re-enacted, and then, over these re-enacted scenes the camera has been brought to play as over actual life, and the result is that same conviction of reality.

This Russian film and the two films we have made must be thought of as experiments. The principle is there. Its development will come.

It is this development, independent of stage, or story, or star, depending on nothing but what is in the camera itself, that I suggest to you as a destiny of the screen. I suggest it as a great destiny, because pictures made from life, of the drama inherent in life, are documentary and philosophic. In them the educational, the religious and the dramatic are blended into one.

COMMENTARY

After filming first in the northern reaches of the world, and then in the southern, Flaherty ended his self-imposed exile from America and attempted a short film about New York called TWENTY-FOUR DOLLAR ISLAND (1927), which has since disappeared. In abbreviated form, it was projected as background for a stage show at the Roxy Theatre in New York in December, 1927. Later it was shown in full at a New York art house (January, 1928).

Flaherty withdrew from the production of WHITE SHADOWS IN THE SOUTH SEAS (1928), and eventually also from a film planned by the German director F. W. Murnau, TABU (1931), because both projects took directions incompatible with his own aims.

Terry Ramsaye was the author of *A Million and One Nights* (1926), a history of the early movies.

1927   "PRODUCER OF NANOOK JOINS METRO-GOLDWYN"

By Donald H. Clarke, *The New York Times*, June 26, 1927, Section 8, p. 2.

Robert J. Flaherty, who has more or less epitomized his adventurous life by making one picture, NANOOK OF THE NORTH, in Arctic snows, and another picture, MOANA, in the tropic heat of the South Seas, and who has recently been trying to catch with his camera the dynamic spirit that is New York's, was in the midst of preparations for his departure for the West Coast the other day, when this writer had a chat with him.

Mr. Flaherty said that he wouldn't know definitely what his plans would be until he reported at the Metro-Goldwyn-Mayer studio to talk over his first dramatic picture.

"About all I can tell you," he replied in response to questions, "is that the tentative plan, as I understand it, is to do *White Shadows of the South Seas*, and that John Colton, who put *Rain* into play form, as you'll recall, will do the story.

"My understanding also is that we will make exterior shots in Tahiti. The idea is to get all of the natural beauty in the picture that is possible."

Then the conversation shifted to the picture of New York City that the traveler-scientist-director has been busied upon for many weeks and about which there has been a deal of discussion in cinema-following circles. Mention was made that this film is

347

regarded as more or less of a mystery, and that no one had been permitted to see any of it thus far.

Mr. Flaherty lighted a cigarette, and laughed.

"It's something of a mystery to me too," was his confession. "It's a more or less experimental job financed by more or less altruistic persons who have no connection with the motion picture business."

A question was interjected, which caused him to shake his head and exclaim:

"No! There are no tricks or stylisms in it. I wandered about 15,000 miles around this town in taxicabs, and shot about 30,000 feet of film in an effort to get these two reels—trying to get a dynamic, impersonal picture of this over-crowded island that is New York.

"It is an attempt to get the achievement of the mass, not the achievement of the individual. Heights of buildings are accentuated: hurry is emphasized; movement is maintained. It is not a story of single individuals, but it is emphatically not a scenic.

"All of the scenes are taken from peaks," Mr. Flaherty continued. "That is, they are taken from what we may call 'unconscious points of view.' And I don't know whether I make myself clear when I express it that way or not. Probably not—at least until you see it for yourself. And then you may get the idea.

The Smoke—Plumes of Smoke!

"I don't know what we've gotten myself, but with an eight-inch lens, and our peaks, we have tried to get the picture story of the most dynamic city the world has ever seen—a city that has more compression, more movement, than ever has been known in history.

"New York is an episode of millions of people. Like the Pyramids and the Panama Canal, it cannot be pictured through an individual, or through individuals. You wouldn't dream of trying to tell the story of the Pyramids by telling the life of one of the architects. Would you?

"But a visualization of sweating humanity streaming like ants with the grains that were the huge blocks which composed the Pyramids would give you some idea of what they stood for. Wouldn't it?

"Yes, there are faces, human beings, in this new film of New York," he said, in response to another question. "A workman or workmen may be glimpsed swinging a girder into place or rushing at some other task, but no faces are recognizable.

"And I mustn't forget to mention the smoke—the plumes of smoke, the smoke that from the peaks is visible everywhere—issuing from the buildings and drifting through them and over them. The smoke is most important. And the constant, the ceaseless motion—the dynamic something that is this monster of New York.

Always Activity Here.

"Everything is moving always. The boats in the harbor, the six millions, the city itself. And over it all, pervading it, is the smoke.

"The idea for such an attempt to make a picture of New York was suggested in a conversation. I went at the job with no idea how I would come out. It fascinated me. It still fascinates me. I would like to spend a lot of time on it—years. I am sure that someone will do it some time. To do it properly, it seems to me that it easily might take three years. And that is only a guess.

"You will understand, of course, that I am speaking of a film in which New York is the central character—not a picture in which individuals are portrayed, which, it seems to me would make New York merely the background for a story. I am talking about the picture in which New York is the story."

1928   "FLAHERTY, GREAT ADVENTURER"

By Terry Ramsaye, *Photoplay Magazine,* Vol. 33, No. 6, May, 1928, pp. 58, 123-126.

The Maker of MOANA is the Last of the Long Pioneer Line that Sought
the End of the Open Road

One merry evening in June of the distant year 1668 His Highness Prince Rupert and a blithe party of friends sat in the captain's cabin of a ship riding at anchor off Wapping Old Stairs dock in London River.

There were toasts in the wind of Oporto, maybe a song or two and farewells. At the turn of the tide the Prince and his party went ashore in a cutter and the brave little ketch-rigged Nonsuch dropped down the Thames.

The first expedition of "The Company of Adventurers of England trading into Hudson's Bay," was off "for the Discovery of a new Passage into the South Sea, and for finding Furs, Minerals, and other Considerable Commodities."

The little ketch Nonsuch was burthened with the fate of empire. "The Company of Adventurers" was made up of sundry "noblemen, knights and esquires," a lusty array of daring, swashbuckling entrepreneurs. In their hands was the exploration and the making of half the New World.

That "Company of Adventurers" lacked yet—by some two hundred and fifty years—one of its proper members, Robert J. Flaherty. He should have been in that captain's cabin aboard the Nonsuch that night.

The adventurers sailed across the Atlantic and through Hudson's Bay down into James Bay. There they found furs and other "Considerable Commodities," such as they sought. For two and a half centuries this went on; then Flaherty came and caught up with the expedition, completing that task of exploration that the crew of the Nonsuch began.

To Flaherty, in dramatic adventure, came the distinction of discovering the last of the unknown lands of the New World. Also there he discovered NANOOK and something of a new career for the motion picture. Fittingly enough, further, in co-incidental fulfillment of that ancient charter with the royal seal of King Charles upon it, this discovery brought Flaherty, in time, a "Passage to the South Sea."

This romantic Flaherty, in spite of the fact of his contemporary existence, in spite of his very modern concern with a new phase of the newest art, the motion picture, is in truth a man of the seventeenth century.

At interludes between his voyagings, Flaherty may be found undergoing the conventionalities of New York—commuting to New Caanan—the restaurants, the night clubs, the theater, the self-conscious sophistication of the Coffee House club, and the studios of Greenwich Village. Here there is a tension of suppression over him. A voice that is used to wide spaces is adroitly softened to an improbable, considerate restraint. And there is that attitude of continuous alertness, bearing testimony to the automatic, continuous vigilance of the wild places. His cool blue-eyed glance is unconsciously penetrating and restless. There is an air of impatient patience under a bearing of the most polite suavity. His very broad shoulders and deep chest dispute the punctilio of his dinner coat. For the time he can be utterly New Yorkly; but it is not really so.

Sometimes when morning begins to break over Washington Square and the company is to his liking, Flaherty lays aside his mask of convention. Then there are songs of the trails and seas; tales of far away campfires, sagas of the trappers and prospectors. Flaherty's real life is out where the world is still young—a seventeenth century world with endless wonders yet to be seen and wide lands and waters yet to be mapped.

It is only for that occasional hour that one meets the actual Flaherty, who just chances to be among us in this effete twentieth century. And it is then that one knows him for a true confrere of Radisson and Groseilliers, for a successor to the traditions of Paul de

349

Chomedy and Champlain and David Thompson. Radisson is merely the name of a hotel in Minneapolis now, and Champlain is a lake in upper New York state. Flaherty is the sole survivor of his clan.

The masters of the movie world do not quite understand this strange Flaherty. And for all his knowledge of men and their ways, from Cree to Kanaka and from Eskimo to Maori, Flaherty does not quite understand the movie magnates.

A strife results. Perhaps it is not very consciously conducted, but it is strife. There is a striving to make Flaherty and his pictures into what they call "box office," by force of movie conventions. Meanwhile Flaherty struggles to record a real world as seen through his eager, earnest eyes.

About seven years ago Flaherty, unheralded and unknown, came down out of the north with his pictures of Nanook. Within a year he had become a conspicuous name in the world of the motion picture, but with a frame which was largely outside of it. With a single picture, simply made and unostentatiously presented, he attained international note.

Now Flaherty has three pictures to his credit, presented to the world through as many conspicuous film corporations, but for all his name, it is just the same. The story of the man himself and the greater personal drama behind his screen attainments has never been told.

Meanwhile the screen works of Flaherty have added importantly to the status of the motion picture as an instrument of expression, as a teller of true tales, more vital than the studio fancies of Hollywood.

The motion picture has drawn its personnel and manpower from many and varied sources—furs, gloves and cloaks-and-suits, medicine shows, newspapers, politics, banks and bars, but Flaherty's background is uniquely iron—iron ore. He is the son of the late Robert H. Flaherty, one of the foremost figures in the history of ore exploration for his day in the Northwest and Canada.

So properly enough young Bob Flaherty was born at Iron Mountain in Michigan. It was in the snowy February of 1884. He grew up in the iron mining regions and the gold camps of the north. He followed the travels of his father, who was made nomadic by his pursuits as a mining engineer. Bob's friends and playmates were the miners. From them and with them he got a hard rock education in the code of give and take. He, as the lone boy of the camps, was given to many devilments.

Up at the Golden Star mine in Ontario the boss of the blasting crew kicked Bob's dog. Off at the edge of the camp was a cabin where dynamite was stored. A stove with a low fire burned all the while to keep the explosive from freezing. There were tons of it there. That night Bob stoked the fire with wet wood and stuffed the chimney. Then he alarmed the camp to view his first motion picture effect.

Smoke poured from every crevice of the building. The camp was in terror. The surrounding hills were filled with wild-eyed miners in sock feet and shirt-tails, running through the snow of a Canada winter night to escape the destruction to come.

When the fugitives got back at dawn they found Bob, with his dog, comfortably asleep in bed. He had turned in as they left, knowing that presently his smudge fire would burn out without harm.

After a series of such episodes as these, Flaherty's father decided to give the young man the influences of civilization. Bob went away to school. With considerable velocity he passed through Upper Canada College in Toronto and the Michigan College of Mines at Houghton. His college life is said to have been more marked by its intensity than its duration. If he ever got a degree from either of these schools they must have thrown it at him as he went past.

350   Bob was in a hurry, being at least two hundred and fifty years behind that "Company

of Adventurers" which sailed on the Nonsuch. Out of school he took to the woods and waters of the Canadian wilderness, working with his father in the exploration of the mineral resources of northern Ontario. He learned to paddle a canoe like a Cree and to carry a pack like an Ojibway.

There was romance and a feeling for life in the youth. He carried a violin, along with the transit and geologist's hammer. They were all instruments of his career.

By the light of a thousand campfires he heard the lore of the north country, the weird tales of "La Chasse Gallerie," and the adventures of voyageurs in all the wildernesses from Nanaimo to the Straits of Belle Isle. With them he drank and fiddled and sang: "En Roulant ma Boule" and "J'aimerai Toujours."

Soon he added a kodak to his pack, along with the violin. He wanted some way to record and interpret this fascinating world of the Big North. And even his first amateurish snapshots had something of poetry in them.

Far out on the west coast of Vancouver Island Flaherty found an out-crop of wonderful marble. He spent three years quarrying there and trying to develop a business. His marble was too far from the monument trade. The northwest coast is healthy. Flaherty did not mind much. He was not so anxious to be a businessman anyway.

Flaherty turned east to Toronto. He was looking about. His real career was still ahead of him. The Canadian government was projecting a railway that would carry the wheat of the prairie provinces to ships on Hudson Bay, a short cut to European markets. Sir William Mackenzie was building the Canadian Northern railway. With this talk of Hudson Bay development in the air he conceived the possibility that, if reports of mineral deposits were true, there would also be a traffic in iron ore from the great bay to the markets of the world. He sent for Flaherty.

One August day in 1910 Flaherty, with one companion, dropped a seventeen-foot canoe into the water of Ground Hog river at the last northern frontier station of the Grand Trunk, and pushed off for the north, down to the Mattagami and on into the big Moose river. At last Flaherty was on his way to complete the work of the expedition of the Nonsuch, in the quest of "Minerals and other Considerable Commodities." He was bound for the Nastapoka Islands where according to rumor there was iron, eleven hundred miles above the rim of civilization.

Up and up into the northland Flaherty with canoe, laden with tea and pemmican and beans and flour, and a fiddle, traveled day upon day. The forest gave way to the open plains of the north with their miles of muskeg, broken only here and there by stunted windbeaten trees. On an island in the great river they came at last to Moose Factory, for two and a half centuries a northern center for the Hudson's Bay Company with its fringe of Indian cabins, little patches of garden, teepees, red church, and everywhere sprawling sledge dogs, lazy in the late summer sun.

But this was only a place of taking breath on the long trail. Seventy miles out in the bay at Charlton Island, Flaherty outfitted for the push north to the Nastapokas. Winter was even then bearing down from the north. At Fort George he waited for the sea ice to spread over Hudson Bay and at last drove out across the frozen wastes to the Nastapoka Islands. Five days of prospecting there revealed the iron strata too poor in metals to offer commercial value. Flaherty was ready to turn back for the long cold journey back to civilization, six hundred miles to the southward, with a report of disappointment.

Nero, an Eskimo dog driver, came up to Flaherty, as he stood looking out across the endless leagues of sea ice. "Big land over there!" The Eskimo pointed out into the emptiness of Hudson Bay.

Flaherty was curious, incredulous, but hopeful. He had come to find iron, and there was not enough iron in the Nastapokas. His maps and charts, with all of the due authority of the British Admiralty and two and a half centuries of navigation of these waters, showed a tiny cluster of dots out there in the big bay, labelled Belcher Islands, mere pinpoints of geography. What the Eskimo said must of course be an exaggeration, a campfire tale. But, there was a chance. Flaherty remembered one Wellatok, an Eskimo at Charlton Island, who had told tales of his one-time home and hunting grounds on a great land up in the bay. Wellatok's stories were always discounted at Charlton Island by the canny fur traders. They knew the maps were right.

But science and the scientific spirit, which is so closely akin to the spirit of adventure, too, will have its way. All that long journey back to civilized Canada, Flaherty was pondering the possibilities and remembering one tempting fact. Years before in the iron prospecting of Ontario, Flaherty and his father had come upon interesting bits of ore, just scraps and shards of it in the tangle of glacial gravel heaps. It had come, ages before, in the big ice sheet, from somewhere north. Never had they been able to find the mother lode, the source of these glacial borne fragments. But there was the tempting certainty that somewhere in the mystery of the Big North that rich ore was sleeping under the snow and ice.

In Toronto Flaherty made his report on the Nastapokas and told Sir William Mackenzie about the rumors of the big unknown land in Hudson Bay. Up at Ottawa the Government officials smiled and pointed to the charts. There were deep sea soundings on the maps where Wellatok had placed his tales of hunting in "the big land."

Mackenzie sent Flaherty back to prospect, and to see about that big land, be it myth or fact. So again Flaherty went into the north, taking a motor to put into a boat for the voyage in quest of the unknown islands. A quest of years, filled with adventure and disasters, had begun. The motor boat was wrecked upon the Great Whale coast. Flaherty waited for the sea ice of deep water, and a storm came and broke up the ice the day he was ready to set forth on the big drive toward Wellatok's land.

Again Flaherty returned south and again had audience with Mackenzie.

"Get a ship," Mackenzie decided. Then one brave day in summer "The Laddie," a stout Arctic schooner sailed from the harbor of St. Johns in Newfoundland, with Flaherty aboard. This time he carried, instead of the kodak, a motion picture camera. It was 1913 and Flaherty had seen the first of the feature dramas on his short sojourn in the cities of Canada.

The cruise of the Laddie brought many new adventures, by shore and sea. The schooner was wrecked, salvaged and repaired. At last Flaherty found the land of his quest, Wellatok's islands. Here was a great domain of some thousands of square miles— and on it nearly a hundred square miles dotted with outcroppings of rich iron ore.

Thus posthumously the mission of the ketch Nonsuch and that company of gentlemen adventurers from London, now after two hundred and fifty years, was fulfilled. And for all those two and a half centuries the annual cruise of the Hudson's Bay Company fur ships into the big bay had passed within a few hours' sail from these unknown islands.

Flaherty was vindicated and honored among geographers. Presently he was to be elected to the Royal Geographical Society, and authorized to write F. R. G. S. after his name.

Meanwhile Flaherty industriously recorded the life of the people of the north, the battle for life of the Eskimos, on film. He had come to know it and understand it on terms no white man had ever shared before. He wanted to bring back to the civilized world that dramatic saga of ice and sea.

At last Flaherty reached Toronto and sat down in the comforts of civilization to put his picture together. Then as the job neared completion, and his picture was all in neat rows of rolls piled up before him on the cutting table, he dropped a cigarette. There was a burst of flame. Flaherty was thrown across the room, burned deep by the blast, scorched as though he had stepped into the roaring vortex of a giant blow-torch. He struggled out of the room and ran to the street in a frenzy of pain, clothes afire. Weeks later he recovered in a hospital. His treasured film record of the life of the northland had vanished completely in that one searing explosion.

But creative zeal was upon this determined, adventuring Flaherty. On his intermittent sojourns in the cities of civilization he had seen the rise of the feature drama. He had watched the screen begin as a recorder of novelty and develop into a medium of expression. Only the screen could tell this wild, sweeping story of the big north which Flaherty had made so completely his own.

At last Flaherty determined to go back north, no longer concerned with iron and other "Considerable Commodities," but with pictures alone. John Revillon and Captain Thierry Mallet of Revillon Frères, the world famous fur concern, agreed to finance the project. One may pause for a parenthesis of whimsy to regard this fact, for what with all the retail furriers who have become the builders of the screen empire it seems oddly coincidental that now at last the great super-trappers and traders of the snowy north should also enter the picture. For twenty-odd years there has been an amazing affinity between furriers and films, from pelt to pellicle.

One August day Flaherty's ship let go anchor in Innusuk river, the harbor for the Revillon post at Cape Dufferin in Hudson Bay. There Flaherty picked a dozen Eskimos and their families for his picture making. Chief of them all was one Nanook—meaning The Bear.

The motion picture which gave Flaherty world fame is a faithful accounting of the battle for existence of the Eskimos. But like most good reporters he kept himself and his personal adventures mostly out of the telling of that story.

No masterpiece was ever achieved under more desperate difficulties.

The Nanook expedition faced all of the perils of the Arctic winter, storm, starvation and disaster.

There was a desperate week when Flaherty had to burn precious rolls of film to melt snow for tea water, out on the barren wastes, blizzard bound and facing death.

Out on the ice a thousand miles from a dental surgeon, Flaherty was stricken with dental trouble involving an abscessed tooth, so painful it made him helpless. With a file and a nail he fashioned a drill, and with that crude instrument and no anaesthetic, he directed an operation performed by a clumsy Eskimo. Infections resulted and the Nanook story came near ending there.

There were technical difficulties without end. Flaherty found that at 37 degrees below zero the brittle film broke into flakes like glass when he tried to put it through the camera. He had to warm the film in the igloo at the camp and wrap it in clothes that could ill be spared to keep it warm until it could be exposed.

After the year-long campaign in the north, Flaherty's ship, the little schooner Annie, sailed into the Innusuk river one August day and a week later he stood at the rail, waving farewell to Nanook, who had followed out to sea in his kayak.

Two years later the once-a-year ship brought back word to Flaherty that Nanook was dead. The annual migration of fish had failed and the Eskimo chief died of starvation. Meanwhile, incident to Flaherty's film labors, Nanook had become the most famous Eskimo in history. His picture had gone all over the world, even to the deserts of Africa and Asia where the magic of snow had to be explained to the amazed native audiences.

The triumph of the pictures of Nanook took Flaherty away from his quest of iron and changed the whole course of his career.

Jesse Lasky, the only film magnate with a feeling of the great outdoors and the adventures of the far places, commissioned Flaherty to go into the South Seas and record   353 the native life of that region as he had in the north. MOANA, an idyll of Samoa, resulted, after a series of adventures quite as remarkable as the filming of NANOOK—but that is yet another story for another day.

Meanwhile the influence of Flaherty's technique in NANOOK OF THE NORTH began to exert itself. There was a quickening of interest in "natural drama." GRASS made by Merian Cooper and Ernest Schoedsack, the spectacular tale of a migration in the Persian highlands, found a release with Famous Players through Lasky's interest. And in sequel Cooper and Schoedsack made that current success, CHANG, in the jungles of Siam, with a parallelism to the Nanook idea.

Again Flaherty is off to the far away lands, in Tahiti now, to make a screen record based on Frederick O'Brien's *White Shadows in the South Seas*. So indeed in this fateful way, Flaherty has fulfilled through the films the quest of his confreres of the ketch Nonsuch, which sailed that day in 1668 "for the Discovery of a new Passage into the South Sea."

Flaherty ashore in Papeete has just landed at the end of the cruise that began two hundred and sixty years ago in London river.

CHAPTER 19

Foreign Invasion (III):
Films from Germany, France,
Scandinavia

COMMENTARY

Lubitsch's PASSION had found America congenial to a German film beyond all expectation, but other films imported from Germany were less fortunate: THE CABINET OF DR. CALIGARI, for instance, flopped at the Capitol Theatre in April, 1921, in spite of careful and intelligent advance publicity. This film was the most complete demonstration of expressionism in drama which America had yet seen, but, offered to an audience of average movie-goers in a big New York house, it almost totally missed that particular public which might have made it a success from the start. Broadway, after all, had just barely begun to flirt with plastic expressionism in Robert Edmond Jones' stage settings for *Macbeth,* produced only a month and a half earlier.

CALIGARI was directed by Robert Wiene (1881-1938), from a script by Carl Mayer and Hans Janowitz; sets were done by Hermann Warm, Walter Reimann and Walther Röhrig. These credits do not appear in *The Times* review; they had been given, however, in three advance notices in the same paper, all of which quoted from Herman George Scheffauer's extensive discussion of the film in a two-part article, "The Vivifying of Space," originally printed in *The Freeman* issues of November 24 and December 1, 1920.

It is significant that in connection with CALIGARI *The Times* should mention, without reproach, "Nude Descending a Staircase," Duchamp's wildly provocative painting of the Armory Show in 1913, even if only to point out that CALIGARI was relatively less extreme. Modern art was gaining greater acceptance, and exactly a month later the august Metropolitan Museum was to stress Post-Impressionists for the first time, in a big loan collection. Some years earlier, in May, 1915, a movie-goer who enjoyed fast, jumbled editing, had even called Mack Sennett's Keystones "The Cubists of the Movies" (42), but a more common attitude was expressed by the editorial entitled "Art and Democracy," in *Photoplay Magazine* for April, 1918: ". . . The moving picture art is not the art of the cubist, the futurist, the synchronist, the vorticist or any other what-d'ye-call-it-ist. It does not base its reputation upon obscurity of meaning. It is an art which uses simple language and direct statement. . . ." (43)

The musical score for CALIGARI seems to have been a staggering advance over the usual film accompaniments. Willard Huntington Wright, whose *Photoplay* article follows below, was an author, editor and critic, who toward the end of his life wrote a series of detective-story novels under the pen name of S. S. Van Dine.

355

After initial exposures, CALIGARI disappears for five years, then reappears to clinch the new art house movement, and to become, with THE BIRTH OF A NATION, another of the three most famous of all silent films.

In the last half of the decade, three more films by Wiene were shown here: CRIME AND PUNISHMENT and THE GUARDSMAN (both 1927), from Dostoievsky and Molnar, respectively; and THE HANDS OF ORLAC (1928), with Conrad Veidt, the somnambulist of CALIGARI. Wiene's film of DER ROSENKAVALIER (1926), for which Richard Strauss wrote a little extra music and conducted the orchestra (during the performance he could not keep pace and the music fell behind the film), seems not to have been imported.

THE CABINET OF DR. CALIGARI   FILM 1921

Excerpt from "The Screen," *The New York Times*, April 4, 1921, p. 18.

Opinions about THE CABINET OF DR. CALIGARI, at the Capitol this week, will probably be sharply divided—and that's the first thing that recommends the picture, for, although individuality so pronounced that it breeds active disagreement does not necessarily denote peculiar excellence, it is bound to have a strong appeal for habitual motion-picture spectators depressed by stock stuff.

The most conspicuous individual characteristic of the photoplay is that it is cubistic, or expressionistic. Its settings bear a somewhat closer resemblance to reality than, say, the famous "Nude Descending a Staircase," but they are sufficiently unlike anything ever done on the screen before to belong to a separate scenic species. A house, for instance, is recognized as a house, but with its leaning, trapezoidal walls, its triangular doors, and its bizarre floor patterns, it does not look like any house anybody ever lived in—likewise the irregular alleyways between inclined buildings, the crazy corridors and the erratic roofs.

Doubtless these expressionistic scenes are full of meaning for the specialist in the form of art they represent, but the uninitiated, though they will now and then get a definite suggestion from some touch here or there, and enjoy it, are not asked to understand cubism, for the settings are the background, or rather an inseparable part, of a fantastic story of murder and madness such as Edgar Allan Poe might have written. This story is coherent, logical, a genuine and legitimate thriller, and after one has followed it through several scenes the weird settings seem to be of its substance and no longer call disturbing attention to themselves.

The two principal characters in this horrific story are Dr. Caligari, an uncanny old wizard, and Cesare, an unearthly somnambulist completely in his power, who is his agent in the commission of crime for crime's sake. Werner Krauss as the doctor gives one of the most vivid performances recorded on the screen, and Conrad Veidt is no less the embodiment of the ghostly, ghastly sleep-walker. The others in the cast are also effective, and if they all act with exaggerated gestures and facial contortions, this, too, is in keeping with the story and its settings. Everything is unreal in THE CABINET OF DR. CALIGARI. There is nothing of normalcy about it.

So the film, then, is a shocker for those who like such to revel in. It is a feast for those who want their fiction strong and straight.

But none of this bears directly on the importance of DR. CALIGARI as a motion picture, for it is not likely that it will establish a vogue of cubistic films, unless, indeed, it is commercially successful, as it may be, and the enterprising "fillum" men, accustomed to making "mother-love," "homespun" and "religious" pictures in pursuit of the popularity of other successes so catalogued, suddenly discover that "the public wants cubistic stuff," and grind out terrible imitations of this original work.

356   The picture is significant, though, not because it is expressionistic in any special sense,

47. Robert Wiene's THE CABINET OF DR. CALIGARI took audiences by surprise, an experience most of them did not enjoy. German it was, to be sure, but what else? "Cubistic, or expressionistic," one critic wrote. Werner Krauss, as the doctor, enticing Lil Dagover, as Jane.

but because it is expressionistic in the general sense that all of its elements, its settings, its plot, its people, are expressive, eloquent, and, for the most part, harmoniously so. Sometimes the more nearly normal characters in their unnatural surroundings give an impression of incongruity, but this wears off after a time, and in most of the scenes there is unity and vitality. Herman George Scheffauer, who saw the picture in Berlin, wrote about it in *The Freeman* under the caption, "The Vivifying of Space," and this indicates its importance as a work of cinematography. It gives dimensions and meaning to space, making it an active part of the story, instead of merely the conventional and inert background for the performance of puppets. It leaves literalness behind, and leaps into the field of creative imagination.

The picture has been skillfully titled by Katherine Hilliker, who has not only inserted well-selected words where they are needed, but, with restraint rare among expert title writers, has not stuck in words where they are not needed, though she has used "fakir" when, apparently, she means "faker."

As presented at the Capitol by S. L. Rothafel, with a prologue and epilogue calculated to supply an atmosphere of usualness and a happy ending for those who demand them, and with stirring interpretive music by the orchestra, the picture's effectiveness is materially increased. [*The prologue and epilogue consisted of "live" stage action.*]

It should be stated further, perhaps, for the benefit of those who have not yet added the word "European" in its new sense to their motion-picture vocabulary, that the film comes from Germany, where it attracted considerable attention before it was brought to this country. . . .

"COMES STRAVINSKY TO THE FILM THEATER" 1921

By "B. R.," [Bernard Rogers], *Musical America,* Vol. 33, No. 25, April 16, 1921, p. 5.

Music of the Ultra Modernists Employed to Accompany Remarkable Motion Picture at the Capitol Theater—Distortion as Principle in Adapting Motives to Nightmare Mood of Screen Play—Latter an Original Treatment of Psychopathic Theme—Impressionism in Two Arts Synchronized—A Genuine Musical Departure Effected

At that point the young man left off his eerie recitations. . . . Together with his solitary auditor he entered the marmoreal house that rose from the wet and twining shubbery. . . .

With the opening of that mad-house door the creators of THE CABINET OF DR. CALIGARI let in the light of imagination upon the movies. With a gesture, bold and admirable, they raised the blazing flag of futurism where the prosaic has from the first held title. At last the camera promises to inherit its rich and rightful portion.

THE CABINET OF DR. CALIGARI is to the regulation film play as a canvas by Cézanne to a Meissonier. One shows you a viewpoint and personal vision, the other holds up the microscope of the many. One is art, the other artifice.

The makers of CALIGARI have taken as a springboard the premise that the principles of modernism applied in the plastic arts are perfectly applicable in motion pictures. In the strange domain where Dr. Caligari plies his grisly trade, the windows and doors and rooftops are joined at crazy and disturbing angles. The "lighting" proceeds from strange planets; the shadows are extra-somber and intense. Of the terrestrial as we understand it there is virtually nothing. Extraordinary as all this is, it is seen to have its logic, its inevitability, as the film spins on. For all that one sees on the sheet is the puppets which dance in a diseased brain. The play, in short, is a psychopathic study.

Properly, the American première of CALIGARI employed music calculated to heighten its exotic character, to underline its fantastic aspects. At the Capitol Theater, where the film was introduced, the admirable symphony orchestra played a special score arranged from the writings of the modernists Debussy, Strauss, Stravinsky and others. Of the compiling and adapting of the music let S. L. Rothafel—in charge of the artistic destinies of the big theater—speak.

"In handling the musical problem presented by THE CABINET OF DR. CALIGARI Mr. Rapée (the conductor) and I felt that the orthodox thing would not do. A film conceived along revolutionary lines called for a score faithfully synchronized in mood and development. We took psychology into reckoning—the psychology of the audience no less than of the play. In the phantasmagorical scheme of DR. CALIGARI people move and live in a world out of joint. The cracked country is dotted with grotesque houses, skinny twisted trees, enormously steep and rutted pathways. . . . The key principle of this sprawling architecture and wild terrain is, distortion. With that steadily in mind we built up the score. We went to Schönberg, Debussy, Stravinsky, Prokofieff, Richard Strauss for thematic material. We assembled our themes, assigned characteristic ideas to the principals of the play, and then proceeded to distort the music. The music had, as it were, to be made eligible for citizenship in a nightmare country.

"The score is built up on the leitmotif system; quite in the Wagnerian manner. For Caligari's motif we went to Strauss's 'Till Eulenspiegel.' His idea recurs, or is suggested, whenever Caligari or his influence is at work on the screen. To identify Cesare, the Somnambulist, Mr. Rapée and I borrowed a bit from Debussy's 'Afternoon of a Faun.' These main ideas appear singly or together, whole or in part, as the psychology of the tale demands. The scoring is not that of the original, but has been done here and is contrived to emphasize the *macabre*. Muted brass was resorted to for most of the sinister sounds.

"I think I may confidently, and justly, say that the whole represents the most daring musical achievement in the history of the American motion-picture theater. We tried very hard with this picture, because we think so much of it. CALIGARI is, to my mind, an imaginative masterpiece and a triumph as directing. Musically no less than pictorially it opens up a virgin country."

As briefly back as five years Stravinsky or Schönberg in the movie-house belonged to the inconceivable. Today it calmly happens, and the audience calmly swallows the pill. It would have been far simpler, in preparing accompaniment for this film, to dish up the old safe and sickening potpourri. The more admirable, then, is the departure made by Messrs. Rothafel and Rapée. The thing took more than courage; it meant double labor and it meant considerable expense. Four rehearsals were called. But the tune was worth the toll. The acrid air of Stravinsky has been borne into the film theater. It may clear the sweet murk before the last reel is run.

(Signed) B. R.

1921   **Los Angeles Protest**

Excerpt from "California Chatter," Hazel Simpson Naylor, *Motion Picture Magazine,* Vol. 22, No. 7, August, 1921, p. 99.

. . . There is one theater which is going to stand up for the exclusion of the German films which the critics have so enthusiastically applauded. When Miller's Theater in Los Angeles tried to show the German-made THE CABINET OF DR. CALIGARI, a mob of wounded soldiers and members of the American Legion stormed the place and created such a riot outside the theater that the management gave up and showed an American-made film instead. . . .

"THE ROMANCE OF THE THIRD DIMENSION"   **1921**

By Willard Huntington Wright, *Photoplay Magazine,* Vol. 20, No. 4, September, 1921, pp. 41-42, 105.

> How the photoplay found the artistic goal of all the centuries—
> THE CABINET OF DR. CALIGARI, was really an American triumph!
>
> EDITOR'S NOTE: Mr. Wright is recognized both in Europe and America as one of the foremost authorities on painting and aesthetics. He has been intimately associated with the modern evolution in Europe, and is almost equally well known as essayist, novelist, critic and editor.

It is a matter of record that no picture, not even THE BIRTH OF A NATION, ever created quite as much comment, argument and speculation in one month's time as did THE CABINET OF DR. CALIGARI. It was lavishly praised in most quarters, "patriotically" banned in some and hugely talked about everywhere.

And why?

Because, answer the thoughtless, "it had such crazy scenery."

But why did it have "such crazy scenery?" To be eccentric—unusual—bizarre? That sort of quest, merely, would have landed it in the cutting room's waste-barrel.

The wiser heads tell you, with a concluding and all-summarizing nod, that here was the first film exploit of the futurists, the impressionists, or the post-impressionists. And they let it go at that, considering that that is the beginning and likewise the end of the answer; and that, probably, the modernists will get along pretty well in the cinema theater if this, their premier experiment, may be taken as a criterion.

But as matter of fact, CALIGARI stirred the film world to its depths neither because it was odd nor because it was German; neither because it was adroit melodrama nor because it was modernistic, but because it was the first sight of land in a motion picture new world—the eastern shore of the continent which has been the quest of every Columbus of the brush—farthest east of that Arcadia of vision, the Land of the Third Dimension.

In many of the sets of THE CABINET OF DR. CALIGARI one received the distinct impression that the action moved in depth; that the picture, unlike other motion pictures, was not merely a flat performance on a two-dimensional screen.

Now the importance of this achievement may be realized in the answer to the question: what, during its centuries of evolution, has been the chief problem of the art of painting? The achievement of the third dimension. From the hectic days of the *Cinquecento,* when old Leonardo, pausing from his bellicose labors of gun-making for the bloody Cesare Borgia, wrote his famous "Trattato della Pittura," down to the most recent manifesto of the latest Neo-Ultimo-Futurist of Greenwich Village, you will find that painters large and small, conservative and revolutionary, famous and obscure, have ever been sedulously hounding the trail of that same Third Dimension. Mere perspective has never been enough. Something more realistic was demanded.

During the horse-hair-settee period of American culture, when all parlors possessed a marble-top center-table, a what-not, a brace of crayon portraits, a cluster of wax flowers under glass, and a carpet-covered rocking-chair mounted upon wooden tracks, there was always to be found a stereoscope for the amusement of callers who had exhausted the fascinations of the family album. This instrument of diversion consisted of a species of huge goggles (similar to those now worn by Ford drivers) with a handle underneath, and a projecting bracket on which was placed a double photograph. By adjusting this photograph and peering through the goggles, one could see the Capitol at Washington, Niagara Falls, Yosemite Valley, or the stalactites of Mammoth Cave, all set off in bold relief and apparently possessing *three dimensions.*

Now, it is exactly this effect which painters have always endeavored to obtain. With but a flat surface to work on, they have realized that depth, or rather the illusion of depth, was needed to give their pictures solidity and form and verisimilitude. They also realized that this third dimension would have to be achieved by optical and other scientific principles applied to the technique of painting; for, in reality, paintings are and can be but two-dimensional.

Now, when we look at an object in nature we do so with two eyes, and we necessarily get two distinct impressions of that object, as anyone can prove by closing first one eye and then the other. These two impressions differ slightly from each other because our two eyes look at the object from slightly different angles; and it is the focusing, or super-imposing, of these two dimensions, which creates the sense of depth—three dimensions—in ordinary vision. The double photograph used with a stereoscope consists merely of these two impressions (each "snapped" at a little different angle) which, when looked at through a certain kind of split lens, become one picture, and appear to have depth. The stereoscope, in other words, is merely a mechanical reproduction of our normal binocular vision.

To a man with but one eye the world is flat. And practically all painting up to modern times has been the vision of the one-eyed man. The modernists, who a few years ago were ridiculed as "communards," lunatics, sensationalists or mere fakers, recently discovered how to produce the effect of a third dimension; and by doing so they solved the profoundest problem of painting, and one which has baffled the greatest artists and investigators for centuries.

Consequently, in order to solve this problem, the modern painters first studied and experimented with the laws of optics, the mutability of related masses, the fluctuability of lines, the functioning elements of tones and colors, the laws of composition and organization, the principles of psychology and physiology, the emotional reactions to external stimuli, and numerous other aspects of the subject. Then they sought to apply these researches to painting, and to express them with a painter's technique—in short, to state the scientific principles which they had mastered in terms of pictorial art. The first experiments were something beyond all human understanding, but at last a few of the greater artists succeeded in producing pictures which gave the impression and the illusion of depth.

The motion picture producer has, from the first, felt the need of this third dimension on the screen, and has made a few unsuccessful attempts to produce it. But he has completely failed for the simple reason that he has never gone to the men who really knew something about the subject from the pictorial and scientific standpoint.

Germans made CALIGARI, but, like the submarine and the first principles of the modern dye industry, CALIGARI was in Germany, but not of it. The Germans merely took the discoveries which other peoples neglected, and faced them with the motion camera.

Do you know that today America leads the world in modern painting? With the exception of the few great experimental artists of the past generation—Renoir, Cézanne, Matisse and Picasso—this country possesses, among its younger men, the truly profound and creative painters of the new art movements, the painters who have gone furthest in mastering the principles of three-dimensional form.

Certain arrangements of lines and masses and tones produce certain moods; and a mere "set," in itself, can be made to evoke the exact emotional effect of an action or situation. There are pictorial laws governing these linear and tonal arrangements, just as there are laws governing the projection of atmospheres and dramatic tensities. The different schools of modern painting have determined and developed these various laws, and in America are those who stand highest in their respective lines of artistic research.

It is possible to produce an infinitely superior picture to CALIGARI in our own   361 country, now. If the right men were chosen for it, it would possess in a much greater degree the illusion of three dimensions. It would be a dozen times as varied as the CALIGARI film, for within these shores we have the leading representatives of practically all the modern art schools. Such an American-made picture would not only be more dramatically effective, but it would be more original, more appealing and more beautiful. It would be as far in advance of CALIGARI as that picture was in advance of the old-time conventional "feature."

Its cost would be about one-third that of the average super-feature today. It would end, once and for all, this silly talk about "German invasion" and "German supremacy." It would set motion picture production ahead twenty years!

COMMENTARY

THE GOLEM, German-made, with sets by Hans Pölzig which struck audiences in 1921 as more expressionistic than they seem to us today, had-sufficient success to keep it running for 16-1/2 weeks at New York's little Criterion Theatre. SHATTERED, a German film without subtitles, and with script by Carl Mayer, was shown to special audiences the same year. A few subtitles were added in this country.

THE GOLEM   **FILM 1921**

From *The New York Times*, June 20, 1921, p. 17.

The black magic of the Middle Ages, sorcery, astrology and all of the superstitious realities of people so legendary in appearance and manners that the unnatural seems natural among them, have been brought to the screen of the Criterion in THE GOLEM, the latest motion picture to come from the explorative innovators of Germany. The photoplay gives the impression of some fabulous old tale of strange people in a strange world, fascinating, exciting to the imagination, and yet so unfamiliar in all of its aspects that it always seems remote, elusive even, when one would like to get closer to its meaning.

Paul Wegener, who directed the production, has shown his greatest artistry, perhaps, in maintaining the consistency of his production. Even his method of telling the story without the usual directness and coherence of modern narration seems a part of the age and subject with which he deals. It will doubtless be disconcerting to some; it will be said that the photoplay does not develop climactically, and in places its lack of direction does leave the mind somewhat at sea, but this is not to say that it is ever dull, for one cannot lose interest in a work so strangely engrossing and with such power as THE GOLEM has in many of its scenes.

This power is derived mainly from a combination of exceptional acting and the most expressive settings yet seen in this country. Resembling somewhat the curious constructions of THE CABINET OF DR. CALIGARI, the settings may be called expressionistic, but to the common man they are best described as expressive, for it is their eloquence that characterizes them. They give impressions of distance, of compactness, of massiveness, of old-world unearthliness that could not be conveyed in any other way. They are as active a part of the story as any of its characters, and afford another striking illustration of how much constructed scenery, furniture, buildings and the like may mean in a photo-dramatic composition. It is not because they are weird, but because they vivify the action of the story, that they are cinematographic works of art.

The acting of the players, too, is of that pantomimic quality essential to the motion picture if it is to be a living thing. None of the players is named, except Mr. Wegener, so individual credit cannot be distributed, but the old Rabbi Loew, his daughter, her betrothed, Rudolph Hapsburg, and the others in the cast, including many who are only vital figures of the crowds, all define their characters clearly. None of them is simply a silenced chatter-box, as are so many supposed screen actors in this country.

The most impressive performance is that of Mr. Wegener as the Golem. This is the name for a huge figure of clay fashioned by Rabbi Loew and brought to life by the insertion of a magic word in a receptacle in his chest. The rabbi employs the monster to propitiate Rudolph, who has ordered the banishment of the Jews from Prague, but, like the creature of Frankenstein's creation, the Golem does not remain obedient and seeks its own dumb satisfaction to the threatened havoc of the Ghetto. He is reduced to the impotence of inanimate clay only when a Christian child whom he picks up playfully unscrews the bright star in his chest which holds the magic word.

The story is said to be based on an old Jewish legend, but it is no part of orthodox Jewish tradition, surely. It is, however, a most absorbing Old World story, most effectively told.

Its effect is heightened by Dr. Hugo Riesenfeld's presentation of it with appropriate accompanying music, an inspiring musical prologue and motion picture views of the still ancient-seeming City of Prague.

By way of light relief the picture is followed by a dance by May Kitchen Cory in Benda masks, another of Tony Sarg's delightful chapters on the merry men of prehistoric times, and a mirthful [Buster] Keaton comedy called HARD LUCK.

FILM 1921   SHATTERED

Excerpt from "Screen: Pictorial Efficiency," *The New York Times*, December 11, 1921, Section 6, p. 3.

. . . Pictorial effectiveness is strikingly illustrated in another German production entitled SHATTERED, which was shown privately not long ago, and, as this is written, is scheduled to be exhibited, with THE CABINET OF DR. CALIGARI, under the auspices of the National Board of Review, at Town Hall, on what will be last night by the time this is published.

The picture suffers from as poor photography as has been seen on the screen in recent years. Furthermore, in the form in which it was first shown, its story often dragged because of the unnecessary prolongation of relatively unimportant scenes, and at various points its action was obscure. But the chances are that those who see it will remember it longer and more definitely than nine out of ten photoplays that come back from the most modern studios, because of the eloquence of its moving pictures. You simply can't forget some of them.

The fact that the picture is practically without subtitles, having only some five or six to indicate passages of time, is important only because in many places where most directors would have put words, Lupu Pick, the director of SHATTERED, has put expressive moving pictures. It may be admitted that the photoplay would be helped if a few subtitles were inserted here and there to clarify doubtful incidents, but it should also be noted that, as in the case of the few other photoplays which have been made without subtitles, the ability of motion pictures to convey ideas and information undreamed of by those who use words freely on the screen is stirringly demonstrated in SHATTERED.

The story is a sombre tragedy. Into the drab home of a plodding railroad track-walker, his methodically hard-working wife, and his daughter, whose life is being smothered in a dull environment, there comes a man from the outside world, an aggressive, well-tailored, metropolitanly toned railway inspector. He easily seduces the girl, fanning to flame the dying spark of life in her, and when the mother discovers them she runs out of

363

the house to find the father, but stops at a wayside shrine to pray and freezes to death in the snow there. The father is crushed by his wife's death and when he learns the real cause of it he proceeds, without any evidence of violent emotion, but with dogged determination, to choke the railway inspector to death. Then he flags the next train and surrenders himself as a murderer, leaving his utterly benumbed daughter in the shattered home.

Can you imagine the verbal embellishments many directors would have given this story? And how futile and how soon forgotten they would be? But who will forget Werner Krauss's impersonation of the old track-walker? He does nothing spectacular, nothing excitedly or to excite the spectator. He just plods along through the dull routine of his life, and when the routine is disturbed he reacts to the disturbance like a dumb beast. But in his slow, uneven walk, in his spiritless attention to the details of the work, in his pitiful agony before his wife's empty bed, he makes the character of the track-walker one of the most vital the screen has had. And the two women, as well as Paul Otto, who plays the role of the inspector, make their characters significantly realistic. Also many scenes are vivified by expressive little touches for which, presumably, the director is responsible, such, for instance, as when the track-walker is called away from his dinner to attend the telegraph instrument in his house, and his wife, after looking at him solicitously a moment, obviously wondering how long he will be, covers up his soup to keep it hot.

If you see SHATTERED you will probably think it a very poor picture in some respects. Its photography and some of its direction are primitive. But you are not likely to forget it. Even with its handicaps, it is efficient to a remarkable degree, because it is substantially pictorial. And if it had the benefit of good photography you would not be able to get away from it for years, the influence of its pictures would be so powerful. As it stands, it's much more worth seeing than all the illustrated novels and plays turned out in a year.

COMMENTARY

The Swedish SIR ARNE'S TREASURE was one of a group of Scandinavian films seen here in the early Twenties, without establishing a regular market for them. This film was directed by Mauritz Stiller (1883-1928), whose THE BLIZZARD was shown here in 1924. His THE STORY OF GOSTA BERLING, a long and important film, and, like the two above, adapted from Selma Lagerlöf, did not arrive until 1928, four years after its European première. It introduced a young Greta Garbo, so plump that she was scarcely recognized by those now familiar with her svelte Hollywood figure. Stiller and Garbo had arrived in New York together, Hollywood-bound, in the summer of 1925.

Victor Sjöström's THE STROKE OF MIDNIGHT (he is already billed as Seastrom in the credits), also from Lagerlöf, was the fourth of his later films to be seen here. Already shown had been THE GIRL FROM THE MARSHCROFT (1919), once more from Lagerlöf, A MAN THERE WAS (1920), after a poem by Ibsen, and YOU AND I (THE OUTLAW AND HIS WIFE) (1921), from an Icelandic drama.

Asta Nielsen's HAMLET, in which she plays the title role not as a man but as a masquerade, was seen at New York's Lexington Theatre in an engagement beginning November 7, 1921. Neither her Dostoievsky nor her Strindberg film mentioned in this article was shown here publicly, and they seem to have vanished utterly. This anonymous critic, from the new audience of the 1920's, assumes that Nielsen had never been seen on American screens before.

SIR ARNE'S TREASURE   **FILM 1921**

Excerpt from "Screen: Two Current Pictures," *The New York Times*, December 25, 1921, Section 6, p. 2.

. . . One of the regrets of the motion picture reviewer's life is that circumstances compel him to see so many photoplays that he doesn't want to see and to miss others that he would really like to look at. It is especially regrettable when conflicting engagements prevent his attending the exhibition of a worthwhile production, and this is the case with respect to the present writer and the Swedish Biograph Company's photoplay, SIR ARNE'S TREASURE. This picture has been shown several times hereabout in recent weeks, and reports have indicated that it is a work of special merit, but the present writer has not yet found himself free to go to see it. There has been no account of it in these columns, therefore.

Now, however, an account may be given, for Mrs. Frances Taylor Patterson, instructor in photoplay composition at Columbia University, having seen the picture and having noticed that it has not been reviewed here, has written concerning it, as follows:

"The Swedish Biograph Company has produced a picture called SIR ARNE'S TREASURE, which seems to me to be a revelation in motion picture production. Since it is based upon a story by Selma Lagerlöf, it cannot be said to be a photoplay in the purest sense of the word—it was not composed in the language of the screen as were THE GOLEM, THE CABINET OF DR. CALIGARI and PASSION. It is an adaptation rather than an original photoplay. Nevertheless, I have never seen a production which approaches more nearly to consummate art. Pictorial beauty, histrionic beauty and dramatic beauty are consistently sustained through all the scenes. The lights and shadows in some of the interiors are reminiscent of Rembrandt. This picture is fluid art. The scenes move with a smoothness and harmony of motion that are admirable. There is an air of quietude, of dignity, in the sequence, with never a note of exaggeration or of over-sustained repose. The characters are not puppets, not mere marionettes who dance as the director pulls the strings. They are living people; they are personalities created in pantomime, which is the language of the screen.

"The play dramatizes the snowy wastes and icy fastnesses of the north country. The ice-locked firths and bays are used symbolically and bring about the unraveling of the plot. Beauty which we usually associate upon the screen with the scenics and nature pictures is here used to dramatic purpose. The play is frankly a tragedy built along the lines of the Greek tragedies, moving inevitably toward catastrophe. But the tragedy is logical; it satisfies our sense of dramatic justice. There could be no marriage between Elsa and Sir Halmar, who is the murderer of her little sister. Little Elsa, thrown over her lover's shoulder, receives the bayonet thrusts of the men-at-arms and gives her life for her lover. But he, after his long vigils with her dead body in the hold of the ship, gives himself up, and the ice breaks and the bays and firths open wide to the sea.

"The picture is a period picture set in a kingdom of the north 350 years ago. The attention to detail in settings, costumes, customs and properties is remarkable.

"I first saw this picture at the Town Hall and was so struck with its beauty that I secured a print to exhibit and analyze before my classes in photoplay composition here at Columbia. A second viewing bears out the impression of the first. I have not yet seen the picture reviewed in your columns or elsewhere. In fear lest such outstanding artistry go unnoticed, I take this occasion to call the picture to your attention. It embodies the Swedish contribution to the gallery of Italian, German, French and Norwegian pictures now being exhibited in our theatres."

FILM 1922   THE STROKE OF MIDNIGHT (THE PHANTOM CHARIOT)

Excerpt from "The Screen," *The New York Times*, June 5, 1922, p. 16.

Based on a story by Selma Lagerlof. Adapted and directed by Victor Seastrom, with a cast including Mr. Seastrom, Hilda Borgstrom, Astrid

Holm and Tore Svennborg, a Swedish Biograph production; HORSE TEARS, a Universal comedy. At the Criterion.

The odds are ninety-nine to one that, if THE STROKE OF MIDNIGHT, the Swedish picture which came to the Criterion yesterday, had been produced by any of the first ninety-nine out of a hundred producing companies you can think of, it would have been stereotyped, dull stuff. The odds are the same that, if it had been directed by any of the first ninety-nine out of a hundred directors you can name, it would have been a cut-and-dried, tiresome thing. But the hundredth company and the hundredth director did it. And it is compellingly interesting.

This is not to say that the other ninety-nine companies and directors do not make interesting films sometimes. Sometimes they do. And, probably, also, the Swedish Biograph Company and Victor Seastrom are sometimes guilty of deadly averageness. But in this particular case the Swedish company and Mr. Seastrom have taken a theme which has been done hundreds of times by others and invariably done to death, and they have made it live as a story on the screen. Hence they are counted as one company and one director out of a hundred.

The story is of a man's redemption. How many times have you seen it done! How many times has it left you wearied and unconvinced! Reforming its puppets is one of the chief functions of the movies, but the foreordained reformation of a mechanical figure, obviously without a will or a character of his own, animated only by the will of an arbitrary playwright, is not interesting. The reformation of a man is interesting, however, and the first fact about THE STROKE OF MIDNIGHT is that its principal figure is a man, a man with a definite character, a man of stubborn will whose strength you admire even when it is manifested in a determination to destroy himself and others. The first premise established by the picture is that this man is worth saving. You never ask, "Why are all these good people wasting their time on such a fellow? Aren't there others who would better repay their efforts?" This fellow is worth saving. He's worth a hundred of the others—as is the film in which he appears.

Thus, then, the story is started logically. It wins your consent to its proposition. And then it proceeds logically. Sometimes its continuity is broken—it has been badly edited for American circulation or Mr. Seastrom has permitted a number of hiatuses—but, except where you are forced to make a mental jump, it takes you from scene to scene convincingly. The tavern to which David Holm and his hard-living, hard-drinking companions resort becomes a real place. The hall of what appears to be the Swedish Salvation Army is likewise real, and real, also, is David's home as it approaches the final destruction which he all but brings upon it. And when it is said that these scenes are real it means that the people in them, as well as the settings, are real. David himself, as played by Mr. Seastrom, and his wife, as played by Hilda Borgstrom, stand out especially. Here is acting that is intense and positively expressive and yet always restrained, as truly forceful acting must be. Astrid Holm, as Edith Larssen, the girl who does most to save David, also makes her character and feelings felt, and Tore Svennborg, as a friend of David instrumental in his redemption, is entirely sufficient for the purpose of his part.

This salvation of David is accomplished through the medium of spiritism. In a dream David dies and his spirit is conducted to the deathbed of Edith Larssen and to his home by the driver of a deathcart, who, according to an old legend, goes about gathering the spirits of those who have died by violence and in the midst of suffering and crime. Although David's awakening leaves the driver and his cart still legendary, the fact that, upon arising, he possesses information gained during his dream and acts upon it, definitely commits the photoplay to the spiritistic hypothesis, and it is the honesty with which it accepts this hypothesis, as well as its imaginative treatment of it, that wins its acceptance by the spectator, who, in his own life, may have no faith in spiritism at all.

These spiritistic scenes employ double exposure, of course, and, for the most part, they are strikingly effective. Sometimes the ethereal objects seem too solid, sometimes too thin, but these technical flaws pass almost unnoticed, so absorbing is the action of the scenes in which they are present. This is true of the photoplay throughout. Photographically, it is not always good, but even poor photography cannot destroy the effect of a scene physically well composed and humanly vivified. There is imagination, too, to take the place of literal-mindedness in the treatment of the film. Some of the sharpest impressions are given by suggestion rather than by explicit picturization. . . .

1922   "SCREEN: THE PUBLIC BE SERVED"

Excerpt from "Screen: The Public Be Served," *The New York Times,* August 6, 1922, Section 6, p. 3.

A couple of Sundays ago there was printed here a query as to the present activities of Asta Nielsen and the whereabouts of the films in which she has appeared in Europe. Surely, no one who saw the Danish HAMLET, which was shown at the Lexington Theatre last November, will fail to remember Miss Nielsen with enthusiasm. Her performance in that photoplay, think what you please of the inevitable and unfortunate conflict with Shakespeare, was one of the most finished pieces of work ever done on the screen. For those who have not seen her before she was immediately revealed as a motion picture actress of the highest rank, an inquiry brought forth the fact that she had been appearing on the European screen for years and was rated abroad at, or very near, the top.

So, naturally, the question came up: Why had only one of Miss Nielsen's pictures been shown in this country? And the publication of the question has brought a letter from R. M. Becker, Secretary of Asta Films, Inc., which firm, it is understood, controls the Nielsen films in America.

Mr. Becker writes that HAMLET was exhibited on Lexington Avenue, and not on Broadway, "because none of the so-called Broadway theatres would show it"; that Asta Films, Inc., has "been unable to arrange for a proper distribution of this picture, notwithstanding that the terms on which distributors handle pictures are such as to insure them against any possible loss or risk"; that the company, in addition to HAMLET, "has ready for American showing Miss Nielsen's other great works, including THE IDIOT, based upon Dostoievsky's great novel of the same name, which Miss Nielsen considers to be her best work, and COUNTESS JULIA, based upon Strindberg's play," and that "these great works are denied the American people, while the most stupid and worthless stuff is dished up to them."

Here's an unsatisfactory situation, then. This department knows nothing of the merits of any differences that may have arisen between Asta Films, Inc., and the distributors and exhibitors whom they have approached with the Nielsen films. And, although any of the Broadway exhibitors, or any of the producing and exhibiting companies which control their theatres, might well exhibit HAMLET even at the present time, it is understandable if none of them is inclined to show a film which has already run publicly for four weeks in New York. But if HAMLET is denied distribution throughout the country, and if THE IDIOT, COUNTESS JULIA and other Nielsen films are kept from the Broadway screens, something is wrong somewhere. It is impossible to say, in the present case, just what is wrong and who is to blame, but it is well known that the machinery of motion picture exhibition and distribution is not efficient. It often fails to get the best pictures to the people who want to see them. Other interests than those of the entertainment-seeking public are largely influential in the determination of what films shall be distributed and where they shall be shown. With "angels" backing certain—as they call them—stars, with producers and distributors pushing their own pictures in   367 groups and series, often in their own theatres, with trade agreements and rivalries effective regardless of the merits of the pictures affected—with these and other purely personal and commercial considerations taking precedence in the minds of those who have the loudest voices and the strongest arms in the motion picture business, not to mention the bumptious ignorance enjoyed by many of those who write, make, buy and sell cinema productions, it is no wonder that the film industry wastes much of its best talent and does not always deliver to the hungry public the best pictures which, despite adverse circumstances, somehow manage to be made.

The Nielsen films, it would seem, serve to emphasize the existing fact. That HAMLET is far and away better than most of the productions widely exhibited in the last twelve months is beyond question. That THE IDIOT and COUNTESS JULIA, unseen, may be counted as well worth seeing, is made probable almost to the point of certainty by the evidence of Miss Nielsen's performance in HAMLET. That the first of these pictures is unable to obtain general distribution, and that the other two are kept from the Broadway screens, means that the public is not being served by the motion picture industry. . . .

COMMENTARY

German imports soared and sank, and Hollywood breathed freely again when it became apparent a) that Germany could make bad films on occasion, and b) that its backlog of usable films was running out. The spotlight was again on Germany, however, at the end of 1924: Mordaunt Hall conveys his excitement over F. W. Murnau's THE LAST MAN, eventually shown here as THE LAST LAUGH, and his boredom over Hepworth's British COMIN' THRO' THE RYE, produced by the same studio which had made THE DRUNKARD'S SON back in 1909.

In THE LAST LAUGH, written by Carl Mayer and photographed by Karl Freund, Jannings was directed by Murnau in a superb performance as the old porter. What to do with this obvious masterwork? It was cut and offered on a double bill for first runs in New York (January-February, 1925), then restored to its original length for art house screenings (January, 1926).

Murnau and Jannings were later signed by separate West Coast studios to come to Hollywood; Karl Freund did not come over until the sound period. Further German films by Murnau (1889-1931) shown in America include: FAUST (1926), TARTUFFE (1927), LOVE'S MOCKERY (1928) and NOSFERATU, THE VAMPIRE (1929), this last an unauthorized version from Bram Stoker's *Dracula*.

CRAINQUEBILLE, mentioned here in Hall's article, was the work of the French director Jacques Feyder.

THE LAST MAN (THE LAST LAUGH); COMIN' THRO' THE RYE   **FILMS 1924**

"Two Foreign Photoplays," by Mordaunt Hall, *The New York Times,* December 21, 1924, Section 7, p. 3.

In the last ten days we have taken the opportunity to view two foreign productions, one of which is a masterpiece and the other an old-fashioned story produced in an old-fashioned way. The first is the German production called THE LAST MAN, and the second is Cecil Hepworth's COMIN' THRO' THE RYE, a British picture.

THE LAST MAN is a story told without titles, except for two or three inserts, and yet one is never in doubt as to what the director wishes to convey. While subtitles are not necessary, there is no doubt but a caption here and there would have done no harm. It seems to us to be rather straining the point to avoid subtitles altogether, even if the picture is clever and one is not actually conscious of the lack of titles. Some of the lines from a play from which a pictorial effect has been adapted never detract from the production. The captions are interesting, but this does not mean we think that each sequence should be boomed by text which is practically only repeating what has been said in pantomime.

Whether producers who have an eagle eye on box-office returns will look with enthusiasm on THE LAST MAN is problematical. The French production, CRAINQUEBILLE, an excellent character sketch, was not received with open arms by the theatre owners. It was the story of an old man, without love, and the comedy it contained was whimsical and delicate. It was very much like O. Henry's "The Cop and the Anthem."

There is real art both in the acting and in the camera work of THE LAST MAN. It has no love story, and the heart interest, like CRAINQUEBILLE, deals with an old man. The present German production has the advantage of more modern ideas in photography and in producing technique. The story grips one from beginning to end and, owing to the author "taking pity on his chief character" and giving him another act [sequence], there is a jubilant finish.

Natural Scenes.

None of the scenes in THE LAST MAN causes one to think of studios, and the action is so natural in many of the sequences that one is quite stirred without words of explanation. Pride and its fall is one idea that can be gleaned from the story, while another is the ingratitude toward old age. One can also look upon it as a story unfolding the theme of the vanity of mortals.

In a striking bit of photography in which the rain seems to be real, one perceives a tall and hefty old porter, with carefully combed hair and mustache, standing at the main entrance of the important Atlantic Hotel, helping persons from taxis and lugging great trunks to the mat in front of the building. His greatcoat is the pride of his existence. It is lavishly trimmed with wide gold braid and set off by a cap. The whole effect would make an Admiral's uniform look like that of a First Lieutenant.

After hauling a trunk in the rain from one vehicle, the old porter enters the hotel for a breathing spell. He settles in a seat. Just at that instant the imposing hotel manager appears, and after observing a conveyance arriving while the porter is resting he makes a note of it in his little book. The porter eventually goes out and again and late that night as usual forges his way to his humble abode in a tenement quarter, where his glittering braid is looked upon as something which gives tone to the whole neighborhood. Women bow to him and men salute to him, each receiving a military touch of the cap from the proud old porter. He is rather pleased with himself.

His Amazement.

Next day when he goes down to work he observes with amazement that there is a younger man, also robed in a greatcoat covered in gold braid, whistling for taxis and escorting persons into the hotel. Emil Jannings gives a wonderful exhibition of the old man's feelings when confronted with the surprise of his life. Soon he is seen in the manager's office where he is told that he is to take the aged menial's place in the washroom, as that veteran has been pensioned. The porter crumples up with the news, but takes advantage of an opportunity to steal the key of the cupboard, in which he is told to hang his glorious coat.

When the time comes for him to go home he remembers that his daughter is to be married that night. He cannot think of appearing at the wedding without his gold-bedecked overcoat, so he stealthily crawls along the corridor, clinging close to the wall, and finally sneaks into the manager's office. Soon he issues forth, bent and much aged by his humiliation, but wearing the treasured uniform.

369

He is no longer his esteemed self on reaching home, but with the aid of wine he holds himself together. A little too much wine sends him into the land of dreams where the whole story comes before him. This section of the story is particularly impressive. One sees the old porter as he had been a couple of days before—straight, strong and filled with honest pride.

It is raining and four or five men are seen trying to lift a trunk. In his dream the porter waves them aside and without any apparent exertion with one brawny arm lifts up the trunk. He pitches it up in the air, exchanges a word with one of the men and then catches the trunk with one hand.

The Porter's Dream.

Next morning the dream was only a dream. Demotion had really happened! He was no longer entitled to the uniform. He sneaks out of the house, gets to the usual road crossing and hurries over toward the hotel, but, being fearful lest he be caught with his coat, he finally checks it at the nearby railroad station. After that one sees him in the shabby clothes which the glorious coat had covered for so long, stealing into the washroom to attend to his new duties.

Mr. Jannings is perhaps a trifle off his guard in one or two places in this picture. He appears too bowed and bent after the humiliation, hardly able to walk, and yet he has sufficient energy to dash across the street like a youth catching a train. His facial expressions are wonderfully indicative of moods, conveying every atom of feeling flowing through the old man's mind, changing here with a glimmer of hope and then to tragic despair at the thought of the horrible humiliation. To serve in the hotel as a humble washroom attendant in a mere white coat was bad enough, but to have to go home night after night and emerge morning after morning in the shoddy clothes, emphasizing his rotundity, was more than he could bear. The cackling females in the tenement quarter are seen delivering the news when one of their ilk has discovered accidentally that the porter, the man of gold braid and pomp, is nothing but a white-coated attendant.

In the picturing of several scenes the director has obtained great effect by the wheeling up of the camera, once actually passing the main objective on the screen. It gives the effect of traveling from one's seat and following the persons on the screen.

We will not dwell upon the happy development in the last act [final section of the film], as the author has decided that this is merely given to the porter in pity, and that the story ought to end with the disappointed old man in his white jacket. Nevertheless fiction readers will delight in this additional chapter, and in the way it is told it is just as clever as the preceding ones. THE LAST MAN is a masterpiece on which it is hoped New York will have the opportunity of delivering its verdict.

THE LAST MAN was filmed in the Ufa studio in Neubabelsberg, near Berlin, F. W. Murnau being responsible for the direction. Carl Mayer, author of THE CABINET OF DR. CALIGARI, wrote the scenario of the current photoplay.

On the other hand, COMIN' THRO' THE RYE is a frayed and clumsy production, in which the players appear to emulate old tragedians rather than persons in real life. Time and again the characters start when it appeared to us that they ought to have heard the footsteps on the grass before the approaching player really appeared in the picture. There is a lot of slow, tedious action, with painful expressions that do not reflect emotions of real life. The heroine might just as well be suffering from the toothache as from the pangs of love. Yet this production has been highly praised in England—which is strange, for it is hardly comparable with ordinary features produced in this country. We had hoped for much in this picture—which is a sweet, old-fashioned love story—with its beautiful English background.

370

48. *Monumental décor in Fritz Lang's German film SIEGFRIED, "produced on a mammoth scale . . . set forth in terms of utter unreality." An earlier film of Lang's was withheld from the American market so that Fairbanks could study its trick effects for use in THE THIEF OF BAGDAD.*

THE LAST LAUGH,

Excerpt from "Drama," Robert Benchley, *Life,* Vol. 85, No. 2209, March 5, 1925, p. 18.

On the evening of the opening of *Cape Smoke*, we finished dinner early, and, tossing off a cordial, decided to spend the hour before theatre-time slumming in the movies watching THE LAST LAUGH.

As a result of seeing THE LAST LAUGH before *Cape Smoke*, we are now completely at sea about everything. Our whole system of dramatic valuations has gone to smash. This movie made the subsequent example of the theatre's art seem cramped, tawdry, and old-fashioned. It made us feel that in a hundred years there will be nothing but movies, and that the spoken drama will then occupy the place that the Punch and Judy show now holds.

Of course, *Cape Smoke* is not a fair example of what the theatre can do, although it is by no means any worse than most of its *genre*. It has its moments, and an occasional not inconsiderable kick. But it does embody all that is clumsy and phony about the spoken word and fabricated scenery (very *well* fabricated in this particular case), while THE LAST LAUGH embodies all that is easy and poignant in the unspoken word. (There is not a subtitle in THE LAST LAUGH. Not one.)

We are told that THE LAST LAUGH is by no means typical of movie art. That makes no difference. Here is a movie which can make almost any play seem like the markings on a Cro-Magnon cave wall. It may be the only movie which has done so, but the fact that it can be done should be a warning to playwrights and actors. We had much the same ominous feeling about written humor after seeing Buster Keaton in OUR HOSPITALITY. If movies can capture humor as it was captured in that picture, and, with no evident effort, express it as it was there expressed, then we old writing-boys had better pack up our leaden words and wooden phrases and learn a new trade. Following our experience at that picture, we secretly began learning glass-blowing, and are ready any day now to duck. . . .

THE LAST LAUGH

Excerpt from "Masters of the Motion Picture," Matthew Josephson, *Motion Picture Classic,* Vol. 23, No. 6, August, 1926, pp. 24-25.

In the modern period of the movies, the films of Messrs. Lubitsch, Chaplin, Stroheim, Vidor, Cruze, have developed a complete character of their own as an art, instead of being a mawkish rendering of cheap theatrical successes in photos.

The eye is struck first by the immense improvement in the quality of the camera work, the cleanness of line, the absence of waste detail. All of them manipulate their groups, their sets, as well as the light they spill over the scene, to get a balance, a form that keeps your eye unswervingly on the things that count most.

Not only have they learned to *paint* with the camera, but also to *suggest*, by the interplay of sequences, by the terrific power of concentration in a close-up, by the shrewd angles they catch, almost a new understanding of life. The modern film, in short, becomes an instrument fit for artists to express the highest flights of their imaginations, their most delicate and subtle fancies.

That Masterpiece Again

The one film out of this rich period which you have doubtless heard critics refer to more than any other is THE LAST LAUGH. It is a German picture, directed by F. W. Murnau, with the great Jannings in the central role.

There is virtually no plot at all, no love interest, no sensationalism of any kind. What is the merit of this picture, which failing, as it did, to become a popular success, appealed to insiders, critics, artists, column conductors, everywhere as most nearly approaching the ideal of perfection?

THE LAST LAUGH gave us the unique feeling of looking into the interior of a man's life through some wholly unaccountable peer-hole. We not only watched this man's expressions and movements, we watched the states of his soul. Jannings, who is possessed with some divine understanding of his business, seemed to know more about how to make *his whole body expressive* than most of the other film folks put together.

The picture forms simply the inside history of a crisis in the life of an old hotel porter who is demoted because of senility to a still more servile occupation, that of lavatory-attendant! And because of the simplicity of his material, because he didn't have to bother with the details of some silly plot, the director was able to bear down upon the pure creation of his character and his awful fix through cinema technique alone. It is one thing to interest you with pictures of pirate ships, knights-at-arms, society gals. It is another to make you feel with the pride, the hope, the passions of an old derelict like this. Within the hour you have a sustained motion picture which through its overtone hands over to you his whole code of living. This idiotic old creature is interpreted with as much *éclat*, sympathy, intimacy, and frankness, as, let us say, Chaplin interprets Chaplin.

Perfect Technique

The background, the group of characters, the labor which fills this life are all drawn with a tremendous effort at reality. There are no subtitles at all to interrupt the mood of understanding into which you are thrown. The pictures as Murnau composes them put the stuffy and artificial-looking studio sets of his expressionistic colleagues to shame. He uses every trick of the modern cinema that will help him trap an idea, an effect, and hurls it at you.

For instance, there is a daring full-length flash of a revolving hotel-door, which with its glassy glitter and whirl recurs in the sequence of the film like a refrain, a dominant motive in music, setting off the whole idea of this proud and cruel hotel. Or, there is a wedding feast in which the camera, itself, seems to go drunk with wine and contentment and, wandering about the meager North Berlin interiors, drops into a brass instrument and brazens out to you the very music of the occasion in a few inspiring mechanical close-ups.

All the "stunts" and tricks of the director followed his material with absolute faithfulness. They did not stick out like useless fandangles, as in CALIGARI. All the shades of joy, grief, desperation, came to you through the insidious *overtones* that caught you in their spell. . . .

COMMENTARY

When Fritz Lang (1890-   ), the German director, made his first visit to the United States in the fall of 1924 to study our motion picture industry, he and Erich Pommer (the producer who was travelling with him) were shown Fairbanks' THE THIEF OF BAGDAD. Lang's reactions must have been mixed, as his own film of several years earlier, THE TIRED DEATH, had been purchased by Fairbanks but withheld from American distribution in order to examine its trick camera work. After the première of THE THIEF OF BAGDAD, Lang's film appeared in New York as BETWEEN WORLDS (1924). In 1925, 373 the first half of his two-part film, THE NIBELUNGEN, called SIEGFRIED, opened first in Rochester, then in New York. It would be three years before its sequel, KRIEMHILD'S REVENGE, was shown here.

SIEGFRIED   **FILM 1925**

"SIEGFRIED," excerpt from "The Silent Drama," R. E. Sherwood, *Life*, Vol. 86, No. 2239, October 1, 1925, p. 24.

The German picture, SIEGFRIED, supplies what to this correspondent has always been a long-felt want: it affords the opportunity to hear operatic music, pictorially interpreted, without having to go to the opera.

For here is set forth the legend of "Siegfried" in all its barbaric splendor, and with all the impressive beauty of Wagner's score, but without the dead weight of fat tenors, fatter sopranos and collapsible scenery. Here the ear and eye may work together, and the one is not offended by the other.

The absence of the human voice, to me, is a negligible loss.

SIEGFRIED has been produced on a mammoth scale—as of course it should be—and is set forth in terms of utter unreality—again as it should be. Its director, Fritz Lang, and its designer, Otto Hunte, have displayed the flawless taste that, for some strange reason, is evident in all German pictures. These men are artists; because of this, they can avoid the obvious pitfalls of ignorance into which the average movie maker of Hollywood must inevitably stumble.

SIEGFRIED, above everything else, is eminently *right*—in tempo, in manner and in design.

There is some magnificent acting by Hanna Ralph, as Brunhilde, by Margarete Schoen as Kriemhild, and by Paul Richter as Siegfried himself; but the greatness of the picture is creditable primarily to the men behind the cameras.

We could use more of them over here, just as we are using Lubitsch and Seastrom and von Stroheim. . . .

COMMENTARY

BACKSTAIRS, directed by Leopold Jessner, whose position as a stage director rivaled Reinhardt's in the Twenties, was, like SHATTERED and THE LAST LAUGH, a German film without subtitles.

In the following article we can see that the web of mis-information about early films had already begun to be spun by 1926: The May Irwin-John C. Rice THE KISS, filmed in April, 1896, was several years too late to be "the first commercial film" produced in the United States, and THE GREAT TRAIN ROBBERY has acquired the quite unjustified label of "the first feature ever made." THE FATAL MALLET dates from 1914, not 1916, and Mary Pickford's GOING STRAIGHT, a one-reeler, was released first in 1911 (not 1912) as THE BETTER WAY.

BACKSTAIRS   **FILM 1926**

"The Screen: Old Films and a Tragedy," Mordaunt Hall, *The New York Times*, June 4, 1926, p. 26.

With Henny Porten, Fritz Kortner and Eugene [sic] Dieterle (43a), a

German tragedy; DRIVEN, with Burr McIntosh, George Bancroft, Emily Fitzroy, Charles Emmet Mack and Elinor Fair, directed by Charles Brabin; GOING STRAIGHT, with Mary Pickford; THE KISS, the first commercial film made and released in America; THE GREAT TRAIN ROBBERY, the first special feature produced. At the Cameo for one evening.

An excellent entertainment was afforded last night at the Cameo, where the International Film Guild presented for its fourth subscription evening several old films, Charles Brabin's powerful drama, DRIVEN, and a German tragedy called BACKSTAIRS, which was produced about seven years ago.

A good deal of mirth was created by such old numbers as GOING STRAIGHT with Mary Pickford, King Baggot and others, and THE GREAT TRAIN ROBBERY, the first feature ever made [sic]. The audience also found an old Chaplin comedy, THE FATAL MALLET, quite amusing, although it proved that the illustrious screen clown has gone a long way since 1916, when this feature was made. Another comic strip was THE KISS, the first commercial film ever produced and released in the United States.

The initial presentation was Mary Pickford's ancient production. It was made in 1912. In it Miss Pickford filled the role of a Salvation Army lass, and King Baggot, who is now a director of repute, figured as the hero who had resolved, come what might, to go straight. The action of the extended flat right hand signified his intentions, and he stuck to his resolution in spite of all temptation that was thrust in his way. It is safe to assert that nobody would recognize in the Salvation Army girl with the big bonnet the charming Miss Pickford of today.

From the viewpoint of merit the picture that proved the most stirring was Mr. Brabin's DRIVEN, which was made in 1922. It is a throbbing narrative of Southern mountaineers in which a mother betrays her husband and two sons to save her youngest boy. Emily Fitzroy gives an amazingly fine performance in the part of the mother and Burr McIntosh is capital as the cruel, godless husband and father. Charles Emmet Mack, who is to be seen this week in THE UNKNOWN SOLDIER, acts the role of the youngest son. George Bancroft, who really came to the front after his portrayal of the smiling villain in James Cruze's production, THE PONY EXPRESS, demonstrates that he ought to have been recognized as an unusually fine screen actor a year or so before he appeared in Mr. Cruze's film.

THE GREAT TRAIN ROBBERY was produced in 1903 and it contained some features that at least show the resourcefulness of the producer. When it comes to throwing the fireman off the engine tender a dummy is quickly substituted, and off it goes to the embankment.

BACKSTAIRS, the German contribution, is a film without titles, in which Henny Porten, Fritz Kortner and Eugene Dieterle are seen. It is a strong, gruesome feature, but the detail is worked out magnificently. Miss Porten officiates as a servant in a large household, and in depicting her daily toil the director does not duplicate any of her activities. Whether it is dusting a piece of furniture, washing the plates or polishing the glasses, it is done in a natural way. The tale concerns the girl's love for a tall young man, who goes away. The servant waits for a letter, and she smiles the first day when no missive is brought. Her smile has partly faded in a few days, and soon she receives the postman with a stare and a worried frown.

The subnormal, semi-paralytic postman, a man of forbidding appearance and actions, has kept back the girl's letters because he is himself in love with her. In the end the postman slays the girl's sweetheart with an axe and the servant in a daze walks to the roof of the building in which she had been employed and falls to the cobblestones below.

The action is told fairly clearly without subtitles, although the players seldom make a   375 move of their lips that might be understood. There is not even an insert of the letters in this film, as there is in THE LAST LAUGH.

Symon Gould, the director of the International Film Arts Guild, was congratulated by scores of the spectators for the exceptionally interesting evening he had afforded by his selection of pictures.

COMMENTARY

In the German-made VARIETY (1926), the elements of filmmaking seemed to reach a perfect balance with the acting of Emil Jannings and Lya de Putti, the script and direction of E. A. Dupont, and the camerawork of Karl Freund.

(The Léger-Murphy abstract film from Paris, BALLET MECANIQUE, mentioned in the first review, had been shown in New York several months earlier.)

VARIETY ran twelve weeks at the Rialto in New York. But, as feared by Evelyn Gerstein, the entire Hamburg episode of the film was dropped for circulation in "the dark corners of this country," presumably to build up greater audience sympathy for Jannings' Boss Huller.

Almost every foreign film was cut, re-edited or both before distribution here, but this was merely an extension of an old American custom even for domestic films. In 1917, the managing director of the Strand Theatre wrote that a film was "very seldom" seen there "in the form we receive it from the manufacturer. Every foot of film is perused very carefully, and lots of cuts have to be made, either for complete elimination or for replacement in some other part of the film. . . ." (44) Perhaps the most extreme example of the abbreviation of a foreign film occurred when the German three-part THE THREE WAXWORKS was reduced to the Jannings episode alone, as part of a Christmas program at the Rivoli Theatre in December, 1925.

VARIETY   **FILM 1926**

"Exceptional Photoplays: VARIETY," *National Board of Review Magazine*, Vol. 1, No. 3, July, 1926, pp. 5-6. (With the permission of the National Board of Review of Motion Pictures.)

Directed by . . . . .E. A. Dupont
Photographed by . . . . .Karl Freund

The Cast

Boss . . . . .Emil Jannings
Bertha . . . . .Lya de Putti
Artinelli . . . . .Warwick Ward
The Wife . . . . .Maly Delschaft

Once in a while a picture so unusual, so strictly a motion picture, comes along, that the critical eye is opened wide, or it seems to be seeing for the first time; the praise that has been bestowed on films in the past seems then to have been overwrought and ill-considered, and to have been poured forth with an enthusiasm either unrestricted by knowledge or due to forgetfulness of what the motion picture can be at its best and is in its purest example. Much praiseful criticism of motion pictures has been of this kind, smacking of the ballyhoo that ever tends to launch itself with the phrase "the greatest yet." We know that few motion pictures, upon second sober examination, yield such large unalloyed nuggets to our analysis as to justify any such cataloging, but that here and there along the long line reaching back into the distance does a film appear that fully reveals what the true nature of the medium is, with intimations of what its further development may produce. VARIETY, now showing on Broadway to audiences in America for the first time, is such a film, and one that makes it seem as if many well-intentioned words of praise vented upon lesser pictures have been too generously or inappropriately bestowed, and not withheld from being given long enough, as seem pearls around the throats of women whose beauty is revealed as undeserving when the true queen of beauty appears. Thus do comparisons become odious.

VARIETY is a simple, tragic tale adorned by the most dexterous and magical camera that has yet captured with its eye for the retina of the screen the movement and meaning of its subject. This is not necessarily to say that it is more interesting or better than CALIGARI or SHATTERED or THE LAST LAUGH. But as a thing of moving pictures reacting on our sensitivity, as a mechanism or a medium or, if you please, as an art operating on our consciousness through the visual channel, making us *see* and therefore feel and know, and, within the limits of what it has to do, in its speed, its energy, its concentration, its ever roving angle of shots like the eye itself roving, and its ability, through camera means alone, to create pure sensation in the spectator, this latest product to reach us from the German studios surpasses anything in film that has gone before it, at least as far as our knowledge goes. The theory of the floating camera, as referred to by report by Murnau, the director of THE LAST LAUGH, is here, in VARIETY, most vividly illustrated, and motion pictures to come that do not in some way embody such technique, when contrasted in memory with this film, must always remain something less than motion pictures. One goes back, by the way, to Léger's and Murphy's BALLET MECANIQUE, through VARIETY's use for certain effects of the abstract method, but where VARIETY uses abstraction it is to tune the nerves and so make us more sensible of the concrete meaning of acting, situation and story. Nevertheless, VARIETY is proof positive that tremendous possibilities are opened up by the abstract method, and such as lie within the true scope of motion camera art.

For both the BALLET MECANIQUE and VARIETY gain their foremost position and distinction as products of motion picture art. Nowhere as in these two films is it so clearly revealed that the art of the motion picture and that of the motion camera are one and the same thing, and that that thing is complete in itself, and to this extent the film constitutes a formula out of which is possible a definition. Here the camera tells all, both implies and is explicit, strikes at the imagination and spurs it on and sets the text for what must be exactly and immediately understood. In the circus the acrobats swing to the trapezes straight up from the eye along the rope whose length stretches vertically to a slender quivering apex based at the camera. The sensations of height, a long climb upward, danger, are at once established. The trapeze artists begin swinging high over the audience; what their sensation is is told by what they see as the camera swings with them and records the swaying blur of faces in the audience gazing up from far beneath in the abyss of the theatre. We understand at once their dizzying peril and their art of agility and precision which allows them to conquer it. As they poise and swing and fly through the air from one trapeze to another and are caught and drawn to safety, we follow their movement because the camera like our gaze travels with it. But the camera sees more than the eye and that more completely. We drop to the audience, circle around, and perceive its various expressions of wonder, interest, fear, of breath held against the half-expected fall, and soar again amid the lofty paraphernalia of the acrobats, the flickering wires and the marvelous rhythmic swinging trapezes. The situation and the psychology of the actors and the audience are absolutely embraced and transferred to us. We are both the acrobats and the audience, swinging by turns from the sensations of the former to the sensations of the latter. We swing, fly, alight, swoop down upon the wings of pictures. When one considers that the situation in this

377

incident is one of uncertainty and suspense, that the central character may reveal himself as such or such a man, that the plot may swing this way or that, since the decision of the head performer is to determine whether he shall allow his fellow acrobat, who has betrayed him with the trapeze girl he himself loves, to plunge to his death at the conclusion of a particularly spectacular and perilous swing, or reserve him for some other fate, the tremendous gain achieved through such photographic technical exposition becomes apparent.

One could go on giving instance after instance of this kind of thing in the picture. The whole film is marked, through this sustained camera technique, with a magical quality affording a succession of exact and pregnant images, telling what must be told and nothing more through selection, enriching, and massing of necessary details analyzed, recorded, and kept in flux.

But while the cineographic quality of VARIETY is thus outstanding, the camera plays upon a brand of acting for which the European screen has become justly noted. Emil Jannings as the Boss, who has been lured back to the "big time," and away from his wife and child, by the young dancing girl whom he has trained on the aerial swings and who rewards his love for her with infidelity with one Artinelli, the third member of the troop, a much younger and more dashing man, is authentic and, except for a slight tendency toward overemphasis, fills the part. It is but another of Mr. Jannings' successes in giving characterization on the screen. Lya de Putti as the beautiful, wily, and utterly unscrupulous girl shares Mr. Jannings' honors. Here is a new face which will prove fully as attractive to American audiences as that of many of our charming ladies of the films, and hers is a temperament more intense in interpreting the kind of role she has to play in VARIETY than any that has come under our observation. Miss de Putti, however, is an artist. Her touch is sure and light and her work is never coarsened beyond the demands of reality and character meaning. Fully abreast of Miss de Putti's and Mr. Jannings' is the performance of Warwick Ward, an English actor, as Artinelli. The suavity of this performance in connection with the character which must be expressed is far above what is usually to be seen in motion pictures. Not a touch is missed to add to the pigment of this portrait of a famous and conceited acrobat, used to the plaudits of the crowd and marred in his personal life by a strain of decadence and cowardice. Every performance down to the smallest role and to the most minute detail which is needed in the picture is finished and distinguished for its entire truth and naturalness.

VARIETY is a picture that should not be missed by anyone who wishes to see what motion picture art is and who is interested in its highest present attainment.

(Screen story by E. A. Dupont. Produced by U. F. A. and distributed by Paramount.)

"... VARIETY" 1926

Excerpt from "The Silent Drama," R. E. Sherwood, *Life,* Vol. 88, No. 2281, July 22, 1926, p. 24.

In its first two showings, in Los Angeles and in New York, VARIETY appears to have rung the bell of popular approval. It seems destined to achieve that degree of financial success which has been denied the other fine German pictures, such as THE CABINET OF DR. CALIGARI, THE GOLEM, SIEGFRIED and THE LAST LAUGH.

This is good news, for the success of VARIETY will inspire with hope those progressive American directors and actors who are ready and able to give the public worthwhile pictures as soon as the public signifies its willingness to receive them.

VARIETY **FILM 1926**

By Evelyn Gerstein, *The New Republic,* Vol. 47, No. 608, July 28, 1926, pp. 280-281.

The first of the German invaders of the cinema was Lubitsch, then came von Stroheim; now there are Murnau, Mendes and Dupont whose VARIETY is his first film to be shown in this country. A dark, stinging tale of life in variety, utterly devoid of the pale puerilities, the sterile conventions, that cabin and confine the cinema, it has yet captured that ephemeral thing—the favor of the populace. Dupont, like von Stroheim, is a realist, ruthless, passionate, Rabelaisian. At some time or other all of this German band have been so. Lubitsch was when he directed in Europe, in GYPSY BLOOD, ONE ARABIAN NIGHT, PASSION; there was a vitality of a different sort, a light Viennese laughter in THE MARRIAGE CIRCLE. But he lost something of it between Berlin and Hollywood. And it is this earthiness, this madness that reaches to ecstasy, this foot-in-the-soil intensity that has given even the least of these German films a dynamism that the watered romances of Hollywood have never approached.

VARIETY is not so exquisitely chiseled or so lyrical as THE LAST LAUGH. Its story is far more commonplace, a melodramatic tale of a crime of passion among vaudevillians. Drama of a different genre, sensual, voluptuous, beautiful in its nakedness as Dupont has done it; a tragedy rich with a low, lusty laughter. It moves rhythmically, relentlessly towards its end, a perfectly coordinated work of art, each detail pertinent, illuminating, carved in the round. There is no gesture that is unconsidered, no planting of the camera that is not arresting and eloquent. Almost titleless, VARIETY is pure cinema, drama wholly dependent on pantomime; on the swift ordering of moving masses, the weird, shunting play of light and shadow, all of that restless, fantastic world of mechanistic device still so little explored.

Objects tearing through space; intangible, phantom shapes; swarming, searing eyes of the audience; chattering hands; white pin points of light that torture "Boss" Huller as his little world collapses about him; chains and machines that leap and revolve with a terrible intensity, destroying, whipping life into a timeless muddle—all this touches on moods too fragile for words, too tenuous to imprison, distorted creations of the unconscious mind. Always, there is that endless motion, charging and rebounding, singing through space, devouring. Faces, machines, inanimate objects even, are alive, plastic, lyrical with a strange animate silence. This is Picasso technique translated to a moving screen, which as yet only Murnau and Dupont, and a few of the experimentalists (Dudley Murphy, Fernand Léger) have carried so far. THE LAST LAUGH used it, too, yet that evolved into a cameo-like melody. But VARIETY is crude, barbaric, pulsing, touched with wildness, like the music of Stravinsky, at times, although it is not so self-conscious.

Unlike THE LAST LAUGH, VARIETY was not written directly for the screen. It is an adaptation of a novel by Felix Hollander, worked into a deft, malleable continuity. The scene is Hamburg, a circus on the waterfront, a dejected caricature of a circus whose frequenters are sad creatures that once were men. Disheveled sluts, still trading their wasted bodies, angle their arms and legs while the audience applauds in beery obscenity. In command is "Boss" Huller, powerful and gentle, a sensualist, the creature of his emotions. His wife, once a trapezist, now sullen and heavy-heeled, thumps the piano. A man with restless eyes and a leery smile, just off the ship, brings a girl to Huller, Berthe-Marie, a young rounded girl who dances. The voluptuous white-armed dancer from the Barbadoes, hips bending sinuously, maddens the half-naked men into a delirium. "Boss" can stand no more; the curtain is rung down; catcalls hurtle up from the pit; he decides to return to the trapeze with the dancer. In Berlin, "Boss," with his new partner, a petulant, untamed creature, an exquisite voluptuary, is in a circus near the Winter Garden. Then, the Winter Garden and "the three Artinellis" (Artinelli, Huller, Berthe-Marie), trapezists pursued by blinding lights and distorted perspectives high above the audience where they saw the air with their leaping bodies, unprotected even by a net below. (This is one of the most amazing stunts that trick photography has as yet manipulated.) Artinelli seduces Berthe-Marie, and "Boss," bull-necked and irresistible, knifes him in the dismal little room of the theatrical boarding house that was the setting

379

of the seduction; then he gives himself over to the police. Then follow ten years in prison. All that has gone before is done on the screen as a flash-back, as the story of Prisoner Number Twenty-eight whose face is not revealed until the end, when he is at last released at the plea of his deserted wife. Freedom, and a bent, shuffling derelict passes through the gates.

In and around this relentless tale Dupont has worked his satire, a satire candescent and pitiless, scorching audience and performers alike. Chinese jugglers, trundling grimacing clowns, a serpentine dancer, a nude girl reflected on a dozen opera glass lenses, fat-chinned women, beery men with protuberant bellies, sycophants, fatuous fools . . . louts . . . the camera shrieks it . . . have been limned with the power and ferocity of a Daumier. And with what rich blacks Freund, camera man also of THE LAST LAUGH, has lighted it, blacks that even Renoir would have envied.

In "Boss" Huller, another emotional instrument of fate, Emil Jannings, for the first time acting without make-up, has once again created a man. There is more drama, more tragic force, more joyous abandon in his broad, powerful back than in the faces of most actors. An actor with an imagination and restraint that transmutes each thing that he touches into something alive and rounded; a man with an unerring dramatic instinct, a leaping sense of humor, he is without an equal, whether it is in the playing of a decadent Louis, an old doorman with querulous eyes, or the passion-ridden bouncer of a circus. Without him it is difficult to imagine VARIETY. Miss Lya de Putti, by now well intrenched in the American movie colony, is an interesting and exotic beauty who ranges inordinately from the luxuriantly oriental, a woman out of Conrad, even to a plain-faced and callous, but always animated, screen actress. She plays with a temper and abandon that none but a European actress ever has, an emotional intensity, that seems always destined to be lost with importation to our shores. Warwick Ward, the hollow-cheeked villain of the piece, will doubtless be made still another of the Byronic permanents of Hollywood as soon as the deliberating movie makers can arrange it.

Here, in VARIETY, the cinema has at last depicted sex without self-consciousness and adolescent pruderies. It is the motif of the piece, riddling, overpowering, the basic theme of this tragedy of the backwashes of the show business; a tragedy that but for the grace of God and Herr Dupont might have passed into another shoddy anecdote of the sort that delights the readers of the journals for "people who think." But through the sardonic and unflinching lens of Dupont and Freund it has been charged with something of genius, warmed with a tormented, vital beauty having nothing at all to do with the feeble, chastened myths that make the "movies."

It is said that when VARIETY descends upon the dark corners of this country, especially the free and censored states of Massachusetts, Ohio and Pennsylvania, the entire Hamburg episode will be dropped. The piece will open with Berlin and the circus where "Boss" Huller and Berthe-Marie, discreetly married, are paired performers. But no one expects intelligence or the toleration of art in dark places. It would be incongruous to countenance VARIETY in hamlets where babies are admitted as naturals only for week-day showings, and even travelogues are stripped of their bathing sequences on Sunday. The great Berlin-to-Hollywood emigration grows more staggering day by day. But, in the face of it, it is wiser to forget what happens to directors in that fleshly paradise by the western sea where studio politics is the only intellectual diversion, and the director is merely an unhappy soul lost among the magnates in a Minotaur's cave.

Evelyn Gerstein.

"CAMERA WORK ON SCENES IN VARIETY"   **1926**

380   By Ewald André Dupont, *The New York Times*, July 11, 1926, Section 7, p. 2.

Its Director Explains Photographer's Ingenuity
By Ewald André Dupont
Director of VARIETY

Wherever VARIETY has been shown, whether in Berlin, London, Athens, New York or Los Angeles, a number of queries have come from persons interested in the motion picture as an art, asking how certain of the effects in the picture were obtained. It is difficult to answer these queries without making a cold-blooded thing of what is, after all, the child of my emotions.

VARIETY to me was a fascinating script to write, an absorbing film to produce, for I had the cooperation of Erich Pommer, who supervises Ufa films, and also of Jannings and Karl Freund, my cameraman. Lya de Putti was enthusiastic and indefatigable. During rehearsals of the scene in which she falls down the stairs she sustained many a bruise.

It is, of course, not yet time for me to write a textbook on VARIETY. Here are some of the questions that have come to me:

"How were the images in the opera glasses photographed?"

"Does Warwick Ward fall from the trapeze?"

"Is the prison scene real?" etc.

At the risk of somewhat destroying the illusion (and after all the motion picture is in the world of illusion) I am going to tell you how some of the scenes were created.

Karl Freund is a resourceful cameraman. I found in him a ready ally for my purpose. He was always experimenting, trying to discover new angles, new approaches to familiar scenes. Thus, our first introduction of Emil Jannings as Boss Huller, manager and ballyhoo man of a Hamburg sideshow, was by not photographing him full-face, but by accenting his occupation, his ringing of a bell to call the crowd about his booth. In the earlier prison sequence Jannings has his back to the audience.

When Jannings comes to the rescue of the girl and drives the audience from his little theatre a feeling of disgust for his life comes over him. He, once the great catcher in a famous trapeze act, to sink to this! Here summations are revealed by the camera taking the place of his eye as it roves over the dilapidated drapings of his sideshow.

Lens Vs. Subtitles

It was my general aim in the picture to show a simple, childish grown-up, devoted, lovable, and his reaction to betrayal and duplicity. I tried to portray the primitive emotions that are in all of us. And I tried to show it, not by subtitles, but by the lens, which, after all, is our true medium. One would as soon think of putting a series of subtitles or their equivalent in one of the galleries at the Metropolitan Museum as adding text to scenes that can be told by gestures and expressions.

The trapeze work, and, indeed, all the shots in the Winter Garden were difficult to make. For one thing we had to bring a great deal more light into the theatre than normally is used. Then we had to construct observation positions for the camera, so as to photograph the entertainment to the best effect.

The Falling Scene.

For one of the scenes we strapped a camera to another trapeze, facing Jannings, and operated it electrically from the ground. To make the falling scene we lowered a camera by cable, slow-cranking all the way. We "shot" from every angle in the theatre, using every device known and a great many that were invented at the moment.

A trapeze act is interesting when one observes the actual trapeze work. There is a natural lull in interest as the performers take their positions. To bridge this gap without causing a break in the action, I had to photograph the artists from unusual angles. Thus, in one sequence, the audience saw the actors from below, climbing like monkeys up their rope ladders. The following scene had to be taken from another vantage post.

Later in the picture, when the very same act had to be shown again, it would obviously have been quite boring to repeat the identical action. Therefore, Freund had to move his camera to still another position.

The festival scene, in which Warwick Ward and Lya de Putti figure, has the appearance of having been an elaborate set. As a matter of fact, by grouping my extras interestingly, dimming my lights, and showing only the sparkle and glow of fireworks, I convey the impression of a great celebration. It was merely the adaptation of the newer stage technique—the use of a pillar to indicate a great edifice.

Jannings used several make-ups for the picture, besides appearing in many of the scenes with virtually no facial aid whatever. Each change reflected a mood.

The scene in the prison courtyard is purely atmospheric. I wanted to show men in prison. It would be best, I felt, to photograph them from above, giving the impression of their hopeless confinement, as if they were actually at the bottom of a pit, like so many caged creatures.

COMMENTARY

FACES OF CHILDREN, by Jacques Feyder (1888-1948), had been preceded in this country by his MISSING HUSBANDS (L'ATLANTIDE) (1922), and BILL (CRAINQUEBILLE) (1923). It was followed by a CARMEN with the Spanish singer and actress Raquel Meller (1928), and by SHADOWS OF FEAR (1928) from Zola's *Thérèse Raquin*. The first film he directed in Hollywood was THE KISS (1929), which was Garbo's final silent motion picture.

PARIS ENDORMI, or PARIS QUI DORT, was the work of the French director René Clair (1898-   ), who directed in Hollywood fifteen years later. A FEUD IN THE KENTUCKY HILLS (1912) has already been reviewed in a previous chapter.

FACES OF CHILDREN   **FILM 1926**

"The Screen: A French Work of Art," Mordaunt Hall, *The New York Times*, June 30, 1926, p. 18.

> A French production, directed by Jacques Feyder; PARIS ENDORMI, also a French film; Thomas Geraghty's FILM WITHOUT PICTURES; Merle Johnson's KNEE-DEEP IN LOVE; David W. Griffith's old melodrama, A FEUD IN THE KENTUCKY HILLS, with Mary Pickford. At the Cameo for one evening only.

France had its innings last night at the Cameo Theatre, where the International Film Arts Guild offered another subscription evening. Among the presentations on the varied program were two French films, one a curious, fanciful affair, known in the land of its origin as PARIS ENDORMI, and the other was a magnificent study in child psychology called FACES OF CHILDREN. Besides these pictures there was exhibited also a film without pictures, a bright idea perpetrated by Thomas J. Geraghty, a scenario writer; Merle Johnson's production, KNEE-DEEP IN LOVE, a film in which the faces of the protagonists do not appear, and an old D. W. Griffith photodrama entitled A FEUD IN THE KENTUCKY HILLS, wherein Mary Pickford figured as the heroine.

382   The principal offering was Jacques Feyder's FACES OF CHILDREN, a pathetic story

woven around the marriage of a widower, who has two children—a boy of nine and a girl of four—and a widow, who has a little girl, eight years old. Jean, the boy, worships the memory of his dead mother, and he can't reconcile himself to the new scheme of things. He resents his step-mother's daughter using his playthings and as time goes on, the bickering between the two older children soon causes Jean to become so bitter that he hates his step-mother's daughter. His belligerent little soul fights against the intruders into his father's household, and he persists in calling his step-mother "Madame." The girl finds herself tormented by Jean, and although she naturally resents his treatment of her, she appears to forgive and forget.

During the winter while they are in a sled, Jean, ever on the alert to hurt the girl's feelings, tosses her doll out of the vehicle. He goes even further, for that evening when the child is weeping because of the loss of her doll, Jean tells her that it dropped out not so far away. The girl thereupon creeps out of the house and while trudging over the snow-covered mountain paths she is forced, utterly exhausted, to take refuge from an avalanche in a shrine chapel. She is rescued eventually after her mother has suffered hours of anguish.

Even this terrifying experience fails to wring any affection out of the boy, and it is only after his step-mother has exhibited marvelous courage that little Jean is finally impelled to call her "Mama."

The acting of the three children is nothing short of marvelous, for, when one anticipates a conventional expression, one beholds something different and thoroughly suited to the situation. The boy narrows his eyes in a childish way. He lies in deep thought over his cruel plot, and after a while he betrays nervousness. He is a good-looking boy with fine, clear eyes, and his face lights up when he gazes upon the picture of his own mother. The girl is wistful and sweet. She shows temper, but it soon fades away. She is a little Trojan, despite the fact that she does not curry favor with Jean. She is willing to enjoy the new domestic arrangement and also the companionship of her stepfather's little son and young daughter.

In the cutting of this production for exhibition there are some jerky places, and in one chapter one is suddenly taken from Winter to a full-blown Summer, while a caption describes merely the passing of a night. These shortcomings can easily be remedied, and the screen will be richer by having this remarkable picture. Incidentally, the exterior scenes for this film were made in the Vosges Mountains.

PARIS ENDORMIS, or PARIS ASLEEP, is concerned with a scientist's invention of rays that not only inflict slumber on the whole population but leave its victims in the posture they held when attacked. Eight persons, including the scientist and his niece, escape the rays. One of them is a night watchman on a high platform of the Eiffel Tower; another is a crook, and then there are a detective, an aviator, a financier and a wealthy travelling woman. The idea is very original. There are touches of genuine humor throughout this eccentric piece of work, especially when the old scientist fathoms the formula for waking up the city.

COMMENTARY

The first film to be shown here by the German director G. W. Pabst (1885-1967) happened to be the first he had ever directed: THE TREASURE (1926). Then came SECRETS OF THE SOUL (1927), through which, about ten years later than the American reading public, movie audiences were let in on the secrets of psychoanalysis (just in case they hadn't seen GRANDMA'S BOY). SECRETS OF THE SOUL was followed by STREETS OF SORROW (1927), a cut-down version of THE JOYLESS STREET (also by Pabst), in which the aging Asta Nielsen gives way to a handsome young woman, Greta Garbo. It was Garbo's second important film. Then came THE LOVES OF JEANNE NEY (1928), and PANDORA'S BOX (1929).

383

This review of SECRETS OF THE SOUL appeared in the fall of 1926, but the film was not shown publicly in New York until April 24, 1927.

SECRETS OF THE SOUL   **FILM 1926**

"Exceptional Photoplays: SECRETS OF THE SOUL," *National Board of Review Magazine,* Vol. 1, No. 5, September-October, 1926, pp. 7-8. (With the permission of the National Board of Review of Motion Pictures.)

Directed by . . . . G. W. Pabst
Photographed by . . . . Guido Seebart

The Cast

The Husband . . . . Werner Krauss
The Wife . . . . Ruth Weyher
The Mother . . . . Ilka Gruning
The Cousin . . . . Jack Trevor
The Doctor . . . . Pawel Lawlow

Freud has at last come to the screen with an adequate exposition through the medium of a dramatic rendering. SECRETS OF THE SOUL, the film made by UFA of Germany in collaboration with Dr. Hans Sachs and the late Dr. Karl Abraham, noted psychoanalysts and confreres of Dr. Freud, is propaganda, in a way, for the Freudian theory and treatment, but over and beyond this it is a surprising cinema, strikingly dramatic at moments, and a pioneer contribution to the art. Again, it is among the finest instances in motion pictures of a blending of the scientific and the instructional with what is primarily entertainment.

It is not the aim of this review to enter into any discussion of the Freudian implications of the film, its authenticity in this respect or its success as propaganda, other than to state that to the lay mind this picturization is vastly more provocative and downright informative and clarifying than any row of books on a shelf could be. For it is a triumph of the pictorial, recorded in a train of vivid visual impressions, sometimes unforgettable and perhaps, to those who dislike to remember their dreams, somewhat painful and disturbing. Here we are concerned purely with its merits as a work of motion picture art, and there the film can stand on its own legs and command attention in the rank of merit.

Cinegraphically it is a projection of the medium on the plane of CALIGARI, SHATTERED, THE LAST LAUGH and VARIETY. That is, it is said with pictures, it contains magnificent acting, it has the reality of the real world and it successfully crosses the bridge into that realm of the disturbed imagination where sanity and insanity are relative matters. As in CALIGARI where the phantasmagoria of sleep and mental aberration lie on the screen like an unquiet glitter breaking into mad whorls, so in this film is a dream quality related to the normal awake world, but troublous and convex and setting up of a conflict between conscious actions and unconscious and half mad motives. And as in SHATTERED and THE LAST LAUGH, the profoundly psychological is probed from the minds of baffled and distraught characters and held by a knife-like camera for the audience to view, in SECRETS OF THE SOUL the hidden and portentious is flicked to the surface, particle by particle, and assembled in a definite and tragic pattern most dramatic in its effect and revealing of the further reaches which the scientific delving of our modern world into the causes of men's actions has given to the province of drama itself. And as in VARIETY the camera receives new and tremendous

49.   *Harold Lloyd (right) and Buster Keaton in Rochester, New York, 1957. By this time, Lloyd had replaced with actual glasses the glassless frames he had worn while filming.*

use in the choice, movement and arrangement of pictures, so in the present film the image structure—the live, articulated frame of visual content—is vibrant, leaping and concentrated in its energy and purpose.

The narration cuts through a story of fear, defeat, and mental anguish on the part of a husband who is unconsciously jealous of his wife's cousin and his best friend for no other reason than that a conflict growing out of the childhood associations of all three has been set at work in his innermost psychic self. This drives him to a mad desire to kill his wife, whom he dearly loves and who loves him, and only the fact that his revulsion at this half-revealed thought of murder gives him a knife phobia which makes him afraid to see or touch a knife, saves him from committing the act. The true cause of his dilemma is revealed to him through psychoanalysis, a cure is worked, and the happiness of his marriage is restored, resulting in his wife's having the child they both want and whose birth was prevented by the psychological failure of the husband. In the unfolding of this story the dream-experience of the patient is ingeniously depicted by the camera with startling reproduction of the dream state, and the unique ability of motion pictures to do this sort of thing is once more impressively recorded.

Werner Krauss, in playing the husband, again bears witness to his outstanding ability as a screen actor, an ability which sets him beside but two others—Chaplin and Emil Jannings. His grasp of the human emotions, his sympathy, and his exact understanding of what he must do to create the portrait wanted with his supreme gift of naturalistic pantomime afford a remarkable characterization. Ruth Weyher as the wife brings an unknown name to the attention of picture goers in this country and reveals an actress of fine talent. All the others of the cast play their parts with that meticulous attention to detail and that faithfulness to nature which the finest German films invariably show.

SECRETS OF THE SOUL is another stride forward—a step in motion pictures to be studied by producers and audiences alike.

(Scenario by Colin Ross and Hans Newmann. Produced by the Scientific Department of U.F.A. Distributed by U.F.A.)

COMMENTARY

Lang's METROPOLIS (1927) was one of the few German films of the period to get wide circulation here. The first reading below, written from Berlin by Herman G. Scheffauer, who had provided advance reports on CALIGARI seven years before, was printed in The Times **the day after METROPOLIS opened in New York. One of the ads for this film stated: "Bulletin! TELEVISION The Newest Miracle of Science See it in METROPOLIS . . ." (45)**

Griffith's INTOLERANCE, which immediately springs to Sherwood's mind for comparison, had been revived in New York for a few showings at the little Cameo Theatre in the fall of 1926. "Capek's Robots," in his review, refers to the Karel Capek play, R.U.R., **seen in New York in 1922, for which the word "robot" had been invented.**

Lang's DR. MABUSE arrived in 1927, then came KRIEMHILD'S REVENGE (1928), and, in 1929, SPIES.

METROPOLIS   **FILM 1927**

"An Impression of the German Film METROPOLIS," Herman G. Scheffauer, *The New York Times,* March 6, 1927, Section 8, p. 7.

Berlin

Fritz Lang, the German producer, has accomplished a monumental task—the placing of METROPOLIS upon the screen. The title is derived from a novel by his wife, Thea von Harbou, who was also the author of two other grandiose films, THE INDIAN

MAUSOLEUM and SIEGFRIED. For almost two years the author and producer have been working on this "light drama"—working with thousands of hands and with millions of German marks and American dollars—for the film is an "Ufa" production, and the "Ufa" is a combination of American capital and German training. The territory of Neubabelsberg, between Berlin and Potsdam, was the scene of tremendous happenings, the rise and fall of a strange iron community, of desperate undertakings, of cataclysms of nature, of eruptions of maddened humanity, of the appalling experiments of an inventor bent upon creating an artificial human being, of the triumph of the Moloch Machine over man and the revolt of Man against the Machine. Now and again whispers made their way to the public—whispers of the great doings at the creation of METROPOLIS—of the epic action and the technical triumphs which were to make this film a masterpiece of masterpieces.

Potpourri of Elements.

The final effect, now that the film has been unloosed upon the public, may justify some of these expectations—others are fated to disappointment—unavoidable disappointment, since the line between the end aimed at and the end achieved is so plainly visible. The positive achievement is, however, so great that it outweighs many of the flaws and failures. These have arisen chiefly through capitulation to making concessions in something that was to be new and unprecedented, to things that were already old and tried—however trivial, however much of a discord they may have represented in the scheme of this great plan. Instead of showing us a real, stark, implacable State or city of the future, we have an astounding, even dismaying potpourri of all the elements which have ever played a part in so-called successful films. Our eyes and minds are not fixed upon the future, we are not engulfed and overwhelmed by the implacable machine State, but are torn hither and thither by scenes and situations that are utterly familiar and that work havoc with the unity of the whole majestic idea. We are flung into the present and catapulted into the past, and our internal sense of gravity is upset and our emotional and intellectual axis displaced.

It may be that Fritz Lang did not intend to build up a film showing a future civilization—industrialism reduced to its last consequences. But as this great city of slaves and masters which he depicts is not of the present and cannot in this form be of the past, it must necessarily deal with the future. There is the air of Jules Verne, of Edward Bellamy, of H. G. Wells about it—and hints of George Kaiser's *Gas*, and even of Mrs. Shelley's *Frankenstein*. A whole cosmos is unloosed upon us. The settings are awe-inspiring, but the people who act, live, love, labor or hate have all the feelings and gestures and posturings of the film people of today. Perhaps that is necessary, perhaps artistic independence is not for the film producer who must work with millions or for millions.

Perplexing at Times.

And yet METROPOLIS is a wonderful film, in many ways one of the most remarkable achievements in the history of the "light play." It is the epic of man and the machine. It is the apotheosis of technics and mechanics. A new wonder seizes us—a new thrill and shudder work upon our nerves. We feel that new forces have been unloosed upon this earth of ours; that man is being enslaved by them, even the man who is master of the human and mechanical slaves. The sinister, demoniacal nature of machinery that has almost become human is brought out vividly, the drab masses of workers, moving in processions to and from their shifts, walking with a rhythmical tread, a lockstep like the motion of a machine itself; the dark, grimy hordes living in an underground city while their masters revel in the sunlight above, and send their towers and campaniles toward

387

the heavens in a vision that outdoes Manhattan—the gigantic life and intricate en-
tanglement of the human and the inanimate—all this is depicted with a masterly touch,
a true creative vision. The fault lies in the fact that the human beings of today cannot be
fitted into an environment such as that shown in METROPOLIS.

The city of strange skyscrapers with its elevated bridges for automobiles, its vast
steam-whistles built up like a temple, its airplanes circling amid the crests of the towers,
its pigmy masses crawling on the far-down streets, was represented with great
ingenuity—the small scale models had much of the effect of reality. Not precisely of
American reality, for America, seen through the temperament of the European, is always
given a strange, exotic touch. It was evidently the intention of the creators of this film to
present a future State founded upon the America of today—or of America's peak
achievement of today—the Tower of Babel of New York. But the Babel, the Paradise and
the Inferno of METROPOLIS are all sublimated visions of the real America, even where
they are meretricious, and that must be accounted as an achievement in itself—a
triumph for the vision and creative power of the German author, producers, and actors.
They see, for better or for worse, America from another angle than ours and this perspective gives the whole a touch of the ideal—just as distance in space often gives us
the detachment which is inherent in distance in time. With some of its excrescences
lopped off, METROPOLIS will bid fair to become one of the master-films of the times.

METROPOLIS, which now is on view at the Rialto, was originally in sixteen reels. For
this country it has been cut down to nine. Some idea of the enormous task of producing
this film can be gathered from figures furnished by Frederick Wynne-Jones, managing
director for Ufa in New York.

Work on this picture involved 310 days and sixty nights. It cost $1,500,000 and nearly
2,000,000 feet of negative was exposed. There were 25,000 men and 11,000 women
extras, 750 children and 25 Chinese. More than 11,000 of the men had shaven heads. The
costumes cost 2,000,000 marks and 3,500 pairs of shoes were bought. Altogether
1,600,000 marks was paid out in salaries. Fifty automobiles were in use during the busiest
moments on this production.

The trimming of this production is said, by those who saw it in its original form, to
have improved it. The names of the characters had been changed for the showings in the
United States.

METROPOLIS   **FILM 1927**

"The Silent Drama: METROPOLIS," R. E. Sherwood, *Life*, Vol. 89, No. 2316, March 24,
1927, p. 24.

The new German picture, METROPOLIS, is undoubtedly the most ambitious effort in
celluloid since INTOLERANCE. It sets out boldly to tear to shreds the expensive fabric of
our materialistic civilization—a fabric woven on vast looms that have been lubricated,
the subtitles explain, with the blood and sweat of the workers.

It tells the story, in fantastic and quasi-allegorical terms, of a fabulous city in which
efficiency is god. Above the street level are towering skyscrapers, elevated boulevards,
marble stadiums and luxurious palaces of shame; below ground are the dark homes of
the bent, haggard workers who tend the elaborate machines.

Carrying efficiency to its ultimate development, a diabolical scientist—the slave of
the moneyed class—develops an automaton which can do a man's work and thus
eliminate flesh and blood entirely from the already soulless scheme of modern creation.
This invention, of course, develops the destructive tendencies of Frankenstein's monster
and of Capek's Robots, and threatens to pull the city of Metropolis down on the heads of

its rulers; but such a calamity is averted, and the picture ends in a glorious outburst of the get-together spirit and the conclusion that, after all, God is love.

There is altogether too much of METROPOLIS—too much scenery, too many people, too much plot and too many platitudinous ideas. There is also some tolerably bad acting. It has all and more of the eloquent pictorial effectiveness of THE LAST LAUGH or VARIETY, but it has none of the simple directness of these great films.

It is perhaps unduly squeamish of me to dwell first on the faults of METROPOLIS; its virtues are manifold and extraordinary. In all my years as a paid guest at movie palaces I have never seen such amazing pictures as are crammed into every reel of this gigantic production.

Fritz Lang, who directed METROPOLIS, and Karl Freund, who commanded the battery of cameras, have combined to produce photographic effects that are not far short of miraculous. They have displayed an astounding knowledge of the art of movie leger-demain, and unlimited imagination as well.

As to the acting, I was considerably more impressed by the extras than by the principals—the latter, with the exception of Alfred Abel and Brigitte Helm, being quite ham.

There is a certain resemblance between METROPOLIS and the hero of one of Stephen Leacock's nonsense novels, who leaped on his horse and rode off furiously in all directions. If the producers of this incredible picture could only have decided on one definite point toward which to travel, the spectator—who, after all, has only two eyes and one brain—would be able to follow their progress much more easily.

As it stands, METROPOLIS is actually too much of a good thing.

FILM 1928   KRIEMHILD'S REVENGE

"The Screen: . . . The Sequel to SIEGFRIED," Mordaunt Hall, *The New York Times,* October 16, 1928, p. 29.

> With Margarete Schoen, Hans Schlettow, Rudolph Klein-Rogge, Bernhard Goetzke, Theodor Loos, George John and Paul Richter, a sequel to the film translation of SIEGFRIED, directed by Fritz Lang. Sovkino news reel; Chaplin's old comedy, THE COUNT. At the Fifty-fifth Street Playhouse.

Rarely does one discover knowledge, intelligence, imagination and expert direction in a picture. Yet these attributes are to be found in KRIEMHILD'S REVENGE, a sequel to the pictorial transcription of SIEGFRIED, which is now on view at the Fifty-fifth Street Playhouse. When one recalls the many fatuous film stories that have been privileged to occupy Broadway screens, it is hardly believable that this fine Ufa picture was passed over for nearly four years, and that despite the fact that hosts of exhibitors had an opportunity to view SIEGFRIED (when it was launched here three years ago at the Century Theatre), and gave a fair idea of the worth of this current offering.

KRIEMHILD is a magnificent piece of work that is not staled by age, and, so far as one can determine, it is a picture that can grin at Father Time. A mint of money probably went into its production, but here it has not been wasted, for the spectacular episodes are worth every mark that has been expended on them—that is, to those who enjoy such works of art. To the vast majority of other films it is like a Tintoretto painting being compared to a novice's effort. Here, Fritz Lang, the director, has happily seized upon the very things that a spectator expects in a scene.

The comedy here is effective without ever being boisterous. There is, for instance, the sequence where the Huns are eager to awaken Attila. They dance and play and sing, something to the effect that Attila is asleep, when it is quite plain that nobody, not even a fierce fighter like Attila, could slumber through the row made by the savage crew.

Kriemhild, Siegfried's widow, makes her revenge complete. To accomplish her end she has a son by Attila. The series of scenes between Kriemhild's meeting of Attila and the birth of the child are screened without giving the audience a conception of the passage of time, which could be done with a slow fade-out or a few extra words in a subtitle. Yesterday afternoon the picture was screened much too fast and this resulted in a few surprises.

One can get an idea of why Attila's Huns were referred to as "shameless." They live like beasts, with their minds constantly on slaughter. The big, hut-like abode of Attila has a flooring of earth covered with hay and the ruddy, bald-headed murderer is ready to use his scimitar at the slightest excuse.

Sometimes this production is just like a story being told in a fanciful fashion and during other passages it is like delving into the distant past. The action may not be any too speedy, but it is sufficiently interesting to hold one's eyes, if not by the action, then by its scenic values, its properties, or the sight of a man on horseback plunging up an imposing flight of stone steps. Nothing is done by halves in this picture and toward the end there is a glorious conception of a blazing household.

Margarete Schoen is a handsome, somewhat idealistic Kriemhild. She is impressive, with big eyes and thick eyebrows, the left one of which she has a habit of raising to register intense interest. The other players are equally good, and after the massacre of the handsome Nibelungen, the few that remain assuredly reveal the marks of the struggle, which, in itself, is a contrast to the average hero of a motion picture, who is supposed to preserve his hair-parting under the most trying ordeals.

The subtitles of this production are of both German and English.

This picture was exhibited in Great Britain under the box-office title of THE SHE-DEVIL.

COMMENTARY

The censors may have achieved their masterpiece of confusion with PANDORA'S BOX, a Pabst film derived from two Wedekind dramas, Earthspirit **and** The Box of Pandora, **with the American actress Louise Brooks as Lulu. Pabst did not film in the expressionistic manner customary for Wedekind, but naturalistically, and the ambiguity of Louise Brooks' reactions throughout most of the film was an intentional effect. Her performance was spoiled in this country by the severe censoring of the miraculous final sequences with Lulu and Jack-the-Ripper, and by the substitution (through re-editing) of an idiotically moralistic ending, in which Lulu, spared encounter with her murderer, joins the Salvation Army.**

PANDORA'S BOX   **FILM 1929**

"The Screen. . . . A Disconnected Melodrama," Mordaunt Hall, *The New York Times,* December 2, 1929, p. 28.

With Louise Brooks, Fritz Kortner, Franz Lederer, Alice Roberte, Carl Goetz and others, directed by G. W. Pabst; SHOULD MARRIED MEN GO HOME, a comedy with Laurel and Hardy. At the Fifty-fifth Street Playhouse.

At the Fifty-fifth Street Playhouse is a German silent film called PANDORA'S BOX, with Fritz Kortner and Louise Brooks in the leading roles. The story is declared to be a combined adaptation of Frank Wedekind's plays, *Erdgeist* and *The Box of Pandora*. In an introductory title the management sets forth that it has been prevented by the censors from showing the film in its entirety, and it also apologizes for what it termed "an added saccharine ending."

Although there are several adroitly directed passages in this production, the narrative is seldom interesting. One is not in the least concerned as to what happens to any of the characters whose nonchalance during certain junctures is not a little absurd. It is a disconnected melodramatic effusion in which there is an attempt to depict a thoughtless, attractive woman and her unsavory experiences.

Lulu, the woman, played by Miss Brooks, is convicted of killing Dr. Schoen, whom she was to wed. As a matter of fact, he forces a pistol into her hand and in the ensuing struggle the weapon explodes with the fatal result. Lulu apparently is not especially perturbed over this happening. In court she directs flirtatious glances at the Prosecuting Attorney and at the presiding judge. In those scenes dealing with her escape there is a suggestion of the melodrama in old serials, except that there is no climbing to housetops or swinging from trees. Lulu and others eventually reach a gambling place in the slums of Paris, where she is blackmailed by those who want money for one reason or another.

Miss Brooks is attractive and she moves her head and eyes at the proper moment, but whether she is endeavoring to express joy, woe, anger or satisfaction it is often difficult to decide.

Mr. Kortner, one of Germany's ablest screen players, adopts slow tactics in this offering. He is precise about sticking a monocle in his eye and also in getting into trouble at the psychological instant.

The scenes in the wings of a theatre are, however, filmed far better than the story deserves and the types for the minor roles are well chosen.

50. Mary Philbin, as the opera singer, pays the penalty for removing the mask of Lon Chaney as he appears in the title role of THE PHANTOM OF THE OPERA (1923-1925). The film was finally released after two years of tampering with its sinister and comic-relief elements.

CHAPTER **20**

The American Film, 1925-1929

COMMENTARY

In 1925, **THE LOST WORLD**, from Conan Doyle's novel about the survival of prehistoric life, combined some exciting with some quite dull footage. **THE UNHOLY THREE** presents Lon Chaney *au naturel*, though he also disguises himself as an old lady, with not at all laughable, but on the contrary, very sinister results. Some found this film reminiscent of **CALIGARI**. For **THE PHANTOM OF THE OPERA**, Chaney has practically discarded his face, which is stretched so taut it is almost immovable.

THE FRESHMAN, one part Horatio Alger, one part satire, and two parts Harold Lloyd's remarkable creation of a trusting character beset by circumstances, is probably his masterpiece.

FILM 1925   THE LOST WORLD

"THE LOST WORLD," excerpt from "The Silent Drama," R. E. Sherwood, *Life*, Vol. 85, No. 2209, March 5, 1925, p. 24.

Mechanically, THE LOST WORLD is marvelous; dramatically, not so hot. It is an attempted reproduction, in terms of celluloid, of a story which, to my mind, is the most thoroughly exciting and imaginative that Conan Doyle ever wrote. It is a weird tale of prehistoric horror, recording the adventures of four Englishmen on an Amazonian plateau which is tenanted by dinosauri, pterodactyls and brontosauri. These colossal reptiles, as Conan Doyle described them, were even more terrifying than his own Dr. Moriarty.

In THE LOST WORLD, as it appears on the screen, the animals have been constructed with amazing skill and fidelity and their movements, though occasionally jerky, are generally convincing. There is one tremendous scene wherein a brontosaurus, imported by the returned explorers as Exhibit A, breaks loose from his moorings and stalks through the streets of London, demolishing buildings, crumbling bridges and even annoying the traffic policeman in Piccadilly Circus.

All this part of the picture is amazing, and I make a mental note to doff my first straw hat to those who were responsible for the animation of the reptiles.

There is, however, a love story in THE LOST WORLD, played by mere mortals, and this is stupid, inconclusive and dull. It was evidently hurled together carelessly after the real technical work had been done. In most cases, the two parts of the narrative don't fit together particularly well.

THE LOST WORLD is worth seeing because of the monsters and in spite of Mr. Lloyd Hughes and Miss Bessie Love, who furnish what is known as the "heart interest.". . .

THE UNHOLY THREE   **FILM 1925**

"THE UNHOLY THREE," excerpt from "The Shadow Stage," *Photoplay Magazine,* Vol. 28, No. 2, July, 1925, p. 51.

(Metro-Goldwyn) If you really enjoy good crook melodrama, be sure to see this. It is one of the finest pictures ever made, due to the able and clever direction of Tod Browning. From the very beginning the story grips you. The opening scene is a freak show. All the freaks are shown—the human skeleton, the fat lady, the sword swallower and many others. Also the midget, the strong man and the ventriloquist—these three forming the main characters of the picture. On account of being engaged in a brawl in the freak show, the three get together to formulate their plans and become united under the title of "The Unholy Three." The ventriloquist is the master mind and naturally you wonder just what trick this queer combination will pull off.

To divulge the remainder of the story would be unfair—it would be just the same thing as taking the cream out of the cream puff.

The cast is exceptional. Lon Chaney gives a perfect performance as the ventriloquist. Perhaps you will appreciate him because of his abandoning his makeup except during the moments of his disguise [as Grandma O'Grady, the old lady who keeps a pet shop]. He wouldn't be a good crook if he didn't have a disguise, would he? Then comes Mae Busch, whose acting is proof that she can handle emotional roles with feeling.

As for the midget, Harry Earles, he is a strange delight. He is quite a source of amusement, for instance, all dressed like a baby and smoking a big cigar. Victor McLaglen is the strong man who doesn't do very much but show his muscles.

And poor Matt Moore is cast as the innocent victim of the gag. However, we don't recommend it for the children.

(Signed) M. B.

"THE PHANTOM JINX"   1926

By Robert E. Sherwood, *Photoplay Magazine,* Vol. 29, No. 2, January, 1926, p. 113.

Some of the troubles that beset the producers with THE PHANTOM OF THE OPERA

By Robert E. Sherwood
(Editor of *Life*)

The fantastic, blood-curdling, spine-chilling tale, THE PHANTOM OF THE OPERA, which has lately come to the screen, has carried with it a jinx as mysterious, as devastating, as fearsome as the very ghost which is its own leading character.

Following the enormous success of THE HUNCHBACK OF NOTRE DAME, the Universal Pictures Corporation cast about for another story which would give Lon Chaney a chance to use more make-up and Carl Laemmle a chance to spend more money.

THE PHANTOM OF THE OPERA was suggested, and approved, so Universal acquired the screen rights to the Gaston Leroux novel—and, at the same time, acquired the Phantom Jinx.

That jinx has subsequently been wrapped around the necks of Mr. Laemmle and his able lieutenants, the Cochrane brothers, and has caused them to wish fervently that they had left the spirit world alone.

In his weird story, Leroux set down an old legend of the Paris Opera House; it seemed that this magnificent temple of music, built on a grand scale by the lavish Emperor, Napoleon III, had once been haunted by a grim specter, who terrorized everyone within the opera house and until finally driven from his deep cellar, made a general nuisance of himself. This character provided good material for spook melodrama on the screen.

The direction of THE PHANTOM was entrusted to Rupert Julian, who had achieved recognition for his fine work in the completion of MERRY-GO-ROUND, and Lon Chaney, Mary Philbin and Norman Kerry were cast in the principal roles.

Then the energetic technical staff at Universal City set to work to recreate the Paris opera house, with its stage, its enormous auditorium, its gilded lobby and its five tiers of cellars complete. Having done this, Mr. Julian started shooting.

The production of THE PHANTOM OF THE OPERA was a terrific job, and for several months an enormous and expensive staff was concentrated on this one colossal enterprise.

Hordes of extras swarmed through the magnificent scenes; color photography was used; ballets were staged; the company was taken out on location for garden parties and duels; and through it all moved the shadow of the phantom—grim, sinister, oppressive.

At last Mr. Julian's work was finished. He was at liberty to pause for breath. The actors, camera-men, carpenters, electricians, continuity writers, cutters, editors, title writers and laboratory experts turned to other productions. THE PHANTOM OF THE OPERA was ready for release.

It was at this point that the Phantom Jinx stalked into the executive offices of the Universal Corporation and started to add a few more gray hairs to the already silvery thatch of Carl Laemmle.

When THE PHANTOM OF THE OPERA was first shown at previews in and about Los Angeles, the critics who were called in to appraise it voiced a vehement desire for more comedy relief. "There's too much spook melodrama," said they. "Put in some gags to relieve the tension."

So Chester Conklin was hailed from the Sennett lot, and the picture went back into production with Conklin prominent in the cast. He contributed a great deal of monkey business, and answered the demand for a few laughs. Then it was found that new subtitles were needed, so one of the most reliable writers in Hollywood, Walter Anthony, was summoned.

Again THE PHANTOM was completed, and sent to San Francisco for display. When it was shown there, it was received with some of the foggy chill for which that city is justly famed.

"There are some gorgeous scenes," was the opinion in Frisco, "but the story as a whole doesn't make sense."

Following this rather discouraging start, THE PHANTOM OF THE OPERA was crated and shipped to New York, where it was viewed by Mr. Laemmle, R. H. Cochrane and P. D. Cochrane, the officials of the organization.

As a result, the film was turned over to a new staff of editors and cutters who proceeded to hack it into a new form, and new title-writers came in to account for the numerous revisions made in the continuity.

One of the elements that came out first was the comedy. Reversing completely the Los Angeles opinion, it was felt that the gags inserted at the eleventh hour merely clouded the issue. THE PHANTOM was essentially a spook melodrama, in which there was no legitimate place for "belly laughs."

So Chester Conklin, and all his scenes, was put under the knife—and his ludicrous face does not appear at all in the finished picture. Another casualty was Ward Crane, who played an important part in the earlier sequences of the picture. All the garden parties and duels were removed and with them went Ward Crane. Thus two large salaries, and a great many incidental expenditures, were wasted.

At the last minute, THE PHANTOM was again subjected to hasty revision, and whipped into final shape, so that Universal's foreign representative, James Bryson, could take the finished print to England for presentation.

Mr. Bryson had done wonders with THE HUNCHBACK OF NOTRE DAME in Great Britain, and he had planned a tremendous promotion campaign for THE PHANTOM. Unfortunately, he planned a little bit too well.

He arranged for a military escort to accompany him and THE PHANTOM from the dock in Southampton to London. His stunt worked beautifully, and occasioned a loud and painful squawk throughout the British press. An American movie person had insulted His Majesty's uniform! It was a frightful offense. British pride was heated to the boiling point, and scalded the unfortunate Mr. Bryson who, after all, had only done what any enterprising press agent would have done in his place.

As a result of this outrage, THE PHANTOM OF THE OPERA was boycotted by many exhibitors in England, and the picture was withdrawn from the British market.

It is possible, however, to write a happy ending to this tale of supernatural ill-luck. THE PHANTOM OF THE OPERA has finally reached the screen and is finding favor with the public. It may even turn into a bigger box-office hit than THE HUNCHBACK OF NOTRE DAME.

It is improbable, however, that Carl Laemmle will make any further excursions into the spirit world. Ghosts are cantankerous creatures; they don't like publicity, they shrink from the spotlight.

Ghosts, therefore, do not belong in the motion picture industry.

THE FRESHMAN   **FILM 1925**

"The Screen: Harold Lloyd as a Football Player," Mordaunt Hall, *The New York Times,* September 21, 1925, p. 12.

> With Harold Lloyd, Jobyna Ralston, Brooks Benedict, James Anderson, Hazel Keener, Joe Harrington and Pat Harmon, written by Sam Taylor, John Grey, Ted Wilde and Tim Whelan, directed by Sam Taylor and Fred Newmeyer; Colony Melody Masters; "Campus Capers," a special prologue to the feature. At the Colony.

If laughter really is a panacea for some ills, one might hazard that a host of healthy persons were sent away from the Colony [Theatre] yesterday after regaling themselves in wild and rollicking explosions of mirth over Harold Lloyd's comic antics in his latest hilarious effusion, THE FRESHMAN. Judging from what happened in the packed theatre in the afternoon, when old folks down to youngsters volleyed their hearty approval of the bespectacled comedian, the only possible hindrance to the physical well-being of the throngs was an attack of aching sides.

In this new production Mr. Lloyd burlesques a young college student with athletic aspirations. While it is a decidedly boisterous affair, it is evident that Mr. Lloyd knows his public. He gives them something easy to laugh at, a film in which the authors could not be accused of dodging slapstick or of flirting with subtlety. It is a story which deserved more gentle handing, but there's no gainsaying that the buffoonery gained its end in its popular appeal. Occasionally this jazz jester rubs in the fun by repeating his action, and he also anticipates laughter.

Harold Lamb (Mr. Lloyd) first is introduced as a deserving youth who idolizes the past year's most popular student at Tate College. Harold's father is a rampant radio enthusiast, and in one sequence is deluded into the belief that he has reached some far-distant country, only to discover that what he hears are the odd yells of his college-mad son, who is practicing as a cheer-leader in a room above.

We see Harold prancing around a ballroom in a basted dinner jacket, the tailor not having had time to finish the job. Subsequently the sleeves part company with the jacket and the trousers streak open at the sides. He is a gullible young man and heeds the flattery of the College Cad, with the result that his first appearance in the institution of learning is made unexpectedly on a stage, which incidentally was intended to be ready for the head of the Faculty. A kitten disturbs him in his speech and crawls up his sweater, finally squeezing itself out of the collar of that garment, while the mother-cat, quite concerned about its offspring, takes her stand at Harold's feet.

The most amusing chapter in this stretch of fun is where Harold succumbs to the notion that he is a possible candidate for the football team. He permits himself to be tackled and bowled about by the husky students, and is eventually permitted to sit on the players' bench at the most important contest of the season. Tate's team fares badly, one after another being put hors de combat. The coach observes the ridiculous Harold aching for his chance, but has no faith in the young man who wears his spectacles under his rubber nose protector. Harold's insistence, however, gives him his chances and all sorts of laughable gags follow, one of them being introduced when Harold is warned by the umpire that he must release the ball when the official whistles. Later one perceives Harold clutching the ball, dashing toward the opponent's goal. Suddenly there is a factory whistle. He is five yards from his destination when he halts and throws down the ball.

A number of subtitles in this picture are quite witty. The football field is alluded to as a place where "men are men and necks are nothing." The coach is described as being so tough that he shaves with a blow torch. The college President is said to be so aloof that he won't marry for fear of hearing his wife call him by his first name.

This is a regular Harold Lloyd strip of fun, which is made all the more hilarious by introducing something like suspense in the sequences on the ball field. It is not quite so good as WHY WORRY, and not really as sharp in its humor as SAFETY LAST.

COMMENTARY

THE BIG PARADE by King Vidor (1895-   ) must have been the film which came closest to the average American's conception of what World War I was like. It ran for nearly two years at the Astor Theatre in New York, breaking all records for the continuous run of a film in an American theatre. Vidor had first gained notice for his THE JACK-KNIFE MAN (1920).

STELLA DALLAS was directed by Henry King (1896-   ), whose TOL'ABLE DAVID (1922) had earned him the *Photoplay Magazine* **gold medal for the best film of the year. As Stella's daughter, Lois Moran, an American girl who had appeared in films in Europe, made her film debut at home. (46)**

Iris Barry catches THE BIG PARADE in London, where it is preceded on the bill by the jazz of Paul Whiteman. She is already worrying about how films survive the passage of time.

THE BIG PARADE

"The Screen: A Superlative War Picture," Mordaunt Hall, *The New York Times*, November 20, 1925, p. 18.

> With John Gilbert, Renée Adorée, Hobart Bosworth, Claire McDowell, Claire Adams, Robert Ober, Tom O'Brien, Karl Dane and Rosita Marstini, adapted from a story by Laurence Stallings, directed by King Vidor; special musical score. At the Astor Theatre.

An eloquent pictorial epic of the World War was presented last night at the Astor Theatre before a sophisticated gathering that was intermittently stirred to laughter and tears. This powerful photodrama is entitled THE BIG PARADE, having been converted to the screen from a story by Laurence Stallings, co-author of *What Price Glory?*, and directed by King Vidor. It is a subject so compelling and realistic that one feels impelled to approach a review of it with all the respect it deserves, for as a motion picture it is something beyond the fondest dreams of most people. The thunderous belching of guns follows on the heels of a delightful romance between a Yankee doughboy and a fascinating French farm girl. There are humor, sadness and love, and the suspense is maintained so well that blasé men last night actually were hoping that a German machine gun would not "get" one of the three buddies in this story.

At the outset there is as much fun as there is in a book of [Bruce] Bairnsfather drawings, and yet there is no borrowing from that artist. It is the natural comedy that came to the American troops in France, men who landed in a foreign country without the slightest idea of the lingo. The incidents have been painted skillfully, from the blowing of the whistles as the signal that America had entered the war to the skirmishing attack in a forest. And even in a large shell hole the three pals find something to joke about.

There are incidents in this film which obviously came from experience, as they are totally different from the usual jumble of war scenes in films. It is because of the realism that the details ring true and it grips the spectator. At this presentation there were men who were not easily moved, men who had seen many pictures and were familiar with all the tricks in making them. Yet these men in the lobby during the intermission spoke with loud enthusiasm about this, a production of one of their rivals.

Just as the scenes are as perfect as human imagination and intelligence could produce them, so the acting is flawless throughout. Nothing could be more true to life than the actions and the expressions of the three buddies in khaki. They are just ordinary United States citizens, one the son of a millionaire, another a rivetter and the third a bartender. John Gilbert enacts the part of the hero, Jim Apperson, the scion of a wealthy family. Tom O'Brien figures as Bull, the jovial Irishman who served drinks across a bar, and Karl Dane is seen as Slim, the fearless rivetter. Renee Adoree impersonates Melisande, the bewitching French girl, who falls in love with Jim, her affection being surely and certainly reciprocated by that young gentleman, in spite of the fact that he had left a sweetheart in America.

Possibly the scenes where Jim enjoys his flirtation are more delightful than any other part of the story, because it seems so natural for the couple to be fond of each other. They sit together, Jim, proud of his dexterity with his chewing gum, while Melisande, being ignorant of the jaw-exercising concoction, in endeavoring to imitate Jim, swallows her piece of gum. When Jim wants to tell Melisande of the trouble that affects his capacious heart, he has to resort to a dictionary, and often he inserts English words to emphasize his utterances, as the foreign tongue strikes him as being so inadequate.

Bull and Slim decide that Melisande is too serious minded, too much infatuated with Jim, so they dodge the idea of romance and become extraordinarily practical. While Jim is upstairs with the French family, pretending to listen to the letters that have come from poilus at the front, Slim and Bull are enjoying themselves in the wine cellar, expressing surprise that any man who has such a wonderful cellar should be content to spend any time elsewhere.

Then comes the time when the call of battle tears Jim away from Melisande. There is a big parade—a parade of lorries filled with American doughboys bound for the fighting lines. Melisande clings to the vehicle carrying her Jim, until she falls in the street, pressing a shoe, he has given her, to her bosom.

Mr. Vidor is painstaking in putting forth the best work possible, with all the artistry of which the camera is capable, and it is a touch worthy of any artist when Melisande is seen crouched on the straight French road.

Guns, guns and guns roar during most of the second part of this picture, and yet these chapters are flavored with touches which create laughter, coupled as they are with clever captions. For instance: Word is sent to the three buddies while they are in a great shell-hole that one of them must go out and silence that "toy gun." Who will go is the question. This is smartly settled by Slim, the champion tobacco chewer and spitter of his contingent. He draws a circle on the wall of the hole and says that the one who spits nearest the center will have the chance to go and put an end to the men with the "toy gun." Slim wins easily, as he knew he would, and he drags himself over the top and along the undulating ground, torn with high explosives.

The very lights rend the heavens and he has to duck to save himself from being spotted. Eventually he is seen with gun-butt uplifted and later he crawls out from the mess with two German helmets. The machine guns are popping at him, making noise like a giant tearing calico, and he is wounded. Jim and Bull have to stay where they are, as it is declared that orders are orders. Eventually the two pals go after their friend, and they find he has been "done in."

Jim sees red as he plunges toward the enemy lines, and there follows a striking human incident. He would kill one of the enemy, who is half gone. He is rough with him, but the German asks for a cigarette. Jim has one, only one, in his tin hat. He gives it to the German, who before he has a chance to take a puff breathes his last. Jim looks at the man, and, with that indifference that is bred by war, he takes the cigarette from the man's lips and smokes it himself.

There is the big parade of hospital ambulances, the long stretches of cots in a church, the unending line of lorries, and all that breathes of the war as it was. The battle scenes excel anything that has been pictured on the screen, and Mr. Vidor and his assistants have ever seen fit to have the atmospheric effects as true as possible.

This is a pictorial effort of which the screen can well boast. It carries one from America to France, then back to America and finally to France again. And one feels as if a lot had happened in a single evening.

FILMS 1925   STELLA DALLAS; THE BIG PARADE

"The Silent Drama," by R. E. Sherwood, *Life*, Vol. 86, No. 2249, December 10, 1925, pp. 24-25.

Once again it falls to the lot of this occasionally grateful reviewer to consider, on the same page, two pictures of unusual worth. They are STELLA DALLAS, directed by Henry King, and THE BIG PARADE, directed by King Vidor. It would be hard to imagine two movies more utterly opposite in type: the first is a simple, ultra-sentimental heart-throb story—the other, a spectacular, harsh, raw-meaty and somewhat sardonic drama of that grim travesty, the Great War.

They are both splendid pictures. They are both worth seeing.

STELLA DALLAS deals with that most popular of all emotions, mother love—the same theme that animated such stalwart box-office successes as OVER THE HILL and HUMORESQUE.

The mother of STELLA DALLAS, however, can not by any stretch of the imagination be confused with the gray-wigged, bespectacled, simpering, holier-than-thou old pest who represents the conventional mother on the screen. Stella Dallas is a coarse, gross woman, painfully devoid of the most ordinary social graces, gaudy but not neat—a ridiculous person and an inexpressibly pitiful one.

She had married a lonely young man, an aristocrat by birth, who had rapidly outgrown her and had left her to care for the daughter who resulted from their brief and none too appropriate union. But the father was unwise enough to bequeath to his daughter the sensitiveness and good taste which had been his own heritage, and when the girl grows up, it is evident that she too has soared above her mother's level of drab mediocrity.

The mother, of course, sees this—and the latter portions of the story are devoted to her laborious attempts at self-sacrifice.

In these two roles—of mother and daughter—Belle Bennett and Lois Moran give performances of great beauty. Miss Bennett approximates perfection in her portrayal of crude vulgarity, and Miss Moran is incredibly lovely as a tender, loyal but vaguely distressed little girl. Another rich characterization is entrusted to the reliable Jean Hersholt, and Ronald Colman and Alice Joyce are acceptably good in neutral roles. Frances Marion has done an excellent job on the scenario.

Henry King again demonstrates the directorial genius which dignified his work in TOL'ABLE DAVID and THE WHITE SISTER (and which has been lost, strayed or stolen ever since). He has endowed this story, which might have been fearfully artificial, with a fine sincerity; furthermore, he has devised almost every scene with a considerable degree of technical skill. The high spot of the picture, to me, was an adolescent love scene between Lois Moran and Douglas Fairbanks, Jr., directed by Mr. King with fine delicacy and restraint.

There are just two bad elements in the picture. Miss Bennett's costumes are at times so grotesquely exaggerated as to destroy all the fine subtlety of her own performance. The weird regalia that she wears appear to have been gathered from the costume trunks of an old *Zaza* troupe. It is a harsh note in an otherwise harmonious production.

Then there is the trite ending, in which the mother stands out in the rain and watches her daughter tremble through the marriage ceremony. This same conclusion has been arrived at dozens of times before. It is stale.

I could not detect a single flaw in THE BIG PARADE, not one error of taste or of authenticity—and it isn't as if I didn't watch for these defects, for I have seen too many movies which pictured the war in terms of Liberty Loan propaganda.

THE BIG PARADE is eminently right. There are no heroic Red Cross nurses in No Man's Land, no scenes wherein the doughboys dash over the top carrying the American flag.

This is due primarily to the fact that Laurence Stallings wrote the story, and was allowed to select the director and the most important members of the cast. Mr. Stallings kept his story down to the simplest possible terms, avoiding anything that might remotely resemble a complication of plot, and he displayed remarkable judgment in choosing King Vidor as director, and John Gilbert and Renée Adorée as stars.

For these reasons THE BIG PARADE is a marvelous picture, a picture that can be ranked among the few genuinely great achievements of the screen. The initial credit must go to Mr. Stallings, but the final honors belong to King Vidor, who thus substantially justifies all the loud salutes that, I am happy to say, have been fired in his behalf in this department. He proves here what he indicated in WILD ORANGES: that he is a director of intelligence and imagination.

51. *Renée Adorée as Melisande accepts the courtly gestures of John Gilbert as Jim (in barrel), in King Vidor's anti-war film THE BIG PARADE (1925). To one observer, the film placed Vidor at the top of the list of Hollywood directors, alone with Lubitsch, surpassing Griffith, DeMille, Stroheim and Ingram.*

He has made war scenes that possess infinitely more than the usual spectacular thrill; he has made war scenes that actually resemble war. When he advances a raw company of infantry through a forest which is raked by machine gun fire, he makes his soldiers look scared, sick at their stomachs, with no heart for the ghastly business that is ahead. What is infinitely more important, he causes the sleek civilian in the audience to wonder, "Why, in God's name, did they have to do that?"

He has shown an American soldier, suddenly wild with the desire to kill, trying to jab his bayonet into the neck of a dying German sniper. He has shown the look on that sniper's face, and the horrible revulsion that overcomes the American boy. I doubt that there is a single irregular soldier, volunteer or conscripted, who did not experience that same awful feeling during his career in France—who did not recognize the impulse to withdraw the bayonet and offer the dying Heinie a cigarette.

Although the war scenes are naturally predominant in THE BIG PARADE, the picture itself is essentially a love story—and a supremely stirring one at that. Renée Adorée, who appears for a very short time in the early part of the story, and again at the finish, manages to impress herself so vitally on the audience that her presence, in the dim background, is never for an instant forgotten. Both she and John Gilbert are brilliantly effective.

There is great work by Tom O'Brien and Karl Dane, as two rough and blasphemous but typical crusaders of the A. E. F.; indeed, the entire army that moves forward with THE BIG PARADE is recognizable and real.

It is recorded that when Laurence Stallings went to Hollywood to write THE BIG PARADE, he failed to endear himself to the denizens of that strange community. In fact, he intimated in print that the great majority of them were dim-wits.

This caused all the local mental giants to pray feverishly that Stallings' maiden effort as a photodramatist would prove to be a flop. It seems that these embittered yearnings are not to be gratified.

The movies need some more men who can insult them and, at the same time, produce pictures like THE BIG PARADE.

R. E. Sherwood.

Vidor Leads Directors   1926

Excerpt from "Close-Ups and Long-Shots," Herbert Howe, *Photoplay Magazine*, Vol. 30, No. 1, June, 1926, p. 117.

. . . Speaking of great directors, where are they? King Vidor stands unchallenged in the lists today, save possibly by Lubitsch. D. W. Griffith has gone stale. Cecil B. DeMille is wandering some place in the dark ages with his flash-backs. Von Stroheim is uncertain, Rex Ingram is sunning himself on the Riviera while gaily thumbing his nose at his bosses back here.

Everyone has been given credit for THE BIG PARADE except King, to whom it belongs. True, he had the cooperation of two exceptionally creative players, as well as Irving Thalberg. But it takes a great artist to recognize cooperation. Griffith used to have a circle of original minds from which he took ideas. So did DeMille. So did the lesser chief, Mr. Napoleon Bonaparte. But directors, as well as players, invariably reach the point where they feel they can go it alone. Like the late Kaiser, they murmur—"Me and God."

King remains humble. He has his ideas, but he can accept others.

THE BIG PARADE germinated from a simple idea. Examine the full-grown product and you'll find that the characters and situations make the entertainment. They are gems on an old cotton string. . . .

FILM 1925   THE BIG PARADE

"The Cinema," by Iris Barry, *The Spectator* (London), Vol. 136, No. 5110, June 5, 1926, pp. 946-947.

A great deal of pleasant expectation had been aroused by accounts from New York of THE BIG PARADE before that film actually appeared at the London Tivoli. It was reported to be deeply moving and altogether brilliant. And as it was a war film, wholly, there was curiosity to see how the American motion-picture people think, in terms of war, of what their army, as typified in one doughboy, represented and did.

THE BIG PARADE opened (after a wildly exciting half-hour of Paul Whiteman's irresistible jazz orchestra), and had not run for anything like an hour when one felt disappointment, occasional lassitude and a creeping irritation mingle with one's delight at the incomparable photography, the admirably human acting, and, above all, the technical brilliance of the picture. All the latest and best cinematographic craft has gone to make this BIG PARADE.

There is a peculiar delight in sitting through a play in which every dialectic skill is used—where the aptness of language to express character, emotion, the interplay of thoughts gives one a pure joy. It is not often that one plucks such delights in a cinema. Here—when one sees INTOLERANCE, A WOMAN OF PARIS, CALIGARI, FORBIDDEN PARADISE, VAUDEVILLE [Dupont's VARIETY] for the first time—one rejoices most at innovations, at a new grasp of the medium, at hitherto untried economies or sensational effects. The perfectly polished film—comparable to a play by Racine, Euripides, or Congreve—is still far in the future. The films that thrilled us yesterday with their brilliance and originality are, seen today, flat and uninteresting. The brilliancies and originalities have meanwhile become the familiar stock-in-trade of motion-picture makers. Only Chaplin and occasionally D. W. Griffith at his best wear at all well. Telling a story by pictures is still a craft to be perfected.

But THE BIG PARADE carries the development of picture-tale-telling much further forward and stands out, and will stand out until it is surpassed, most astonishingly. Raw recruits change to full-trained soldiers, without need of any verbal explanations and in very few "mixed" pictures melting into each other. A French girl and an American boy meet, court, and love. The boy is ordered up to the front line: the platoons fall in, lorries pack up, villagers bid farewell, the brigade is on the march, the French girl seeks her American sweetheart vainly everywhere. Hundreds of uniformed figures pass: motorcycles and lorries: more uniforms: she finds him just as his squad are off and they embrace desperately: all this with no titles and no waste of pictures. The camera is like a searchlight picking out from the moving army what it needs. It is new: it is better done than anything has been done before: it is good.

But unfortunately for all this technical excellence and creativeness, the story told in pictures was not worth telling. A tale of America's war-life, a tale of a doughboy and his pal, a tender love-story could all have been worthy of the camera-work and the masterly direction, but these in THE BIG PARADE are cheap, maudlin and foolish. The hero grows weakly sentimental over his dead comrade ("Can't you even say goodbye?"), the heroine behaves like a barnstorming damsel when her American goes to war, and the American army apparently spent its time in France larking, then went out in its "millions and millions," and broke right through the German trenches, irrespective of any of the ordinary observances that govern contemporary warfare. What is more, though a subtitle asserts that the U.S. troops advanced along "roads never retraced," somehow the Germans take a village miles behind the advancing Americans, in order that the hero may temporarily lose his heroine.

It is a pity from another point of view that Metro-Goldwyn-Mayer, the firm that made this film, did not realize that in sending THE BIG PARADE to England, to France, or any   403

Allied country, large sections of their potential audiences there would certainly resent, not so much the natural if childish insistence on the victory-winning value of the American army on the Western Front, but the military improbabilities, the cool, over-patriotic subtitles, and most of all one title in which the hero, chafing at instructions given him under shell fire, cries petulantly "Do men or orders win war?" It has always been assumed that every army, even transatlantic ones, respect and obey orders, and it is rather stupid of the American firm responsible to test the temper of Allied countries with such poor diatribes. That no single French, English or other troops took any part in the War is perhaps the impression of many Americans—the film seems to point this way. But it does nothing for the cause of Anglo-American amity to insist, as THE BIG PARADE does, on this point. Mr. Will Hays might explain this to the film people.

Mr. Bernard Shaw is being advertised widely as having said that he likes THE BIG PARADE because he is a pacifist. This must be a joke. The War was not a great game ending in twenty-four hours of fighting: no film dare show what it resembled. But to say that a sentimental and romantic war-film like this does anything in the interests of peace is madness. It wreathes machine-guns in roses.

COMMENTARY

The chariot race in BEN-HUR was one of the principal responsibilities of Reeves Eason, directorial associate of Fred Niblo, the director. The session described must have come near the end of the approximately four months of work which were devoted to the race sequence alone.

Gilbert Seldes, whose "Letter" urges a revival of popular as well as esoteric films, had already written The Seven Lively Arts **(1924), in which films are one of the liveliest, and was soon to write** An Hour With The Movies and The Talkies **(1929).**

"FORTY-TWO CAMERAS USED ON SCENES FOR 'BEN-HUR' "   1925

"Forty-two Cameras Used on Scenes for BEN-HUR," *The New York Times*, November 1, 1925, Section 8, p. 5.

Hollywood

Most of the Hollywood picture folk recently took a day off to witness the filming of the most expensive motion picture scene on the largest set ever constructed. This was when Fred Niblo made the Antioch Circus chapter for Metro-Goldwyn-Mayer's film version of BEN-HUR, on a tract of forty-five acres northeast of Culver City.

Douglas Fairbanks and Mary Pickford came to watch the work for an hour, they said. So engrossed were they with the stupendous scene that they remained for six hours. Harold Lloyd left his company waiting in the studio while he stood beside Mr. Niblo [the director] in a high tower for something like eight hours. Other stars and directors were there in such numbers and remained so long watching the photographing of the chariot race that virtually no work was done in many of the great studios. To make up for lost time those busy on THE BLACK PIRATE, Fairbanks's new picture, worked until midnight that night.

Some 10,000 extras were on hand, costumed, bearded and bewigged by 9 o'clock in the morning when they took their places in the vast amphitheatre. They were assembled as early as 6:30 a.m., in order to be ready in time. It required an army of costumers, wig and hair experts, armor specialists, hostlers, commissary help and so forth to support the force working before the battery of cameras.

Forty-eight Horses in Mad Gallop.

With this enormous throng at work, with forty-eight horses galloping around the course in the mad seven laps of the great chariot race, with 150 other horses utilized, the scene was made with precision and without an accident. Not a man, woman or child was even scratched, and none of the horses was injured. The police force of Culver City was on hand to help in guarding the scene, the City of Los Angeles sending a reserve force, and the United States Army came to the aid with a hundred soldiers.

Mr. Niblo worked most of the day from his tower, which was nearly 100 feet high. Beside him stood his chief assistant and the head camera man, who had supervision over forty-two cameras at work grinding on that scene. A total of 53,000 feet of negative was "shot" during the day, which will be analyzed, picked from and reduced to less than a thousand feet for the finished stretch.

The great task, which began early in the morning—that of fitting of costumes, wigs and beards—fell directly upon Adolph Seidel, chief costumer of the Metro-Goldwyn-Mayer studio. This man, who has dressed the companies of the Berlin and Vienna grand operas, worked all the night before, and began sending his finished subjects into the stands as early as 7 o'clock.

Wearing costumes in keeping with the groups they had to direct were sixty-two assistant directors, recruited from many studios and rehearsed carefully for days in advance. These men and women worked in the great grand stands, on the enormous spine or center structure and at the entrance.

The first section was that of the fifty-four Roman Imperial Guard members, who rode into the arena on horseback to clear the course of the rabble of several races and nations. This done, these men made a quick costume change and reappeared as buglers. Incidentally, they were all members of Troop B, Eleventh Cavalry, U.S.A., loaned by the commander at the Presidio at Monterey, Calif., and brought to Southern California with their horses and equipment by special train. They were under command of Captain Adamson and Lieutenant Sand. All were of the same height and build; the horses were all thoroughly matched bays.

Meanwhile many were rushing to and from the stands to the betting corner; Sanballat and his tablet were seen hurriedly recording wagers; Sheik Ilderim with Iras and Simonides with Esther were seen in their box, while all about thousands of Romans, Jews, Egyptians, Assyrians and others gesticulated and chattered in anticipation of the great race.

Mr. Niblo gave orders through his megaphone, and his chief assistant relayed these orders over a specially arranged loud-speaker system. The instructions were audible to each assistant in the various sections of the arena. The crowd of guests also heard every order.

In order that there be no conflict in this regard, Percy Hilburn, the camera man in charge, had to fall back on a primitive system—that of using army and navy signal flags. He had a United States Army Sergeant at his elbow to register these signals for the forty-two camera men at different points.

Scene Taken from Air.

When it is known that the main grandstand was over 3,000 feet in length, and that the other portions of the set extended beyond that limit, it can be understood how important were these signals. It was beyond the realm of possibility to carry these directing orders to the men behind the cameras or the crowds in the stands in costume by the ordinary human voice through a commonplace megaphone. Thirteen thousand feet of direct telephone wire was used in main lines on the set during the scene and 12,000 feet

405

of auxiliary wire was used for connecting links. An airplane even flew overhead much of the time to record high and long shots directly down on the crowd.

The buglers blew their final signal, galloped off to the southeast entrance and drove back the rabble of mixed peoples. Huge tapestries or curtains were flung back and out dashed twelve chariot teams with drivers in gay colors and attendants in more sober effects. The teams came on, four horses to each of the dozen chariots. From the entrance and the subsequent lining up for the start both onlookers and the thousands of workers in the picture realized they were due to see expert horsemanship.

Ready for the Race.

The start was almost perfect, save that Ben-Hur was crowded short and off in ninth position. This was correct, as the story of the picture follows that of General Lew Wallace's book, which has him ninth at the start. Francis X. Bushman, as Messala, was off fourth, as called for by the story.

William Donovan with the Greek team of bays took the inner pole quickly and held it for the first two laps. Bushman came up on even terms at the beginning of the third lap and held that position until the fourth, when he went to the front.

The sixth lap was the most exciting. Mickey Millerick, a famous horseman, driving the Esthonian team of roans, caught the inner rail at the south turn and just behind the Roman team. In doing so he crowded the Greek, Sidonian, Circensian and Athenian teams far wide. The first went down and soon the others piled on top of him. There were actual shrieks from the throngs and it seemed that someone must be hurt, and perhaps fatally.

Ben-Hur (Ramon Novarro) had luckily gone wide and escaped the wreck. He went on to get even at the beginning of the seventh and last lap, and then the great incident of the story was enacted. Messala's wheel was torn off and he was smashed beneath his chariot and team. Ben-Hur went on to win easily amid the cheers of the vast crowd.

"A LETTER TO THE INTERNATIONAL ART GUILD" 1925

By Gilbert Seldes, *The New Republic,* Vol. 44, No. 572, November 18, 1925, pp. 332-333.

GENTLEMEN: You were quite right in assuming that I would be interested in your project, and that, as a writer about the movies, I would be happy to assist you. Your program is a general one. You propose to arrange showings, one night a week, I believe, and for comparatively small audiences, of films which otherwise would be forgotten or entirely unshown. There is, as you know, a Film Guild in England, with Wells and Shaw as the most notable sponsors, which has a similar object; and as you are international, you will probably work with foreign organizations and bring us pictures which, whether popular or unpopular abroad, are destined to be locked in some distributor's safe in America.

It happens that I cannot think of the movie except as a popular art or form of entertainment. What you offer, therefore, seems to me most important as a means for making good films more popular. Just as our small theatres have encouraged new dramatists, and given a field for experimental stage-craft, you may prosper inventiveness and imagination in the movies—two qualities they now sadly lack, or are only beginning to develop. You will build up an audience and this audience, eventually making itself felt at the box-office, will bring interesting films to the big and to the neighborhood houses. Gradually the patrons of the movies will be able to see what you now see; eventually, you may hope, these patrons will recover from the somnolence which years of inferior movies have lulled them into. At the same time there will be new things coming up, and you will continually keep ahead, so that the movie may not degenerate.

All this is to the good; but it would hardly explain why, when you asked me to suggest a list of ten pictures which I feel ought to be shown, I sent you such a mixture of sacred and profane. To the aesthete, CALIGARI and THE LAST LAUGH are sacred; possibly CABIRIA also. But why, next to these and two early Griffith films, should I have suggested three Chaplin pictures, two Keystone comedies, and, worst of all, "any good old serial" and "a western"? The old serials and westerns were nearly all badly photographed; the pictorial beauty in them, the sense of form, the whole plastic value, are nearly nil; the subjects are trivial enough. Why place them side by side with the few works of actual imagination which we possess? Why not rather have made room for the "artistic" SALVATION HUNTERS and SHATTERED?

The reason is that if you only keep alive the unpopular and artistic film, you will do less than half your work; I think you will even defeat your ends, unless your ends are purely arty. I suggest these pictures, and could suggest a hundred others, because what is wanted now, desperately, is to keep alive the *popular* film. The film which runs its week or two on Broadway, on Market Street, at Graumann's, or in the Loop, has its little life. If you are some sort of determinist and think that the owners of movie houses are coerced by popular demand, you may assume that these films stay alive until all the people who want to, have seen them. Even so. Within three years you have a new group of patrons; and within five years the good films enrich themselves in memory, so that they can be revisited and old pleasures renewed. It is the blessing of the film that a revival means only unlocking a deposit vault; the risk is not comparable to the risk of a stage revival. And the virtue of these revivals is that they could undercut the popularity of bad new films while the good new ones would only profit by the comparison.

I am aware that only a very few films have been successfully revived. I saw CABIRIA announced about three years ago; at the Capitol in New York I saw THE BIRTH OF A NATION, perhaps four years ago. Fitfully the old Chaplin comedies appear at out of the way houses. A friend of mine who wanted to arrange a private showing of CALIGARI found that there was not a single print of that picture in America; it had lain idle for so long that it was returned to the European owner. But that is precisely where your work can be most effective. While you are creating an audience for new and unpopular things, try to create one also for the old and the popular. Keep the movies all alive.

It would not be a bad thing to do this merely from historical interest. If you are convinced that the movie is an art (without that conviction most of your work will be sterile) think how remarkable your opportunity is to be aware perhaps for the first time in history, of every movement in the development of an art. The cinema museums preserve in their field all that is lost in the older arts. And just as secrets have been lost, processes died out, in the graphic arts; just as we have only to wonder what the music of the Greeks actually was; so we are likely to lose sight of elements in craftsmanship and technique if we do not continually observe the old movies. Because in addition to being an art, the movie is our great American toy and has to show something novel and tricky every week. And as soon as one trick is developed, the old one is taboo. Even if behind the old trick there was dexterity of handling, neatness, perhaps a strain of artistic propriety.

I put these things hypothetically although I am myself convinced that the best corrective to the display and dullness of most of our new movies is to be found in the simplicity and energy of the old. There is a refreshing movement toward resuscitation of the old type of movies; the western discloses itself in the "epics" and "sagas" of the pioneer days; who knows? perhaps we shall have a thriller presently masquerading as a problem play. THE PHANTOM OF THE OPERA advertised an opulence not quite in keeping with the thrillers of the old days, but essentially it was one. The natural course of development is to use the old material with the new intelligence we have of ways of making films, and adapting them to the possibly greater intelligence of the new movie

407

audiences. This development can be made surer, and the field of available material can be substantially broadened, if we continually go back and see what the old pictures did and how they did them.

Chiefly I think the old movies will help the new ones by indicating the superior suitability to the movies of certain types of stories, and by pointing out the greatest of all chances which the movie passed up—I mean the chance of creating a type of playing which shall not be acting and shall be as linked with the mechanism and the limitations of the camera and screen as ordinary acting is linked with the mechanics and limitations of the stage. A type of playing dissociated entirely from the spoken word and from the gesture which accompanies the spoken word was beginning to develop. You see it frequently in the serial picture where everything is related, or grows from, the exaggerated activity of the story, an activity which the screen supremely records. I have noticed that in recent pictures the bane of the close-up is not so fearful; in another dozen years we shall see it properly used. To assure ourselves that Mr. Griffith's discovery (he claims it, I believe) is not necessary to the film, let us look at the early ones in which it does not occur. To get rid of stereotyped gestures (imitated from the stage in too many cases) let us look at the films when the gestures were awkward, but self-developed.

In my list I have included two spectacular pictures, and in this category there are others, of more recent date, which might be substituted. In the hands of a few directors the spectacle has developed nobly; in others it has become an extravagant bore. I put the old ones in because they are good in themselves and because the spectacle is a good thing in the movies. I have added an old psychological film. Do not smile; THE AVENGING CONSCIENCE [1914] is one in a simple way; and in the hope that Mr. Griffith may attend your evenings, I put it in for him to see, as a mute request for him to consider whether he might not do it or a similar picture again. Conscience, like everything else in the movies, must be made visible; here is the proof that there was a time when it seemed possible to do this, in America, in the early days.

The reasons for putting in the Chaplin pictures are obvious; I have added two of my favorite Keystones because they are good and because the comic line seems always to have something to teach its more serious parallel. And for lack of places I have omitted extremely important films. Some drawn comics ought to be preserved (you might even find a Krazy Kat from Herriman's own hand); and some news reels; and any quantity of trick photography. The elements in the films which are fruitful are the ones to cherish; and the artistic movies are only a small portion of these.

Gilbert Seldes.

COMMENTARY

The World Premiere of THE SEA BEAST in New York in 1926 revealed the industry's first try at Herman Melville; it is *Moby Dick* (1851), and a terrible disappointment. John Barrymore had been making films since 1914, and had attracted critical attention especially for DR. JEKYLL AND MR. HYDE (1920). He was always more interested in the stage, however, and usually betrays his lesser interest in films by the performances themselves.

The comedian Raymond Griffith (normally in silk hat) was greatly admired by certain critics, among them, Robert Sherwood and John Grierson. Sherwood preferred this Civil War comedy (HANDS UP) to Buster Keaton's later film, THE GENERAL (1927).

THE AMERICAN VENUS celebrated the Atlantic City Beauty Contest, and introduced an actress, Louise Brooks, who was later to play Wedekind in Germany. Rex Ingram's MARE NOSTRUM, filmed out of his studio in Nice, contained a startling love scene by the octopus tank in an aquarium, which is now missing from prints of the film.

52. Louise Brooks and Ford Sterling in THE AMERICAN VENUS (1926). In her first major role, Miss Brooks was spotted immediately by the reviewers. Later, after Hollywood had made only mild use of her capacities, she travelled to Germany to make two films under the direction of G. W. Pabst.

THE SEA BEAST   **FILM 1926**

"Exceptional Photoplays: THE SEA BEAST," *National Board of Review Magazine*, Vol. 1, No. 1, March-April, 1926, p. 14. (With the permission of the National Board of Review of Motion Pictures.)

Directed by . . . . Millard Webb
Photographed by . . . . Byron Haskins

The Cast

Ahab Ceeley	John Barrymore
Esther Harper	Dolores Costello
Derek Ceeley	George O'Hara
Flask	Mike Donlin
Queequeg	Sam Baker
Perth	George Burrell
Sea Captain	Sam Allen
Stubbs	Frank Nelson
Mula	Mathilde Comont
Rev. Harper	James Barrows
Pip	Vadin Uranoff
Fedellah	Sojin
Daggoo	Frank Hagney

THE SEA BEAST is a stirring melodrama of a whaler's life on the open sea with John Barrymore in the title role and a certain amount of literary tradition behind it. The last of these qualities is derived from the fact that the story is to some extent based upon Herman Melville's *Moby Dick*, for a long time one of the most talked about but not much read of all American novels. But the resemblance between book and picture is none too great when it is considered that in the original Moby Dick, the whale, remains the unconquered hero and that the dour whaler was hardly a matinee girl's idea of a lover.

But the picture shows at its best some real feeling for the sea with a salt water flavor which an Old New England whaling community would appreciate. It shows also something of the vague terror, the haunting fascination of desolate ocean spaces and the lurking terrors of storms or deadly tropical calms when the sea beast challenges man's fragile supremacy over the waves. The old romantic impulse to go to sea which the inlander, deep in the heart of a continent still feels occasionally, will undoubtedly be stirred in many hearts when this picture is shown.

The interpolated love story is not without its charm, with Dolores Costello playing the part of Esther Wiscasset [sic] and giving it not only beauty but the flavor of an old time courtship. The scenes of the whaler's departure from the little New England harbor when the two brothers, Ahab and Derek, are taking leave from Esther and again when they meet in the far off harbor of Surabaya in Java, have the true romantic atmosphere of the sailor and his lass and the sea that always comes between them.

The story of the picture may be recapitulated briefly. It concerns two brothers, both in love with the same girl, who go off on a long whaling trip. The younger brother is consumed with jealousy and in a fit of revenge pushes his older brother out of the boat just as Moby Dick, the fabulous whale, is attacking. The big monster bites off Ahab's leg who, feeling that he has lost the love of Esther through having become a cripple, vows eternal hatred for Moby Dick whom he now hunts relentlessly over the Seven Seas. After many years, during which he is the half insane captain of the whaling ship, he at last

410

finds Moby Dick and succeeds in harpooning him to death. Just before this he has discovered that it was his brother who pushed him out of the boat into the whale's mouth and in the fight that ensues the brother is drowned by falling into the sea. Esther and her father are wrecked and picked up by Ahab's ship and the childhood lovers are reunited.

THE SEA BEAST, aside from its own picturesqueness as a story of life aboard an old fashioned whaler and its authentic atmosphere of the sea, is carried to success largely through the performance of John Barrymore as Ahab. We are quite willing to agree that John Barrymore is a whale of an actor in more senses than one. He is both excellent as a straight actor and his command of convincing make-up is on a level with Lon Chaney's. But his screen work frequently shows a tendency towards exaggeration and an indulgence in virtuosity for its own sake. His registration of pain when his lacerated leg is being seared with hot irons is certainly overdone as regards artistic effect, aside from probably being untrue to the life of those times. So much screaming and contortion would have been greeted with derision by the other members of the crew whose life was such as to inure them to pain. This scene is one of the sensational features of the picture which for the sake of artistry might well have been toned down.

FILM 1926   MARE NOSTRUM

"Exceptional Photoplays: MARE NOSTRUM," *National Board of Review Magazine,* Vol. 1, No. 1, March-April, 1926, pp. 15-16. (With the permission of the National Board of Review of Motion Pictures.)

Directed by ....Rex Ingram
Photographed by ....John F. Seitz

The Cast

The Triton ....Uni Apollon
Don Esteben Ferragut ....Alex Nova
His son, Ulysses...Kada-Abd-el-Kader
Caragòl ....Hughie Mack
Freya Talberg ....Alice Terry
Ulysses Ferragut ....Antonio Moreno
His wife, Dona Cinta ....Mlle. Kithnou
Their son, Esteban ....Michael Brantford
Their niece, Pepita ....Rosita Ramirez
Toni, the mate ....Frederick Mariotti
Doctor Fedelmann ....Mme. Paquerette
Count Keledine ....Fernand Mailly
Submarine commander ....Andre von Engelman

It is nothing new to report that Rex Ingram has produced a beautiful film; this is expected of him by his admirers and he still persists in not disappointing them. The element of beauty is always the basis of his pictures' exceptionability. This beauty is both pictorial and physical—a correct richness of movement against a carefully chosen scenic splendor.

Having gone to the cities of the Mediterranean for the background of his latest film,   411 he has come back with his reels of beautiful, delighting pictures. His screen version of Ibanez's *Mare Nostrum* photographically fills the eye and again satisfies us that Mr. Ingram knows how to point the camera at his scenic material.

Ulysses Ferragut, a Spanish sea captain, is persuaded by the love of Freya Talberg, an Austrian spy, to carry supplies to a German submarine which afterwards becomes the cause of his son's death. He refuses to take Freya away when she is tracked by the police, and sails off leaving her to an inevitable execution. His ship is then attacked by the submarine, which killed his son, and torpedoed, but Ferragut, managing to crawl to the gun at the up-tilted bow, takes one last effective shot at the under-sea boat, which completes his revenge.

The story runs through in an entertaining way despite some sluggish spots, and achieves an effect of serious undertaking on the part of Mr. Ingram. A certain, far-fetched mystery is added to the character of Freya by her close resemblance to a painting of Amphitrite, the sea-goddess, and gives excuse for a rather horrific scene in the Naples Aquarium—the one in which Freya, who is known to the attendants here, with an apparent fascination for death as it is associated in her subconscious with the destroying monsters of the deep, bribes the keeper to stir up a fight between two oc-topuses, and gazes greedily till the end when she falls upon Ulysses with a violent kiss. This is interesting as spectacle, of course; likewise it shows that Mr. Ingram has adhered closely to the Ibanez method of creating interest in some of his heroines by endowing them with the proper modern psycho-pathological tendencies. That the motion picture is beginning to recognize these in its character-treatments indicates that it is progressing in an interest in, and a technique to handle, situations in which subtle psychological values play a part, and is thus enlarging its discernment and scope.

The most dramatic scene of all is at the execution. All the lost hopes cherished by a woman who has tried to serve her country are focused in Freya's last forced effort to present an example of imposing heroism. Jewels, furs and even the unnecessary military grandeur all fit into what seems to her more than just a killing. She is determined to die like a soldier, little realizing till the last minute that a soldier's death is as horrible as anyone else's. Then all the ceremony and heroism fade away leaving only the black holes of aiming barrels. A look of childish, pleading fright comes over her as the officer, with his last grain of nerve, drops the sword and the shots are fired.

At the end we seem for the moment to be on the verge of the old slush when Ulysses is shown, after the ship's sinking, sliding deeper and deeper below the surface into the arms of Amphitrite, or Freya, the goddess and the woman having at this point become symbolically fused. But then it is seen that such an illusion is perfectly permissible in the mind of a man dying in what is supposed to be the most pleasant way, especially one who has been violently kissed by the lady he loves beside a tank of fish. A cut-back to the sea pounding on the rocks makes an effective climax and leaves a thrill which is seldom felt in the time-worn clinch.

MARE NOSTRUM goes a long way toward redeeming two stars. It has taken Alice Terry out of the petted blond class into one where characters are created, and has shown that Antonio Moreno is good for more than the serial-type sheik stuff.

But it is a question whether the alien members of the cast—Mlle. Kithnou and young Michael Brantford, as Ferragut's uncherished wife and son, Mme. Paquerette as the woman head of the Teutonic spys in Italy, and one or two others in minor roles—do not furnish the best understanding of the picture's histrionic needs and bring a training better equipped to meet them.

MARE NOSTRUM's success will lie in its appreciation by those who see deeply enough to recognize a physically beautiful, entertaining and well done motion picture, but not too deep to have a suspicion that Mr. Ingram, by exceptional direction and the ingenuity of some unusual incidences, has saved what, notwithstanding Ibanez, is not

such a very extraordinary story from being a not too ordinary film.

FILM 1926   HANDS UP

"HANDS UP," excerpt from "The Silent Drama," R. E. Sherwood, *Life*, Vol. 87, No. 2258, February 11, 1926, p. 26.

At this particular moment in the history of the Silent Drama, Raymond Griffith leads all comedians in point of ingenuity, imaginativeness and originality. Since he became a star he has appeared in three consecutive pictures—PATHS TO PARADISE, A REGULAR FELLOW and HANDS UP—which are definitely in the sure-fire class. They have all been funny, and they have all been progressive. Griffith seems to have faith in the idea that the best gags are those that have not as yet been used, and he is on a continual voyage of discovery into new fields of humor.

HANDS UP is a Civil War story, in which Griffith appears as a Confederate spy. The most notable and most daring feature of the entertainment is the presence of two heroines, who share every love scene with the hero, and in the end—but it would be a low trick to spoil this refreshing laugh by attempting to explain it in cold, uninteresting type.

Raymond Griffith deserves enthusiastic encouragement. He is flying in the face of movie tradition and getting away with it beautifully. . . .

FILM 1926   THE AMERICAN VENUS

"THE AMERICAN VENUS," excerpt from "The Shadow Stage," *Photoplay Magazine*, Vol. 29, No. 4, March, 1926, p. 55.

(Paramount) This picture has all the elements of motion picture entertainment: an interesting story, excellent cast, good performances, able direction and pictorial beauty.

It is the much heralded picture of the Atlantic City beauty pageant of last year, in which Miss Fay Lamphier won the title of "Miss America."

Miss Lamphier plays a part in this film, but leaves much to be desired in photographic beauty. She won't go far, we fear.

Esther Ralston and Lawrence Gray are so good-looking and full of pep that the romance of the story romps along at a very gratifying rate.

The story is generously sprinkled with gags that are refreshingly simple and quite funny. Watch Louise Brooks, a new face. That gal's there. . . .

COMMENTARY

"Lesser Glories" of the American film, under scrutiny by Iris Barry in London, foretells that these will receive due attention when she forms the important museum collection in New York. Felix the Cat and Krazy Kat were cartoon characters.

Lon Chaney by-passed the use of one eye in THE ROAD TO MANDALAY. In MAN-TRAP, from Sinclair Lewis' serialized novel, Clara Bow caught the eye of the authoress Elinor Glyn, who said she would be perfect in IT.

With Warner Brothers' DON JUAN, which opened in New York on August 5, 1926, there arrived the first of the sound-film systems to become temporarily practical: Vitaphone, confined here to the humble role of providing musical accompaniment. Sound was soon to revolutionize Hollywood, send home most of the foreign actors [the crude early equipment exaggerated their accents], and lead films into "that roar which lies on the other side of silence."

Warner Brothers also got there first with THE LIGHTS OF NEW YORK in July, 1928,   413

advertised as "the first 100 Per Cent 7-Reel 'All Talkie' Motion Picture." In the last years of the decade, Hollywood was chaotic — continuing the production of silent films, and at the same time, trying to improve its "talking" product, which at first was awful.

All the readings in this book pertain to silent films, even when the films in question were, like DON JUAN (1926), SUNRISE (1927) and THE WIND (1928), fitted with mechanical accompaniment. An exception which is barely an exception is THE JAZZ SINGER (1927), having only a bit of song and dialogue.

"THE CINEMA: LESSER GLORIES" 1926

By Iris Barry, *The Spectator* (London), Vol. 136, No. 5097, March 6, 1926, p. 415.

The more intelligent cinemagoers seem to be divided into two; those who go seldom and only when they can be sure of seeing an exceptionally good picture, and those who go frequently to take the bad with the good. The latter, however, are naturally the best informed, because the most experienced, and are able to detect in our peculiarly ill-differentiated and often excrutiatingly managed cinemas certain ingredients which will give them the minor if not the major pleasures.

There are certain constants in any picture programme. There is, for instance, the news reel with its laying of foundation stones, sports events and Cabinet Ministers. One knows certain things about Sir Austen Chamberlain after seeing the Locarno film which otherwise escaped even the most assiduous reader of political news. And there is not only the topical interest of these pictures. Sometimes they are triumphs of camera work. In fact, I should like to express the firm opinion that the English news reel photographers are far and away the best of their craft in this country. Working under immense difficulties they surpass their studio brothers in getting the maximum visual and dramatic values out of events. Particularly in the scenes of a recent royal funeral was the camera-man exquisitely successful, the procession of black-clad servants through a snowy lane was given, by sheer photographic skill, the elements of drama, not of actuality at all.

Then there is Felix and his new relation, Krazy Kat (not forgetting the mouse, Ignatz). Of their rivals Bonzo, Terry and so forth, the less said the better. But Felix is a joy. He is one of those nursery tales which become funnier and more enjoyable the oftener they are told; he is, of course, the Cat that Had an Idea. You can actually see him having it, in the form of dots.

It seemed sad when the old familiar flowers that used to open (often in garish hues) for our delectation years ago disappeared from the screen. However, slow-motion pictures came to take their place and we never tire of the divers falling as gently as clouds into cream-flecked water, the dogs who sail like feathers through the air, the tight-rope walkers whose movements are so gentle that they seem to stand stationary in mid-air. Now the old kind of photography has come back into fashion, the quick-motion kind. The Film Society recently showed one of these marvels of patience, THE LIFE OF A PLANT, in which a nasturtium germinated, grew up, flowered, was cross fertilized, languished, shot its seeds off and died in five minutes. Gigantic on the screen, this plant ceased to have any vegetable attributes and became the most temperamental of creatures, dashing itself about, waving its "arms" like a prima donna in a rage. This fascinating little picture has yet to come to the theatres, but when it does shortly, it will certainly repay a visit to see it, even if there is nothing else noteworthy in the programme.

Constance Talmadge is one of the better-known phenomena of the cinema; all her pictures are light comedy, shapely in construction and wittily conceived. A newer figure is Reginald Denny. His films are definitely delightful and extremely funny, not farces like those of Lloyd and Keaton, but real, light comedy, from which the plaguey humor of dress suits, dance partners and domestic and business life in general is deftly extracted. I warmly recommend WHAT HAPPENED TO JONES and SKINNER'S DRESS SUIT, two of his films now imminent.

A word for Tom Mix again. A man's man is Mix, with his horse and his gun, brooding over the canyons and galloping over the prairies. There is a rapidity of action in all his films which is tonic. He is the absolute hero, outwits his enemies and triumphs over the most impossible odds with the ease of dream life. You can tell by the roars and moans of appreciation which the small boys in the cheap front seats emit that he is appreciated by them as nothing else is. For I recommend the smaller and obscurer of the picture houses to the film lover's attention. They have a way of springing surprisingly good and little advertised pictures on one, and they also teach one how incredibly bad the worst films can be. There is a sort of perverse pleasure to be got out of a really unspeakable film. Joys unknown to the casual frequenter of picture houses are open to habitués who note with glee how many famous stars are shockingly inept. Norma Talmadge and Milton Sills are probably the two worst: Norma Talmadge's film, GRAUSTARK, is a triumph of folly and bathos. But whenever it has been shown, the audience has probably, as a whole, liked it because Norma Talmadge is "popular," and so they will continue to like her, and the young ladies who so selfishly recline their heads on their young men's shoulders just in one's line of vision will always murmur at the end, "Isn't she lovely?"

Iris Barry.

FILM 1926   THE ROAD TO MANDALAY

"THE ROAD TO MANDALAY" and "MANTRAP," excerpts from "The Shadow Stage," *Photoplay Magazine* Vol. 30, No. 4, September, 1926, p. 54.

(Metro-Goldwyn-Mayer) Not so much as a story, but lifted to melodramatic interest by the highly colored performance of Lon Chaney as Singapore Joe, keeper of the toughest dive on the whole China coast. Chaney affects another of those bizarre make-ups. This time he plays a gent with a cataract in one eye, and, to get the effect of the white film over the optic, dropped a dangerous preparation into his eye between scenes. This necessitated short scenes to guard against permanent blindness. Singapore Joe has his good brother, a priest, bring up his beautiful daughter without knowledge of her father. The story doesn't hold water, but you will be impressed by Chaney's work and you will like Lois Moran, as his daughter, and Owen Moore, as the regenerated waster.

MANTRAP

The erudite Mr. Sinclair Lewis should present his gratitude to Clara Bow. For it is Clara's performance, rather than his plot, that makes the film version of his latest novel such fine entertainment.

Undoubtedly, the story was intended to center around Percy Marmount, as a New York divorce lawyer, who goes to the great open spaces to escape women. Ernest Torrence, as a backwoodsman and husband to an ex-manicurist, befriends him. And then Clara Bow steps into the picture as a wife who couldn't make her eyes behave, and runs away with everything. When she is on the screen nothing else matters. When she is off, the same is true.

The backgrounds are perfect for summer—cool and inviting. Victor Fleming's direction is sufficient. But it's Clara's triumph. She is personality and sex appeal plus. . . .

Robert Sherwood on the Silent Drama

"The Silent Drama: DON JUAN and The Vitaphone," R. E. Sherwood, *Life*, Vol. 88, No. 2286, August 26, 1926, p. 26.

DON JUAN

Some press matters issued in connection with the showing of DON JUAN assures us that, in the course of this lengthy film, John Barrymore receives or delivers exactly one hundred and ninety-one kisses.

This figure is probably correct, but it seems extremely conservative to me. Certainly, Mr. Barrymore has established a new record for running broad osculation over the twelve-reel route. As the most celebrated lover in history, he literally leaps from lip to lip, with optional stopovers at each point of interest.

Among the actresses who are favored by his lingering caresses are Estelle Taylor, Mary Astor, Jane Winton, Phyllis Haver, June Marlowe, Helene D'Algy, Hedda Hopper and various unidentified but luscious extra girls.

More darned fun. . . .

DON JUAN has been as liberally panned by the United Brotherhood of Movie Critics as has any picture within my memory. Strain my ears as I might after its New York opening, I could hear no kind word for it from any one.

For all that, I confess that I enjoyed it. The backgrounds are awful, and the costumes grotesque in their inaccuracy; Mr. Barrymore himself is almost as bad, at times, as he was in THE SEA BEAST; the story is dragged out and frequently confused. But the fact remains that DON JUAN engaged my humble interest and provided me with considerable entertainment.

Much of this merit is traceable to good direction by Alan Crosland, and to the efforts of a generally good cast. There is one splendid performance by Nigel de Brulier, and some effective work by Willard Louis, Warner Oland, Phillipe de Lacy and Myrna Loy.

As the father of Don Juan, Mr. Barrymore is his old self. When he steps down a generation into the title role, he becomes the movie Barrymore, with a few flashes of brilliance and a great many glints of supreme silliness.

You may take or leave DON JUAN, as you yourself may choose. I hesitate to recommend either course.

THE VITAPHONE

In connection with the "world première" (as it is fatuously called) of DON JUAN, there was a demonstration of the Vitaphone, a new device for the synchronization of shadow and sound.

There can be no doubt that the Vitaphone is a real triumph. It is as far ahead of De Forest's Phonofilm as the Phonofilm was ahead of Edison's ill-fated Kinetophone (I think it was called that).

The Vitaphone has reproduced speeches, songs and instrumental numbers by Marion Talley, Will H. Hays, Mischa Elman and others. On the female voices, the choruses and the violin solos it is a trifle unsure of itself, but in a solo by Giovanni Martinelli and a ukulele number by Roy Smeck it proved to be extraordinarily impressive.

DON JUAN was accompanied by the New York Philharmonic Orchestra via the Vitaphone, indicating that it will be possible in the future to dispense with orchestras and organists in movie theatres.

Well, I for one will shed no tears. I'm tired of hearing "Hearts and Flowers" during the views of the United States Cavalry riding to the rescue, and "Horses—Horses—Horses" during the tender love scenes.

R. E. Sherwood.

COMMENTARY

These six articles by John Grierson (1898-1972) were one result of the Rockefeller Research Fellowship in Social Science, awarded him in 1924, which brought him from Britain to America for three years to study American motion pictures, press, radio, etc. Grierson's observations during this period [which found him concentrating more and more on film], his excitement at seeing the Russian film POTEMKIN here in 1926, his meeting with Robert Flaherty, and their agreements and friendly disagreements, all led to the documentary movement which he eventually launched in England.

THE EXQUISITE SINNER (1926) is a puzzling case. Josef von Sternberg (1894-1969) had directed it for M.G.M., but the film was not put into release immediately, apparently because there was some dissatisfaction with it in the front office. Von Sternberg says it was entirely remade by another director, but it was reviewed as his own, and Grierson refers to it here as such. This was the film which followed von Sternberg's THE SALVATION HUNTERS (1925), already referred to in my chapter on Chaplin (p. 270), who praised it.

Fairbanks' THE BLACK PIRATE (1926) was filmed in color. THE TOWER OF LIES (1925) with Lon Chaney, and THE SCARLET LETTER (1926) were both directed by Victor Seastrom. THE VANISHING AMERICAN appeared in the fall of 1925.

1926   "THE PRODUCT OF HOLLYWOOD"

By John Grierson, *Motion Picture News*, Vol. 34, No. 19, November 6, 1926, pp. 1755-1756.

Let us get the proper proportions at the outset. Here is an industry which caters to the dramatic needs of ninety million people a week in the United States alone; to the plain people of all the world in the upwards of fifty thousand theatres; to people of different race, rank, religion and culture! It risks a production outlay of $125,000,000 a year and a taxable property of $2,000,000,000 in the process. Very obviously there are two factors determining its life from the start. It faces as nothing before ever did a popular and indeed a universal audience. It cannot experiment too rashly, nor can it lose sight of the plain every-day people to whom it belongs.

Yet the industry (for all the pack it bears on its back) is only twenty-five years old, and the consideration of the cinema medium as a vehicle for serious matters five or ten years old at most. Out of its youthful bowels (somehow, anyhow) it has to produce more than 800 features a year and more than 2,000 short subjects. If the industry is more like a gigantic cabbage than anything else—mostly leaves—who can wonder? Its growth has been forced as no growth was ever forced. Before it had time or occasion to know what it was about, the orders were pouring in and had to be met. The cabbage has scarcely had time to set. To use another metaphor, this great sprawling youngster has been out trying to do a giant's job with its bones still soft. Ninety per cent of the criticism it has met with is due to this fact alone.

But now is the beginning. The cinema industry has to set down and realize how great is its destiny in the modern world, and plan how the quality of its product will be upsides   417 with the quantity. That is what all the present fuss about movies means. It is a logical development.

THE RECORD OF THE YEAR

Of course everybody knows that there are bad movies, and the limitations to human talent will always provide for bad movies. But, remembering the cabbages and sprawling youngsters, the record is fair enough for the year.

Item in drama: THE BIG PARADE, BEN-HUR, THE BLACK PIRATE, THE MERRY WIDOW, THE TOWER OF LIES, THE DARK ANGEL, THE VANISHING AMERICAN, BEAU GESTE.

Item in comedy: THE GOLD RUSH, TRAMP, TRAMP, TRAMP, THE STRONG MAN, HANDS UP, BROWN OF HARVARD.

Item in light farce: KISS ME AGAIN, SO THIS IS PARIS, THE CAVE MAN, THE GRAND DUCHESS AND THE WAITER.

These pictures were all good in some respect or another. They had that extra quality in them of inspiration or of power, which separates a special picture from an ordinary one. But the important thing is this: the list is longer and stronger than ever before. I am not satisfied with it; nobody with any feeling for the destiny of the cinema ought to be satisfied with it; but it does mean that the cinema is pushing its roots deeper. There is a welter of critical nonsense poured into the industry's ears, there is a buzz of fools and falsities, of cheap people and cheaper ambitions in and about it, enough to drive it distracted; but, like Topsy, it goes on growing. Whatever its weaknesses, it has a constitution.

The development has been along the line. The talents are riper, the plans larger, the themes more ambitious, the handling more powerful.

DEVELOPING TALENT

Here is Chaplin with his GOLD RUSH, a step ahead of the old Chaplin. The picture has moments of weakness and a bad ending, and it is not without stray elements of slapstick, but Chaplin's pyrotechnics on the borderline between tragedy and comedy are profounder than before. Langdon goes on developing his talent amazingly. "The Christian Innocent" has graduated into a full-size role and THE STRONG MAN is better than the TRAMP, TRAMP, TRAMP of a moment ago. Raymond Griffith, with his HANDS UP, starts a vein of impudent irony that will land him, if he keeps to the sticking point, in a world with George Bernard Shaw. Lloyd retains his excellent sense of craftsmanship.

Among the actors, new faces and new names. Among the directors, old talents developing still, and new ones shooting the cinema sky to pieces. Lubitsch, subtler than before in SO THIS IS PARIS; the small town comedy Cruze better than ever in MARRY ME; von Stroheim less lugubrious, if not so strong, in THE MERRY WIDOW; King Vidor with his BIG PARADE; St. Clair with his GRAND DUCHESS; Donald Ogden Stewart getting a fresh touch of nose-thumbing comedy into BROWN OF HARVARD. People from the other side, arriving with reputations already made: Murnau of THE LAST LAUGH, Dupont of VARIETY, Stiller, and others. There is no end to the happenings if one is in a mood to be generous.

What has been stirring in the industry chiefly is ambition. Only a moment ago one was satisfied with a program picture; now nothing will do but that vague thing called a "special," a picture which will grip the imagination and take hold. The drive for specials has been fevered and fitful but has accomplished some things for a beginning. It has brought about one or two great pictures (too few) and it has made so many nearly-great, that almost anything can happen if the drive goes on and gathers momentum.

53. Alverna (Clara Bow) attempts to stir up the party in MANTRAP (1926), made from a minor Sinclair Lewis novel. It was this appearance that led to her performance in IT, written by that magnetic novelist Elinor Glyn.

WHY SO MANY NEAR-GREAT PICTURES?

It is at this point precisely that the problem of criticism arises. One must sympathize with the industry and even be generous with it, as with a youngster whose respon- sibilities are too great for his young shoulders, and whose brain has not yet had time to put away undeveloped attitudes. But it has arrived at a point where the most important thing is that it should get clear about itself. It is trying hard. All this continuing and accumulating fuss, the noise of the critics, the hectic plotting and planning of the producers, the feverish hunt for inspiration and guidance from authors and artists and even (it seems) social psychologists—is the sign and symbol that it is realizing its destiny and trying to understand it.

The main problem of the whole industry is the problem I stated a moment ago. With all its efforts the product of Hollywood consists of two or three great pictures, a bunch of nearly-great pictures and a mass of average or worse than average pictures. The problem is to have more of the nearly-great pictures actually great. The problem is to define their weaknesses and to have them stated brutally.

After a year's wanderings in the infield and the outfield of the movie world I find this "nearly great" business more annoying than anything else. Why are there so many pictures good one moment and bad the next? Why are so many huge cinema effects spoiled by hokum emotions? Why are so many great themes spoiled by moments of vulgarity and cheapness? Why are so many pictures plainly unequal?

GOOD THINGS ARE NOT-SO-GOOD

The questions are fair questions when you think of it. There were three obviously great pictures over the year: THE GOLD RUSH, THE BIG PARADE and THE MERRY WIDOW. These were inspired, and they held their grip to the end and they left that glow in the spectator which only great drama gives. Other things too were in their way perfect. Harold Lloyd is a fine craftsman and his stuff is always equal. Lubitsch's work or Cruze's work is always equal. St. Clair's work in THE GRAND DUCHESS was equal. The loveliness of Flaherty's work in MOANA and of von Sternberg's work in THE EXQUISITE SINNER continued from the beginning to the end. But consider the others. Think of how THE BLACK PIRATE was spoiled by its pretty-pretty drawing-room atmosphere and by those underwater pirates who were more like fairies. Think of that vulgar and impossible dinner scene in THE DARK ANGEL, of the hokum plot that desecrated the wonderful setting of MEN OF STEEL, of the aeroplane slapstick which spoiled the gentle satire of A REGULAR FELLOW. Or, ask yourself why THE TOWER OF LIES was not another VARIETY, or why THE SCARLET LETTER was not another VARIETY. They had the stories, but they lacked the continuing nerve, the continuing abandon, the continuing smash of vitality that put the big things over.

I am going to illustrate my point more fully with an example. I believe that by all the laws of cinema, THE VANISHING AMERICAN might have been with THE BIG PARADE and THE GOLD RUSH, one of the great pictures of the year, one of those pictures that make the world of cinema a roaring place to live in. We know it was not.

SAD CASE OF THE VANISHING AMERICAN

THE VANISHING AMERICAN had only an average foundation to build on: In its primitive Zane Grey version, it was a simple Western. Paramount, however, worked on the story, magnified it, and for a moment it looked as though it would prove a far greater picture than THE COVERED WAGON. For a moment only, however; in the end it drooped and fell, and what greatness there was in the picture fell with the rest of it. THE

VANISHING AMERICAN, like the Indian it recorded, started magnificently and finished miserably.

Yet THE VANISHING AMERICAN had a great story; there is no greater story than the passing of the Indian. And it had a love theme; the impossible and tragic love of an age-old Indian for a twentieth century white girl is a great love theme. Then think of the setting: the picture had the desert, the canyons and the plains to conjure with. It had the night rain-gods and the night luck-gods to conjure with.

It began finely. The Valley of Vanishing Men took hold of the spectator and gripped him from the beginning. The primitive races came out from the rocks, they built their cave houses, they fought and were beaten. The Indians rejoiced in their victory; the Spaniards came and the horses and the muskets; the advancing American of the new era came, and the soldiers, and the artillery. That was noble stuff. There was something of the wilderness of space and of the infinity of time written on it, that took one's breath away. The whisper of the winds of history was on it.

HAMLET AND THE VILLAGE MAIDEN

But something failed at that moment. The last episode was the twentieth century story of how grafters took advantage of the Indian and stole his lands and how the twentieth century Red Man ([Richard] Dix was amazing) loved the little schoolmistress. But how cheap and how trivial they made that story! The punch of the picture faded, the dignity of the theme vanished, the story lost the atmosphere of the valley and the sense of fate and became like any other story of gentle, gentle heroines and nasty, nasty villains. Dix did a grand job; he caught the spirit of the thing and lived and died like a god; but he hadn't a chance.

How could he have a chance? What sort of drama can you get into a love story when the heroine is just another of these Hollywood smilers, just another of these Hollywood schoolmistresses who are good and kind to the school children in the goodest and kindest way, but haven't any other significance in the world? And how can you get dignity into a love theme when you have this Hollywood smiler treating a magnificent fellow like an imbecile, sitting him down on the floor to tell him how once upon a time, long, long ago in the village of Bethlehem, etc., etc. . . . ? Especially in these days of Indian universities. How can you keep the audience from being diappointed when the director hasn't the courage to let the love story run its course? You say it is impossible and tragic that a magnificent red man should love a little Nordic, but let that be the story. Say it is true that east is east and west is west, but let that be the story. What happened, however, was that the director flunked. Dix was not permitted to make love to the lady at all except by innuendo, by bringing along flowers and calling the lady "little white rose," etc., etc. And in case of trouble, a nice American army officer was held in the background as a standby, so that when the great American vanished, a very average Hollywood schoolmistress should have a fade-out under the moon. Who cares a damn if the real story is about the Vanishing American? It is like finishing *Hamlet* with the kiss of a servant girl.

WHOSE THE RESPONSIBILITY?

These are not the only daggers that slew THE VANISHING AMERICAN. But they will serve for illustration of the kind of blow that kills. The weakness of THE VANISHING AMERICAN is the weakness of Hollywood. Too often it does not hold to its theme, or it does not realize the logic of character. And far too often it lets dignity slip through its fingers into the gutter. There are, I believe, many reasons for this. Sometimes the fault is not Hollywood's. I don't believe the weakness of THE VANISHING AMERICAN was Hollywood's fault. Paramount bought a second-rate story and failed in a brave effort to

421

turn it into a first-rate story. The element of hokum was there to dog the picture from the start.

But often, it is decidedly Hollywood's fault. There are too many cooks and they spoil the broth. They don't pull together. A picture has to be a composite effort, granted, but the spirit of co-operation is not developed to the point of producing consistently good things. Then again, people are too haphazard in the making of pictures, too scrappy. Above all, they are not serious enough about their job. They are energetic enough, but in the real sense of the term they are not serious enough.

These matters (and the remedy) I shall develop in my second article.

"THE INDUSTRY AT A PARTING OF THE WAYS" 1926

By John Grierson, *Motion Picture News*, Vol. 34, No. 20, November 13, 1926, pp. 1842-1843.

The growing need in the movie industry is an atmosphere of genuine criticism. The industry is at a parting of the ways. It is seeing itself in a new light, as having a destiny which demands larger plans and greater ambitions than it dreamed of ten years ago. It is trying to get a new sense of itself and to realize its true proportions. And it needs all the help it can get from the critics (within and without) if it is to accomplish its task.

The industry has kept pace in some respects with the growing interests of people all over the world in matters cinematic. It has realized that the modern masses have come to depend more and more on the cinema theatre as their one continuing and habitual place of entertainment and release. The industry has catered to the greater demand as well as it knew how.

The producers have realized roughly that people wanted something more than mere invitation and entertainment in their cinema theatres. The notion of "bigger and better pictures"—the distinction between mere program pictures and "specials" indicates a feeling for the larger needs of the public. The producers, however, have never gone very intelligently into the question of what makes a "bigger and better picture" or what makes a "special." They have been haphazard often, and stupid often. They have mis-estimated petty pictures and thought them great (Laemmle's opinion of HIS PEOPLE is a case in point). They have thrown away great pictures by vulgarizing and pettifying them with hokum. They have imitated big successes like THE COVERED WAGON without realizing at all what made pictures like THE COVERED WAGON big. And they have naturally failed.

THEATRES OFTEN TOO GOOD FOR PICTURES

The industry has been far more sensitive in the matter of theatres. The highbrows may complain about the vulgarity of some of the deluxe theatres (they are as over-decorated sometimes as an old lady with a past), but the deluxe theatre was the first big idea that came to the cinema world. It showed that the industry was getting a sense of its own importance; it gave promise that sooner or later the industry would get a sense of its own dignity. There is much in knowing how big you are, and more still in believing how great you can become.

Walking over the great red carpeted spaces of some of these deluxe theatres, one can forget for a moment the "business angle." The people of this modern maelstrom needed a great scarlet carpet to walk on. In these days of dolls' houses and miniature vestibules, they needed a great entrance hall where they could feel good. It made the weekly visit to the cinema theatre something of an "event." In this higglety-pigglety modern world, half organized and wholly distracted, people needed "events."

Yet I think the big theatres have dislocated the cinema world for the moment, and I have a mind to say that the pictures are not good enough for the theatres. Too often I have been ushered into one of these great palaces like a princelet, and mounted the great staircase like a modern Jacob, only to find the picture so trivial that I had to unusher myself and descend five minutes after. The hospitality was excellent, the meal terrible. The mountain was laboring hugely and giving birth to mice.

THE SMART YOUNG MEN

I have felt the same disproportion in another field of the industry. I made a zig-zag voyage to Hollywood, and my zig-zag way took me to theatres and distribution centers all over the country. There, if you like, was the unadulterated "business side" of the industry. It was in touch with the people, and was in the business of serving the people. Now when I think of the really big side of the industry I think of neither the directors nor the producers. Their job is more exacting certainly, and they ought to receive more latitude from a critic. But my point is this: the movie managers and the salesman were a deal more efficient in their job than the production people were in theirs. The salesmanship was better as salesmanship, the showmanship was better as showmanship, than the direction of pictures was as direction. In fact, these smart young men out and about the country were more energetic and original, they were more preoccupied with their work and had a more complete command of it than the people in Hollywood. The Hollywood people were playing all sorts of futile side games and (I suspect) getting vain on the job and too blown up with easy reputations to put their backs into big and ambitious things.

HOW SET THE STUDIOS ALIVE?

This criticism is commonplace. The producers themselves are coming to be painfully aware of this great disproportion within the industry. They realize (to put the matter in an extreme form) that the movie industry is a Fifth Avenue store selling Fourteenth Street bargains, and they are getting concerned about it. They feel, as I have noted already, that the logical urge of the industry at the moment is toward greater films. The emphasis of interest has come off theatres and is going on to production. The producers are all for intensifying and deepening the world of production. They are all for setting the studios right. I may be wrong, but there is something almost feverish about Famous Players' hankering after new blood and new energy in the creative field.

But how? The only thing that will set the studios alive is an atmosphere of genuine criticism, an atmosphere of discussion: talking about pictures and analyzing them, plotting, planning, thinking, dreaming twenty-four hours of a day, if need be, in terms of cinema. It is all very well to have turned out a good picture and to have made a pretty reputation and earned a lot of money, but that is scarcely an excuse for getting comfortable on the job and lying around on the cushions of flattery and self-conceit. I fear me, there is too much of that in the production end of the cinema world, and it saps its strength more than anything else.

A HUNDRED MILLION MUST PARTICIPATE

I know an atmosphere of genuine criticism, one that will really help the industry, is a tall order. Where begin? What are the essentials, the fundamentals?

The very first thing to realize is that all productions, certainly the big ones, must be popular productions. The movie world is being jostled and crowded just now by the highbrows, and while highbrow criticism is often helpful when properly diluted and reapplied, it is at the moment doing far more harm than good. For two reasons. (a) It is

423

prompting wrong themes, themes that can only have a specialized appeal. (b) It is spreading a contempt for the dramatic sentiments of the masses.

Now, the problem of the producers is really a simple one. It is to realize how widespread is their world of spectators. It is to realize how simple and fundamental are the dramatic needs of the world crowd which goes to the cinema. It is to take universal themes, or themes as universal as may be, and give them a simple, strong, dignified treatment. Let the treatment be ever so brilliant, let the kick and the flash of the treatment be as powerful as energy and inspiration can make them, but in the end the world crowd (a hundred million of them) must participate in the story, belong to the story, and the story must belong to them. That was always the way with the great popular stories, the great simple stories that commanded men, and they are the best stories.

THE HARMFUL HIGHBROWS

In fact, one must begin, not by despising this world crowd which makes up the audience in the cinema but by believing in it. One must believe that a simple story can be made great, that a simple story does not necessarily mean a collection of hokum. One must believe that this world crowd's demand on the cinema is profound, for all its seeming crudeness and simplicity. That way lies the true future of the cinema. It must forget the special pleas of the little, specialized culture groups. It belongs to the people as no other social institution in the world before. It is the only genuinely democratic institution that has ever appeared on a world wide scale. It is the Internationale of sentiment and emotion.

But listen to the critics. Hicks, they call this world public, lowbrows, cripple wits, sex-seekers. The London *Times* vies with the *American Mercury, Harpers* with *Vanity Fair*, to encourage the movie producers to despise their people. Unfortunately, Hollywood listens. A score of times in Hollywood, I found it affecting men's judgments and spoiling their efforts. I would ask some director about some particularly bad piece of work, ask why it was there when it was quite obvious the director could do better. "Oh," the director would say, "you've got to for the crowd, you must put in the hokum." In fact, the attitude of contempt has paralyzed some of the directors. It gives them an excuse for bad work, it allows them to go easy and save themselves trouble, it enables them to substitute automatic anyhow-work for genuine powerful work.

FOR BETTER OR FOR WORSE

I would say this: so long as the theme is simple and understandable and near to the heart, there is nothing too good and too dignified for the public. If THE BIG PARADE has a lesson for the producers, it is just that. It is a simple thing, treated with honor and dignity.

An atmosphere of genuine criticism must begin with the actual conditions of the movie industry. You must say: here we are with this world public for better or for worse: what can we do with it? Just because the cinema industry is what it is, an institution for the millions, it simply cannot play the hole and corner games of the drawing rooms and the cultural talking shops. It belongs to the strange and primitive animal with lusts in its body and dreams in its eyes which we call the mob.

DISCUSSION OF TECHNIQUE NECESSARY

This opens up the second aspect of genuine criticism. Having got the necessity of making things simple and fundamental into our heads, the job is to get a kick and a flash into the treatment. That is where discussion of the ways and means of cinema dynamic

424

comes in. That is where discussion of technique comes in, discussion of tempo, composition, screen metaphor and a host of other things. There is too little of it. The newspaper critics might help, but they are too busy gossiping. Of the more ambitious critics I can think of only two or three who have contributed something practically helpful. Taken as a whole, the critics have left the industry in the lurch. They have cursed aplenty, but they have seldom contributed an analytic understanding of the medium that might help directors in their work. So bad and unhelpful has been the criticism of movies, that nearly all the credit for the development of the cinema as a medium must go to the industry itself. That development, heaven knows, has been haphazard and accidental enough. With an atmosphere of clear thinking it would have been much greater.

THE CUSHIONS OF COMPLACENCY

The worst of it is that Hollywood does not step in and do its own thinking. It progresses, it adds something here and something there, and the movies get better, but there certainly isn't a wind of critical thinking that would blow their stars away. Hollywood takes life easily. I had imagined that I would find there a set of adventurers, men young and eager in a young and eager popular art, working by day and planning and plotting by night, seizing like young eagles on every new method, analyzing, developing, asking themselves questions at all times, why this was good, why this was bad, and how the good might be better. But not on your life! The limousines flashed on the boulevards, and the sun was hot and flannels were white, and everything was for the best in the best of all bourgeois worlds. Reputations were easy and money was easier, and men grew soft on their unexpected wealth and hung around in the purple livery of perfect content. They were good fellows and largely inclined to say pretty things to each other. I missed something. I missed the fever that goes with creative work. I missed the appetite for criticism that goes with ambition. I suspected that instead of craving discussion and asking always for more, they discouraged it, were frightened for it. I suspected, in the end, that they were often not so much concerned with making the cinema great as with serving their own private interests. I talk generally and there are great exceptions like Chaplin, Fairbanks, von Stroheim, von Sternberg, King Vidor, [Harry] Langdon, Raymond Griffith, John Gilbert and others. But I found far too few with ambitious ideas. And worse still, I found that these men were inclined to keep their ideas to themselves. There was no steady atmosphere of critical discussion that was worth more than a nickel or two to the future of the industry.

This it is that must be righted.

1926 "WHAT MAKES A SPECIAL"

By John Grierson, *Motion Picture News,* Vol. 34, No. 21, November 20, 1926, pp. 1933-1934.

Why is THE BIG PARADE a greater picture than BEN-HUR? Why is BEAU GESTE, which started out as a simple mystery story, more satisfying than THE VANISHING AMERICAN, which started out as an epic? Why was VARIETY the most surprising Broadway hit of the year? Why is GREED for all its sincerity of treatment and greatness of direction a failure with average audiences, and should we get pessimistic about its failure? The function of helpful criticism is to answer such questions, and give producers a proper understanding of what makes for greatness in a picture and what makes for success. Greatness and success are equally important. Despite the evidence of GREED, they are not mutually exclusive.

425

There are two understandings necessary in the world of cinema. The first is the understanding of what makes a big theme, a gripping theme, an entertainment-plus theme. The second is the understanding of how to put over the gripping theme, how to make the story take possession of the many millions who see it. The reception of the pictures I cited will serve to illustrate how necessary both are. BEAU GESTE was a picture with a fair theme (it was almost a great theme), but it was given powerful treatment. THE VANISHING AMERICAN had a magnificent theme, but it was given poor treatment or at best mixed and unequal treatment. VARIETY had an average theme, but the treatment of it was brilliant. GREED, with all the greatness of its direction, had a theme that was bound to be unpopular; it presupposed a sophisticated analysis of life. BEN-HUR had no clear theme at all, and its pretentious treatment was everything by starts and nothing long. Only THE BIG PARADE came near to having both requisites: a clear, simple, universal and dignified theme, and a powerful treatment.

I shall explain first what I mean by a simple, universal and dignified theme, and in subsequent articles consider treatment under such headings as tempo, visual composition, screen metaphor, etc.

THE ROLE OF THE CINEMA

No one can understand this matter of theme (as no one can understand what movies are all about) who has not a sense of the world public which the cinema serves, and who does not comprehend the role that the cinema is coming to play in the modern world. The world public involves so many people, so many average people, that themes have to be universal themes, stories of fundamental and (in the high sense) common emotions. The movie theatre is coming so much to be the one place where the average people of the modern world have their imaginations fired, that these simple and common stories should be as strong and inspiring as art and artifice can make them. The modern public, now that so many of the old dream places are passing out of its life, is coming to depend on the cinema for its deepest imaginative experience.

The modern multitude craves a release from the everyday as all other multitudes did before it. It craves participation in a world where dreams come true, where life is more free, more powerful, more pungent, more obviously dramatic. That is the common and continuing craving of the average mind (or the average mood) at all times. It craves mythical figures (ideal figures, significant meaningful figures) whose fortunes and successes it can identify with its own. It craves the knowledge (or the illusion) that people like oneself can also be wonderful and that a life somewhat like one's own can also be great. In the meanwhile the old folk worlds, the worlds of established heroes and familiar romances, are so dead and so distant that the multitude has lost touch with them and the imaginations of average people are without a sticking point. The modern world rooted up more than the fields and cut down more than trees. The old dream paths and the old dream places have been submerged.

THE PRECIPICE OF THE PRIMITIVE

The cinema theatre, as I suggested, is fulfilling this great need of the modern populace for a place to dream in. It is not so much a mere place of entertainment as an institution integral to modern society. It is already much more important than the theatre, and almost as important as the theatre once was to the people of Athens, for the world of cinema has a special relation to its public. It is an ideal world for capturing the imaginations of common people. It is visual, it is silent, it is non-intellectual, it can capture the vivid simplicities of romance and adventure as no medium ever did before. It can idealize, it can mystify, it can make heroes really heroic, it can haunt the great spaces and walk on the precipice of the primitive.

426

These things men will always love, because men in their everyday mood are incurably simple and unsophisticated. They don't want an intellectualism like Shaw's and they don't want a haggard realism like von Stroheim's in GREED. They don't want a play of ideas, they don't want a devastating and lugubrious account of everyday miseries; at least they don't want them as a regular diet. They want stories of those simple interests which are nearest to their hearts, and which make them feel good and brave; they want stories of beauty, ambition and achievement.

ULTIMATE VIRTUES

They want to believe too that the simple emotions they understand are somehow profound emotions; they would have them set in great and glorious places. The setting cannot be too grand for a simple story of love, or for a simple story of courage. The greater the setting, the greater it seems is the love and the greater is the courage. If the mystical atmosphere of the unknown or the uncertain communicates itself to the simple theme, all the better. If the width of the plains and the height of the mountains and the breadth and the depth of the sea become the dimensions of the simple emotions, all the better. The winds of the unknown and the dimensions of the great places are peculiarly dear to the common heart. There men display more plainly those ultimate virtues which the affairs of civilization tend to conceal. The common heart is peculiarly concerned with ultimate virtues. Courage above all things, simple strength, power to achieve, honor, ultimate manliness: these are the stuff of its admiration. Perhaps ninety per cent of the power of the cinema over its people lies in the fact that it is the medium most suited to recording such things. It is the only medium which can adequately and simply record the dimensions of the great places.

Finally, it is of the essence of this commonday mind that it dreams positively; it has small concern with tragedy, and does not enjoy thinking of demoralization and destruction. It dreams steadfastly of better things and never stops sadly or cynically to analyze the misery of the actual. GREED hadn't a chance as a popular film. Vividness was in it, but not the brightness, not the breath of honor nor the simple splendor of life which the populace wants continually to be reminded of. VARIETY with its sordid theme had a brightness and a gaiety in its movement, a kick and a flash of originality in its lovemaking, which carried it over; at least on Broadway. The camera, in the last instance, must make the world it shoots, a dazzling place.

THE THREE ESSENTIALS

The successes and failures of the cinema world may seem more explicable now in the light of what I have said. The points to emphasize if one is talking of "specials" are these:

1. The theme must be simple, it must be near to men's more primitive and common interests.

2. The theme must be positive rather than negative: it must refer to achievement, not to failure.

3. It must take people away from the pettiness of everyday life. It must be a significant theme with something of the atmosphere of distinction and fate, it must smell of ultimate things. The setting must be heroic.

THE BIG PARADE had all the qualities necessary or nearly all. From some points of view the ending was trivial, but the essentials were fine. In the tremendous atmosphere of war a boy loved a girl, nothing more, nothing less: the theme simple, the setting heroic and huge: the whole thing done magnificently so that the love and the heroism and the hugeness recorded itself indelibly.

427

THE CONFUSION OF BEN-HUR

BEN-HUR, on the other hand, had no clear theme at all. Again a boy loved a girl, but spasmodically. He saw her, he forgot her. There was no great reason that they should come together, there was nothing in particular to hold them together. The hero and the heroine were two dolls who went through the usual Hollywood flipflap of mutual interest. There was nothing grand, nothing of fate or of destiny, nothing inevitable and dramatic about their love. For the life of me I cannot remember if Novarro ever kissed the lady. If he did, there certainly wasn't one fundamental gesture attached to the episode.

This, however, was not the main theme of BEN-HUR. There was a second: a story of rivalry between two men interlaced with the general hatred of Roman for Jew and Jew for Roman. This in turn was bound up with the story of Christ. The boy hoped that Christ was the great King come to deliver the Jews from bondage, only to find that Christ's kingdom "was not of this world." The theme so stated was a great theme, the setting tremendous: oppression, rivalry, hatred, revenge, the hope of emancipation and that defeat of Christ which was also triumph. But did it come over? Not simply, nor greatly. The boy was no Monte Cristo in the hugeness of his hatred and the magnificence of his revenge. The hatred was not piled up until it became a colossal and tremendous thing. The will for emancipation was not nurtured till the whole hope of the race shown through it. The atmosphere of the Christ story was not woven in as something inevitable and necessary to the story.

SECOND-HAND GESTURES

Simplicity, clearness (or lucidity) and hugeness were lacking in BEN-HUR; the story was mixed, the setting failed of its purpose. There was some colored spectacle (too consciously arty and unnatural to be really impressive) and there were two great episodes: the slave ship and the chariot race. These latter belonged to the big world, but the story did not take hold, it did not possess the audience, it was something they looked at, not something in which they participated. How could they participate when they did not see what the issue was? There must always be an issue, a simple noble issue with which people can identify themselves. And how could they get excited when the story was not told with any feeling for freshness and originality. The slave ship and the chariot race were good, but the rest was a sequence of second-hand gestures and second-hand episodes. The spectator had seen their like a million times. The boy approaches the lady in the time-old way, snaps his fingers in the villain's face in the time-old way, struggles with his captors and vows theatrical vengeance in the time-old way. The villain tosses his head and snarls and smirks and sticks out his chest in the time-old way. The heroine simpers and plays around with white pigeons in the time-old way. Not a variation.

BEAU GESTE

I could go on giving instances. Consider for contrast the simplicity and strength of the central theme of BEAU GESTE. Here was a film of quality, not quantity, and though quantity may earn money for a time (BEN-HUR and MARE NOSTRUM are quantity films) it is quality that wins finally. It is quality that gets under people's skins and makes them remember. The theme that caught in BEAU GESTE was the loyalty of the three brothers under the tyranny and brutality of their officers. Both elements were transcribed simply and vividly without affectation of any kind. The sweltering sun and the mad stand in the desert made them all the more elemental. If ever purely cinema values had a play it was here. The elemental atmosphere of the desert heat and the desert spaces, life on the edge of the unknown, the fundamental emotions of hatred and

54. *Lon Chaney appears with relatively little disguise as Alonzo the Armless in Tod Browning's "unadulterated shocker," THE UNKNOWN (1927). It could be argued that this is the most disquieting of Chaney's surviving films. The girl is Joan Crawford.*

affection, courage and sacrifice, were present. There was, however, an ultimate weakness in BEAU GESTE which not even the great scenes could overcome. Colman did not single out so that people might attach themselves to him and travel with him. (The third brother almost did.) The mystery of the blue water and Mary Brian were stray elements that did not belong to fate. They were not worthy of the great scenes and primitive feelings in which the real part of the picture was centered. The picture had its elements of shoddy. My curse is not on the director but on the author. As in too many cases the director was bigger than the author. To let loose the whole immensity of human greatness (as BEAU GESTE for a moment did) in the name of a sapphire (and Mary Brian) was a disproportion too obvious to be quite satisfying. The picture failed to scale the biggest heights because of it and it had the wherewithal to scale almost anything. A picture is like a chain: it is no stronger than its weakest link. And you cannot make big stuff with missing sapphires and hidden hands or with meaningless women: they are too flimsy to be associated with elementals. The Renée Adorées are worth the noise. They stand up to it and contribute something. They actually seem for a moment the stars for which men might fight, and these are the only stars worth talking about.

Elemental non-sophisticated themes, simple, lucid and pungent themes developed with strength and dignity, elemental non-sophisticated themes of courage, love, sacrifice and achievement caught in the roar and swing of great settings: of war, of adventure, of the plains, of the city: these are the stuff of the big pictures.

NOTE ON VARYING AUDIENCES

There are certain differences between audiences. The German mind is not the same as the American mind and the Russian mind is identical only with itself. The sense of drama (whether it involves story, acting or treatment), is different in each case. The European mind probably has a more developed sense of tragedy than the American. The American mind has certainly a better sense of pure comedy and a better sense of epic.

COMMENTARY

At the time that Grierson was writing these articles, Eisenstein's POTEMKIN had still not been shown publicly in the United States.

Charles Brabin, husband of Theda Bara, had directed DRIVEN (1922), and had begun BEN-HUR for M.G.M. before he was replaced by Fred Niblo.

Von Sternberg's THE WOMAN OF THE SEA (or THE SEA GULL) (1926), which had nothing to do with either Ibsen or Tchekhov, was made for Chaplin, but was never released. It followed THE EXQUISITE SINNER. THE TREASURE was a G. W. Pabst film.

"PUTTING PUNCH IN A PICTURE"   1926

By John Grierson, *Motion Picture News,* Vol. 34, No. 22, November 27, 1926, pp. 2025-2026.

There is no use having a big and grand theme unless the director can bring out the bigness and the grandeur of it. The story must be told visually with accumulating power and flash.

Visual story telling is so much an art that it might well be the greatest of the arts. It is certainly the most complicated. It involves a manipulation of character and acting and stage as in legitimate drama; it involves a manipulation of visual composition as in painting (the composition is a moving composition with varying dramatic effect and

430

therefore much more complex); it involves a manipulation of tempo as in music; it involves a manipulation of visual suggestion and visual metaphor as in poetry. Beyond all that, it involves a manipulation of such effects as are peculiar to itself. This includes (under camera) the manipulation of dissolves, double exposures, trick shots, etc., etc.; (under continuity) the manipulation and juxtaposition of long shots, close-ups, medium shots, truck shots and so on, and of recurring visual themes (as in music).

THE PLAY'S THE THING!

The various elements of cinema technique (tempo, composition, and the rest) must of course begin and end by subserving the dramatic purposes of the story. From one point of view they are the instrumental effects out of which one might compose a visual symphony as abstract as one pleases. We might have a "pure visual flow," a "cineplastic poem," a "symphony of masses" without any representational element whatsoever, as certain advanced critics have suggested. Or we might have an abstract film built up of representational elements as in the case of the BALLET MECANIQUE, which told no story but was simply a sequence of similar, complementary and developing movements. But for ordinary purposes this won't do. The art of the cinema for practical purposes is grounded in the needs and desires of simple people (i.e., all people at their simplest) and can never throw over the plainly human element. The directors might experiment among themselves with tempo films (the BALLET MECANIQUE was little more) and films which played with a scale of pure forms (heavy masses to delicate masses, dark to light, hard angular patterns to graceful sweeping patterns, etc., etc.). This would be useful as any other laboratory experiments are useful in helping the director's sense of construction when the real dramatic problem presented itself. But in the end the play's the thing.

So, I repeat, all the elements must be handled to the single end of giving the story a visual character and a visual wonder commensurate with its dramatic essence. And the telling of the story is half the battle. It gives accumulating power as it emphasizes, lights up, darkens, colors, atmospheres, and generally dramatizes what there is to dramatize.

TREATMENT MORE THAN HALF THE BATTLE

Indeed, the telling of the story is often more than half the battle. THE WANDERER had a great story (the parable of the prodigal son) but the telling made it rather less than great. THE SEA BEAST had a magnificent story (the greatest story in American literature, *Moby Dick*) but the telling made it nothing at all. On the other hand, VARIETY had a very unoriginal story, but the telling made it one of the great successes on Broadway. THE MERRY WIDOW was a musical comedy trifle to begin with, but the telling made it one of the more powerful things of the year. BEAU GESTE was a simple mystery story, but the telling made it jump for a while into epic. THE VANISHING AMERICAN was a Zane Grey Western, but the telling made it for a couple of reels great history. THE LAST LAUGH was the simple story of an old man who was deprived of a uniform, but the telling made it the tragic little bijou of the highbrows.

On the whole, however, great story and great handling are best when they travel in company. All the pictures I mention are not finally so satisfying as THE BIG PARADE and THE GOLD RUSH (or, if I may for a moment go Russian and realist, and leave the world public out of the argument) POTEMKIN and GREED. The point of these pictures was that the issues were as great as the handling. On a less pretentious level there is a unique satisfaction where the treatment catches exactly the inner quality of the story, be the story ever so slight. This is the level of perfect (but not necessarily great) art. MOANA, THE THIEF OF BAGDAD, THE EXQUISITE SINNER, the Lubitsch comedies, the Cruze small-town comedies, THE GRAND DUCHESS AND THE WAITER, Langdon's

431

SATURDAY AFTERNOON and some of the Aesop cartoons have more or less this perfect proportion.

TEMPO

Here follow some notes on the technique of story telling: principally on the manipulation of tempo and visual composition. The manipulation of camera I must leave to those technical experts who have also a dramatic sense (I only wish the camera man of POTEMKIN and Karl Freund of THE LAST LAUGH and VARIETY would talk a little).

This about tempo: tempo is the means by which movement and energy are disciplined and directed, to give the maximum dramatic effect.

(a) *Crescendo of Tempo.* Gradually and steadily raising the speed and power of movement. This is what gives power to the scene in THE BIG PARADE, where the alarm is given and the wagons go off to the front. Wagons begin to accumulate, pile up on one another; men get more excited and hurried. The movement becomes still more frantic and disordered, then finds a direction. The boy and the girl have lost each other and are searching crazily, and the directed movement, more and more powerful, more and more inevitable, must carry them away from each other. The suspense grows; they meet when there is scarcely a moment to say good-bye. The movement, at last directed, is so terrible that it cannot be stopped; it must separate them inevitably. The girl tries to stop it and can't; she hangs madly to the wagon and tries to stop it; she is dragged in the dust of the road. It goes on; she falls beaten.

(b) *Diminuendo of tempo.* Same scene. The wagons go past, the men march by, the movement dissipates itself and disappears. The shouting dies, the gesticulation becomes quieter. The rearguard is quiet, the stragglers separate. Soon there are only one or two figures hurrying on after the rest and finally, there is the girl only, left in the deserted road by herself. She waves, waves, she gives up waving; she hugs a shoe, kisses it, sinks to her knees, she falls fainting on the ground. The show is over and the screen is still. The action has been stepped down from absolute intensity to absolute quiet, just as in the first case it was stepped up.

Other instances of crescendo well done: The chariot race in BEN-HUR, the chase in THE EXQUISITE SINNER, the discovery of the old man's fraud and the awakening of the slum quarter in THE LAST LAUGH, the smashing of the table in VARIETY. Most American directors know nothing about varying tempo. They start at top speed and keep going. This is the case in Westerns and in such pyrotechnics as are served in DON JUAN.

Other instances of *crescendo and diminuendo* together: The chase in THE EXQUISITE SINNER, the two dances in MOANA, especially the second one that finishes with the boy asleep. THE EXQUISITE SINNER showed the first conscious and deliberate use of crescendo and diminuendo from Hollywood. Without being a classic in the matter of strong drama, it shows more general knowledge and command of movie technique than 90 per cent of the pictures that have struck Broadway. But King Vidor is the most powerful exponent of tempo in American movies and, possibly, the most conscious student of it.

(c) *Drum-tap tempo.* One beat, two beat, three beat, as in primitive music, with never a variation. Tempo of the heart beat. The movement goes on one beat, two beat, three beat, as though the universe were a gigantic clock ticking. It is what gives the punch. It is responsible for the power of the slave-ship scene in BEN-HUR, of the attack in THE BIG PARADE. It gives the atmosphere of madness to the movement of Jannings in VARIETY after he has knifed the villain. One beat, two beat, three beat, the movement goes on in each case with no variation, despite the disturbances of shot, shell, and frantic females. One beat, two beat, three beat, remorselessly, relentlessly, altogether inhumanly, till it becomes ghastly with emphasis. O'Neill used the technique in *The Emperor Jones*. It is the emphasized time-beat of the "Blues."

POTEMKIN, THE SUPER TEMPO FILM

Tempo was varied on the scale of the entire picture in the Russian film, POTEMKIN. Herewith the analysis:

POTEMKIN is the story of the 1905 mutiny in the Black Sea Fleet. From the point of view of tempo the action is set in continuing waves, and these I shall for the moment call Acts. The mutiny is Act 1. Act 2 is the entry of the cruiser Potemkin into the port of Odessa at night. Act 3 is the lying-state of the dead leader, the working up of the populace, and the demonstration of revolution. Act 4 is the massacre of the people by the Czarist troops. Act 5 is a second night-scene of the crew of the Potemkin awaiting the dawn. Act 6 is of the Potemkin getting under way, clearing for action, and preparing, in all nervousness, to fight it out with the rest of the fleet. In the final shot, after the other ships have unexpectedly joined the mutiny, the cruiser Potemkin comes crashing through the picture, head-on, lifting her gigantic prow like the head of a god.

Act 1. There is a first crescendo of discontent, but this is troubled and as yet un-directed. The note of doubt is struck in a swinging pendulum movement (of hammocks, of tables, of skilly-cans) which is repeated at intervals like a theme. When the direction is taken and the action proper begins the tempo climbs in intensity from the short staccato rushes of groups to the continuing and unrelaxed madness of the mood in which the officers are hunted down and killed.

Act 2. But, in the Shakespearian manner, there is a knocking-at-the-door scene for the murder of Duncan, i.e. a scene for catching one's breath. After the peak, there is a diminuendo of movement which has the effect of dramatic (or cinema) relief. The intensity of the mutiny is reduced and reduced in purely visual terms, by the movement of a cutter, by the movement of a barge creeping into harbor, by the vaguer motion of ships by the quayside, till the action is almost dead and the scene is a night-scene of ships at anchor and of the oily water moving sleepily against a float.

Act 3. The second crescendo of movement begins at dawn. The dead leader is alone, under an improvised tent on the wharf; an old woman comes to weep, others come, a dead stairway comes to life with crowding spectators, there is a procession of people on the long breakwater, another on a bridge, a double movement of people above and below. The action piles up till there is agitation and a lynching scene and finally the concerted demonstration of the populace and the bewildering burst of sailing boats as they go out to greet the Potemkin.

DRUM-TAP TEMPO, JUNGLE TIME

Act 4. At this minor peak there is a sudden step-up of intensified movement. The massacre is under way. It grows quickly and steadily, then at the topmost level of horror it falls into the drum-tap tempo, jungle time, that made the advance in THE BIG PARADE and the scene after the murder in VARIETY so powerful. But the Russians have known a little more. They have staged the advance of the Czarist troops as a descending movement on a long flight of steps (cf. the funeral march in THE MERRY WIDOW) and the mechanical remorseless time-beat is more terrible, the contrast of frantic women and mad appeal more ghastly. The people are gradually, consistently, and completely blotted out in a continuity of insane and sometimes lovely detail. A woman is shot in the abdomen, a boy is shot in the head, a benevolent old lady with spectacles is smashed in

433

the eye, and the scene goes screaming with blood; but weaving in and out is the detail of a baby carriage and a chuckling infant lost in the mob.

Act 5.   The movement diminishes in the slow smash of bursting shells. It passes into the quiet of night again, into the uneasy stillness of the watch on deck and the watch below. There are the dim movements of a lookout on the bridge, of men going to rounds, of men sleeping fitfully. The ship is only alive with weariness and a vague uneasiness. The movement finished in the shot of a logline turning. The shot punctuates the quiet of the sleepers. It is repeated.

Act 6.   The signal is given from the bridge in the quiet of the morning as the enemy ships come over the horizon. The last movement begins, and it is probably the most amazing demonstration of cinema art that has appeared anywhere. Perhaps only those who have had ships in their bones can comprehend it properly. The Potemkin opens her eyes like a man asleep and comes gradually to life. The technique is similar to Murnau's in the waking of the slum quarter in THE LAST LAUGH, but there is a greater orchestration of visual effects. The still dials of the engine room and the stokehold, the gauge glasses, the ship's telegraph, the engine-room telegraph, the signal and answer, the first jolt of the engines, the taking in of the ladder, the fuss on the foc's'le head, the water that goes faster along the clean line of the side, the plunging of the engines, the still, swifter movement of the auxiliary, the feather at the bow, the streaming of smoke at the funnels, are all used as themes, repeated, stepped-up to the racing intensity and smashing solidity of full speed. The movement becomes bound up with the process of clearing for action and goes intenser still; the shell locker, the shell-chain, the scamper for stations, the burst of signal flags from the halyards. The dreadful elevating and ranging of the guns in the turrets is the leit motif of foreboding.

The Potemkin, as it happens, sails into a wild and enthusiastic reception. It is the note on which the film closes; she comes smashing down on the camera, a conqueror. But the important thing is not the story; it is the fact that this variation in the flow, from quiet to intensity and from intensity to quiet, is a visual flow; and this visual flow makes the picture the powerful thing that it is. It is constructed in terms of cinema. It is achieved by an appreciation of the relative dramatic values of different movements.

"PUTTING ATMOSPHERE IN PICTURES"   1926

By John Grierson, *Motion Picture News,* Vol. 34, No. 23, December 4, 1926, pp. 2141-2142.

Tempo gives punch to an episode, it piles up the dramatic effect of the action. In crescendo it gives gathering intensity; in monotone or drum-tap it gives inevitability, brutality, the spirit of the elemental, the feeling of destiny; in diminuendo it gives relaxation and relief. Stills, the lowest limit of tempo, are for the beginning or the ending of a wave of action (e.g., the ending of the tragic sequence in THE LAST LAUGH). Spectacle may be included with stills. Mask effects (acting stills) are for pungent emphasized fade-outs, or for moments of suspended action where the director takes the emphasis away from the action and plays up the human effects of it (e.g., Chaplin's mask as he enters the dance hall in THE GOLD RUSH, his mask as he looks in the window of the dance hall at midnight). Tempo in fact is the secret of manipulating movement toward the dramatic ends of the story.

On the other hand, visual composition (the making of strong and noble compositions, or lovely compositions, or fantastic and fairy-like compositions, or distorted and mad compositions, or hard and angular compositions or flowing and varied compositions) is the secret of atmosphere. Tempo gives dynamic to the action: composition gives solidity and spaciousness and atmosphere to the action. Both together give character to the action.

THE GOOD ONES: THE DANGER OF PRETTINESS

So far as visual composition goes, the German directors (in their limited field of tragic effects)· are far ahead of the American directors, but the best visual composer today, taken all in all, is Eisenstein, the Russian director of POTEMKIN. The only directors in Hollywood who have a consistent visual sense and a feeling for composition are von Sternberg, von Stroheim, Cruze, Tourneur and (in a polite way) Brabin. These men have a sense of pictures. Von Sternberg and Brabin, however, show only a sense of photographic beauty and do not show a marked sense of dramatic beauty. Their pictures are beautiful but soft, and they indicate no great capacity to vary their sense of visuals from soft to hard, from gentle to brutal, from simple to complex, with the demands of the action.

A sense of photographic beauty may often do more harm than good. A picture that is merely beautiful is nothing (hence the futility of continuous spectacle). The composition must be integral to the action and must add something definite to the story. Von Sternberg is a case in the negative. His unreleased picture for Chaplin (THE WOMAN OF THE SEA) is in some respects the most beautiful film ever produced in Hollywood, but it is undramatic. Its beauty goes for naught; it does not pile up to anything, it does not lead anywhere: it is just good to look at. So is a picture gallery good to look at, but a picture gallery is not cinema.

THE PINK PIRATE

A familiar case of visual composition false to the action (and therefore useless) is THE BLACK PIRATE. The light and airy atmosphere which suited the spirit of THE THIEF OF BAGDAD, and helped it, is actually harmful to this later Fairbanks film. THE BLACK PIRATE is a pretty enough picture, with a more or less exquisite sense of design. The ships, the sails, the masts, and the rigging are all neatly arranged, and would look rather well, say, on drawing-room panels. But the picture is about pirates, and black pirates at that. It is about murder, and rape and walking the plank, about desperadoes with grim secrets in their skulls, dark desires in their bellies, and sinister knives in their teeth. It is not about drawing-rooms, but about the open sea where women are angels and men are shaggy brutes and the winds of heaven blow art and artiness all over the place. The pretty-pretty drawing room atmosphere makes it a nice-nice picture, but (to be brief) it takes the guts out of it.

And, note you, the same studied prettiness extends from end to end of THE BLACK PIRATE. It isn't simply a case of having pretty designs and a fairy-story atmosphere for the lovely-lady scenes. When Fairbanks swings through the rigging in hair-raising parabolas and demonstrates that he is one hell of a fellow, that too is done a trifle prettily. And when the boarding party swim under-water to capture the schooner and stick knives in the pirates' innards, they might be a bunch of fairies swimming in the moonlight.

THE CASE AGAINST THE GERMANS

So the first point about visual composition is this: unless it is complementary to the spirit of the action and at all times subservient to it, it is a dangerous affair to play with and is very liable to spoil things. When the picture is too consciously and deliberately arty, it takes the breath of life out of the story. And the breath of life is the cinema's specialty.

435

Much of the American objection to German films is based on this fact. American films (for all their faults) have tended to be natural; their very ignorance of aesthetic matters has helped them. The Germans, on the other hand, have tended to studio-mania; they have forgotten the camera's capacity for recording the natural, and they have become theatrical in the bad sense of that word. THE LAST LAUGH was a trifle theatrical. In a recent picture, THE TREASURE, the dramatic atmosphere of the sets was so deliberate and the visual composition so conscious, that the action was over-shadowed and lost. People wandered about in desperate passage ways; they did something or other against powerful exteriors, or pungent stairways; they lay around on billowy bedsteads under tremendous ceilings; yet I cannot remember very clearly (and indeed I did not follow as well as I should have) what it was all about. One couldn't see the wood for the trees.

To take instances. No one felt anything deliberate about the sweeping movements of THE COVERED WAGON. No one felt that the advance to the front in THE BIG PARADE (the swinging line of wagons and aeroplanes) was anything but fine and fitting. No one could object to the Sahara scenes in BEAU GESTE, and say they were forced into the picture. Yet all these moving designs which lent themselves so well to the dramatic feeling of the story were carefully composed. They were deliberate, and yet they were natural. They belonged to the story and took it somewhere; they didn't hog the picture to the exclusion of the main purposes of the story.

THE RANGE OF VISUAL DRAMATICS

But this problem of visual composition is not merely a matter of nice designs or even of grand designs. It is really a very complicated matter, and I propose for a moment to be quite complicated about it. Visual effects can be scaled and organized like any other dramatic raw material (sound, for example) and sooner or later this will have to be understood by directors even though the pictures they make are popular pictures. In the world of jazz the great step forward did not come till Paul Whiteman and others took jazz seriously enough to make an analytic study of it.

There are several possible variations in visual effect, each with its capacity to pile up or diminish the dramatic feeling of the story. There is the variation in light, from light to dark; the variation in solidity from delicate masses to strong masses; the variation in proximity from long shots to close-ups; the variation in direction, to the spectator and away from the spectator; the variation in pattern from light and graceful patterns to the brutality of straight lined or angular pattern, or from flat and shallow pattern to majestic and sweeping pattern; and finally, the variation in the tempo of movement which I have discussed in a previous article. These different scales must of course be orchestrated together; they are separable only in theory.

EXAMPLES FROM VARIETY

VARIETY illustrates the powerful use of all these variations and the flash of VARIETY is largely due to its use of them. There are tremendous contrasts in the picture. The atmosphere of the roundabouts is light and airy as befits the happiness of the two lovers; the movement is free, the dark solidity of close-ups is not emphasized. The scene in [the] caravan with its atmosphere of physical freedom and physical happiness is shot through with light: with the flashing of light on the towel, with the flashing of light on the lady's naked body, etc. Similar effects are gained in the first acrobatic display at the Winter Garden when, as yet, there is no note of tragedy in the air: the dancing of dwarfs becomes a shimmering of silk and a spinning of circles, the trapeze swings back and forward airily in gentle rhythm.

On the other hand, when the atmosphere is set in primitive mould for the killing, the emphasis is laid on solids, close-ups, and hard angular pattern; the movement is chained

436

55. *Greta Garbo as Anna Karenina in her first film version of the Tolstoi novel. Perhaps no one since Chaplin has ever seized and amassed a screen following so quickly. This Tolstoi film was equipped with alternate happy endings. Edmund Goulding directed, and with broad simplicity the film was renamed LOVE (1927).*

and stiff and deliberate. When Jannings stood ready to murder, he was a gigantic shape in the foreground that stood mesmerically still and kept its face away. Against his dark certainty the victim fluttered punily in the light. After, when the man was dead, Jannings was a figure that moved forward slowly and regularly in a straight corridor. The screaming contortions, the body bewilderment of the woman, could not halt or vary the continuing movement. It kept its monotone in the monotonous straight-line regularity of the corridor, it kept it down the blinding similarity of the steps. There was a shot at the beginning which demonstrated the same powerful relation between setting and story. Jannings shambled with head bent and back bowed to the warden's office. He passed down a corridor of brutal uprights that made hard black angles with the beams of the roof. The uprights and the beams, with their stiff, unyielding spirit of mechanism, spoke as loudly as the bent head and the bowed back and the shambling feet. Against them, the movement seemed slower and the spirit of the man more crushed.

THE POWER OF THE CLOSE-UP

I know of no picture where the power of the close-up has been so well illustrated. In most cases proximity was used to give physical thrill, and this is entirely as it should be. It was used too for moments of extreme emotional tension in the individual. At such points the general scene does not matter; the effect on the individual, and therefore the mask of the individual, is everything. The big close-up of the picture, however, was the one in which Jannings moved slowly down on the hairy-chested longshoreman. The neck was arched bull-fashion; the camera went with the neck; then the face came forward slowly and threateningly into the very eye of the camera. The piling up of tension in the audience was so tremendous that when the mouth snapped the words "the show is over," it had all the effect of a shot from a gun. A similar use of close-up is found at the end of POTEMKIN, where the cruiser crashes head-on through the picture, and in those familiar scenes where railroad trains rush down on the audience. This utter annihilation of space has so powerful an effect on the nerves that I have heard women scream at it. Going over the camera (as in the BEN-HUR chariot race) has the effect rather, of flight.

PRIMITIVE EFFECTS AND MAGNIFICENT EFFECTS

Primitive unintelligent masses and slow and certain directions are fairly terrible things to work with in cinema. There is a stupid impressiveness about railway trains, motor buses and street cars. Something of the same character of mechanical impressiveness comes into the movement of such things as bull-necks and backs, or big guns and engines, or battalions and crowds in action.

Both mass and movement, in fact, may be said to vary from the level of primitive effects and crude purposes to the level of free and spiritual achievement, and the dramatic appeal may be gauged accordingly. Direction without variation is primitive. Given many primitive bodies moving in regular tempo in an identical direction, it is cumulatively primitive. Set primitive bodies in an unvarying direction to a primitive purpose: move, say, motor-buses and railway trains and battalions similarly to war: and it will seem as though the earth's foundations themselves must go. The effect will be cumulatively impressive of blind and threatening power.

Of magnificence? Vary. Let the motor-buses and the railway trains and the battalions move in a swinging curve (as in THE BIG PARADE); let the aeroplanes wheel overhead like birds instead of driving ahead like machines; let the tempo be varied so that the tramp, tramp, tramp of one movement is contrasted with the freedom of another; let the entire movement vary for all its set purpose, and there will be magnificence. Oppositions held together in visual orchestration make for splendor. Mountains and forests

438

and sea have an air of foreboding and oppressiveness when there is darkness about them. But, great impending masses that they are, when they are shot through with light, and clear skies are over them, and their variation of shape and contour and movement is apparent, the effect is of expansion and freedom. Set gloomy cliffs alive with sea birds, and there is a similar shift in dramatic feeling.

MASSES AND MOVEMENTS USED IN CONTRAST

Where primitive effects are held together with free effects: where dark is held together with light, solidity with airiness, slow and regular tempo with free tempo: where certain direction and purpose are held together with varied movement and changing purposes, and this contrast is emphasized, the dramatic effect can be very great. In the massacre scene of POTEMKIN, the regular movement of the advancing troops is opposed to the frenzied movements of the escaping women and children, and the brutality of the first and the frenzy of the second are thrown into relief. The same opposition is apparent in the corridor scene of VARIETY, where the steady movement of Jannings is accompanied by the feverish gestures of the girl.

Heavy still masses when set in contrast give added life to what is already alive. In POTEMKIN the contrast between primitive enslaved masses and things of freedom and life was used throughout the picture. A gun or a stanchion or a rail or a davit broke through heavily in the foreground and set in relief the liveliness of the action beyond. The vicious black and white of iron ships was thrown in with the softer effects of sailing ships as a dramatic variant. Von Sternberg shows a similar sense of visual contrast in the market scenes of THE EXQUISITE SINNER: there are always the heavy masses of carts, booths and cattle-pens in the foreground to light up the happenings beyond them. The murder scene in VARIETY, with Jannings' back looming up in the foreground is a perfect instance of the value of contrast.

VISUAL FLOW NOT EVERYTHING

In the last instance, one must imagine the moving shapes which make up a cinema story as in process of ebb and flow. They come up from the sheer nothingness of light and space and take form and solidity; they arrange themselves in one pattern or another, and shift from pattern to pattern; they speed up, they slow down; they surge into the impressive proximity of close-ups; they annihilate space; they sink back again with diminishing vitality into the distance. All these processes, if cinema is being handled properly, ought to be utilized in the deliberate and coherent manipulation of the spectators' emotions. They represent an unexploited gold mine of cinema effects.

But (I must repeat) the main thing about visual composition is not fine design, nor is it that this ebb and flow I speak of, be in itself beautiful. These things are necessary as a pleasant voice in the telling of a story is necessary, but there are more important things still. First and last, the composition (whatever it is) must help the story; the story is paramount.

1926   "THE SEVEN OBSTACLES TO PROGRESS (I)"

By John Grierson, *Motion Picture News*, Vol. 34, No. 24, December 11, 1926, pp. 2225-2227.

In drawing my series of articles to a close, it may be the better part of valor in a cautious critic to make some appropriate gesture of humility. It frequently happens that a theory (be it ever so blue-eyed and blonde) can be very neatly stabbed to the heart by the fact of the matter; and a critic must forever be fearful of the rod of correction 439 wielded by practical men and practical circumstances. I am not unaware of that. Cinema criticism is nothing if it is not sufficiently mindful of the practical difficulties laid on a young industry, and of the ghastly complexity of the labor of actual production.

I may as well emphasize this gesture of humility at the beginning, because in this last article I have elected to put down all the weaknesses of the industry together and exaggerate them; and it may be that before the end, I shall have dropped into the style of the easy knocker whom the industry has good reason to detest. But in this matter I crave privilege. I believe in the industry. I believe that it is getting nearer and nearer to its public and falling gradually into its destined place in modern society. And it is doing so, not because it is being forced from the outside, but because it has the secret of growth within it.

Its energy and ambition are two principal factors in its growth. There is another. The policy of box office to which the industry is committed is in the end a stepping stone to the best service of the public; to the recognition of its wants and the fulfillment of its dreams. It is, in fact, a better stepping stone to a realistic service of the public than the patronizing attitudes of the Highbrows and the Uplifters. This has been abundantly apparent in the more recent history of cinema.

But I believe cinema has a huger part still to play in modern life. It has not reached the point of saturation nor near it. It has to get closer still to the life of its public, it has to go deeper still in the service of its public, it has to become even more indispensable to its public. As I have suggested, it is the destiny of cinema to be the source of imaginative release and every-day inspiration for the common people of the world. And that is not only an ideal of service, but a pointer to commercial success such as no other business has dared to dream of.

It is in the light of this belief that I emphasize the weaknesses of the industry. An institution with so great a destiny cannot afford to take its existence sloppily. With this explanation, I go about my business.

THE SEVEN OBSTACLES TO PROGRESS

There is one outstanding problem. It is the problem of how those very actual talents which Hollywood has at its command can be set a-going harmoniously, how they can be integrated to the end of better production. There is the complementary problem of how the industry can best utilize those outside talents which are necessary to it. Briefly, there is a great amount of creative energy in and around the movie world, but there isn't the integration and use of it that there ought to be. The unit is troubled with negative elements, and false elements, and cheap elements, and catch-as-catch-can elements, and there are times when it doesn't look altogether healthy to the wandering stranger. The theory that it's a tough world, and that the stranger's stomach ought to be correspondingly stout is poor theory, because the elements I think of are unnecessary elements that keep back the greater success of the industry—and that is paramount. They are the monkey wrenches in the cinematic machinery that gum up the works.

Taking all the good sides of the cinema world for granted and the progress of the industry as a whole for granted, I shall cite the negative elements together and then take them singly. I list them under the general heading of the Seven Obstacles to Progress.

(1) The *gimcrack reputations*, with the resultant big-man vanities and little-man vanities—the penny balloons that publicity has blown into the semblance of size.

(2) The smart-aleck *complacency* and self-satisfaction of the tenth rate—the disheartened carelessness (the pulling of punches) on the part of the first-rate—the let-it-slide spirit which limits initiative.

(3) The provincial narrowness and *superficiality* of outlook, the unashamed ignorance, the hick-town nervousness of big feelings and big ideas. This with regard to

the motivations of human drama and the destiny of cinema as the source of inspiration for the common people of the world.

(4) The blatant under-estimate of the public's wants and the public's capacity—the *disrespect for the public.*

(5) The lack of hospitality to criticism—the die-hard *resentment of outside ideas.*

(6) The pestiferous *individualism*—the nursing of the job at all costs, playing off catch-as-catch-can politics, getting ahead on the principle of opportunism rather than by genuine contribution to the good of the whole and the future of cinema.

(7) The *lack of the spirit of investigation* within the industry itself—the nervousness about experiment in technical effects and dramatic effects. With this goes the exaggerated spirit of specialization which often leaves one man in the studio unit ignorant of what his neighbor is doing and not very eager about asking. With this, too, goes the failure of production people to talk cinema. They talk shop (personalia, politics, etc.) but not cinema. The silly fear about being exploited and having one's ideas stolen (as if ideas were as rare and exclusive as diamonds) and the canny spirit which prevents the proper exchange of ideas may be included.

THE GIMCRACK REPUTATION

The first obstacle is the gimcrack reputation. It eats at the vitals of the industry, and the very conditions of the industry today help to nourish it more and more, rather than to kill it. The system of salesmanship especially nourishes it. What can you expect when you sell pictures before they are made? You are selling a pig in a poke; or worse still, you are selling a pig that hasn't had a chance to go into the poke, for the good reason that it doesn't even exist. The result is that you have to sell a picture on its pedigree; you have to sell it on names; on the name of the director, or the name of the star. And what does picture pedigree amount to except in a few exceptional cases? Who makes the picture? Does the author, or the continuity writer, or the general supervisor, or the director, or the assistant director, or the art director, or the camera-man? Or is it not just possible that the director's wife has something to do with it? Save in a few cases I would as soon say the man in the moon as any of them, for a picture, save when one outstanding figure dominates (Chaplin say, or von Stroheim), is a composite production, and the product of the studio unit working as a whole rather than of any single figure. What's more, as the range of effects in a single picture widens, it will become more and more only possible for a composite unit to produce it. Even Chaplin will have to bring in an advisor on art and a first-rate photographer one of these days. Even von Stroheim will have to be kept away by somebody or other from his narrow-gauge and slightly perverse realism.

As I see it, the studio unit of the near future will not only have a decent director and a star to boss it, but a decent musician and a decent expert on costume and a decent poet and a decent expert on visuals to boss it, too. This means that there will have to be more and more an integration of different energies rather than a dependence on one or two.

And that will mean a good riddance of the gimcrack reputation. Up till now, the salesmen have been selling names, and the publicity men have built up a mythology around the names to serve their immediate purposes. But the publicity has boomeranged. The names have frequently grown fat and lazy and arrogant and so entirely credulous of the spurious reputation that has been thrust upon them, that they have lost all sense of proportion. Shakespeare—there are quarters in Hollywood you wouldn't get a hat off for Shakespeare! Bernard Shaw—there are quarters in Hollywood that feel so innocently superior to the good Bernard that they would enter naively into argument with him and give him the lie! And all because of the publicity made necessary by the condition of sales. Why, out in Hollywood the publicity men made one man so much higher than the angels, that everybody around had to call him God.

The important point, of course, is that these gimcrack reputations become a hin-   441 drance to the industry rather than an asset. They hog the road of progress and all the honking of honest men won't shift them.

When you think of it, what stage of the industry is this for people to get puffed up? Twenty-five years from now all but half-a-dozen of today's reputations will have vanished and sunk like the movies of ten years ago into the dust. And the half-dozen will remain because their actual pictures live, and have something in them fundamental enough for people to see again. Today's vanity won't matter so much.

THE CURE FOR HIGH-HATS

I realize that proper publicity is necessary and indeed, one of the intriguing aspects of the cinema manifestation. The public demand it and need it. They need figures to worship, and the mythological reputations of stars can be as fair an aid to the imagination as any. I merely object to the stars claiming the power of miracle for themselves, and deceiving themselves. A billboard is one thing and an honest mirror another. Fan mail and the worship of the humble are fine things, but stars should perceive that they are a part of dream-life (the dream-life of the publicity man and the public), and not confuse them with waking reality. They are to be treated with all respect, but by no means to be taken seriously.

The cure for the gimcrack reputation is obvious. (1) Sell pictures. Build up pictures ahead. Show them on Broadway and State Street and sell them on their actual box office effect. I leave a qualification for those pictures for which box office reputations on Broadway and State Street are no criterion.

(2) Go on improving the honor system in the studios, and make it certain that the people really contributing to a picture (be they ever so unknown) are given the proper credit for their work. Let the stars and the directors *et al* leave their billboards outside. This will lift the hoodoo of Job that is at present on the industry. In Job, if you remember, the just were stricken and the unjust flourished. There was something in Job, too, about the "flattering tiles" which destroy honesty.

(3) By a little self-discipline it ought to be possible for the industry to disbelieve its own exaggerations. The producers and publicity men start a ballyhoo about somebody or other, and to begin with, they are not deceived about the reality of the matter. In less than no time, however, they are as much the victim of their own repetition as their audience. Chloroform is an excellent beverage but there is no fun in committing a nice chloroform murder if you finish by catching an overdose yourself. The industry might find it worth while to keep a tribe of professional cynics and pay them generously for keeping people brutally conscious of the simple laws of personal arithmetic. It should be compulsory under the rules of contract for every high-hat of the cinema persuasion to visit one of these professional cynics once a week, for his (or her) soul's sake and the industry's.

COMPLACENCY, PROVINCIALISM, ETC.

The second obstacle is complacency. I met it frequently in Hollywood. In some cases it was the complacency of the stupid; in other cases it was the more dangerous complacency of the talented and apathetic who have got to the mental pass of saying, "O, let it ride—who gives a damn?" Or alternatively, "Good God, of course, it's a three-ringed circus—what did you expect?"

Stupid or talented, the gesture is identical and the effect harmful. It involves a snap of the fingers at the future. In the case of the stupid it amounts to carelessness in pictures which takes them no further than the obvious. In the case of the talented, it involves the pulling of punches which might be grand. Raymond Griffith is, I believe, one of those

who is pulling his punches. He has much more in him than most people realize, and so much, that I set him down as one of the greatest potentials in the industry, and one of those most likely to bring it prestige. For reasons which are frequently no fault of their own, others are having their punches pulled for them. Dix is in this category. He has some of the things that Fairbanks has, and many of the things that Fairbanks needs; for instance, a command over sober seriousness and the more majestic mask and gestural effects. But the public have had only one superb glimpse of his real power in THE. VANISHING AMERICAN.

The curse of this complacency business is that the cinema world has, as yet, no conscious traditions of attainment; and this fact I have exaggerated for present purposes into the charge of provincial ignorance. The industry is young and not quite out of the baby clothes of its pioneering years. It is born of a new democratic public whose demands in drama have never been properly ascertained. One of its traditions is a vaudeville tradition of catch-as-catch-can entertainment and quick returns. It has no tradition in art; it has no tradition of real fame behind it to haunt it, as has the craft of poetry and the other aesthetic crafts. It has, for no fault of its own, few standards.

Then the personnel of the industry is mixed. Part of it (and a somewhat important part) is in the business tradition, pure and simple, and cannot be expected to be the last judge of the terms of public appeal. Dramatic motivation, let us say, is not their specialty. The other section of the industry comes from anywhere and nowhere, with and without knowledge of the arts, but frequently without. In Hollywood they tell you that the number of wise men is fifteen and they will not raise you by one. This, however, is slight evidence. The art shops and book shops of Hollywood are a little better. The level of average discussion in Hollywood of how perfectly wonderful, etc., etc., is better evidence still.

WHAT MIGHT BE DONE ABOUT IT

Nobody is to blame. Cinema is young and easily rich, and sorrow has not come into its gay twenties to temper its youthful lack of discipline. And Hollywood is itself a provincial town, set by a provincial sea, in a provincial climate. Intellectually speaking, it is in the midst of rustic seclusion. It is far away from New York, far away from Chicago, far away from poverty and stress (physical or mental), and a little lost to the world, where the storms blow and the winter rages. With no tradition in the arts to stir it, and no knowledge of how cinema is the child of all the arts and dependent on them, Hollywood denies itself even that continuing connection with the common people which is the taproot of art. The very system by which stars are placed on pedestals isolates them from the every-day life whose dreams they have to fulfill. It happens so.

As a partial cure for this state of affairs (I shall suggest other cures later) an arrangement might be made by which the personnel should not be permitted to isolate themselves too long in Hollywood. There might be a greater exchange between studios; with studios in the East, with studios in England, France, Italy, Germany and Russia. I feel that the introduction of outsiders, from Germany and Russia especially, will have excellent effect.

The proper discussion of cinema, and the proper criticism of cinema (without regard to publicity or place-hunting) ought to start shortly. This might take the form of a periodical circulated *within the industry* which will gather together cinema criticism from all parts of the world, bring out the contribution that painting and poetry and the other arts can make to cinema, discuss and encourage new dramatic effects, technical advancements and camera, lighting, etc.

The encouragement of an interest in paintings and the running of a first-rate art gallery in Hollywood with continuous exhibitions from the more established galleries (German color facsimiles will serve for the rest) might accomplish a little improving in the general sense of composition.

DISRESPECT FOR THE PUBLIC

Still another aspect of Hollywood's complacency is the disrespect for the public which prevails in certain quarters. I have heard it said that Hollywood divides its reading too exactly between the trade papers and *The American Mercury*. The trade papers too often preach the gospel that hicks are hicks the world over and that you have to play down to them. At least, they suggest it. *The American Mercury* preaches likewise. The result whether among the lowbrows of the industry or the pseudo highbrows is identical. There is no sufficient belief in the capacity of the public to understand, there is no sufficient belief that the cinema public, while it won't stand for the hole-and-corner values of special classes and art in the arty (or emasculated) sense, does at all times stand for whatever is simple and noble and genuine.

As I noted in a previous article, time and time again the incapacity of the public was served up to me as sufficient excuse for bad work and low standards of achievement. A conversation with Chaplin was interesting in this regard. He felt low one night and the burden of his tale, for a while, was "what's the use! There's the crowd cheering for dumb stuff, as well as for good stuff, and often enough not for good stuff, at all." Then with one of those parabolic changes of mood which are characteristic of him, Chaplin changed his tune. Perhaps, he suggested, if it's simple enough and big enough in that honest-to-God way that goes only with simplicity, they get it. Or, perhaps, what they really get isn't what they cheer about but what they get subconsciously and are only properly aware of after. Somebody added (perhaps it was Chaplin himself or Donald Ogden Stewart) that there was a point in audience reaction where people cheered as if they had seen God; not knowing it, but with that sort of feeling. A feeling of delight, he called it. I recommend the distinction as a guide to the biggest box office reaction the cinema (or any other entertainment) can ever achieve. It is the reaction in which an audience gets a trifle in the way of inspiration. The condition of it, however, is not disrespect for the public and the theory that any old hokum will serve it, but that the public has to be taken into partnership in those simple, dramatic matters that go deep.

A proper understanding of social institutions and their growth and of the place of the cinema as a social institution, would make this plain. It would be a sufficient cure for the attitude of disrespect if the industry made a proper study of its own audience reactions and got a dozen really competent social psychologists (with cinema good will) to report on them. It might not find a desire for complexity on the part of the public and often it would find an uncritical stomach for hokum. Nor would it find the desire for subtle drama or arty drama or far-away-fantastic drama, even if that drama is surpassingly fine for a few. But the experience with pictures like THE BIG PARADE and BEAU GESTE and THE COVERED WAGON is sufficient to point out the taste for the more simple and ennobling effects.

FOOTNOTE

This is the point Lasky is driving at when he says (in *The Film Daily Year Book*) that the day of the mere program picture is gone forever. "It is not enough," he says, "that a picture be well made. It is not enough that it tell an interesting story or that it be enacted by a good cast. *Every picture should have some basic theme or element which lends itself to exploitation.*"

In my estimate Lasky's analysis is excellent and clears the way for a profounder attitude to box office values; the basic themes of human life are easily discernible. It is my contention that the basic theme is one which is near to the people, simple enough to be understood, and at the same time one which searches out their intensest desires and deepest ambitions and inspires them. This is not so much a matter of boy-girl-and-motor-car as some producers seem to think. It means big things pictorially and big things psychologically. A basic theme is more likely to be one of ambition, pride, and achievement of distinction. Pride, I believe, is one of the biggest box office themes. It involves such things as pride of self, pride of family, pride of country, pride of race, etc. Pride of self is that complex of human values which includes self-command, self-sacrifice, loyalty, and above all, dignity; in common parlance it means "standing up to it," "sticking it," "showing guts." THE VANISHING AMERICAN (pride of race and pride of self); BEAU GESTE (pride of family and pride of self); BEN-HUR (pride of race); THE DARK ANGEL (pride of self); THE BIG PARADE (pride of self, pride of country), were pride pictures.

("The Seven Obstacles to Progress" will be concluded next week.)

1926   THE SEVEN OBSTACLES TO PROGRESS [II]

By John Grierson, *Motion Picture News*, Vol. 34, No. 25, December 18, 1926, pp. 2321-2322.

This brings me to the fifth obstacle to progress. Hollywood's provincialism in knowledge and attitude makes it inhospitable to outside ideas. This is a difficult subject because, frankly, some of the outsiders who touch Hollywood are (consciously or unconsciously) on the make; and as not a few of the insiders are also on the make, a certain natural clash of personal interests is inevitable. But the matter goes deeper. The overblown vanity that comes with gimcrack reputations, the complacency of the rich, the ignorance of higher standards in art and deeper standards in drama, and the catch-as-catch-can self-seeking natural in a business which has not yet given itself the dignity of a profession—all these things make for an atmosphere of nervousness and suspicion when a stranger presents a card written in another language. It comes indeed to be a matter of talking different languages. How can a painter of note get a show in Hollywood when few have the sense to see the value of composition to cinema? How can a poet of note have graceful entrance when few have read him and fewer still realize how near the poetic imagination is to one side of cinema production? Who was it told Maeterlinck he might one day be as great as Rex Beach? And how even can a critic have proper entrance when it is bad manners in Hollywood to discuss a picture's weaknesses in the presence of its director or its star? In fact what chance has any outsider when in all my stay in Hollywood I met but one person (Raymond Griffith), who was humble enough in his art (and great enough) to curse his bad work to his own face.

SAD TALES FROM HOLLYWOOD

Here I might cite the private stories of some authors who have been unfortunate in Hollywood. Most of them, however, come out speechless and their record is so inarticulate as to constitute poor evidence. The stories boil down to this. Hollywood speaks a language incomprehensible to men from the other arts and they in turn talk a language incomprehensible for the most part to Hollywood. The main reasons for this (so far as Hollywood is at fault), I have cited in my list of sins. But there are more immediate reasons.

An artist or author who goes out to Hollywood has, to begin with, no great feeling of humility before businessmen and the like. Every artist (be it plainly) secretly and inevitably despises the businessman; and every businessman secretly and inevitably despises the artist, for the artist in practical matters is generally a clown. Now the author or artist is either scared of these businessmen or administrators because they are so wise in matters practical, or he is as trusting as an infant. The result in the one case is suspicion and sensitiveness to insult. The result in the other sometimes is just as   445 negative. I think of one occasion where a too-trusting author had his titles side-tracked on their way to the main office. Somebody, scared that the author was going to take his job, was having them put presto in the waste box, and after the best laws of studio politics was spitting innuendo to the effect that the author was laying down on the job. Not knowing the maze of studio ropes it was a week before the author realized what was happening. A pester of petty incidents of this sort puts a crook in a man's attitude. Here is another case. A producer had a picture sold to the exhibitors and the picture had still to be made. He put a very well-known author on the job of writing the scenario. Not content with that he put another, and still another on to alternative scenarios. Not one of the three knew what was happening. The author in question went ahead in blissful ignorance. He finished his scenario and presented it only to find that one of the others had been accepted and indeed had been reckoned on from the beginning. He himself had been doing useless work for weeks, but nobody had seen fit to tell him that it was going to be useless.

DEMORALIZING EFFECT OF THE CHEAP BALLYHOO

Now from one point of view (a business point of view) everything was all right. The author was being paid for his work, or at least for his name. But from the author's point of view everything was all wrong. He had been deceived into wasting his energy; he had been the victim of an atmosphere of secrecy and half-truth. He had been treated like a servant, and his time and work and personality had been slighted; he had been denied an open and above-board partnership in the production. Any one who knows the exaggerated independence of artists knows how that author felt. It lost Hollywood right at the start the good-will which is necessary in an artist if he is to give anybody anything.

Then again an artist with any sensibility has a poor time when the atmosphere is full of cheap ballyhoo and spurious celebrity and comical airs of superiority. Playing the publicity game with the others he loses that detachment which is necessary to him. Not playing it, he is stifled, and voted a poor stick and a sad squirt and a dead nothing-at-all. I still think sadly of how it happened with one honest author who took to publicity. He joined up with the pack and inserted his advertisements in the trade papers, saying how-d'y'-do to this magnate and the top o' the mornin' to the other magnate, as the commemoration numbers came along. And to make matters worse he got swallowed up by the party system. When I saw him last he had staged a comeback and was doing honest work again. "Gawd, the place nearly choked me," he said, and authors a-plenty have said the same with sundry and sometimes eloquent embellishments of their mood. In fact, the present atmosphere stunts a lot of good things, and until the Nessus shirt of ballyhoo and publicity and playing the cheap game of spurious importance is taken from its back, Hollywood is going to be sicker than it ought to be.

POLITICS AND THE NEED FOR CO-OPERATION

All this, however, is not just another curse on Hollywood. Hollywood is simply the victim of its own natural origins and its own natural circumstances; and these no man can blame. I merely detach them as a basis for my plea for greater integration and smoother lubrication in the processes of production. In the end, the clash of the businessman and the artist will be avoided as each learns to understand the other and compromise a little. The businessman will have to learn that to treat an artist as a second-rate clerk is to bring the wrath of the gods on him. And the artist will have to humble himself before the proper demands of the common people as the none-too-believing artists of the Renaissance once humbled themselves in the service of the commercial princes and the church. He will have to fit himself into the essential conditions of cinema as a popular art and a composite art, in which every contributor must

446

56. George O'Brien, as The Man, begs forgiveness from Janet Gaynor, as his wife, in SUNRISE (1927), F. W. Murnau's first American film. They are shortly to participate in that lengthy trolley ride toward the city which constitutes one of the finest passages of the film.

be prepared to sacrifice something of his more specialized intellectual preoccupations. The net cure for the whole matter is the spirit of co-operation. As the war cry for 1926 was "greater co-operation between producer and exhibitor," the war cry for 1927 should be, "greater co-operation within the studio unit."

This brings me to the sixth sin—the sin of the studio politics. I have said enough to suggest how it works in cinema. It means capitalizing [on] the confusion of the young industry, for one's own cheap purposes. It means playing the ballyhoo and having one's name writ as large as may be, by hook or by crook. It means playing favorites or playing for favoritism. It means playing for the personal favor of the big businessman at the expense of art and initiative and honor. It means getting in right and keeping in right when it might be a better service to the producer to get in wrong for a change and suggest something. It means the underground bickerings of directors with supervisors and supervisors with directors and the silly school-kid jealousies of directors and stars, and the resulting atmosphere of innuendo. It means the spirit of secrecy and distrust in which producers cannot let their left hand know what their right hand is doing. It means the spirit of secrecy in which a man is so fearful of his neighbor and so fearful of being quoted in his private and honest opinion (whether through fear of his job or of adverse publicity) that he gradually stops behing honest about anything. The haphazard nature of success and the spirit of "let well enough alone—I might spoil it" encourages this. Almost everyone I met in Hollywood conjured me with something approaching tears in his eyes, not to say anything about this, that or the other opinion he had given me. The fear of being critical even for a moment was so overwhelming that it became touching. Certainly it was the most idiotic note in the Hollywood symphony, and the most frequent.

WHAT IS WANTED

This spirit of secrecy which prevents discussion, and the ignorance of critical standards which makes a great deal of what discussion there is a petty matter of personalia and flip-flap, must be broken down, something more must be done to give the general personnel of the industry a basis in idea and a sense of common purpose. Standards of criticism must be formulated and a proper language of criticism made familiar, so that cinema possibilities may be made more articulate and actual efforts less haphazard and casual. Something should be done, in the first place, to encourage articulacy on the part of each of the many crafts engaged in production. Their attitudes to production should be formulated and their problems, their difficulties and their responsibilities should be made generally known. Something, in fact, should be done to encourage an exchange of ideas between the different crafts engaged in production. The mystic atmosphere in which each, at present, veils its doings has become silly enough.

The idea I have in mind is of some common ground of discussion where the relation of one part of the production process to the others could be made plain. A photoplay, as I have tried to suggest in my series of articles, has many relations. It has certain relations to the other arts, and a complete directorial talent involves an imagination which has a point of contact with each. Production, too, involves some comprehension of the peculiar relation which the cinema has to its world-public, of the place of cinema in modern society, of the demand of the public for day-to-day inspiration, of the sort of themes which will meet that demand. It involves an understanding of box office values less flippant than the casual understanding which has ruled up to the present. Then, again, there are special attitudes for story-writer, cameraman, art director and so on. Some mechanism must be found for disseminating a common knowledge of these relations and for the exchange of these special attitudes.

448

NEED FOR A CINEMATIC SOCIETY

I hesitate to offer the analogy of journalism and the discovered necessity for universities of journalism, but there is, at least, room for a university of cinema in Hollywood in which directors and cameramen and the various experts of the industry could formulate the terms of their work. This they might do first to each other, then to those beginners in cinema who want to take their profession seriously. From such a common ground of discussion something of the common understanding I spoke of might easily develop.

There is a further possibility. It is the general custom for every profession of importance (academic and commercial) to have a society which will bring together the inquiries and experiments which light the way to greater knowledge and further progress. There are engineering societies, scientific societies, geographic societies, and even (in Old England) Aristotelian societies. If a mining engineer finds out a new trick of mining in Western Australia or a professor in Newcastle devises a new signal lamp for fire-damp, each writes a monograph about it that can be read in New York. Indeed, by means of these societies knowledge is shared and the way paved for the general application of new knowledge.

There is, however, no Cinematic Society and, indeed, no encouragement either of the formulation of ideas or of the pushing of investigation and research as these affect cinema. Investigation and research would, of course, be the special cares of such a society. Men should be encouraged to investigate new developments of camera and lighting and report on them. Men who have studied audience reaction ought to be invited to place their findings before the society. Experimental films, or films which involve experiment of one kind or another, ought to be reported on. All matters brought before the society would, of course, be published in monograph form and placed at the disposal of the general personnel of the industry.

SUMMING UP

What does it all come down to? As I gave warning at the beginning, I have purposely exaggerated the weaknesses of the industry by isolating them from the strengths of the industry. I have, in orthodox movie fashion, played them up, and I am personally and privately no more a pessimist about the cinema world than the showman who exaggerates a picture's good points is an optimist about it. I feel that no good purpose is to be served at the moment by taking out a monopoly in hallelujahs. The attitude that all is for the best in the best of all possible worlds and that Hollywood (like anything else) is nothing to lose one's sense of humor about, is a good attitude on occasion. It helps to preserve balance, and it is an impregnable defense against cinema crusaders and cinema nuts. It is fine, too, for those after-dinner moments when honest men may reasonably expect a let-up from labor and a release from the knowledge of their responsibilities. But, meanwhile, the industry has a lot of growing to do, and it can grow one way or another slowly or speedily, as it is directed. This is a matter of plain, common sense.

As I suggest, the industry is still at sixes and sevens in some respects, and in no proper state to take life easily. It must be so keyed at its various points that it not only expands but expands to its fullest potentials. It must see to it that the mechanism for expansion is running properly. It must see to it that such arrangements are made as will (on a long-view policy) bring results in more successful pictures. This is entirely a matter of more enlightened organization. It means, in the last instance, organization for a better all-round understanding among the people who do the actual work of production. I have set down some specific methods by which this might be accomplished. They may be suggestive.

449

In Hollywood, Mauritz Stiller was taken off THE TEMPTRESS (1926), in which Garbo was acting, to make two films with Pola Negri: HOTEL IMPERIAL and THE WOMAN ON TRIAL (both 1927). It is further evidence of his uncertain position that he had been slated to direct Emil Jannings' first American film, but instead directed his third: THE STREET OF SIN (1928), from a story by von Sternberg. Stiller returned to Europe in 1928 and died there that same year. For two years his great talent had been either wasted or partly thwarted by those only partially satisfying films which invariably seemed to result from the mingling of Europeans with Americans in Hollywood.

FLESH AND THE DEVIL (1927) was Garbo's third American film, following THE TORRENT and THE TEMPTRESS (both 1926).

Rather than include an only so-so review of Buster Keaton's THE GENERAL, which opened in New York in February, 1927, I have left it out entirely. Why this marvelous Civil War comedy should have been unenthusiastically received by the critics is a mystery.

Chaney was minus arms in THE UNKNOWN.

On F. Scott Fitzgerald's first visit to Hollywood in 1927, his boredom and restlessness are already apparent in an interview. Clara Bow, high on his list of flappers, had filmed IT, which opened in New York on the same day as THE GENERAL.

HOTEL IMPERIAL   FILM 1927

"HOTEL IMPERIAL," excerpt from "The Silent Drama," R. E. Sherwood, *Life*, Vol. 89, No. 2308, January 27, 1927, p. 24.

The German production, FAUST, tended to prove that camera angles, lap dissolves and other photo-acrobatics are, in themselves, insufficient to make a picture a work of art. HOTEL IMPERIAL now comes along to make that proof conclusive.

HOTEL IMPERIAL has all the visual qualities that made MERRY-GO-ROUND and VARIETY great; its "shots" are extraordinary, and establish its director, Mauritz Stiller, as a genius in the manipulation of camera effects.

But it lacks that homely quality which is known as guts—and all the trick lighting, all the twisted lenses in creation would be unable to atone for the fundamental vitality that isn't there.

Pola Negri is the star and is very good; so, it may be added, is the entire cast, down to the most inconspicuous extra. . . .

FLESH AND THE DEVIL   FILM 1927

"Exceptional Photoplays: FLESH AND THE DEVIL," *National Board of Review Magazine*, Vol. 2, No. 2, February, 1927, pp. 11-13. (With the permission of the National Board of Review of Motion Pictures.)

Directed by . . . . Clarence Brown
Photographed by . . . . William Daniels

The Cast

Leo Von Sellenthin . . . . John Gilbert
Felicitas Von Kletzingk . . . . Greta Garbo
Ulrich Von Kletzingk . . . . Lars Hanson

Hertha Prochvitz	Barbara Kent
Uncle Kutowski	William Orlamond
Pastor Brenckenburg	George Fawcett
Leo's Mother	Eugenie Besserer
Count Von Rhaden	Marc MacDermott
Minna	Marcelle Corday

FLESH AND THE DEVIL is a compelling story convincingly told. The theme with which it deals is a mature one whose appeal will be most appreciated by adult audiences. It is exceptional in its portrayal of that theme both through a wealth of good acting and high directorial skill.

The story is based upon Hermann Sudermann's novel, *The Undying Past*. A comparison between the adaptation and the original is greatly in favor of the picture which gains in strength by its simplification of a rather elaborate plot. The theme of Sudermann's novel, dealing with the devastating effect of an alluring but unprincipled woman, coming between two men who have been united since childhood by bonds of the firmest friendship, verges upon the melodramatic, always an outstanding characteristic in this novelist's work. Cut down to its essentials it is after all only another variation of the familiar vampire plot. Ordinarily that would in itself be enough to make the discriminating picture-goer sniff suspiciously.

How refreshing, therefore, to find that the picture overcomes this handicap and emerges as a fine and self-sufficient piece of screen art. Slightly less expert management combined with a little more lurid detail might well have brought out the melodramatic aspects of the story and have weakened the general impression to the point where the picture could no longer be taken seriously. Burlesque is the nemesis ever threatening to overtake the vampire plot, screen vampires of the past having been what they have been.

The success of the picture lies in the avoidance of that pitfall by making the lady in question both real and unreal until she finally becomes a symbol of sexual appeal rather than any particular bad woman. Felicitas is a woman such as might well have been. She is believable. She is possessed of the beauty which must always make its primary appeal, and she has the refinement and culture which may allow her to maintain herself in her social sphere without being found out and exposed. The usual stage vampire is represented as being cruel and relentless, a strong and sadistic personality. The very perfection of her vices brings on a titter as one suddenly realizes that she is an automaton, a stuffed simulacrum not unlike the unbelievable giraffe which prompted the immortal remark "There ain't no such animal."

Felicitas is not of this species. She is human and weak even though her weakness becomes a destructive force for the men who yield to her. When she falls in love with Leo Von Sellenthin, she does so without circumspection. When the intrigue is discovered by her husband, the military code of honor which held sway in Germany comes into operation and results in a duel in which the husband is killed.

Thus far Felicitas is merely a woman who, presumably no longer loving her husband, becomes passionately enamored of another man, a situation from which the necessary consequences follow. But now she proceeds to interfere in another relationship in which the sanctity of a great friendship is involved. Leo receives an unofficial command to absent himself on colonial service for five years until the scandal of the fatal duel blows over. He leaves her in the care of Ulrich, his friend and boyhood chum. Again the same fatal enchantment ensues and Leo returns after four years only to find Ulrich married to Felicitas. He still loves her and she gradually breaks down his code of honorable aloofness which he tries to hold for the sake of Ulrich, who had been unaware of Leo's infatuation, until these two friends in turn are about to face each other in another deadly duel.

451

But when the two men are confronted with the stark issue of death, they find that their friendship is a stronger and cleaner thing than the selfish passions that have come between them.

The success of such a picture, in these days when audiences have become more sophisticated about ladies of vampirish repute, depends, as we have been at pains to point out, entirely upon the credibility of the lady in question. She must be "believable." And it must also be "believable" that men of standing should fall in love with her and not recognize her for what she is. The old hollow formula of "a fool there was" who was undone by "a rag, a bone and a hank of hair" has slowly yielded to character emphasis.

The leading contributor to the success of FLESH AND THE DEVIL is Greta Garbo. This remarkable Swedish actress has, of course, been groomed for this sort of role ever since her debut in America, as her previous work in THE TORRENT and THE TEMPTRESS clearly shows. She is both physically and emotionally the seductive, appealing type. A very good indication of the changing values and emphasis in the vampire picture is brought home to us if we compare Miss Garbo with the most famous screen vamp of yesteryear, Theda Bara. Miss Bara, with her robust voluptuousness, her relentless eyes and her encircling arms, was the accepted prototype of the lady who has made men uneasy, from St. Anthony to Rudyard Kipling. Her appeal was nothing if not frank, and wise and sober men could be on their guard against her. Miss Garbo, in her later day impersonation, shows a frail physique and a fragile, ethereal air. She is infinitely more civilized and all the more subtle for not being so deliberate. When to these gifts of appearance and suggestion is added the real histrionic power of Miss Garbo, the memorable impression which FLESH AND THE DEVIL is leaving upon contemporary audiences is already to a great extent explained.

To her portrait of Elena—the fine lady, enshrined but emotionally struggling, of the first few reels of THE TEMPTRESS—is thus added, in her Felicitas, a fuller length, richer colored portrait that carries its truth to character clear to the end of the photoplay. Miss Garbo's art is both instinctive and imaginative; it is therefore revealing and consistently right.

The directorial skill of Clarence Brown, the cinegraphic slickness of the photography, and the careful attention given to detail, do the rest. Great care has been taken in the scenification of the whole picture to create an atmosphere in which duels and a society whose social codes are tinged by a military regime, will seem natural. The picture begins in the military training school for officers in which Leo Von Sellenthin and Ulrich Von Kletzingk are students. We see them as part of that life and then follow them on their home vacation in the attractive German town where Leo is to meet the fatal Felicitas. It is all so enchantingly done, with not a little of the charm that recently endeared THE WALTZ DREAM to American audiences.

Then follows the brief interval of happy, undisturbed love with Leo youthfully abandoned in his first infatuation for a woman obviously so much experienced in love, no less enraptured because it is evidently not her first adventure. The sequence of the duel with the husband that follows is also managed in a less strident key than usual in such scenes and the actual duel itself, by being presented in a beautiful silhouette under a few tall romantic linden trees, loses its air of reality so that it is removed from our everyday criticism which has outlawed the duelling code from our everyday life.

John Gilbert and Lars Hanson respectively play the parts of Leo and Ulrich. They succeed in suggesting their deep friendship and comradeliness with a rare combination of conviction and restraint.

John Gilbert impersonates the romantic young German officer without ceasing to be the appealing type of American lover that he is—or bothering to crop his hair too short and to wear a monocle. He retains the air of boyish bewilderment in the midst of the maelstrom of passion that threatens to engulf him. It is pleasant to see that Mr. Gilbert continues to work hard in the interpretation of his part rather than resting upon his mere

452

attractiveness as a male star with already an enviable record behind him. Lars Hanson is, of course, at home in his part and gives excellent support to all who play opposite him.

(From the novel *The Undying Past,* by Hermann Sudermann. Adapted by Benjamin F. Glazer. Produced and distributed by Metro-Goldwyn-Mayer.)

FILM 1927   THE UNKNOWN

"THE UNKNOWN," excerpt from "The Shadow Stage," *Photoplay Magazine,* Vol. 32, No. 3, August 1927, p. 53.

(M.G.M.) Some of the New York critics said that Lon Chaney has overreached himself in playing the armless Alonzo of THE UNKNOWN. (No punning intended, of course.) We think you will like it as an unadulterated shocker.

Alonzo is the armless star of a small circus. He isn't really armless, for he keeps his real ones strapped to his sides. Still, he has developed great skill in using his toes in place of his fingers.

In fact, he is the star knife thrower of the show.

Estrellita, a beauty of the circus, is loved by Alonzo. The girl has a complex against arms, grown out of her hatred of men.

So she is drawn to the "armless" Alonzo.

To gain her heart, the knife thrower hies himself to a hospital and forces a surgeon to amputate his arms. Thus his distorted mind fancies to win the girl. When he returns to the circus, he finds that Malabar, the circus strong man, has overcome Estrellita's complex. In fact, she is in love with Malabar. So Alonzo starts out to eliminate the strong man.

See THE UNKNOWN and follow the story from there.

Like the other Chaney pictures directed by Tod Browning, this has a macabre atmosphere. If you wince at a touch or two of horror, don't go to THE UNKNOWN. If you like strong celluloid food, try it. It has the merit of possessing a finely sinister plot, some moments with a real shock and Lon Chaney. Besides, Joan Crawford is an optical tonic as Estrellita. . . .

1927   "HAS THE FLAPPER CHANGED?"

By Margaret Reid, *Motion Picture Magazine,* Vol. 33, No. 6, July, 1927, pp. 28-29, 104.

> F. Scott Fitzgerald Discusses the Cinema Descendants of the Type He
> Has Made So Well Known

The term "flapper" has become a generalization, meaning almost any *femme* between fifteen and twenty-five. Some five years ago it was a thing of distinction—indicating a neat bit of femininity, collegiate age, who rolled her stockings, chain-smoked, had a heavy "line," mixed and drank a mean highball and radiated "It."

The manner in which the title has come into such general usage is a little involved, but quite simple. A young man wrote a book. His heroine was one of the n. bits of f. referred to above. "Flapper" was her official classification. The young man's book took the country by, as they say, storm. Girls—all the girls—read it. They read about the flapper's deportment, methods and career. And with a nice simultaneousness they became, as nearly as their varied capabilities permitted, flappers. Thus the frequency of the term today. I hope you get my point.

453

The young man responsible for it all, after making clear—in his book—the folly of flappers' ways, married the young person who had been the prototype for the character and started in to enjoy the royalties. The young man was F. Scott Fitzgerald, the book was *This Side of Paradise*, and the flapper's name was Zelda. So about six years later they came to Hollywood and Mr. Fitzgerald wrote a screen story for Constance Talmadge. Only people don't call him Mr. Fitzgerald. They call him "Scotty."

But we don't seem to be getting anywhere. The purpose of this discursion was to hear Mr. F. Scott (or Scotch) Fitzgerald's opinion of the cinema descendants of his original brain-daughter, the Flapper.

It was with an admirable attempt to realize the seriousness of my mission that I went to his bungalow at the Ambassador. Consider, tho! By all literary standards he should have been a middle-aged gentleman with too much waistline, too little hair and steel-rimmed spectacles.

And I knew, from pictures in *Vanity Fair* and hysterical first-hand reports, that instead he was probably the best-looking thing ever turned out of Princeton. Or even (in crescendo) Harvard—or Yale. Only it was Princeton. Add "It," and the charming, vibrant, brilliant mind his work projects. My interest was perhaps a bit more than professional.

There was a large tray on the floor at the door of his suite when I reached it. On the tray were bottles of Canada Dry, some oranges, a bowl of cracked ice and—three very, very empty Bourbon bottles. There was also a card. I paused before ringing the bell and bent down to read the inscription—"With Mr. Van Vechten's kindest regards to Scott and Zelda Fitzgerald." I looked for any further message on the other side, but there was none, so I rang the bell.

It was answered by a young man of medium height. With Prince-of-Wales hair and eyes that are, I am sure, green. His features are chiseled finely. His mouth draws your attention. It is sensitive, taut and faintly contemptuous, and even in the flashing smile does not lose the indication of intense pride.

Behind him was Mrs. Fitzgerald, the Rosamund of *This Side of Paradise*. Slim, pretty like a rather young boy; with one of those schoolgirl complexions and clear gray eyes; her hair as short as possible, slicked back. And dressed as only New Yorkers intangibly radiate smartness.

The two of them might have stepped, sophisticated and charming, from the pages of any of the Fitzgerald books.

They greeted me and discovered the tray hilariously.

"Carl Van Vechten's going-away gift," the First Flapper of the Land explained in her indolent, Alabama drawl. "He left this morning after a week's stay. Said he came here for a little peace and rest, and he disrupted the entire colony."

In the big, dimly lit room, Mrs. Fitzgerald sank sighing into a chair. She had just come from a Black Bottom lesson. F. Scott moved restlessly from chair to chair. He had just come from a studio conference and I think he'd rather have been at the Horse Show. He was also a trifle disconcerted by the impending interview. In one he had given to an avid press-lady the day before, he had said all his bright remarks. And he couldn't think up any more in such a short time.

"What, tho, were his opinions of screen flappers? As flappers? As compared to his Original Flappers?"

"Well, I can only," he began, lighting a cigarette, putting it out and crossing to another chair, "speak about the immediate present. I know nothing of their evolution. You see, we've been living on the Riviera for three years. In that time the only movies we've seen have been a few of the very old pictures, or the Westerns they show over there. I might," his face brightening, "tell you what I think of Tom Mix."

"Scotty!" his wife cautioned quickly.

"Oh, well. . . ."

Having exhausted all the available chairs in the room, he returned to the first one and began all over again.

"Have flappers changed since you first gave them the light of publicity? For better? For worse?"

"Only in the superficial matter of clothes, hair-cut, and wise-cracks. Fundamentally they are the same. The girls I wrote about were not a type—they were a generation. Free spirits—evolved through the war chaos and a final inevitable escape from restraint and inhibitions. If there is a difference, it is that the flappers today are perhaps less defiant, since their freedom is taken for granted and they are sure of it. In my day"—stroking his hoary beard—"they had just made their escape from dull and blind conventionality. Subconsciously there was a hint of belligerence in their attitude, because of the opposition they met—but overcame.

"On the screen, of course, is represented every phase of flapper life. But just as the screen exaggerates action, so it exaggerates type. The girl who, in real life, uses a smart, wise-cracking line is portrayed on the screen as a hard-boiled baby. The type, one of the most dangerous, whose forte is naïveté, approximates a dumb-dora when she reaches the screen. The exotic girl becomes bizarre. But the actresses who do flappers really well understand them thoroughly enough to accentuate their characteristics without distorting them."

"How about Clara Bow?" I suggested, starting in practically alphabetical order.

"Clara Bow is the quintessence of what the term 'flapper' signifies as a definite description. Pretty, impudent, superbly assured, as worldly wise, briefly clad and 'hard-berled' as possible. There were hundreds of them—her prototypes. Now, completing the circle, there are thousands more—patterning themselves after her.

"Colleen Moore represents the young collegiate—the carefree, lovable child who rules bewildered but adoring parents with an iron hand. Who beats her brothers and beaus on the tennis-courts, dances like a professional and has infallible methods for getting her own way. All deliciously celluloid—but why not? The public notoriously prefers glamor to realism. Pictures like Miss Moore's flapper epics present a glamorous dream of youth and gaiety and swift, tapping feet. Youth—actual youth—is essentially crude. But the movies idealize it, even as Gershwin idealizes jazz in the 'Rhapsody in Blue.'

"Constance Talmadge is the epitome of young sophistication. She is the deft princess of lingerie—and love—plus humor. She is Fifth Avenue and diamonds and Catalya orchids and Europe every year. She is sparkling and witty and as gracefully familiar with the new books as with the new dances. I have an idea that Connie appeals every bit as strongly to the girls in the audience as to the men. Her dash—her *zest* for things—is compelling. She is the flapper *de luxe*.

"I happened to see a preview the other night, at a neighborhood movie house near here. It was Milton Sills' latest, I am told. There was a little girl in it—playing a tough baby-vamp. I found that her name was Alice White. She was a fine example of the European influence on our flappers. Gradually, due mostly to imported pictures, the vogue for 'pose' is fading.

"European actresses were the first to disregard personal appearance in emotional episodes. Disarranged hair—the wrong profile to the camera—were of no account during a scene. Their abandonment to emotion precluded all thought of beauty. Pola Negri brought it to this country. It was adopted by some. But the flappers seem to have been a bit nervous as to the results. It was, perhaps, safer to be cute than character. This little White girl, however, appears to have a flair for this total lack of studied effect. She is the flapper impulsive—child of the moment—wildly eager for every drop of life. She represents—not the American flapper—but the European.

"Joan Crawford is doubtless the best example of the dramatic flapper. The girl you see at the smartest night clubs—gowned to the apex of sophistication—toying iced glasses,

455

with a remote, faintly bitter expression—dancing deliciously—laughing a great deal with wide, hurt eyes. It takes girls of actual talent to get away with this in real life. When they do perfect the thing, they have a lot of fun with it.

"Then, inevitably, there is the quality that is infallible in any era, any town, any time. Femininity, *ne plus ultra*. Unless it is a very definite part of a girl, it is insignificant, and she might as well take up exoticism. But sufficiently apparent, it is always irresistible. I suppose she isn't technically a flapper—but because she *is* Femininity, one really should cite Vilma Banky. Soft and gentle and gracious and sweet—all the lacy adjectives apply to her. This type is reticent and unassuming—but just notice the quality of orchids on her shoulder as she precedes her reverential escort into the theater.

"It's rather futile to analyze flappers. They are just girls—all sorts of girls. Their one common trait being that they are young things with a splendid talent for life."

COMMENTARY

WINGS appeared in New York in the summer of 1927. Directed by William Wellman, it was the first big film about aviation in World War I. Gary Cooper is visible only for seconds in it; Clara Bow's part is longer, but not very typical. It is described here at the time it went into general circulation, the following year. Note the competition in Maine from a nearby town playing the film with sound effects.

UNDERWORLD established von Sternberg without reservation as "one of the real creators for the screen." Is "Buck" Mulligan a tribute to the character in Joyce's *Ulysses*?

Young Beaumont Newhall made study notes on THE CAT AND THE CANARY (1927), by Paul Leni (1885-1929), who had designed sets and directed in Germany. Leni also made in Hollywood a film with Conrad Veidt: THE MAN WHO LAUGHS (1928), and THE LAST WARNING (1929).

Murnau's SUNRISE (1927), which some regard as a masterwork, was entirely planned in Germany, from a Carl Mayer script, but was made for Fox in California with no budget. Murnau had instructions to take his time and use what money he needed to produce a great film.

His second Hollywood film was FOUR DEVILS (1928), and his third, OUR DAILY BREAD, which, begun later that year in Oregon, was apparently abandoned when nearly finished, for fear that a silent film, even by a master director, would be lost in the growing roar of sound. Even so, TABU (1931), Murnau's next and final film, released just after his death, was also silent.

WINGS   **FILM 1927**

"WINGS," excerpts from "Box Office Record," *The Motion Picture Almanac—1929*, The Quigley Publishing Company, Chicago, Ill., 1929, p. 209.

(Paramount, Clara Bow, Charles (Buddy) Rogers, Richard Arlen, Gary Cooper, James Hall, 15 [reels]—*October 21-22-23 [1928].*) A great production. Satisfied very well and did a fair business. Nothing sensational, however, as I had expected to break the house record. (Empress theatre, Akron, Ia.—General patronage.) *October 16-17.* Of course, the greatest picture of aviation. Although the percentage is low it was because of a sound equipped house 15 miles from me playing it two weeks ahead of me. I estimate 75 per cent of my patrons motored away to see it. It's great though. Have seen it three times and I'd see it again. (Town Hall theatre, Carmel, Me.—Small town patronage.) Good entertainment, well directed and it pleased crowds on four nights. Our only objection was that Paramount (figuratively speaking) met us at the door with shotguns in the form

57. *Emil Jannings, the great German character actor, as the Russian general attacked by the mob of revolutionists in Josef von Sternberg's THE LAST COMMAND (1928). This actor-director team, which achieved this "brilliant performance" in Hollywood, was to function once again, in Germany, in THE BLUE ANGEL (1929-1930).*

of a coupla checkers who seemed willing enough to extract the shirts from our backs in order to satisfy the insatiable demands of the producers, after the split was reached. Exploitation expenses, with overhead and too close a split caused us to record a poor showing at the box office, hence our "net" wasn't much, and "prestige," that intangible and illusive thing the film peddlers prate about, fails utterly to provide beefsteak for our tables. (B. B. theatre, Ashland, Neb.—General patronage.) . . . Great picture that pulled fair, but too long. The chickens were crowing each morning when we got home. Let's kill the next guy who goes over 10 reels. (Crystal theatre, Wayne, Neb.—General patronage.) . . .

UNDERWORLD

"Exceptional Photoplays: UNDERWORLD," *National Board of Review Magazine*, Vol. 2, No. 8, August, 1927, pp. 10-11. (With the permission of the National Board of Review of Motion Pictures.)

Directed by	Josef von Sternberg
Photographed by	Bert Glennon

The Cast

"Bull" Weed	George Bancroft
"Rolls Royce"	Clive Brook
"Feathers"	Evelyn Brent
"Slippy" Lewis	Larry Semon
"Buck" Mulligan	Fred Kohler
Mulligan's Girl	Helen Lynch
Jaloma	Jerry Mandy
"High Collar" Sam	Karl Morse

UNDERWORLD is just about the best underworld picture that has come along. Melodrama it is, but melodrama that is human, that keeps its actors people while unraveling a plot developed through the interplay of human temperaments, passions, feelings. Cinematically it is modern, in the stride of the art. Imaginatively it is frequently of the first rank, a finely visualized selection of touches that reveal not only the fabric of the characters but as well the predicament of their lives, intensified as they are by the decent instincts that urge them upward despite the dragging impulses that are the result of their conditioning in society's darker strata. As important, it stamps an American actor, George Bancroft, with finality as of the elite among screen artists, a power like Jannings and Krauss, and it brings a director, Josef von Sternberg, very definitely into his own as among the real creators for the screen, thus fulfilling a prophesy more than hinted by THE SALVATION HUNTERS.

Isn't this all pretty high praise for just another picture? we seem to hear it said. And to boot: Doesn't the picture deal with criminals and isn't it melodrama? If it is artistic in places, how about its moral tone?

We answer categorically: Certainly it is another picture, but not one, just. For all that it is a melodrama with characters, fascinating as they will always be, of the underworld, it is that rare thing on the screen, a film wrought on the iron of truth, on a framework of understanding visualized in telling, conclusive movement that is the target reached by all good art, and seldom reached, at least so unerringly, in motion pictures. And for its moral values (and may the censors and the criers-out for "better" pictures perceive them in this film!), they are coursing in the very veins of the story picture; fortunately, neither

458

skin deep nor washed on with a smirk. It is the story picture of a man coming from darkness into light, surrendering at the last gasp the kingdom of his world to gain the kingdom of himself. As the film travels, we watch the coarse clay refining in a fierce burning. It is a parable of the primitive child-man attaining the civilized state, facing the moral problem, perceiving it, finally redeeming himself and the others of his tribe. The purely sentimental is untouched by the film. "Bull" Weed is set down for what he is, and his personal story is ended as it inevitably must end—at the hands of himself as much as at the hands of the law.

"Bull" Weed is a Napoleon of the underworld. He has a vast superiority feeling. He cannot imagine anything overpowering him. His girl "Feathers," his chief friend and retainer one "Rolls Royce," whom "Bull" has taken in from the streets, provided with money and clothes befitting the thing "Bull" perceives he once has been—a gentleman. "Bull" nicknames him "Rolls Royce" because, like the super automobile, he has the pleasing and trustworthy quality of silence. Thus "Bull" is disclosed as being of a philanthropic turn of nature in a wholly fascinating, illogical way. He has a real instinct for saving. Sin he can perceive in others, although hardly in himself—a cunning reading of not only the man, but also perhaps of the so-called criminal type.

"Feathers" and "Rolls Royce" fall in love with each other, impelled by mutual recognition of the pathetic residue of decency left in both. At the same time, they remain true to "Bull," taught by the decency he has shown to them.

Then "Bull" kills "Buck" Mulligan, a gang leader, for insulting "Feathers." He is taken by the police, tried, and condemned to be hanged, leaving "Feathers" and "Rolls Royce" soon to be free to follow their love. They make plans to go away together, while "Bull," in the death cell, is agonized by the rumor that they have turned traitors to him, double-crossed his love for the one and his trust of the other.

But "Feathers" and "Rolls Royce" cannot turn back on "Bull." At the last moment, they plan to rescue him. "Bull," surreptitiously acquainted with the plan, is torn by hope and suspicion that it is only a cock and bull story, another turn of the doublecross.

The plan of "Feathers" and "Rolls Royce" is discovered by the police and broken up. "Bull" from his cell window, awaiting his execution, sees the ominous hearse, in which his gang were to be hidden in order to rescue him, drive into the jail yard without disturbance. He does not know that it has been surrounded by the police, and his friends captured. While "Feathers" waits in the road with a car and "Rolls Royce" waits in the railroad station, acting as a decoy, "Bull" breaks jail and escapes to his hideaway, determined to kill "Rolls Royce" and "Feathers" for their fancied treachery.

Meanwhile "Feathers," hearing that the plan to save "Bull" has gone amiss, returns in sorrow to the hideaway, thinking "Bull" has been hanged and expecting to meet "Rolls Royce." She finds "Bull" there. Her murder at his hands, despite her protestation of innocence, is prevented by the arrival of the police, who besiege the place and bombard it with machine-gun fire. "Bull" barricades doors and windows and shoots back, determined to sell his life dearly. Then "Rolls Royce," wounded in running the gauntlet through the firing area, enters by the secret passage that "Bull" has found locked from the outside. "Rolls Royce" has returned at the risk of his life to save his friend.

Confronted by this evidence of "Feathers's" and "Rolls Royce's" fidelity, confounded by the knowledge that though they love each other with a better love than any he has known, they have yet been willing to sacrifice themselves in order to stand by him to the end, "Bull" makes his expiation, gives generosity for generousity, makes return for the assurance thus gained of mankind's essential meaning of love, the meaning that blindly he has always hungered for and that life has at last brought to him. He sends "Feathers" and "Rolls Royce" out through the secret passage to safety and honest happiness together, and signals his surrender to the police outside. As they lead him away, an officer remarks to him, "Do you think your extra hour of life was worth it, 'Bull'?" "Bull" answers, "I have learned something I always wanted to know—now, come on."

459

Out of this simple pattern of action, the full portrait of "Bull" emerges—the coarse, brutal, jovial, ignorant, conceited, generous, loving, pathetic, in the end self-redeeming man—done to a shade, a glint of the eye, by George Bancroft. On each side of that picture stands a smaller, less complete, a bit more "movie," portrait of "Feathers," played by Evelyn Brent, and "Rolls Royce," played by Clive Brook, but each stamped with sincerity, the effort toward creation for a single end—that of making an honest picture.

The pattern of action, cinematically concentrated at point after point, blots out such minor weaknesses as occur, even the old stuff such as the police chase in automobiles. When it weaves around the figure of "Bull," it is often superb. "Bull" playing checkers through the bars with his prison guard, listening for the wagon of death, keeping up his manhood, hoping and assailed by miserable doubts, his hands at last gripping for the guard; "Bull," pacing in the hideaway, desperate, murderous at heart, taking in the little kitten from the hallway and feeding it from the finger half unconsciously wetted in the stolen cream-bottle. Nothing is overdone here; one says, He would do just that; that is the way he would look; it is right on the screen. Such details as the underworld ball, the impression of mounting orgy given by the fast cutting, quarter-foot flashes of contorted faces as various guests peer drunkenly in a contorting mirror hung on the wall, can teach many a director how to do these things in true motion picture fashion, so that sensation darts from the screen to the spectator and the senses run with the picture. UN-DERWORLD opens with beautiful economy and swiftness, plays with its camerawork around each situation until it is complete, and brings them to a focus in a perfect ending.

UNDERWORLD is a film of integrity on the part of director, scenario writer, actors and cameraman, done with back-bone, which is to say, strength and grit. Best of all, at least for those looking for cinema growth on our native screen, it is a film made in America, with an actor and a director who need take off their hats to none.

(*From the story by Ben Hecht. Adapted by Charles Furthman. Produced and distributed by Paramount-Famous-Lasky.*)

THE CAT AND THE CANARY   FILM 1927

"THE CAT AND THE CANARY, à la Caligari," unpublished study notes by Beaumont Newhall, written about a screening at the Olympia Theatre, Boston, in December, 1927.

The story: does not matter at all, for it is an asinine mystery tale, handled by the director as well as possible. From John Willard's play of the same name.
The cast: Laura La Plante, Creighton Hale, Tully Marshall, Martha Mattox, Flora Finch, Gertrude Astor.
Produced [and directed] by Paul Leni.

THE CAT AND THE CANARY is a mystery tale, and extremely good if you like that sort of thing. It is not my idea of the best stuff from which to make a cinema. Nevertheless Paul Leni succeeded in putting a lot of punch and suspense into it, and I do not hesitate to call his work commendable. As to the photography, the criterion of a good moving-picture, it was far above par. The first scene showed some bottles, and a cat tearing a canary apart, or rather fighting with it, these bottles then changed in a startling manner to a castle high upon a hill. Here is where the scenes were enacted. There was a series of remarkable dissolves, the opening of a door, the entrance of a person to the assembled multitude. Mr. Leni was not at all wary about using that most valuable asset in the cameraman's bag of tricks, the trucking of the camera around the scenes. It seems that the will was to be read at twelve o'clock, so at twelve we see the mechanism of a clock striking out the hour, this slowly dissolves, or is superimposed upon the scene showing the crabby lawyer reading the will. Mr. Leni places his camera near the floor and thus heightens the weird effects. A hand seizes a jewel around the sleeping woman's neck. She screams, and bolts upright in bed, a truck-in to her mouth, followed immediately by a title "Help!", very effective. The doctor examining the young heiress was inevitably a scene from the famous CABINET OF DR. CALIGARI, there was the same type of cold impassionate mental doctor, spreading fear and mental disorder more than curing it.

I have called this film "à la CALIGARI" because there is so much insanity in it, and this feeling of insanity is heightened by the crazy sets. All honor to Mr. Leni for making a presentable photoplay from a maudlin stage thriller.

1927   "TRUE TO THE MEDIUM"

By Louise Bogan, *The New Republic*, Vol. 52, No. 673, October 26, 1927, pp. 263-264.

Mr. Murnau's talent as it appears in his direction of SUNRISE (Times Square Theater) is a talent that takes the camera on neglected rather than new terms, making it primarily an eye for motion-beside-within-motion, a retina reflecting an intricately flowing world. The camera moves as the eye, and the eye, with the camera, makes journeys, steering gently along the path of the subject it follows, is caught into long perspectives that plunge into the screen, swerves around corners, becomes involved in elaborate fleeing lights and shadows, all the exciting mixture and quarrel of vision. Here is camera technique pushed to its limits, freed from pantomime and parade against a world as motionless as a backdrop. In the same way that a man walking becomes a more complicated and dramatic mechanism when seen from a moving train than from an open window, so the people in this adapted Sudermann story are heightened and realized in their joy and despair by having their action set against action.

Not since the earliest, simplest moving pictures, when locomotives, fire-engines, and crowds in streets were transposed to the screen.artlessly and endearingly, when the entranced eye was rushed through tunnels and over precipices on runaway trains, has there been such joy in motion as under Murnau's direction. He slaps down the cramping cubes of sets and makes, whenever possible, walls of glass and steel that imprison in their clear geometry the intersection of long smooth lines of traffic, people walking, trains gathering speed. When the rare shot shows human gesture against a static background, the stillness is an accent, after the rush of a full and moving screen. He knows every complication and subtlety of his method—his people walk over uneven rather than level ground, along paths always slightly devious. The earth has mist over it, and breath comes visibly from nostrils. Distortion he uses but rarely, and then only as the object naturally might be distorted against the eye.

The story of the young peasant who is seduced into the thought of murdering his wife by the woman from the city is given in unbroken sequences, a continuity of the eye, throughout half its length. The husband and the city woman embracing in the dark fields, the wife in her clumsy dress seated in the boat with rocking water behind her, the blind face of the husband as he rows back to the land after his murderous resolution breaks, and, above all, the two agonized young creatures huddled on the platform of the trolley car with the landscape pouring by them through the car windows—all these scenes have a plasticity, a beauty not easily named or described. They have economy as well as reckless daring in presentation, and are, at the same time, completely true to their medium.

The last half of the picture moves more heavily. It has less freshness and more obvious invention. The episodes of the photographer's studio and the barber's shop are ordinary in conception and detail. Fortunately, however, here the emphasis is laid upon the   461 young peasant couple, and the energy and youth of George O'Brien and Janet Gaynor make even the duller moments come alive. Murnau's imagination is whetted by speed and confusion; his camera should always be taxed to its capacity. His real power again comes through when, at the end of their day, the young pair are set against every conceivable effect of light on darkness. Rockets leap upward; bonfires burn on the water's edge; there is monstrous lightning; and, at the last, a crowd of lanterns is held up over still black water. Night and storm revolve behind the frightened man and woman, and the picture springs back to an intensity hardly to be believed.

SUNRISE is not fortunate in its art director. It has had contrived for it a village evidently molded from marzipan, artificial trees—one remembers the real tree blowing beyond the prison window in VARIETY—and a claptrap moon. Mr. Murnau does not need this "art" superimposed upon his reality.

UNDERWORLD, a melodrama concerned with Chicago gangsters, has little to recommend it save the neat sense of economy and brisk timing on the part of its director, Josef von Sternberg. His sequences are worked out crisply and with dispatch, without soggy lapses in which nothing in particular happens. He presents a conversation by a series of close-ups—not a new device, but one seldom managed cleverly. Each face speaks and is really concerned with the face seen but a moment since, and does not merely stare dully or furiously out of the screen. The jewelry-store hold-up is done in four flashes: a pistol shot smashes a clock set above shelves full of silver; a frightened clerk turns; a hand scrapes diamonds from their cases; a crowd is seen through the store's plate-glass window. Police on motorcycles and in long shining cars are handled vigorously. The fight at the hideaway has thrilling disorder but no waste motion. This kind of incisiveness, this giving of the part for the whole, when used imaginatively, not spottily or as a trick, is a method exactly suited to the screen, and one little used.

George Bancroft as Bull Weed is excellent. His big mouth opened in a laugh gives liveliness and gusto to a picture otherwise lacking in intelligent characterization.

Paul Leni, a German director imported by Universal Pictures, has done his best for THE CAT AND THE CANARY, a story full of complicated disappearances and such box-office horrors as long taloned hands appearing from wainscoting. He has invention—a turn for grim lighting and sinister composition not ineffective even when applied to this thin material—which should come through magnificently, given a picture of really terrifying implications. THE CAT AND THE CANARY has several sets done in the best *Castle of Otranto* feeling. One, a long corridor lined with tall Gothic windows whose heavy pale curtains blow out in the wind like shrouds, is shot from every angle—from above, as a woman moves along it carrying a lamp, from below, when figures seen against the narrow arches lean back in alarming distortion. Leni suggests action by shadows sliding against bleak bright walls; he breaks up his scene into patterns by placing his actors behind barred chairs and lozenged windows. His talent, more discreet and less violent than Murnau's, is yet one that can save sets from their three-walled monotony, switch them into impressive design, give them tenseness and angularity.

The possibilities of motion pictures as a medium for projecting horror have never been fully realized. THE CABINET OF DR. CALIGARI pointed the way, with its use of backgrounds pulled into the color of the action. Without screams or pistol shots, by arrangement and pattern alone, by a combination of pure realism and grotesque dream, the picture of pure horror is still waiting to be made. If any company wants to produce Poe, Paul Leni might very well be the man to take the work in hand. *The Narrative of A. Gordon Pym*, under his direction, should be a full adventure for the startled eye.

The maneuvering of men and machines in war has always been perfect grist for the camera. WINGS carries the panorama of war from the ground into what appears to be an
infinite sky. There are some almost visionary scenes of planes engaged in attack and

escape in a wilderness of clouds, of enormous clouds and great trees with little men under them. The magnascope, a device which widens the screen, making, at some intense moment perspectives seem endless and figures hugely stereoscopic, has possibilities here disclosed only in part. Its properties could intensify landscape to such an extent that the painted drops, now so often used so dully, would never be considered feasible by any intelligent director.

Each of these four pictures recognizes in some degree both the limitations of, and the properties that are claims and demands upon, the camera. Two of them have been made by native directors; all have been photographed in America with native actors. It is to be suspected that the leaven of authentic excitement has definitely been dropped into the lump of the American motion picture industry.

Louise Bogan.

FILM 1927   SUNRISE

"SUNRISE," excerpt from "Box Office Record," *The Motion Picture Almanac—1929*, The Quigley Publishing Company, Chicago, Illinois, 1929, p. 207.

Fox, George O'Brien, Janet Gaynor, Bodil Rosing, Margaret Livingston, Farrell Mac-Donald, Ralph Slipperly, Jane Winton, Arthur Housman, Eddie Boland, 10 [reels].— Artistic, probably, from a directorial point of view, but the plot was too simple and dragged out to excessive length. Small town patrons not very enthusiastic regarding its merits and there were as many knocks as words of praise. The intelligentsia of the large cities may go wild over Mr. Murnau's art, but the people in small towns don't appreciate it quite as much. O'Brien's, Gaynor's, Livingston's acting was good. (Amuse-U theatre, Melville, La.—General patronage.)

COMMENTARY

THE JAZZ SINGER, so full of significance for the future, opened in New York October 6, 1927.

LOVE was the first of the two films Garbo made from Tolstoy's *Anna Karenina*; **the second belongs to the sound period (1935).** *Time*, **which was rarely enthusiastic about films in those days, makes an exception here.**

FILM 1927   THE JAZZ SINGER

"THE JAZZ SINGER," excerpt from "The Silent Drama," R. E. Sherwood, Vol. 90, No. 2347, October 27, 1927, p. 24.

There is one moment in THE JAZZ SINGER that is fraught with tremendous significance.

Al Jolson, appearing as a Jewish youth, returns to his old home after years of wandering around the Pantages circuit. His strictly orthodox father has disowned him because he chose to sing mammy songs in music halls rather than chants in the synagogue; his mother, however, welcomes the prodigal with open arms.

Al sits down at the piano and sings "Blue Skies" for his mother. Thanks to the Vitaphone attachment, his marvelous voice rings out from the screen, the sound agreeing perfectly with the movements of his mobile lips, the wriggling of his shoulders, the nervous tapping of his feet.

463

After the song, there is a brief bit of spoken dialogue and then Al bursts into "Blue Skies" again. When he is halfway through the chorus, his father enters the room, realizes that his house is being profaned with jazz, and shouts, "Stop!"

At this point, the Vitaphone withdraws and THE JAZZ SINGER returns to a routine of pantomime punctuated with subtitles.

Such is the moment referred to in paragraph one—and when it came, I for one suddenly realized that the end of the silent drama is in sight, that I shall have to find a new name for this department, and that several attractive heading designs by John Held, Jr., will have to be thrown out.

There is no question of doubt that the Vitaphone justifies itself in THE JAZZ SINGER. Furthermore, it proves that talking movies are considerably more than a lively possibility: they are close to an accomplished fact.

THE JAZZ SINGER isn't much of a moving picture, as moving pictures go. It has a good idea (taken from Samuel Raphaelson's play), but it has been hoked and sugared to a regrettable extent; and Al Jolson as an actor on the screen is only fair.

But when Al Jolson starts to sing . . . well, bring on your super-spectacles, your million-dollar thrills, your longshots of Calvary against a setting sun, your close-ups of a glycerine tear on Norma Talmadge's cheek—I'll trade them all for one instant of any ham song that Al cares to put over, and the hammier it is, the better I'll like it.

In view of the imminence of talking movies, I wonder what Clara Bow's voice will sound like. And I wonder whether the speeches that the Hollywood subtitle writers compose will be as painful to hear as they are to read.

Perhaps the silent drama had better remain silent until Miss Bow and the other stars have taken a few lessons in voice culture, and until all the present subtitlers have died or something. . . .

LOVE   **FILM 1927**

Excerpt from "Cinema: The New Pictures," *Time*, Vol. 10, No. 24, December 12, 1927, pp. 43-44.

LOVE is certainly a poor translation of the title *Anna Karenina*. It would be natural to suppose that the rest of famed Leo Tolstoy's novel would suffer similarly; that it does not, is due in part to the direction of Edmund Goulding and in even larger part to the acting of Greta Garbo.

The story definitely follows the outlines of what has been called the "greatest novel in the world." Anna Karenina meets Count Vronsky one snowy day, has an affair with him that reaches its climax when she leaves her husband and its conclusion when she accepts a defeat (which is totally inevitable) by stepping in front of a fast train. That any film producer should begin by calling his picture LOVE and end it with this necessary but cinematically unconventional tragedy is only one of the many contratictions, which in their sum, make this one of the most striking adaptations yet effected.

There are four moments upon which the focus of the story falls: the snowstorm in which, after an accident to her sleigh, Anna meets Count Vronsky; the steeplechase in which he rides with the gay officers of his regiment; the moment when Anna Karenina, after she has gone away with her lover, creeps into the bedroom where her son is asleep; and the moment when, a vague figure in veils, she vanishes as silently as a bird's wing in the brightness of a locomotive's headlight.

These moments belong mostly to Swedish Greta Garbo whose beauty infuses the **464** picture with a cold white glow; John Gilbert as Vronsky is too frequently exposed to a

58. Domestic tension: Eleanor Boardman and James Murray as the husband and wife in THE CROWD (1928) by King Vidor. The resolution of this fine American film presented problems. Vidor shot a whole group of alternate endings. Perhaps a series of previews determined the ending that now completes the film.

highly approximate lens, he is too willing to act only with his teeth or his hair, to duplicate the excellence of his performance in THE BIG PARADE. But his inadequacies are minor and partly made evident by contrast. Good handling of minor parts by George Fawcett, Brandon Hurst, Emily Fitzroy and Philippe de Lacy, intelligent photoplay, brilliant direction are enough for any picture that includes such a performance as that supplied by Actress Garbo. . . .

COMMENTARY

THE LAST COMMAND (1928), in which von Sternberg directed Emil Jannings, must have been by far Jannings' best American film. Gloria Swanson's SADIE THOMPSON, with Raoul Walsh (1892-   ) directing and also acting the role of the sergeant, came through very well, after some compromise with the censors. Unfortunately, the final reel is missing in the only known print. With THE CROWD, King Vidor surpassed his BIG PARADE.

THE LAST COMMAND   **FILM 1928**

"His National Anthem," excerpt from "The Screen," Mordaunt Hall, *The New York Times*, January 23, 1928, p. 18.

> With Emil Jannings, Evelyn Brent, William Powell, Nicholas Soussanin and Michael Visaroff, based on a story by Lajos Biros, directed by Josef von Sternberg; Miriam Lax, soprano; HAVE A DRINK!, a Pathé novelty scenic. At the Rialto Theatre.

From the standpoint of its narrative, Emil Jannings's latest picture, THE LAST COM-MAND, now at the Rialto Theatre, is one of the most satisfactory of shadow stories. It is logical throughout. It was inspired by the experiences of a Russian General, who fled to this country after the revolution in his own land. This production has its forced moments, its sluggish incidents, but the chronicle is equipped with a double strain of suspense. It strikes one as a good short story turned to excellent account in film form. It is a far more plausible account than that of THE WAY OF ALL FLESH, but in the older picture the detail was more carefully filmed than that of THE LAST COMMAND.

This current offering has a clever finish, an ending that is particularly skillfully devised, and one that is most effective. And if there are moments when Mr. Jannings holds the same expression and pose too long, you are rewarded for the most part with a brilliant performance in which there is a wealth of imagination. In the closing scenes, Mr. Jannings gives a highly gifted and gripping portrayal of the last moments of the bent and bowed czarist generalissimo working as an extra in a motion picture studio. You see General Dolgorucki meet his death in the same uniform he wore with pomp and confidence of his high office before the red flag flew from Moscow's Kremlin, and the fiddle, a piano and a 'cello are rendering the old Russian National anthem.

Just before the General crumples up on the salt-covered, barbed-wire battleground of the studio, he hears his militant hymn and the director, a Russian who had no reason to love the General, gave the old man the words of comfort that caused the extra, in his unbalanced mental state, to believe that the Russia that was had come into power again.

Mr. Jannings does not wear a cap in this scene, as he realized that it would conceal to a certain extent his various expressions. He is magnificent as he straightens up at the sound of his militant hymn and then drops to the studio "snow."

"He was a great actor, that old guy," observes the casting director.

"And a great man, which is more," adds the picture director, who incidentally in Russia had felt the General's riding crop on his cheek.

The motion picture end of this feature is wonderfully good, even to the selection of the players. There are the "yes men," the light experts, the electric wires like eels around the studio floor. The instructions are done to a T, without anything being too extravagant. The story opens up with the choosing of a General for the battle scene, and Dolgorucki's photograph is brought out. It results in his selection and soon the casting director's assistant is on the wire calling Dolgorucki on the telephone at his shabby abode. He is told to report at 6:30 the next morning.

As the broken Russian military commander, Jannings gives a hint of the man's sufferings. He wears a beard. His face is that of an aristocrat, but every half second he shakes his head, like a man suffering from shell shock. They gibe him about this in the studio and scoff at him when he tells them, the other extras, that the Czar gave him his military cross. Jannings is perceived gazing at his make-up box, the cover of which is a mirror. He looks, every so often shaking his head. Then comes a fade-out and soon one sees the General as he had been before the Kerensky or Soviet days. He is a man of courage, one who may use his riding crop occasionally, but who is not cruel. He loves his fatherland and even sneers at the Czar for taking a division of troops from the battle front to satisfy the Little Father's vanity.

More might have been accomplished with these Russian scenes to give a better idea of the General. His style appears to be cramped at times, for while one is told that he is a cousin of the Czar and commander of the Russian armies, he does not appear to be doing much more than the work of a captain.

There is pictured the flaring up of the rabble, and Jannings is shown with swollen lips, blood-smeared, standing against a wall of a railway station. In some of these flashes Mr. Jannings—who, as the General, admittedly has suffered frightful punishment—could nevertheless have shown in his eyes some fire when the men and women goad him and spit water in his face. His strength may have been ebbing, but he now and again lifts some coal to the locomotive's fire, and subsequently he musters up enough strength to bang the locomotive driver over the head with a shovel, and then to leap from the locomotive to the snow. But it is Mr. Jannings's splendid work that causes one to want just a bit more. He lives the character and the most trifling shortcoming makes one wonder at it.

After the chapters in Russia, wherein there is quite a good portrait of the last Czar, the story goes back to the studio.

Evelyn Brent is pleasing as a girl who helps the General. William Powell gives a sterling portrait of a motion picture director and also as one of the ringleaders of the infuriated mob. . . .

FILM 1928   SADIE THOMPSON

"Exceptional Photoplays: SADIE THOMPSON," *National Board of Review Magazine*, Vol. 3, No. 2, February, 1928, p. 9. (With the permission of the National Board of Review of Motion Pictures.)

Directed by . . . . Raoul Walsh

Photographed by . . . . Oliver Marsh
George Barnes
Robert Kurrle

The Cast

Sadie Thompson . . . . Gloria Swanson   467

Oliver Hamilton	Lionel Barrymore
Sergeant Tim O'Hara	Raoul Walsh
Mrs. Hamilton	Blanche Friderici
Dr. McPhail	Charles Lane
Mrs. McPhail	Florence Midgley
Joe Horn, the trader	James A. Marcus

Story, "Miss Thompson," by W. Somerset Maugham.

A serious dramatic motion picture is always an event. SADIE THOMPSON serves as an excellent example, for we have here a screen production far exceeding the average in telling a story of meaning and interest to the mentally adult motion picture-goer. Except for the change in the name of one character and the omission of a few unessentials, the transcript of the Somerset Maugham story as exemplified by its stage version *Rain* has been carried out with vivid accuracy.

The propriety of producing SADIE THOMPSON is fully proven by the result, for here the screen is again vindicated as a serious and legitimate purveyor of ideas. SADIE THOMPSON says something. Sifted to its essentials, if you are looking for morals, what it says is persuasive of good rather than bad. Morally it is constructive, as all revelation of life in terms of human action must be. This story of the persecuted, tawdry Sadie battled with for the salvation of her soul by the fanatic reformer deluded as to his real and far from holy motives is a sermon compounded of several themes, among which are, "Know thyself" and "Judge not, lest ye be judged." Further, human love is shown to be quite as divine as any in purifying the heart and leading a bruised life into new and healing pastures. When Sadie leaves the mire and rain of Pago Pago where her tattered pride has received its last crucifixion, and takes ship with her Marine lover and future husband, you have the feeling of coming out into the sunshine of a fresh day where souls and bodies are made over. And here Miss Swanson is mightily successful in convincing you that innocence can survive the most formidable obstacles and can be resurrected even from the shadows of the ignoble alleys where our blind sentimentalization would have it irretrievably lost.

Miss Swanson, with only minor exceptions, is very fine as Sadie. Tempted at first to act, she soon feels and lives the part; emotionally she rings true; her portrait of the deplorable, hardboiled, courageous Sadie struggling for the smallest crumbs of human joy, finding herself at the moment of escape caught in the darkest net of her life—a net which neither she nor its weaver, the fanatical saver of souls, Mr. Hamilton, can, in the slightest degree understand until the final struggle rends the net and lets in the horrible light of revelation—this portrait is among Miss Swanson's best. Here for the first time one feels that she has been given a character and a story worthy of her mettle. To the raw, true nature of Sadie she has risen with a discriminating art, so discriminating that even more than in the original story and the play made from it, Sadie emerges an object not only of pity but of essential grace, a human being struggling for a fuller life, and worthy of it.

Beside Miss Swanson's portrait stands that of the reformer, known in the picture as Hamilton, done superbly by Mr. Lionel Barrymore. Mr. Barrymore's work is exceptional in every way, in intelligence and in execution. At the first glance he is recognizable as an individual as well as a type—a professional saver of souls, a fanatic enduring a vision of demons and angels whose secret seductiveness lures him and frightens him back to the path of salvation, the narrow, thorny way which, since it is so hard for himself to travel he must make hard for others. For him holiness as well as sin is a misery from which he can only escape by punishing others. In Mr. Barrymore's slightly bent body, carried upright on the legs slightly bent themselves by their eternal toil up the stony hill; in his facial mask behind which dance libidinous images, flickering up from the darkness of his being against the will that would drive them down into that darkness; in the stern mouth

468

with its looseness of lower lip; the sharp, sniffing nose with its profile of emaciation; in the eyes that are ready to burn with the fire of the zealot and the horror which they reflect from the inner depths of his soul, you have the perfect picture of a tortured spirit struggling with itself and torturing others.

The performance of Raoul Walsh as Sadie's Marine lover is also worthy of honorable mention. Mr. Walsh introduces just the right note of rugged health, of real impending salvation for Sadie from the abnormal shadow that pursues her under the delusion of saving her soul. You understand how this humble soldier loves Sadie and how she loves him, and that is something you often cannot understand about the hero and heroine of the average picture.

The remaining cast are adequate although their parts are cut down. The production values are good, but the atmosphere of the rain-smothered little town of the tropics could have been made more vivid by adroiter cinematic means. The film also depends upon very many subtitles. These are minor criticisms. The thing that stands out and makes SADIE THOMPSON a portent is that it has a real story to tell and tells it with artistic restraint and, as far as it needs to be told, with courageous clarity. It is a picture which will perhaps accomplish that miracle—make people think.

(*Produced and distributed by United Artists.*)

FILM 1928   THE CROWD

"A Fine American Movie," Gilbert Seldes, *The New Republic,* Vol. 54, No. 692, March 7, 1928, pp. 98-99.

In the long time that has passed since King Vidor directed THE BIG PARADE, he has done, I believe, some small pictures; his heart and his mind have been in THE CROWD, a picture originally released on the regular programs, not advertised as a super-feature, and to me the most interesting development in the American movie in years. (After a week at the Capitol, it has been put on as a special at the Astor.)

It is not entirely a fine picture; either Mr. Vidor or his collaborator, Mr. John V. A. Weaver, has given it scenes which are feeble or vulgar, and he has fumbled the handling of emotions in an attempt to get a laugh. Yet negatively the picture is extremely important because it breaks completely with the stereotype of the feature film. There is virtually no plot; there is no exploitation of sex in the love interest; there is no physical climax, no fight, no scheduled thrill. The characters, all commonplace people, act singularly unlike moving picture characters and singularly like human beings; there is no villain, no villainy, no success. THE CROWD is absorbingly interesting, at moments charged with tremendous emotional excitement, exceptionally intelligent and satisfactory.

It condenses a few years in the life of a boy who comes to New York persuaded that he will get somewhere, do big things, be somebody, if he ever gets an opportunity. He becomes one of a hundred clerks in an insurance office; with thousands of others he kisses a girl at Coney Island; even his marriage does not isolate him, and the birth of his first child brings him to a maternity ward where hundreds of beds are aligned. He gets a raise of eight dollars a week, his second child is killed, he gives up his job, he can't succeed at any other, his wife starts to leave him but cannot carry it through, they go to the theater together, and as they rock and roar with laughter they are again submerged in a crowd which also rocks and roars.

In the movie sense, this is no plot; the absence of romance in the treatment is equally unlike the movies. But it is Mr. Vidor's triumph that he can make precisely this absence of romance seem actually tender and beautiful. The boy goes out, while his wife's family waits for Christmas dinner, to borrow some gin; he gets drunk and returns only after all

469

have gone except his wife, who is in bed. The tradition, the romantic tradition of the movies, demands here a scene; Mr. Vidor gives the wife a smile of sympathy, the husband a moment of contrition, and the scene ends with them quarreling lightly over the propriety of her raising the umbrella which is one of his presents to her. When the child is run down by a motor truck, the father, driven mad by the city noises which he thinks are preventing the baby's return to consciousness, rushes into the street beseeching passersby, motorists, fire engines, crowds, to be quiet; almost mad with the noise of the crowd, he returns to the room; the doctor has meanwhile removed his instrument from the child's heart; the father learns the news from the mother's face. So in everything fine in the picture, the treatment is fresh, credible, creative of intense emotion.

It is clear that, to make these things fresh and moving, the technique must be out of the ordinary. It is. But before coming to that, I must indicate Mr. Vidor's two errors. When the boy and the girl are married, they go to Niagara Falls, and there is a long sequence of pictures on the sleeper. I have never thought jokes about the bridal night funny in themselves, and Mr. Vidor has worked the old ones to death; the taste is quite bad here, the gags are tedious. The purpose was to give Mr. Vidor a scene on a knoll, with the falls as background, where the desire of the boy and girl manifests itself the next day. It was a good scene, but the business in the sleeper was romantic in the tawdriest way, a serious blemish.

The second fault baffles me to explain. Possibly Mr. Weaver, having once written a bit of verse about a Victrola, thinks that instrument really the machine out of which the god of drama springs; possibly Mr. Vidor, perplexed about his ending, took the easiest way. The wife has left the house; she returns on a pretext and the husband, who has got a job that day, asks her to go to the theater with him, and gives her some flowers. Their reconciliation is barely begun; they hardly know how to go about it. And so a talking machine, which has not appeared before, is started by the husband; they dance to "There's Everything Nice About You," the child joins them in laughter, and this scene dissolves into them laughing at the vaudeville show which ends the picture. Did Mr. Vidor mean to suggest that even in the expression of their deepest emotions they have to call on a standardized mechanical aid? It is the most flattering explanation, but if it is true it points to another defect—lack of preparation, lack of significant emphasis. As the picture stands, it looks more as if Mr. Vidor himself had to call in mechanics.

And of mechanics he is a master. Here is a man who knows how to take moving pictures—an excessively rare thing in the moving picture industry. He takes them so that they have movement, so that they have beauty, and, rarest of all, so that they have meaning. A little boy comes up a flight of stairs to discover what has happened to his father: the stairs, the walls, the ceiling, form a long tapering rectangular box through which we look upon the little figure; by the time he is three-quarters of the way up, the father has died for us, although we have seen nothing of him, and Mr. Vidor breaks the movement by having another figure come down to meet the boy. The grown lad comes to New York on a ferry; we are not limited to his view of the city; we see what the city *means* to him, from his early confusion, his bewilderment at regular blocks of buildings, its speed, its carelessness, its unapprehended rhythm. Then the city engulfs him. The camera sweeps the city, picks out a building, miraculously describes all its majesty, beauty, and aloofness. A shot is taken so that the tier after tier of window and stonework lies flat before us, slowly it rises like a painted cardboard wall pushed from behind; we approach the pinnacle breathlessly, the building absorbs us physically, leans over, takes us in, and when it is righted the camera begins to pick out a floor, a series of windows on that floor, a separate window, and we are inside, on an anonymous floor, of an anonymous company, and our hero—ourself—sits at one of a hundred desks.

Mr. Vidor has avoided the complete stylization of the crowd—the method of

470   METROPOLIS. Endless doors open and endless crowds come to endlessly moving

elevators; but there is no machine-like precision. It is, to me, poignant enough—that people in their own way still do the same things. So the different crowds have varying rhythms and pace, are friendly or menacing or indifferent. They have not only their own meaning, but their function in the picture.

James Murray, who plays the boy, is a genuine find—the story of his siege of Hollywood is highly romantic and absolutely true; he reminds me of the young Charles Ray, and is beautifully suited to Mr. Vidor's quiet method of expression. The great player of the film is, however, not the lead but Eleanor Boardman, who plays the girl. Except for a few moments when she imitated the Mae Marsh of years ago, everything in her creation was personal, worked out from within, and terribly affecting. She brought me close to tears more than once; she satisfied my inner sense of the decorum and rightness of methods all the time. She grew up in the brief hour of the movie from a cheap little girl to a suffering and tender woman, with weaknesses and powers. It is altogether a beautiful performance.

THE CROWD does not follow precisely the outline Mr. Vidor gave to me about a year ago, when it was almost finished. I should like to think that the one really bad spot was not left in at his order, and that his neutral ending—the boy getting back his original job—was not omitted at the command of his employers. Whatever the truth may be, the Metro-Goldwyn-Mayer corporation is to be congratulated on having Mr. Vidor and on giving him his head; and he is to be congratulated on courage and intelligence and the mastery of his art. His future is bound to be interesting; what remains to see is whether he can achieve greater freedom in production, and get material even more amenable to his powerful and delicate hands.

Gilbert Seldes.

COMMENTARY

Relieved of its original noisy music-and-sound-effects, and run with a straight musical accompaniment, OUR DANCING DAUGHTERS is probably a better film today than it was when it was first released.

THE WIND was another of those films which gave M.G.M. troubled hours trying to figure out when to release it. Seastrom had directed it, with Lillian Gish and Lars Hanson, in the spring of 1927, but it did not reach the theatres until November, 1928.

FILM 1928   OUR DANCING DAUGHTERS

"Mad Youth," excerpt from "The Screen," Mordaunt Hall, *The New York Times,* October 8, 1928, p. 14.

> With Joan Crawford, John Mack Brown, Dorothy Sebastian, Anita Page, Kathlyn Williams, Nils Asther, Edward Nugent, Dorothy Cumming, Huntley Gordon, Evelyn Hall and Sam de Grasse, written by Josephine Lovett, directed by Harry Beaumont; Fox Movietone News; Van and Schenck via the movietone; "Under the Sea," a stage spectacle, with Walters and Ellis, Mario Naldi and the Chester Hale dancing girls. At the Capitol Theatre.

Hundreds of girls and young women were attracted yesterday to the Capitol Theatre and their presence probably was due chiefly to the title of the film feature, OUR DANCING DAUGHTERS, a chronicle concerned with the wild young people of this generation. The Capitol now is equipped for the reproduction of sounds, which fact was

471

only too patent yesterday, for while OUR DANCING DAUGHTERS is not furnished with dialogue, it has a musical accompaniment, several love songs, stentorian cheering and, at the end, a chorus of shrieks.

Whether this audible mixture adds to the entertainment value of the picture is a matter of opinion. It assuredly detracts from the action of the picture in some of the sequences. The romantic melodies that accompany the love-sick looks and the violent embraces of the principal characters are reminiscent of the old-time singing to lantern-slides. The enthusiastic cheering impresses one as though the producers wanted to make the most of sound, and the shrieks in the closing scenes come from mute figures to whom terror has suddenly given tongues.

There is nothing startlingly novel about OUR DANCING DAUGHTERS, for while there is an undeniable vivacity to many of the scenes, the action is not particularly well portrayed and it is frequently anything but conservative. Cocktails, flasks and mad dancing appear in quite a number of episodes. It is quite unnecessary to depict an intoxicated girl, as is done for considerable length in this film. Presumably it is to point a moral, for the young woman falls to her death down a flight of stairs.

The wide-eyed Joan Crawford, who is attractive in many of the scenes, figures as one of the dancing daughters. After an unusually violent terpsichorean performance [she dances "The Wobbly-Walk"], this young woman, known as Diana, suddenly takes an interest in Ben Blain, a stranger to the hectic life but the son and heir of a multi-millionaire.

Harry Beaumont, the director, has among his worthy sequences in this film, one in which the fractious Diana tells her companion, Beatrice, that she is in love. This incident is quite appealing and it caused great glee yesterday afternoon.

But Diana is doomed to be disappointed, for a little blonde, the daughter of a mercenary mother, succeeds in capturing the heart of the peculiarly susceptible Mr. Blain. This fair-haired minx, named Anne, soon leads Mr. Blain to the altar and Diana is left to brood over a blighted life. Josephine Lovett, who wrote OUR DANCING DAUGHTERS, cannot be accused of much subtlety in ridding Mr. Blain of his tempestuous bride.

John Mack Brown is sympathetic as Mr. Blain. Dorothy Sebastian is appealing as Beatrice. Anita Page gives a fairly good portrayal of her idea of a dancing daughter.

"Under the Sea," an elaborate and effective stage contribution and a movietone of Van and Schenck are among other numbers on the program.

THE WIND   **FILM 1928**

"Exceptional Photoplays: THE WIND," *National Board of Review Magazine*, Vol. 3, No. 12, December, 1928, p. 9. (With the permission of the National Board of Review of Motion Pictures.)

Directed by . . . . .Victor Seastrom
Photographed by . . . . .John Arnold

The Cast

Letty . . . . .Lillian Gish
Lige . . . . .Lars Hanson
Roddy . . . . .Montagu Love
Cora . . . . .Dorothy Cumming
Beverly . . . . .Edward Earle
Sourdough . . . . .William Orlamond

Cora's Children . . . . Laon Ramon,
Carmencita Johnson,
Billy Kent Schaefer

From the novel by Dorothy Scarborough

This latest film vehicle of Miss Lillian Gish's marks one of the most interesting productions in which the star has appeared.

It is a study of psychological reaction to atmospheric environment, and as such employs cinematic effects in more abundance than is to be found in the usual photodrama. Its attempt is to be more mature than the average picture, to dwell on mood of scene and state of mind as essentials in plot and to envisage both as forces in the secret springs of action of human beings. All this has not been altogether successfully done, but at moments one does get glimpses of the inner nature of things, of the psychology of fear and escape, and in these moments as they touch upon the heroine, the effect is dramatic and poignant.

Miss Gish plays the part of Letty, a young girl who goes west to join the household of a cousin in a place where the wind always blows. It is the wind, its sound, its implications, its effect of growing menace on the mind of this girl that provides the motif for the story and its cinematic treatment. The jealousy of Cora, the cousin's wife, toward Letty, her attempt to drive Letty into the hands of the traveling man whose purpose is none too reputable, as a means of getting rid of her, Letty's marriage with one of the ranch hands to escape from this predicament, his advances to her and her repulse of him, her final love for him and her killing of the libidinous suitor who intrudes again into her life, are movements of the wind that, constantly beating on her ears and senses, beats up fears, forebodings and strange impulses in her inner self, until her mind verges on collapse.

Anyone who knows how effectively Miss Gish with her fugitive hands and agitated mobility of bodily gesture, at times so strikingly effective and so peculiarly hers among screen actresses, can do this sort of character, will perceive that THE WIND gives her an opportunity to act which she is able to take full advantage of.

Other characters well done are those of Cora played by Dorothy Cumming. Letty's husband played by Lars Hanson, and her amatory pursuer acted by Montagu Love.

The film shows one bad tendency of our directors and scenarists, its atmospheric chord is twanged too often. In the present case in their anxiety to make the wind felt and heard (and sound synchronization will only make matters worse), they have blown the bellows and shoveled the sand over-long and with too much energy. It is surprising that Victor Seastrom, noted in his Scandinavian days for his eerie touch and delicate hintings, should so far have lost sight of the art of suggestion in a story made exclusively to his hand as to have, so to speak, piled it on until the illusion is well nigh buried under and winnowed away. What might have become imaginative cinema has been made obvious movie, no matter what excellent movie it may be.

(*Produced and distributed by Metro-Goldwyn-Mayer.*)

COMMENTARY

Four Garbo films were released in 1929, twice as many as in any previous year. They were all silent: M.G.M. was taking no chances on a possibly unfavorable reaction to her voice, and presented a soundless Garbo to the last allowable moment. Among the four were A WOMAN OF AFFAIRS, from Michael Arlen's book and play, *The Green Hat*, directed by Clarence Brown, and the farewell to silence: THE KISS, directed by Jacques Feyder.

But, in 1930, the sound of Garbo's voice proved to be a magic sound, and her career 473

was not terminated but extended. When this interview was conducted, she had just returned from Sweden, where Lars Hanson, playing on the stage in O'Neill's *Strange Interlude,* **had arranged a special performance just for her.**

"THE HOLLYWOOD HERMIT"   1929

By "M.H." [Mordaunt Hall], *The New York Times,* March 24, 1929, Section 10, p. 7.

That languid screen enchantress, Greta Garbo, was at the Hotel Marguery, Park Avenue, last Wednesday, having arrived the day before from Sweden. Her mere presence appeared to have its effect upon the room clerk, for most of the conversation was either uttered in a whisper or by signals. The Metro-Goldwyn-Mayer representatives could not have acted with greater deference had a visiting potentate been the object of their attentions, for Miss Garbo, like Charlie Chaplin or Sir James M. Barrie, is a shrinking violet when it comes to being interviewed.

The telephone bell broke the silence and the room clerk lifted a finger as a signal to the elevator operator that Miss Garbo would receive a representative of *The New York Times.* Soon the door of Miss Garbo's apartment was flung open and the sinuous figure of the alluring actress appeared as if from a ray of sunlight. In a low-toned voice that suited her bearing, she greeted the caller, whose eyes fell from her face to a bouquet of flowers on a table and then to the carpet.

"Won't you sit down?" she asked.

The visitor's eyes once more challenged the chance of being caught staring and forthwith became aware that Miss Garbo wore a black covering on her head, like a skull cap, with two tassles of hair bursting forth from each side. It was quite obvious after she had answered a few questions that Miss Garbo's magnetism was just as impressive off the screen as on. Like Pola Negri, whom she greatly admires, she is natural, being more amused than embarrassed by her none too extensive knowledge of English.

She wore a pink silk sweater with a short black velvet skirt, and coils of smoke rose to the ceiling from the cigarette she held in her long fingers.

When she first came here, three and a half years ago, Miss Garbo knew hardly any English, but now she succeeds fairly well in expressing herself and, in spite of occasional lapses, that are quite captivating, she declared that she was quite willing to try acting and dialogue in a talking picture.

Wants to Do the Unusual

What would she like to do as a pictorial story? She puffed her cigarette, threw back her head, lowered her eyelids and vouchsafed:

"Joan of Arc. But it probably wouldn't go so well. I would like to do something unusual, something that has not been done. I would like to get away from the usual. I don't see anything in silly love-making. I would like to do something all the other people are not doing. If I could get von Stroheim! Isn't he fine?"

Miss Garbo said that she liked the screen translation of Arlen's *Green Hat,* which was called A WOMAN OF AFFAIRS, better than any other of her films. Her first picture, one of the only two she made in her native Sweden, was the film version of *The Legend of Gosta Berling,* which was exhibited here in 1928. She was then 17 years old and, according to her own description, "twenty pounds bigger, or was it ten pounds?"

Crowds greeted her when she returned to Sweden this last time. She did not make much of the reception, but admitted that throngs had been at Guttenborg when she landed. She did not know, now that she was back in America, whether she was homesick or not. In Stockholm she said that she loved to wander along the streets looking in the

380-3

59. The Garbo of *A WOMAN OF AFFAIRS* (1928-1929), her favorite of her own films up to this time, anticipates the image she will give from the screen in the early 1930's. John Mack Brown is reduced here—as were almost all of Garbo's leading men, but through no intentional act on her part—to a small adoring boy. Clarence Brown directed.

smaller shop windows and then going off to dinner without returning to change her clothes. Her blue-gray eyes lighted up as she referred to this.

All Alone

When she was asked whether many people recognize her in this city, she replied, as she has a habit of doing to other questions:

"I don't know."

What did she do on her first evening in New York?

She had dinner alone.

"All alone?"

"Yes, quite alone, and I loved to look at the—what you call—shyscrapers—No, what it is?"

"Yes, skyscrapers. Let's not talk about me, let's talk about New York and the skyscrapers. They look so beautiful from this window. It is true I was invited to go to dine somewhere in the country at a house where Captain Lundborg was a guest. He, you know, is the man who flew over to Nobile and brought him back. But, as I said, I dined alone and looked always at the gorgeous, unreal skyscrapers—did I have it right, then?"

This would-be hermit admits that she knows very few people in Hollywood. She occasionally plays a little tennis and owns only one car, but drives in others belonging to friends.

The talk of necessity switched back to Sweden, when Miss Garbo was asked whether she had ever appeared on the stage. She said she had not, but that a friend of hers asked her to act in *Resurrection* while she was in Stockholm. She, in evidently a rash moment, consented.

She went on so far as to memorize her lines and study the part. She was confident of herself, but the night before the dress rehearsal she began to be very nervous and she could not sleep a wink. She asked her friend to come and see her and she told him that she could not appear after all. She had not slept. No amount of pleading could change her mind. She simply could not appear before the footlights.

One would be almost inclined to believe that no matter where Miss Garbo goes she has a pretty dull time. But that seemed impossible. She takes about six weeks to make one of her pictures and so far has appeared in eight Hollywood productions.

She studies her stories before she appears before the camera.

"And when are you returning to Hollywood?"

"I don't know. Tomorrow perhaps."

Then the conversation turned to talking films, and Miss Garbo said: "If they want me to talk I'll talk. I'd love to act in a talking picture when they are better, but the ones I have seen are awful. It's no fun to look at a shadow and somewhere out of the theatre a voice is coming."

She was asked whether she knew Charlie Chaplin and answered that she knew him "very little."

There is no longer any Swedish coterie in Hollywood, for Victor Seastrom is no longer there. Lars Hanson is back in his native land, to which lesser lights have also flown.

Miss Garbo has a profound admiration for Pola Negri. She said that she loved the way in which Miss Negri kept to the old-world atmosphere.

"There's hardly no one so good as Pola Negri," said Miss Garbo. "She is so amusing. It is always amusing to see her."

Amusing as used by Miss Garbo means a combination of interesting and inspiring.

She repeated, "Delighted to have met you," and then turned her head in the direction of her beloved skyscrapers.

(Signed) M.H.

CHAPTER **21**

"Thunder Drum for All Four Horsemen": Presentation

COMMENTARY

Although a few were fortunate enough to hear private thumpings on parlor keyboards, many of the multitude in America learned about the "light classics" and "classics" of music from what they heard in moving picture theatres. Films were never shown in silence: at the very least there was a piano; at the most, an orchestra.

After ragtime gave way to fancier quotations in the piano scores of early films, "cue sheets" with musical suggestions appeared in the trade magazines. The score for Bernhardt's CAMILLE, as given here, is loaded with old chestnuts, but it is handy for telegraphing the mood of a scene at its very opening, a practice that is still followed today by makers of sound films.

When THE BIRTH OF A NATION was revived in New York in 1921, the original score was considered too elementary—a measure of the movie-going public's increasing familiarity with a certain portion of classical music repertory—and a new one was substituted. S. L. Rothafel had presented ambitious film programs in Minneapolis, using a 15-piece symphony orchestra and a vocal quartet (1911). In New York, where he successively managed the Regent, the Strand, the Rialto, the Rivoli, the Capitol, and, in 1927, the Roxy (with his nickname now adopted as the name of his theatre, an elaborate place also called "The Cathedral of The Motion Picture"), he programmed stage acts, ballet, and symphony concerts, along with the films.

1912   "MUSIC FOR THE PICTURE"

Excerpt from "Music for the Picture," Clarence E. Sinn, *The Moving Picture World*, Vol. 13, No. 9, August 31, 1912, p. 871.

Our old friend, Will H. Bryant, writes: "I have moved from Indianapolis to this city (Terre Haute, Ind.), and have been managing the house and leading the orchestra since June 3. Am enclosing my program for the Sarah Bernhardt film CAMILLE. The manager of these pictures was good enough to ask for a list, saying it fit the picture better than any yet found. Hope it may be of use.

CAMILLE

1. Waltz lento until Camille and Armand alone, then:

2. "The Flatterer" (Chaminade) twice through.

3. "Scarf Dance."

4. "Serenade" (Puerner) or "Spring Song" (Mendelssohn).

SECOND ACT

5. "Confidence" (Mendelssohn). Twice.

6. "Berceuse" (Godard) or Waltz lento until title:

"CAMILLE'S HOME IN THE COUNTRY"

7. "Evening Star" (*Tannhäuser*), until Armand's father leaves Camille.

8. "Calm as the Night" (Bohm), until next title.

9. "Song Without Words" (Tchaikovsky). To end of act. Tempo according to action.

10. "*La Bohème* Fantaisie" (Puccini), until Camille out of bed.

11. "Barcarolle" (*Tales of Hoffman*), until Camille's arm drops to her side.

12. "Ase's Death" (*Peer Gynt Suite*—Grieg), until end. . . .

THE BIRTH OF A NATION (Revival)   **FILM 1921**

"The Capitol," excerpt from "Musical Comedy-Drama-Motion Pictures," *The Musical Courier*, Vol. 82, No. 19, May 12, 1921, p. 69.

Anyone who might have felt a doubt as to the advisability of reviving D. W. Griffith's THE BIRTH OF A NATION received his answer, very emphatically given, in the long lines which daily besieged the Capitol last week, and resulted in its holding over for another week. Owing to the length of the film itself, of necessity there was no program other than the overture and an interlude which introduced its second part after a brief intermission.

In connection with this film, S. L. Rothafel adapted a special musical setting, in the arrangement of which he was aided by Erno Rapée, William Axt and Hermann Hand. The overture was compiled of excerpts from Hosmer's "Southern Rhapsody," with interpolated negro melodies and Southern tunes descriptive of the life and general atmosphere of the period. The scene opens with the restless days of the South before secession and carries one through that desperate period which culminated in the formation of the Ku Klux Klan. The picture, which is an adaptation of Dixon's *The Clansman*, is replete with thrills enough to satisfy even the most insatiate, and the splendid musical setting heightens these effects until at its close one returns with a thump to

60. *Sarah Bernhardt prepares to die in CAMILLE, a screen transfer—seen by Americans in 1912—of her long-lasting stage success. In Terre Haute, Indiana, the exhibitor and orchestral conductor suggested this scene should be accompanied by part of the "Peer Gynt Suite."*

present day affairs. If any criticism were made, it might be that in some of the war scenes the orchestra played too loudly. But then there is certainly nothing soothing or peaceful about war, anyway.

An example of the care and effort lavished on the score is found in the accompaniment to the scenes of Sherman's march to the sea. In these, Mr. Rothafel has used four distinct themes with unusual fine effect. There was the trumpet call—from the extreme top of the balcony, then from the orchestra, then off-stage—the tread of marching feet, the agitato of the battle itself, and finally the tragic motif which tells of the desolation which invariably follows. Another theme which was especially interesting was the "Clan Call," of which acknowledgment was made in the program to Joseph Carl Breil, who, it will be remembered, was the composer of the score used with the original production. Its weird accents are well calculated to strike terror to hearts even more courageous than those which beat in the timid breast of the ignorant and superstitious negro. The second half of the story deals entirely with the Ku Klux, and immediately preceding this, the heavy curtains parted to disclose a member of this body, with the flaming signal cross raised—a figure which might well strike terror to the guilty. Erno Rapée, conductor, and David Mendoza, associate conductor, had the forces well in hand at all times and deserve special words of praise for their excellent work. . . .

The Second Week's Run   1921

"The Capitol," excerpt from "Musical Comedy-Drama-Motion Pictures," *The Musical Courier*, Vol. 82, No. 20, May 19, 1921, p. 65.

There seemed to be no lack of interest during the second week of the revival of THE BIRTH OF A NATION at the Capitol. The large theater was filled for every showing and reports have it that about $45,000 was paid during the first week of admissions. That this master picture of David Wark Griffith is for all time has been proven conclusively. Yet, with all, THE BIRTH OF A NATION still remains a great picture and through inspiration and execution seems modern. There have been very few pictures made six years ago or more recently that can stand a revival without depreciating their former glories.

Not having heard the original music score by Joseph Carl Breil, there can be no comparison with the musical accompaniment arranged by Mr. Rothafel. They do, however, use his clan call from the original work, and if all of the score is as powerful as this call, it would appear useless to have arranged a new and more modern one. He seemed to have caught the spirit of the Ku Klux Klan, for the trumpet call is thrilling, has a mysterious, determined sound that is quite inspiring. Mr. Rothafel arranged many old Southern melodies to suit the scenes, and in most cases they were effective. There were times when the music seemed too loud, but this is of little matter. The organ came in for full share; in fact, it seemed to play a greater part of the time. By the way there seemed to be a perfect synchronization between organ and picture with an invisible organist. The handsome console seemed deserted, electricity and perfect timing doing the trick. At any rate it was splendidly done whatever the method. The Capitol management is to be thanked for giving the city the opportunity of seeing this picture again, and doubly so for some of us who saw it for the first time. . . .

"S. L. ROTHAFEL DEFENDS MUSICAL SCORE"   1921

"S. L. Rothafel Defends Musical Score," excerpt from "Musical Comedy-Drama-Motion Pictures," *The Musical Courier*, Vol. 82, No. 22, June 2, 1921, p. 64.

480   There was considerable discussion over the musical score S. L. Rothafel arranged for

the revival of THE BIRTH OF A NATION at the Capitol Theatre two weeks ago. Mr. Rothafel has the following to say in defense of his action in arranging his own musical accompaniment rather than use the original music that was composed by Joseph Breil for the Griffith picture:

"A score is nothing more or less than a musical adaptation or interpretation of the dramatic values of the picture. The art of musical presentation has progressed so markedly during the seven years since THE BIRTH OF A NATION was first produced, that different standards and methods of adaptation have educated the public to new musical values. In the original adaptation such selections as *Rienzi, Freischütz*, "Ride of the Walkyrie," and "Light Cavalry" were used. The movie going public has since then become familiar through the medium of the motion picture theater and popular opera with these operas and the stories of these works, and their usage today in the accompaniment to THE BIRTH OF A NATION would have seemed inadequate and misrepresentative. The Clan Call, which is an inspired bit of composition, was retained, but in the body of the setting it was thought in better taste to utilize the airs which are contemporaneous with the period of history covered by this American screen classic. . . .

COMMENTARY

The cocoanut shells for horses hoofs, and the pistol shots for pistol shots, which echoed through nickelodeons in 1907, had by 1921 developed into such intricate arrangements for presentation that long instructions were necessary for THE FOUR HORSEMEN OF THE APOCALYPSE.

But the managers of small town theatres either retained their pianos, or, in bursts of extravagance, replaced them with organs. The foreword to a 1924 compilation of movie music gives encouraging instructions for procedure.

1921   "MUSIC PLOT AND SUGGESTIONS"

Excerpts from "Music Plot and Suggestions," FOUR HORSEMEN OF THE APOCALYPSE, Ernst Luz, Metro Pictures Corporation, n.d.

with instructions for Playing Music Score

to

Rex Ingram's Super-Production

FOUR HORSEMEN OF THE APOCALYPSE
By Ernst Luz. . .

[Cue Sheet with 110 musical citations in sequence follows]

Stage Effects of THE FOUR HORSEMEN. . .

Act II

Thunder Drum and Thunder Sheet after Angel on screen, and Brass Call in Orchestra, for Red Scenes and for First Horseman and Second Horseman. Soft rumble when Russian on screen. Nothing for Third and Fourth Horseman. Heavy Thunder Drum and Sheet when all Four Horsemen ride across screen. Nothing until Russian looks into sky. Then

481

Thunder Drum and Sheet for all Four Horsemen and continue Thunder Drum alone through Red Scenes and subtitle, "For fourteen days, etc." until after music starts.

Cannon Shots until subtitle "The ceaseless rumble, etc." then medium thunder. Drums accenting Beast and Cannon Shots until subtitle, "His family, etc." then soft rumble to subtitle "Only the old lodgekeeper, etc." Short tacet until subtitle "Only a flimsy shell, etc." then Thunder Drum softly, accent Cannon and Explosions. Second man at shot pad to get two rifle shots as man on roof shoots two Uhlans. Continue Thunder Drum for big battle until all Four Horsemen cross screen second time. Accent all Four Horsemen with Thunder Sheet.

Long tacet until after scene moves after, "A grim warning," then a volley of shots immediately second close-up of German soldiers with rifles shows. . . .

Stage Plot for THE FOUR HORSEMEN

Necessary Props:

Rain Machine, Thunder Drum for Cannon Shots, Wind Whistle, Triangle, Chimes . . . Rack and Hammer . . .

Curtain and Lights for Act I

Add foots (pink and blue) to house lights before Overture starts. After about three minutes at brass accent in Overture take off house lights. About 15 seconds later take pink out of foots leaving only blue: at tympany roll solo, without orchestra, take out foots quickly for Curtain. . . .

Curtain and Lights for Act II

. . . At first beat of drum in Orchestra Pit take off simultaneously all foots and house lights and open with a fast curtain. Draw screen curtain immediately after operator flashes picture on screen.

For end of Act 2 [end of film] close in slowly on screen curtain after long subtitle after Four Horsemen ride across the screen. Quick to Proscenium Curtain and drop quickly. House lights on after Curtain down. . . .

"FOREWORD AND INSTRUCTIONS FOR USE OF THIS MANUAL"   1924

Arranged by Erno Rapée: *Motion Picture Moods for Pianists and Organists,* "Foreword and Instructions for the Use of this Manual," G. Schirmer, Inc., New York, 1924, p. iii.

In preparing this Motion Picture Manual for Piano and Organ, I tried to create the necessary bridge between the screen and the audience which is created in the larger motion picture houses by the orchestra. If we consider that the theatres of the size and standard of the Capitol Theatre in New York have half a dozen or so musical experts under the direction of the Musical Director working out the music to fit the action on the screen, we realize what a very hard task it must be for any single individual, either at the piano or at the organ, to go through with music selected at random and generally at very short notice, and supply good musical accompaniment to pictures.

This collection is meant to do away with the aforesaid haphazard collection of music and its use for synchronizing pictures. Inasmuch as most pianists or organists in the smaller theatres do not get a chance, or a very poor one, to review the pictures before the public performance, you can readily see the difficulty under which they work with quickly changing scenes, different psychological situations chasing each other, back-shots, close-ups, close-ins, etc. In creating fifty-two divisions and classifications in this

Manual, I tried to give the most numbers to those classes of music which are most frequently called upon to synchronize actions on the screen. Let me say here for the information of every man attempting to use this Manual to the best of his advantage that you can't always portray action; one-third of all film footage is used to depict action; another third will show no physical action, but will have, as a preponderance, psychological situations; the remaining third will neither show action nor suggest psychological situations, but will restrict itself to showing or creating atmosphere or scenery. If it is action that the organist or pianist wants to portray, he will find a sufficient variety of headings in the index to satisfy almost any aspect of his musical taste; should the portrayal of psychological situations be necessary, he will find it under the heading of Love, Horror, Joyfulness, Passion, etc. In the music of 'Nationalities,' Chinese and Japanese music has been treated as a unit; the less known national airs of Honduras, Uruguay and Venezuela I enclose only for the rare use in news reels; for Tournaments, Skating, or any exhibition of individual skill where the action is not too fast, I advise the use of concert waltzes by Waldteufel, Strauss, etc.; should the action be rather rapid, a galop or lively one-step would be suitable. One-steps and fox-trots have not been included, as most of them are of passing interest and can readily be had in any quantity from all dealers. Under the caption of 'Neutral' you will find seven different numbers which are meant for use in situations where none of the aforesaid three situations are present—that is, where *there is neither action*, nor atmosphere, nor the elements of human temperament present in any noteworthy degree. The music found under the caption 'Sinister' is meant for situations like the presence of the captured enemy, demolishing of a hostile aeroplane or battleship, or for the picturing of anything unsympathetic. The eleven pieces included under the caption 'Parties' will be found suitable also for the portrayal of social gatherings in gardens.

I advise every one trying to get the best use out of this Manual not only to read these instructions carefully, but also to acquaint himself thoroughly with the contents of the whole Manual; only in that way will he derive the benefit I have striven to give every user of this book through the condensing and summing up of my six years' experience in the Motion Picture game.

Erno Rapée.

COMMENTARY

In the Twenties many sumptuous motion picture theatres were built, heavy with ornament, yearning after the periods of Louis XVI and the Italian Baroque, after styles Hindu, Chinese, Spanish, Arabian Nights. But the latter half of the Twenties also saw the rise of the little art house, given impetus by the revival of THE CABINET OF DR. CALIGARI, which opened the Fifth Avenue Playhouse in New York October 29, 1926, and ran for six weeks.

This film had vanished into legend in the five years it had remained unseen, and now, seen again, became to the art house movement what THE GREAT TRAIN ROBBERY (which was 23, not 15, years old in 1926) had become to the early nickelodeons; in both cases the perfect film had been found for each of their purposes.

Mary Pickford's GOING STRAIGHT really dates from 1911. L'Herbier's THE NEW ENCHANTMENT, and the Léger-Murphy BALLET MECANIQUE, had been seen together at a special performance in New York on March 14, 1926.

Another result of CALIGARI's revival was the encouragement of film societies, which slowly began to form at the end of the Twenties.

1926   "THE RISE OF THE LITTLE CINEMA"

By Matthew Josephson, *Motion Picture Classic*, Vol. 24, No. 1, September, 1926, pp. 34-35, 69, 82.

Like the Little Theater Movement—the Little Cinema Idea Is Spreading Rapidly. Film Guilds Are Sprouting Everywhere and Picture Patrons Are Taking Up the New Art of the Future.

A Wave of Revivals is on—Revivals of Worth-While Pictures, Which Are Being Shown With New Impressionistic Ideas. The Public Taste is Changing—It Demands Intelligence and Quality in Its Films.

Under the surface, one of the most exciting events of the year in motion pictures has been the spread of the "little cinema" idea. We have had our art theaters and theater guilds; now we are to have Film Guilds and "salons of the cinema."

"A little theater for the films in every community, reviving and introducing only the best American and foreign pictures. Minority of true screen devotees to be organized. Skeptics to be converted." So run the manifestoes of these new film-phobes and pioneers.

The *intelligentsia* is taking up the films. Society is taking them up too—not as a secret sin, but frankly, avowedly, as the New Art of the Future!

Invited to one of these "film art evenings," I elbowed my way into a pretentious theater lobby thru a cultured mob in evening dress and eight-cylinder cars. It was more like Carnegie Hall or Russian Ballet night at the Metropolitan Opera: artists, professors, all the younger generation and the smart "New Yorkers" were there talking at the top of their voices. As the great foreign film with its famous stars went on the screen, there was wild applause; or, hisses, laughter, organized cheering as some new wrinkle or fandangle appeared on this ultramodern screen. Verily, like a first night at the Opera! And here were—well several hundred people who had paid some ten dollars in advance to see a few films that were heralded as examples of the modern art of the cinema, not because there were specimens of feminine or masculine pulchritude displayed therein.

They've Come to Stay

Observing this new movement toward "little cinemas" for artistic and seriously wrought pictures, I have been struck not so much by the strangeness of the idea as by its vitality, its staying power. This season we are to have four "little cinemas" in New York instead of two; and a chain of them in other large cities such as Boston, Washington, Chicago, Los Angeles.

The idea of little theaters for exhibiting new, experimental, and unpopular films offers so many possibilities for the future (if it persists and grows as it seems to be doing) that it is time to look over the field and meet some of the leading figures of this movement which has started from the outside.

Symon Gould, the mainspring of the International Film Arts Guild, has, for instance, never been connected with any of the big producing companies. His group has been the most successful, the most aggressive. It has gained a foothold on Broadway and is at the very moment regaling chosen audiences of New York with film masterpieces of the past, or box-office flops, or foreign films of great beauty which might never otherwise see the light here—were it not for the Film Arts Guild.

Gould is a little man with horn-rimmed spectacles, but big with ideas for livening up the motion pictures. His Film Guild has the charming little Cameo Theater which seats only five hundred. Here among the screaming electric signs of Broadway by night the passerby, drawn by the magic name of Lubitsch or Stroheim or Griffith, may turn in for a quiet hour with some enduringly beautiful work of the screen. THE LAST LAUGH, THE MARRIAGE CIRCLE, THE MIRACLE MAN and many other immortal works which I have tried to call back to the mind of readers of *Classic* as outstanding achievements of this new art live again. How absurd that such things should lie rolled up on shelves in dusty storehouses!

The Public Must Be Educated

"I have realized from the beginning," Gould said to me, "that our growth would have to be slow and gradual. I have felt all along that there was a place for really fine pictures which are not box-office attractions on a large scale, and that there is a special public for such things. It is slow work because we have to educate more of the general movie-going public into going out of their way to view these fine things.

"However, results in the first year have been surprisingly good. Beyond our hopes. We have arrived, and now we are going to expand. Prominent writers, painters, musicians, film-executives came to our programs. Society people came. Some of our subscription evenings had to be repeated because of the overflow."

"How are you going to expand unless you have a distributing system," I asked. I was thinking of how many well-intentioned ventures of this kind drop into the red-ink side of the ledger. Motion pictures cost so much to make that they have to be seen by a lot of people somehow.

Like the Little Theater Movement

"We are going to build up on the framework of the Little Theaters thruout the country. In scores of cities there are small groups which are seriously devoted to the stage and good drama. They have theaters and followings. We are interesting them in the better films with the plan of building them up into a distributing system on a small scale. Programs shown in our New York Theater will be shipped around this circuit. To pay the expenses there will be subscription showings. In this way, instead of being seen by a few hundreds, our programs will be seen by thousands."

Symon Gould believes that the work of the Film Guild will eventually be of great value to motion pictures as a whole. Revivals interfere in no way with the work of the big producers and exhibitors. In fact, a new market is created for films which have been rolled up and forgotten. In a way he is simply taking advantage of an awakening interest in movies on the part of another section of the public. Small exhibitors with their tiny financial risks can try new ideas and experiments that big organizations dare not attempt. The very bigness of the film companies has been against their making rapid progress with new ideas. Once there is a small public of say ten thousand with a developed appetite for new ideas in pictures, or for tragic or "serious" film works, it is possible that new talent may be encouraged along more adventurous lines. Men like young von Sternberg, who turned out the SALVATION HUNTERS for a few thousand dollars, might get their chance for a public showing much more readily.

Would the "little films" and the "little cinemas" compete in any way with the field of the big companies?

New Ideas for the Big Producers

No, it was pointed out. No more than the Neighborhood Playhouse in New York competes with the Shubert Theaters. The one interested in the art of the drama; the others in entertaining the public. The latter have a public ten-thousand times greater. But when the little theater has an actor or an idea that the public take up, the Shuberts will buy them.

So with the Little Cinemas. Their risks will cost little, and their discoveries of new ideas (which anyone who has the interest of the films at heart prays fervently for) will be common property for the motion picture industry and serve to liven up things.

In the meantime the taste of their highbrow public, if it may be called such, is very curious. Chaplin and Harold Lloyd slapsticks are mingled with German expressionist films, and are equally liked.

One of the most enjoyable programs was a showing of old pictures of a dozen or 485 fifteen years back—"antiques" they had become by now. Nothing could have better illuminated the big strides which movies have taken since these old thrillers, nor the improvement in the taste of the general public itself. The directors were bright young men then, but their little tricks were so elementary! There were no "fadeouts." There were all sorts of funny skips and jumps. Titles took the place of action or scenery; everything was done in haste. A dummy instead of a man, is thrown from the train in THE GREAT TRAIN ROBBERY of fifteen years ago, and he is very much a dummy, altho the train is going at five miles an hour.

It was delicious to see Mary Pickford and King Baggot, for instance, in GOING STRAIGHT (1913). The pantomime was primitive. Mary Pickford very pretty, in one of those wide-sweeping skirts, or whenever you could see her face under a huge bonnet. King Baggot most touching as he claps his hand to his head or waves temptation away with his other hand in brisk gestures. That which was sad and tragic is all fun now!

If only some of these old thrillers could be revived with their titles touched up. They would be the most side-splitting farces.

It is only thru looking at these old pictures and comparing them with what we have done since that we will know the true nature of the moving picture. When we know this, there will be films that will never grow old.

Rhythmic Motion Essential

Dudley Murphy thinks that the chief character of the film is motion, or the rhythm of things in motion. I must stop and tell something about Dudley Murphy. He is one of the figures in the art-film movement. His revolutionary BALLET OF THE MACHINE [BALLET MECANIQUE] was booed and hissed and laughed at. A lanky young man, soft spoken and visionary. He is home talent which has absorbed the ideas about modern art that are current in Europe. But some day he may come back from his wild exploits and experiments to give a vision of the great American scene.

"New York, in fact, the whole sweep of the American scene, fascinates me," he said. "Nobody realizes how strange the life that is going on right under our noses is. I am trying to get the fantastic speed and rhythm of this jazz age into a film."

He is working now on a feature film of New York life. It has never been done yet, as Flaherty has done the Eskimos or the South Sea Islanders. Dudley Murphy, if he can work out his ideas, may be heard from in a big way.

His opinions are worth noting:

"One of the greatest films made here was James Cruze's HOLLYWOOD. Cruze came closer to the very feeling of American life today than anybody I know. King Vidor is probably our greatest director right now. The first half of THE BIG PARADE had some of the finest motion picture technique ever done. The 'business' between Gilbert and Renée Adorée was marvelously carried out and conceived. Vidor has a miraculous sense of timing."

Worthy Revivals and New Ideas

The other "Little Cinema group," the Film Associates, is headed by a Mr. Montgomery Evans, 2nd. Also an outsider. A young man who likes to dabble with the arts, and finds more art in the films now than in anything else. The Film Associates do more in the way of introducing new pictures than revivals. On their programs have been some very curious French films, in fact, more French than German. The French have lots of ideas, and some great painters. Among the pictures shown here, THE NEW ENCHANTMENT, directed by l'Herbier, was a fake on a detective thriller and built along the crazy lines of DR. CALIGARI. It had the aid of one of France's greatest modern painters, Fernand Léger, in the making of the sets, which were often very jolly. It was received, however,

486

with mixed feelings and its authors showed on the whole less natural genius for the film than the Germans do. I have not doubt, tho, that American directors viewing this and other films of its like can derive some new ideas for their own work. That is, perhaps, one of the most valuable things about a group like the Film Associates. They too are counting on a bigger and more ambitious season, and will show ROSE BERND, an Ufa picture, featuring Emil Jannings, Werner Krauss and Henny Porten, as their first offering.

Another group headed by Joseph Lawren and Robert A. Sanborn, have secured the tiny Fifth Avenue Playhouse at 66 Fifth Avenue. Lawren is a publisher, and Sanborn an old film hound, once associated with the scenario department of Universal. They have taken over a theater in Greenwich Village which was started with the idea of giving modern drama and will present in it only modern films. Exhibiting rights to THE CABINET OF DR. CALIGARI have been secured, and they are counting on a long run.

It will be amazing if CALIGARI does draw the public. Three or four years ago it was a flop; but taste has changed and things that were impossible then are being tried now. CALIGARI has been referred to so many times by screen critics that it has become a by-word and the public knows much more about it than when it was first shown. Its revival in a theater of its own may have quite an effect.

Uplifting the Public Taste

The Little Cinemas are doing a great deal of educational work among the public and I know that their efforts are being keenly watched by the big producers and distributors. The "top-price" features which Famous Players, Metro-Goldwyn and the others have developed have done much to raise the public taste. Their greatest worry has been the changing taste of the public; it has been a nightmare for them to spend millions catering to some new fad or craze which will be forgotten next season. Now it looks as if the really great films of the past few seasons have a permanent quality about them that will not be put out of date by some new fad. It is comforting to think that pictures like THE BIG PARADE, THE MERRY WIDOW, THE GRAND DUCHESS AND THE WAITER, can be revived and exhibited successfully many years from now. The time is coming when certain feature films will so have mastered their art that they have the eternal value of, let us say, a play by Shakespeare. They will not have to be acted over again; merely taken off the shelves and revived.

The director of the International Film Arts Guild has devised a code for the appreciation of films. With this bright little measure-stick you may decide infallibly whether the movie you have just seen is a "classic" or a nuisance:

SUGGESTED CODE FOR CRITICS AND PUBLIC

1. Faithfulness to the individuality of the cinema art. To what degree does the film make use of the particular intrinsic character of this new art?
2. Story. Is it a mere transposition of a novel or a play, or does it attempt to create its tale in terms of true cinema?
3. Cast. Are they merely transposed from the stage with all the routine tricks of the stage, or have they developed the art of pantomime with a true and inspired talent?
4. Photography. Has the cameraman made full use of his instrument, extracting from situations and groupings of characters certain "angles" and "shots" which set off the scene and action most vividly?
5. Composition. Have the groupings, backgrounds, arrangement of objects, etc., been carefully composed to support the full significance of

487

a situation? Do the scenes etch themselves in the memory, or are they merely stereotyped?

6. Direction. To what extent has the director utilized these suggestions in his work? To what extent does the picture bear the imprint of his individuality? To what degree does it differ from the work of any other directors?

THE CABINET OF DR. CALIGARI (Revival)   **FILM 1926**

"The Somnambulist Awakens," "A.B.K." [Alfred B. Kuttner], *National Board of Review Magazine,* Vol. 1, No. 7, December, 1926, p. 3. (With the permission of the National Board of Review of Motion Pictures.)

When we first reviewed THE CABINET OF DR. CALIGARI after a special showing of the picture to the Exceptional Photoplays Committee in the Capitol Theatre, we wrote in part as follows:

> "THE CABINET OF DR. CALIGARI is a revelation and a challenge. It is a revelation of what the motion picture is capable of as a form of artistic expression. It challenges the public to appreciate it and challenges the producer to learn from it. The revelation is there for all to see. If the appreciation falls, the motion picture itself, and all that it has promised, is in danger of failing.
>
> "In THE CABINET OF DR. CALIGARI the motion picture for the first time stands forth in its integrity as a work of art. It is one of the paradoxes of art that it is at the same time an abstraction and something tangible in terms of our bodily senses. It is form and idea.
>
> "The story of Doctor Caligari is a phantasy of terror told with the virtuosity of a Poe, in terms of the screen. Its emotions appeal directly to a universal audience. Even if stripped to its barest outline it would still compel our attention, for it deals with the fascinating problem of one person's supernatural control over another person. But it acquires the irresistible quality of all true art because it is told with such complete mastery of medium that its terror becomes an aesthetic delight. We find that we have shared the experiences of a madman without suspecting that he is mad; we have been transported into that sphere where man creates his own imaginative realities as an escape from the realities of life which constantly overwhelm without ever completely satisfying him."

This high encomium was written in 1921. Today after a second viewing nothing has happened to make us change that unreserved judgment. For now again after a lapse of over five years the picture shines forth in its artistic integrity. With a minimum of advertisement or paid publicity THE CABINET OF DR. CALIGARI has been running to packed houses for over four weeks at the Fifth Avenue Playhouse. It still dwarfs contemporary pictures of artistic pretentions and in its own field it has never been surpassed. Now more than ever we feel assured that it will go down as a landmark in the history of artistic pictures.

In concluding our review we also said:

> "In THE CABINET OF DR. CALIGARI the motion picture has proved its kinship with the other arts. Its popularity ought to be assured. It comes to us at a critical period of our motion picture industry when the

public is jaded by many inferior domestic pictures and our producers themselves are still at a loss as to how to get out of their rut. It should give the public a new standard and imbue the producers with the courage to live up to it. Is it too much to assume that the American public can appreciate the best when it is given a chance to see it?"

This also, is no less true today. The motion picture industry is still groping. It still pursues popularity to the exclusion of quality, and seeks to dazzle a jaded public by extravagantly spending money for flashy pictures on the plausible theory that the more money spent on a picture, the better it will be. But THE CABINET OF DR. CALIGARI was made for a trifling sum under the most penurious war conditions. Why not try giving a director as little money as possible, instead of as much as possible, so that he must give something of his imagination too?

The present success of THE CABINET OF DR. CALIGARI also answers the last question of our paragraph. A sufficiently large part of the American public *will* appreciate the best if given a chance to see it. The Cameo repertory and the more modest Fifth Avenue Playhouse experiment prove that up to the hilt.

In the inevitable extension of the Little Motion Picture Theatre movement to other communities in the United States, THE CABINET OF DR. CALIGARI deserves the post of honor in the vanguard of artistic pictures. It has done most to give that movement form and substance, to bring it from the realm of Utopia to the world of practical possibility.

(Signed) A.B.K.

FILM 1926   THE CABINET OF DR. CALIGARI (Revival)

"THE CABINET OF DR. CALIGARI," unpublished study notes by Beaumont Newhall, written May 17, 1927.

Last night [May 16, 1927] the Shady Hill Film Guild brought that most remarkable film, THE CABINET OF DR. CALIGARI to a crowded house at Brattle Hall [Cambridge, Mass.]. This cinema is well known as an attempt to use the movies as an interpretive art rather than as a reproductive art. In considering it we have to remember that it was produced many years ago, which is a long time, cinematically speaking. I will not attempt to tell the story, for it is much beyond me. Let it suffice to say that I left the hall in a frame of mind that no other movie has left me in, with the exception of VARIETY, which, one might say, stands upon the shoulders of CALIGARI. Photographically speaking, there were no tricks, to which the Germans have striven in the last few years. No double exposure, no truck-ins, simply straightforward shooting. Almost every scene ended in . . . [an iris-out], circling out on the principal character of the scene. Few close-ups. One scene would circle out in the upper right hand corner, and another would circle in in the lower left hand corner, undoubtedly the predecessor for the dissolve, which yields such remarkable transitions from scene to scene, if handled well. The settings were most modern in their treatment, and smacked a little bit too much of the scenic art that we see at Revere Beach, from the standpoint, not of design, but of construction. Especially good were the scenes at the stairs to the police station, the sleepwalking scene, the town clerk's office, the insane asylum and the bedrooms. The picture suffered from faulty projection, and the lack of proper music, and the obvious American addition of "art" titles, in a style of print that evaded all attempts at legibility. In spite of its shortcomings, the film was well worth the rather exorbitant price that was asked, and was a far cry from the sentimental slush that is overruling the screens of the myriads of American movie houses.

489

61. SALOME, the controversial film of 1922 with Nazimova, the Russian actress, and décor after Aubrey Beardsley. Was it "a really fine moving picture" or "degrading and unintelligent," a work which "cannot by the most liberal extension of terms, be called artistic"?

CHAPTER 22

The Experimental Film

COMMENTARY

The experimental film was not a popular form with general audiences (witness IN-TOLERANCE and the first run of THE CABINET OF DR. CALIGARI), but this failed to discourage some film-makers, who were endeavoring to shape films to new forms and purposes.

NEW YORK, THE MAGNIFICENT, a short film by the painter-photographer Charles Sheeler (1883-1965) and the photographer Paul Strand (1890-   ), was first shown publicly at the Rialto Theatre July 24, 1921. In Paris, as THE SMOKE OF NEW YORK, it was included two years later on a Dada-group program. When revived in New York, in 1926, the film was called MANHATTA.

As the Twenties progressed, Alberto Cavalcanti (1897-   ), a Brazilian, continued the cycle of "city" films with his four-reel RIEN QUE LES HEURES. *The New York Times* reported from Paris about this in the fall of 1926, finding it momentarily the most impressive achievement in the arts: "It races past electric signs, luxurious breakfasts, slaughter houses, sordid streets. It rushes past the miserable derelict . . . as she sits on a curb swaying to its rhythm; it rushes past the street-walker with her eager, ready-made smile. It reveals every mad, distorted perspective. . . . It is the city of the artists . . . and testifies to the truth of their vision, from the enchanted street of Utrillo to the savage street of Chagall. . . ." (47)

And shown here in 1928 was BERLIN, SYMPHONY OF A BIG CITY, the result of collaboration between the director Walther Ruttmann (1887-1941), who came to films from painting, and the cameraman Karl Freund (THE LAST LAUGH, VARIETY). Ruttmann worked for a "symphonic 'curve' " in his five-reel film, using no actors, but directing all his cameramen to film random individuals and street crowds, in an attempt to depict morning, noon and night in the German capital. At the editing stage, he realized that "Many beautiful individual scenes had to be cut out to avoid the effect of a series of static pictures," and he kept altering his script to make room for the addition of effective shots in order to achieve "related incidents fitted to each other which would grip one by their intensity." (48)

In New York, one reviewer noted: "It is what Robert J. Flaherty tried to do with his film, THE TWENTY-FOUR DOLLAR ISLAND." (49)

The Russian actress Alla Nazimova (1879-1945), who in 1905 had been the first to play Strindberg's *Miss Julie* and Dostoievsky's *The Brothers Karamazov* on the American

491

stage, appeared in films as early as 1916. The sets and costumes for her SALOME (1922) were adapted from the drawings of Aubrey Beardsley by Natacha Rambova, who married Rudolph Valentino.

Thomas Craven, who disapproves of the film, later wrote a widely-read book, *Modern Art* **(1934), in which Matisse is described as "superficial" and Picasso as "perhaps the cleverest man in the history of art."**

"THE ART OF THE CAMERA, AN EXPERIMENTAL MOVIE"   1921

By Robert Allerton Parker, *Arts and Decoration,* Vol. 15, No. 6, October, 1921, pp. 369, 414-415.

A few weeks ago the Rialto exhibited a short series of motion pictures of New York. These motion pictures were the work of Charles Sheeler and Paul Strand, two American artists. Sheeler is well-known as one of our modern painters whose works are in the collections of discriminating connoisseurs and galleries. He is also a photographer of great distinction—an artist in photography. Strand is likewise a master in photography, an experimenter and a pioneer in this youngest of the arts. In entering the field of the motion picture, Sheeler and Strand sought to apply the technical knowledge gained from their experiments and achievements in "still" photography to the more complex problem of the motion picture—"to register through conscious selection and space-filling those elements which are expressive of the spirit of New York, of its power and beauty and movement."

The results have fully justified this daring adventure in a new art. Short as this film was in the showing, it suggested all sorts of glorious possibilities in the development of the movies. It was not merely artistically satisfying. It was a great stimulus to thought. At a time when our motion picture critics are shouting the praises of DR. CALIGARI and the rest of the German importations, it is strange that they should neglect such a significant achievement as this one of two American artists. But perhaps these critical gentlemen can register only the merits of imported art and of the demerits of domestic.

In spite of this critical apathy, the Sheeler-Strand pictures mark a turning point in the development of the art of the camera. The direct, expressive, unashamed photography, the salient selection and discrimination by which these "cameramen" managed, with the most effective economy, to capture the very spirit of lower Manhattan, the eloquent silence of these brief "shots," all lead one to claim that in the hands of such craftsmen the camera becomes truly an instrument of great art.

Such pictures possess that uncanny power of awakening and kindling our interest in that neglected beauty that crowds in upon us from all sides, and through which too many Americans walk with blind and unseeing eyes. It is always the exalted function of the true artist to make us see things through his eye, to reveal beauties undiscovered. In the fulfillment of this mission, he legitimatizes the means at his disposal. And so the camera of Sheeler and Strand dramatizes such a commonplace routine event as the entrance of a Staten Island ferryboat into the South Ferry slip, with its crowd of commuters suddenly released into the streets of lower Manhattan. The docking of the Aquitania, surrounded by those busy Lilliputian tugs; the pencil-like office buildings stretching upwards for a place in the sun—"High growths of iron, slender, strong, splendidly uprising toward clear skies." They give us the vision of Whitman in plastic poetry, viewed always from unsuspected points of vantage: the restless crowds of lower Broadway, for instance; view from balustrades hundreds of feet above; plumes of silvery smoke and steam; curious geometry of massive shadows and sharp sunlight; the molten silver of surging waters at dusk; all that dynamic power and restless energy of the metropolis. All of these were captured in the motion photography of the American artists. There was no heroine, no villain, no plot. Yet it was all thrilling, exciting, dramatic—but dramatic in the language of plasticity. It was honestly, gloriously photographic, devoid of trickery and imitation. They used no artifice of diffusion. They did not resort to the aid of the soft-focus lens. They did not attempt to make pictures that looked like paintings. They did not "retouch" to produce the effect of a spurious etching. Always were they vigorously, rigorously, photographic. These artists avoided the well-known "points of interest." Instead, they gave us, by a brilliant emphasis of its own way of speaking, the spirit of Manhattan itself, Whitman's "city of the world," Whitman's "proud and passionate city." The city, they discovered, reveals itself most eloquently in the terms of line, mass, volume, movement. Its language is plastic. Thus it expresses its only true individuality.

How does this experiment, this glorious adventure, differ from the ordinary movie? It emphasizes anew the art of the camera. Properly understood and used intelligently, the motion picture camera, like the ordinary camera, becomes an invaluable instrument, registering the vision of the creative artist. With it he is endowed with a new power of capturing on the wing, as it were, all that fleeting and evanescent beauty of places and people. At last the artist can register those strange accidental moments when light, lines, form and movement seem by chance to combine into an unearthly divine beauty, transmuting everyday objects into plastic poetry.

Of course, there are complex difficulties, obstacles almost impossible to overcome. But to dismiss the camera as a mere "machine," to deny it a place in the realm of legitimate art, is to cast away forever the possibility of discovering its latent potentialities and secrets. But to accept it, as these American artists have, with respect and reverence, to use it as an instrument of art, is to acquire the key to a vast and unexplored treasure house of expression. A comparison with another art may illuminate this point. Both for the creation and the interpretation of great music we accept without question the legitimacy of the musical instrument. The piano of a Chopin, the 'cello of a Casals, the violin of a Kreisler, are never considered as "music machines." In the hands of a Sheeler the camera should likewise be accepted as an instrument of art, objectifying the creative vision of the artist. The difference between the camera and the musical instrument is a difference in degree, not in kind.

Photography still remains the Cinderella of arts. Once its legitimacy is recognized, once we awaken to the urgent duty of developing its latent potentialities, it may become an essential in any adequate art-education. Perhaps the time is far distant when photography may be taught in the schools, or schools of photography as an art established and endowed. Mr. [George] Eastman, we read, has endowed a music school in Rochester. Might he not, with singular appropriateness, likewise establish a school of photography through which the art of the camera might be elevated to its legitimate place among the arts?

The Sheeler-Strand experiment brings up another question. Is there no place in the motion picture world, as organized at present, for such pioneering experiments? At least two answers to this question have been offered.

The first is that there should be a "little movie" movement, paralleling the so-called "little theatre" movement, which has a beneficial influence upon native American drama, releasing new talents, and demonstrating that the public will support worthy plays. In the field of the motion picture, such a movement might take the form of a small producing group of directors, scenarists, actors and photographers. The "release" of a film produced in this manner might be effected through the regular exhibitors. Or it might be shown in theatres especially rented for that purpose. In either case the expense would be enormous and the profits small. In view of the uncertainty of results, the

493

almost insuperable obstacles in the way of any widespread exhibition, this plan is hardly feasible. In an art in which the studio and laboratory costs are so high, it is to be doubted whether the experimenter could ever attain even the technical excellence of the professional producers. And without this excellence the experiment would fail.

The second suggestion is the organization by the most firmly established and reputable producers of a research or experimental department, in which true artists of the camera would be free to carry out their adventures and experiments. Occasionally, perhaps often, they would attain results that might be used with the greatest artistic benefit in the regular productions. In this way the art of the motion picture would be developed from within. A great variety of methods might be attained. And instead of submitting every scenario to one cut-and-dried method, each picture would be screened in a highly individual and novel manner. It might then be interpreted in a manner best suited to the realization of its values. Such a research department would eventually do away with the hit-and-miss methods at present employed. It would in time prevent the enormous waste of effort, the conspicuous expenditure on non-essentials, of which the press-agents now, for some strange reason, actually boast. All the inherent powers of the motion picture camera might thus be developed into eloquent expression, and the motion picture industry would be assured of continuous novelty and artistic vitality. The lamentable evidences of repetition, imitation and conventionalization would disappear.

If it be objected that such a suggestion is wildly idealistic and "highbrow," we need in reply only point to the example set by other highly successful industries and commercial organizations. Professor Soddy, the great English authority on radio-activity, recently declared that the department of scientific research established by the General Electric Company was doing more for pure science than the majority of British universities. Such a department, based on far-sighted commercial policy, is recognized as essential to the health and growth of the electrical industries. A similar department, we are informed, is supported by the Bell Telephone system. In the more immediate field of the industrial art, we may point to the eminent example of one of our foremost manufacturers of American silks. The Cheney Brothers Company have long supported an experimental studio, in which a staff of artists, designers and weavers are given the freedom to pursue unhindered their artistic adventures in the realm of design. There are no directions, no prohibitions, no insistence upon turning out work that may be immediately gauged in terms of dollars and cents. In this fashion the art standards are upheld and the public is assured of the artistic quality of the finished product.

An insane passion for immediate profit in any industry may in the long run become the most unprofitable of policies. And it is precisely this mad passion that has worked to the detriment of the motion picture. The geese that lay the golden eggs are beginning to rebel. Millions have been spent, often unwisely and without appreciable result. The "camera men," who really hold the strategic key to the situation, are only beginning to be recognized. Few directors have the "camera" sense. Light too often is used merely as a necessary evil, when it should be used to enhance and vitalize the movement. When the producers awaken to the fact that the "camera men" must be artists of intelligence and discrimination, educated and efficient in their craft, the art of the motion picture will attain its maturity.

Without this co-operation of science and art, no permanent progress in the field of the motion picture can ever be effected. A far-sighted policy, looking not merely to immediate profits, nor resting on the miraculous success of the past, must recognize and protect the new art of the camera. Once this Cinderella of the arts is recognized by our Princes of the Celluloid, the latter may discover the only true way in which motion pictures may become not merely more artistic, but more popular and profitable as well.

FILM 1922   SALOME

"SALOME," excerpt from "The Silent Drama," Robert E. Sherwood, *Life,* Vol. 80, No. 2071, July 13, 1922, p. 22.

When a really fine moving picture flashes across the film heavens, it is customary for the critics to bare their heads in wondering awe, murmur a prayer of devout gratitude—and then wait for the dull, sickening thud which inevitably occurs when any meteoric masterpiece lands in the box office.

I shall therefore preface my remarks concerning Nazimova's SALOME with the statement that it will probably be a flat financial failure. By doing this, I can forestall the courteous movie exhibitors who will write in to say, "Thank you for praising that picture; I now know that it would be suicidal for me to book it at my theatre."

Having discharged this important obligation, I can go ahead with a clear conscience.

Nazimova's production of SALOME is exceptional in every noteworthy sense of the word: it is extraordinarily beautiful to look at—its backgrounds, costumes, lighting and composition being designed with a fine sense for pictorial values; it is well acted; it is intelligently directed; it is faithful to the play by Oscar Wilde, from which it is taken; and its action is continuous. By this last, I mean that there is no break in the sequence of events. There is no necessity for explanatory subtitles like, "Spring came—and once more did the roses bloom in those wan cheeks that had been ashened by the searing breath of Fate."

The persons responsible for SALOME deserve the whole-souled gratitude of everyone who believes in the possibilities of the movies as an art. Nazimova, of course, is the first. Here, indeed, is an artist—a great one. Without recourse to any over-energetic spasms of emotion—with no attempt at muscular calisthenics—she creates Salome more vividly than Mary Garden ever did on the operatic stage.

A few laurels must also be planted upon the brows of Charles Bryant, the director, Charles Van Enger, the camera man, and Natacha Rambova, who adhered closely to Beardsley's drawings in designing the costumes and scenes.

Regardless of the Olympian wrath of the Great Gods of the Box Office, I emphatically recommend SALOME to everyone who loves beauty. . . .

1923   "SALOME AND THE CINEMA"

By Thomas Craven, *The New Republic*, Vol. 33, No. 425, January 24, 1923, pp. 225-226.

Nazimova's SALOME has been offered to the public in the name of art. The press-book compiled to exploit the film is one of the most extraordinary sidelights on the infirmity of the human mind that I have ever seen. Amongst the Special Teaser Designs and the Catch Lines for Ads or Program Use I find this typical and preposterous statement: "Nazimova's SALOME stands out as a triumphant rebuke to those critics of the Screen who have said 'Art cannot come out of a camera.'" It is a common practice, in advertising a moving picture, to proclaim its aesthetic virtues, but in the present instance there seemed to be more than usual warrant for such an assertion: the text, according to the producers, was based on Oscar Wilde's tragedy, a play so simple in its general outline as to make impossible the elaborate and incoherent waste of the average film; and the sets and costumes, according to the producers, were taken from the drawings of Aubrey Beardsley.

Let there be no mistake about this performance—it is degrading and unintelligent, and cannot, by the most liberal extension of terms, be called artistic.

The limitations of the moving picture are, of course, the limitations of photography, but there is one way in which the aesthetic can incontestably enter the film—through the "still," or the composed background. By reproducing literally the designs of the creative artist the camera performs its most valuable service. In the case of *Salome* the designs were to be had for the asking, the flat decorations of Aubrey Beardsley being strikingly adapted to the screen.

Now although Aubrey Beardsley is not the great artist he is popularly supposed to be, still he is an artist, and a very serious one; and furthermore, he was, of all the brackish precocities of the decadent nineties, the most brilliantly endowed in strange satire. His work is literary, but it is intense and intelligent. His drawings for the Wilde play, despite their obvious Japanese influence, are truly original, and at times approximate pure design of a distinguished order. But the American director must improve upon them! And to improve upon them he must obliterate them! I defy anyone to show a single point of resemblance between the unimaginative stupidity of the Nazimova production and the work of the English artist. What a smiting scene The Climax would have made! To have rendered it as large as life, identical with Beardsley's black-and-white conception, would have stirred the dullest sensibilities into a shout. Instead we have the simplicity that is not art—stark eccentricity and drab nonsense.

Wilde, also, has been completely eliminated. French titles would not have been feasible, but even the translation of Lord Alfred Douglas has been garbled beyond recognition. The value of the French drama lies, not in its plot—the story is the Biblical legend as modernized by Flaubert—but in the highly charged poetic atmosphere. It matters little that Wilde's imagination was hypertrophied and lascivious, and it is hardly necessary to emphasize the physical artifices and repulsions of his genius; the important fact to remember is that he created within his own narrow scope a curiously consistent and powerfully effective play. I grant that without words most of the power is incommunicable, but with the aid of Beardsley's linear art and with appropriate characterization the general atmospheric tone of the Wilde version might have been maintained. In the pictures all is lost—the fantastic precision of the imagery, the tragic sensuality and the religious terror. The scenes are not elaborate; they are barren, inarticulate and meaningless.

Nazimova, as the daughter of Herodias, has attempted a part for which she has no qualifications. She flits hither and thither with the mincing step of a toe-dancer; she has the figure of a boy, and in her absurd costume, a satin bathing suit of recent pattern, she impresses one as the old Tetrarch's cup-bearer. Try as she will she cannot be seductive— the physical handicap is insurmountable; she tosses her head impudently, grimaces repeatedly and rolls her eyes with a vitreous stare. The effect is comic. The deadly lure of sex, which haunts the Wilde drama like a subtle poison, is dispelled the instant one beholds her puerile form. The Dance of the Seven Veils, used by the poet to release the hideous consequences of lust, is wholly innocuous. Not that one expected, in these censorial days, a danse du ventre, but had Nazimova appeared in the garb contrived by Beardsley she might at least have given a touch of reality to her epicene antics. The other characters can be disposed of summarily. Herodias is a drunken charwoman with frizzy hair; Herod resembles nothing so much as a fat clown; John the Baptist is ascetic and canonically lean, but his leprous debility is not likely to inspire the salacious Princess of Judea with any ideas, either impure or holy. Salome runs from the gluttonous Tetrarch to the moonlit terrace, and thence to the gaping cistern to peer at the Prophet; she arches her slender brows, stretches flexuously, and tries in vain to hold together a succession of irrelative details.

The present inchoate condition of the cinema makes it almost impossible to determine the aesthetic value of a medium which gives the illusion of physical movement by a projected sequence of flat planes. Any motif, either in the world of phenomena or of ideas, is too complex to be presented exhaustively by one art, and it may be that in the film of the future we shall see revealed by some unexpected combinations of silhouette, color and background, states of the soul, which shall play upon our emotions with a force equivalent to the sting of actual experience. If so, the moving picture will have arrived at true art.

But this seems improbable. At best it will always be a bastard art. Pictorially it has no significance in its own right; it may, as I have indicated above, serve to reproduce the designs of plastic artists—the tempest aroused by the CALIGARI experiment was the result of the bizarre modern decorations; and its literary merit is negligible. It remains then to be seen whether the film can convert pantomime into genuine drama. To be sure there are people who weep over pictures, and people who clap their hands; but tears and laughter are false witnesses of art. I refer to an imaginative conception, the dramatic effect of carefully planned and deliberately ordered forces operating toward an inevitable conclusion.

I confess that I am not greatly disturbed over the aesthetics of the question. What is demanded of the moving picture at present is not art or the claptrap released in the name of art, but plain intelligence. Nazimova's SALOME is not more unintelligent than most films—it is only more pretentious in its claims. So long as the debasement of literary and artistic ideas continues to fill the theatres, just so long will the moving picture remain at its low and insufferable stage of vulgarity.

Thomas Craven.

COMMENTARY

"The Cinema," by the British novelist and essayist Virginia Woolf, had appeared in *The Arts* **magazine for June, 1926, and was subsequently reprinted in** *The New Republic*, **as "The Movies and Reality." Gilbert Seldes' comments came a few issues later.**

The Léger-Murphy film is, of course, BALLET MECANIQUE (50). OF WHAT ARE THE YOUNG FILMS DREAMING? was directed in France by Henri Chomette. Chomette was the brother of René Clair, whose PARIS ENDORMI, as noted in Chapter 19, had been preceded by ENTR'ACTE (for which, yes, the music was written by Erik Satie). When Seldes wrote this article, CALIGARI was within a month and a half of its famous New York revival.

OF WHAT ARE THE YOUNG FILMS DREAMING? had been screened at a special performance in New York in April, 1926. Beaumont Newhall saw it a year later in Cambridge.

The film by Man Ray (1890-   ), an American painter and photographer living in Paris, arrived in 1927, and with it came Pirandello's THE LIVING DEAD MAN, directed by Marcel L'Herbier (1890-   ), whose THE NEW ENCHANTMENT had been seen earlier.

1926   "THE ABSTRACT MOVIE"

By Gilbert Seldes, *The New Republic*, Vol. 48, No. 615, September 15, 1926, pp. 95-96.

In Mrs. Woolf's essay, The Movies and Reality (*The New Republic*, August 4), there occurs this sentence:

> Something abstract, something which moves with controlled and conscious art, something which calls for the very slightest help from

497

words or music to make itself intelligible, yet justly uses them sub-
serviently — of such movements and abstractions the films may, in time
to come, be composed.

The keen intelligence of the whole essay ought to tempt every one who has been
thinking about the movies to write an extensive commentary; but the sentence quoted
has peculiar interest because it is apparently written without knowledge of the abstract
films which have been made in Paris in the last two or three years, films which already
make the conditional future unnecessary. At least a part of the films of tomorrow will be
composed of the elements Mrs. Woolf mentions.

Of the three films I have seen, two at least have been shown in New York by the Film
Guild and the Film Associates, the film made by the French cubist painter Fernand Léger
collaborating with the American Dudley Murphy, and the film sponsored by Comte
Etienne de Beaumont, OF WHAT ARE YOUNG FILMS DREAMING (an unhappy
flavorless translation of the French title which was a pun on the name of de Musset's
play). The third was made to be shown between the two parts of the last of the Swedish
ballets under Rolf de Maré, and is called ENTR'ACTE. Of these, the Beaumont film seems
to me to be the most completely realized, the Léger-Murphy film which was the pioneer,
the least; but as the three films are identical in essence and in significance, I shall not try
to judge among them, nor to identify the separate points of interest by name.

It is extremely difficult for the American, accustomed to an involved plot dominating
even such films as exploit a dominant player, to gather by word of mouth the actual
content of these films; that they can be interesting passes belief. Fortunately for the
critic he has only to write down what he has actually seen; these films are made for pure
visual enjoyment. In general the spectator has seen objects in motion; the objects may
be easily identified — a straw hat, a boat on the Seine, a row of bottles, a shoot-the-
chutes; or they may be distorted, seen through a prismatic glass, through smoke, at
unusual angles, upside down. The movement may be accelerated or retarded, shown
backward, repeated, tricked in a hundred ways. There may be a swelling blot of ink on a
pane of glass, a shadow endowed with proper life, mysterious darkness or twilight on the
screen; human beings may be present, as actors, as masses, as incidentals. There may be
a mock funeral with the mourners in slow motion and the hearse running off by itself, or
a green triangle may leap under and through a red circle, faster and faster in a
geometrical struggle for supremacy, or the city of Paris may rush headlong to perdition
as the airplane from which the picture is taken nose-dives around the Eiffel Tower.

Anyone familiar with the pictures will recognize some of these elements: the cleverer
news reels, the trick pictures in which a cow walks into itself, added to a touch of the
Clavilux will supply at least half of the sensations in seeing an abstract film. Until the
abstract picture arrived, in fact, the trick movie was the "purest" in a technical sense.
What the abstract picture had added is deliberate intention. The repetitions, the
changes of pace, the variations in the form projected in the Léger picture were intended
to create cumulative emotion, coming to a climax. It was not wholly successful; I have
noted before that the only actually moving part of that picture was concerned with a
woman bearing a burden up a hill, and being eternally shifted back to the bottom just as
she reached the crest. To make the film theoretically successful this suggestion of
human emotion ought to have been omitted; yet it, too, was entirely cinematographic,
and did not depend upon story. ENTR'ACTE was vaguely connected with the ballet,
Relâche, and Borlin, the principal dancer, appeared too regularly; in the Beaumont film
the only persons one recalls at all are a few well-known Parisians whose faces are distorted
as in the comic mirrors at Coney Island. In each of the films the most significant part
was that played by the variation of movement and the variation of forms. There was
excitement in the changing speeds at which bottles moved about each other; there was

extraordinary pleasure to the eye in watching a tiny object spinning round on a moving phonograph record and seen through a distorting glass; there was a prime thrill in the dip and sway of the roller coaster, a movement which took in the whole visible world and was felt at the pit of the stomach. In two of the pictures there appeared the most beautiful scenic shots I have ever seen, with the color-scheme reversed, so that trees were white against a black sky.

None of these pictures is entirely successful; all three are exceptionally fine movies and important in the progress of the movie. They all have created images on the screen and proved that these images can call our emotions into being; but none of them has tried to be specific. None of them has tried to use a definite image for the communication of a definite thought. They have proved that symbols can be evocative on the screen; it is enough.

Until recently THE CABINET OF DR. CALIGARI has been uniquely the art-film, and it is interesting to note that Mrs. Woolf's thoughts on the movies were inspired by this hardy outrider. There were several important things in CALIGARI, most of them noted so often as to cause nausea to our good American directors. CALIGARI used expressionistic (i.e., entirely unrealistic, but emotionally correct) settings for its action, and would have been an entire failure if the rhythm of the principal players had not also been cast in a mode of unreality. The shape of an attic or of a window, the bizarre unexplained appearance of a patch of sunlight without a source, the use of levels, inclines and curves, all contributed to the intensity of emotion which the story was to call up. It was in no sense an abstract film, but indicated, years before the abstract film was made, to what ultimate use it may be put. Because I think it quite unreasonable to suppose that we shall give up the story-film; the film, properly handled, tells a story magnificently, and so far has been a disappointment only because it has found no way to tell more than the outside of a story, telling it blatantly and vulgarly. CALIGARI succeeded at moments in suggesting thought and feelings without always depending upon action. ("A kiss is love. A broken cup is jealousy.") The abstract film which will give the director symbols and images will give him at the same time a hundred times his present capacity to tell his story, to give it the third dimension it has so far been lacking, an intellectual and emotional content.

The abstract film, like the trick film and the news reel, has worked severely within the limitations of the machinery of taking and projecting; it has called in few outside aids. (I believe that Satie wrote the ballet music, and that part of it accompanied ENTR'ACTE; but I saw it alone and heard nothing beyond the ordinary piano; the other two films I saw in small projection rooms, without music.) That means that as soon as the director feels free to do so, and brings his technique up to the required point, he can embody all that these films teach him. In the actual taking of pictures the American director is probably unexcelled; the technical proficiency he needs is in knowing how a thing will look when taken, in knowing how to displace or distort his object in front of the camera; I should also think that a knowledge of psychology would not be inappropriate. He will displease the fanatical amateurs of the abstract picture by using a few hundred feet here and there to heighten an emotion; but he will gradually enlarge the available field for the movie and teach the movie-going public to look for more and care for more than he has previously given.

In writing about THE BIG PARADE in this journal I noted that its finest moment was the reappearance of a line of soldiers advancing through a wood—a line seen perhaps twenty minutes earlier in the picture. The line reappeared in the midst of barrage fire; its contribution to the narrative was far less than that of many other sequences. Yet it had tremendous emotional effect because it made contact in our minds in the electrical circle of image-imagination. I am convinced that the soldiers purely as soldiers were not the cause; it was the appearance of a known line, it was the pace, the timing, the rhythm of that appearance which counted.

In all such speculations we who are not actually engaged in making movies assume   **499** one thing which the professionals instantly deny. We think that the movie can be made great by ceasing to be realistic; we insist that the camera is not a mere recorder—even the still camera is more than that, and when you add motion we feel we have scientific backing in our claim that the camera can and should transpose its objects. In short we want the moving picture to be an *art through its mechanism*, not an art through literature and not a mechanism alone. The professionals tell us we are slightly mad; and it has been left for amateurs to prove that we are sane. But the last word is still in the field of commerce. The non-realistic, the actually imaginative or creative movie will not sell. That is, I believe, true. But it is impermanently true. Our audiences have been starved of imagination so long that they may fail to recognize it and care for it. The usual method, after starvation, is to begin to feed the victim slowly indeed.

Gilbert Seldes

A Film by Man Ray 1927

Excerpt from "MAN RAY AND METROPOLIS," Gilbert Seldes, *The New Republic,* Vol. 50, No. 643, March 30, 1927, p. 170.

. . . The first of the Film Guild's Sunday showings [March 6] was devoted to Man Ray's abstract movie, EMAK BAKIA, and a film made by Marcel l'Herbier out of Pirandello's *The Late Matthias Pascal.* The film is called THE LIVING DEAD MAN, and all of Pirandello's exceptional tediousness in fiction or drama has been faithfully transferred to the screen. The direction of the dull story is commonplace, the mugging distasteful. Miss Lois Moran appears in the second half of the picture, and may help it on; I cannot report, because the first half wearied me so that I went away.

Man Ray's film has gone straight to hell with good intentions. It has its source in the same feeling for the cinematic, the same protest against "literature," as the Léger-Murphy BALLET MECANIQUE and Beaumont's A QUOI REVENT LES JEUNES FILMS? In Man Ray's experiment you get the usual elements: objects in motion, objects seen at unusual angles, distortion; at rare moments a few feet of film create a startling, almost ravishing effect, and clearly do this by means of movement, not statically. The changes of pace, the rhythm, are occasionally effective. But as a whole this film does not come up to the level of the Beaumont forerunner, because the whole and most of the parts lack significance. There is almost no relation between any hundred feet of film and the preceding or subsequent hundred; it is a camera man's holiday without the single idea and the single effect of a good abstract or even a good commercial movie. A picked audience hissed it a little and then settled down to enjoy the dullness of Pirandello. . . .

A QUOI REVENT LES JEUNES FILMS? **FILM 1927**

Unpublished study notes by Beaumont Newhall, written May 17, 1927.

Along with the remarkable THE CABINET OF DR. CALIGARI [shown May 16, 1927, at Brattle Hall, Cambridge, Massachusetts, by the Shady Hill Film Guild] was a laboratory experiment by the Comte de Beaumont. I cannot begin to give all the effects that were thrown upon the screen, so I shall only give a very few. Here we see the true possibilities of that most versatile machine, the motion picture camera. Crystals. Kaleidoscopes. Soap bubbles. Dynamos. Shells. Lights everywhere. And best of all a trip through Paris. First we went at breakneck speed through the subway. Lights looked like white lines, in fact that is all that there was on the screen for several feet. Then a square light in the distance. Just the merest speck. Nearer, and nearer, until it looked like a newspaper.

Bigger and bigger, until at last we realized that it was the entrance to the tunnel. Railroad tracks, shooting by and merging one into the other, or rather melting. A double exposure of two tracks, the one going, so I heard, at two-four time, the other at two-three time. Subway cars rushing at you, upside down, or pointing to the sky. Under bridges in the Seine, until you thought that you had been under all the bridges in the world. The negatives of foliage, queer white branches against a black background. A profile, repeated across the screen to make a pretty pattern. A series of studies in dissolves. Distorted motion pictures, and again crystals, and bubbles and wheels, all, not symbolic of anything as the audience would have us believe, but simply as pretty and interesting things, revealing, as it were, of the remarkable possibilities of the camera as something more than a mere machine for reproduction. American photographers might sit up and take notice. Most interesting for one interested in the future of the movies and the possibilities of the motion picture camera, most boring for one seeking sentiment and a story. So these experiments fail in America.

COMMENTARY

The Hungarian Paul Fejos is reported to have made THE LAST MOMENT (1928) in Hollywood in 28 days for $5,000. Under contract to Universal, he directed LONESOME (1928), THE LAST PERFORMANCE (1929) and the sound film BROADWAY (1929).

FILM 1928   THE LAST MOMENT

"Exceptional Photoplays: THE LAST MOMENT," *National Board of Review Magazine*, Vol. 3, No. 2, February, 1928, pp. 5-6. (With the permission of the National Board of Review of Motion Pictures.)

Directed by . . . . Paul Fejos
Photographed by . . . . Leon Shamroy

The Cast

He . . . . Otto Matiesen
Innkeeper . . . . Lucille La Verne
First Wife . . . . Isabel Lamore
Second Wife . . . . Georgia Hale
A Woman . . . . Anielka Eltar
An original screen story by Paul Fejos

From Hollywood at last comes the experimental film. In Europe this sort of thing has been going on for a long while, ever since CALIGARI startled us (and still startles us) with its expressionistic fantasy, its stylized sets and acting, followed by the abstractions of Beaumont, Léger and others, until the Russian film POTEMKIN, in the sequence of the ship getting under way for action, utilized the mechanizing of objects to create suspense and dramatic movement. It is a matter for celebration that the methods of technique used in those laboratory efforts have been combined exclusively for pictorial narration in a film made in an American studio, and that this film now affords clearer speculation on the dynamics of the motion picture, and further, on its proper essentials as an expressive medium. Our patriotic impulses are somewhat thwarted by the fact that its director, Paul Fejos, hails from Hungary. But then we have adopted Lubitsch, von Stroheim, and von Sternberg, not to mention Seastrom, Murnau and others—Charles Spencer Chaplin, for instance. When our creative powers are questioned we do not hesitate to hold up their works as shining refutations of any hint thrown at the progress of our domestic cinema art. Perhaps it is more fortifying to be able to state that Mr. Fejos' American-made film was financed by native private capital not hitherto put in circulation in making artistic and worthwhile motion pictures, or any motion pictures at all. To Mr. Spitz, the new comer in this necessary financing branch of the business, goes therefore all due recognition for not only having given Mr. Fejos his money but also unobstructed leaway in carrying out the director's ideas. So Mr. Fejos, a bacteriologist, with only this assistance, has made one of the most remarkable and interesting films to appear on this side of the Atlantic. It would seem that ideas and the freedom to use them count after all, as some have insisted, just as much as studio experience and adherence to standardized studio practice.

The film is, briefly, the history of events in a person's life at the moment of that person's death. It has thus a psychological import, although we have scant evidence at best of what a man can think about while he dies. But the theory is familiar to everyone, and it is an interesting theory which in this case has been used in a way to provoke the imagination and in a medium peculiarly suited to its artistic expression. In any event, the only subtitle in the film is the one at the beginning that sets forth this psychological assumption, and it is the only one that is necessary.

The first scene shows bubbles rising from the pond as a man's hand vanishes beneath the water. Then follow, with lightning-like rapidity, flashes—faces, objects, snatches of scenes—an apparently disconnected phantasmagoria of life. These slow down to connected rhythmic sequences of action which compose the experienced incidents and situations out of which arose these mind images of the drowning man. These again, at the end of the picture, speed back into the lightning flashes of the brain. Thus, at the beginning and ending, the mechanism of the mind is plausibly and vividly exposed, the effect being that of peering into the secrets of cerebral action, while throughout the intervening stretches of the film the sense is preserved of a dream interlude, not quite real, but real enough, like reflections in a dark strange mirror before which a human life passes at its illuminating and crucial moments.

Nothing quite like this film has been done before. The significance lies in the fact that its method is the chiefly interesting and compelling thing about it. The story it tells is hazy, sketchy, nothing in itself extraordinary. But the method allows the medium to hold sway in a technical virtuosity. This manipulation of pattern and image, light and shadow, in a constant shifting and convolution, is of itself enough to cast a thralling spell. The pictures alone count—or rather the *moving* pictures. In short, it is cinema on its own, distinct, like painting, poetry, music. The medium is permitted to achieve its own results.

Here we see a motion picture cut free of its established mould and striving for a purer form. We see that the acting, which, even interpreted as stylization, could for the most part be improved, is not after all of prime importance, the idea being, not to represent characters, but to present them as a part of the mood, movement and intention of the film. They are but images used like objects to hold the sequences together. Perhaps they may be likened to pervading notes in a harmony, something that threads the production like a theme. Again the relationship of music and cinema is suggested, not as mediums that go hand in hand, as supplements or complements, but as distinct, independent ways of awakening emotions and evoking imagination. So too with the story. It is simply an outline that gives the pictures cohesiveness. One technical feature is extraordinary. The film may be said to have been cut in the camera box. There is little splicing together of scenes. Continuity is photographed not assembled, separate shots dissolve one into the other. This gives an unusual flow to the composition. One can only assume that a very perfect continuity was worked out and closely followed by director and camera man.

THE LAST MOMENT is another milestone at which our hopes for the motion picture can be replenished and our enthusiasm renewed.

502   (*Produced by Freedman-Spitz. Distributed by Zakoro.*)

COMMENTARY

The two-reel THE FALL OF THE HOUSE OF USHER (1929), filmed in Rochester, New York under the direction of J. S. Watson, Jr., is noted here in several stages of progress: first as its work began, and later at a showing on the West Coast, when the picture was only half-finished. When finally completed, it opened the new Film Arts Guild theatre in New York, along with a Russian feature film.

This theatre incorporated darkened planes on "the side walls, which will be employed in the future, according to announcement, as part of the screen. By flashing pictorial matter upon the side walls the management hopes to create more of an illusion of three dimensions than the flat screen can hope to give. But nothing of this sort was tried last night." (51)

NINETY SEVEN DOLLARS, the film Dr. Watson mentions, was made for that amount in 1928 by Robert Florey, working in Hollywood with Slavko Vorkapich and the camera man Gregg Toland. This one-reeler has also been called both RHAPSODY OF HOLLYWOOD (perhaps in recognition of its supposed source of inspiration, Gershwin's "Rhapsody in Blue") and THE LIFE AND LOVES OF A HOLLYWOOD EXTRA.

The concluding review is from *The Dial*, the magazine which Dr. Watson published and co-edited from 1920 through 1929. A second film by Watson, also made in Rochester, and entitled LOT IN SODOM, was not released until 1933, even though it was silent.

1928   A Poe Film in Rochester

Excerpt from "Amateur Movies," Frederick James Smith, *Photoplay Magazine,* Vol. 33, No. 6, May, 1928, p. 74.

. . . A great deal of amateur interest is centered in the production of Edgar Allan Poe's THE FALL OF THE HOUSE OF USHER, now being filmed by a Rochester group of non-professionals.

The Rochester amateurs are taking plenty of time with their production. It was started a year ago, and is now half finished. When completed it will be in two reels.

The photography is in the hands of J. S. Watson, Jr., who is also directing. In the last named task he is being assisted by Louis Siegel. Melville Webber has contributed the continuity and the scenery. Hildegarde Watson is playing Madeline Usher, Herbert Stern is acting the role of Roderick Usher and Melville Webber plays the Traveller.

"We decided to work first of all on scenery," writes Mr. Watson to *Photoplay*. "The *Fall of the House of Usher* seemed to us to be a suitable story because its intense mood and atmosphere depended more upon background than upon good character drawing.

"We first constructed a thirty-foot mansion out of painted wallboard. This, of course, proved to be worthless, but it furnished us with one scene and some experience. After that we stopped painting wallboard and tinted the surfaces with light only. To make these surfaces more interesting, we break them up with various shaped prisms. When we want a flight of stairs or a landscape we introduce it by double exposure.

"Films must have movement, of course. For movement we have the actors walk about, the camera moving about on a rubber tired truck and the scenery also in movement. This all requires expert timing and we are getting better at it with practice.

"Sometimes we resort to double printing, but only when absolutely necessary. With a Duplex printer this is no joke. We do our own finishing—and our film looks it. The Standard Bell and Howell is one of the few cameras which will take backwards and still register perfectly. We are fortunate in having one available. As we are limited in our light power, we use a 43 mm. F 1.5 Ernemann lens for most long shots. We use arcs and Kirby lights, but not many at a time because of lack of juice. On account of the Kirby lights we use panchromatic film.". . .

"AN AMATEUR STUDIO PICTURE"   1928

By J. S. Watson, Jr., *Transactions of the Society of Motion Picture Engineers*, Vol. 12, No. 33, meeting of April 9-14, 1928, Hollywood, California, pp. 216-223.

A great many people have said recently, and some of them may have believed it, that the artistic future of the motion picture was in the hands of the amateur. They were of course using the word amateur as an antithesis to everything bad in professional practice. The word professional can be used outside of its proper meaning either as a compliment or as an insult, either to designate seriousness of purpose and knowledge of means, or on the other hand, standardization at the expense of feeling, perfunctory haste in production, and callous and inappropriate imitation of known commercial successes. But really there are only three kinds of pictures, good, bad, and medium. Everyone has seen bad films with plenty of the latest professional surface glitter and good films in which every drawback known to photography has not upset the well-conceived plan or the good luck of the director. Certainly what is called the amateur spirit, the desire for sincerity and freshness of treatment, is not incompatible with a professional desire to have your film a success. More good amateur films have been made by professionals or semi-professionals than by strict amateurs, the strict amateurs having only the one slightly disheartening advantage that their films do not have to be cut up and titled by ill-disposed distributing organizations.

In November, 1926, Melville Webber, a painter and archaeologist, told me that he would like to try his hand at sets for a photoplay. We had an empty stable, plenty of wall board, and 12 KW of direct current, but neither of us felt able to write an original story. We finally selected Poe's *Fall of the House of Usher* which neither of us had read for 10 or 15 years, and which we therefore felt all the more able to treat as raw material. The liberties which we have taken with the story, although hair raising, are not unprecedented in the annals of the motion picture industry. They will be explained later.

Aesthetic Theories

We suffered from the pseudo-scientific prejudice, the essence of modernism, which makes people believe that each medium of expression can and should be isolated and purified just as a chemical compound is isolated in the laboratory. You say to yourself that the cinema is not theater or the dance, and certainly not the novel, and then you begin to wonder what it is. You think of camera tricks as essential, of oppositions of movement, changes in size, changes in lighting and sharpness, accelerations and contrasts of speed, distortions of shapes and perspectives. You decide to play any number of tricks on time and space. Then you remember that the worst picture you ever saw had all of this and nothing else; that every possible trick was invented the same year as the camera; that ideas have nothing to do with art and that there are too many ideas anyway.

But just the same, suppose one could take the old tricks and use them not only to illustrate the story, as double printing is used to show Pharaoh in the Red Sea, but to improve the flow of the picture, gathering force from scene to scene, so as to make the spectator feel not with any particular hero or heroine as one does in a cheap novel, but to make him feel the whole piece like a piece of poetry.

Practical Difficulties

Thus far our aesthetics would have affected our procedure no more than a list of good intentions. The cumulative effect which we hoped to get is the most important effect produced by any first class picture no matter how little the average spectator may be aware of it. We went on, however, to a thought which has occurred before to a great many people, namely that the crucial point in a motion picture is the point where one scene changes into another. There is not only the action to be made coherent, but also there are matters like speed, composition, and photographic quality which must not be suddenly interrupted without good reason. An inappropriate change of scene is probably much more serious than an illogical sequence of ideas in writing. Scenes to the sensitive eye frequently appear to annihilate one another, and a picture in which this occurs repeatedly, however meritorious it may be from other points of view, will give you a headache.

In feature pictures these transitions from scene to scene are supposedly taken care of by the director and the photographer and what escapes them has to be looked after by the cutting department. We decided to eliminate the difficulty once for all at the very start. Our first scenario called for continuous action during 1000 feet of film. This was to be accomplished mainly by keeping the camera moving from one part of the set to another, photographing successively wheels, doors, windows, actors, and pieces of actors. Anyone who has tried to make a sequence of lap dissolves in the camera will know how difficult it is not to be able to cut the film. And this sequence did not permit even dissolves. We had taken about fifty feet of it when somebody made a mistake. It appeared impossible to recapture the exact position and pose. We began over again and only got to thirty feet. After spoiling a good deal of film, we settled down to the cross reference system of the ordinary feature, where you jump from the cellar to the attic, and where the hero lights a match in a long shot and throws it away in a close-up.

Scenario

In *The Fall of the House of Usher*, the plot is of little consequence; the importance of the piece lies in its mood—in a development of emotional tone almost without action. We decided to make a picture with a mood rather than a story. It became clear at once that for this the literal representation of a sequence of events in time would not be appropriate. The characters and their relations to one another became thematic material, in the organization of which movement and progression were essential. For example: the visitor to the House, the I of Poe's story, has been used as a motive, running (often literally) through the whole picture and supplying a key to the arrangement, which falls into three main divisions.

In the first part he is seen entering the house, becoming affected by the weird atmosphere of the place, and gradually being subordinated until only his hat suggests his presence.

The second part has to do with the Lady Madeline of Usher and her brother Roderick, her fall into a cataleptic trance, her entombment (which is represented as a mental submission) and subsequent escape from the burial vault, and the effect of all this on her brother's mind. In this episode the visitor is suggested shortly after the burial by the shadow of a hat on the wall and again by a more definite recurrence of the hat.

In the third part the sister and the mad brother destroy one another and the house falls. At this point the hat becomes the visitor again, and he flees from the scene of destruction.

Effect Scenes

As for our very numerous tricks, or more properly (since there is no attempt at deception) our effect scenes, probably not one of them is new or even fresh. I think, however, that by a digression I can show why they seemed to us to be an important and even a necessary part of our picture.

Several years ago a member of the Society of Motion Picture Engineers stated that the motion picture was not then an art and probably never would be, but that theater presentation with colored lights, music, and personal appearances was certainly an art and a very important one. To this another member replied that if the Broadway prologue is an art, the motion picture ought to be happy to remain an industry. . . . In spite of which, the word "art" continues to be used by almost all the speakers at motion picture banquets.

Now without getting involved in metaphysics one can perhaps say that an art is quite simply a means by which the human spirit expresses itself. Action is also a means of expression, but imperfect and at the mercy of circumstances. The artist prefers colors, words, or sounds, over which, with practice and talent he gains a wonderful and intimate control. The perfect example of an art medium is modeling clay. The artist can actually feel his idea take shape, and if he does not like the feeling of what he has done he can change it immediately.

As an art medium, the motion picture lacks plasticity, sharing a great many of the drawbacks of war and politics. You take advantage of happy accidents and use your ingenuity to cover up unhappy ones. The animated cartoon is about the only sort of picture over which the worker has really intimate control.

In studio pictures, a moderate degree of control is exercised by the professional director, and this is obtained mostly *in the set*. The scenery is built, with or without miniatures, and lighted, the actors trained, and the results transferred as directly as possible to the screen. A few years ago the directors were so pleased with their results that the camera came to be looked upon as a mere recording instrument and it was generally believed that effect photography as such was unworthy of a part in the making of a serious picture. Lately, due to the popularity of films like THE LAST LAUGH, effects have come back. Half of our feature pictures are now decorated with "musical" sequences of lap dissolves which threaten to last the rest of the evening.

Nevertheless the professional photoplay continues to aim primarily at story interest put over by realistic pantomime. The flexibility of the medium continues to depend on the expertness of actors and on the ability to manipulate realistic settings. Control over details of the latter sort is obtained as a rule only at great expense. The careful lighting of a drawing-room 30 ft. high and 100 ft. long, even though half of it is painted on glass, is quite beyond the amateur; yet this appears to be exactly the sort of clay in which the professional director is working.

Is it necessary then for the amateur who wants to make a studio picture which shall exploit the wonderful possibilities of studio lighting and of screen acting, to content himself with even less control than is enjoyed by the professional director? Not at all. Although he cannot afford the expensive control of the setting, there is another and surer method of control, the possibilities of which have scarcely been touched. I refer, of course, to camera and printer control, which the professionals use for economy, or safety, or for a laugh, or to jazz up a dull sequence, but which could be used just as readily for serious purposes.

I do not suggest that the amateur undertake the enormous labor after realistic effects of the professional trick department. The important thing for the amateur is that the medium be flexible not that it be realistic. One should be able to control the rhythm of a sequence in space and time, and then if the sequence has not exactly the right feeling, one should be able to change it in the darkroom. The more control a medium permits the better art medium it is, and in this respect a pencil still has it all over a camera.

Scenery

In THE FALL OF THE HOUSE OF USHER we started with painted scenery, but we have come more and more to depend, for effects of depth and weight on surfaces of plain cardboard broken with moving prisms and tinted with light. We have also used the familiar slow, stop, and reverse motion, multiple exposures, and double printing. Shadows naturally appeal to the amateur as being easily controlled and effective. We have used them a little but not half so effectively as the makers of the film NINETY SEVEN DOLLARS, recently released by F. B. O. This film was made in Hollywood by a painter in collaboration with a professional director, and the cost is indicated by the title. The lighting equipment consisted of one 400-watt lamp. Some magnificent shadow effects were obtained by moving the lamp behind cardboard silhouettes. The film was also very ably cut. It is all in the way you do it.

Another spare time film is being made after working hours in one of the big studios by the art director of the studio and the director of NINETY SEVEN DOLLARS. They are especially proud of the small amount of electricity used on their sets. Apparently the production of super features no longer appeals to professionals with a real interest in the motion picture as being fun, and they are descending to amateur methods to get a little satisfaction out of their work.

The Picture

The picture is supposed to illustrate the mood or atmosphere of the House of Usher rather than the story. We have taken liberties with the story which is hair-raising, but that is not unprecedented in the industry. Unfortunately, the picture is only half finished and an unfinished picture is considerably worse than an unfinished book. (Showing of the picture.)

1929   **Usher and Caligari**

Excerpt from "The Theatre," Padraic Colum, *The Dial*, Vol. 86, April, 1929, p. 352.

. . . THE FALL OF THE HOUSE OF USHER produced by the Film Guild develops from THE CABINET OF DR. CALIGARI. In that memorable photoplay the settings were made accessories to the story; they expressed the fantastic mood of the play. In THE FALL OF THE HOUSE OF USHER an experiment is made that goes further in this direction: the cast is of the smallest and the settings quite dominate the people in the film. What goes to establish the mood is the interior of the strange house, with its corridors and vaults, its dimly lighted rooms, its toppling walls and arches. Motion is given to things which should be inanimate and the strange shapes that fill the interior are made more sinister by this device. No picture that I have seen seems as much related to music as THE FALL OF THE HOUSE OF USHER—it is as if it was the expression, not of Poe's story, but of some music that accompanied that story. As I see it there are some defects in this very interesting production: the photoplay is too brief—it is over before the mood of fantasy and horror has been definitely established; the parts of the players are not stylized sufficiently: for instance the scene in which Usher and his sister sit together at table is altogether too representational. The photoplay is remarkable for the effect got from the strange, toppling architectural forms, and for that weird scene at the end with the moon gleaming in the tarn.

62. *Slaughter on the Odessa steps, the most famous sequence in the Russian film POTEMKIN of Sergei Eisenstein. John Grierson analyzed: "The massacre is under way. It grows quickly and steadily, then at the topmost level of horror it falls into the drum-tap tempo . . . and the scene goes screaming with blood. . . ."*

CHAPTER **23**

Foreign Invasion (IV): Films from Russia; Films of Carl-Th. Dreyer

COMMENTARY

The great shock of the decade in films was the slaughter on the Odessa steps in POTEMKIN (1926), directed by the Russian Sergei Eisenstein (1898-1948). Its musical counterpart was the Sacrificial Dance at the climax of Stravinsky's ballet *Le Sacre du Printemps*, revived in London in 1921 (T. S. Eliot covered it for *The Dial*), and first heard here in 1922 as a musical score, without the dancing. By the summer of 1926, now losing its shock power and gradually emerging as a masterpiece, *Le Sacre* was played to its largest and most popular audience at a Stadium concert in New York. This was just a month before Mary Pickford and Douglas Fairbanks returned from Europe, with excited praise for POTEMKIN.

An invitational showing of this film within days of their return left viewers impressed, but convinced that it would strike the censors as Soviet propaganda, and thus be forbidden circulation. Nevertheless, the film did open in New York in December, eventually joining THE BIRTH OF A NATION and THE CABINET OF DR. CALIGARI as one of the three most famous of all silent films.

Eisenstein found his players not at the Moscow Art Theatre, as advertised, but in all sorts of non-acting jobs. The false mention of connection with Stanislavsky's troupe, which had appeared in America with tremendous acclaim several seasons before, was considered helpful publicity for a doubtful film venture.

Although part of *Le Sacre* parallels, in music, part of POTEMKIN, there was no equivalent shock in painting during the Twenties, but Picasso, the man who was to provide it in the following decade, was already attracting more and more of the attention formerly focused on his great rival, Matisse. In 1937, two days after news came that German planes flying for Franco had bombed the Spanish town of Guernica and its inhabitants out of existence, Picasso began to paint his 11-foot canvas protesting the massacre. In the silent uproar of "Guernica," a figure at the left of the canvas—a woman screaming over the inert body of her child—bears an astonishing resemblance to the woman who with the slain child ascends the Odessa steps in POTEMKIN, to challenge the rifles of the descending line of soldiers.

FILM 1926   THE CRUISER POTEMKIN

"THE CRUISER POTEMKIN," excerpt from "The Silent Drama," R. E. Sherwood, *Life* Vol. 88, No. 2290, September 23, 1926, p. 26.

Soviet Russia has at last deposited a moving picture on these shores. It is called THE CRUISER POTEMKIN, and it presents the official record of a mutiny aboard a warship after the Russo-Japanese war.

In this picture we are supposed to see the awakening of the rebellious spirit in the Russian soul; we are supposed to hear the first faint murmurs of that voice, which, ten years later, was to burst into a violent full-throated roar of protest against the tyrannies of the Romanoff régime.

Such is the object of THE CRUISER POTEMKIN; so far as this observer is concerned, it failed almost entirely to accomplish that object. I saw in it a few marvelous examples of the director's and photographer's art—notably the deliberate, ruthless advance of a company of soldiers upon a hysterical, mutinous mob; but I found the picture as a whole to be so utterly confused, so disorderly, as to be practically incomprehensible.

THE CRUISER POTEMKIN proves that a movie may have magnificently effective long shots and still fail as coherent drama because its close-ups fail to hit the mark. The director here has handled his mobs with unbelievable skill, but when he gets down to individual cases, he is lost.

Look at a von Stroheim, a Lubitsch or a Chaplin production and you will find that the long-shots make the picture, but that the close-ups tell the story.

This review of THE CRUISER POTEMKIN is of purely academic interest, as the film will never be permitted to get by the National Security League, Secretary of State Kellogg and other defenders of the faith.

R. E. Sherwood

POTEMKIN   **FILM 1926**

"First Thoughts on POTEMKIN," "W.A.B." [Wilton A. Barrett], *National Board of Review Magazine,* Vol. 1, No. 6, November, 1926, p. 5-6. (With the permission of the National Board of Review of Motion Pictures.)

Sometime in 1905 there was a mutiny on board the Russian armored cruiser Potemkin. The crews, having been steadily rationed on bad meat, protested to the officers but without effect. Their resentment due to this treatment growing, they refused to eat the meat. Violence on their part threatened, and the commander of the ship ordered a number of the crew to be executed. This resulted in a general revolt and slaughterous attack on the officers by the maddened men, who then assumed command and brought the ship into the harbor of Odessa.

When news as to the cause and outcome of the mutiny reached shore, where the body of the mutineers' leader was brought for burial, a sympathetic spark of revolution was fired among the inhabitants of the town, who revitualed the cruiser and joined, high and low, at the harbor side, in a demonstration of approval of the crew's action. For this act they were massacred by the Czar's Cossack Guard. The Potemkin's crew then put to sea, escaping the Czar's fleet, perhaps by some connivance on the part of their brother seamen on board the other vessels, and later interned their ship in a neutral port. They were promised immunity at the hands of the Czar by the Navy Department if they would return to Russia. Acting in good faith, they did so. Whereupon their leaders were sentenced and executed, and the rest sent into Siberia.

The history of this incident has now been recorded in a motion picture by the Moscow Art Theatre players, presumably with the cooperation of the present Russian government and its Navy Department. It is said that each step of the production follows facts as established in official documentary evidence long hidden in the archives of the defunct government and recently brought to light, and that therefore the film is an exact cinematic re-creation of what really happened.

Whether or not the above is entirely correct, THE CRUISE OF THE BATTLESHIP POTEMKIN, to call the film by its full and provocative name, bears the stamp of something that is actually occurring before our eyes, as if the screen on which it is projected were a square hole through which we looked at human events in the making — at the whole phenomenon, as it were, of man's thought and will to be free taking fire under repression at an infinitesimal central point and spreading conflagration to the great human mass, so that we not only understand what the spirit of revolution is, but see it being set in motion and that motion explained through a visual impact of all the facts as they happened as well as of the passions at the roots of the facts before happening. Reality as it swiftly occurs appears to have been caught and photographed, and likewise its foundation. In this regard no other motion picture but the news reel has approached POTEMKIN, and the film leads us to a reconsideration of the cinema as an art and to a new evaluation of its architectonics.

We seem to remember someone once saying that the art of the motion picture resided in the news reel. That is, that the immediacy of the news reel to the subject presented, with its fast cutting from shot to shot over territory covered, applied more carefully, selectively, and rapidly so as to gather up all the essential facts of reality and fix embracingly and swiftly the attention upon them would provide a result analogous to creation itself, and that this method carried on to themes of the creative imagination would be the artist's use of motion pictures as an expressive medium. The probability of this being true comes to us strongly in looking at this remarkable Russian film and afterwards pondering over why it affects us as it does.

Let us take one characteristic sequence of its action for illustration, that in which the congregated people of Odessa are murdered by the soldiers.

Here we see the populace standing massed on the long, seried flights of white steps leading down from the town to the quay, and waving to the crew on the ship.

The camera passes swiftly, picking up this group and that — friends and strangers mingled, whole families, men, women, children, babies in their carriages, the prosperous and the poor, fine ladies in holiday dress and women from the hovels in shawls, men of business, idlers, working men and sailors from the water-side — the characteristic conglomerate mass of a city's dwellers, talking, laughing, looking, jostling for a better view, on their eager faces and in their attitudes various motives and emotions expressed — curiosity, sympathy, hope, intenseness — a revolutionary crowd touched by something up the wind, gathered together by the message of rebellion, of the overthrow of long oppression felt by everyone there, borne into it from the grim ship lying at anchor in the harbor just beyond. Something terrible in this crowd, something pathetic, something instantly human and absolutely real, nothing staged. Yes, the work of the news reel camera man sent to cover a great public happening. If one thinks at the moment, one certainly says it is his work; he has been very busy with his box and tripod scurrying rapidly around. He has done a great job, he has gotten everything that it is important and right to get.

High on the steps, descending slowly in long, even lines, suddenly appear the soldiers in their white, immaculate tunics, splendid tall fellows, loading their rifles as they come. Every now and then the lines stop, fire, reload, descend again — nothing hurried, still nothing staged. And the steps before them, swept by that cold, casual rifle fire! A terror-stricken, bullet-stricken multitude, shorn in a breath of all enthusiasm, all revolutionary fire, resubmitting to the old tyranny — a mob stumbling, falling, dodging, lying flat, rising again, pitching, huddling still, dwindling, fleeing, fleeing down those terrible, unescapable, everlasting steps, pursued grotesquely, almost humorously, by a bumping baby carriage bearing its unwitting infant, which has broken away from the mother's dying grasp. Most of this has been done by a swift, flickering assortment and throwing together of little pieces of pictures, a face here, a slipping body there, a flopping arm or leg, a pair of eye-glasses, a bit of torn clothing, a shuddering group or a convulsive body, as if the camera were dancing down the steps in that dance of death—as if the news reel camera man were running about madly, stumbling and falling himself at times, but ever busy with his crank. Nothing approaching the reality of these scenes has ever occurred in cinematics before. It is superb "motion picture"—the medium is disclosed as being separate and distinct, words cannot do it; the photograph of an actual massacre, yes— the photograph of a tragic happening, yes, like that shot taken in Paris of the man who jumped from the Eiffel Tower with a bat-winged parachute which crumpled and let him plunge, a fluttering shape down the depth of the screen; like some authentic shots of men being killed in trenches under fire taken in the war, shots made by the news reel, and his military brother, the signal corps, camera man.

Yet this thing in POTEMKIN—and the same technique is seen everywhere else in the film—has been manipulated, gauged and directed. Perhaps the finest art yet put upon the screen has resulted, an art in its effect swifter, more inclusive, more accurate and absolute and directly expressive than the effect to be had from the sense of seeing itself. Is the art of the motion picture, then, precisely this seeing of things for us beyond our own power of sight? Is it a synthesis of selected observations through the eye of the camera? Is it the director's function to study only reality in substance, form and movement and then reproduce its essentials for us? And is it the camera man's business—the business of a very busy camera man who will scurry about with great speed—to record the result as news? POTEMKIN seems to tell us so.

(Signed) W.A.B.

POTEMKIN in Hollywood   1926

Excerpt from "Studio News and Gossip East and West," Cal York, *Photoplay Magazine,* Vol. 30, No. 5, October, 1926, p. 94.

. . . There's one little foreign masterpiece that will never be shown at your neighborhood theater. It's called THE CRUISER POTEMKIN, and it was made under the auspices of the Soviet government of Russia. The picture is one of the greatest ever filmed, and it has had a long run in Berlin. Nevertheless, you won't see it, because it is Bolshevik.

James Creelman, scenario writer for Famous Players-Lasky, obtained a print of THE CRUISER POTEMKIN and showed it to a few of his friends, as a little lesson in picture-making. After witnessing it, nobody went Bolshevik, but a lot of people left with some revolutionary ideas of film making.

The events pictured in the film took place in 1905 in the harbor of Odessa, on the Black Sea. The film tells of a mutiny on board the Potemkin, and pictures the revolt of the sailors against the filthy meat offered them as food. At the time the motto of the Russian navy was, "Join the Navy and See the Worms." This little mutiny was one of the first of many small outbreaks that led to the Revolution. The city of Odessa sympathized with the mutineers, and the Cossacks, so the film tells us, were ordered to train their guns on the crowd that assembled to cheer the men of the Potemkin and shoot down the civilian populace.

There is no story to this film, or no leading actors. If you weren't told that it was staged, you'd swear it was a prehistoric news reel. The photography is beautiful enough to enchant an artist and the action is vivid enough and swift enough to satisfy any box office demand for melodrama. The scene in which the Cossacks pursue the populace down a long flight of steps, shooting in the crowd, is unforgettably impressive. When enough of our directors have seen this episode, you'll find it duplicated in home-made dramas.

And yet, alas, the ugly head of propaganda intrudes itself to mar an artistic triumph.

The Imperialist officers of the Potemkin are represented as brutes, when, as a matter of fact, they were probably as helpless in the situation as the men themselves. And, with a great disregard for the facts of the case, the ending has been changed. In the film, other ships of the Russian navy are sent to punish the Potemkin. But instead of firing on her and her crew, the sailors sent up a great shout of "Brother!" No such love feast took place back in 1905. The Potemkin escaped from the Black Sea, but its crew were captured and interned in Bulgaria. . . .

FILM 1926   POTEMKIN

"Exceptional Photoplays: POTEMKIN," *National Board of Review Magazine*, Vol. 1, No. 7, December, 1926, pp. 11-12. (With the permission of the National Board of Review of Motion Pictures.)

Directed by . . . . S. M. Eisenstein

Acted by members of the Moscow Art Theatre and the Proletkult.

It was good news to hear that POTEMKIN would at last be given a public showing at a New York theatre for all to go to see. This definitely puts an end to the private petting parties to which this picture has been treated both abroad and in this country. For now the public will be able to judge for itself and incidentally to judge whether Max Reinhardt and Douglas Fairbanks were right, and also many prominent critics and art lovers.

When the preliminary notice of POTEMKIN which appeared in our last issue was written a public showing for the picture had not yet been assured. But this advance review had been written in hopeful anticipation of just such an event and for the sake of stimulating a discussion which might accelerate the time of its coming. For as soon as the Exceptional Photoplays Committee of the National Board of Review had viewed POTEMKIN it realized that it had seen a unique entertainment and one which contained important contributions to the theory of motion picture making.

POTEMKIN is innovational both in subject and in treatment. In 1905 the crew of the battleship Potemkin, anchored off Odessa, mutineed after vain protest against contaminated meat rations and either slew or drove off its officers. The people of Odessa sympathized with the crew and were massacred by a suddenly arriving detachment of the Czar's Cossacks. The Potemkin took refuge in a Roumanian port and surrendered to the Czar's Government upon the promise of immunity. This promise was broken and the crew was partly executed and partly exiled to Siberia.

The picture is a faithful reproduction of this historical event. It is neither fictional nor fictitious, seeks in fact to avoid this quality altogether, by adhering as much as possible to a literal transcription and reproduction of officially documented facts. Thus it assumes, as was pointed out in our preliminary notice; the aspect of an enlarged news reel, as if a news reel camera man had anticipated the occurrence and had gone to cover it.

POTEMKIN therefore has no story thread in the ordinary sense of the word, and no hero. The action is carried by groups of people, the crew, the officers, the population of Odessa, the Cossacks. Our interest does not become attached to any particular individual. It is entirely absorbed in the idea of the picture, the revolt against tyranny, the happiness of sudden freedom, and the release of generous impulses that well up in the breasts of those who have suffered oppression. Then, as a counter movement, the tragic motif enters to say, as Shakespeare said in his tragedies, that in this world of ours the good and the innocent often perish.

513

The real hero of this picture is humanity. When Max Reinhardt, the most noted European stage impresario, saw POTEMKIN he is reported to have said that "Now, for the first time, I am willing to admit that the stage will have to give way to the cinema." It is easy to understand what Reinhardt meant. He had specialized in mass drama on a huge scale both in large theatres and in open air arenas. The effort broke down from its own cumbersomeness. The spectator could not take in the whole spectacle anymore than you can really take in a three-ring circus. His magnified theatre suffered from two major handicaps which do not apply to pictures. The theatre spectator is stationary and the movement of a spectacle can only go forward; it cannot freely go back and repeat a previous effect. In a picture the spectator can be moved about at will as the camera moves and any effect can be instantly re-enacted.

POTEMKIN plays rings around the stage spectacle; it achieves its desired effects with the apparent effortlessness characteristic of all good art. It plays havoc no less with our previous notions of what constitutes proper material for making a picture. We had just arrived at the notion that pictures must cease to borrow from literature and must be made from original scenarios cinegraphically conceived. POTEMKIN seems to say that not even this is necessary. It fosters the revolutionary idea that anything, cinegraphically photographed, can be made to fascinate the eye. A clerk, getting up in the morning, washing, dressing, breakfasting, on his way to business, at work during the day, returning home to supper and in the evening going to a movie, could be made into an absorbing picture.

One wonders what would have been the history of pictures if the first directors, instead of going in for trick effects and photographing train robberies, had set out to photograph simply what they saw, had allowed the camera to lead them into its virgin field of new wonders instead of harnessing it to the treadmill of the jaded drama. Perhaps POTEMKIN indicates that the motion picture will have to go back to this age of innocence, that it must, like the Romantic Movement of the early Nineteenth Century, recapture its innocence if it is to avoid the same death which is gradually stiffening the theatre.

The attempt was made in our comment on the picture last month to convey some idea of the technical theory on which, apparently, it was produced. Perhaps the most notable device was the shortness of the sequences and their continuous change; some of them are only ten frames long. This is responsible for the extraordinary "liveness" of the picture, its vibrant quality. The camera roves about with a sort of gasping haste as a person actually on the scene might do in a vain attempt to remember everything that is passing before his eye, with the only difference that the camera never loses what has once passed before its lens. A further effect is achieved by preferring the part to the whole, constructing the sense of the whole by emphasizing the parts. Thus the whole cruiser Potemkin is rarely shown but we get a marvelous sense of it by seeing what each part is there for and how it works. The ship becomes animated for us, it becomes active to the point of acquiring a personality. The same technique is applied with equal success to the mob scenes. Here again the effect is never studied; the people move oblivious of any megaphone; their gestures are never tuned in unison. The naturalistic quality of these mass movements is a distinct advance over even the best German achievements in this important part of motion picture art. When we consider that S. M. Eisenstein, the director, is only twenty-eight years old and that this is only his second picture, the promise of further contributions from him to the art of the screen seems bright indeed.

(Produced by the Moscow Art Theatre. Distributed by Amkino Corp.)

COMMENTARY

514   **Vsevolod Pudovkin (1893-1953) was considered by some critics of the Twenties to be a**

63. *Kozinstov and Trauberg's Russian film* THE NEW BABYLON, *which deals with the period of the Paris Commune at the end of the Franco-Prussian War. Elena Kuzmina as The Girl. Reviewer: "Fortunately for the motion picture as a form of art, there is no restriction put upon the Russian director about how he shall make his picture, once the subject and its ideological treatment have been decided."*

director superior to Eisenstein. His MECHANICS OF THE BRAIN, a scientific film made with Pavlov, and an early effort, was shown in the United States in 1928, but MOTHER, THE END OF ST. PETERSBURG and STORM OVER ASIA, which Pudovkin thought of as his first three real films, did not reach here until 1934, 1928 and 1930, respectively. MOTHER, a story of the 1905 eruptions, was held up eight years by the American censors.

Speaking about his early years, in a 1929 interview, Pudovkin stated: "About that time I happened to see Griffith's great film, INTOLERANCE. In that wonderful work I saw for the first time the possibilities of the epic picture. Yes, Griffith was really my teacher. Later on I saw BROKEN BLOSSOMS, and I fell more and more under the spell of Griffith. My first three pictures, therefore, were really influenced by this great American director." (52)

Eisenstein's POTEMKIN was followed here at intervals by his TEN DAYS THAT SHOOK THE WORLD (1928) (a film celebrating the tenth anniversary of the revolution, like Pudovkin's ST. PETERSBURG) and by OLD AND NEW (1930), which had been begun as THE GENERAL LINE. Eisenstein's admiration for Griffith is well documented.

THE END OF ST. PETERSBURG   FILM 1928

"Exceptional Photoplays: THE END OF ST. PETERSBURG," *National Board of Review Magazine*, Vol. 3, No. 6, June, 1928, pp. 7-9. (With the permission of the National Board of Review of Motion Pictures.)

Directed by . . . . W. J. Pudovkin
Photographed by . . . . A. Golownia

The Cast

A Peasant . . . . Alexis Davor
His Father . . . . Peter Petrovich
His Wife . . . . Olga Korloff
His Mother . . . . Anna Baranowska
A Worker . . . . Paul Petroff
His Wife . . . . Katrina Kaja
Factory Manager . . . . Natan Golow
Capitalist . . . . W. Obelensky
Kerensky . . . . Serge Alexandrowski
Field Marshal . . . . Feodor Varvarow
Original screen story by Natan Zarchi

Those who are claiming that the motion picture is the most powerful medium for expressing the world of today, have another example to point to in the latest film to come to us from the Russians—from the same studios of Sovkino that produced POTEMKIN and CZAR IVAN THE TERRIBLE. Of the three films, THE END OF ST. PETERSBURG, as a ribbon stamped with cinema dynamics, will be thought by many to be the most impressive.

THE END OF ST. PETERSBURG stems from POTEMKIN, but branches farther. Like POTEMKIN it raises the question as to which, between this type of film and the type of CZAR IVAN, approaches closer, artistically speaking, to the thing the screen in its dramatic aspect should concern itself with—whether it should reveal life, in the drama-structure of the stage play, through the dynamic visualization of characters pursuing or pursued by fate, or, as absolutely distinct from the theatre, through the dynamic depiction of forces where mere character movement is subordinated to the representation of tidal elements that all but drown the individual forms of men. Perhaps, because THE END OF ST. PETERSBURG combines both types, humanizes the machine more than does POTEMKIN, and wraps all mankind in the folds of fate more than does CZAR IVAN, the chief justification is to be found for calling it the superior film of the three, the most powerful in its attack on the core of the emotions, the furthest along on the path to terror, beauty and truth. And in this direction no film yet produced has exceeded it.

Yet this is strange, for the picture embodies to the furthest degree the theory of art as a social utility which seems to be the aim of present day Russian creators. It is gospel of their social order. POTEMKIN and CZAR IVAN might quite possibly be propaganda for the Russian people—the latter a warning of what return to the Czars would mean, the former a terrifying reminder of an event that left a memory of oppression and flame. Both were re-creations in terms of legends and therefore to be filled in by the imagination in order to make them real. But THE END OF ST. PETERSBURG is fresh from the palette of experience, it is a record of passions not yet faded from the hearts of those who made the picture, it is a proclamation to the world of those passions and an acknowledgment of the whirlwind they caused, and it is a manifesto of belief in their righteousness.

Confronted with this picture, those who animadvert on propaganda—especially the brand put out by the Soviets—have now the opportunity to weigh its dangers, to ask themselves if revolutionary partisanship is menacing to those parts of the world where revolution does not exist. Sober-minded reflection on THE END OF ST. PETERSBURG is likely to teach the conclusion that, for all its scenes destructive of the reputation of the Czarist regime, for all its titles solidifying the Soviet theory as it pertains to Russia, it is probably the greatest preachment against war yet delivered from the screen, just as it is the most forceful argument, in its intellectual as well as emotional appeal, for man's brother feeling for man. For hatred is here washed away in the flood of defilement, misery and fury, and the pale dawn that rises over the sad splendor of the trampled city shows men only in their loneliness and desolation, weary at the beginning of a new road. It is a light tinged only with that fragile brightness that is symbolic of the universal hope for better things, in this case all but fearfully felt.

Though it be overburdensome, the propaganda of the picture is strangely enough not wholly inartistic, possibly since it springs both as a need and a creed from the very chaos of the historical circumstances which are so powerfully and convincingly presented. However that may be, it fades from view in the explosive, terrifying and beautiful flower of the film's achievement as a well-nigh perfect thing of pure motion picture representation—a thing that rises, grows, and shimmers with colors of smoke, blood, steel, flying clouds and foaming heartbeats in a pattern and convolution of images tendrilling from the soil of life itself and plucked by the artist's hand to be held as a trophy—enduring as long as the film it is printed on endures. For what Carlyle's French Revolution did in words, THE END OF ST. PETERSBURG does in cinematics.

Beginning with the St. Petersburg of Czar Nicholas, and the oppression of the workers by the aristocrats and capitalists, the action joins swiftly to the entrance of Russia into the World War, centering in a munition factory where the men are driven to the last gasp to supply the ammunition by which lives are to be taken and fortunes reaped. The war draws off the revolutionary fever of the oppressed workers into the channels of patriotism. The soldiers are recruited and marched, prisoners and agitators are thrown into the ranks. The factories grind on. The workers sweat. The privileged classes fatten on their labor. At the front the soldiers fall—on the one side the soldiers of the Czar, on the other the troops of the Kaiser. All is horror, waste. And the social order behind the lines still remains heedless, cruel, greedy. At last the fury of the workers breaks. The Czar is forced out. Kerensky rises to lead the new government, to lead the troops again into battle, playing his role of puppet to the old regime of aristocrats who hail him as savior. 517

But the fire has started. The soldiers revolt and march on St. Petersburg. There they join their comrades, and the city is bombarded and captured. In the shadow and amid the splendors of the surrendered Winter Palace, soldier, worker and peasant meet exhausted to contemplate the future, to begin the work of the new order.

The film is panoramic rather than focused as was POTEMKIN. But each sequence is so extraordinarily condensed, vivid and emphatic, that when chained together in an even drive of dynamic images, the whole creates a sensation of exhaustion similar to the emotions of the masses depicted—the exhaustion of completing an immense experience of events. More than in POTEMKIN our sympathies go out to individuals, we are liberated at moments from the whirl and fury of crowds and from the things of iron that surround them like a cage. Some of the acting is utterly moving—it is not acting, like much of Russian histrionic art, it is the spectacle of experience, human, truthful to the last degree. The character of the boy who becomes a revolutionary leader in the army, of the woman bearing with unyielding fortitude the malice of the slums, of her husband, the factory worker, heroic in his urge to overthrow oppression—they live in the memory and make a story shrouded in the smoke and crashing dust of the cataclysm.

Nowhere has there been a flight of the camera such as went into the making of this film, such sheer power of pictures, circling, soaring and dipping to strike kinetically at the nerves.

Patterns of steel, cranes, jagged edges of iron, hot metal whose fumes float past battered, stoical faces; long fields gray with the white disastrous clouds driving over them; the furious bourse, men gambling for the spoils created by sweat, starvation and anguish; the madly waving flags of a city sending off its armies to war, a thousand banners fluttering along the balconies beneath the glorious cornices lined with the colossal statues of the nobility; these statues, always photographed gigantic against the little figures of tired, bewildered men and women in the streets—great height, great depth, and ever the sense of the depth rising to absorb the height; the utter horror and misery of the battle shots—mud, slime, pools, all gray and sucking, with a body like putty sinking here and blobbing up there—no glorification, just the hideous thing itself, a nightmare of reason; the fine dusk and night shots of troops moving back on the capital, silhouettes of guns waiting to fire, the first sputtering of machine guns, the huge equestrial statues beginning to fall; and finally the superb and deeply moving sequence where a woman moves through the conquered streets among the soldiers giving them cold potatoes from a tin pail, which emptied she carries up the staircase of the palace, between the ornate walls laden with marble and fresco.

It is realism intense and something more; the art of the motion picture lives in this film.

(Produced by Sovkino. Distributed by Hammerstein Attractions.)

"SOME RUSSIAN FILMS" 1929

By Gilbert Seldes, *The New Republic*, Vol. 59, No. 761, July 3, 1929, pp. 179-180.

It is clear that if the silent movies are going to make any stand against the talkies, they will find their firmest ally in the films made by the Russians; and it is barely possible that the persistence of the silent film, if it does persist, will be due to the incorporation in American movies of something of the spirit and something of the technique of these comparative newcomers in the field.

Several of these films are already familiar; one, MOTHER, is not to be shown here—as the moral problem does not enter, the censorship must have been exercised on political grounds; another, STORM OVER ASIA, the reputed masterpiece of Pudovkin, who made THE END OF ST. PETERSBURG, is scheduled for elaborate presentation next season; and

THE NEW BABYLON, a film of the Franco-Prussian War and the Commune in Paris, will probably appear shortly. These films, with POTEMKIN and TEN DAYS THAT SHOOK THE WORLD, tell us enough about the general direction of the Soviet films, and what they tell us is extremely important.

The first point is that all of them are possessed of moral fervor far more intense than we are accustomed to, not only in our films (which almost entirely lack any element of morality), but in all of our arts. All our satire on the stage, all our "grim realism" in fiction, is trivial in comparison. The Russians who make these films have a new religion, and their religion is a constant force in their artistic expression; these films dynamically illustrate the truth of Dr. Dewey's essential observation on Soviet Russia, that the real revolution took place in the souls of Russian men and women.

Obviously, the films are propaganda. I dislike propaganda in works of art and am not excessively sympathetic to the principles of communism; if I were I might not be annoyed at the silly omission of Trotsky from historical pictures, nor quite so amused at the speeding up of the film to show that, as soon as the exploiters are dethroned, sewing machines run more easily and speedily, and bent and haggard sempstresses sing at their work. The propaganda is a nuisance; but it gives all these pictures their force, and even their integrity. Our films have usually been made without passion, without conviction of any sort; THE BIRTH OF A NATION was exceptional in its time, and Griffith tried once again, in INTOLERANCE, where his passion fell over into a sort of fanaticism against fanatics.

The reason the Russian propaganda is acceptable is that you never feel the picture being twisted to give a communist happy ending. While the pictures unroll you feel intellectually what the directors obviously feel spiritually: that the triumph of Soviet Russia is the single desirable thing in the world, making all things right. Except in the historical films, the directors seem to come to their conclusions by internal necessity; and that is why you can say that the pictures are prejudiced and argumentative and moralistic—and still have artistic integrity. If you do not share their theories of economics, you may find that passion misdirected; but you will not find it feeble.

Enthusiasts for the Russian films have often been unable to separate the cinematic from the economic, and so have apparently been willing to start a red revolution in Britain and America, in order to produce an Eisenstein or a Pudovkin. If the revolution could be localized in the Balkan territories of Hollywood, I should think it worthwhile; otherwise, I fancy we can learn from Pudovkin and Eisenstein without accepting Stalin as an article of faith. The one thing we cannot learn is to have passion, to have religion, and to have no sequence in any film without that. That is a gift from God.

The two great directors I have mentioned are profound students of cinematics and good theorists; yet, seeing their work and that of their compatriots, one fancies that the freshness of these Russians comes from not having seen too many other films. Take a specific instance. In all American films since THE BIG PARADE, if a regiment is marching away, or a thousand trucks roll by, the hero or heroine staggers through the lines, fighting off the men or trucks, trying to make his or her way to the beloved and departing one. The scene even occurs in THE SINGING FOOL, where Jolson battles with taxicabs. In THE NEW BABYLON there are ranks of marching soldiers—and one man standing absolutely motionless, his soul trampled while his body remains erect. I do not say that this is better than the hysterics of the American parallel; but it is fresh, individual; you feel again the emotion which repetition has staled.

In TEN DAYS, at a Soviet congress, people sat and talked for what seemed to be hours. I suspect that this was due to a desire to allow a representative of each of the nationalities of Great Russia to appear; it made a pretty bad central section of what should have been a good movie. Here you had freshness of the most amateur kind—by the maker of POTEMKIN! In almost all Russian films of the last year a statue figures, sometimes a few dozen statues. That of Peter the Great on horseback has fallen again 519 and again; Justice appears frequently; Love, also; and in THE NEW BABYLON a socialist hammer strikes a single blow and the Vendome column falls. These are the weaknesses of film symbolism. But in MOTHER, a river breaks through its covering of ice, and when the hero is about to escape from prison his mind turns to the river over which he must go, and you have definite imagery, profoundly moving. In THE VILLAGE OF SIN, a single exquisite shot of peasants mowing the waving wheat expressed everything one wanted to know of the aspiration of simple Russians for security, ease, and earnestness of life.

The directors are creating movies to influence the lives of simple and emerging souls. Their contrasts are all black and white: the bourgeois with his clean cuffs and cigar is as monotonous as the moustached villain and the doctor looking at his watch, in American films. In TEN DAYS the strangled horse hangs from the top of the drawbridge through almost half the picture; in STORM OVER ASIA you have alternating shots of Mongolian priests being arrayed for a ritual and a general and his lady (looking as British as can be) being decked in social finery; in THE END OF ST. PETERSBURG you have alternating shots of the front and the Bourse. This system of cutting, which is one of the many things called *montage*, is so overdone that the essence of the picture escapes, for the unit of cinematic utterance is not a single picture or a single foot of pictures, but whatever length of film constitutes a sequence. The Russians have alternated rhythms so rapidly that all rhythm escapes.

Yet their essential idea is correct; the film must be so made, cut, and arranged as to impose a series of emotions on the spectator. They give you the effect of the lapse of time by showing you a blacksmith at his anvil and, showing the hammer at various points of the descent, interpolating other events, near or distant; their principle, a correct one, is that the more distant the interpolated event, the greater the lapse of time in the feeling of the spectator; but when too many events intervene, one loses the sense of the action of the hammer on the anvil.

The flickering of the camera back and forth, from one event to a contrasting event, reached its extreme in TEN DAYS, where Kerensky's walk up endless stairs (an over-worked piece of imagery) was broken into hundreds of little pieces. The eye refuses to follow unless it has a sequence. But in STORM OVER ASIA this technical trick is in a secondary place. The film has more of a definite story, it has a hero; were it not for its abiding passion, one would say that STORM OVER ASIA marks a slight Americanization of the Soviet's film ideas. Pudovkin has a new method of bringing things up to the camera by three stages, through which the spectator progresses as he used to progress in watching the old films of a railroad track taken from the back of a train. He mingles his realism with straight adventure—fist fights, machine-guns blazing; he throws his picture out of balance by over-documented photography of a Mongolian religious festival, and restores it by the passion and irony of his story. There is no missing the solid feeling of life in this picture, no missing the powerful rhythm, as simple as heartbeats, on which it is built.

The hero of STORM OVER ASIA is played by a professional actor, himself a Mongolian, attached to one of the Russian theatres. His performance will instantly rank him with Jannings, perhaps higher. The rest of the Mongolians are non-professionals, like the mobs in the historical films, like nearly everyone, including the leading actress, of Eisenstein's new film, THE GENERAL LINE, which is not yet finished. A great deal is made of these amateurs, and they are compared to our professional movie stars and mobs. There is a confusion of ideas here. First, because the grizzled faces and toothless gums and odd-shaped skulls of the *moujik* and the Russian factory worker or beggar are unfamiliar to us, they impress us excessively. Second, hardly anyone in the American movie has learned movie-acting. When we compare the Russians to them we are comparing fresh players who do what good directors tell them, to pretty girls or hand-some men who are still under the influence of stage-acting. The amateurs in Russia are

64. *Carl-Th. Dreyer's* THE PASSION OF JEANNE D'ARC, *with Falconetti in the leading role. Probably no other film up to this time contained so many large-scale close-ups of faces. Acknowledging that this technique is magnificently right here, The Times added: "It is doubtful whether this . . . would be as effective for any other story."*

being made temporarily into movie players; the professionals in America are still acting on the stage.

Gilbert Seldes.

COMMENTARY

Each of three Russian films shown here in the last half of 1929 seemed to add something new; Dziga Vertov's LIVING RUSSIA OR THE MAN WITH THE CAMERA prompted Mordaunt Hall to a comparison with BERLIN, but he found the editing in the Russian film bewilderingly abrupt. Concerning this "disjointed array of scenes," he wrote that Vertov (1896-1954) failed to realize that "the human eye fixes for a certain space of time that which holds the attention." However, he liked the device "of having everything come to a sudden stop . . . especially when one discovers that the reason is that a motion picture joiner is pausing at her work. The slow motion passages of athletes diving, throwing the shot and other physical exercises are well conceived." (53)

The other two films, by different directors, were ARSENAL, and THE NEW BABYLON, the latter already mentioned above by Gilbert Seldes.

ARSENAL   FILM 1929

"Exceptional Photoplays: ARSENAL," *National Board of Review Magazine,* Vol. 4, No. 9, November, 1929, pp. 8-9. (With the permission of the National Board of Review of Motion Pictures.)

Directed by . . . . Alexander Dovzhenko
Photographed by . . . . D. Demutzki
Starring . . . . S. Svashenko
Screen story by Alexander Dovzhenko

ARSENAL is a poem, created in the motion picture medium by a Ukrainian who is both an idealist and a realist, and above all what is often called a modernist. In a way that seems peculiar to the Russian temperament he is disillusioned and mystical, tragically pessimistic and fierily optimistic. The picture he has made of the revolution in Ukraine is spiritually akin to *All Quiet on the Western Front.* It reveals horrors and beauties, with a fierce kind of pity.

It is suggestive of Eisenstein and other Russian directors in some of its use of the camera, but in all other ways it is different from, and beyond, anything else that the Russians have done. For its particular kind of thing, that means it is beyond anything else that anyone has done.

It is singularly free from the thing we usually call propaganda in the Russian pictures, the thing that is put there for the education of the Russian people because their motion pictures are a part of their educational system. There is only one injection of politics and policies—an argument over the possession of the land after Ukrainian independence was obtained. Otherwise there is almost nothing of a purposeful nature. It is merely the director's vision of the human struggle.

There is no story to it. One man—a soldier, magnificently acted by S. Svashenko—has a kind of individual existence in it, in the sense that we are permitted to follow him through some of the episodes of the revolution and we know what he is after. But he is a symbol far more than he is an individual—the symbol of man's struggle with his own ignorance, his blind flight for some driving ideal of knowledge and freedom that he feels with his soul but cannot define with his mind. He is continually defeated, and eternally undefeatable.

The whole picture is a continuous use of symbolism, but the symbols are people and actions, never the inanimate objects that we are accustomed to. Over and over again we see motionless figures—in a house, in the streets, in fields—which are signs of the way normal human living utterly ceases in times of war. A one-armed peasant with an old horse crosses a meadow and stops before a field of grain—a woman stands in the center of a room with crying children pulling at her skirts. A still picture of misery. Suddenly the peasant is beating his horse, the woman is beating the children, with a quick interchange of scenes that marvelously pictures the emotion of helpless people slashing out furiously at their own wretchedness.

A train carrying soldiers stops—the engineer explains that he cannot go farther because there is a dangerous down-grade ahead and the brakes are not working well. The soldier leader says confidently that they'll run the train themselves—they will be able to manage the brakes all right. The train is wrecked—and out of the smoking wreckage the soldier stumbles to his feet, muttering, "I'll learn to run these things yet!" Never in even the most violent anti-Soviet propaganda has there been such a vivid example of the disasters that follow power in ignorant hands.

The incidents of the picture are mostly unrelated, in the accepted continuity sense. We see a group of people—they do something and vanish from the screen, quite unconnected with what went before or comes after. Horses speak in titles. Spoken titles appear as if they were themselves pictures—their meaning is entirely within their words and it does not matter who spoke them: therefore we do not see, or know, or care, who spoke them.

All of this is a kind of technique that no other picture has prepared us for. It is difficult to adjust one's self to, because unconsciously everyone in a movie audience is all set for something at least approaching the usual kind of screen play. It is pretty sure to leave one bewildered at the first seeing of it, though the emotional power is even more sure to make an impression that is far stronger than the bewilderment. It is a picture that, like sublime music or poetry, gives up its meanings slowly, more and more eloquently and movingly the more often it is seen. It is so fine that repetition and familiarity do not dull it. The episode in which galloping horses carry a dead soldier across snow-covered plains to his home—and at the end of the ride there is a motionless woman standing by a new-dug grave as if she had always been waiting there, always knowing that only thus would her son come home—such an episode is as lovely and moving and eternally fresh as a movement in a Beethoven symphony. And it is only one among many episodes that put ARSENAL in a niche all its own among motion pictures. It reaches a goal that only the silent screen could achieve. It makes one hope that its director will go on, along his own way, and leave the development of new inventions to others.

Produced by Wufku; Distributed by Amkino.

FILM 1929   THE NEW BABYLON

"Exceptional Photoplays: THE NEW BABYLON," *National Board of Review Magazine*, Vol. 4, No. 10, December, 1929, pp. 8-10, 23. (With the permission of the National Board of Review of Motion Pictures.)

Directed by . . . . G. M. Kozintsov,
                                                                                L. G. Trauberg
Photographed by . . . . A. N. Moskvin

The Cast

The Soldier . . . . P. Sobolerski
The Girl . . . . Elena Kuzmina

523

In this picture the Russians have gone outside their own land for their subject, but their ideology—their social philosophy and social passions—remains, of course, the same. They have undertaken to represent the efforts of communism to establish itself in France at the close of the Franco-Prussian War, when the Paris Commune fought its vain fight against the rest of France, under the eyes of the German conquerors.

We have become accustomed, in these Russian films, to the fact that they are all made with a definite educative purpose. That sort of thing is called propaganda, which is a word with sinister and aggressive connotations. The propaganda of Russian films can be summed up and disposed of in one statement—Russian films are made for Russians, to spread among them, with all the power of which the motion picture medium is master, the social and political principles which the Soviet leaders know must become part of the mentality of every citizen before they can become a completely living force in the national life. Therefore every motion picture they make is a picture with a purpose, a frankly ulterior purpose—not to paint the whole world red, but to help the people of Russia to understand the form of government under which they are living. Which may be dangerous and wicked, or not, as you happen to feel. The only point about it that interests us for the time being is that it determines the subject matter and the "message" of all Russian films.

Fortunately for the motion picture as a form of art, there is no restriction put upon the Russian director about how he shall make his picture, once the subject and its ideological treatment have been decided. And he has no box-office bugaboo to set a low standard of intelligence for him to appeal to. His hand as an artist is free.

It is this freedom that has given the Russian directors the means to go the extraordinary distance they have covered in motion picture technique. Perhaps the removal of other considerations—subject, story and such—has increased this freedom. It certainly has not hampered them any more than it hampered Michael Angelo and Raphael to be assigned definite subjects to paint.

THE NEW BABYLON belongs without any doubt in the group of remarkable pictures which we first became aware of in CZAR IVAN THE TERRIBLE and which includes the Eisenstein pictures—POTEMKIN and TEN DAYS THAT SHOOK THE WORLD—the Pudovkin END OF ST. PETERSBURG and Dovzhenko's ARSENAL. There is a habit in Russia of lining up their directors according to their leftness or rightness—the directors of THE NEW BABYLON would come somewhere not far from Pudovkin: much more radical in their artistic procedure than the man who made IVAN, but not nearly so far to the left as Eisenstein and Dovzhenko.

They have frankly avoided much in the way of plot by calling their picture "episodes from the Franco-Prussian War and the Paris Commune." But these episodes are sufficiently held together by two characters who are rather more individualized than most of the left-wing directors go in for: a soldier, weary of war and anxious to get back to his home village, and a girl who works in La Nouvelle Babylone—the huge department store that symbolizes the Paris of its time and gives the film its title. These two people have almost a story, an unfulfilled love-story. They meet for a few minutes in the wild whirl of gaiety that came with the beginning of the war when all Paris was confident of victory and the army was supposed to be sweeping victoriously toward Berlin. Again during the siege of the city they come together—he is bitterer against war now, and she is beginning to feel that distrust of the government which later, when it became widespread, flamed into the Commune. Later still they confront each other on the barricades in the midst of the fighting—he still sticking by the national army because he sees no other way of bringing the fighting to an end and getting home—she taking her place beside the men and battling against what she feels to be the tyrannous incompetence that has lost the war for France. The last meeting is at the end—she among the rebels who are lined up to be shot—he, not allowed to go home, set with other soldiers to digging graves for the executed criminals.

These two people are individuals—all the others are types and symbols: types of the aristocracy and rich bourgeoisie, or of the idealized poor. The two individuals are magnificently successful, because the parts are splendidly acted and everything that they do is in character. Most of the others hover close to the mark that borders on caricature, and caricature of a particularly bitter kind. Probably never in a motion picture, even in some of Eisenstein, has there been such a gallery of violent cartoons.

This is hardly a dramatic weakness: it is a fault only in the eyes of those who are looking for fairness and neutrality. There is nothing of either quality in this film. It is a passionately one-sided affair, for the people who made it are convinced, to the bottom of their souls, that they are right, and this profound conviction gives their passion a stamp of truth that carries it to a point which, if it does not terrify you, carries you off your feet until a quiet after-moment allows you to think the whole thing over with cooler judgment. "Vive la Commune," scrawled upon a wall by a dying rebel at the end, wakens a sympathetic thrill for the moment, and a temporary belief that all that was really noble in France was snuffed out in the last vengeful executions of the nationalist army.

It is no reflection on the artistic power of this picture to say that what it presents is biased and therefore mixed with falsity. It must be admitted, though, that the repeated contrasts between the rich and the poor, the sunshine and the rain, get to have the effect of a mannerism—they lose the hold on the essentials of truth-telling, by which I mean telling the truth to the best of one's ability according to one's vision of it, and become artificial, almost sentimental. It is rarely that Russians become sentimental in this particular way.

There is extraordinary photography, of a kind, in this picture. It is fuzzier than Russian films are wont to be—it often has almost a Hollywood beauty—the honest blacks and whites, clear-cut and uncompromising, are used only for the communists, while the festivities of the wicked bourgeoisie are befogged in a softness that American directors often use as the acme of loveliness. Whatever its effect on different spectators, it is all done with intention, and reveals only another aspect of the Russians' many-sided mastery of the camera.

Produced by Sovkino; Distributed by Amkino.

COMMENTARY

The faith of the Fifth Avenue Playhouse in the Danish director Carl-Th. Dreyer (1889-1968) was not borne out by the critical response in 1926. His CHAINED was picked to follow the important revival of CALIGARI at the new house; elsewhere entitled both THE INVERT and MIKAEL, it was said to have been suggested by the life of Rodin ("dull"). His second and earlier film, LEAVES FROM SATAN'S BOOK, was directly influenced by Griffith's INTOLERANCE, but though it had been screened privately in New York for exhibitors in January, 1922, it failed to find a taker.

The remarkable THE PASSION OF JEANNE D'ARC (1929), filmed in France, changed his reputation considerably, although many found it difficult to adjust to such frequent use of large-scale close-ups of faces, generally reserved for climactic confrontation.

In general, however, silent film audiences settled for Dreyer as a one-film man. His THE WITCH WOMAN (THE PARSON'S WIDOW), shown here in 1929 after JEANNE D'ARC, apparently drew little attention ("tedious").

FILM 1929   THE PASSION OF JEANNE D'ARC

Excerpt from "Poignant French Film," Mordaunt Hall, *The New York Times*, March 31, 1929, Section 8, p. 7.

Maria Falconetti Gives Unequaled Performance as Jeanne d'Arc
By Mordaunt Hall

France can well be proud of that great picture, THE PASSION OF JEANNE D'ARC, for while Carl Dreyer, a Dane, is responsible for the conspicuously fine and imaginative use of the camera, it is the gifted performance of Maria Falconetti as the Maid of Orleans that rises above everything in this artistic achievement. Like the others in the cast, Mlle. Falconetti is a member of the Comedie Francaise. She, it is true, has been guided with veritable genius by Mr. Dreyer, but as one witnesses her eyes filling with tears or perceives a faint grateful smile crossing her appealing countenance, one feels that it would be difficult indeed to elicit from any other actress such an eloquent interpretation as she gives in this production, which deals only with the trial of Jeanne d'Arc and her terrible fate.

Mlle. Falconetti's portrayal actually reveals that faith that guided the girl knight of France. Her sadness seems very real and sometimes, as a tear courses down her cheek, her eyes widen at hearing something from the aged, erudite men who question her pitilessly. It all happened 500 years ago, but nevertheless as one sits in the Little Carnegie Theatre, gazing upon this remarkable motion picture, one is constantly torn between pity and hate.

The face of this French actress with her closely cropped hair is at first compelling but startling. Her eyes are staring; her lips, untouched by rouge, seem dry and her skin is brown, like that of a girl of the soil. But as the picture continues one finds in the sensitive features something truly magnetic, especially the occasional glance of hope. When the startled eyes fill with tears, this Maid of Orleans permits only the merest suggestion of expression from her sometimes slightly quivering lips. Her expression never tightens a feature, and while she is unswerving in her faith, it is not portrayed by any movement of the jaws, but invariably by the eyes. She is not bitter or vengeful, but she is sure of herself in her replies to her inquisitors.

The Questioning.

This girl is clad in a military uniform, on which not even a button glistens. It is like that of a private who has been neglected. Her boots are clumsy, and as she staggers in to face Bishop Cauchon and the others one notices that her ankles are shackled.

She admits she was born to save France. Not only one question is put to her at a time, but several by different prelates. They come to the vision of St. Michael and ask her for a description of the angel. She is asked whether the apparition had hair and her reply is:
"Why not?"
"Why does she wear men's clothes?" and "Would she like a gown?" She replies that she will wear women's clothes only when she has fulfilled her God-given mission. What does she expect from God? Her answer:
"The salvation of my soul."
She is told that she blasphemes and the aged heads and wrinkled faces shake as some of them mumble "Shame."
"Has God made a promise to you?"
"It is not for you to judge me," says the girl, "lead me before the Pope."

Original Direction.

Mlle. Falconetti is superb during this questioning and Mr. Dreyer darts here and there with his camera, sometimes revealing Jeanne in a corner of the room with the big heads and smaller heads in the foreground. He reminds one of something that is occurring and then flashes elsewhere to other heads. And all this is accomplished without dissolves or

526

65. *THE PASSION OF JEANNE D'ARC: Antonin Artaud (right) makes an unforgettable appearance. This was the man who as critic, playwright and actor was later to urge the creation of a "Theater of Cruelty" in France.*

fadeouts in such an effective way that no matter what the angle from which the scenes are pictured it is always satisfying and not, as one might suppose, tricky or impressionistic. It is, as a matter of fact, a curious feat, for while the manner in which this film is pictured, with its many close-ups, is so thoroughly suited to this particular subject, it is doubtful whether this screen technique would be as effective for any other story.

Mr. Dreyer makes the most of the long lines of the priest's garments; in the foreground on one side is the wheel of a barrow. There is sycophancy written on one face, on another there is admiration in the eyes, which is however denied by the sneer on the lips. For a second there may be a close-up of a shorn priest who is evidently not at all sure of himself, and then Mr. Dreyer turns his lens on another visage, on which is a contrasting expression.

There are the English soldiers with "tin hats," which are curiously like those the Americans and British wore in the World War.

If exception could be taken at any sequence it is where the English soldiers are perceived tormenting Jeanne, by snatching a ring from her finger, putting a straw crown she had made in prison on her head and by sticking their arrows in her arms. This seems too brutal at this stage of the proceedings for even a callous warrior of that day.

A Wonderful Face.

This picture, which shows Warwick watchful that the girl shall not escape her tragic fate, gives a sane impression of the trial.

The scenes where Jeanne is finally led to the stake in the Place du Vieux Marché, Rouen, are agonizing in their remarkable realism, and this is, of course, one of the reasons that Britain has banned THE PASSION OF JEANNE D'ARC. America benefits where Britain loses, for as a film work of art this takes precedence over anything that has so far been produced. It makes worthy pictures of the past look like tinsel shams. It fills one with such intense admiration that other pictures appear but trivial in comparison.

When one leaves the theatre the face of that peasant girl with all its soulfulness appears to leap from one to another in a throng. Long afterward you think of the tears welling from the eyes, of the faith that seemed to stay any suggestion of irritation. Then comes the return of that scene where the nineteen-year-old girl who saved France is bound to the stake and surrounded by a pile of faggots and as the smoke streaks up birds are seen in the heavens.

Mlle. Falconetti is now appearing in scenes of a picture called CATACOMBS, which is also being directed by Mr. Dreyer. In order to meet the demands of the part of Jeanne d'Arc, Miss Falconetti agreed to have her luxuriant hair shorn, and when she is returned to a prison cell, before she repudiates her abjuration, she submits to having part of her hair clipped even shorter.

Bishop Cauchon is acted with marked intelligence and appreciation by M. Sylvain. Others in the cast are Maurice Schutz, Ravet, André Berley, Antonin Artaud, A. Lurville, Jacques Arnna, Mihalesco, R. Narlay, Henry Maillard, Michel Simon, Jean Ayme, Jean d'Yd, L. Larive, Henry Gaultier and Paul George. The work of these skilled players is true, restrained and earnest.

THE PASSION OF JEANNE D'ARC was filmed in Clamait studio in France. The scenario is based on a book on the Maid of Orleans by Joseph Delteil, who also assisted in the direction. The settings were designed by Jean Victor Hugo and Hermann Warm. Mr. Warm is responsible for the weird backgrounds of THE CABINET OF DR. CALIGARI.

When this production was first released in Paris the Archbishop asked for a startling number of eliminations, but eventually the film was permitted to be circulated without any exclusions. . . .

NOTES

(1) Eadweard Muybridge: *Animals in Motion* (Third Impression), Chapman and Hall, Ld., London, 1907, pp. 4-5.

(2) Ibid., p. 2.

(3) "Mr. Muybridge at the Royal Institution," *The Photographic News*, Vol. 26, No. 1228, March 17, 1882, p. 129.

(4) "Edison's Invention of the Kineto-Phonograph," Antonia and W.K.L. Dickson, *The Century Magazine*, Vol. 48, No. 2, June, 1894, p. 208.

(5) Eadweard Muybridge: *Animals in Motion* (Third Impression), Chapman and Hall, Ld., London, 1907, pp. 4-5.

(6) Edison letter printed as preface to "Edison's Invention of the Kineto-Phonograph," Antonia and W.K.L. Dickson, *The Century Magazine*, Vol. 48, No. 2, June, 1894, p. 206.

(7) "The American Biograph," advertisement, *The New York Clipper*, Vol. 48, No. 44, December 29, 1900, p. 988.

(7a) The Biograph had been seen previously at Hammerstein's Olympia Music Hall in New York.

(8) "Copied Films," *Complete Illustrated Catalog of Moving Picture Machines, Stereopticons, Slides, Films,* Kleine Optical Company, Chicago, Ill., November, 1905, p. 210.

(9) "Edwin S. Porter," George Blaisdell, *The Moving Picture World*, Vol. 14, No. 10, December 7, 1912, p. 962.

(10) "Too Near the Camera," *The Moving Picture World,* Vol. 8, No. 12, March 25, 1911, pp. 633-634.

(11) "Edwin S. Porter," George Blaisdell, *The Moving Picture World*, Vol. 14, No. 10, December 7, 1912, p. 961.

(11a) This is a mistake — it would have to be frames of film per second.

(11b) An examination of the only surviving print reveals a small boy who observes the burglar and then runs to summon the police.

(12) "Our Visits," *The Moving Picture World,* Vol. 2, No. 5, February 1, 1908, p. 71.

(13) "Browning Now Given in Motion Pictures," *The New York Times,* October 10, 1909, Part 2, p. 8.

(14) Review of Biograph's A RICH REVENGE, *The New York Dramatic Mirror,* Vol. 63, No. 1634, April 16, 1910, p. 18

(15) "Reviews of Licensed Films" *The New York Dramatic Mirror,* Vol. 64, No. 1653, August 27, 1910. p. 26.

(15a) As a matter of fact, Griffith was doing this even earlier. THE LONEDALE OPERATOR, released March 23, 1911, contains 97 separate shots.

(16) "Earmarks of Makers," *The New York Dramatic Mirror,* Vol. 60, No. 1560, November 14, 1908, p. 10.

(17) "MILLS OF THE GODS," *The Moving Picture World,* Vol. 5, No. 11, September 11, 1909, p. 345.

(17a) "Feature Films of the Week: JUDITH OF BETHULIA," "F.," *The New York Dramatic Mirror,* Vol. 71, No. 1839, March 18, 1914, p. 24.

(18) "Griffith Signs Stars," W. E. Wing, *The New York Dramatic Mirror,* Vol. 73, No. 1888, February 24, 1915, p. 33

(19) "Frank Powell," advertisement, *The New York Dramatic Mirror,* Vol. 70, No. 1825, December 10, 1913, p. 39.

(20) "D. W. Griffith," advertisement, *The New York Dramatic Mirror,* Vol. 70, No. 1823, November 26, 1913, p. 26.

(21) "The Riddle of America," Guglielmo Ferrero, *The Atlantic Monthly,* Vol. 112, November, 1913, p. 707.

(22) Foreign dispatches to *The Musical Courier* from Hamburg (Vol. 65, No. 19, November 6, 1912, p. 22) and Dresden (Vol. 65, No. 22, November 27, 1912, p. 8).

(23) "Editorial," *Camera Work,* Special Number, August, 1912, p. 3.

(24) Gertrude Stein: *Lectures in America,* Random House, New York, 1935, p. 176.

(25) "Recent Reflections of a Novel-Reader," *The Atlantic Monthly,* Vol. 115, April, 1915, p. 501.

(26) Quoted in Lincoln Kirstein: *Dance,* G.P. Putnam's Sons, New York, 1935, p. 290.

(27) Charles Dickens: *Christmas Stories,* Household Edition, Harper and Brothers, New York, 1876, p. 5.

(28) "Comments on Film Subjects," *The Moving Picture World,* Vol. 4, No. 4, January 23, 1909, p. 94.

(29) "Queen Elizabeth," advertisement, *The Moving Picture World,* Vol. 13, No. 4, July 27, 1912, p. 311.

(30) "QUO VADIS," advertisement, *The New York Dramatic Mirror,* Vol. 70, No. 1803, July 9, 1913, p. 32.

(31) Letter from Mrs. Thomas Ince to the author dated August 29, 1955.

(32) "THE SINEWS OF WAR," *The New York Dramatic Mirror,* Vol. 69, No. 1788, March 26, 1913, p. 25.

(33) "AN INDIAN MARTYR," *The Moving Picture World,* Vol. 10, No. 13, December 30, 1911, p. 1074.

(34) "BATTLE OF THE REDMEN," *The Moving Picture World,* Vol. 11, No. 12, March 23, 1912, p. 1063.

(35) "Great Expenditure at Triangle Studios," Henry MacMahon, *The Triangle,* Vol. 1, No. 1, October 23, 1915, p. 5

(36) "Ince: Rodin of Shadows," Harry C. Carr, *Photoplay Magazine,* Vol. 8, No. 2, July, 1915, pp. 81-84.

(37) "What Does the Public Want?", Thomas H. Ince, *Photoplay Magazine,* Vol. 11, No. 2, January 1917, p. 66.

(38) "Along the Pacific Coast," *The New York Dramatic Mirror,* Vol. 73, No. 1906, June 30, 1915, p. 22.

(39) "The Seven Arts" Department, James Huneker, *Puck,* Vol. 80, July 29, 1916, pp. 12, 21.

(40) "Radio Getting Results from Home Sets," *The New York Times,* May 21, 1922, Section 6, p. 4.

(41) As James Card says about films, "Never say 'never,' never say 'first.' " FLAMING YOUTH cannot possibly have been the first Jazz Age film. In looking back, Fitzgerald telescoped the period. What about THE BEAUTIFUL AND DAMNED, for instance, filmed from his own Jazz Age novel and released at the end of 1922?

(42) Reply to "S.E.R.," Answer Department, *Motion Picture Magazine,* Vol. 9, No. 4, May, 1915, p. 137.

(43) "Art and Democracy," editorial, *Photoplay Magazine,* Vol. 13, No. 5, April, 1918, p. 19.

(43a) Usually listed in Germany as Wilhelm Dieterle. In America, as a director, he was known as William Dieterle.

(44) "Putting the Pictures Before the People," Harold Edel, *The New York Dramatic Mirror,* Vol. 77, No. 1988, January 27, 1917, p. 46.

(45) *The New York Times,* April 9, 1927, p. 17

(46) F. Scott Fitzgerald, fascinated with Lois Moran, later wrote her into his novel *Tender is the Night* (1934) as Rosemary.

(47) Excerpt from "Paris Notes," *The New York Times,* October 31, 1926, Section 8, p. 11.

(48) "The Filming of BERLIN," Walther Ruttmann, *The New York Times,* May 20, 1928, Section 8, p. 8.

(49) "Ireland and Spain," Mordaunt Hall, *The New York Times,* May 20, 1928, Section 8, p. 5.

(50) This film does not seem to have been shown here in the Twenties in conjunction with the score which the composer George Antheil (about whose work Ezra Pound was so pleased) wrote for it. The music alone was played at a Carnegie Hall concert April 10, 1927, Eugene Goossens conducting.

(51) "Film Arts Guild Opens New Theatre," *The New York Times,* February 2, 1929, p. 15.

(52) "Russian Film Expert," P. Beaumont Wadsworth, *The New York Times,* May 12, 1929, Section 9, p. 5.

(53) "The Screen: Floating Glimpses of Russia," Mordaunt Hall, *The New York Times,* September 17, 1929, p. 36.

LIST OF ILLUSTRATIONS

APPENDIX

DATES OF NEW YORK CITY OPENINGS

Unless otherwise noted, the following are the dates of the New York City openings of the feature films discussed in this book. Shorter films from these later years are marked with an asterisk.

1913 Feb. 17   THE MIRACLE.
          Feb. 18   THE PRISONER OF ZENDA, Invitational Showing.
          Oct. 4   DAVID COPPERFIELD reviewed, *The Moving Picture World*.

1914 Feb. 2   *MAKING A LIVING.
          Mar. 23   *THE PERILS OF PAULINE: Sixth Episode.
          June 1   CABIRIA.
          Nov. 4   TILLIE'S PUNCTURED ROMANCE reviewed, *The New York Dramatic Mirror*.
          Dec. 3   THE BARGAIN released.

1915 Jan. 12   A FOOL THERE WAS, Invitational Showing.
          Feb. 8   Los Angeles. THE CLANSMAN (THE BIRTH OF A NATION).
          Mar. 3   New York. THE BIRTH OF A NATION.
          Apr. 12   *THE TRAMP.
          Sept. 5   ESMERALDA.
          Dec. 26   DESTRUCTION.

1916 Feb. 20   POOR LITTLE PEPPINA.
          Sept. 5   INTOLERANCE.
          Dec. 24   THE AMERICANO.
          Dec. 25   JOAN THE WOMAN.

1917 May 13   A ROMANCE OF THE REDWOODS.
          June 18   *THE IMMIGRANT.

1918 Oct. 20   *SHOULDER ARMS.
          Dec. 22   THE GREATEST THING IN LIFE.

1919 Mar. 23   THE GIRL WHO STAYED AT HOME.
          Apr. 13   THE ROARING ROAD.
          May 13   BROKEN BLOSSOMS.
          July 21   THE FALL OF BABYLON (from INTOLERANCE).
          Aug. 18   THE MOTHER AND THE LAW (from INTOLERANCE).

1920 Apr. 24   WHY CHANGE YOUR WIFE?
          Sept. 3   WAY DOWN EAST.
          Nov. 14   THE PENALTY.
          Dec. 12   PASSION (MADAME DUBARRY).

1921 Jan. 2   THE LAST OF THE MOHICANS.
          Jan. 21   THE KID, Special Benefit Performance.
          Feb. 27   THE OLD SWIMMIN' HOLE.
          Mar. 6   THE FOUR HORSEMEN OF THE APOCALYPSE.

Apr. 3	THE CABINET OF DR. CALIGARI.	
May 1	THE BIRTH OF A NATION, Revival.	
June 19	THE GOLEM.	
July 24	*NEW YORK, THE MAGNIFICENT (MANHATTA).	
Nov. 26	SIR ARNE'S TREASURE, Special Performance.	
Dec. 10	SHATTERED, Special Performance.	

Jan. 3	ORPHANS OF THE STORM.	**1922**
Jan. 11	FOOLISH WIVES.	
June 4	THE STROKE OF MIDNIGHT.	
June 11	NANOOK OF THE NORTH.	
Aug. 27	THE THREE MUST-GET-THERES.	
Sept. 3	GRANDMA'S BOY.	
Oct. 30	ROBIN HOOD.	
Dec. 31	SALOME (Nazimova).	

March 16	THE COVERED WAGON.	**1923**
Sept. 2	THE HUNCHBACK OF NOTRE DAME.	
Sept. 3	ROSITA.	
Oct. 1	A WOMAN OF PARIS.	
Nov. 25	FLAMING YOUTH.	
Dec. 4	Hollywood. THE TEN COMMANDMENTS.	
Dec. 9	ANNA CHRISTIE.	

Feb. 3	THE MARRIAGE CIRCLE.	**1924**
Feb. 21	AMERICA.	
Mar. 18	THE THIEF OF BAGDAD.	
May 25	SHERLOCK JR.	
July 1	MONTMARTRE	
Aug. 28	THE IRON HORSE.	
Oct. 5	THREE WOMEN.	
Oct. 12	THE NAVIGATOR.	
Nov. 9	HE WHO GETS SLAPPED.	
Nov. 30	ISN'T LIFE WONDERFUL?	
Dec. 4	GREED.	

Jan. 25	THE LAST LAUGH, Cut Version.	**1925**
Feb. 8	THE LOST WORLD.	
Apr. 13	Rochester, New York. SIEGFRIED.	
Aug. 2	THE UNHOLY THREE.	
Aug. 16	THE GOLD RUSH.	
Aug. 26	THE MERRY WIDOW.	
Sept. 6	THE PHANTOM OF THE OPERA.	
Sept. 20	THE FRESHMAN.	
Oct. 15	THE VANISHING AMERICAN.	
Nov. 5	Hollywood. THE BIG PARADE.	
Nov. 16	STELLA DALLAS.	
Dec. 26	LADY WINDERMERE'S FAN.	
Dec. 30	BEN-HUR.	

Jan. 10	THE LAST LAUGH, Uncut Version.	**1926**
Jan. 15	THE SEA BEAST.	
Jan. 17	HANDS UP.	
Jan. 24	THE AMERICAN VENUS.	
Feb. 7	MOANA.	
Feb. 15	MARE NOSTRUM.	
Mar. 14	THE NEW ENCHANTMENT and *BALLET MECANIQUE, Special Performance.	

	Apr. 4	*A QUOI REVENT LES JEUNES FILMS?, Special Performance.
	June 3	BACKSTAIRS and *THE GREAT TRAIN ROBBERY (Revival), Special Performance.
	June 27	VARIETY.
	June 27	THE ROAD TO MANDALAY.
	June 29	FACES OF CHILDREN and PARIS QUI DORT, Special Performance.
	July 11	MANTRAP.
	Aug. 5	DON JUAN, Invitational Showing.
	Aug. 14	SO THIS IS PARIS.
	Aug. 31	POTEMKIN, Invitational Showing.
	Oct. 29	THE CABINET OF DR. CALIGARI, Revival.
	Nov. 3	INTOLERANCE, Revival.
	Dec. 5	POTEMKIN.
1927	Jan. 1	HOTEL IMPERIAL.
	Jan. 8	FLESH AND THE DEVIL.
	Mar. 5	METROPOLIS.
	Mar. 6	THE LIVING DEAD MAN and *EMAK BAKIA, Special Performance.
	Apr. 24	SECRETS OF THE SOUL.
	June 11	THE UNKNOWN.
	Aug. 12	WINGS.
	Aug. 20	UNDERWORLD.
	Sept. 9	THE CAT AND THE CANARY.
	Sept. 23	SUNRISE.
	Oct. 6	THE JAZZ SINGER.
	Nov. 29	LOVE (ANNA KARENINA).
	Dec. 3	*TWENTY-FOUR DOLLAR ISLAND, Cut Version.
1928	Jan. 7	*TWENTY-FOUR DOLLAR ISLAND, Uncut Version.
	Jan. 21	THE LAST COMMAND.
	Feb. 3	SADIE THOMPSON.
	Feb. 18	THE CROWD.
	Mar. 11	THE LAST MOMENT.
	May 12	*BERLIN, THE SYMPHONY OF A BIG CITY.
	May 30	THE END OF ST. PETERSBURG.
	Aug. 17	THE PATRIOT.
	Oct. 6	OUR DANCING DAUGHTERS.
	Oct. 12	THE WEDDING MARCH.
	Oct. 13	KRIEMHILD'S REVENGE.
	Nov. 3	TEN DAYS THAT SHOOK THE WORLD.
	Nov. 3	THE WIND.
1929	Feb. 1	*THE FALL OF THE HOUSE OF USHER.
	Mar. 28	THE PASSION OF JEANNE D'ARC.
	Sept. 14	LIVING RUSSIA or THE MAN WITH THE CAMERA.
	Nov. 8	ARSENAL.
	Nov. 30	THE NEW BABYLON.
	Nov. 30	PANDORA'S BOX.

INDEX
Illustrations are cited by page number

538

539

541

542

543